Selected Master Lists (contin...)

Master List	URL
Planet Access Networks	http://www.planet.net/
Planet Earth	http://white.nosc.mil/info.html
Point Communications Top Sites	http://www.pointcom.com/gifs/topsites
Starting Point	http://www.stpt.com/ or http://stpt.com/
Surfing the Net—Resources Galore	http://www.whittier.edu/www/surfing.html
Today.Com	http://www.today.com/
TradeWave Galaxy	http://www.einet.net/
W3 Search Engines	http://cuiwww.unige.ch/meta-index.html
Whole Internet Catalog	http://gnn.com/wic/wics/index.html
World-Wide Web Virtual Library: Subject Catalogue	http://www.w3.org/pub/DataSources/bySubject/Overview.html or http://www.w3.org/hypertext/DataSources/bySubject/Overview.html

Cool and Hot Sites

Site	URL
Cool Places	http://www.com:80/webnet/webnet1.html
Cool Site of the Day	http://cool.infi.net/
Dynamite Site of the Nite	http://www.netzone.com/~tti/dsotn.html
Hot Sites	http://www.amdahl.com:80/internet/general/sites.html
HOT Web Sites	http://www.refdesk.com/tablehot.html
What's Hot and Cool	http://kzsu.stanford.edu/uwi/reviews.html
The WinMagWeb HotSpots	http://www.winmag.com/flanga/hotspots.htm

The Internet Business-to-Business Directory

The Internet Business-to-Business Directory

Sandra E. Eddy

Michael M. Swertfager

Margaret M.E. Cusick

SYBEX

San Francisco • Paris • Düsseldorf • Soest

Associate Publisher:
Amy Romanoff

Acquisitions Manager:
Kristine Plachy

Developmental Editors:
Brenda Kienan, Pat Coleman

Editor:
Pat Coleman

Project Editor:
Bonnie Bills

Technical Editors:
K. Miles Pratt, William Pinto

Book Designers:
Emil Yanos, Alissa Feinberg

Book Design Director:
Catalin Dulfu

Desktop Publishers:
Alissa Feinberg, Deborah Maizels

Production Coordinator:
Kim Wimpsett

Indexer:
Matthew Spence

Cover Designer:
Design Site

Cover Illustrator:
Hank Osuna

Acknowledgments

Writing a computer book is most definitely a team effort. The authors cannot get through a long and detailed project without a great deal of help from editors, family, friends, and other support. In this section, we would like to thank all the people whose efforts have been so important.

Our interviewees contributed their important insights and knowledge. Thanks to Jerry Yang, Chris Lopes, Bob O'Keefe, Wayne Marr, Mark Williams, Scott Yanoff, and Terry Brainerd Chadwick.

We can't thank Steve Davis enough for his masterly job of writing Appendix A.

We especially thank the people at SYBEX for all their help and encouragement. Special thanks go to Developmental Editor Brenda Kienan, who started this project, and especially to Pat Coleman, who saw it through to the end and became a friend. Thanks also to Bonnie Bills, Project Editor; Kim Wimpsett, Production Coordinator; and a very special thanks to Alissa Feinberg, Desktop Publisher, and her colleagues.

For accuracy and attention in reviewing every site of the thousands in this book, a special thank you to Technical Editor Miles Pratt, and to William Pinto for pitching in.

A special thanks to Sean Cusick, who provided Internet information and links at the beginning of this project.

As always, thank you to the folks at Waterside Productions, especially Matt Wagner and Margot Maley.

For their continued encouragement, my family and friends—you know who you are. Special thanks and wishes for continued success to Brian Robb and Denise Robb.

Particular thanks to Stephen Connors at NETCOM, Donald L. Nicholas and Dick Rubenstein at Blue Dolphin Communications, and Donna Loughlin at NetManage. Thanks also to Lucy Ventresca at SoftQuad, Paul Uhlhorn at ViaCrypt, Jerome N. Gould at Crazy Bob's, Ann M. Krauss at Frontier Technologies, Carsie McCarty at Walnut Creek CDROM, Suzanne Koumantzelis at Information Access Technologies, and Deanna Leung at Spry.

For their special and continuing contributions—Toni and Bart. And in loving memory—Indy. We miss you more each day.

S.E.E.
73510.3154@compuserve.com

To all my close friends and family who have helped me through tough times: Mark Williams, Rob Swertfager, Sally McNeil, Dave Engelbrecht, Dave Wyllie, John Schroeder, Keith Krohn, and Mike Ryan. And especially to Sandy Schnyder.

M.M.S.

Thanks to the technical staff at Netscape for the patience they showed in helping me go online. I sometimes felt that they were speaking in a foreign language, but they were able to translate it for me.

The work on this book was very time-consuming, and I appreciate the understanding of my family. They put up with late dinners and a dirty house and patiently listened as I told them about yet another fascinating find on the Internet. My teenage daughter was even willing to give up the use of our phone!

M.M.E.C.

Table of Contents

Introduction

Welcome to *The Internet Business-to-Business Directory*, a comprehensive guide to thousands of business sites on the Internet—with a few wildcards thrown in here and there. Consider this your new desktop reference to the Internet.

During the months that this book was under development, we have seen evolutionary and sometimes revolutionary changes. At the beginning of the project, pages on the World Wide Web were drab combinations of gray background, large black text, blue links, and often large photographs that loaded very slowly. Just a few months later, graphic designers and artists have exerted their influence. Now, Web page design and programming often incorporate fill-in forms and clickable image maps. It's been an amazing advance over a matter of months.

When we started this book, we were worried that we wouldn't find enough sites to fill the pages. Instead, we almost always found more than we could use. And every day, we were happily surprised by at least one new discovery that may or may not have had anything to do with the subject of this book—business. The planning, imagination, and intelligence that make for the best sites on the Internet simply boggles the mind. We are looking forward to seeing even more advances.

Who Should Read This Book

The Internet Business-to-Business Directory is designed for businesspersons, academics, students, and all others who want one central Internet business resource. Its thousands of Internet sites can help you locate the latest economic statistics and demographics, get information about government agencies and their business programs, learn about corporations from which you might want to buy or with which you may want to do business, arrange a business trip (including after-hours activities), move into the international marketplace, and much more.

Although this book assumes that you have some knowledge of the World Wide Web and other Internet features, you can always refer to Appendix A for basic information.

The Contents of This Book

This book is a directory of thousands of Internet business sites, presented in two ways: as short evaluations or as table entries. Also included are two appendixes—an Internet primer and a Web page development tutorial—and a glossary of terms.

You'll also find these special features:

Sidebars cover a variety of Internet topics—from how to find a provider to how to compress and decompress files that you download.

Interviews provide questions and answers with Internet experts.

Interesting Sites highlight sites that are not to be ignored—for content, entertainment, and/or design.

Notes emphasize important information about a site.

Tips provide shortcuts and easy-to-use methods for performing functions.

Text Conventions Used in This Book

In this book, italicized text represents both variables (for example, a *filename* or a *value to be typed*) and new terms.

This font

http://www.yahoo.com

indicates URLs that you type to go to a particular site.

How to Use This Book

Each entry in *The Internet Business-to-Business Directory* is a snapshot of a site—at the time that an author wrote about it, when a technical editor checked it, and possibly when an author changed it. One thing that we have learned is that the Internet is always changing: students graduate, professors move on to other interests, webmasters change folder and file naming conventions, and businesses switch to new providers or get a new domain name. During this project, we have seen URLs change from one day to the next, and sites that we thought would be permanent just disappeared.

Below are some of the ways that you can search for a site that has moved from one part of the Net to another without leaving a "forwarding" link. Most of the time, one of these methods results in success.

Finding a Site: Part One

If you are willing to try a shortcut, think of a logical name for a site. For example, when we couldn't find the Federal Aviation Administration (FAA) at http://web.fie.com/web/fed/faa/, we successfully tried http://www.faa.gov/. Starting with http:// is a no-brainer, following with www is a good bet, using an abbreviation such as .faa is an excellent first (and probably only) first try, and .gov represents the government domain. However, there are exceptions to every rule: Not every address includes www; some just start with the company or agency name, and others start with web or some other identifier. To confuse things more, not all government agencies use the .gov domain; the agency may be an organization (.org) or even a private-public commercial (.com) site. If you try this with Gopher sites, the best bet for the first part of the URL is gopher://gopher.

Finding a Site: Part Two

One way to find a missing site is to take apart its URL piece by piece. Let's say that the address for which you are looking is http://networth.galt.com/www/home/insider/publicco.html. (This URL actually changed during this project.) You can either remove all the address after the main domain name (leaving http://networth.galt.com/) or remove the address in stages from one slash to the next (for example, http://networth.galt.com/www/home/insider/ to http://networth.galt.com/www/home/ to http://networth.galt.com/www/, and so on) until you see a link that looks as though it might work. Sometimes you find yourself looking at the folders that form the understructure of a site, but sometimes you hit pay dirt. This works for both Web and Gopher sites.

By the way, for this example, we started from the domain name http://networth.galt.com/ and clicked on buttons with familiar names to find the new URL, http://networth.galt.com/www/home/info/insider.

Finding a Site: Part Three

If guessing a URL or taking it apart and putting it back together again doesn't work, use a search index (for the best of them, see the inside front cover or inside back cover of this book). In the text box, type the title of the site, the name of the author, or a keyword you think will clearly identify the site. Then, click on the button to start the search. On the page of results, look for the link that most closely resembles the site for which you are looking, click, and hope for the best. If the first results don't pan out, try a new search with a different keyword.

Chapter One

Business Management

A t the sites in this chapter, you can obtain all sorts of information about business and supplies—particularly helpful for those running small businesses or just starting out. Managing a business is tough enough today with demands on your time, new technologies coming down the pike, and worries about cash flow. The sites in this chapter can help you get both general business help and answer specific questions.

General Resources

Many all-purpose business sites, from several comprehensive online books to all types of business resources, are from the pioneers of the Internet—those that can help the rest of us get comfortable with the Net. In many ways, you can consider this section the cornerstone of this book. Here you will find a place at which you can barter your goods and services, order office supplies, link to research centers and investment sources, and get marketing and sales information.

The Barter Network

http://www.shicho.com/shicho/barter/barter.html

The Barter Network is a clearinghouse for goods and services that can be bartered. To register your goods or services, click on either Register Products or Register Services. To browse the goods and services of others, click on either Browse Products or Browse Services.

On one visit, the available goods included video and audio tapes, retread and used tires, latex exam gloves, summer clothing, used medical equipment, PVC, polyethylene bags, computers, and cellular phones and service. Services included real estate trades, communications consulting, and trade consulting.

BizPro Online Business Services

http://www.bizpro.com/

This commercial site not only provides information about itself, but also includes links to a directory of servers, integrated services digital network (ISDN) information, Internet information, and travel information for Austin, Texas.

Click on Main Listing for Interesting WWW Pages (http://www.bizpro.com/other.html) to go to a long list of sites, ranging from Internet manuals to travel information.

A Short History of the Internet

The Internet is the "network of networks" that has links in every continent. Born in the middle of the Cold War (1969) and initially a nuclear defense communication system developed by the U.S. Department of Defense, ARPAnet (Advanced Research Projects Agency NETwork) was the Internet's predecessor. According to some sources, at the very beginning, ARPAnet consisted of four mainframe computers.

Over the years, colleges and universities that were doing defense research and defense contractors were added to the network. And, as you know, in recent years, individuals, organizations, other educational institutions, and commercial establishments have joined the network in vast numbers.

In 1986, the National Science Foundation Network (NSFnet), with five supercomputing centers at universities, replaced ARPAnet. NSFnet went out of business in 1991.

Business and Commerce Links

http://galaxy.einet.net/galaxy/Business-and-Commerce.html

This very large and comprehensive site provides links to many business resources, separated into categories and subcategories. Categories include Business Administration, Business General Resources, Consortia and Research Centers, Consumer Products and Service, Electronic Commerce, General Products and Services, Investment Sources, Management, and Marketing and Sales. Articles, announcements, collections, directories, and organizations are in a separate category.

Business Directory from Texas A&M

gopher://gopher.tamu.edu:70/11/.dir/business.dir

At this site you'll find 25 business links— from economic development to finance sources, from international business resources to news. Here are links to some of the most popular Internet business resources: Business Resources at Nijenrode University, the Economic Bulletin Board at the University of Michigan, and the Occupational Outlook Handbook. Geographic areas covered include Asia, Israel, Russia, Japan, and Singapore. Also included is a link to DOS finance software.

The Business of the Internet

http://www.rtd.com/people/rawn/business.html

This long and well-written article about the Internet and how to use it for your business contains "chapters" to which you can jump and links to footnotes. This document includes Internet history, what you and your business can and cannot do on the Internet, and how to connect.

Business Sources on the Net

gopher://refmac.kent.edu:70/1D-1%3A2577%3ABusiness

This site contains an up-to-date edition of a comprehensive online book, in text format, with many Internet business resources. Click on BSN.README to read an introduction and to view the table of contents. Folders include INTRO, which contains Internet Guides and Common Definitions; GENERAL, which has general business Internet sources; and GREEN, which has information about business and the environment. Generally, you can guess the content of a folder from its name.

A typical entry contains a title, author(s), description, and Internet addresses. The emphasis is on academics, but you can find many top business sites here.

Business Sources—Global Network Navigator (GNN)

http://gnn.com/gnn/wic/bus.toc.html

This section of the GNN, a very large and excellent index of Internet resources, is dedicated to business and finance. At this site, you'll find links to other GNN pages and Internet newsgroups in these categories: Agriculture, Career and Employment, Government Information (Business), Internet Commerce, Investment, Management, Marketing, Nonprofits, Personal Finance, Real Estate, Small Business, Taxes, and Yellow Pages. The two largest sections are Career and Employment and Investment.

The Commerce Page

http://www.charm.net

This commercial site provides many of the same links that you will find at other addresses and several unique links that make a visit worthwhile. Click on Business to get started. Sample links include Dun and Bradstreet, economic data from the University of Michigan and the U.S. Department of Commerce, and Quote.Com financial market data. In addition, you can track a UPS or a FedEx package, look at the Fortune 500 Online, look up zip codes, and go to a variety of online periodicals.

Document Center

http://doccenter.com/doccenter/home.html

At this commercial reprint service, you can search and purchase business-related documents from its catalog. Document categories include engineering, plastics, International Standards Organization (ISO), and so on. There are three search indexes—Inventory Database, Catalog Database, and History Database—but very little information as to the contents.

Jerry Yang on Starting Yahoo

Jerry Yang and David Filo, two Stanford University Ph.D. students studying electrical engineering, are the founders of Yahoo (http://www.yahoo.com/). Yahoo (Yet Another Hierarchical Officious Oracle) is the most popular online World Wide Web directory system, accessed an amazing two million times each day.

When and why did you create Yahoo?

We created Yahoo in late March 1994. We created it because we were beginning to be overwhelmed by the number of sites on the Web even then, and we wanted our way of organizing life and information around it.

What do you think of your creation now that it is a roaring success?

We still think that it's a long way from being the useful, everyday resource that we would like it to be. I think we have a lot of work ahead of us to make it continually useful and beneficial.

Electronic Commerce

gopher://gopher.texas-one.org:70/11/ecommerce/refs

If your company does business on the Internet, you will want to visit this site. Here you will find links to electronic commerce resources, Internet adver-tising FAQs and guidelines, the Internet Business Journal, telecommuting information, and an article (by Internic) on what businesses can get out of the Internet, survey results, and Babson College marketing resources.

Electronic Democracy Information Network (EDIN)

gopher://garnet.berkeley.edu:1250/11/.econ

At this site, you'll find a variety of business and other information: California and other economic resources; the current U.S. budget; and articles on credit unions, economic resources, and the Economics Bulletin Board, among others. Note that some links at this site were inactive at the time of this writing.

Enterprise Integration Technologies (EIT)

http://www.eit.com/

EIT develops software for the World Wide Web, electronic commerce services, and collaboration tools. Clicking on About EIT presents company information, a description of the technology it is developing, and its place on the Internet.

Click on the links in the EIT Creations section to view demonstrations, presentations and papers (some can be downloaded), technical information, reports, software, and a short page of mailing lists on Zoomer personal digital assistants, World Wide Web courseware, and World Wide Web literature.

Foundation for Enterprise Development (F.E.D.) Employee Ownership

http://www.fed.org/fed/

At this site, you can obtain information about employee ownership, equity compensation, employee involvement, and other new business strategies. You'll find links to What's New, Introduction to Employee Ownership and Equity Compensation, Equity Compensation Methods, Employee Motivation and Empowerment, International Employee Ownership, Case Studies of Successful Companies, Best Practices Profiles (from the U.S. Department of Labor), Government Policy & Legislation, Employee Ownership Research, and F.E.D. publications.

GNN (Global Network Navigator) Business Pages

http://gnn.com/gnn/bus/index.html

The GNN Business Pages list companies and organizations—both large and small—that have Internet sites. At this address, you can access an alphabetically arranged list, or you can choose from categories that contain company and organization links. Many categories list a single entry; others contain quite a few.

To list your organization at this site, send e-mail to market@gnn.com.

Harvard Business School Publishing

http://www.hbsp.harvard.edu/

This site not only publicizes Harvard Business School Press books and periodicals, but also provides abstracts and previews of *The Harvard Business Review*, an excellent source of business articles, and gives you access to the International Directory of Business and Management Scholars and Research. Other links include the Best of HBS Press Online and Business History Review.

Interesting Business Sites on the Web

http://www.owi.com/netvalue

Bob O'Keefe, a professor at Rensselaer Polytechnic Institute and interview subject in this book, presents an ever-changing list of some 50 links that demonstrate interesting business uses of the World Wide Web and pinpoint coming trends.

This site, at Net.Value, is formatted like a monthly magazine—with an editorial, a case-studies section, and a forum.

Internet Business Information

http://www.ibos.com/pub/ibos/buslinks.html

This page of business information includes links to the Small Business Administration and other business-related federal agencies, articles on incorporation, and business services: a 1-800 directory, area code lookup, FedEx Airbill Tracking Form, and stock quotes from Security APL and QuoteCom. It also contains business resources, indexes, and master lists.

The home page (http://www.ibos.com/pub/ibos/busops.html) provides a few links to franchise and small business opportunities and multilevel marketing.

internetMCI Small Business Center

http://www.mci.com/SmallBiz/

This well-organized site provides many links to business financing sites: venture capital and franchising; finding employees using recruiters and Internet job bulletin boards; and professional services and associations, including such categories as legal, marketing/advertising, finance/accountants, human resources, entrepreneurial associations, government agencies that provide help to business, and news and information services. As with other MCI Internet pages, the links are up to date as well as comprehensive.

The only strictly commercial page here is MCI small business solutions.

Note
internetMCI is one of the few sites to use security features. If you see https:// rather than http:// at the beginning of a World Wide Web URL, you are about to visit a secure site.

How Does the Internet Work?

Information sent over the Internet is accumulated into groups of data, called *packets*. A packet consists of the bits representing data, identifying information, and information that might prevent errors from being added to the packet. Thus, an entire message does not have to be sent as one unit; instead, the packets making up the message are sent along the most accessible lines at a particular time. In fact, packets can travel separate routes to the destination computer.

Using data packets allows more traffic to flow through the linked networks and automatically routes packets around extremely busy lines or links or computers that are out of service.

IOMA (Institute of Management and Administration) Business Page

http://starbase.ingress.com/ioma

This comprehensive and very long list includes a wide range of business links: news (many to ClariNet news, a for-a-fee service), administration (accounting and taxation, human resources, insurance and risk, regulatory issues, and corporate law), finance (banks and banking, stock firms, corporate profiles, and filings), and many electronic periodicals and articles on business practices.

Joe Walker's Hot List

http://www2.bae.ncsu.edu/bae/people/faculty/walker/hotlist.html

Your first impression of this site might be that it contains much information but is somewhat disorganized. Once you select a category, however, things change. For example, the business page contains more than 30 alphabetically arranged links to all types of business resources, from Auction Directory & News to Taxing Times, and includes exchange rates, financial economics, business directories, stock quotes, and law.

The NetCenter

http://netcenter.com/

This commercial site is the home of the Interactive Yellow Pages, a long, alphabetically arranged list of all types of links—from graphics to health to government resources. This site bills itself as the Center of the Internet and claims to have more than 100,000 visitors a day. Here, you'll find downloadable Web browsers, links to advertisers, a beginner's online guide to the Internet (a sample of a for-pay book), an online trade show, a shopping mall, and so on.

As a business site, the Interactive Yellow Pages includes links to many companies. For example, under business services, you can find a management consulting firm, printing services, checks by phone, an investigator, a business information center, and more. Some addresses are strictly text pages without links; others provide very good links.

Nijenrode Business Resources

gopher://gopher.nijenrode.nl:70/11/Business

Nijenrode University in the Netherlands presents a list of general business resources. Topics include strategic management; human resource management; management for public and nonprofit organizations; corporate, international and business law; management science; and operations management and statistics.

Project Management Programs— Frequently Asked Questions (FAQ)

http://www.cis.ohio-state.edu/hypertext/faq/usenet/proj-plan-faq/faq.html

This 31-page text file contains questions and answers about using project management software. Pete Phillips, who maintains this site, is a Unix specialist; he acknowledges that PC and DOS coverage is sketchy.

PurchasingWeb Articles

http://www.catalog.com/napmsv/pwhead.htm

From the National Association of Purchasing Management—Silicon Valley, Inc., comes a list of articles that provide information for supply managers and purchasing managers. The information here is useful for small business operators who must tackle many diverse tasks.

Rice Economics Business Links

gopher://chico.rice.edu:70/11/Subject/Economics

Rice University provides a wide variety of business and other links at this address. Resources include accounting, economics, and marketing links; a trade library; industrial sections; a bibliography; several versions of the *CIA Factbook*; the *Commerce Business Daily*; U.S. government sources; United Nations sources; World Bank sources; business statistics; quality assurance; and much more.

Sam Sternberg's Internet Business Guide

http://www.interlog.com/~bxi/diamond3.htm

This 11-chapter downloadable and very large (308 kilobytes) book about using the Internet as a business resource is an excellent example of an individual giving something back to the Internet community. Chapters cover communications, operations, global commerce, developing an office on the Net, research, small business, and the future.

Just go to the site, which automatically starts the download process.

The author is the publisher of the *Global Business* newsletter, which provides its readers current Internet business resources.

Small Business Innovation Research Program (SBIR)

http://nctn.oact.hq.nasa.gov/SBIR/SBIR.html

gopher://asc.dtic.dla.mil:70/11/SBIR%20-%20Small%20Business%20Innovation%20Research%20Program

The SBIR takes proposals from small high-technology firms and makes awards to support their continued research. To continue receiving awards, a company must successfully pass three stages of evaluation.

The Gopher site gives you the names, addresses, and other contacts at each winning firm as well as a description of the firm's work, allowing other companies to apply for subcontracts. This U.S. government program is available until at least the year 2000.

The World Wide Web site describes SBIR and the Small Business Technology Transfer Pilot (STTR) Program. To search SBIR abstracts, click on Click Here. On the search page (http://nctn.oact.hq.nasa.gov/scripts/SBIRabs.cgi), type one or more keywords and press Enter.

State Economic Development Resources

gopher://info.babson.edu:70/11/.bus/.ec-dev

At this site is a short list of links to departments of economic development: ASEDD (Arizona State Economic Development Database), the Economic Democracy Information network (EDIN),the Institute of Urban and Regional Development (IURD), the Nebraska Department of Economic Development, the New England Electronic Economic Data Center, the Texas Marketplace, and the Tucson Economic Development Gopher. In addition, you will find a variety of information, demographics, and indexes about Arizona.

Jerry Yang on Converting Yahoo to a Commercial Site

You two initially created Yahoo for personal use. Then you opened it up to the Web, and it grew quickly. At what point did you decide to drop Yahoo as a personal directory and begin developing it for its commercial value?

We didn't really think of designing it for commercial value until very recently. We always thought that building the most easy-to-use and informative guide to the Net was going to be the best thing, whether it's commercially successful or not.

Nonetheless, we started to look for a commercial home for Yahoo in early 1995. It's apparent to us that we need to develop a commercial focus so that Yahoo will be self-sustaining and profitable.

TEXAS-ONE

http://www.texas-one.org/

TEXAS-ONE, one of the best business sites on the Internet, provides information particularly for companies located in Texas.

Click on Business Information Collection to get to a page of 20 categories of Internet links, from Agriculture to Weather Reports. (At the bottom of each page are text boxes for using a search index.) Clicking on a link provides several new links.

The Texas Marketplace provides business directories (not only for Texas), a market exchange, trade and procurement opportunities, and technology transfers.

Click on General Information to view links for these categories: Internet, News and Comment (about TEXAS-ONE), Information about the TEXAS-ONE Project, and Projects Related to TEXAS-ONE.

Thomas Ho's Favorite Electronic Commerce WWW Resources

http://www.engr.iupui.edu/~ho/interests/commmenu.html

http://webster.cadcam.iupui.edu:80/~ho/

This expanded curriculum vitae (and one of the most popular links on the World Wide Web) contains pages of information. Topics include Ho's education, projects, and memberships; favorite online publications, foods, TV stations and shows, movies and places (good tourist links, especially to Hawaii); and many Asian and Singapore links.

The best part of this site is the Membership link. Not only will you find many useful Internet resources and tutorials, but also entertaining sites, such as two classics: Uncle Bob's Kids' Page (http://gagme.wwa.com/~ba/kids .html) and The Awesome List (http://www.clark.net/pub/journalism/awesome.html).

Interesting Site

Uncle Bob's Kids' Page, at http://gagme.wwa.com/~ba/kids.html, is undoubtedly one of the best sites on the Internet—for both kids and grownups. With links to a variety of Internet resources, you could live on the Kids' Page for days. When you arrive at the home page, click on the graphic (see Figure 1.1), the only element on the page, to get to the real first page. Then scroll down to the Section Index and make a selection. This site consists of seven sections, each with many entertaining and educational links.

Other Bob Allison sites include BOBAWORLD, Bob Allison's Home Page (at http://gagme.wwa.com/~ba/home.html), The Spider's Web (http://gagme.wwa.com/~ba/spider.html), The Scarecrow's WWW Link (http://gagme.wwa.com/~ba/scarecrow.html), and a Newsgroups page (http://gagme.wwa.com/~ba/news.html).

UUNET Primer and Business Guide

http://www.uu.net:80/primer.htm/

This small commercial site provides links to Introduction to the Internet and the Internet Business Guide, a short article on doing business on the Internet. Simply click on the links to jump to specific locations. Consider this a good introduction to business on the Internet; documents at other sites are longer and more informative.

At this site, you also will find the Glossary, definitions of Internet terms, and the Directory of On-line Resources, which includes links to searchable directories, newsgroups, Internet guides and resources, and FTP sites.

Web Sites for Logisticians

http://www.telebyte.com/atsg/www.html

This very large site is for logisticians, which the author of the site states "are generalists with an emphasis in a particular functional area." This describes many owners of small businesses and heads of departments.

Figure 1.1 Click on the graphic to reveal the real home page.

This one-page site provides seven groups of functions: General Resources, Economics, Government, Logistics, Management, Maritime Issues, and Quality. Simply scroll down the page and see links that you can use every day: Internet information, business directories, U.S. and international economic information, publications, government, and much, much more.

Ethics

Ethics should be an important part of every company's mission. Ethical treatment of other companies and employees is the topic of this section. Here you will find information about the Business Ethics Teaching Society (BETS), online guides to ethical and socially responsible business and investment, and links to ethics, socially responsible business and investment, and human resources sites.

Business Ethics Teaching Society (BETS)

http://www.usi.edu:80/bets/index.htm

BETS is the center of ethics education on the Internet. At this site, you can fill in a form to subscribe to the Business Ethics Teaching Society's BETS-L mailing list, read the answers to frequently asked questions about policies and procedures, browse the BETS Web archive (under construction at the time of this writing), or see the Management Archives. Also included are three links to ethical and social business listings in the United Kingdom and a link to the Socially Responsible Business Organizations site.

ethicalBusiness

http://www.bath.ac.uk/Centres/Ethical/

This site consists of links to World Wide Web resources relating to "ethical and socially responsible business and investment in the UK and elsewhere." Here, you will find a Directory of ethicalBusiness

---

Interesting Site

When I first surfed the Net, The Awesome List was just a single list. Now this textual list of links has grown to The Awesome Lists: Truly Awesome and Awesome. The Truly Awesome list consists of 40 entries: from famous all-purpose sites, such as Yahoo, EINet Galaxy, City.Net, and the WWW Virtual Library, to single-purpose sites, such as the Virtual Frog Dissection Kit and Games Domain. The Awesome List consists of entries that are just as important: Virtual Tourist, Town Hall, Submit It!, The Best of the Web, the Monster Board, and the InterNIC directory—to name just a few.

You'll learn more about many of these sites as you read through this book.

---

and links to Ethical Investment Resources, Organizations and Projects, Articles, and Books and Magazines.

Books and Magazines includes links to the full text of *The Shareholder Action Online Handbook* by Craig Mackenzie, one chapter from *The Ethical Investor* by Russell Sparkes, two book lists, and two magazines: *Green Money Journal* and *Multinational Monitor.*

Internet Sites of Relevance to Ethical Business is a long list of links to organizations, including Amnesty International, the Carter Center, Friends of the Earth, Greenpeace International, OXFAM, and several United Nations sites.

Socially Responsible Business (SRB) Mailing List

http://envirolink.org/archives/srb/

The SRB mailing list is a large site, with an archive of messages from the socially responsible business Listserv. This site also links to other socially responsible business information: publications, books, and articles from the *Green Money Journal*; community development loans; FAQs about socially responsible business and investing; and company information.

Jerry Yang on the Future of Yahoo, Filo, and Yang

Yahoo was developed while you two [David Filo and Jerry Yang] were going for your Ph.D.s at Stanford University. Since then, both of you went on "leave" to concentrate your efforts on Yahoo. What are the future plans for yourselves and for Yahoo?

We would like to take Yahoo as far as we can—hoping that the outcome is successful. As for ourselves, for both of us, the next few years will be devoted to making Yahoo successful.

What is the feedback from the people and companies that list their sites on Yahoo? Do they report an increased audience on their Web sites?

For the most part, yes. All the responses that we have heard have been extremely positive.

Socially Responsible Business Organizations

http://www.srb.org:80/orgs.html

This nicely designed and fast-loading site provides a good mix of links to ethics- and human resources-related addresses and business resources. Links to socially responsible sites include environmental legal information, a meta-index for nonprofit organizations, and women and minority sites. In addition, there are energy efficiency and waste management sites. Business-related sites include government resources, business and investing, mailing lists and publications, and Internet etiquette.

Franchising

Do you want to start your own business with a little help from experts? When you're not interested in starting a business from scratch or when you need training in operating a small business, buying a franchise may be the answer. Top franchise companies provide training and equipment, look for financing sources, provide or find a good location, and supply much advice.

In this section, you'll find franchising information: links to franchise companies, an online course on franchising, checklists, articles, and conference schedules.

Franchise Opportunity SuperStore

http://franchise.com

This service provides you with information about franchise opportunities, submits applications to franchise companies, assists with financing, and suggests locations—all free. The company supports itself by producing a franchise guide for about 2,250 franchise companies. You must fill out a questionnaire to use this service and obtain information.

Franchise Table of Contents

http://www.teleport.com/~ryton/fran/tablfran.html

At this site, you will find a very long list of franchise opportunities organized in three levels: categories, subcategories, and franchise names. At the top level, choose from an alphabetically arranged list of 22 categories of franchises: from apparel and accessories to travel businesses. Then select a subcategory to narrow your choice, and, finally, click on the name of a franchise to obtain a list of brief descriptions

How does Yahoo make revenues to pay for the equipment and miscellaneous expense needed in a business?

We will keep Yahoo free for the end user. Therefore, we'll be focusing on developing a sponsorship/advertising program for Yahoo on which advertisers can pay to appear.

Have companies asked you to sell Yahoo? If so, why haven't you sold it?

Several reasons, I guess. We haven't sold it because we didn't really want to part with Yahoo just yet—and we didn't want to work for a larger company at this time.

Have you received offers from investors?

We took on some venture capital investment in April 1995.

---

and to inquire about the franchise. Except for clickable buttons in the left margin, this is an all-text site.

Franchising Links from Kim Software

http://www.strmsoln.com/fransba.htm

This self-paced online workshop on franchising, from the Small Business Administration (SBA), comprises modules that explain franchising, allow you to explore whether franchising is for you, identify the franchiser's responsibilities, describe the franchise package, and explain the typical franchise contract. The appendix contains a small business entrepreneur's checklist.

A bibliography (at http://www.strmsoln.com/franbib.htm) links you to franchise books, documents, and resources and to a list of U.S. Library of Congress publications and books. Franchise Offerings on Web (at http://www.strmsoln.com/franweb.htm) provides 10 links to franchise information or companies that franchise.

Online Franchise Handbook

http://www.franchise1.com/

This commercial site contains a great deal of free information. Here you will find franchise checklists, articles about franchising, trade show listings, and brief news stories about franchising worldwide.

Advertising and Marketing

A substantial number of new businesses fail because of inadequate marketing and advertising. You may have the most unique business in the world, with a product or service that many need, but if you don't make yourself known, you are doomed to failure.

In this section, you can get advice from experienced advertising and marketing experts, learn about marketing over the Internet, and discover links to advertising and marketing agencies.

General Resources

Many advertising agencies no longer specialize in particular industries or specific types of advertising. They also provide marketing, market research, and public relations services. In this section, you'll find sites that provide a variety of links to all types of advertising, marketing, public relations, and market research sites. You'll also find articles and links to academic papers.

Academic Advertising and Public Relations Links

http://sage.cc.purdue.edu/~penkoff/Welcome.html

Professor Diane Penkoff of Purdue University has provided links to interesting communications, public relations, advertising, and writing sites—primarily academic. Topics include computer-mediated communication (CMC); organizational communication, business, and management; public relations, advertising, and journalism; qualitative and quantitative research methods; scholarly and professional organizations; virtual libraries, catalogs and journals; and writing resources.

AdMarket

http://www.AdMarket.com/

This well-designed and attractive site has links to advertising agencies, marketers, public relations firms, organizations, resources, a forum, and archives. The best pages at this site are Advertising Agencies and Resources, especially World

Wide Web Resources. Other categories were rather sparse at the time of this writing.

Advertising and Public Relations (A&PR) Center

http://www.apr.ua.edu/Center.html

This site consists of a long list of links to advertising, marketing, and public relations topics, including academic sites, papers, guides, media research, Internet advertising, advertising agencies, and examples of good World Wide Web sites.

Journalism and Communication Online Classes

http://jcomm.uoregon.edu

At this site, you'll find links to recent and current classes in advertising, marketing, journalism, and communication. Explore classes such as Advanced Editing, Information Gathering, Communication Law, and Online Marketing and Advertising Resources.

Purple Paper on Internet Advertising Messages

gopher://gopher.cni.org:70/11/cniftp/forums/cni-modernization

These archives include many papers and message strings about advertising and marketing on the Internet. Many are related to a paper entitled *Draft "Purple" Paper on Internet Advertising* (gopher://gopher.cni.org/00/cniwg/modernization/adpaper-draft.txt). This is an important site for those who are planning to advertise or are already advertising on the Internet.

Usenet Marketplace FAQ

http://www.phoenix.net/~lildan/FAQ/

At this site, you can learn all about buying and selling on the Usenet Marketplace (the misc.forsale and biz.marketplace newsgroups). Categories of questions include Advertising on the Marketplace, Newsgroup Information and Other Ad Sites, Conducting Transactions over the Internet, Other Frequently Asked Questions, and And, For Your Convenience (other newsgroups' FAQs).

What Public Relations Is All About

http://www.interlog.com/~jjlinden/prsabout.htm

This long text document explains public relations and how public relations firms work for their clients. You can adapt the ideas when publicizing your own organization or decide whether the public relations firm that is working for your company is doing a good job. Headings include:

- Press Agent/Publicity
- How Good Public Relations Works
- Marketing
- Image Management
- A Good Public Relations Company Can Limit the Damage of Negative Publicity
- Event Creation
- Integration into the Total Effort

Yahoo Marketing Pages

http://www.yahoo.com/business/marketing/

Yahoo, the gigantic Internet index, offers links to marketing-related and other sites: from mass-mailing to advertising agencies and from newsletters to lists of Internet resources.

Advertising

There are many advertising resources on the Internet—links to agencies, articles on the right and wrong ways of advertising on the Internet, and the nuts and bolts of establishing an Internet presence. In this section, you'll find links to an established advertising organization, an advertisers' blacklist (with some excellent advice), an advertising agency with pages that you can try to emulate, reports and articles, and many other advertising resources.

Audit Bureau of Circulations (ABC)

http://www.accessabc.com/

ABC, established in 1914, is an organization of 4,225 publishers, advertisers, and advertising agencies. ABC provides audited-circulation information, reports, and services. Click on <u>What's New at ABC</u> to access News Bytes, the organization's press releases. At the time of this writing, the reference library and other sections of this potentially valuable site were under construction.

Blacklist of Internet Advertisers

http://www.cco.caltech.edu/~cbrown/BL/

This site is not only a blacklist of Internet advertisers who have broken the unwritten rules but also a valuable advertising resource—presented with a wry and sometimes sarcastic sense of humor. Articles include how advertisers get on the blacklist, how to deal with commercial junk, what terms such as *spam* (the widespread sending of the same message to many Usenet newsgroups many times) actually mean, and how to advertise on the Internet in an appropriate manner.

The most famous case of "bad advertising" involved the famous green-card lawyers (who shall be nameless here) who were guilty of EMP (Excessive Multi Posting) and then proudly taught others how to follow their example. Other cases involve the person who advertised desktop publishing services to rec.food newsgroups, an

Internet access provider who advertised his services to 792 newsgroups, and the spammer who sometimes wants $5 for removing a recipient from his mailing list.

Chiat Day Idea Factory

http://www.chiatday.com/factory/

This commercial advertising site is worth exploring for its imaginative use of graphics, design, and ideas. Just as a start, you can learn about the principles behind Chiat Day's virtual office (click on Virtual on the home page) and posttelevision media (click on Emerging Media). (See Figure 1.2.)

At this site, you also can get your thought for the day (see Figure 1.3) from Jay Chiat, the head of the firm. Just click on Vision, click on Quotes, and click on the red book, or go to http://www.chiatday.com/cd.www/vision/quote/quote.html and click on the red book.

Figure 1.2 Click on a part of a graphic or on a text link to reveal a new page.

Figure 1.3 Get your thought for the day from Chairman Jay, the head of Chiat Day.

Electronic Billboard on the Digital Superhighway

http://www.cni.org/projects/advertising/www/adpaper.html/

This report by the Coalition for Networked Information covers advertising on the Internet. With quotes from both academics and professionals, the report includes six categories: endorsements, billboards, yellow pages, penny shoppers, newspapers, and junk mail.

How to Advertise on the Internet

gopher://gopher.internet.com:2200/00/News/cmd-ibiz/

This site contains an online article entitled "Advertising and Promoting on the Internet" by Daniel P. Dern, an Internet author and expert. The article is a valuable overview of advertising on the Internet. Topics include:

- Advertising On-Line
- Making Info Available
- How People Get Your Stuff
- Getting the Word Out
- The Usenet
- Is It OK to Advertise on the Internet?
- Some More Final Advice

Internet Advertising with Mercury Center

http://www.sjmercury.com/howtoadv.htm

From the *Mercury*, an Internet newspaper (its home page is http://www.sjmercury.com/), this short article answers questions about advertising on the Internet: Why advertise on the Internet? Doesn't the Internet hate advertising? How do I advertise on the Internet? Who's the audience? Who's using the Internet and how do I audit? Also included is information about advertising in the *Mercury*.

The Internet Advertising Resource Guide

http://www.missouri.edu/internet-advertising-guide.html

This well-designed site provides many links to advertising resources on the Internet. The first set of links contains a bibliography, articles, FAQs on Internet advertising, and messages on the Internet Marketing Discussion List, on the Net-Happenings list, and so on. Other links are arranged by university advertising departments, interactive media (which also includes some nonadvertising business resources), commercial storefronts, directories, and World Wide Web utilities.

Leasing a Server and More

http://union.ncsa.uiuc.edu/HyperNews/get/www/leasing.html

This very useful site provides links to servers, both large and small, on which you can advertise or create a storefront. A typical link includes a brief description of the server and, many times, its address. At some of these sites you can advertise at no charge.

Links to other Internet service providers, Internet presence providers, and other business resources appear at the bottom of this long page.

Marketing

Marketing is the process of evaluating your product's or service's potential customers and planning the best way to approach and win them. Marketing incorporates advertising, research, and evaluating the customer base both now and for the future.

In this section, you will find links to both specific and wide markets, articles to expand your marketing knowledge, information for marketing professionals, direct mail information, examples of good Internet marketing efforts, and much more.

Abbott Wool's Market Segmentation

http://www.asb.com/usr/awool/

This unique site provides lists of links for marketing to particular segments of the U.S. population: African-American, Asian-American, Hispanic, Lifestage, and Lifestyle . A typical page contains resources arranged by category: advertising agencies, research services, marketing services, media, media planning/buying services, and government/academic.

Allen Marketing Group

http://www.allen.com/

At this nicely designed commercial site, you can read useful online articles: How to Market Your Products on the World Wide Web, Generating Quality Leads, Effective Use of Direct Mail, and more. You will also find an in-depth guide to high-tech marketing: Successful High-Tech Marketing.

American Marketing Association (AMA)

http://www.ama.org/hmpage.htm

The AMA site contains a great deal of information for marketing professionals, especially for AMA members. Here you'll find the AMA conference calendar, information about becoming a member, staff names, journals, local chapters, and special interest groups.

Despite the large graphics, these small pages load quickly.

ASI: The Market Research Center

http://www.asiresearch.com/

At this site, you can investigate these marketing topics: Industry News, Free Publications (downloadable documents in Adobe Acrobat format), Market Research Industry, Surveys, and Links to Other Places, which is particularly useful.

Business to Business Marketing Exchange

http://www.btob.wfu.edu/b2b.html

At this site, you will find information about the American Marketing Association (AMA); Business to Business news, conferences, and jobs; business, academic, and other Internet resources; and the Reference Desk, which is a combination of academic and marketing resources.

Some of the links are quite valuable. For example, click on Institute for the Study of Business Markets (ISBM) to learn about ISBM and to link to other business-related sites. Click on Marketing Resources to view a list of links to business resources of all types. When you click on the Media Web Sites link, you'll be able to link to a variety of advertising, television, radio, and other sites.

Direct Mail Guide

http://mainsail.com/dmbook.html

The Direct Mail Guide, by Name-Finders Lists, Inc., is an online book about direct

mail and effectively selecting and using mailing lists. Among the topics are Response Lists, Evaluating a List, Selecting a Mailing List, What is a List Broker, Analysing Test Results, The In-House List, List Management and Maintenance, and a Glossary.

Direct Marketing World

http://mainsail.com/dmworld.htm

At this commercial site are links to all types of marketing resources. Here you will find information about and directories of mailing lists, mailing list resources, advertising agencies, and direct marketing services. Also at this site is a link to Maxwell Sroge Publishing, which offers company profiles and newsletters.

Five Top Internet Marketing Successes

http://arganet.tenagra.com/tenagra/awards.html

This site presents annual awards to the best Internet marketers of the year. Click on a link to see what makes the company a marketing success.

The 1994 winners were Pizza Hut (http://www.pizzahut.com/), id Software (the creators of the game DOOM, at http://doomgate.cs.buffalo.edu/), Netscape Communications Corporation (found at http://home.netscape.com and at http://www.mcom.com), Randy Adams and Bill Rollinson for the Internet Shopping Network (http://internet.net/), Gleason Sackman and Glenn Fleishman for Net-Happenings (http://www.internic.net/internic/lists/net-happenings.html), and the Internet Marketing (http://galaxy.einet.net/hypermail/inet-marketing/) mailing lists.

High-Tech Marketing Communicators (HTMARCOM)

http://www.usa.net/wolfBayne/htmarcom/default.html

HTMARCOM is an e-mail discussion group with plenty of links to Internet marketing resources (click on <u>HTMARCOM Showcase</u>) and a newsletter (<u>HTMARCOM Newsletter</u>).

Note

Be sure to visit the well-designed and unique home page (http://www.usa.net/wolfBayne/) of wolfBayne, the firm that manages this site.

The Internet Marketing Archives

http://www.popco.com/hyper/inet-marketing/

This site reviews and provides information about marketing on the Internet. Click on a range of dates to see the archives for that time period. Then click on the title (link) to read the message or part of the thread. WEB DIAMONDS are new sites.

Be aware that some titles are not really representative of the contents, but if you look around, you'll find some valuable information.

Internet Marketing Blackbook

http://www.legion.com/books/

http://www.gate.net/books/

This commercial site, which advertises the "Internet Marketing Blackbook," presents excerpts that might help you market your product or service. Useful links include <u>The FAQs about Marketing Your Business on the Internet</u>, <u>Internet Marketing Insights</u> (for an essay entitled "Internet Marketing Reality Check"), and <u>Directory of Internet Marketplaces and Web Space Providers</u>.

Internet Marketing Discussion List

http://galaxy.einet.net/hypermail/inet-marketing/

At this site, you can find the archives for the Internet marketing discussion list. You can access information by selecting the current discussion or searching the archives using keywords. Click on <u>General Information</u> to see Frequently Asked Questions (FAQs) for this site.

Marketing on the Internet

http://www.tig.com/IBC/White/Paper.html

This online document describes how a small business can compete with larger businesses using the Internet as a marketing tool. "Chapters" include The Information Superhighway, Changes in Business Communication, Internet Culture and Its Impact on Business, The Three Intermarketing Components, Summary, and Appendix.

Multilevel Marketing (MLM)

http://www.cis.ohio-state.edu/hypertext/faq/usenet/mlm-faq/faq.html

Multilevel, or network, marketing uses many people to sell a product. People are recruited to sell, and they in turn recruit others. Bad MLM is known as a pyramid scheme. However, there are legitimate ways of using MLM to market products.

At this site, you'll find frequently asked questions (FAQs) about multilevel marketing from the alt.business.multilevel newsgroup. Also included is an appendix, a directory of MLMs.

New South Network Services (NSNS) MouseTracks

http://nsns.com/MouseTracks/

This site provides a variety of resources, from the <u>Hall of Malls</u> collection of electronic malls to the <u>List of Marketing Lists</u>, which is composed of marketing-related Internet mailing lists. Of special interest are <u>Nuts and Bolts</u>, which provides links to Internet learning materials, and <u>MetaMarket</u>, which lists marketing companies. It is well worth exploring the resources at NSNS MouseTracks.

Successful Marketing Strategists

http://www.successful.com/cyberinfo.html

This commercial marketing site and each of its pages feature slow-loading graphics. However, don't avoid this site—you can find a great deal of useful information. Just go directly to a page, thereby avoiding as many graphics as you can. Good pages include Articles, Tips & Assessments, and PR in Cyberspace.

Advertising Promotion Products

For those of us who have not completely grown up, attending trade shows and conferences is highlighted by the T-shirts, umbrellas, and other goodies that we can pick up. In this section, you'll learn about some of the advertising promotion products that you can pass on to your customers and potential clients. These online catalogs, for the most part, include illustrations of products, price lists, other product information, and online order forms.

Advantage Solutions

http://www.bestbuys.com/bestbuys/

At this site, you'll not only find advertising promotion products but also you can add your business to Advantage Solutions' Business-to-Business Directory.

Click on Catalog to see a list of products, including alarm clocks, business card items, bath thermometers, calculators, telephone calling cards, keychains, mugs, puzzles, paperweights, pens, T-shirts, and so on. On a typical page, you'll see a complete product description (imprint information, prices, colors, and so on). See Figure 1.4 for an example.

Even/Anna, Ltd.

http://www.ais.net/evenanna/

At the Even/Anna site, you can order promotional products that send your message to potential clients. Even/Anna offers computer-related gifts: mouse pads, disk keyrings, computer mice, a diskette alarm clock, and mugs (see Figure 1.5), each illustrated on these pages. With each product is additional information: prices per quantity, sizes, colors, and other charges.

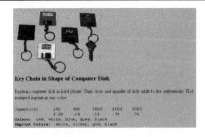

Figure 1.4 You can see a picture of the merchandise and get other product information at this advertising promotion products site.

Figure 1.5 Even/Anna, an advertising promotion products firm, shows its merchandise and product information.

Graphiti

http://libertynet.org/
~graphiti/

With Graphiti's help, you can use your own designs to decorate T-shirts, sweatshirts, tote bags, caps, jackets, mugs, or aprons. At the time of this writing, items must be ordered in quantity (usually at least a dozen), but soon Graphiti will offer single items. Discounts are available on purchases of four items or more.

You can send your graphics to Graphiti via FTP, which then uses a thermal wax-transfer process to print. To place an order, you must have a forms-capable browser. This site does not include illustrations.

Powerhouse Advertising

http://www.infi.net/powerhouse/

Powerhouse Advertising specializes in advertising promotional products, such as coupons, pompoms, and pennants for educational institutions and mugs, auto safety kits, desk sets, and so on for companies (see Figure 1.6). Order information and prices are provided for each item, and you can order online. Although the graphics are large and slow-loading, this site is carefully designed; the background allows you to read the text quite easily.

From this site, you also can access a text page of advertising-related terms. Under each category—adver

tising, art, business, and product—is a list of alphabetically arranged terms described in a phrase or brief sentence.

Figure 1.6 See an illustration of a product before you buy it.

Market Research and Surveys

Many companies are evaluating the size and characteristics of potential customers using the Internet. Now, several academics and commercial firms are surveying those who visit certain commercial sites. In fact, any time you fill in a registration form at a commercial site, you are providing market research information that will, in part, determine the content of new pages.

This small section includes an online survey and links to market research, surveys, and other sites.

World Wide Web User Survey

http://www-survey.cc.gatech.edu/cgi-bin/Entry/

At this site, you'll find the results of the third World Wide Web user survey, including data, graphs, and lists, with more than 13,000 responses to 5 sets of questionnaires for one month in spring 1995. Categories included General Demographics, WWW Browser Usage, Authoring Information, Consumer

Attitudes, and Preferences. All the data at this site is important for those planning to conduct an advertising and/or marketing campaign on the Internet.

Entrepreneurship

According to the experts, an *entrepreneur* is a business person, usually starting a business with his or her own money, thereby remaining independent and in control. Starting a business is difficult, and there are many obstacles to success. Using the resources in this section, you can obtain information about starting a business, keeping it running, and optimizing your effort.

Babson Entrepreneurship Gopher

gopher://gopher.babson.edu:70/11/.entrep

Babson College is a small Boston institution that encourages entrepreneurship. Its Gopher server provides many links to entrepreneurship resources. At this site, you can learn about Babson's Center for Entrepreneurial Studies, and you can link to Entrepreneur Interest Groups and bulletin boards, the Listserv ENTREP-L, and the misc.entrepreneurs and misc.entrepreneurs.moderated newsgroups.

Business Start-Up Information Database

http://galaxy.einet.net/hytelnet/OTH053.html

The Business Start-Up Information Database is a searchable index of information for new businesses: licensing, a checklist for starting up, employment, business development centers, and business financing.

To search, type a search term, and press Enter. The search software rates and ranks the results in the order in which it "agrees" with your query.

Cyberpreneur's Guide to the Internet

http://asa.ugl.lib.umich.edu/chdocs/cyberpreneur/Cyber.html

This text guide features Internet resources for entrepreneurs: an introduction, Listservs, newsgroups, information available through Gopher, and World Wide Web resources. Entries contain name, address, description, and author comments.

You can search this guide using Resources by Tool, links by category, or All Resources, which is an alphabetically arranged list of links at the University of Michigan. Clicking on About This Guide displays a page covering the history of the guide and information about the authors. Click on Related Guides for a short but very useful list of links to business and finance resources on the Internet.

Entrepreneur NET (E-NET)

http://www.cyberzine.org/html/Entrepreneur/enetpage2.html

E-NET provides a long page of links to resources that entrepreneurs and small business operators will find useful. Here you can find links to advertising (both on E-NET and other locations), World Wide Web information servers, tax resources, Usenet and mailing lists, incorporation, online publications, general entrepreneurial sites, government, associations and clubs, Internet, and commercial sites. As of this writing, this site was under construction. Despite some glitches, you can find a great deal of useful information here.

At this site, you can advertise at a very low cost—$15 a month for a page that can include as many as 6,000 bytes of graphics.

The Entrepreneur Network

http://BizServe.com/ten/

http://www.bizserve.com/ten/

The Entrepreneur Network has links to Business Opportunities, New Products wanted,

Public-Sector Resources and Private-Sector Resources, Membership Organizations, and articles on entrepreneurship.

Clicking on Business Opportunities reveals a text list of primarily investment-wanted advertisements. The New Products wanted section lists brokers and manufacturers. Public-Sector Resources, primarily for Ohio and Michigan, includes Small Business Administration, Small Business Development Center (SBDC), Service Corps of Retired Executives (SCORE) offices, government bookstores, and recommended books. The Private-Sector Resources page is composed of technical services and business services offered by both organizations and individuals. The Membership Organizations page lists organizations: names, addresses, and meeting times.

Entrepreneur Network Articles

http://bizserve.com/ten/art.html

At this site, you'll find useful articles or series of articles arranged under these topics: For Aspring Entrepreneurs (7 articles and 1 series), For Aspiring Inventors (13 articles), Marketing & Sales (3 series and 2 articles), and General Business (2 series and 1 article). A typical article is one or two text pages.

Entrepreneurship Gopher (EGOPHER)

gopher://sluava.slu.edu:70/11gopher%24root%3A%5Bdata21._general._entrepreneurship%5D

From St. Louis University comes the Entrepreneurship Gopher (EGOPHER). Click on About EGOPHER and then click on About the SLU Entrepreneurship Gopher to learn all about this site.

To find the Internet Entrepreneur Guide, click on EGOPHER and other Internet Entrepreneur Guides and then click on Internet Entrepreneur Guide. The next page to appear is a document with all types of Internet resources for entrepreneurs and an overview of all the services, forums, and databases for small business people.

Click on Other Guides in Entrepreneurship and Business to reveal entrepreneur and small business guides, bibliographies, resources, lists of Listservs, and other valuable links. Click on Functional & Topical Business Resources on the home page to go to folders of specific information about accounting, finance, management, and so on. This site is rich with information for all types of businesses.

Entrepreneurs on the Web

http://sashimi.wwa.com/ ~notime/eotw/ EOTW.html

At this site, you'll find business information resources as well as available goods and services. Click on Business Information Resources to access links for a variety of information: Entrepreneur Weekly newsletter (this link did not work at the time of this writing), U.S. Patent and Trademark Office, the Legal Information Institute, CommerceNet, Trade Law, Ecash (electronic cash), Law of Electronic Commerce, InterQuote (stock market information), <u>Home Business Solutions</u>, <u>Capital Investors Directory</u>, <u>Stellar Business</u>, <u>Corporate Agents, Inc.</u>, <u>The Internet Business Center</u>, <u>Advertising on the Internet FAQ</u>, <u>Brookfield Economics Institute</u> newsletter, free listings or publicity, laws, <u>A-ha</u> newsletter, <u>IDEAbase</u>, and online support for new business.

MIT Entrepreneurs Club

http://www.mit.edu:8001/activities/e-club/e-club-home.html

At this site, you can obtain all types of information about starting a new business. You can participate in a contest or an e-mail list, attend meetings, and learn about entrepreneurial courses at the Massachusetts Institute of Technology. Also included are links to other business and Internet resources.

San Diego Business Resource Center

gopher://gopher.electriciti.com:70/11/archive/sdbrc

The San Diego Business Resource Center, for California business operators, provides information for those starting new businesses. Included is information about using a fictitious name, getting the seller's and a variety of other permits, computing, paying business tax, hiring the right people, and so on.

Incubators

Incubators, a relatively new phenomenon, provide office space and help for start-up businesses, primarily high-tech. An incubator can provide information about obtaining venture capital and running a business as well as secretarial services and telecommunications hookups. This section provides information about specific incubators as well as a table of World Wide Web addresses for the members of the National Business Incubation Association (NBIA), an international organization.

Incubator Program — Rensselaer Polytechnic Institute

http://www.rpi.edu/dept/incubator/homepage/

This site describes the Incubator Program at Rensselaer Polytechnic Institute (RPI). It has links to information about the program, goals, staff, history, policies, and so on. Be sure to click on <u>Useful Links</u> to access links to venture capital firms, matching companies, directories, and other information.

Long Island High Technology Incubator

http://www.lihti.org/

Started in 1986, the Long Island High Technology Incubator is at the State University of New York (SUNY) Stony Brook campus. Currently, 32 companies are part of the program. At this site, you can get information about the incubator, its management, and its tenants.

One of the outstanding features of this site is the link to regional economic development activities, services, and opportunities. Click on <u>Here</u> to jump to a long page of links under these categories: SUNY Stony Brook, Long Island, New York, small business, biotechnology, general, international, and governmental sites. Note that, under International Items and Federal Agencies, the STAT-USA links are out of date; this service is now by subscription.

North Central Idaho Business Technology Incubator

http://www.fsr.com/
Moscow/business/b/bti/

The North Central Idaho Business Technology Incubator is the host for 15 companies or organizations. This site briefly describes the facility and manages a newsgroup (http://www.moscow.com/news/moscow.html). At the bottom of the page are links to other small business resources: Lexis-Nexis™ Small Business Advisor, National Technology Transfer Center, National Science Foundation, and U.S. government information. Note that the National Trade Data Bank is an old link that cannot be accessed.

The National Business Incubation Association (NBIA), listed under Professional and Membership Organizations on a following page, provides links to incubators. Those having World Wide Web sites are shown in Table 1.1.

Small Business Resources

Perhaps you're an entrepreneur or a franchiser. Or you might be thinking about starting a business. Using the resources in this section, you can decide whether to start a business, or you can obtain training to keep your business successful. If you want your very small business to grow, see the links to Internet resources here.

In this section, you can get the address of your local Small Business Administration (SBA), Small Business Development Center (SBDC), and Service Corps of Retired Executives (SCORE) offices, which can provide great

Table 1.1: Selected National Business Incubation Association (NBIA) Incubators

Incubator	URL	Location
Association of University Related Research Parks (AURRP)	http://www.siue.edu/AURRP/	Tempe, AZ
Austin Technology Incubator	http://www.utexas.edu/depts/ic2/ati.html	Austin, TX
The Ben Craig Center	http://avery.chatweb.org/organizations/bencraig/	Charlotte, NC
Ben Franklin Technology Centers	http://infoserv.rttonet.psu.edu/bf/bf.htm	Pennsylvania
Birmingham Business Assistance Network	http://www.tech-comm.com/customer/bban/bbn0000.html	Birmingham, AL
Boulder Technology Incubator	http://www.metzger.com/bti/	Longmont, CO
Bozeman Technology Incubator	http://bti1.alpinet.net/incubator	Bozeman, MT
Colorado Bio/Medical Venture Center	http://www.frontier.net/MEDMarket/tenants/cobiomed/cobiomed.html	Lakewood, CO
Communications Research Centre Technology Incubator	http://www.crc.doc.ca/crc/innov-clients/innov-e.html	Ottawa, Canada
Cornell Office for Technology Access and Business Assistance	http://www.research.cornell.edu/COTABA.html	Ithaca, NY
Evanston Business & Technology Center	http://www.birl.nwu.edu/RESEARCHPK/1840oak.html	Evanston, IL
Incubadora de Empresas con Base Tecnologica	http://www.cicese.mx/tech/docs/iebt.html	Baja California, Mexico
Instituto de Engenharia de Sistemas e Computadores	http://www.inesc.pt/index-eng.html	Lisbon, Portugal
Manoa Innovation Center	http://www.htdc.org/mic/mic.html/	Honolulu, HI
North Central Idaho Business Technology Incubator	http://www.fsr.com/Moscow/business/b/bti	Moscow, ID
Otaniemi Science Park	http://www.otech.fi	Otaniemi, Finland
Rensselaer Polytechnic Institute Incubator	http://www.rpi.edu/dept/incubator/homepage	Troy, NY
The Turku Technology Center	http://www.utu.fi/org/ttk/	Turku, Finland
Virginia Biotechnology Research Park	http://opal.vcu.edu/html/biomede/vbrp.html	Richmond, VA
Western New York Technology Development Center, Inc.	http://cosmos.ot.buffalo.edu/www__azte/TDC.html	Amherst, NY

(and free) advice and information for a small business; read several articles about running a business; learn about running a business from home; and find out how to deal with the unique problems of running a family-owned business.

Association of Small Business Development Centers Membership Directory

gopher://gopher.sbdc.ba.ttu.edu:70/00gopher__root%3A%5B._ASBDC%5D._Mem

At this site is a text file listing small business development centers (SBDCs), which are sponsored by the U.S. Small Business Administration (SBA) and local colleges and universities. SBDCs provide both one-on-one help and seminars for small and new businesses.

A typical entry at this site includes the state in which the center is located, the name of the director, the sponsoring college or university, address, telephone number, and fax number.

Business Advice Articles

http://www.mit.edu:8001/activities/e-club/articles.html/

For small business owners and entrepreneurs, here are eight useful articles by Joe Hadzima of Sullivan & Worcester:

- ◆ A Little Advice on Advising: Three Models of Success Will Help

- ◆ Beware Capital-Gains Gift: New Companies Should Take Care

- ◆ Questions of Copyright: Another Weapon in Property Arsenal

- ◆ Paying the Founding Piper: It's Not As Simple As Writing a Check

- ◆ Leasing Tips

- ◆ The Importance of Patents: It Pays to Know Patent Regulations

- ◆ Pinpointing That Critical Entrepreneurial Spark

- ◆ Of Kleenex and Cheez Whiz: Trademarks Are Nothing to Sneeze At

Business Resource Center

http://www.kciLink.com/brc/

Khera Communications presents links to text articles about business, especially good for start-ups. This is a good source of marketing and management information.

At this site, you will find links to the Government Contractor Newsletter (http://www.govcon.com/periodicals/contractor), Government Contractor Glossary (http://www.govcon.com/information/gcterms.html), two professional associations, and total quality management (http://www.dbainc.com/dba/).

Home Business Solutions

http://netmar.com:80/mall/shops/solution/

The main focus of this site is on businesses that you can start at home and solutions for home-based businesses. This is a commercial site, but you can get free information if you look around.

Links include Advertising and Marketing Solutions, Financial Solutions, Business Resource Solutions, Services, Business Reports, and Business Shareware, which provides business-related shareware that you can buy for $4.95 a disk for IBM-compatible computers.

IDEAS DIGEST

http://www.ideas.wis.net/contents.html

This is an online small business center that provides articles and forums for learning how to use your ideas to succeed and innovate.

The very useful feature articles, which are one or two pages, treat topics such as protecting trademarks, how to name products, and using video for marketing. Other categories at this site include Experts Online—Resource Center, INNO-LINKS: Worldwide Innovation Links, Young Inventors' Fair Society, and NEW...IDEAS MART, the path to the online magazine. Once you are on the NEW...IDEAS MART page, you can access Feature Articles, Inventors Corner, Calendar of Events, Action in the News, and Classified Ideas.

help you choose an appropriate business that matches your past experience.

To find your closest SCORE office, click on the map. Then either click on the next map or select an item from the menu: local Small Business Administration (SBA) offices, calendar of events, Small Business Development Centers (SBDCs), small business investment companies and loan participants, information centers, and disaster area offices.

Information for Emerging and Family-Owned Businesses

http://www.netmarquee.com/

At this site, you'll find a variety of information about running a new or family-owned business. Every two weeks, you can read a column by Paul I. Karofsky, director of the Northeastern University Center for Family Business, read about recent conferences and events, and access a library and other Internet resources. To take full advantage of this free site, you must register.

Service Corps of Retired Executives (SCORE)

http://www.sbaonline.sba.gov/regions/regionmap.html

SCORE is composed of volunteers who have varied backgrounds in executive work and are now retired. SCORE volunteers can help solve your business problems, plan your next strategy, or even

What Is an Internet Address?

An address on the Internet may not make any sense to you at first, but it is very logical when broken into its individual components. For example, one of my addresses is 73510.3154@compuserve.com.

Component	What it is
73510.3154	The name that identifies me to the network, in this case, CompuServe. Many networks assign a name or allow you to choose one (for example, eddygrp, jimstock, or sheila55).
@	Located at
compuserve	The Internet service provider
com	Its domain (see the next sidebar)

When you string an address together, each component is separated from the next with a period (in Internet-speak, a *dot*). Some addresses consist of more elements. For example, companies or educational institutions can have more than one location at an address. Each location is known as a *server*. Typically, a server is a single computer or workstation. However, several servers can be located on a specific computer. For example, if an organization provides both World Wide Web and Gopher sites, each can be a server. Or, a university can provide one or more servers for each of its departments.

Underlying the names in the address are IP (Internet Protocol) addresses, which consist of 4-byte fields of 32 bits. A *bit*, or a binary digit, is the 0 (off) or 1 (on) in computer instructions; a *byte* is a grouping of 8 bits. So, for example, holonet.net's actual IP address is 157.151.129.196, and sover.net's is 204.71.16.10. Since it's easier for humans to remember names, most Internet sites use names rather than IP addresses.

Small Business Administration WWW Site

http://www.sbaonline.sba.gov

gopher://www.sbaonline.sba.gov/11/

The Small Business Administration (SBA) home pages—both World Wide Web and Gopher—include links to pages listing SBA offices, Business Information Centers, SBA Disaster Area Offices, Service Corps of Retired Executives (SCORE), Small Business Development Centers, Small Business Investment Companies, and Veterans Affairs Offices. Also included are training aids, SBA publications, loan programs, calendars of events, and approved lenders. A special feature at this site is a list of major government contractors seeking subcontractors. Here you can read federal acts and regulations, learn about classes and events at SBA offices, and get FTP access to the SBA Online Bulletin Board. You also can obtain local information (SBA offices, business information centers, cal-

endars of events, certified-preferred lenders, microloan lender participants, and much more).

Small Business Advancement National Center (SBANC)

http://www.sbaer.uca.edu/

This site contains small business links: Small Business Advancement Electronic Resource, a Gopher site, an FTP server, and links to the SBANC newsletters. Here you will find links to proceedings containing papers on small business.

At this site, you have the choice of going to graphical or nongraphical pages.

Small Business Publications

http://www.gsa.gov/staff/pa/cic/smbuss.htm

From the Consumer Information Center, you can order five free or inexpensive short publications for small business:

◆ Basic Facts About Registering a Trademark

◆ General Information Concerning Patents

◆ Guide to Business Credit for Women, Minorities, and Small Businesses

◆ Reporting and Disclosure Guide for Employee Benefit Plans

◆ Small Business Handbook

Small Business Resource Center

http://www.webcom.com/~seaquest/welcome.html

At this commercial site, you will find online text reports about starting a small business and links to business resources on the World Wide Web.

The online reports (about 30 at the time I visited) are about writing business plans, raising money, buying a franchise, running a home business, starting and operating particular businesses, surviving as a businessperson,

---

Interesting Site

If you are into computer and video games, you'll want to visit Games Domain (at http://www.gamesdomain.co.uk/). According to information on the home page, this well-designed site was accessed more than 2 million times in the first eight months of 1995. It provides all types of information for all types of games. Use the FAQ (frequently asked questions) to get started; win games software in the Competition area; read the *GD Review*, an online gaming magazine that is updated daily; and visit Direct Download, from which you can download games, patches, and demos. In addition, you can access Games Information, which points to FAQs, strategies, Internet sites, online magazines, and gaming company sites, and Games Programming, which discusses how games are programmed.

advertising without paying, selling, and getting public-ity. A typical report concludes with links to reviews of books that you can order at this site.

smallbizNet: The Edward Lowe Small Business Network

http://www.lowe.org/

At this site, entrepreneurs, small-business owners, and consultants can obtain impor-tant information, usually for a fee, that will help their businesses grow. The founder, Henry Edward Lowe, who invented KittyLitter®, wants other entrepreneurs to "bring down the brick walls" that prevent success.

Click on smallbizNet SERVICES to display a table of contents from which you can access a variety of small-business information: databases (full-text searching and business periodicals), a bulletin board (BBS), a fax-on-demand system, links to other business resources, and a feature in which you can ask a human being a reference question.

Tucson's Small Business Financial Info Guide

gopher://econ.tucson.az.us:70/11/biz/

The Small Business Financial Info Guide provides links to both national and Arizona economic information, including Economics and Business from the Library of Congress, foreign exchange rates, the text of the North American Free Trade Agreement (NAFTA), the Arizona State University Economic Database (all Arizona information), Tucson area business directories, and the City of Tucson's Small Business Financial Info Guide. Note that some links at this site are old and no longer work.

Yahoo Small Business Resources

http://www.yahoo.com/Business/Small_Business_Information/

At this site, you'll find links to information and commercial sites for small businesses.

Among the links are entrepreneurial organizations and information about business opportunities, conferences, franchises, home offices, publications, and more. As always, Yahoo is a good starting point for any Internet search.

Package Delivery Services

As a small-business person, on average I send or receive one or two packages a week. Large organizations give the package delivery companies a great deal of busi-ness—not only within the borders of the U.S. but also around the world. The entries in this section cover major commercial U.S. package delivery services, the U.S. Post Office, and the Canada Post Corporation.

Canada Post Corporation

http://www.canpost.ca/english/enghome.html

"Canada Post Corporation (Société canadi-enne des postes) provides postal services to over 28 million Canadians, 900,000 businesses, and most public institutions." This large, well-designed site (see Figure 1.7), with both English and French pages, provides a variety of services and information: What's New, Postal Code Lookup, Postal Services, Post Rates, For the Collector, Post Office Locations, Electronic Services, Sales and Services, Business Centre, Direct Marketing Centre, Corporate Overview, and Hot Links. Clicking on Postal Services provides a list of links to ser-vices along with a brief description of each. The Hot Links page provides links to Internet search engines and other postal services (in the U.S. and Japan, and a link to Stamp Collecting Hot Links) and links to the Yahoo government page, City Net, and government depart-ments and agencies in Canada, the U.S., and Japan.

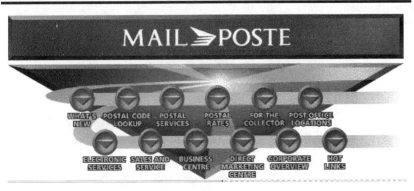

Figure 1.7 Click on a button to obtain information about the Canada Post Corporation and its offices.

DHL Worldwide Express

http://www.dhl.com/

This corporate home page provides information about DHL, which was started in 1969 by Adrian Dalsey, Larry Hillblom, and Robert Lynn, the D, H, and L of the company. Click on Using DHL to find out how to use DHL's services to ship packages internationally. You can choose a particular company by selecting a country from a list of regions and countries (click on Choose a Country) or by clicking on part of a map (click on View by Map). After selecting a country, you can view a list of national holidays and information about local DHL offices.

FedEx

http://www.fedex.com/cgi-bin/track_it/

The well-designed and attractive FedEx site provides company information, downloadable tracking and airbill preparation software, and online tracking. Click on Info Central to open a page with a table of contents for the site.

You can track a FedEx package quite easily. Click on Services Online on the home page, and then click on Track a FedEx Package. Then type the package tracking number (found at the upper right corner of the airbill) in the text box, select the destination country, and click on the Send Request button (see Figure 1.8). A new page opens, showing the final disposition of the package and all its stops from the drop-off point to the delivery site.

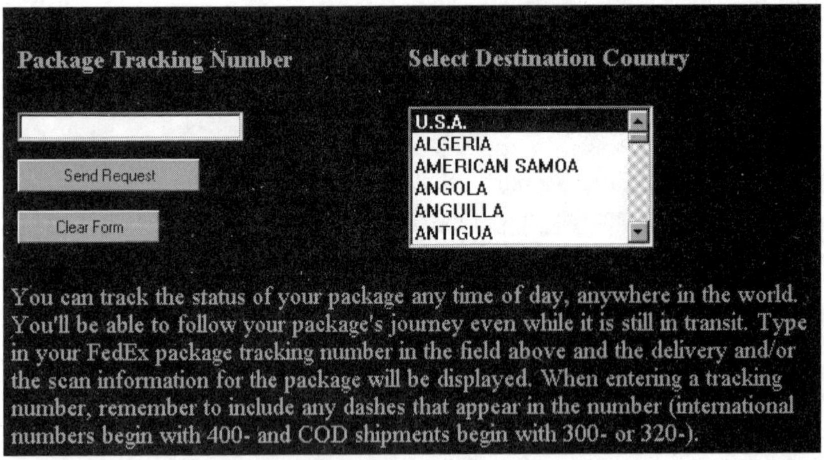

Roadway Online

http://www.roadway.com/rps/prf_rps.htm

Roadway Online is the home page of Roadway Services, Inc., the parent organization of Roadway Express, Roberts Express, and the Roadway Package System. Perhaps the best known of these, "Roadway Package System (RPS) serves customers in the small-package market throughout North America."

Package Tracking Number

Select Destination Country

U.S.A.
ALGERIA
AMERICAN SAMOA
ANGOLA
ANGUILLA
ANTIGUA

Send Request

Clear Form

You can track the status of your package any time of day, anywhere in the world. You'll be able to follow your package's journey even while it is still in transit. Type in your FedEx package tracking number in the field above and the delivery and/or the scan information for the package will be displayed. When entering a tracking number, remember to include any dashes that appear in the number (international numbers begin with 400- and COD shipments begin with 300- or 320-).

Figure 1.8 Fill in the online form to trace a FedEx package.

To access the RPS page, click on <u>About Roadway Package System</u> or the RPS graphic on any page at this site. The RPS page, which includes an overview and description of services, also includes a link to <u>RPS ACCESS</u>, information about Windows-based package-tracking software that you can order if you are a customer of Roadway Services.

United Parcel Service (UPS)

http://www.ups.com/

At the good-looking and informative UPS site, you can learn about the company, read press releases, and get packaging tips.

Of particular interest is <u>Using UPS</u>, which provides the <u>Quick Cost Calculator</u>, <u>UPS Service Mapping</u>, <u>Ground Time in Transit Estimator</u>, and <u>Package Tracking</u>. Here, you also can access service guides for the U.S. and Canada and download tracking software that runs under Windows or the Macintosh.

To track a package, click on <u>Package Tracking</u>, type the tracking number in the text box, and click on the Track This Package button.

United States Postal Service

http://www.usps.gov/

The United States Postal Service, Internet Branch, online branch office offers several services: <u>Today's Features</u>, <u>Your Post Office</u>, <u>The Business Section</u>, and <u>F.Y.I.</u> (For Your Information). The text menu, at the bottom of the home page, is more informative than the graphic links at the top of the page. So scroll down and click on a link at the bottom of the page. For example, under <u>Your Post Office</u>, you can look up zip codes, get the latest postage rates, and find other consumer information. In the <u>Business Section</u>, you can download business forms, view business publications, and learn about opportunities selling to the Postal Service. Through the <u>Postal Information Locator</u> in the F.Y.I. section, you can link to a zip code directory and state abbreviations list. This site is well worth exploring for its information and services.

Note
Look in the *Human Resources* chapter for information about zip codes and other mailing codes throughout the world.

Incorporation

Part of growing a business should be to investigate the types of corporate structures and determine whether your firm should be a sole proprietorship, partnership, or corporation. Each has advantages and disadvantages.

In this small section are two commercial sites that can answer corporate structure questions and, if you decide to incorporate, quickly provide that service.

The Company Corporation

http://www.service.com/tcc/

The Company Corporation, located in Delaware, one of the most popular states in which to incorporate, incorporates your business in 48 hours or less. Also included at this site are articles on incorporation and corporate structures, a price list, and a list of Internet-based business resources.

Corporate Agents, Inc.

http://www.corporate.com/

This commercial site, run by a company that specializes in setting up corporations, provides articles about the advantages and disadvantages of incorporating, the types of corporations, and how to incorporate.

If you want to incorporate, you can fill in a comprehensive form using a Web browser that supports forms.

Interesting Sites

After you have used the Internet for a while, you know that you can find any type of information—sometimes too much. For example, look for information about movies, and soon you'll locate many sites. Two of the best are The Internet Movie Database (at http://www .msstate.edu/Movies or http://www.cm.cf.ac.uk/Movies/) and Clamen's Movie Information Collection (at http://www-cgi.cs.cmu.edu/afs/cs.cmu.edu/ user/clamen/misc/movies/README.html). Each of these sites provides links to many other movie sites. So if you want to read a variety of reviews about films or videos before seeing them, visit these two sites regularly.

If you are willing to wait for a gigantic graphic to load, The Buena Vista MoviePlex from Walt Disney (at http://bvp .wdp.com/MoviePlex/MooVPlex.html?LO=D&GL=V) is a highly commercial but sometimes entertaining site. From the home page (see Figure 1.9), click on the Press Room icon to see film clips in Quick Time format or learn more about a particular new Disney film. Click on the question mark icon to answer technical questions about this site, to link to sources of World Wide Web browsers, or to download a test version of Apple's Quick Time for Windows, a JPEG (graphics) viewer, and other helpful software.

Other film-related and worthwhile Internet sites are Early Motion Pictures (http://lcweb2.loc.gov/papr/mpixhome.html), Film and Theatrical Web Links (http://www.catalog .com/media/sd/film.html), and the Mirror Movie Guide (http://mirror.wwa.com/mirror/reviews/movies/ guide.htm).

Figure 1.9 Click on the marquee to go to a particular movie page.

Prices are listed at the bottom of the form. After you send your form (just click on the Send button), Corporate Agents will send you a corporate kit.

Management Skills

Successfully running a business requires organizing your time, planning ahead, and a lot of good luck. Starting a business or running a department for a "lean, mean" firm adds to the pressure, filling up all your time and forcing you to work day by day. To work efficiently, use the resources in this section. The first entry provides links to many management ideas and information; the other two cover project management.

100 Rules for Project Managers

http://pscinfo.pscni.nasa.gov/ online/msfc/project_mgmt/ 100_Rules.html

This worthwhile site presents 100 rules for NASA Project Managers, compiled by Jerry Madden, the Associate Director of the Flight Projects Directorate at NASA's Goddard Space Flight Center. At the top of the page is a table of contents from which you can select a link in order to jump to that topic on this long page. Among the topics are The Customer, Decisionmaking, Professional Ethics and Integrity, Project Management and Teamwork, and <u>Treating and Avoiding Failures</u>. Probably the best way to use this site is to scroll down the page, reading rules as you go.

Decision/Risk On-Line Resources

http://www.lumina.com/DA/

When making a business or personal decision, you must analyze the risks and the benefits. This large site provides many Decision Sciences resources—from educational institutions, organizations, laboratories, and private businesses. Some links provide papers and reports, software, publications, and sources of help.

The Management Archive

gopher://ursus.jun.alaska.edu/

This difficult-to-reach site provides academically related management ideas and information of all kinds: working papers and preprints in management and organizational sciences, recent calls for papers, course syllabi, teaching materials, conference announcements, archives of the Academy of Management, and management-related discussion lists.

Planning and Scheduling Benchmarks

http://www.neosoft.com/~benchmrx/

This online document discusses project scheduling based on large-scale assembly, but you can apply its 12 downloadable problems to your own projects. After the introduction, the document contains these headings: The Focus, The Challenge, The Physical Problem, and The Data File. At the bottom of the page are links to the downloadable files (in PostScript, ASCII, and Microsoft Word formats), an ASCII data set, and C++ programs that read and write

Domains

Domains are two- or three-character specifications of the type of organization or the region in which the organization is located.

Domain name	What it is
com	commercial organization (for example, a corporation or company)
edu	educational institution (for example, a college, university, or secondary school)
gov	government unit (for example, the White House or a city department)
int	international organization (this is quite rare)
mil	military unit (for example, an Air Force base or research office)
net	networking organization (for example, an Internet service provider)
org	nonprofit organization (for example, The Internet Society or Electronic Frontier Foundation)

Sometimes, domains are abbreviated to two-character codes, especially when followed by an international domain code (see Table 1.2). For example, an educational institution in Japan may be identified as ac.jp, where ac represents academic institution and jp identifies Japan. Or, an organization in Thailand ends with the codes .or.th. See Table 1.2 for more information about international and regional domains.

routines in the data set. Some problems have been solved; so you can compare your results with those.

Project Management Glossary

http://www.wst.com/projplan/proj-plan.glossary.html

This long, single-page document is a useful guide to project-management terminology. Some links send you to the top of the page rather than to a term; if this happens, simply scroll down the list.

Table 1.2: International and Regional Domains

Domain	Where it is	Domain	Where it is
am	Armenia	it	Italy
ar	Argentina	jp	Japan
au	Australia	kr	South Korea
at	Austria	kw	Kuwait
be	Belgium	lu	Luxembourg
bm	Bermuda	lv	Latvia
br	Brazil	mx	Mexico
ca	Canada (although California, U.S. is .ca.us)	my	Malaysia
ch	Switzerland (Confoederatio Helvetia)	nl	The Netherlands
cl	Chile	no	Norway
cn	China	nz	New Zealand
co	Colombia	pe	Peru
cr	Costa Rica	ph	Philippines
cz	Czech Republic	pl	Poland
de	Germany (Deutschland)	pt	Portugal
dk	Denmark	ro	Romania
ee	Estonia	ru	Russia
eg	Egypt	se	Sweden
es	Spain (España)	sg	Singapore
fi	Finland	si	Slovenia
fr	France	sk	Slovakia
gr	Greece	su	Soviet Union (mostly Russian sites)
hk	Hong Kong	th	Thailand
hu	Hungary	tr	Turkey
id	Indonesia	tw	Taiwan
ie	Northern Ireland	uk	United Kingdom
il	Israel	us	United States
is	Iceland	za	South Africa

World Wide Project Management

http://www.idt.unit.no:80/~njaals/PS2000/Home/welcome.html

The World Wide Project Management site presents a variety of project management information and resources: information about PS 2000 (a research and development program based in Norway), project management software and associated parent companies, and links to other project management sites.

WWW Project Management Forum

http://www.synapse.net/~loday/PMForum/contents.htm

This site contains many project management and other business links in one place. The major headings under which you will find links are Project Management Resources, Communications/Information Sharing, Cyberia (that is, cyberspace matters), and User Input (posting to the forum and the forum evaluation sheet). Click on a subheading under a major heading to reveal a page of links. To get the true value from this site, thoroughly explore the links in your area of interest.

Organizations and Associations

One of the best ways to get new ideas for running a business or doing a better job or to interact with colleagues or peers is to be an active member of an organization. This section provides information about many organizations that have established Internet sites. Here you'll find organizations for all types of people, from engineers to advertising executives, from scientists to feminists to graphic artists.

At the top of this section, you'll find organizations with interesting or important links. The remaining part of the section is composed of a table of many organizations, their Internet addresses, and the major links on each home page.

American Communication Association (ACA)

http://cavern.uark.edu/comminfo/www/ACA.html

The ACA is an organization of "students and practitioners in the field of communication studies." It is concerned with communications law, including academic freedom, copyright and intellectual property, human rights, freedom of speech and information, and privacy rights.

Also at this site is a gigantic electronic reference desk with links to many bookstores, communications departments, libraries and archives, online books, reference resources, and so on. This section, by itself, is well worth your visit to this site.

AutomationNET Technical Society PhoneList

http://www.automationnet.com/associat.htm

At this site, you can find engineering and technical associations. Each entry includes a telephone number, fax number, and sometimes an e-mail or World Wide Web address.

Helpful Organizations for Professional Writers

http://www.cloud9.net/~kvivian/proforgs.html

At this site, which was very much under construction at the time of this writing, are links to organizations that can help professional writers one way or another. Here you'll find links to the International Association of Business Communicators (IABC), National Writers' Union (NWU), International Women Writers' Guild (IWWG), Society for Technical Communication, American Marketing Association, Women in Communications (WICI), Public Relations Society of America (PRSA), International Public Relations Association (IPRA), the Alliance for Computers and Writing (ACW), Association of Teachers of Technical Writing (ATTW), Society of Professional

Writers (an empty page at the time of this writing), Broadcast Professionals Forum, American Society of Journalists and Authors, and the Conference Board.

International Organization for Standardization (ISO)

http://www.iso.ch/

The home page for the ISO explains the organization, its structure, and membership—in both English and French. Click on Your Guide to ISO Online to learn about this site. The ISO catalogue is a page from which you can order books and other materials. Click on How to Use the Catalogue to access an index in which you can enter keywords to find ISO publications. The ISO 9000 Forum provides information about quality management and quality assurance. Note that you can find other quality entries in the Quality Assurance section of the *Engineering and Manufacturing* chapter.

The Internet NonProfit Center

http://www.human.com:80/inc/

At this site, you can link to many nonprofit and human rights organizations, arranged alphabetically, geographically, or according to purpose. When you link to an organization, you can read, in a staff member's own words, an abstract of its work. In addition, you can add your own nonprofit organization to the "gallery of self-portraits."

National Business Incubation Association (NBIA)

http://ra.cs.ohiou.edu/gopher/dept.servers/aern/homepage/nbia.html

Business incubators are buildings and business parks in which new businesses can get a good start.

An incubator's management typically provides advice, management services, and sometimes office staff and other resources. The NBIA is an international organization of business incubators.

The NBIA's long page is packed with links, not only to the association, its mission, and services, but also to conferences and meetings, the member incubators (more than 50 at the time of this writing), and other organizations. Table 1.2, in the *Small Business Resources* section of this chapter, lists incubators and their Internet addresses.

Web-sters Net-work

http://lucien.SIMS.berkeley.edu/women_in_it.html

At this site for Women in Information Technology, you can learn about women in information technology, engineering, and computer science. Note that the large home page graphic takes a while to load. One of the best features at this site is a group of links to other Internet sites for women and technology.

Who Cares Resource Directory

http://www.whocares.org/resources/rsrcdir.html

The Who Cares, Inc. site provides a searchable index and a list of many organizations that offer support to social programs. Organizations include NOW, Greenpeace, ACLU, National Audubon Society, and so on. Each entry includes the name of the organization, its address, and telephone numbers.

Table 1.3 is composed of selected professional and membership organizations that have Internet sites. Each entry includes the name of the organization, its URL, a brief description, and its major links. As a rule, many organizations not only provide detailed information about themselves and their members but also include links to valuable Internet resources.

Table 1.3: Selected Professional and Membership Organizations on the Internet

Organization	URL	Description	Major Links
Academy of Family Mediators	gopher://gopher.igc.apc.org:70/00/orgs/afm/1	An educational organization that supports professional and public mediation education; founded in 1981; about 2,500 members.	AFM Brochure, Joining the Academy, AFM Membership Application, AFM Resources, AFM Educational and Marketing Products
The Acoustical Society of America	http://asa.aip.org/	"Increase and diffuse the knowledge of acoustics and promote its practical applications"; founded in 1929.	Audio Samples, An Introduction to the Society, A Brief History of the Society, Future Meetings of the Society, Abstracts, Membership Information, Technical Committees and Technical Groups, Regional Chapters, Awards and Fellowships, Sustaining Members of the Society, Officers, Members of the Executive Council, Members of the Technical Council, Office Staff, Publications, Acoustical Standards, More about the Society, An Introduction to Acoustics and Sound, Links to Other Sites of Interest to Acousticians
AFL-CIO	http://www.aflcio.org/	"A federation of 79 labor unions representing some 13.6 million working men and women."	AFL-CIO Policy Statements, Press Releases, Boycott List, Organizing Institute, Stand UP Campaign, News On-Line, Links to other Internet Resources
Alaska Wilderness League	gopher://gopher.igc.apc.org:70/0ftp%3Aftp.igc apc.org@/pub/orgs_on_igc/awl	An environmental organization serving as a "watchdog on Alaskan environmental issues."	A text page of information
American Association for Artificial Intelligence	http://www.aaai.org/	"A nonprofit scientific society devoted to the promotion and advancement of artificial intelligence."	Descriptive Contents of This Web Site, AAAI Membership and Programs, AI Resources

Table 1.3: Selected Professional and Membership Organizations on the Internet (continued)

Organization	URL	Description	Major Links
American Association for the Advancement of Science	http://www.aaas.org/	"A nonprofit professional society dedicated to the advancement of scientific and technological excellence across all disciplines"; founded in 1848; more than 143,000 members throughout the world.	AAAS Information, Membership, Science, Science's Next Wave, Focus on Science Journalism as an Alternative Career, Next Wave Correspondents Network, Education & Human Resources, Kinetic City Super Crew, Science & Policy, Latest Data on Congressional Appropriations for R&D, International Directorate, Project 2061, News & Information, Meetings Information, AAAS Headquarters Information, AAAS Affiliate Information, Washington, D.C., Information
The American Association for the Advancement of Science (AAAS)	gopher://aaas.org/	Furthers the work of scientists, engineers, science educators, policymakers, facilitating cooperation, fostering scientific freedom; more than 134,000 members; founded in 1848.	Welcome, About AAAS, Directorates and Program Activities, Meetings, Membership, Publications, SCIENCE Magazine, Affiliate Gopher Servers and Other Server Connections, Telephone Directories and Other Services
American Association of Advertising Agencies (AAAA)	http://www.commercepark.com/AAAA/AAAA.html	The "national trade organization representing the advertising agency business." Founded in 1917, AAAA is composed of advertising agencies that represent about 75 percent of the advertising volume in the United States.	Fourteen reasons for choosing an A.A.A.A. agency, Benefits of Membership, Fact Sheet, Member Services, Washington, Roster of Members, Publications (The cost of publications ranges from free to more than $100), Federal Trade Commission, Better Business Bureau, Backchannel newsletter, Calendar of Upcoming A.A.A.A. Events

Table 1.3: Selected Professional and Membership Organizations on the Internet (continued)

Organization	URL	Description	Major Links
American Astronomical Society (AAS)	http://www.aas.org	"The major professional organization in North America for astronomers and other scientists and individuals interested in astronomy."	What's New, Committees, Council, Divisions, Education, Astrophysical Journal On-Line, Electronic Publishing Projects, FTP Archive, Grants Program, Job Register, Meeting Information, Membership, Other Astronomical Resources, Publications, Public Policy, Feedback Form
American Automatic Control Council (AACC)	http://web.eecs.nwu.edu/~ahaddad/aacc.html	"An association of the control systems divisions of seven member societies" and the U.S. member of IFAC (International Federation of Automatic Control)	ACC Conferences, AACC, IFAC, About the AACC
American Bar Association (ABA)	http://www.abanet.org/home.html	The organization for attorneys-at-law.	What's New, About the ABA, Events & Education, LAWlink, Technology, ABA Entities, Public Information, ABA Store (You can find many other law resources in the Law and Government chapter of this book.)
The American Ceramics Society	http://www.acers.org/	An organization of ceramic professionals in the U.S.	Contact ACerS, E-Mail ACerS, Ceramic Bulletin, Advertising, Book Sales, Ceramic Information Center, Meetings and Calendar, Expositions, Rental Lists, Ceramic Correspondence Institute (CCI), Ceramic Futures Employment Database, Precollege Education Program, Press Kit, Membership
American Chemical Society	http://www.acs.org/	The "world's largest scientific society" has 150,000 members—chemists and chemical engineers.	About the American Chemical Society, Chemical Abstracts Service, ACS Departments and Services, New on ACSWeb, Event Calendars, Search the ACSWeb

Table 1.3: Selected Professional and Membership Organizations on the Internet (continued)

Organization	URL	Description	Major Links
American College Personnel Association	http://www.acpa.nche.edu/	An organization of professional student affairs educators.	American College Personnel Association, ACPA Member Benefits, Convention 1996, Publications, Teleconferences, Specialty Conferences, Regional Workshops, Commissions, Standing Committees, State Divisions of ACPA, Other Internet Resources
American Electronics Association	http://www.aeanet.org/	A trade organization of the technology industry; founded in 1943; comprises 3,000 member companies.	About AEA, Public Policy, Hot News, Members, AEA Offices, Calendar of Events, Programs & Conferences, Publications, Services (Note: These are not links, but headings. Links are found under these headings.)
American Foundation for the Blind (AFB)	gopher://gopher.afb.org:5005	A nonprofit organization, which is a "leading national resource for people who are blind or visually impaired; the organizations that service them, and the general public"; founded in 1921.	About the American Foundation for the Blind (AFB), AFB Information Center, AFB Technology Center, AFB Press: Journal of Visual Impairment & Blindness, Literacy for People Who are Blind or Visually Impaired, Governmental Relations Group, Policy and Position Papers, Research and Technical Reports, Connections to Other Internet Resources
American Geophysical Union (AGU)	http://earth.agu.org/kosmos/homepage.html	An international scientific society with more than 32,000 members in more than 115 countries; founded in the mid-1920s.	News and Announcements, Science and Society, Meetings, Publications, Inside AGU
American Institute of Aeronautics and Astronautics (AIAA)	http://www.lmsc.lockheed.com/aiaa/sf/home.html or http://www-leland.stanford.edu:80/group/aiaa/national/	"A national professional society with over 34,000 members serving the aerospace engineering community." The AIAA "addresses the needs of scientists, engineers, and allied professionals who conceive, design, develop, test, construct, and operate air and space vehicles."	National General Information, Membership Information, Meeting Information, Publication Information, AIAA Regional and Student Chapters, Places that Specialize in Related Links, Other Links, Searching the Web

Table 1.3: Selected Professional and Membership Organizations on the Internet (continued)

Organization	URL	Description	Major Links
American Institute of Biological Sciences (AIBS)	gopher://aibs.org/	"Provides the biological sciences community national representation on pressing public issues involving biological considerations, enhances biological education and research, and improves interactions among biology societies and disciplines"; founded in 1947 as part of the National Academy of Sciences; more than 80,000 members.	Welcome to the AIBS, AIBS-Mission and Goals, 1995-2000 AIBS ACTION PLAN, AIBS Office/Staff Directory/Telephones/E-Mail Addresses, AIBS Officers/Board of Directors, Membership Information, Membership Directory, AIBS 1995 Council, Committees, Corporate Sponsors, Delegates to Other Organizations
American Institute of Chemical Engineers (AIChE)	http://www.che.ufl.edu/aiche/	"Provides leadership in advancing the chemical engineering profession" and "promotes excellence in the development and practice of chemical engineering"; founded in 1908.	Welcome to AIChE (Mission Statement, History, Headquarters Operations, How to Contact the AIChE), Announcements, Programs and Activities, Open Discussion Forums, Web Spinners Corner, Guest Book, Related Webs
American Institute of Graphic Arts (AIGA)	http://www.dol.com/AIGA/	The "national non-profit organization that promotes excellence in graphic design"; founded in 1914.	Welcome to AIGAlink, What is AIGAlink?, AIGA, Events, Gallery
American Institute of Mining, Metallurgical, and Petroleum Engineers (AIME)	http://www.tms.org/AIME/AIME.html	A "leader in the exploration, extraction, and production of the Earth's minerals, materials, and energy resources"; founded in 1871.	What is AIME, History, Organization and Activities, Honors and Awards, WAAIME, For More Information

Table 1.3: Selected Professional and Membership Organizations on the Internet (continued)

Organization	URL	Description	Major Links
The American Institute of Physics (AIP)	http://aip.org/	A membership corporation that promotes the "advancement and diffusion of the knowledge of physics and its application to human welfare"; founded in 1931.	New and Different, Announcements, AIP, The 1994 AIP Annual Report, The AIP Corporate Associates HomePage, AIP Press, Archival Journals, Translations Program, Computers in Physics, The Industrial Physicist, Physics Today, Announcement & New Developments, Author Services, Publishing Services, Applied Physics Letters Online, PINET (Physics Information Network), Subscribe Online, Electronic Newsletters, Gopher, FTP, Electronic Products (SPIN Bibliographic Database, etc.), Jobs, Physics Career Bulletin Board, Center for History of Physics Newsletter, Congressional Science Fellowships, Inside Science, Links, Search the WWW, Positions, Contact
American Mathematical Society	http://e-math.ams.org/	A membership organization for research mathematicians, publishes results of mathematical research.	Frequently Used Services, e-MATH Update, List of Services, About the AMS, Secretary's Page, Mathematics on the Web, AMS Publications, Science Policy, Education, Meetings and Conferences, Professional Information and Services
American Medical Informatics Association (AMIA)	http://amia2.amia.org/	A nonprofit membership organization, founded in 1990 and dedicated to the development and application of medical informatics; 3,700 members, especially academically based health-care professionals	Meetings, Membership, Working Groups, Overview, Strategic Plan, Structure and Operations, Publications

Table 1.3: Selected Professional and Membership Organizations on the Internet (continued)

Organization	URL	Description	Major Links
American Meteorological Society	gopher://atm.geo.nsf.gov:70/11/AMS	An organization of meteorologists; programs include education, employment, publications, professional programs and accreditation; headquartered in Boston, Massachusetts.	How to Contact the AMS; Meeting Calendar; Announcements/Calls for Papers; Information about AMS K-12 Education Programs; Information on Manuscript Submission; AMS Council; Committees, and Boards; Listing of STAC Committees and Their Members; Scholarship and University Information
American National Standards Institute (ANSI)	http://www.ansi.org/	A private organization that establishes and coordinates standards for U.S. industry and represents U.S. standards internationally; founded in 1918.	SID: Standards Information Databases Network (fee-based), ANSI: Mission and Role, News: Latest Developments in the ANSI Federation, Calendar: Upcoming Events, The ANSI Catalog: Standards and Standards Related Information (and order information), IISP: Information Infrastructure Standards Panel, People: Your Contacts at ANSI, ANSI Reference Library: Information Online or by eMail, Links: Other Internet Sites with Standards Information, ANSI Membership Information
The American Nuclear Society	http://neutrino.nuc.berkeley.edu/ans/ANS.html	An international organization of more than 17,000 engineers, scientists, educators, students, and others.	Bulletin Board; Conferences, Meetings, Workshops; ANS Professional Divisions Home Pages; ANS Local Sections; ANS Student Chapters; Nuclear Engineering Resources and Information; Other Professional Societies

Table 1.3: Selected Professional and Membership Organizations on the Internet (continued)

Organization	URL	Description	Major Links
The American Physical Society (APS)	http://aps.org/ or http://www.aps.org/	Publishes physics research journals, holds meetings, and offers education, international and public affairs, and public information programs; founded in 1899; has a membership of more than 41,000.	The American Physical Society; Recent Additions; Membership Information; Journals Information; Meetings Information; Careers/Employment Information; International Affairs; Prizes, Awards, and Fellowships; Education and Outreach; APS Divisions, Topical Groups, Sections, and Forums; APS Governance; APS News Online; What's New; Related Scientific Societies; Physics Related Internet Resources
American Political Science Association (APSA)	gopher://apsa.trenton.edu/1/	An academic organization that studies the American political system.	About the American Political Science Association Gopher; Computers, Software, and Data; APSA Information and Services; Conference Information; Scholarships, Fellowships, and Grants; Journal Information; and many non-APSA links
American Psychological Association (APA) PsychNET(SM)	http://www.apa.org/	Provides information for psychologists, media, and the general public.	Automatically Informed by eMail (update), URL-Minder, Bragging Page, What's New (on Congressional bills), Public Policy Office, Classified Ads for the APA Monitor, News, What's New (PsychNET), Information on Psychology for the General Public, Media Information, Public Policy Office—Advocacy Information, Selected Stories from the APA Monitor, Science Information, Practice Information, Education Information, Books, Journals, PsycINFO (database), APA Conferences, Information for APA Members, Division Information, Other APA Services, Contacting APA, Search

Table 1.3: Selected Professional and Membership Organizations on the Internet (continued)

Organization	URL	Description	Major Links
American Society of Quality Control (ASQC)	http://www.asqc.org/	"The leading quality improvement organization in the United States, with more than 130,000 individual and 1,000 sustaining members worldwide."	About ASQC, Quality News, Membership Services, Publications, Education, Other Programs and Services, Society Alliances and Collaborations, Other Quality Related Resources, What's New in This Home Page
American Wind Energy Association	gopher://gopher.igc.apc.org/11/orgs/awea	Founded in 1974, the American Wind Energy Association (AWEA) "has worked to further the development of wind energy as a reliable energy alternative."	About the American Wind Energy Association (AWEA), AWEA Publications Catalog, AWEA's 1994 Wind Industry Status Report, Technical Information, Frequently Asked Questions (FAQ) about Wind, Legislative/Regulatory Issues Affecting Wind (U.S.), Recent AWEA News Releases
Amnesty International	gopher://gopher.igc.apc.org.70/11/orgs/ai	Observes "throughout the world of human rights as set out in the Universal Declaration of Human Rights."	Amnesty International's Mandate, Universal Declaration of Human Rights, Amnesty International Office Addresses, What is Amnesty International?, Hagase Miembro de Amnistia Int'l, Join Amnesty International USA, AI Statistics 1994, News, Announcements, AIUSA Publications catalog 1994, Amnesty International Offices in North America
ASM International	http://www.asm-intl.org/	A society, formerly named the American Society for Metals, that "fosters the understanding and application of engineered materials and their research, design, reliable manufacture, use, and economic and social benefits."	About ASM, ASM Awards, ASM Chapters, ASM Events, ASM Products, Search ASM's Web, About ASM's Web Server, Directory of Materials Suppliers, Materials Information, Links to Materials Sites, ASM Headquarters Photo, Access ASM BBS via Telnet

Table 1.3: Selected Professional and Membership Organizations on the Internet (continued)

Organization	URL	Description	Major Links
Association for Computing Machinery (ACM)	http://info.acm.org/	An international organization "dedicated to advancing the art, science, engineering, and application of information technology"; founded in 1947.	About ACM, What's New, Membership, Publications, Special Interest Groups, Classic of the Month, Key People, Catalogue, Conferences and Events, Serving the Community, Enhancing Your Career, Chapters and Local Activities, Text-Only Home Page, Other WWW Resources
Association for Education in Journalism and Mass Communication (AEJMC)	http://www.aejmc.sc.edu/online/home.html	"An international association of more than 3,000 journalism/mass communication faculty, students, administrators, and professionals"; founded in 1912.	Message from AEJMC's President; Membership Information; Publications; Conventions and Meetings; Calls for Papers and Articles; Divisions, Commissions, and Interest Groups; Placement Ads (Help Wanted); Officers, Editors, and Staff; Reports from Committees and Task Forces
Association for Educational Communications and Technology (AECT)	gopher://sunbird.usd.edu:72/1	An international organization for instructional technology professionals: academics, instructional designers, trainers, curriculum developers, television producers and directors, and communications specialists.	About the AECT Gopher, New on the AECT Gopher, About AECT, Announcements/Calls for Papers, AECT Vision 2000, Conferences/Meetings, AECT Awards Program, Publications, AECT Position Papers and Other Papers of Interest, Committees/Divisions/Affiliates/Chapters, Assembly, Placement Center (Job Announcements), Other Resources Related to Instructional Technology
Association for Process Safety Research (IPF)	http://wwwce1.kat.lth.se/rot/ipf/ipfe.htm	"Provides a platform for reach and education in the field of process safety research in Sweden."	IPF Programme, STOA Documentation System (free software), IPF Mailing List

Table 1.3: Selected Professional and Membership Organizations on the Internet (continued)

Organization	URL	Description	Major Links
Association for the Study of Literature and Environment (ASLE)	http://faraday.clas.virginia.edu/~djp2n/asle.html	Promotes the exchange of ideas and information pertaining to literature that considers the relationship between human beings and the natural world"; founded in 1992.	What's New, About ASLE, Membership, Officers, Publications, Conferences, Archives, Related WWW Resources
Astronomical Society of the Atlantic (ASA)	http://www.america.net/~erg/asa.html	"One of the largest amateur astronomy clubs in the southeastern U.S."; founded in 1989.	Monthly Meeting Information, Observing Sessions and Location, Membership Information, The 1995 Georgia Star Party Information, How to Contact the Society, Finding Astronomical Information on the Internet
Audio Engineering Society (AES)	http://www.cudenver.edu/aes/index.html	Over 50 years old, the "only professional society devoted exclusively to audio technology; an international organization of engineers, scientists, and others."	AES Info, Sections, Education, Events, Listserv, Links, Companies, Careers, Information (AES Publications, AES Standards Committee, Membership, Events)
The Biophysical Society	http://molbio.cbs.umn.edu/biophys/biophys.html	A society that encompasses "theoretical, experimental, and methodological problems arising from the attempts to understand physical aspects of biological systems."	About the Biophysical Society, Annual Meeting, Biophysics Subgroups, Biophysical Journal, Biophysical Journal Gopher/ftp Server, Employment in Biophysics, Graduate Programs in Biophysics, Granting Agencies and Information, Meetings of Interest to Biophysics, Newsgroups for Biophysics, Other Biophysical and Scientific Societies, Related Sites of Interest for Biophysics, World Wide Web/Internet Information
Biotechnology Industry Organization	http://www.bio.com/bio/biohome.html	"The largest trade organization to serve and represent the emerging biotechnology industry in the United States and around the globe"; a federation of biotechnology companies.	BIO Press Releases, Information about BIO, BIO Publications Online, Regulation Comments, Testimony, BIO Membership Information, BIO Members List, BIO Online Industry & Government

Table 1.3: Selected Professional and Membership Organizations on the Internet (continued)

Organization	URL	Description	Major Links
The British Computer Society (BCS)	http://www.gold.net/bcs/	"The Chartered body for Information Technology professionals"; "offers its professionals the opportunity to participate in the development of their profession"; founded in 1957; nearly 34,000 members.	The BCS, BCS Diary of Events, News Stand, Branches, Specialist Groups, Students and Young Professionals Group, Professional Development, BCSNet, Quick Contents Guide, HQ Contact List
CFI (CAD Framework Initiative, Inc.)	http://www.cfi.org/	"CFI is an international not-for-profit consortium to improve product design and Electronic Design Automation (EDA) integration productivity through open information, standards, and technology"; founded in 1988; has a membership of more than 40 companies "comprised of end-user and design tool, workstation, and semiconductor suppliers in North America, Europe, and Asia."	EDA Industry Council Home Page, EDA Industry Standards Roadmap, Glossary of Standards, Delay Calculator Language (DCL), EDA Industry Events, Using EDA CAD Tools, Search Index, Interactive "Plug–Play" Demos, CFI Issue Tracking Service, CFI Standards On–Line, RASSP (Rapid–Prototyping of Application Specific Signal Processors) Home Page, Frequently Asked Questions, CFI Servers, What's New, Management Brief, Membership Directory, Initiative Newsletter, CFI Corporate Profile
Committee on Data for Science and Technology (CODATA)	http://www.cisti.nrc.ca/codata/welcome.html	"An interdisciplinary Scientific Committee of the International Council of Scientific Union (ICSU), which seeks to improve the quality, reliability, management, and accessibility of data of importance to all fields of science and technology."	CODATA's Organization and Activities; CODATA Reports, Newsletters, Conference Reports, and Task Group Reports; CODATA Membership, National, Union, Co-Opted, Affiliated, and Supporting Organizations; CODATA Publications and Databases; CODATA Task Groups, Commissions, and Working Groups; What's New; News

Table 1.3: Selected Professional and Membership Organizations on the Internet (continued)

Organization	URL	Description	Major Links
Committee to Protect Journalists	gopher://gopher.igc.apc.org:5000/00/int/cpj	A "nonpartisan, nonprofit organization founded in 1981 to monitor abuses against the press and promote international press freedom."	About the Committee to Protect Journalists, Dangerous Assignments Quarterly, News and Alerts, Press Freedom Violations This Year, CPJ Publications, Attacks on the Press: An Annual Survey, Journalists Killed & Imprisoned This Year, a search index
Computer Professionals for Social Responsibility (CPSR)	http://cpsr.org/home/	An organization that studies the "impact of computer technology on society."	Select this to join CPSR; Organizational Information; Current Hot Topics; Program Areas; World Wide Web; Gopher; FTP; Coming Events; Links to Organizations, Resources, and Individuals; Annual Meeting
Consumer Action	gopher://gopher.igc.apc.org:70/0tp%3Altp.igc.apc.org@/pub/orgs_on_igc/consumeraction	"A non-profit advocacy and education organization serving consumers since 1971."	A text document with information about the organization and its programs
Council of Better Business Bureaus (BBB)	http://www.cbbb.org/cbbb/	An organization that promotes the "highest ethical relationship between businesses and the public through voluntary self-regulation, consumer and business education, and service excellence."	Index to This Server, What's New, Directory of BBB Offices, Better Business Bureau Programs and Services, Member Directory, Publications for Consumers and Business, Media Room, About the BBB, About the CBBB, Links to Local BBBs, Other Resources, Frequently Asked Questions about the BBB
The Director's Guild of America (DGA)	http://leonardo.net/dga/	"Represents more than 10,000 members working in U.S. cities and abroad." Members are represented in "theatrical, industrial, educational, and documentary films, as well as television, radio, videos, and commercials."	A Message from the President, A Short History, Membership Benefits, Special Projects, DGA Awards, DGA Magazine, DGA Publications, Artists Rights Foundation, Frequently Asked Questions, Contacting the DGA, Other Internet Resources

Table 1.3: Selected Professional and Membership Organizations on the Internet (continued)

Organization	URL	Description	Major Links
Earthwatch	http://gaia.earthwatch.org/	Founded in 1972, Earthwatch has "mobilized over 40,000 people to spend one to three weeks assisting noted scientists and scholars on projects that range from coral reef surveys to public health studies."	Mission to Earth, Mission and History, The Center for Field Research, Join Us, The Global Classroom, Comments, The Earthwatch Hotlist
The Electrochemical Society	http://www.electrochem.org/ecs.html	An international organization "concerned with a broad range of phenomena related to electrochemical and solid state science and technology"; more than 6,000 members in more than 60 countries; founded as the American Electrochemical Society in 1902.	What's New on the ECS Home Page?, Society Information, Society Office & Staff, Individual Membership, Contributing Membership, Divisions and Groups, Student Services and Information, The JOURNAL, Interface Magazine, Meetings, Electronic Meeting Abstract Submission, Awards, Publications, Committees, Local Sections, Short Courses, Guidelines, Web Pages of Interest
Electronic Design Automation Companies (EDAC)	http://www.edac.org/	A consortium of companies that "provide fundamental development technology to the world-wide electronics market"; the underlying foundation technology for the development of electronic projects.	EDAC, Search, Mail, Events, News, Jobs
Electronic Frontier Foundation	http://well.eff.org/	"A non-profit civil liberties organization working in the public interest to protect privacy, free expression, and access to online resources and information."	EFF Info; Alerts; Current Newsletter; Archives; Sponsors; For-Sale/Wanted; Click This Button to Change the World; Document & File Archives; EEGttl (Eff's (Extended) Guide to the Internet); Usenet (News and Discussion); Images, Animations, and Sounds; Other Publications; Board, Staff, and Volunteer Homepages; Other (Interesting Internet Sites & Resources)

Table 1.3: Selected Professional and Membership Organizations on the Internet (continued)

Organization	URL	Description	Major Links
Electronic Frontiers Houston (EFH)	http://www.efh.org/	"An independent, non-profit corporation in Houston, Texas. EFH's agenda includes advocacy of civil liberties on-line, development of ties within the on-line community, and provision of education about the on-line world."	Upcoming Events, Communications Decency Act of 1995 News, Speakers, List (of related organizations), EFH Archive, EFH Membership Form, Houston Information Server, Internet Service Providers, Internet Consultants, Yahoo, Texas List, Board of Directors of Electronic Frontiers Houston
Engineering Foundation	http://www.engfnd.org/engfnd/	"A department of the United Engineering Trustees, a non-profit corporation; provides funds for research in science and engineering."	Grants for Exploratory Research and the Advancement of Engineering, Engineering Journalism Reward, Conference Calendar and Conference Information, Conference Fellowships, Foundation Overview, Founder Societies
Environmental Bankers Association (EBA)	http://envirolink.org/orgs/eba/	A federation of more than 40 commercial banks "that represent both lending and trust activities"; "a clearinghouse for information, a technical resource, a forum to exchange ideas, and a network of multi-disciplinary bankers."	What We're All About; A Media Release; A Letter from the EPA; EBA Membership Application; Survey of Interests; Your Bank, Your Business, and the Environment
Environmental Law Alliance (E-LAW)	gopher://envirolink.org:70/00/.EnviroOrgs/.eorgs/E-Law	An international network of public interest attorneys and scientists defending the environment and human rights; established in 1989; has offices in Australia, Ecuador, Indonesia, Japan, Malaysia, Peru, the Philippines, Sri Lanka, and the U.S.	Text paper with these headings: What Is E-LAW?, What Does E-LAW Do?, About E-LAW U.S., E-LAW Public Interest Conference

Table 1.3: Selected Professional and Membership Organizations on the Internet (continued)

Organization	URL	Description	Major Links
EXACT	http://exact.fmv.se/	"An international technical association concerned with the exchange of information on the technology of electronic components"; founded in 1967.	General Information, Type of Reports, Scope of EXACT Reports, 1996 Press Release, I would like to know more, Directory of Test Equipment, EXACT Reports on CD-ROM, Subscriber Sites, Other WWW References, National Centres
Federation of Nova Scotia Naturalists (FNSN)	http://ccn.cs.dal.ca/environment/FNSN/hp-fnsn.html	"Supports the common interests of naturalists clubs and represents those clubs at the provincial level."	More about FNSN, Member Groups, SPACES, SPECIES, SUSTAINABLE USE, FNSN Event and Notices List, What's New, Other Conservation Organizations
Forever Wild Tree Conservancy	http://emall.com/wild/wild.html	"A grass-roots membership organization designed to preserve and maintain the integrity of the Deep Forests bordering state land within the 6,000,000 acre Adirondack Park of New York State."	About Conservation (who we are and what we do), Just the FAQs, Great Gifts that Everyone Will Appreciate, Sponsor a Tree Now, Weekly Tips, eMall Directory
Global Network of Astronomical Telescopes (GNAT)	http://www.gnat.org/~ida/gnat/index.html	"A non-profit organization dedicated to being a catalyst and information source for all those interested in research and education using relatively small astronomical telescopes."	What's New, GNAT Meetings, GNAT Information, GNAT Disclaimer, Other Astronomical Online Resources
Greenpeace International	http://www.greenpeace.org/	"An independent, campaigning organisation which uses non-violent, creative confrontation to expose global environmental problems, and to force the solutions which are essential to a green and peaceful future."	Greenpeace International, Hot Items, International Campaigns, Greenpeace International Index, WebChat, Greenpeace's Photo and Video Galleries, National Offices, The Greenpeace Ships, Gopher Menus, Non-Greenpeace Environmental Home Pages
Human Rights Watch	gopher://gopher.igc.apc.org:3000/00/int/hrw	Investigates human rights abuses worldwide; founded in 1978.	About Human Rights Watch, Human Rights Watch reports, Human Rights Watch Arms projects, Human Rights Watch Film Festival, Catalog of Publications, Search Index, Support the Work of Human Rights Watch

Table 1.3: Selected Professional and Membership Organizations on the Internet (continued)

Organization	URL	Description	Major Links
Industrial Computing Society (ICS)	http://www.ics.org/ics/	"An organization of computer professionals working in industry"	Our Technology, Our Society, Not Elsewhere Classified (Note: these are not links; links are found underneath each of these items.)
International Building Performance Simulation Association (IBPSA)	gopher://nisp.ncl.ac.uk/11/lists-f-j/ibpsa	"An organisation devoted to the improvement of the built environment through simulation."	Description of IBPSA, Members, Moderators, Owners, Mail Archives, Other Files, Search IBPSA Archives and Files
Institute for the Study of Business Markets (ISBM)	http://www.smeal.psu.edu/isbm/	An organization that emphasizes business-to-business (industrial) marketing; members include both corporations and academics.	What's New, What is ISBM?, List of ISBM Member Companies, People at ISBM, ISBM Locations, ISBM Seminars & Conferences Schedule, Membership Information for Corporations, Membership Information for Academics, Recent Working Series Papers (members can order them), Executive Summaries of ISBM Research Projects—Abstracts, 1996 Business Marketing Doctoral Support Award Competition, Guidelines for Research Proposals, Marketing Related Sites

Table 1.3: Selected Professional and Membership Organizations on the Internet (continued)

Organization	URL	Description	Major Links
Institute of Electrical and Electronics Engineers (IEEE)	http://www.ieee.org/	"The world's largest technical professional society" with more than 320,000 members in 147 countries.	About the IEEE, Search the IEEE Web Pages, Events and Newcomers, Member Services (Joining, Financial Advantage Program, Job Listing Service, Standards (SPA), Education, Electronic Communications), IEEE Bookstore, IEEE's Technical Societies (New Technologies, Web Pages, Technical Activities Guide), Student Activities (Newsgroups, Membership Info, Register, Student Pages), Local Activities and IEEE Officer Information, IEEE Publications (Spectrum Magazine, THE INSTITUTE, Transactions/Journals/Letters Preview, Electronic Products Home Page, Standards, Author Info, Copyright, Logo Request), United States Activities Home Page, Education Home Page, IEEE Standards Process Automation (SPA) System, IEEE Quick Guide to Help, IEEE Gopher, IEEE Women in Engineering Home Page, IEEE Staff 'Whois' Searchable Index, IEEE Web Documentation, IEEE Mailer
The Institute of Physics (Gopher)	gopher://gopher.iop.org/	A "leading learned society and professional body" that "undertakes a wide range of activities on behalf of physics and physicists", founded in 1874; more than 20,000 members.	Welcome, About the Institute of Physics, About Institute of Physics Publishing, What You're Missing on the World Wide Web, Frequently Asked Questions, Classical and Quantum Gravity, Physics World Jobs Online, Physics World Electronic News, Institute of Physics Publishing Publications, Digests of the Latest Issues of our Magazines, Information for Authors

Table 1.3: Selected Professional and Membership Organizations on the Internet (continued)

Organization	URL	Description	Major Links
The Institute of Physics (World Wide Web)	http://www.iop.org/ or http://www.iopublishing.com	A "leading learned society and professional body" that "undertakes a wide range of activities on behalf of physics and physicists; founded in 1874; more than 20,000 members.	Journals, Books, Reference Works, Magazines & Newsletters, Conferences & Exhibitions, Electronic Journals Update, PhysicsNet, Latest from The Institute of Physics, Electronic Products and Services, Full Index, Contacts
Institution of Electrical Engineers (IEE)	http://www.iee.org.uk/	"The largest professional engineering society in Europe with a worldwide membership of over 130,000"; founded in 1871.	Overview of the IEE, Membership Requirements and Procedures, INSPEC and Publishing, Index, News
International Advertising Association	http://www1.usa1.com/~ibnet/iaahp.html	An international organization of advertisers, agencies, and media.	IAA Profiles & Services, Communiqués, Campaign for Advertising, Education, Advocacy Programs, Conferences & Congresses, Communications, Speech Bank, Membership, American Association of Advertising Agencies

Table 1.3: Selected Professional and Membership Organizations on the Internet (continued)			
Organization	*URL*	*Description*	*Major Links*
International Association for Business and Society (IABS)	http://cac.psu.edu/~plc/iabs.html	"A learned society devoted to research and teaching on the relationships between business and society"; founded in 1990; 300 professors are members.	Click here for an overview of IABS in English/French/Spanish, 1996 Annual Meeting, IABS Membership, IABS Email List, IABS Phone and Address List, IABS and SIM (Social Issues in Management Division of the Academy of Management) Newsletters, IABS Officers, Constitution, Bylaws, BETS (Business Ethics Teaching Society) Web Page (http://www.usi.edu/bets/), Academy of Management HomePage (http://www.usi.edu/aom), Academic Positions Available in Business and Society and Ethics, Society for the Advancement of Socio-Economics (at the time of this writing, this link is not active), Syllabi for Business and Society Courses, Home Pages of Some IABS Members, Programs from Previous Conferences
International Association for Management of Technology (IAMOT)	http://mot.cprost.sfu.ca/~iamot/index.html	An academically oriented site without an adequate description of the organization (under construction at the time of this writing).	Newsletters, Conferences, Resources, People, Journals (Technology Management)
International Association of Business Communicators (IABC)	http://www.hooked.net/iabc.com/welcome.html	The successor to both the American Association of Industrial Editors and the International Council of Industrial Editors; more than 12,500 members; founded in 1970.	Click on About IABC to learn more about the organization. To view an alphabetically arranged index of resources at this site, click on Main Index.

Table 1.3: Selected Professional and Membership Organizations on the Internet (continued)

Organization	URL	Description	Major Links
International Astronomical Union (IAU)	http://www.lsw.uni-heidelberg.de/iau.html	A "forum where astronomers from all over the world can develop astronomy in all its aspects through international cooperation"; founded in 1919; has approximately 7,800 members in 60 countries.	World Wide Web, International Astronomical Union, Announcements, Most Recent IAU Information Bulletin, Previous Issues of the IAU IB, IAU Members, Nomenclature, Services
International Chamber of Commerce (ICC)	http://www1.usa1.com/~ibnet/iccbp.html	An organization that promotes trade, investment, and open markets; founded in 1919; more than 7,000 companies and business associations in 140 countries.	Introducing the ICC, The ICC Index, The ICC Worldwide, Your Business and the ICC, Central Working Bodies, ICC Int'l Court of Arbitration, Institute of Int'l Business Law & Practice, Commercial Crime Services, IBCC (World Forum of Chambers of Commerce), ICC Publishing, National Committees and Direct Members, Public Statements, IBCC Chambers
International Computer Music Association	http://cnos.dartmouth.edu/~rsn/icma/icma.html	An international organization of computer music creators, technicians, and performers.	A text page that provides information about the organization and lists its board of directors.
International Council on Monuments and Sites (ICOMOS)	http://www.icomos.org/	An "international organization of professionals dedicated to the conservation of the world's historic monuments and sites"; founded in 1965 and in more than 80 countries	National Committees, International Scientific Committees, Gopher, About ICOMOS and This Server, ICOMOS Charters and Other Documents, Forthcoming ICOMOS Conferences and Meetings, ICOMOS Partners in the World Heritage Convention, Other WWW Resources Dealing with the International Protection of Cultural Property, Related WWW Pages

Table 1.3: Selected Professional and Membership Organizations on the Internet (continued)

Organization	URL	Description	Major Links
International Dark-Sky Association (IDA)	http://www.darksky.org/~ida/index.html	A nonprofit organization that educates people on the" value and effectiveness of quality nighttime lighting" and in "stopping the adverse environmental impact of light pollution and space debris."	What is the IDA, How to Join, What's New, IDA Newsletters, IDA Information Sheets, Images, Links and Web Resources, Relevant Newsgroups
International Ergonomics Association (IEA)	http://turva.me.tut.fi/iea97/iea.html or http://www.spd.louisville.edu/~ergonomics/iea.html	"The association of ergonomics and human factors societies around the world."	A text document with these headings: Goals and Objectives, Organization, Activities, including information about committees and lists of names, addresses, and telephone numbers. Note that the two home pages are not exactly the same.
International Federation for Information Processing (IFIP)	gopher://IETF.CNRI.Reston.Va.US:70/11/ifip	An international "federation of professional and technical organizations concerned with information processing."	Articles, Books, Conferences, IFIP Information, IFIP Lectureship Program, IFIP Member Society Information, Newsletters, README, Technical Committees, The Internet Society, Working Groups
International Federation of Accountants (IFAC)	http://aix1.uottawa.ca/~josephlj/ifac.html	An international federation of more than 110 accountancy organizations in 82 countries and with more than 1,200,000 accountants.	Council of IFAC, Education Committee, Ethics Committee, International Auditing Practices Committee, Financial and Management Accounting Committee, Public Sector Committee
International Federation of Automatic Control (IFAC)	gopher://gopher.eunet.es/11/ifac	Founded in 1957, a "multinational federation of National Member Organizations representing the engineering and scientific societies concerned with automatic control in its own country."	General Information about IFAC, IFAC National Member Organizations, IFAC Organization, IFAC-96, Journals, Meetings, News, The IFAC Information Server
International Linear Algebra Society (ILAS)	http://gauss.technion.ac.il/iic	An international organization, founded in 1989; assists the development of linear algebra.	ILAS - The International Linear Algebra Society, which reveals a text page of information

Table 1.3: Selected Professional and Membership Organizations on the Internet (continued)

Organization	URL	Description	Major Links
The International Society for Measurement and Control (ISA)	http://www.isa.org/isa/	"A non-profit engineering society with nearly 50,000 members around the world"; founded in 1945; "offers programs and activities of interest to anyone involved in measurement and control in the process and discrete manufacturing industries."	ISA in the News, Membership, Journals, Training, Reference Publications, Directory of Instrumentation, Certification, Measurement & Control Standards, Technical Divisions, Sections, ISA Staff Contacts, Today's World News, Career Moves, Related Organizations and Resources
International Society for Optical Engineering (SPIE)	http://www.spie.org/	A nonprofit professional society dedicated to advancing research, engineering, and applications in optics, photonics, imaging, and electronics	Text-Only Page, What's New, Publications, Online Publications Order Form, Education, Events, Employment, Optical Standards, About SPIE, Other Links
International XAFS Society	http://xafsdb.iit.edu:80/IXS/	Represents those "working on the fine structure associated with inner shell excitation (near edge and extended) by various probes (e.g., x-rays and electrons)."	Charter and Bylaws, Executive Committee, Facility Contacts, Minutes, Subcommittee Reports, Related Resources, IXS XAFS Database
Internet Engineering Task Force (IETF)	http://www.ietf.org/	"A large open international community of network designers, operators, vendors, and researchers concerned with the evolution of the Internet architecture and the smooth operation of the Internet."	Internet Engineering Task Force (IETF), Working Groups, Mailing Lists, Meetings, Instructions, The Tao of IETF, Hypertext Proceedings, Gopher Proceedings, Hard Copy Proceedings, Internet Engineering Steering Group (IESG), Internet Society, Internet Architecture Board (IAB), Guidelines to Authors of Internet-Drafts, Internet-Drafts Index, IETF Structure and Internet Standards Process, RFC Editor Web Pages, RFC Index, Internet Assigned Numbers Authority (IANA), Ways to Access IETF Information, CNRI (Corporation for National Research Initiatives), IETF Secretariat

Table 1.3: Selected Professional and Membership Organizations on the Internet (continued)

Organization	URL	Description	Major Links
The Internet Society (ISOC)	http://www.isoc.org/	A "non-governmental International organization for global cooperation and coordination for the Internet and its internetworking technologies and applications."	What is the Internet Society; Information Services; Internet Society Chapters; Administration, Ops, & Security; Conferences; What's New at Isoc Web?, Papers & Presentations; Internet Standards; Secretariats; Other WWW Sites; Join the Internet Society, Text (a nongraphical alternate page)
Izaak Walton League of America	gopher://ecosys.drdr.Virginia.EDU:70/00/information/cville/issac	A 50-year-old organization that serves as the "defenders of the soil, air, woods, water, and wildlife"; more than 51,000 members.	Text description of the organization
The Materials Research Society (MRS)	http://dns.mrs.org/	"A non-profit organization which brings together scientists, engineers, and research managers from industry, government, academia, and research laboratories to share findings in the research and development of new materials of technological importance"; founded in 1973; has more than 11,500 members.	What's New, What is MRS, Membership/Career Services, Meetings. Symposium Tutorials, Publications, Sections and University Chapters, Awards, Fellowships, Corporate Participation Program, Advertising Opportunities, Equipment Exhibits, Public Affairs, Materials Related Links, The MRS ftp Archives
Microscopy Society of America (MSA)	http://146.139.72.10/Docs/nonanl/msa/MSA.html	"An organization dedicated to the promotion and advancement of the knowledge of the science and practice of all microscopical imaging."	General Information about MSA, Application Form, Society Officers, Video Tape Library, Sustaining Members, Annual Meetings

Table 1.3: Selected Professional and Membership Organizations on the Internet (continued)

Organization	URL	Description	Major Links
The Minerals, Metals, & Materials Society (TMS)	http://www.tms.org/	An organization of materials science and engineering professionals and students; mor than 12,000 members.	Search the TMS World Wide Web Server, What Is TMS, Membership Information and Application, Honors and Professional Recognition Information, Divisions of the Society, International Society Home Pages, Publications Information, Meetings Information, Services for Students, Finding Information on the Internet, TMS OnLine Service
National Association for Community Mediation (NAFCM)	gopher://gopher.igc.apc.org:70/00/orgs/nafcm/1	"An organization of community mediation programs and volunteer mediators that serve as a national voice an advocate of community mediation."	National Association for Community Mediation, Preamble, Mission Statement, Definition of Mediation, Organizational Goals, Characteristics of Community Mediation, Initial Board of Directors
National Association of Broadcasters	http://www.nab.org/	A District of Columbia–based group that provides lobbying, legislative, and regulatory help for the broadcast industry.	Member Services, Regulatory Representation, Greeting from NAB President/CEO, Index to NAB, NAB'96, Membership, Library & Information Center, Conventions & Exhibitions, Science & Technology, NAB Store, On-Line@NAB Newsletter, NAB News Releases, Broadcast JobLinks
National Center for Appropriate Technology (NCAT)	gopher://envirolink.org:70/00/.EnviroOrgs/.eorgs/.ncat	A nonprofit organization with three programs: sustainable energy, resource-efficient housing, and sustainable agriculture for disadvantaged Americans; founded in 1976.	Text paper with the address, telephone, and email address; Who We Are; Energy; Housing; Sustainable Agriculture; Information about NCAT

Table 1.3: Selected Professional and Membership Organizations on the Internet (continued)

Organization	URL	Description	Major Links
National Center for Nonprofit Boards (NCNB)	gopher://ncnb.org:7002/1/	Encourages the effectiveness of nonprofit organizations of all types by "strengthening their boards of directors"; founded in 1988.	About the National Center for Nonprofit Boards; About This Gopher; Answers to Common Questions about Nonprofit Boards; Articles, Checklists, and Tools; Current Issues in Governance; NCNB Publications and Resources; Upcoming Workshops and Conferences; How You or Your Organization Can Become NCNB Members; Other Resources on Nonprofit Management; Other Gophers of Interest; What's New on This Gopher
National Consortium for Environmental Education and Training (NCEET)	gopher://nceet.snre.umich.edu:70/1	Fosters environmental consciousness through education; founded in 1992.	Using EE-Link, the Environmental Education Gopher; NCEET, The National Consortium for Environmental Education; NCEET's Environmental Education Toolbox; Curriculum for EE; Activities/Lesson Plans/Programs for EE; Literature, Articles, and Newsletters on EE; Grants and Awards; Conferences, Courses, Workshops/Higher Ed/Employment; Projects/Organizations/People; Regional Information: EE/Environment; Education Resources on the Internet; Environmental Resources on the Internet; Environmental Facts and Data/General Reference; Search EE-Links

Table 1.3: Selected Professional and Membership Organizations on the Internet (continued)

Organization	URL	Description	Major Links
National Fire Protection Association (NFPA)	http://www.wpi.edu/~fpe/nfpa.html	An international nonprofit organization whose mission is "to reduce the burden of fire on the quality of life by advocating scientifically-based consensus codes and standards, research, and education."	What is the NFPA, Contact Us; United States, Outside the U.S.A., NFPA Membership Information, Product Information, Calendar and Meetings, News Releases, NFPA Journal Table of Contents, Fire Technology Table of Contents, Library, One Stop Data Shop, Fire Investigations, National Fire Protection Research Foundation, Public Fire Education Program, Resources of Interest to the NFPA
National Multimedia Association of America (NMAA)	http://nmaa.org/	"The country's largest non-profit multimedia trade association."	America's Multimedia Proving Ground (a little about NMAA), Visitors Center NMAA, NMAA's Corporate Webstorage Members, NMAA Member Web Pages, What's Cool, NMAA Member Announcements
National Organization for Women (NOW)	http://now.org/now/home.html	An organization that promotes equality for women.	General Information; History; Chapters; States; Regions; National Officers; You: Join NOW; Chapter and State NOW Contacts; NOW Action Center; What Issues Is NOW Involved in?; NOW's Organization; National NOW Times; Notes for Participants, Lincoln-Douglas Debate Topic on Feminism; Feminist Resources on the Internet

Table 1.3: Selected Professional and Membership Organizations on the Internet (continued)

Organization	URL	Description	Major Links
The National Public Telecomputing Network (NPTN)	http://www.nptn.org/	A nonprofit corporation that "serves as the parent organization for Free-Net community computer network systems worldwide."	Organize Committees, Rural, Metro, Cybercasting Services, Academy One Program, Teledemocracy Program, Health & Wellness Center, Legal Information Center ("CyberSolon"), Resource Center, Professional Support Services, Who is an NPTN Organizing Committee and/or Affiliate, Who works at NPTN and what they do here, Where NPTN is located, NPTN, Free-Net systems, What NPTN's current thrust into rural communities is all about
National Society of Black Engineers (NSBE)	http://drum.ncsc.org/~carter/NSBE.html	An organization whose mission is to "increase the number of culturally responsible black engineers to excel academically, succeed professionally, and positively impact the community."	National Long Range Strategic Plan of NSBE, NSBE Region II, The NSBE Mission, The NSBE Vision, The NSBE Journal Publications, The NSBE Email Directory, More NSBE Information
National Trust for Historic Preservation	http://home.worldweb.net/trust/	A nonprofit organization, which is "committed to saving America's diverse historic environments and to preserving and revitalizing the livability of communities nationwide"; more than 250,000 members.	What Do We Do, What's New, Join the Trust, Historic Places, Calendar of Events, Books and Videos, Preserving Communities, Courts & Congress, Resource Directory, Internet Resources, PRESERVE link (members only), Main Street Program
New England Light Pollution Advisory Group (NELPAG)	http://cfa-www.harvard.edu/~graft/nelpag.html	Educates "the public on the virtues of efficient, glare-free outdoor night lighting"; a volunteer group founded in 1993.	Outdoor Lighting Bill text, Good Neighbor Outdoor Lighting brochure, NELPAG Circulars, International Dark-Sky Association
North American Vegetarian Society (NAVS)	http://mars.superlink.com/user/dupre/navs/index.html	"A nonprofit educational organization dedicated to promoting vegetarianism."	Vegetarian Summerfest, Vegetarian Voice, VEGETARIAN EXPRESS, Independent Affiliates, Booklets and Flyers, Booklets

Table 1.3: Selected Professional and Membership Organizations on the Internet (continued)

Organization	URL	Description	Major Links
NYSERNet	http://nysernet.org/	"A not-for-profit 501(c)(3) corporation, NYSERNet has provided Internet connectivity since 1986 and has unequalled experience within New York State."	Products and Services, CYBERCentral - NYSERNet's Web Commerce Directory, Customer Support, About NYSERNet (and Job Opportunities at NYSERNet), Public Services and Special Projects Area, Contact NYSERNet Webteam
The Optical Society of America (OSA)	http://www.osa.org/	An international organization of more than 12,000 optics and photonics professionals in about 50 countries; founded in 1916.	What's New, Links to WWW Sites, Search OpticsNet, News from Washington, Employment, Online Reference, Bulletin Boards, Awards, About OSA, OSA Products, Publications, Conferences, Text-Only (page)
Peace Action	gopher://gopher.igc.apc.org:70/0ftp%3Aftp.igc.apc.org@/pub/orgs_on_igc/peaceaction	A "grassroots peace and disarmament organization, with 55,000 members in 30 states and 100 chapters."	A text document with information about the organization
PEN	gopher://gopher.igc.apc.org:5000/00/int/pen/	A "membership assocation of prominent literary writers and editors; founded in 1921 by John Galsworthy; membership of more than 10,000.	About PEN, Appeals, Bulletins, Reports, Awards, Other PEN Information
Pesticide Action Network North America (PANNA)	http://www/panna.org/panna/ or gopher://gopher.igc.apc.org/11/orgs/panna	An international nonprofit organization that "advocates adoption of ecologically sound practices in place of pesticide use."	What's New, Other PANNA Information and Services; at the Gopher site, a long text page: Information Packet; Online Resources; 1994 Annual Report; address, telephone, email, and Internet information

Table 1.3: Selected Professional and Membership Organizations on the Internet (continued)

Organization	URL	Description	Major Links
Physicians for Human Rights (PHR)	gopher://gopher.igc.apc.org:5000/11/int/phrpx/	"An organization of health professionals, scientists, and concerned citizens" that "investigates and prevents violations of international human rights and humanitarian law."	About Physicians for Human Rights (PHR), Medical Action Alerts, Landmines: Reports and Campaign Activity, PHR War Crimes Investigations, Forensic Science and Human Rights, Projects and papers, PHR Membership Information, Catalog of Publications
Project Management Institute (PMI)	http://www.pmi.org	An international organization of project management professionals; founded in 1969.	Seminar Symposia, Education/Training, Publications, PM Products & Services, Considering Membership?, Executive Office, Chapters, SIGs (Specific Interest Groups), PMI Officers, PMP (Project Management Professional) Certification Information, Member Info, Job Listing, Special Projects, PM Catalog (links to other project management sites), PMI Web Survey
Public Relations Society of America	http://www.prsa.org/	An organization of more than 16,000 public relations professionals; based in New York City.	What's New, General Information, Membership, Chapters, Information Center, Publications, Seminars, Leadership, Directory, Accreditation, Professional Interest Sections, Professional Development, PR Student Society of America, National Conferences, CyberSpace
Radiological Society of North America (RSNA)	http://www.rsna.org/rsnahome.html	"Promotes and develops the highest standards of radiology and related sciences through education and research."	What's New, About RSNA, Research, Education and Practice Resources, Annual Meeting, Radiologic Technology Marketplace, RSNA Launch Pad, Outline of RSNA Link

Table 1.3: Selected Professional and Membership Organizations on the Internet (continued)

Organization	URL	Description	Major Links
Save Our Seas	http://204.182.49.10/sos.html	An Hawaiian nonprofit organization "dedicated to ending all ocean pollution."	Your Comments or Questions, More SOS Information (Page two), SOS Newsletter, Surf, Contents
Sierra Club	http://www.sierraclub.org/	"A non-profit member-supported, public interest organization that promotes conservation of the natural environment by influencing public policy decisions."	Current Sierra Club SC-ACTION Alerts; New Member Information and Application; Regional Sierra Club Chapters; National Sierra Club Outings, Inner City Outings, and Lodges; Sierra Club Books; Critical Ecoregions Program; Sierra: The Magazine of the Sierra Club; The Planet: Sierra Club News for Activists; Sierra Club Mission and Conservation Policies; Sierra Student Coalition (SSC); Affiliated Sierra Club Organizations; History; Miscellaneous Documents; What's New; Keyword Search; Sierra Club Web Server Pages; Other Environmental Resources
SIGGRAPH	http://siggraph.org/	A graphics arts arm of the Association for Computing Machinery (ACM).	ACM, General Information, Organizational and Membership Information, Constitutional Documents, Local Chapter Information, Conferences & Workshops, Educational Resources, SIGGRAPH Professional Chapters, SIGGRAPH Art and Design Resources, SIG-GRAPH Publications, The SIG-GRAPH Calendar, Search the Archives, What's New
Society for Applied Spectroscopy (SAS)	http://esther.la.asu.edu/sas/	"Advances and disseminates knowledge and information concerning the art and science of spectroscopy and other allied sciences."	The Society, The Journal, The Newsletter, Spectroscopy Conferences/Events, SAS Short Courses, Submission/Subscriptions/Membership, Other Spectroscopy Related Sites

Table 1.3: Selected Professional and Membership Organizations on the Internet (continued)

Organization	URL	Description	Major Links
Society for Industrial and Applied Mathematics (SIAM)	gopher://gopher.siam.org/1/	An organization of more than 9,000 mathematicians, engineers, and scientists in 300 institutions; founded in 1951.	1995 Graduate Student Fellowships, 1995 SIAM Student Paper Prizes, About SIAM, About the SIAM Gopher Server, American Mathematical Society Gopher, Book Reviews, Books, Conferences, Journals, Mathematics Awareness Week, Membership Information, NSF Science & Technology Information System, New SIAM Books: Contents and Excerpts (PostScript), Other Gopher and Information Servers, Prizes and Awards, Reports, SIAM News, Special Interest Activity Groups
Society for Technical Communication (STC)	http://stc.org/	An organization that "includes writers, editors, illustrators, printers, publishers, educations, students, engineers, and scientists", "more than 20,000 members worldwide, the largest professional organization serving the technical communication profession."	Chapters and Regions, Society Office, STC Sponsored Research Page, Chapter and Regional Links (What's New, Chapter Home Pages, Conferences, Competitions, Educational Resources, Employment, Publications, Special Interest Groups and Professional Interest Committees, Seminars, Technical Communication Resources)

Table 1.3: Selected Professional and Membership Organizations on the Internet (continued)

Organization	URL	Description	Major Links
Society of Architectural Historians	http://ccat.sas.upenn.edu/~jsmith/sah.html	An international organization, founded in 1940, that "encourages scholarly research in the field and promotes the preservation of significant architectural monuments that are an integral part of our worldwide historical and cultural heritage."	Introduction, Architecture Resources on the Internet, Job Opportunities
Society of Building Science Educators	http://brick.arch.vuw.ac.nz:85/index.html	An international "association of university educators in architecture who support excellence in the teaching of environmental science and building technologies."	General Introduction, Benefits of Membership (Education, Research, Service, Information Exchange), Subscription
The Society of Professional Journalists	http://town.hall.org/places/spj/index.html	"The largest journalism professional organization in the United States", more than 13,500 members.	SPJ-L (listserv), File Directory, Other Journalism Info, Membership, Benefits, Contact, Mission, Ethics Code, Quill, FOI (Freedom of Information), DMV Campaign, Hot News
Society of Women Engineers (SW)	http://www.thesphere.com/SWE/	Based in New York City, SWE encourages women to "achieve full potential in careers as engineers and leaders" and demonstrates that women have a place as engineers.	About the Society of Women Engineers, Organization, Member Services (Member Profiles), Student Services, Special Services, Other Web Sites of Interest, Image Viewers for PC and Mac Users (not active at the time of this writing)

Table 1.3: Selected Professional and Membership Organizations on the Internet (continued)

Organization	URL	Description	Major Links
Software Publishers Association (SPA)	http://www.spa.org/default.htm	A trade organization of more than 1,150 international members from the personal computer software industry: publishers, developers, distributors, retailers, consultants, and other companies.	Visit SPA Member Companies, News Stories and Announcements, Overview of the SPA, Hot News, SPA Addresses and Contacts, Additional Membership Information and Benefits, SPA Publications, Market Research, Press Releases, Anti-Piracy Programs (Download SPAudit/KeyAudit), SPA Education Section, Certified Software Managers Program, SPA Member Companies, SPA Membership Services, SPA Codie Awards, SPA Conferences, Government Affairs, MPC (Multimedia PC) Working Group, SPA After Hours (information about its baseball league)
United States Institute of Peace	gopher://gopher.igc.apc.org:7001/1	"Promotes education and training, research, and public information programs on means to promote international peace and resolve international conflicts without violence", founded in 1984; an independent federal institution.	About the United States Institute of Peace, News, Events, Publications, Work in Progress, Grant and Fellowship Information, National Peace Essay Contest Information, Jeannette Rankin Library Program, Data Sets
User Society for Electronic Design Automation (USE/DA)	http://www.cerf.net/useda/	An international organization of those using electronic design automation tools or those who manage them.	Radio Free CAD CAE, Survey, Archives of Radio Free CAD CAE, Join USE/DA, More Info on USE/DA, Papers, Other User Group Info
VHDL International	http://www.e2w3.com/vi/	Promotes the "Very High Speed Integrated Circuit (VHSIC) Hardware Description Language (VHDL) as a standard worldwide language for the design and description of electronic systems."	About VHDL International, VHDL TIMES Newsletter, Membership Information, VHDL International Internet Services, Recent Announcements, VI Contacts

	Table 1.3: Selected Professional and Membership Organizations on the Internet (continued)		
Organization	*URL*	*Description*	*Major Links*
Women in Science and Technology	http://www.anl.gov/WIST/Wist.html	An outreach program to female students who may be interested in a science career.	News, Focus, Organization, Activities, Other Information on Women in Science and Technology, Contact
Workflow and Reengineering International Association (WARIA)	http://www.waria.com/waria/	"Identifies and clarifies issues that are common to all users of workflow and those who are in the process of reengineering their organizations."	Book Store, WARIA Academy, WARIA Database, Web Places, WARIA Benefits, Conferences, Click Here to Join WARIA
Workflow Management Coalition	http://www.aiai.ed.ac.uk:80/WfMC/	A "non-profit international body for the development and promotion of workflow standards"; founded in 1993.	Workflow Management Coalition Overview, Press Releases, Country Contacts, Members, Events Involving the Coalition, Links to Other Relevant Pages, Workflow Management Coalition Reference Model, Workflow Management Coalition Glossary, Workflow Process Definition Read/Write Interface: Request for Comment. (At the time of this writing, there is only one link (PDM Information Center at http://www.ideal.com:80/pdmic/) in the Links to Other Relevant Pages list.)

New Products and Inventions

For every Thomas Edison and Alexander Graham Bell, there are thousands of people who invent new products. The Internet provides valuable information for inventors and for those who want to sponsor new products.

Note
You can find information about patents in the ***Patents and Trademarks* section and information about copyrights and intellectual rights in the** ***Copyrights and Intellectual Rights* section—both in the** ***Law and Government* chapter.**

In this section, you'll find articles about invention and design, links to resources for inventors, and archived messages for those interested in new product development.

Invention and Design

http://jefferson.village.virginia.edu/~meg3c/id/id_home.html

This large but relatively fast-loading site provides links to an academically related essay on invention and design divided into five sections: Intro, Index, Modules, Resources, and Education. Click on Index to get an overview of the contents, including an overview of the sections, learning modules, outside resources, and so on.

The most valuable part of this site is the Resources section, which includes links to many Internet resources, especially Invention, Patents, Alternative Energies, and Environment. Note that links do not change color to indicate that you have used them.

NEWPROD Mailing List Archives

gopher://ftp.std.com:70/11/archives/newprod/messages/

At this site, you will find up-to-date archives for the NEWPROD (New Product Development) mailing list—for both product and service industries. Click on a folder to read the messages for a particular month and year. Messages are wide ranging, from market research to conferences, from home banking to software.

Chapter Two

Computing and Software

B efore the Internet became a popular location for business users, software developers used the Net to send and receive software and programming modules, to trade news about upcoming applications and new methods of coding, and even to play games and get to know one another.

At the sites in this chapter, you can get general information about computing or details about a particular language or piece of hardware. You can also find the sources of freeware and shareware that you can use when surfing the Internet—for business or for pleasure. Tired of that old screen saver? There are plenty from which to choose in this chapter.

The Internet is a hotbed for new programming developments—virtual reality (VR), Virtual Reality Modeling Language (VRML), artificial intelligence, and so on. If you are on the cutting edge of software development, want to code World Wide Web pages using the newest techniques, need to learn Unix in order to operate your Internet server efficiently, or just want to keep up to date, many of the resources in this chapter should help.

General Resources

Many sites on the Internet serve as general but valuable resources to users who are not necessarily computer software or hardware experts. In this section, you can go to repositories of computing information and software, find articles about new developments and upcoming applications, and get answers to some general computing questions.

Free Database List

http://cuiwww.unige.ch:80/~scg/FreeDB/

This site contains many, if not all, of the free databases on the Internet—at the time of this writing, approximately 80. Most of the databases are related to programming, with an emphasis on Perl and flavors of SQL.

Global Network Navigator (GNN) Computers Page

http://gnn.com/wic/wics/comput.new.html

From this long list of links, you can travel to many of the top Internet computer resources and see the most popular sites for the current week. Links are arranged in the following categories: Computer & Video Games, Computer Dictionaries, Graphics, Hardware Manufacturers, Languages & Programming, Macintosh, Magazines, Microsoft

Windows, Miscellaneous Indexes, OS/2, Publishing & Multimedia, Software & Shareware, Unix and Linux, and Virtual Reality. All the links are within the Global Network Navigator.

To add a site to your Bookmarks list, click on the link and then click in the actual page.

MacLinQ

http://www.maclinq.com/

This Macintosh site provides many resources (see Figure 2.1): Shopping (computers and peripherals, stores, updated price lists), Reference (Mac reference pages, online bookstores, graphical browsers, HTML editors, Internet software, desktop publishing, and programming) Magazines (periodicals of all types and newsgroups), FTP software (downloadable software), MacTalk (a message forum), Products (both software and hardware links), User Groups (a directory of alphabetically arranged software and hardware links from the Products section), Cool Sites (Internet sites that may not be Mac-related), and much more.

PC Lube and Tune

http://pclt.cis.yale.edu/pclt/default.htm

PC Lube and Tune provides introductions, tutorials, and education on technical computer subjects. Through this site, you can learn about the following topics and more:

- ◆ Configurations for using Internet applications with Windows
- ◆ Current and future operating systems
- ◆ COM ports and modems
- ◆ PC hardware
- ◆ Multiple operating systems on the same PC
- ◆ SNA (Systems Network Architecture)
- ◆ TCP/IP
- ◆ APPC
- ◆ Ethernet

The articles written by PC Lube and Tune are complete and easy to understand. This site is an excellent place for users at any level to learn more about computers.

PC SoftDIR— The DOS/Windows Software Reference Guide

http://www.netusa.com/ pcsoftDir/start.htm

If you are looking for a type of program or have selected the program but want more information, this site is for you.

Figure 2.1 Click on the graphic to find a Macintosh resource.

Each entry provides the name, platform, media, price, description, and requirements. This comprehensive online directory is composed of three major categories: Company Names, Software Categories, and Software Titles. Clicking on Company Names displays a page with company information followed by entries for its software. Note that you can't order software here.

Programs Are Programs: How to Make Money in the Software Business

http://www.fourmilab.ch/documents/ProgramsArePrograms.doc

This very interesting 1993 article, written by John Walker, the founder of Autodesk, predicts the future of the software business. To summarize, he says that by 2003, successful companies will be producers of recurring subscription revenue (that is, people will subscribe to computer programs as they subscribe to cable TV services today).

Software Publishers Association (SPA)

http://www.spa.org/

The SPA, founded in 1984, "is the principal trade association of the PC software industry." Comprising 1,150 member companies from all over the world, SPA provides data about the industry and enforces antipiracy measures. At this site, you'll find information about SPA, links to member companies, press releases, downloadable antipiracy programs, conferences, and so on.

Surviving the Next OS

http://pclt.cis.yale.edu/pclt/opsys/default.htm

This interesting article, dated June 1995, can help you learn more about the operating systems that have been designed to replace DOS

(disk operating system). Topical links at the bottom of the page are Microsoft and IBM, There Is No Hotel in Chicago, The Bare PC, DOS, and Windows 3.1 Programs. Although Windows 95 is covered in a cursory manner, it is called Chicago in this article, showing that the article was probably written in the first few months of 1995 or earlier.

UCS Knowledge Base

http://scwww.ucs.indiana.edu/kb/index.html

Sometimes finding an answer to general computer questions can be very trying and time consuming. The University of Indiana provides an online database that may help you quickly find the answers you need. The database, named UCS Knowledge Base, contains more than 3,000 text files that address common computing questions.

With the UCS Knowledge Base search index, you can enter a simple or complex search request into a field on the page. After typing your entry, simply press ↵. Voilà! A new page is presented to you with links to text files that might contain the answer to your question. The Knowledge Base determines which text files will be useful by counting the number of times your entry or entries appear in the text file. For instance, if you enter the word *DNS* as your search request, the first text file you'll see will be the one containing the most occurrences of the word *DNS*.

The Ultimate Macintosh List

http://www.best.com/~myee/ultimate_mac.html

This site from Michael K. Yee is an excellent and well-designed resource for Macintosh users. All in one long page, you'll find an extensive number of links to information and resources: What's Hot (including news about Apple and its products), Apple and other corporate sites, hardware and software, programming, publications, games, other Mac sites, and newsgroups. At the top of the page, you can link to

Michael Yee's Macintosh directory from which you can download Internet and Mac programs.

VMS Operating System WWW

http://www.hhs.dk/vms/index_grp.html

This site provides links to a variety of Internet resources for VMS (Virtual Memory System), a product of the Digital Equipment Corporation. Here you will find several sources of free VMS software, VMS forums and FAQs, a searchable index, and links to Digital and online VMS manuals and to other VMS-related sites. To learn more about VMS, go to ftp://ftp.digital.com/pub/DEC/dec-faq/vms.

Yahoo Computer Directory

http://www.yahoo.com/Computers/

The Yahoo site, from David Filo and Jerry Yang, is a popular online directory system. Originally hosted on the computers at Stanford University, Yahoo provided hundreds of sites to its users in a table of contents arrangement. Today, Yahoo hosts more than 50,000 links to World Wide Web sites. In your search for informative sites about computers, Yahoo will not let you down. It has many valuable links to informative Web sites about computers.

Shareware and Freeware

You can find shareware and freeware all over the Internet. From the beginning of the Internet, universities were among its main users, and much shareware and freeware has accumulated on many university computers.

- *Shareware* is software that you can test before buying. If you use shareware, you are expected to pay for it. Normally, shareware is quite inexpensive.

- *Freeware*, as you can imagine, is completely free—either because the developer is altruistic or wants to introduce you to a "lite" version of a product, hoping that you will eventually buy the complete version.

In this section, you'll find just a few of the many shareware and freeware resources on the Internet for general users as well as for computer specialists. The sites in this section provide applications for specific platforms (for example, Windows 95, Windows 3.1, Windows NT, OS/2, DOS, Unix, and Mac), for particular purposes (such as business, utilities, multimedia, science, communications, screen savers, language tutorials, and games), and, obviously, for using the Internet.

Whenever you download files from any source, you risk introducing a virus to your system. Therefore, it's a good idea not only to have an up-to-date virus checker on your computer but also to run it regularly.

Anonymous FTP Sites with MS-DOS or Windows Materials

http://proper.com:70/0/pc/files/long-ftp

This text document contains a list of the most popular FTP sites for obtaining MS-DOS or Windows programs. The top part of the page contains a description of the site and a few recommended programs. Farther down the page, under Contents is a "terse" list of FTP sites arranged by geographic location. Following that is additional information about each site: its Internet address, name, main program categories, directories, indexes, and the names of the people who manage the list.

Best Windows 95 Software

http://biology.queensu.ca/~jonesp/win95/software/software.html

This site, maintained by Phil Jones, provides tested Windows 95 freeware and shareware. Categories of programs include Internet applications, games, graphics, and utilities. Click on a link on the home page to see a list of program descriptions and links.

At the time of this writing, this promising site was relatively new and contained only a few programs.

The Consummate Winsock Apps (CWSApps) List

http://cwsapps.texas.net/

http://cws.wilmington.net/

Do you need Windows 95, Windows NT, or Internet shareware? If so, you might want to visit this site. Forrest H. Stroud has compiled a variety of shareware programs that are mainly Internet related. The applications are categorized as follows: communication clients, Gophers, mail clients, terminal applications, utilities, WAIS, Windows 95/NT Apps, auxiliary viewers, Winsocks, FTP/Archie/Finger, HTML editors, newsreaders, Winsock utilities, virus scanners, World Wide Web utilities, and World Wide Web browsers. (See Figure 2.2.)

CorelUSA! Software

http://corel-usa.com/software/index.html

This site provides software demos, shareware, and freeware under the headings DTP Utilities and HTML Utilities. Available programs include Kenny's Color Mixer (with which you can define colors for backgrounds and text on World Wide Web pages), HTML Easy PRO (an HTML editor), GIFTRANS.EXE (with which you can create transparent GIF files), and Corel's CMS Plugin Viewer (with which you can view and use vector art when using an up-to-date version of Netscape).

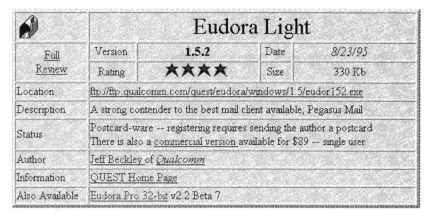

Figure 2.2 A typical program entry from Stroud's CWSApps List

COSMIC Information Services

http://www.cosmic.uga.edu/

COSMIC is NASA's Software Technology Transfer Center, located at the University of Georgia.

At this site, you can view an online catalog of more than 850 program abstracts. Programs, mostly for a fee

but some for free, range from ADA and aerodynamics to Unix utilities, scientific visualization, and satellite communications. You can search for programs by type of application, by NASA subject code, by keyword, by author, and by Silicon Graphics or Sun Microsystems workstations.

You also can download or order the catalog on disk through FTP (ftp://ftp.cosmic.uga.edu) or through e-mail (listserv@cosmic.uga.edu).

Other Internet resources are available at this site. Click on COSMIC Launchpad to access links to NASA centers, Georgia universities, Graphics, Weather, and New Pages.

CSUSM (California State University, San Marcos) Windows World

http://coyote.csusm.edu/cwis/winworld/winworld.html

CSUSM presents an impressive archive of Windows shareware. Click on Top 50 to see the top 50 downloads of the previous week. Here you can find shareware business programs, utilities, specialty calculators, custom calendars, Internet software, screen capture, graphics, games, and much more (see Figure 2.3). Choose a category and click on its link to see a list of links to programs along with the program's description, file size, and the date it was made available at this site. To download a program, click on its link.

The Father of Shareware

http://www.halcyon.com/knopf/jim

Jim Knopf, the Father of Shareware, gives us a World Wide Web page with links to 20 or 30 other sites that host shareware programs. Sites include shareware games, Macintosh shareware, and much more. At this site, you can also download freeware programs for Windows—from multimedia software to a program that displays possible word combinations from an entered phone number. Also at this site is information about Jim Knopf—how he earned the Father of Shareware title, how he developed his first shareware programs, and how he marketed them.

Freely Available Digital Unix Software

http://www.digital.com/info/misc/pub-domain-osf1.txt.html

This site is composed of links to free Digital Unix software—from bug fixes for games to programming languages and utilities—for the Alpha computer system. Although Digital has tested and verified these links, the software has not been tested. Digital customers provide this software. At the time of this writing, 52 links were listed for one or more programs. Each entry contains the name of the program, the link, a description, and the name or e-mail address of the submitter.

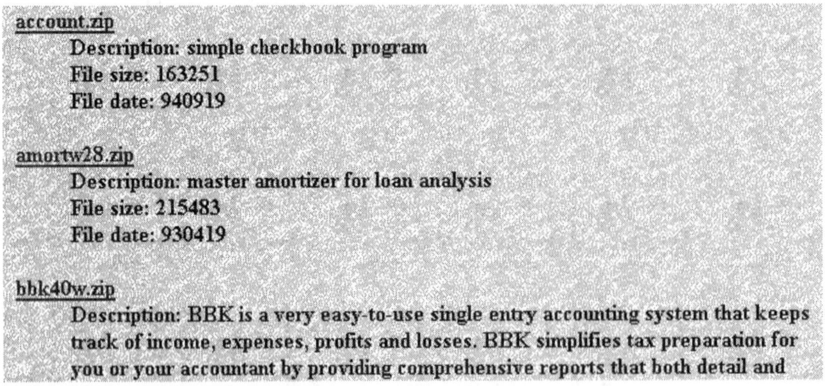

Hobbes OS/2 Software Archive

http://www.teamos2.org/hvm/Hobbes/

This directory includes documents and 20 folders containing downloadable OS/2 software arranged by category. Each folder also shows the date and time it was posted or updated and a short description of its contents.

---

account.zip
  Description: simple checkbook program
  File size: 163251
  File date: 940919

amortw28.zip
  Description: master amortizer for loan analysis
  File size: 215483
  File date: 930419

bbk40w.zip
  Description: BBK is a very easy-to-use single entry accounting system that keeps track of income, expenses, profits and losses. BBK simplifies tax preparation for you or your accountant by providing comprehensive reports that both detail and

Figure 2.3 Click on a filename link to download a program.

Info-Mac HyperArchive

http://hyperarchive.lcs.mit.edu/HyperArchive.html

From this root page, you can search for Macintosh programs and see folders with particular categories of software of all types, from games to utilities.

A good way of getting started is to click on Info-Mac Help, which offers text files that you can read to obtain information and lists of files. When you click on a particular folder, you can click on an Abstract link to find out more about the program, and you can click on Download to download the program. To use the search index, type a keyword, and click on Search.

InternetU Software Library

http://www.iu.net/software.html

At this deceptively small site, you can search for Windows, Macintosh, MS-DOS, and Unix software as well as other software archives: from Washington University (http://wuarchive.wustl.edu/) and from Nova University (http://www.nova.edu/Inter-Links/software/find.html, http://www.nova.edu/Inter-Links/software/multimedia.html, and http://www.nova.edu/Inter-Links/software/stats.html). Note that two links are on the second line.

When you click on a platform, a page listing links to programs appears. The links lead to software manufacturers' sites. Programs are mostly Internet utilities (mail, graphical browsers, Usenet news, chat, Telnet, and so on). However, you also can find file transfer programs, video and document viewers, and links to other software archives. Note that the Windows and Macintosh pages offer more software than the MS-DOS and Unix pages.

Jumbo! The Official Web Shareware Site

http://www.jumbo.com/Home_Page.html

This impressive site claims to have 24,582 freeware and shareware programs for Windows, DOS, Macintosh, OS/2, and Unix. Categories of software include Business, Games, Home and Personal, Programming, Utilities, and Words & Graphics. If you are a first-time visitor, click on Click Here for Special Jumbo Getting Started Kit to get decompression and antivirus programs as well as general instructions on loading and running programs after downloading them.

Learning Japanese

http://www.uwtc.washington.edu/Computing/Japanese/JapaneseResources.html

If you are interested in learning Japanese, this is an excellent site to find shareware and demo software tools to assist you. Through this site provided by the University of Washington, you can find Japanese word processors, translation software, games, tutorials, kanji flash cards, and much more. This site is highly recommended for beginners through intermediate Japanese speakers.

Note

This site has links to other sites—usually FTP sites—from which you can download software. To access an FTP site, you need either an FTP browser or a World Wide Web browser with FTP capabilities.

Mac-FTP-List

http://rever.nmsu.edu/~bgrubb/macp-ftp-list.html

This comprehensive site not only provides links to FTP sites, at Apple and elsewhere, at which you can find shareware and freeware for the Macintosh, but also contains hints and tips for downloading and decompressing compressed files. If you can't find a particular file here and want to look in other parts of the Internet, the managers of this site have thoughtfully included links to Archie and World Wide Web search indexes.

NCSA (National Center for Supercomputing Association) Software

http://www.ncsa.uiuc.edu/SDG/Software/SDGSoftDir.html

The NCSA provides software for Macintoshes, PCs, and Unix operating systems. From this site, you can download many products for free. One of NCSA's most popular products, Mosaic (the Web browser), is also available at this site.

OAK Software Repository

http://www.acs.oakland.edu/oak/

OAK not only is a repository for its own large collection of software but also is a mirror site for SimTel, the Coast to Coast Software Repository for MS-DOS, Windows 3.1, OS/2, Windows 95, Windows NT, and other platforms and program types. This site is easy to use; on the home page, click on a link to go to a page at which you can browse for the desired application.

The Papa Site

ftp://papa.indstate.edu/winsock-l/

This very large site has Windows Sockets and other shareware for Windows 95, Windows NT, and Windows 3.x. Programs range from diagnostics and utilities to World Wide Web browsers and Internet shareware. Click on a folder link to reveal a list of compressed programs. Along with most program files is a text file that describes the program and states system requirements and registration requirements.

PC Magazine's Shareware Files

ftp://ftp.pcmag.ziff.com/pub/pcmag/share/

At this very busy site, PC Magazine lists more than 70 shareware products in the following directories: Business, Education, Games, Graphics, Home, Multimedia, Personal Information Managers, DOS Utilities, and Windows Utilities. To learn more about a program before downloading it, read the README.TXT file, which describes all the shareware programs in the folder.

PC Software—Harvest Demo

http://www.town.hall.org/Harvest/brokers/pcindex/query.html

This site, a demonstration of the Harvest search broker, enables you to search six large Internet software archives at CICA, Garbo, Hobbes, Lowell, Oakland, and the University of Michigan. To search, type a keyword in the text box, specify search criteria, and click on the Submit button. Almost immediately, the results appear, in order of a rank that Harvest assigns to each entry. A typical entry contains the URL, a linked filename, the host and path, ranking information and file length, and sometimes a very brief but helpful description.

Project GeoSim Geography Software

http://geosim.cs.vt.edu/index.html

Tests have indicated that Americans are significantly less educated in geography than those from outside the U.S. This site, created by joint research projects between the Geography and Computer Science departments at Virginia Tech, may help. This site contains tutorials, simulations, and quiz programs on geography topics such as human population, migration, country names, congressional appointments, U.S. counties, and U.S. states. These freeware programs run on MS-DOS, Macintosh, DEC stations with the X Window System, and SPARC stations with the X Window System.

Retail Plus Small Business System

http://www.brainlink.com/~north/menu.html

When starting or even operating a small business for a while, your budget can be pretty tight. Finding the correct software to help you run your business can be costly and difficult. True North Computer Services offers a shareware version of its product, Retail Plus—a PC inventory, invoicing, and point of sale system. You can download Retail Plus and evaluate it before deciding whether to order it.

Screen Savers from CSUSM (California State University, San Marcos)

http://coyote.csusm.edu/cwis/winworld/screen_saver.html

From the very popular CSUSM site, you can choose from 135 screen saver files, mostly in zipped (compressed) file format. For each entry, there is a brief description, file size, and file date. Included are single screen savers, collections, screen saver utilities, and After Dark modules.

Screen Savers for the Macintosh

gopher://userserve.ucsd.edu:70/
11ftp%3APublic%3AScreen%20Savers%20folder%3A/

This site provides a variety of screen savers for the Mac, including Barney Blaster, CleenSaver, BugOff, BlackOut, DarkSide, and Tiny Saver. Simply download one or more screen savers and then test them before deciding to keep them.

Screen Savers for Windows

http://www.sirius.com/~ratloaf/

Entries at this screen saver site are alphabetically arranged by filename. Simply click on a letter at the top of the page to move around the sections. Each entry includes the filename, screen saver name, the file size, and a short description. (See Figure 2.4.)

Shareware Central Interactive Catalog (SCIC)

http://www.q-d.com/swc.htm

The excellent SCIC site describes various shareware files on the Internet. Not only are the shareware files on this page described in detail, but they are available for immediate downloading. The catalog also has embedded e-mail addresses to the authors of the shareware programs. So, if you want to order a manual for one of the programs, simply click on the e-mail address, fill out the e-mail message, and send it.

Business software includes invoicing, employment timekeeping, and an electronic in and out board.

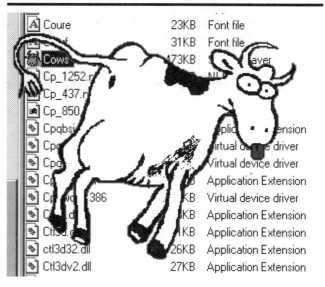

Figure 2.4 Cows is just one example of the screen savers that you can download from the Optimum site.

About Compressed Files

Cruising the Internet viewing World Wide Web pages and reading articles can be both entertaining and educational. After all, accessing information from thousands of the most informative computer users in the world is not a small accomplishment. However, there is no need to stop here. You also can download files and software via the Internet.

Use your World Wide Web browser to copy state-of-the-art computer graphics, download the latest shareware from an FTP site, or retrieve an image posted on a Usenet news server. The Internet hosts more downloadable files and programs than you can count. But, before you begin to fill your hard drive to its maximum capacity with downloaded games from around the world, it is useful to learn about compressed files.

A compressed file is composed of one or many files that have been reduced in size by a utility program and saved as a single file. For instance, the files README.TXT (4 kilobytes) and TEST.GIF (125 kilobytes) can be compressed into one file, SMALLER.ZIP (31 kilobytes). Compressed files are useful for several reasons. For one thing, they take up less disk space. For another, they upload and download faster. And for yet another, they are handy for packaging multiple

files. For these reasons, compressed files are very popular on the Internet. Many Internet servers contain multiple programs and files in the same folder. For example, if you use an FTP program to visit ftp.ulowell.edu and go to the /msdos/games_uwp/arcade/ directory, you will find many compressed files such as CYBOX423.ZIP, DRRIP.ZIP, JET-PACK14.ZIP, TUNNEL.ZIP, and ZM3.EXE. Each of these compressed files contains a complete software game program made up of multiple files. If the games were not compressed into a single file, placing more than one in the same directory would be impractical. It would be almost impossible to distinguish which file belonged to which program. But because programs with multiple files are compressed into a single file, downloading programs is simple.

Finding compression and decompression files on the Internet can be a daunting task. If the links provided in the remaining sidebars in this chapter don't work or are too slow, look for the files elsewhere. One of the best ways to do this is using FTP Search, located at http://ftpsearch.unit.no/ftpsearch. Type the filename in the text box, and click on the Search button. In seconds, results appear on your computer screen.

 ### Shareware.com

http://www.shareware.com/

 Shareware.com contains "over 160,000" PC and Macintosh shareware programs. You can either browse the database (if you don't know the specific program name) or search the database (if you do). Links under which you can find programs are Demo, Desktop, Drivers (other, printer, and video), Dskutil, Games, Misc, Misutil, Netutil, Pim (personal information manager), Programr, Programr vbasic, Sounds, Sysutil, Txtutil, and Winword.

TheYellowPages Programs

http://theyellowpages.com/shareware/default.htm

 TheYellowPages is a great site for downloading shareware. Programs are categorized by the following subjects: business, database, educational, games, graphics, Internet, music, personal information managers (PIMs), religion, and utilities. What makes this site particularly special is that it provides a complete description of a program; so you can read about it before deciding to download.

TUCOWS: The Ultimate Collection of Winsock Software

http://www.tucows.com/index2.html

This well-designed and attractive site provides Windows Sockets (winsock) and many other programs for Windows 3.*x* and Windows 95. Click on Catalog to reveal a window (see Figure 2.5) loaded with icons representing program types. Click on an icon to reveal a page of programs. Each entry consists of a linked heading, version number, revision date, filename, size, license type (that is, shareware or freeware), additional information, and a brief description of the program.

University of Michigan Software Archives

gopher://gopher
.archive.merit.edu:70/
11/.software-archives/

At this site, you'll find "collections of public domain, freeware, shareware, and licensed software" for the Macintosh, Atari, MS-DOS, and Apple 2. At the time of this writing, there were approximately 14,000 files, from business to programming to games. Before accessing a folder, click on Archive Introduction for an overview of the archive. At the bottom of that page is a list of mirror sites.

After going to an archive, click on 00README.TXT to read instructions about finding and downloading files, and click on DIR.LST to see a list of directories of files (the rightmost column tells you the subject matter).

University of Wisconsin— Parkside Archives

http://archive.uwp.edu/

This archive of MS-DOS software consists of a variety of programs, from compression utilities and drivers to games and educational programs. Entries are arranged by program type: Clicking on a folder icon on the home page results in a page of document icons representing specific programs or folder icons representing a group of programs on other

Figure 2.5 Part of the "window" from which you can select categories of shareware programs

pages. Entries for particular programs include the name, the last date modified, size, and sometimes a description.

Note
When you get down to pages containing only programs, you'll find an index file on which you can click to learn more about the programs in the folder.

Virtual Software Library (VSL)

http://vsl.cnet.com/

This site, provided by clnet, is a searchable index that enables a user to find software from the "22 largest shareware and freeware archives on the Internet." More than 130,000 files are available. To find the mirror site closest to you, click on About VSL and then click on Front Desks.

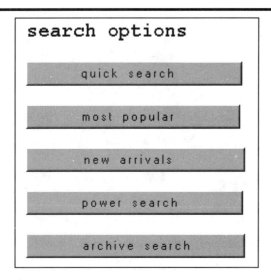

Figure 2.6 Click on a button to find software at the VSL.

Just click on a button to search for the most popular and new arrivals (see Figure 2.6), and you can perform a quick search, power search, or archive search. For example, click on Most Popular to start a search. Select your operating system, and then click on the Show Most Popular button (see Figure 2.7).

Washington University's Data Archive (WUARCHIVE)

http://wuarchive.wustl.edu/

This slow-loading site, sponsored by Washington University, has links to both software and organizations: Digital Equipment User's Society, Documentation and Other Textual Information, Educational Programs and Materials, Graphics Programs, Programming Language-specific Archives, Multimedia: Audio Video and Images, Packages running on many different systems, Public Access, System-specific Programs and Data, and the USENET News Archives. This very popular site is difficult to reach.

Select a link, and you go to a page with folders. For example, in the Programming Language-specific Archives, you can select folders for Ada, C, C++, Elisp, and Smalltalk, among others.

The Well Connected Mac

http://www.macfaq.com/

The Well Connected Mac provides a variety of information and resources for the Macintosh. Here you'll find links to Bookmark lists, contests, the Mac Site of the Moment (not updated on a particular schedule), What's New, a vendor information directory with more than 1,400 entries, Mac FAQs, freely distributable software, trade shows, reviews, periodicals, mailing lists, and much more. If you use a Mac, put this site on your Hot list.

Windows Shareware

http://world.std.com/ ~bhs/share.html

You can add spice to Windows using the shareware applications at this site. For example, pressing Alt+Print Screen in Windows copies the current image of the screen to the Clipboard, from which it can be saved or pasted elsewhere. Beacon Hill's program Snapshot provides the same capabilities plus more. By simply clicking the right mouse button, Snapshot captures the window or a portion of the window and saves it to the Clipboard.

Do you spend much time on the Windows Calculator figuring out how long it will take to pay off a loan? If so, PayOff may be the shareware software for you. PayOff is a calculator program with added functions to quickly handle loan calculations. Other software at this site includes Launcher, Yass, Runner, and Walker.

Windows Shareware Archive

http://www.csusm.edu/cwis/winworld/winworld.html

This is a great site for finding and downloading Windows shareware products. California State University of San Marcos (CSUSM) provides a wealth of applications—hundreds of files in more than 70 categories—for Windows users.

Adding to the value of this site, CSUSM makes searches easy with Windows World Shareware Search. Simply type a keyword in the search field and press ↵.

```
Most Popular

Select the category of files:
MS-Windows(all)  ▼

        show most popular

hints

The Most Popular lists are based on download requests through the VSL in
the last three weeks.
```

Figure 2.7 Select a category and click on a button to see names and other information about VSL shareware programs.

In moments, you will know a program's exact location, its size, and what it does.

WinSite™ Freeware and Shareware

http://www.winsite.com/

gopher://gopher.winsite.com

WinSite, "the planet's largest software archive for Windows," enables you to find software in a couple of ways: You can click on Hot Software to view a list of the last 100 uploads for Windows 3.*x*, Windows 95, and Windows NT archives. Or click on Browse Archive to see a list of subdirectories in a particular directory. You also can use keywords in the WinSite™ SuperSearch search tool.

Winsock 1.1 Freeware

http://www.webcom.com/~llarrow/wsapps.html

Many Internet surfers use a Windows-based application to connect and use the Net. Most Windows Internet applications subscribe to a standard called Winsock 1.1.

Web Communications provides an excellent selection of free Winsock 1.1–compliant software: Eudora, Pegasus, WS_FTP, WinVN, Nxpress, Free Agent, WSGopher, WSArchie, WinQVT, Ewan, WS_Ping, Finger, WSIRC, HTML Writer, MS Word Internet HTML Editor, and Lview Pro. If the freeware application you want is not at this site, Web Communications provides links to other sites containing Winsock applications.

To install one of these applications on your system, simply download the desired application, "uncompress" the files if they are compressed, and execute the installation file. If you are not familiar with expanding compressed files, see the sidebars about compressing and decompressing files in this chapter.

WInvoices 1.0d Invoicing Program for Windows

http://www.q-d.com/winv.htm

Created by Q&D Software Development, this shareware Windows-based invoicing application is an accounts receivable program for small- to medium-size inventory-based companies. Working from a customers, parts, and resources database, you can select a customer by name, choose the purchased inventory, and choose the amount that the customer is being billed. After displaying and editing a record, simply print the invoice.

Also at this site is an online demo for users who want to learn more about the product before downloading it.

Yahoo Screen Savers

http://www.yahoo.com/text/Computers_and_Internet/ Software/Screen_Savers/

Yahoo provides a list of 15 sources of screen savers, many of which are free, either individual programs or libraries. Free screen savers include the Beastie Boys Screen Saver, British Columbia FREE Screensaver, and Calendar Plus for Windows with

Screen Saver. Also included are After Dark screensaver modules for the Macintosh.

The number of shareware and freeware sites on the Internet seems to be endless. Tables 2.1 and 2.2 provide additional shareware/freeware sites and several more screen savers that you can try.

Commercial Software

Until recently, the Internet hosted only free information and software for government employees, professors, and students. In the late '80s, however, the Internet became open to the general public. Since that time, the Internet has become more and more commercialized. Now businesses are marketing their products and services through the World Wide Web.

In this section, you can find commercial software to download and test before ordering. Here, you will find software for real estate and insurance professionals, for retailers, and for your own personal financial planning.

Financial Planning and Investment Software

http://www.moneynet.com/

Reality Online, Inc., offers personal financial planning and investment software. Two of the software programs offered here are Wealth Builder, a personal financial planning program, and Reuters Money Network, a portfolio manager with connectivity to an online finance network.

Insurance Software

http://www.infowest.com/clientchek/index.html

This site describes Client Chek Software, a contact manager program for insurance

Table 2.1: Selected Screen Savers from the Internet		
Site name	*URL*	*Description*
Astronomy-Related Screen Savers for Windows	http://www.fourmilab.ch/	Windows screen savers with an astronomy theme: Craters (http://www.fourmilab.ch/index.html#craters), which "simulates cratering of initially flat terrain," and skyscrsv (http://www.fourmilab.ch/index.html#skyscrsv), which shows a constantly changing view of the sky from your time zone. This site is well worth exploring for computing, astronomy, and other resources.
Convergent's Screen Saver	http://www.convergent.com/convergent/3_3.html	A commercial Windows screen saver (606 kilobytes) advertising Convergent.
Giveaway	http://www.delphi.com/giveaway.htm	The Delphi Internet's Spinning Globe and The Delphi Machine screen savers, both for Windows. (Other multimedia may be at this site in the future.)
GolfSave for Windows and Slideshow for Windows	http://www.xnet.com/~cbone/cmbsoft.htm	Two screen savers from CMB Software. Downloadable evaluation copies are available.
Moroccan Screen Savers and Wallpapers	http://www.dsg.ki.se/~v95-mel/Software/screen.html	Seven screen savers and a wallpaper package in both Windows 3.*x* and Windows 95 formats, downloaded with or without the runtime module or for one floppy disk at a time.
Super, Natural British Columbia Screen Saver	http://www.tbc.gov.bc.ca/tourism/screensaver/	A series of travel posters centered on your computer screen. Click on New Release to download the file.
Unofficial Brady Bunch Screen Saver	http://www.teleport.com/~btucker/ubbpmss.shtml	A free beta version of The Unofficial Brady Bunch Screen Saver (about 350,000 bytes).

producers. Using this software, you can track your clients, policies, and commissions. At this site, you can gather information about the software, download a shareware version of the product, send e-mail to the company, or complete an online form requesting information.

Point-of-Sale Software

http://www.netaxs.com/people/bsc/index.html

Business Systems Communications (BSC) offers point-of-sale software for retailers. This site describes the Birds of Prey software and BSC. You can download a demo of the software directly from this site.

Table 2.2: Selected Shareware Sites on the Internet		
Site Name	*URL*	*Description*
The BioCatalog	http://www.ebi.ac.uk/ biocat/biocat.html	A directory of molecular biology and genetics software arranged under domains.
DEC OSF Freeware	ftp://ftp.uni-koeln.de/ decosf/freeware-cd/ .cd/kits/Prebuilt	A library of freeware for DEC OSF/1 for Alpha AXP computer systems (read README.1ST at ftp://ftp .uni-koeln.de/decosf/.freeware-cd/.cd/README.1ST).
Educational Software	gopher://gopher.ed.gov/ 11/software	Educational software for Amiga, Apple, Atari, IBM, and Tandy computers.
Enterprise Integration Technologies (EIT) Software	http://www.eit.com/ software/software.html	Software for World Wide Web site developing and for both desktop and Internet publishing.
Instructional Software	gopher://isaac.engr .washington.edu:70/11/ software/instruct	Educational programs, especially science, math, foreign language tutorials, astronomy, and much more.
Softsearch	http://www.gdb.org/Dan/ softsearch/softsearch .html	A page of links to biology software, the European Molecular Biology Laboratory (EMBL) software archive, and graphics and general software plus tutorials on Perl and HTML.
TeX and LaTex Archives	ftp://kth.se/pub/tex/	Archive for the Royal Institute of Technology, Stockholm, Sweden. Software: drivers (dviware, fonts, graphics, language, macros, tools, etc.).
University of Texas Mac Archive	http://wwwhost.ots.utexas .edu/mac/main.html	Macintosh freeware and shareware archive: <u>Anti-Virus, Apple Talk, Applications, Communications, Compression/Translation, Development, Games, Graphics, Information, Internet Software and Services, Sound, System Folder Additions, Extensions, Control Panels, Desk Accessories, System Software, Untested Software, Utility Software.</u>
University of Michigan Software Archives	http://www.www.tocnet .com/aron/umich	A searchable index of University of Michigan Macintosh freeware and shareware. Type a title, select search limitations, select a mirror host, and click on Begin Search.
Virus Checker	ftp://zebra.cns.udel.edu/ pub/dos/fprot/	A library of shareware (read the README file at ftp://zebra.cns.udel.edu/pub/README.shareabl before selecting programs). The dos/ and tex/ folders are the best sources of programs.

Software.Net

http://software.net/index.htm

Through CyberSource Corporation's Software.Net (see Figure 2.8), you can browse, evaluate, demo, and purchase more than 7,800 titles for Windows, OS/2, DOS, Macintosh, and Unix. Simply navigate through the menu system until you find what you want. If you choose to purchase the software, place your order on-screen and pay via credit card online or over the phone.

Decompressing Compressed Files

Decompression is a necessary routine when using a compressed program or file. While a file is compressed, your computer's operating system or application on which the file is meant to be run cannot read it. This happens because a file has been altered to reduce its size. Therefore, you must use a decompression utility to expand the file to its full size.

Several compression/decompression utilities are available. You can determine the utility by looking at the extension of the compressed file. For instance, if a file has the ZIP extension, PKZIP was used to compress the file. Therefore, you conclude that PKZIP's counterpart, PKUN-ZIP, will decompress the file. The most common extensions are explained in the sidebars in this chapter. If an extension you need is not discussed in this book, visit the Ohio State University World Wide Web server (at http://www.cis .ohio-state.edu/hypertext/faq/usenet/compression-faq/part1/faq-doc-2.html), which

has links to sites from which you can download and read about more than 100 compression/decompression utilities.

When you download a decompression utility from an FTP server, it may also be compressed. For example, to download the lha decompression utility for a Unix computer, you might transfer the file lha101u.tar.u. This file is compressed with the tar and Z utilities to conserve space on the server. However, the tar and Z utilities are standard on Unix computers; so you will be able to decompress the decompression utility. (Sounds odd, doesn't it?) Most files that you download from a particular computer are compressed with the utility that is standard for the operating system on that computer. Decompression utilities for DOS are either saved on the servers in a ZIP format or as self-expanding executable (EXE) files. Decompression utilities for the Macintosh are saved on the servers in the HQX format.

Windows 95

Windows 95 is the big news of the mid-'90s. In this section, you'll find Internet resources that provide many links to Windows 95 information, files, and hints and tips. For example, new and experienced Windows users can link to newsgroups to read how others solve their Windows 95 problems and get up and running, download Windows 95 utilities, and link to other Windows 95 sites throughout the world.

Dylan Greene's Windows 95 Starting Page

http://cville-srv.wam.umd.edu/
~dylan/windows95.html

This outstanding site provides many links to Windows 95 programs, newsgroups, settings, other Windows 95 sites, help, and programming pages. Click

on a link on the left side of the page to reveal links to resources. Figure 2.9 shows part of the Software page.

Windows 95 Stuff

http://fub46.zedat.fu-berlin
.de:8080/~banshee/win95/soft.html

The primary value of this German-based site is its many links to Windows 95 sites throughout the world. Click on the links under the heading Software to access the software links. Once you click on a link, the color changes so that reading the text is almost impossible because of the dark background.

Graphics

Graphics can be an important part of desktop-published documents as well as World Wide Web pages. This section presents Internet sites that focus on computer-generated graphics—especially technical issues for graphics professionals. You will find papers and professional reports on the creation of computer graphics, handy if you are designing your own images. For example, you can learn about image merging, texture mapping, and optical triangulation. Also included are many incredible computer-generated images for your viewing pleasure. If you are one of the many designing a World Wide Web site, you can get some great ideas by looking at three-dimensional graphics and award-winning images.

Figure 2.8   Software.Net is a multipurpose store with support services, software, magazines, and more.

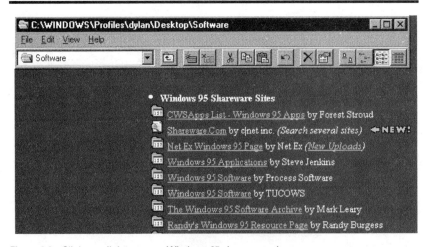

Figure 2.9   Click on a link to go to a Windows 95 shareware site.

 Note
For more information about graphics specifically for home pages and for a directory of graphics sites, see the *Graphics* section of Appendix B.

 FAQ on Computer Graphics

 http://www.cis.ohio-state .edu/hypertext/faq/usenet/ graphics/faq/faq.html

Do you have questions about computer graphics? This site from the comp.graphics newsgroup and presented by Ohio State University supplies answers to many frequently asked computer graphic questions. Pages and pages of topics are covered here, but no graphics are included.

Grafica

 http://www.sgi.com/grafica/

Silicon Graphics offers a site full of graphic creation tips, technical notes, pictures, and essays—a treasure trove for those who create computer graphics. This site covers topics such as Properties of Light, Image Merging, Image Interpolation and Extrapolation, Texture Mapping Applications, and more. Many of the essays are very technical and written for those who are well-versed in graphical design and implementation.

Image Gallery

http://www.sgi.com/Fun/free/gallery.html

At this Silicon Graphics site, you can view images of DNA strands, 1993 contest-winning graphics, posters, and even rastergrams (three-dimensional graphics that are not visible until you relax your eyes completely).

As can be expected, some graphics on this World Wide Web site can be very large. To save load time, the images appear as small GIF files, which you can click on to view in full scale if desired.

Imaging on the Internet

http://netlab.itd.nr/.navy.mil/imaging.html

This long list of scientific and industrial graphics resources on the Internet is based on a listing from an article by Shari L.S. Worthington, president of Cirrus Technology. Links—which include graphics, software, and discussion groups, among others —are organized under these headings: Newsgroups; Mailing Lists; WWW Archives; FTP Archives; Gopher Sites; Public Domain Image Processing Packages; Chemical and Biomedical Imaging (including Mailing Lists, Telnet Archives, FTP Archives); Machine Vision; Engineering (including Newsgroup, FTP Archives, Gopher Sites, and WWW Sites); Meteorological, Oceanographic, Geophic, Geophysical Imaging (Newsgroup, Mailing List, Telnet Archives, FTP Archives, and Gopher Sites); and Astronomy and Space Exploration (Newsgroup, Electronic Journal, Telnet Archives, FTP Archives, and Gopher Sites).

Decompressing Zipped (ZIP) Files

Zipped files, which have the extension ZIP, seem to be the most popular form of compressed files on the Internet. An excellent DOS utility to decompress a zipped file is PKUNZIP, a freeware program created by PKWARE or a shareware program if bundled with PKZIP. PKUNZIP has powerful capabilities such as low memory usage and placement commands. To acquire PKUNZIP, FTP to garbo.uwasa.fi. If you are using the DOS operating system, download the file pkz110eu.exe from the /pc/goldies/ directory.

Macintosh and Unix users can use a program called UNZIP to decompress ZIP files. Macintosh users can FTP to mac.archive.umich.edu. Then download UNZIP2.01.CPT.HQX from the /MAC/UTIL/COMPRESSION/ directory. Unix users can FTP to garbo.uwasa.fi. From the /UNIX/ARCERS/ directory, download the source code UNZIP512.TAR.Z. Another source of UNZIP512.TAR.Z is to go to ftp://ftp.pacificcorp.com, the .L/, FREEBSD/, and DISTFILES/ directories.

Stanford Art Demos

http://www-graphics.stanford.edu/

Stanford University's Computer Graphics Department provides publications and images for the general public to access. If you design and create your own computer graphics, the publications available here may be what you need. Through old and recent publications, you can access reports such as "Better Optical Triangulation Through Space-time Analysis" and "Real-Time Volume Rendering on Shared Memory Multiprocessors Using the Shear-Wrap Factorization."

Or, maybe you are one of the many who just appreciate looking at fine art. If so, you will not be disappointed by the quality of the images at this site. Displayed are many breathtaking computer graphic images created by Stanford students.

 Note
If you visit this site, don't miss Maneesh Agrawala's and Apostolos Lerrios' Lipton tea bottle. Choose Demos, and then go to the Winter '94 page.

Virtual Reality

Used for everything from flight training to aversion therapy to games, virtual reality (VR) is a major phenomenon in the computer world. Through Virtual Reality Modeling Language (VRML), a three-dimensional language, it's making a big impact on the graphics of the Internet.

In this section, you'll discover how NASA used VR to repair the Hubble Space Telescope; find VR sites that provide much information, many links, and samples of VR; and learn about VRML, a cutting-edge technology.

Client/Server Services Branch (CSSB) Virtual Reality Lab

 http://www.jsc.nasa.gov/cssb/vr/vr.html
At this site, you can learn how virtual reality plays a part in NASA's program. Click on

Interesting Site

The Green Egg Report (http://ibd.ar.com/GreenEgg-Report.html) doesn't provide information about green eggs or even Green Eggs and Ham. This site lists links to newsgroups of all kinds—from business to pleasure. Browse through the list of links until you see something that interests you. Then click and get information about the newsgroup, a link to it, or both.

Hubble Space Telescope to find out how astronauts used virtual reality to train for the repairs they would make (see Figure 2.10). Then click on VR equipment and tools and either Hardware or Software to view lists of text items and links.

On the Net: Internet Resources in Virtual Reality

 http://www.hitl .washington.edu/ projects/knowledge_base/onthenet.html
This exhaustive list of virtual reality links, from Toni Emerson, provides hundreds of sites arranged by category: Art and VR; Bibliographies, Indices, Compilations; Commercial Resources; Conferences; Definitions of VR; Electronic Publications; Games and Entertainment; VR Net Guides; Research Centers; Sound; Software; Special Interest Groups and Associations; Newsgroups, FAQs, etc.; VRML Resources and Sites; and Who's Who in VR.

Virtual Reality Modeling Language (VRML) Forum

 http://vrml.wired.com:80/
The VRML Forum provides a place for discussion of the design and standards of a virtual reality language. At this site, you'll find links to four VRML sites, two articles on the history and theory of VRML, and information about joining the VRML Mailing List.

VRML Repository

 http://sdsc.edu/SDSC/Partners/vrml/
Virtual Reality Modeling Language (VRML) is a programming language with which you define three-dimensional scenes on the Internet—making the Internet more viable for architects, engineers, and scientists.

This site provides information about VRML. Among the items that you can explore are a bibliography, calendar of events, documentation and specifications, examples, mailing lists and newsgroups, other sources of information, press releases, projects, software, and a VRML Repository FTP site. If you are interested in exploring VRML, this is a good introductory site.

Hardware

What are the specifications for a Maxtor 210 megabyte hard drive? Does Apple still sell the Macintosh Classic? What is PCI? These and many other hardware-related questions are addressed in this section. Using the information in this section, you can visit specific companies to obtain brief or detailed information about their product lines, you can learn about specific pieces of hardware and how they will fit with your computer system, or get up and running with new hardware technologies. Also in this section are names and addresses of vendors of computer peripherals and overviews of general computer information. The resources in this section are valuable for both computer professionals and those who want to learn more about computers and how they work.

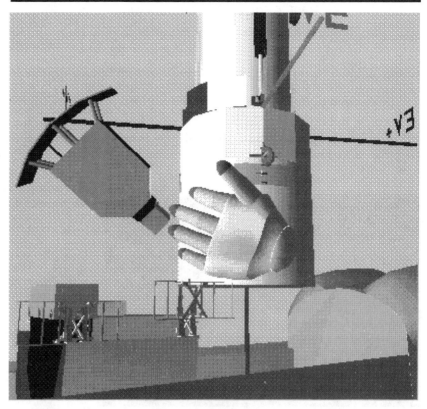

Figure 2.10   An illustration from the NASA virtual reality site

Decompressing Executable (EXE) Files

Often files are compressed with an EXE extension. This form of compressed file is the simplest to decompress because you do not need a decompression utility to do so. A compressed EXE file is referred to as a "self-extracting" file; to expand it into its original file or files, you simply execute the file. For example, you download the file TEST.EXE. If you are a DOS user, you need only type the filename at the DOS prompt and press ↵ to decompress the file. If you are a Windows 95 user, you could decompress the file using the Run utility or by double-clicking on the filename in Windows Explorer or in a My Computer window. If you are a Windows 3.1 user, you could execute and expand the file by choosing File ➤ Run from the File Manager or Program Manager and then typing the filename, with or without the EXE extension. Self-extracting EXE files are supported for DOS and VAX/VMS computers.

Apple Product List

http://support.info.apple.com/aboutapple/prodlst.html

This site provides a list of all products that Apple is currently shipping. The list, which is broken into product lines, provides a brief description of each product and its part number. Although this site is an excellent resource for specific parts, it does not provide enough information for those trying to decide which products to purchase.

Decompressing Archive (ARC) Files

Many files on the Internet are compressed with the ARC extension. ARC is an abbreviation for archive. To decompress an ARC file, you need a decompression utility. DOS users can FTP to garbo.uwasa.fi and download the file PK361.EXE from the directory /PC/ARCERS/. Unix users can FTP to garbo.uwasa.fi and download the source code ARC.TAR.Z from the directory /UNIX/ ARCERS/. Macintosh users can FTP to ftp.noaa.gov and download the file ARCMAC.HQX from the /SYSTEMS/ MAC/MISC/ directory.

CD-ROM Drive Specifications

http://www.cs.yorku.ca/People/frank/cd_specs.html

York University provides technical specifications on CD-ROM drives ranging from 2x ATAPI to 6x SCSI CD-ROM drives. The data, which is categorized by manufacturer, contains specifications on issues such as transmission rates, warranties, seek time, photo CD capabilities, and more. Because the data in this site is not described and is presented in a table format, it is most useful to those familiar with CD-ROM technical issues.

Compaq Product Information

http://www-es.compaq.com/cgi-bin/present/productinfo/product_info.html

Compaq Corporation's product information page provides what you need to know about Compaq's computer products: desktops, laptops, notebooks, servers, monitors, and more.

Except for the price of a product, the information provided to you through this site is comprehensive. After selecting a product, you can read pages of information about it.

Note
Other computer companies provide computing information for their hardware and software products. For a list of computer companies on the Internet, see the *Computer Companies* section in the *Corporations and Industries* chapter of this book.

Data Communications and Networking Links

http://www.racal.com/networking.html

This valuable page is loaded with telecommunications and networking links, organized under these categories: General Resources/Other Telecom Link Pages, References (including acronym lists, books, bibliography/documents/standards, dictionaries, glossaries, and reference navigators), Tutorials, Usenet FAQs, Companies/Organizations/Services, Magazines/Journals/News, Conferences/Events/Expositions/Trade Shows, The Internet, Good FTP Sites, Mailing Lists, Usenet News, and Network Projects. If you have anything to do with networking or you want to learn more about it, this is the site for you.

Hard Drive Specifications

http://www.cs.yorku.ca/People/frank/hd_specs.html

For technical specifications on hard drives, visit this site. York University has posted technical specifications for many drives, ranging from 540 megabyte IDE to 9 gigabyte SCSI drives. The specifications for these hard drives are categorized by manufacturer and provide statistics such as number of sectors, capacity, warranties, rpm's, physical size, transmission rates, and much more. The information is provided as straight statistics in a table format.

Introduction to PC Hardware

http://pclt.cis.yale.edu/pclt/pchw/platypus.html

This site presents part of an article entitled "PC Selection and Support," which explains how to choose a computer based on speed, memory, and behavior of the components, such as keyboard and screen. At the bottom of the article are links to four hardware topics: The CPU and Memory, The I/O Bus, Video Adapters, and IDE or SCSI Disk.

PCI Buses

http://www.intel.com/product/tech-briefs/pcibus.html

PCI, developed by Intel (the sponsor of this site) and other computer industry leaders, is the latest in local bus technology. This site provides an informative briefing on PCI technology, covering topics such as the definition of a bus, bottlenecking, PCI's future, industry acceptance, backward compatibility, and benchmark performance ratings.

Peripheral Suppliers

http://www.ua.com/hardware/peripherals.html

If you are interested in purchasing computer peripherals, from DAT drives to network cables, consider visiting this site, which contains a list of vendors specializing in new and used hardware peripherals. Information includes the company name, address and phone numbers, and type of peripheral.

PowerPC Products

http://www.mot.com/SPS/PowerPC/

If you have or are planning to purchase a computer based on the PowerPC chip, you'll want to visit Motorola's excellent site, which is the "most

---

Decompressing Unix GNU GZIP (ARC) Files

A file with the extension GZ is compressed with the Unix GNU gzip utility. However, you can decompress it using special DOS or Macintosh utilities. Remember, the Internet began primarily on Unix workstations. But, today, all computers, regardless of their operating systems, can access the Internet. Therefore, many utilities make conversions between Unix and computers running other operating systems.

Unix users can download a decompression utility for GZ compressed files by FTPing to garbo.uwasa.fi and then downloading the file GZIPIZ4.TAR.Z from the /UNIX/ARCERS/ directory. DOS users can FTP to aol.com and download the file GZIP124.ZIP from the /PUB/COMPRESS/IBMPC/ directory. Macintosh users can FTP to ftp.cdrom.com and find their decompression utility MACGZIP1.0B0.SIT.HQX in the /.12/MAC/UMICH/UTIL/COMPRESSION/ directory.

---

comprehensive collection of information about Motorola's Power PC products." You'll find links to news, contacts, products, newsletters and technical papers, updates, support, and miscellaneous information.

Sun Microsystems

http://www.sun.com/

For the latest and most complete information on Sun Microsystems, begin at this well-designed and imaginative home page (see Figure 2.11). It is presented in a magazine format; each month, the home page changes (like the cover of a magazine) and links you to Web pages that address special issues of the month. At this site, you also can access standard information that may not change monthly: products, sales policies and contacts, technology reports, and a corporate overview. You also can connect to past editions of the home page.

Telecommunications Suppliers

http://www.ua.com/hardware/ telecom.html

If you are in need of telecommunications hardware, you'll want to visit this site. This list provides a dozen or so company names, phone numbers, fax numbers, addresses, and products. Although most of these vendors sell new telecommunications hardware, some sell used hardware as well.

Networks and Telecommunications

Networks and telecommunications are common in many businesses today. The demand for network and telecommunication specialists is very high and increasing. One of the main reasons is that the field is complex and constantly changing and typically intimidating to the nontechnical user.

This section covers modems and how they work and answers many general questions about networking, setting up and fine-tuning local area networks (LANs) and wide area networks (WANs), using Ethernet cards and cables, and various communications protocols and technologies (such as Ethernet, SNA, TCP/IP, Kermit, and so on). It also provides networking terms and terminology.

Black Box Online Catalog of Networking

http://www.blackbox.com/bb/index.html/tig86e?

Black Box Corporation is a supplier of network communication equipment and information. With more than 6,000 products, it claims to offer in-depth technical support and efficient customer service. Its home page, the Black Box Online Catalog, is stuffed with networking reference materials and product information. Through its catalog, you can read about products, and you can place orders. So that you can easily find what you want, you can view the products alphabetically, or by category, application, or product code.

The Black Box Online Catalog is also a great resource for network information. Through this home page, you can reference technical connectivity information on LANs (local area networks) and WANs (wide area networks), local data transmission, remote data transmission, mobile/wireless communication,

Figure 2.11 The Sun Microsystems site offers valuable workstation information as well as a creative interface.

switches, video/ multimedia, and cables/connectors. This is an excellent resource for anyone installing a network.

Data Communications and Networking Links

http://www.racal.com/networking.html

This comprehensive site is loaded with links to communications and networking sites. Look here for topics such as ATM, Ethernet, modems, ISDN, LANs, PPP, and much more. Links are arranged in these categories: General Resources/Other Telecom Link Pages; References, including acronym lists, books, bibliography/documents/standards, dictionaries, glossaries, reference navigators; tutorials (ATM, ISDN, modem, SNA, and so on); Usenet FAQs; Companies/Organizations/Services; Magazines/Journals/ News; Conferences/Events/Expositions/Trade Shows; the Internet; FTP; Mailing Lists; Usenet News; and Network Projects.

If you're involved in any way in setting up networks or telecommunications, you'll find more than enough information at this site.

Ethernet 101

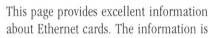

http://pclt.cis.yale.edu/pclt/comm/ether.htm

This page provides excellent information about Ethernet cards. The information is presented in such a way that even non-network experienced users can understand it. The page discusses Ethernet history, components for a complete network, performance, tips, and troubleshooting. Whether you are learning about Ethernets or need a refresher, this page is a must visit.

Decompressing HQX Files

Macintosh computers can produce compressed files that have the extension HQX. HQX decompression utilities for DOS and Unix computers are at ftp://garbo.uwasa.fi. HQX decompression utilities for DOS computers are at ftp://garbo.uwasa.fi; download the file XBIN23.ZIP from the /PC/UNIX/ directory. For Unix computers, utilities are at ftp://ftp.cuhk.hk; download the file MCVERT-215 .SHAR from the /PUB/MAC/CMP/ directory.

If you are a Macintosh user and don't have a decompressor for HQX files, FTP to cdrom.com, and then download the file BINHEX4.0.BIN from the /.12/MAC/UMICH/00HELP/ directory.

Ethernet 102

http://wwwhost.ots.utexas.edu/ethernet/ethernet-home.html

If you are setting up an Ethernet network and need to know all the technical details, this University of Texas site will suit your needs. It provides information about Ethernet systems (10-Mbps and 100-Mbps Ethernets) as well as readings, software, frequently asked questions, technical papers and reports, troubleshooting, Usenet Lists, and vendors. You can even see the drawing of the Ethernet system by its inventor, Dr. Robert M. Metcalfe.

Decompressing LHA Files

Many compressed files on the Internet have the extension LHA. LHA is a popular freeware compression program. To obtain LHA decompression utilities for DOS and Unix, FTP to garbo.uwasa.fi. DOS users should download the file LHA255B.EXE from the /PC/ARCERS/ directory, and Unix users should download the file LHAL01U.TAR.Z from the /UNIX/ARCERS/ directory. Macintosh users should FTP to israel.nysernet.org and download MACLHA2.0.CPT.HQX from the /ISRAEL/COMPUTERS/ SOFTWARE/MACINTOSH/ directory.

Decompressing Tape Archive (TAR) Files

Unix computers can compress files in the TAR format, which stands for Tape ARchive. This decompression utility is built into the Unix environment. However, DOS and Macintosh users must use decompression utilities to decompress these files. DOS users should FTP to ftp.cdrom.com and download the TARREAD .EXE utility from the /.1/CDROM/SAMPLER/DISCS/ STARTER/ directory. Macintosh users can FTP to ftp.cs.athabascau.ca and download TAR-30.HQX from the /MAC/UTIL/ directory.

Introduction to SNA

http://pclt.cis.yale.edu/pclt/comm/SNA.HTM

H. Gilbert at Yale University developed this site to describe SNA (Systems Networking Architecture) networking, which was developed in the '70s by IBM to ensure the reliability of large data transfer. This site provides a solid introduction to SNA. While providing valuable information, Gilbert presents this complex topic in an easy-to-understand manner.

Introduction to TCP/IP

http://pclt.cis.yale.edu/pclt/comm/TCPIP.HTM

Those who want to learn how the Internet works on a technical level should understand TCP/IP (Transport Control Protocol/Interface Program or Transmission Control Protocol/Internet Protocol, depending on the computer dictionary that you use as a resource), the network protocol of the Internet. This site, by H. Gilbert of Yale University, provides a good foundation. Like Gilbert's essay on SNA networks (see the prior entry), this Web page delivers the valuable information in an easy-to-understand manner. Gilbert covers TCP/IP's history, architecture, node addressing, subnetworking, LANs (local area networks), WANs (wide area networks), and routing.

ISDN: A User's Guide

http://www.pacbell.com/isdn/book/toc.html

It is astonishing how much there is to know about computers. And by the time you learn about the current technologies, the successor technology has already arrived. This site explains ISDN (Integrated Services Digital Network), which is becoming more and more popular in the business world and is the next generation of telecommunications service. ISDN, a general digital telephone network specification (or standard) used for transferring data from one location to another, was formulated to be compatible with the telephone and telecommunications equipment already in existence.

This site provides an excellent explanation of ISDN technology with chapters on information exchange, information searching, cost effectiveness of ISDN lines, and how to set up your own ISDN line.

Kermit

http://www.cc.columbia.edu/kermit/

Many universities and businesses require you to connect to their servers using Kermit, a popular modem communications software that provides file transfer, terminal emulation, script programming, and character-set conversion. You can obtain Kermit at this site, hosted by Columbia University. Although Kermit is freeware, it is recommended that you purchase the manuals to help fund the project.

Modem FAQ

http://www.cis.ohio-state.edu/hypertext/faq/usenet/ modems/top.html

If you have a modem manufactured by Digicom, NetComm, Practical Peripherals, or ZyXEL, keep this address handy. Here you can read frequently asked questions (and answers) about these brands of modems. The information is presented in a chapter format categorized by modem type. The questions are open-ended with complete and informative answers. Even if you don't use one of these modems, some of the more generic questions and answers may help you solve your modem problems.

Modem Tutorial

http://www.racal.com/dcom/modem.tutorial.html

Wouldn't it be nice to have a stronger understanding of how modems work? This site, sponsored by Racal Datacom and consisting of excerpts from the book *The Joy of Telecomputing*, written by Patrick Chen, is an excellent place to begin your quest to become modem-literate. Information is presented with minimal technical jargon while still being useful. This site is excellent for both beginners and intermediate users.

Networking Information Virtual Library

http://src.doc.ic.ac.uk/bySubject/Networking.html

Finding information about a particular network can require painstaking effort. Sites such as the Networking Information Virtual Library, which provides links to other network-related sites, can save you hours of research. Through this online library provided by Sun Microsystems, you can gather information about types of networks, network hardware, networking organizations, research, and commercial companies.

Telecom Information Resources

http://www.spp.umich.edu:70/telecom-info.html

Created and managed by Jeffrey MacKie-Mason at the Institute of Public Policy Studies, University of Michigan, this gigantic site includes a searchable index and table of contents to a

Decompressing Z Files

The files that Unix machines compress have the Z extension. Many of these Z files are run in conjunction with the tar compression utility; so the file is essentially compressed twice, creating, for example, a file such as TEST.TAR.Z. To decompress this type of file, run the Z decompressor and then run a tar decompressor. However, if the file has only the Z extension, such as TEST.Z, run only the Z decompressor.

You can find Z decompressors for DOS at ftp:garbo.uwasa.fi. Download the file COMP430S.ZIP from the /PC/SOURCE/ directory. Macintosh users should FTP to ftp.pht.com and download the file MACCOMPRESS-32.HQX from the /.2/MAC/INFO-MAC/CMP/ directory.

Decompressing ZOO Files

Often you will find files from Unix machines compressed in the ZOO format. This compression format, like ZIP and LHA, is very popular. If you run into a ZOO file and don't have the appropriate decompression utility, you can download it from various FTP servers.

DOS users can FTP to garbo.uwasa.fi and download ZOO210.EXE from the /PC/ARCERS/ directory. Unix users can FTP to garbo.uwasa.fi and download the file ZOO210.TAR.Z from the /UNIX/ARCERS/ directory.

Macintosh users can FTP to ftp.cdrom.com and download the file MACZOO.SIT.HQX from the /.12/MAC/UMICH/UTIL/COMPRESSION/ directory.

variety of telecommunications links. Topics in the table of contents are:

- Technical Information and FAQs
- Telecom Policy and Regulation
- National Information Infrastructure (U.S.)
- Global Information Infrastructure

◆ Associations, Nonprofits: Foundations and Professional, Trade, and Interest Groups

◆ Telecom Operating Companies, Standards Bodies

◆ Research Labs

◆ University Research Centers

◆ Research Testbeds and Projects

◆ Government

◆ Mailing Lists and On-line Publications

◆ Usenet Newsgroups

◆ Network Commerce

◆ Companies

◆ Announcements, Event Listings

◆ Other Starting Point

Videoconferencing

http://ppd.gems.com/

When communicating over long distances, the ability to hear as well as to see the person with whom we are communicating adds a new dimension. This World Wide Web site, sponsored by PicturePhone Direct, describes its videoconferencing products and services as well as beneficial ways to apply the technology to your business.

Unix

The Internet was and still is designed around Unix machines. Only recently has the Internet become accessible through PCs and Macintoshes. With the growth of the Internet, the role of the Unix machine is becoming more important every day. This section discusses sites that focus on the Unix environment.

This section covers Unix operating systems and commands, gives names and addresses of sites from which you can download software, and provides learning resources: user groups, tutorials and other documents, FAQs, and magazines. Also included is important information about security—documents, advisories, and downloadable software.

BSD/OS

http://www.bsdi.com/

Berkeley System Design, Inc., specializes in the BSD/OS Unix operating system. BSD/OS is a Unix-compatible operating system for the 386, 486, and Pentium architectures. At this site, you can read a corporate profile, read about company and product information, access BSD/OS manual pages, and download patches for programs. If you are running BSD/OS Unix, you might want to keep the address of this site handy.

FreeBSD

http://freefall.cdrom.com/

FreeBSD is a Unix operating system that runs on 386, 486, and Pentium computers. At this site, you can read about the FreeBSD product and its developers, read frequently asked questions about FreeBSD, download a free copy of FreeBSD, download software for FreeBSD, and learn about future releases.

Linux and Unix Links

http://vinny.csd.mu.edu/linux.html

This page lists many links to Linux and Unix sites. Here you can find articles, projects, user groups, online computer manuals, reference desks, sources of shareware, and other Linux and Unix Internet sites.

Linux Documentation Project and Other Resources

http://www.linux.locus.halcyon.com/

Linux is a free Unix clone for PCs. This long, fast-loading, and well-designed page documents Linux and has links to many Linux resources. Links are arranged according to the following categories:

◆ News

◆ General Information (including FAQs, technical papers, a software map, and security information)

◆ Linux HOWTOs (tutorials) that you can either read online or download

◆ Linux Documentation Project Manuals and other guides

◆ Development Projects (programming aids and more)

◆ Products, Companies, and Organizations (commercial sites of all types)

◆ User Groups worldwide

◆ Links to Linux information and World Wide Web servers using Linux

◆ Downloading the Software from which you can download Linux files

◆ Linux Journal magazine

◆ Other Documents, which are miscellaneous files

Interesting Site

Almost anyone who processes words these days also desktop-publishes (that is, makes a document look better than it does in plain text with the default formats). The DTP Internet Jumplist (http://www.cs.purdue.edu/homes/gwp/dtp/dtp.html) provides links to downloadable fonts, downloadable clip art, discussion groups, and miscellaneous desktop publishing resources on the Internet.

When you reach the home page, click on Topic Oriented Search List, which opens a page with links by subject: General Topics, Specific DTP-related Software, and DTP-related Hardware.

The Linux Operating System

http://www.ssc.com/linux/linux.html

Linux is a free Unix operating system for 386, 486, and Pentium computers. This site has links to Linux information, a downloadable version of Linux, FAQs and how-tos, online manuals and documentation, and other Linux resources: commercial sites, conferences, distribution information, general information, user groups, technical issues, and Linux for other platforms.

Solaris Environment

http://www.sun.com/cgi-bin/show?sunsoft/solaris/index.body

Sun Microsystems offers in-depth information on its Unix environment, Solaris. At this site, you can move through several hierarchical layers of data sheets, white papers, and press releases. In addition, you can download the latest Solaris patches. This is a required site if you are using the Solaris environment on your computer.

Stranger in a Strange Land— Getting the Hang of Unix

http://redwood.northcoast.com/savetz/articles/unix.html

Switching to Unix from the PC or the Macintosh world is not easy. This site provides an article entitled "Stranger in a Strange Land— Getting the Hang of Unix," written by Kevin Savetz. It has links to frequently asked questions about Unix, a list of recommended Unix books, and a sidebar about selecting passwords and maintaining security.

Unixhelp for Users

http://coos.dartmouth.edu/~pete/Unixhelp/TOP_.html

This popular site, designed to help new Unix users, is an online document written in easy-to-understand, nontechnical language. At the top of the home page are links to an index and glossary of terms. Categories to which you can link are <u>Tasks</u>, <u>Commands</u>, <u>Concepts</u>, and <u>Utilities</u>.

Unix Reference Desk

http://www.eecs.nwu.edu/unix.html

The Unix Reference Desk, run by Jennifer Myers at Northwestern University, is an excellent source for almost any type of Unix information, categorized as follows:

◆ General

◆ Textinfo Pages

◆ Applications

◆ Programming (including several languages)

◆ IBM AIX Systems

◆ HP-UX Systems

◆ Unix for PCs

◆ Sun Systems

◆ X Windows

◆ Networking

◆ Security

◆ Humor

All the material is presented on one long page. This is a must page for all levels of Unix users.

Unix Security Information

http://www.alw.nih.gov/Security/security.html

This site, at the National Institutes of Health, provides information about computer and network security. Here you'll find FAQs, advisories about security breaches and solutions, publications and documents, links to Usenet newsgroups, public domain and commercial security software (links to sites from which public domain programs can be downloaded), requests for comments (RFC) on security, and links to World Wide Web security sites.

Unix Tutorial

http://www.css.itd.umich.edu/docs/tutorials/UnixHelp

This tutorial covers a great deal of information about Unix, including a <u>Manual Index</u>, <u>Glossary of Terms</u>, and <u>Searchable Index</u>. The home page presents a table of links organized by chapters: Tasks, Commands, Concepts, and Utilities. Click on a link to reveal another page of text that has some links or to get just links to other pages.

UnixWare Frequently Asked Questions

http://www.calvacom.fr/Unixware/

UnixWare, released in 1992, is Novell's commercial version of Unix for the PC. This very large site (more than 129,561 bytes and slow to load) is the FAQ archive for the Usenet newsgroup comp.Unix.Unixware. Included are links to other versions of the archive document. The FAQ is categorized as follows: General, User, SysAdmin, and Developer.

Other Programming Languages

Although most people in the world speak only one or two languages, computer programmers often need to know three or more computer languages and how they apply to different technologies. The programmer needs vast amounts of informative resources. Books pile up on the shelves, and magazines and journals tower on desks. Put simply, programmers need the most current information and lots of it. The Internet is an excellent resource for programmers, and it doesn't take up desk space!

This section provides information about C, C++, Motif, Virtual Basic, Ada, and object-oriented languages. Also included are general links to programming language resources, such as magazines, computer manuals, books, computer companies, suppliers of programs and modules, and other programming language sites.

Carl & Gary's Visual Basic Home Page

http://www.apexsc.com/vb

Visual Basic, a Microsoft product, is used extensively for programming Windows screen elements: buttons, boxes, dialog boxes, menus, and so on.

At this comprehensive and well-designed site, you can get started with Visual Basic (if you are a rank beginner) or obtain technical support (if you have any level of experience with Visual

Basic). Included are links to other Visual Basic and Windows sites, user groups, news, newsgroups, tips and tricks, a directory of consultants, and much, much more.

Dynamic Languages for the Mac

http://www.cambridge.apple.com/other-langs/dynamic-languages.html

Dynamic languages are object-oriented languages that change whenever a program is edited. Programmers can test and edit the programs as they are running rather than recompiling and then checking the results.

This site provides links to scripting and multimedia languages (such as AppleScript, Frontier, Hypercard, and Lingo), general-purpose programming languages (such as APL, Basic, Forth, and Lisp), and PostScript. At the bottom of the page, you can also read the narrative on programming languages, link to surveys, articles, and other sites, and read about language research at other sites.

Home of the Brave Ada Programmers (HBAP)

http://lglwww.epfl.ch/Ada/

This site, from Magnus Kempe in Switzerland, has links to anything you ever wanted to know about Ada, a software engineering language first developed by the U.S. Department of Defense in 1974. Included are programming resources; the advantages of using Ada; and links to tutorials, textbooks, free downloadable compilers, and examples of programming code. (See Figure 2.12.)

Internet Resources for Windows Developers

http://www.r2m.com/windev/

This site, in a tabular format, has links to magazines, book sources, and other programmer resources. Also included are links to the Microsoft, Borland, Symantec, and Watcom corporate sites as well as a variety of other Internet programming resources.

The author, Robert Mashlan, also provides information about other programming languages, operating systems, and topics: WinHelp, Windows Sockets, Turbo Pascal, Visual Basic, and Borland's OWL.

Introduction to C Programming

http://www.iftech.com/classes/c/c0.htm

If you are beginning to learn C programming, this site by Interface Technologies may be just what you are looking for. The site breaks your training into 16 modules. Simply start off with the first module (Introduction), read through it, and then move to the next.

Although this is an introduction to C programming, it is recommended that you have previous experience in a procedural language such as Pascal or FORTRAN.

Introduction to Object-Oriented Programming Using C++

http://www.quadralay.com/www/CCForum/CCForum.html

This excellent site, provided by Quadralay Corporation, provides a wealth of C++ information. Here, you can read through frequently asked questions, stroll through library listings, learn C++ through an online tutorial, study object-oriented programming, link to other programming resources on the World Wide Web, and more. This is a site for both novice and experienced C++ programmers.

Java: Programming for the Internet

http://java.dnx.com

Sun Microsystems presents Java™, a programming language for World Wide Web pages. Links at this very popular site include About Java, What's New?, Downloading, Documentation, The HotJava Browser, Applets, Developer's Corner, Licensing, and Getting in Touch. Also included are links to a Search index and Mirror Sites.

Tip
Getting into this very busy site can be a hassle. If you plan to visit often, keep a record of the addresses for two or three of the mirror sites.

Figure 2.12   A portrait of Lady Augusta Ada Byron, also known as Ada Lovelace, the namesake of the Ada programming language

MW3: Motif on the World Wide Web

http://www.cen.com/mw3/

This comprehensive site is dedicated to Motif, a graphical user interface (GUI) that was created by the Open Software Foundation (OSF) for the X Windows Unix interface. The table of contents includes the following:

- ◆ FAQs
- ◆ Widgets, toolkits, libraries, and GUIs
- ◆ Organizations, Motif commercial and non-commercial sites
- ◆ Multimedia
- ◆ Examples of codes
- ◆ Publications, tutorials, and references
- ◆ Security
- ◆ Conferences

Online Computer Manuals

http://www.nova.edu/Inter-Links/misc/manuals.html

This small nongraphical site, from Nova University, has links to computer manuals for both languages and programs. Here you can link to manuals on PostScript, C++, and Perl. You can learn about the Minitab, SPSS, and SAS statistical packages, and you can obtain information about Kermit and anonymous FTP.

Pouring the Java

http://www.pointcom.com/gifs/home/java.html

Java is a World Wide Web programming language from Sun Microsystems. On this page, you can learn more about Java and see how some developers work with it. For example, click on Nizze's HotJava Applets to see an animated analog clock that shows the current time with a moving second hand. Note that some of the demonstrations are very slow to load and obviously under development. Note also that you must have the latest version of Netscape to see them.

Programming Languages

http://www.cis.ohio-state.edu/hypertext/tech-docs/CID/languages.html

This site has links to Internet resources for Modula2, Pascal, COBOL, C, C++, FORTRAN, and the Make utility. Click on a link to read frequently asked questions (FAQs), language reference, and/or sample code. This site is not for beginners; you must have some experience to understand the content of the resources.

Programming Languages Resources

http://www.mind.net/jfs/proglang.html

This site consists of links to and brief descriptions of programming sites. Languages covered are Ada, C/C++, Pascal, Perl, and Visual Basic.

Smalltalk Archive Base Page

http://st-www.cs.uiuc.edu:80/

The Smalltalk Archive provides code for experienced Smalltalk developers. You can access the files in the archive by location (the FTP- or HTTP-based site) or by Smalltalk version (Hierarchical Index of Smalltalk Archive).

Software Developer's Resources

http://www.mind.net/jfs/devres.html

This site is an excellent and well-designed source of many links for developers of Internet applications and other programs. Here you'll find articles; source code archives; graphics information; software and recruiting companies; other developers' pages; programming languages; World Wide Web author and developer information; and specifications, standards, and protocols.

Software Engineering Resources

http://iag.net/~m2tech/se.html

This excellent site contains many links to online documents and tutorials, downloadable software, and software libraries for several programming languages: Unix, Linux, C, C++, and more. Also included are Internet tutorials, games programming, and graphics information.

Sponge on the Web

http://http://isx.com/~dsupel/www/sponge/

This site contains "a collection of reuseable C++ classes" tested and compiled by three C++ compilers: CenterLine-C++ Release 2.1.0, SPARCompiler C++ Release 4.0.1, and Microsoft Visual C++ Release 4.0. On the home page, the author has created a table with the header name, implementation, and last date modified. You are encouraged to contribute to this site.

Standard Template Library (STL)

http://www.ualberta.ca/~nyu/stl/stl.html

The STL, which will eventually be incorporated into all C++ compilers, "consists of generic algorithms operating on generalized data structures." In other words, you can use the code in the library to develop C++ programs without writing original code. Headings at this site include STL Implementations and Related FTP Sites, STL Documentation and Reference, C++ Related Information, and Notes on Updates.

User Interface Software Tools

www.cs.cmu.edu/afs/cs.cmu.edu/user/bam/www/toolnames.html

Created by Brad A. Myers of Carnegie Mellon University, this site provides a list of and some links to major user interface programming tools. At this site, you can download the following for free: Amulet, Andrew User Interface System (AUIS or ATK), CanAda, Chimera, Chiron, Forms, Fresco, Garnet, GINA, Groupkit, MrEd, Serpent, SUIT, Tk/Tcl, Theseus++, VXP - Visual X Windows Programming Interface, WIN-TERP, wxWindows, and YACL.

Be sure to go to the bottom of the page to view other programming resources to which you can link.

The WWW Virtual Library: Computer Programming Languages

http://src.doc.ic.ac.uk/bySubject/Computing/Languages.html

This single-page site provides links to information about many common and obscure computer programming languages: ABC, Ada, Visual Basic, BETA, C, C++, Elisp, Cecil, COBOL, Dylan, Eclipse, Elf, Erlang, Forth, FORTRAN, Haskell, Lisp, Occam, Oz, Perl, PostScript, Prolog, Python, REXX, SGML, Sisal, TCL/TK, TeX, VHDL, and Z. At the bottom of the page are links to miscellaneous sites, including Programming Language Research, Language List, and Computing Languages Lists.

The WWW Virtual Library: The Java Programming Language

http://www.acm.org/~ops/java.html

Java is a new object-oriented programming language developed by Sun Microsystems and dedicated to Internet programming. At this site, you can obtain an overview of Java; link to upcoming events, reference materials, documents, and resources; and view applications and examples.

Yahoo Computer and Internet Languages

http://www.yahoo.com/Computers_and_Internet/Languages

From Yahoo, the supreme Internet index, comes a page of links to many programming languages, from ABC and Ada to VRML and Z. At the bottom of the page are indexes that point to other Internet programming resources.

Research and Development

By the nature of the work, computer science is always at the cutting edge of technology. Areas such as artificial intelligence, knowledge engineering, virtual reality, and so on are rapidly developing—with help from academic institutions, government laboratories, and commercial research and development departments. Using the resources in this section, you can always stay up to date with the latest developments in computer science.

Computer Science Technical Reports Archive Sites

http://www.rdt.monash.edu.au/tr/siteslist.html

This site lists worldwide academic and laboratory sites that produce technical reports in computer science. A typical entry includes the name of the educational institution, the address (usually FTP)

from which you can download reports, e-mail contacts with humans, and other links. To view a list of reports at a particular site, click on available.

Knowledge Systems Lab (KSL)

http://www-ksl.stanford.edu/

Stanford University's KSL investigates artificial intelligence. Among its current projects are How Things Work, Knowledge Sharing Technology, Network-based Information Brokers, CommerceNet, and Adaptive Intelligent Systems. Here, you can read papers about these projects and link to other artificial intelligence resources on the Internet.

MIT Artificial Intelligence (AI) Lab

http://www.ai.mit.edu/

MIT's Artificial Intelligence Laboratory provides information about its research in learning, vision and robotics, and new computer development. Links at this site include Our Research, Events at the MIT AI Lab, Our People, and Our Publications. Also included are other MIT links: Around MIT, Reference (other AI resources on the Internet), Other Topics, and Around the Lab. You can find online AI publications (in a 255 kilobyte file) at http://www.air.mit.edu/publications/bibliography/BIB-online.html. Publications also are available via FTP.

Chapter Three

Corporations and Industries

Using the sites in this chapter, you can investigate an industry into which your company might grow and look for a corporate partner or resource.

Every day, major corporations as well as small businesses decide to get on the Internet—particularly the World Wide Web. Doing so is a cost-effective way to make a company known to a very large audience through electronic advertisements, company information and press releases, job listings, and even free or low-cost promotional products. Professional, membership, and nonprofit organizations and industry groups can publish online journals and magazines, enable visitors to participate in forums, and provide important information (such as suppliers and vendor lists) for both members and visitors.

Industries

Have you always wanted to open a restaurant? Or do you want to research a particular industry before investing in it? Using the resources in this section, you can investigate an industry, get marketing tips, and discover how to get started: selecting a site, setting prices, and evaluating the competition.

In addition, you can find a code with which you can look up entire industries or subgroups, and you can review the U.S. government's 1993 and 1994 predictions about the future of many industries.

Internet Industry Resources

http://mfginfo.com/htm/industry.htm

Manufacturers Information Net provides links to resources in these categories: business-related, manufacturing, petroleum, resources, and Internet search indexes. When you select a category, you'll get a table of links (sometimes not obviously related to the category).

Small Business Administration Industry Profiles

gopher://UMSLVMA.UMSL.EDU:70/11/LIBRARY//GOVDOCS/INDPRO

For an in-depth look at a small group of industries (restaurants, subdividers and developers, dental services, advertising), visit this site.

A typical "chapter" thoroughly describes the industry as a whole (primary functions, size, economic performance and future outlook, trends, advertising regulations, and organizations) and a standard life cycle (from starting the business to the condition of the mature business) and provides tips on how to start this type of business (site analysis and selection factors, pricing, export trade potential, government sales opportunities, competition, strategies, and more).

Standard Industrial Classification (SIC) Codes

gopher://info.babson.edu:70/11/.bus/.sic

When contacting a group of companies for business purposes or researching a particular industry, a good first step is to check the SIC system. In the SIC, a two-digit code is a major group (for example, construction is 15), and a four-digit code is an industry within a major group (for example, single-family housing construction is 1521).

Babson College provides the best SIC code site on the Internet. Here, you will find SIC codes from County Business Patterns (an annual U.S. Census Bureau publication that provides economic data about certain U.S. industries), and you can search for SIC codes using either an SIC code or a keyword. This site also has links to other SIC resources and information about alternate or possible replacement codes: FIPS (Federal Information Processing Standards) and NAIC (North American Industry Classification). The University of Virginia provides another important SIC site (gopher://gopher.lib.virginia.edu:70/7waissrc%3A/socsci/other/codes/sic_cbp.asc), some of which are pointed to from this site.

Interesting Sites

At RedStar's Page of Net Fame (http://www.cyberspace.com/chronos/netfame/legends.htm), you can browse a list of almost 200 links to famous Net personalities; just click on <u>Top Nominees</u>. The serious (Tim Berners-Lee, who created the World Wide Web) and the not-so-serious (Christine Carline of The Timewaster Page) entries make this page a pleasure to visit. Two examples of what you can find are Jason R. Heimbaugh's Urban Legends Archive (http://cathouse.org:80/UrbanLegends/) and Sandra Loosemore's Clip Art Server (http://www.cs.yale.edu/homes/sj1/clipart.html). Figure 3.1 shows an example of clip art from Sandra Loosemore's Clip Art Server.

Figure 3.1 Public domain clip art from Sandra Loosemore's Clip Art Server

TEXAS-ONE Business Information Collection

http://www.texas-one.org/ind-sect.htm

This well-organized site has links to articles and miscellaneous industry information arranged by industry sectors: General (miscellaneous industry statistics and predictions), Aerospace, Chemical, Computer and Software, Energy (includes Oil and Gas), Environmental, Insurance, Medical, Microelectronics, and Telecommunications.

U.S. Biotechnology Industry: Facts and Figures

http://www.bio.com/bio/2toc.html

This online table of contents provides links to chapters in a 1994–95 document about the biotechnology industry. Here you can get an industry profile and statistics: Sales; Markets; Number of Companies, Company Size, and Age; Research and Development; Financing; a 1994 Statistical Summary; Products and Patents; Use of Stock Options; and Geographic Area Demographics and Financial Highlights. If you are interested in investing in a biotechnology company or are running or working for one, be sure to visit this site.

U.S. Industrial Outlook

gopher://una.hh.lib.umich.edu:70/11/ebb/industry/outlook

gopher://UMSLVMA.UMSL.EDU:70/11/LIBRARY//GOVDOCS/USI094

The 1994 U.S. Industrial Outlook online book, from the U.S. Department of Commerce, presents forecasts for more than 200 U.S. industries, organized by SIC code. Select the Program Description folder to view an introduction to the Industrial Outlook document. Select Getting the Most Out of Outlook to read about the background and assumptions.

A typical entry for a major group (two-digit SIC) describes the sectors that make up the group, predicts what this group will do in the current year, discusses markets for the products, and then reviews the previous year's activities of industries within the major group. Discussion points for some industries are environmental impact, international competitiveness, outlook for the current year, long-term prospects, and references to related government documents.

Look for the 1993 U.S. Industrial Outlook, which includes forecasts for 350 industries, at gopher://UMSLVMA.UMSL.EDU:70/11/LIBRARY//GOVDOCS/USIO. The Department of Commerce does not plan to issue a 1995 U.S. Industrial Outlook.

Company Reports and Filings

A reliable way of learning a company's plans for the future is to look at its Securities and Exchange Commission (SEC) filings, read its annual reports, and study its press releases (even reading between the lines). Although you might not be able to predict a takeover, you can identify potential targets by studying the materials in this section (also remember to look at the market results in the *Finance and Accounting* chapter).

In this section, you will find the sources of corporate filings, annual reports, press releases, and other company information.

New York University EDGAR Project

http://edgar.stern.nyu.edu/

This enhanced version of EDGAR (Electronic Data Gathering and Retrieval Project) not only presents corporate filings and forms that publicly held companies have sent to the Securities and Exchange Commission (SEC), but also includes links to Get Corporate SEC Filings, Mutual Fund Database Prototype, Search and View Corporate Profiles, Link to Alternate Edgar Site at SEC, Frequently Asked Questions, The R. R. Donnelley Library of SEC Materials, Software and Data, Advanced Software

Chris Lopes on Internet Connections

Chris Lopes, a Lead Communications Consultant at Lotus Development Corporation, has a master's degree in mathematics from Columbia University. He has worked for a number of large companies as a communications software development engineer, has worked with a number of start-up businesses trying to develop communications products, and teaches TCP/IP and SNMP.

What sort of advice can you provide to a business connecting to the Internet?

Depending on the size of your company, there are two ways of getting connected to the Internet: You can either hook in through a service provider, or you can have your own Internet address or many addresses. Then anybody who knows your address can at least get to the front door of your system.

Small businesses can simply buy services from a provider or an online service. Basically, they would have a terminal and connect to the provider's system, and the provider's computers would connect to the Internet.

Larger companies have to think about security. Employees may need to access the Internet to get information or to communicate with people at other companies, but having those capabilities means that people can

---

PART I. FINANCIAL INFORMATION
ITEM 1: FINANCIAL STATEMENTS
LOTUS DEVELOPMENT CORPORATION
CONSOLIDATED STATEMENTS OF OPERATIONS
(in thousands, except per share data) (unaudited)

Three Months Ended

	April 1, 1995	April 2, 1994
Net sales	$202,615	$246,992
Cost of sales	39,146	46,408
Gross margin	163,469	200,584
Expenses:		
Research and development	42,067	34,484
Sales and marketing	133,075	117,820
General and administrative	18,128	16,248
Other (income)/expense, net (Note D)	(2,449)	(1,314)
Total expenses	190,821	167,238
Income (loss) before income taxes	(27,352)	33,346
Provision (benefit) for income taxes	(9,847)	12,005
Net income (loss)	($17,505)	$21,341
Net income (loss) per share	($0.36)	$0.45

Figure 3.2 A page from an SEC report on Lotus Development Corporation

Course, Reciprocal Links, Other Interesting Links, Introduction, and What Is EDGAR?

To search the database, click on Company Search, type a company name, set the maximum number of reports to be found (100 hits is the default), and select a debugging option (no debug—smooth sailing! is the default). Then click on Retrieve Filings. After the search results are on your screen, click on the company name in the row that contains the information you want. Figure 3.2 shows a sample of the results. You can find company profiles in the DEF_14A forms, which also can include graphs (see Figure 3.3).

get to your systems, and that can be dangerous. So there are a number of configurations that one can set up, depending on the requirements.

Some companies just connect to the Internet for e-mail; they don't need to allow every employee to have direct connectivity to the Internet. Sometimes they'll get a single address from the Internet and have an e-mail server that is restricted to outbound only. Anybody from the Internet sending a message or a file to an employee would only be able to drop it off at this front doorstep, and the people inside the company would go and pull it off that machine. This would filter those in the company who could go out and also prevent anybody from the outside coming into your company.

Then there's another technique that's a little more sophisticated. For example, if you need to have e-mail and file transfer or other services, you could have a number of servers that would be isolated from your internal system; you'd have routers sitting between your system and the line of servers, and the Internet would be on the other side.

The most sophisticated implementation is firewalls, the most exotic and the most costly, which control access in and out. Basically, you configure the firewall to do what you need it to do. That would be the most solid security.

Press Releases and Corporate Reports

http://www.yahoo.com/
Economy/Markets_and_
Investments/Corporate Reports

The Corporate Reports section of the Yahoo index has links to corporate home pages. For most companies, the corporate reports are actually press releases. However, in addition to the press releases, you may find some other interesting information: product descriptions, Internet links, and even free downloadable software.

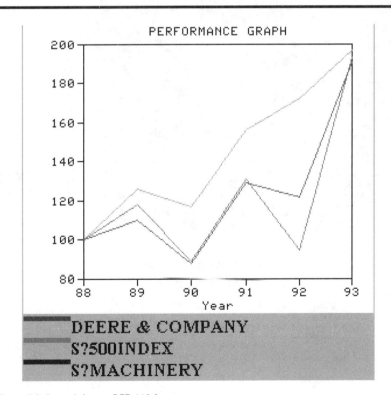

Figure 3.3 A graph from a DEF_14A form

Finding Out What's New on the Internet

Because the Internet is such a dynamic place, sites are constantly coming and going. Here are some of the best places to find out about new sites. Add them to your Hot list, or place a bookmark on them and visit them once a week. You can find other Internet search indexes, master lists, and what's new sites on the inside front cover and inside back cover.

Amdahl's WWW Hot Sites	http://www.amdahl.com/internet/general/sites.html
Internet Scout Report	http://www.internic.net/scout-report/
NCSA What's New Archive	http://www.ncsa.uiuc.edu/SDG/Software/Mosaic/Docs/old-whats-new/footer.html
NCSA What's New Page	http://www.ncsa.uiuc.edu/SDG/Software/Mosaic/Docs/whats-new.html
Top Ten Most Popular Fields of the WWW Virtual Library	http://www.w3.org/hypertext/DataSources/bySubject/TopTen.html
Useless Updates	http://www.primus.com/staff/paulp/useless/whatsnew.html
What's New	http://home.mcom.com/home/whats-new.html
What's New at internetMCI	http://www2.pcy.mci.net/whats-new/index.html
Xanadu What's New	http://xan.xan.com/whatsnew.html
Yahoo What's New	http://www.yahoo.com/yahoo/new/

SEC (Securities and Exchange Commission) EDGAR Archives

http://www.sec.gov/edgarhp.htm

Using this index of SEC documents, you can gather corporate filings and forms from nearly three-quarters of U.S. publicly traded companies.

Click on Search the EDGAR Database to start a search. Then click on Search the EDGAR Archives. Before you start a search, click on Here is a sample header file to see what a typical document looks like. If you are a first-time visitor, click on Here to see a page of instructions, valid operators (AND, OR, NOT, ADJ), rules, and examples. Then type a company name in the text box.

When the results of the search are returned, each found document is ranked according to its relevance to the search string—the number and location of matching keywords in the document and the number of times the keyword appears in a document compared with the total words in the document. Click on a company name to display the form (see Figure 3.2). You can find a description of each form at http://www.sec.gov/edaux/forms.htm.

Using this version of EDGAR, you can see the size of the find results as it loads. At the New York University EDGAR Project site, you can't. So, if you suspect that the results of the search will be gigantic and might take a long time to load, use this version for your search.

Note
You'll find these and other what's new sites on the inside of the back cover of this book.

Major Companies on the Internet

Although commercial activity on the Internet is still in the early stages, many major noncomputer companies are establishing home pages—primarily for marketing and product information but sometimes to provide a few entertaining minutes or some freeware.

In this section, you'll find a searchable directory of company Internet addresses and large companies with sites that do more than tell about goods and services. At the end of the section is a table of large companies whose pages, at the time of this writing, offer almost only company information and sometimes employment listings.

However, given the dynamic nature of the Internet, it is very likely that some of these companies might have added new features by the time you visit them.

Ameritech

http://www.aads.net/

At this site, you'll find company information (but not an overwhelming amount) and many Internet resources. Links include the Quick Index, a text table of contents; News and Information, press releases, a 1994 annual report, biographies, investor update, advertising; and Small Business Marketplace, an online brochure of Ameritech small-business products.

The best information at Ameritech is in The Internet InfoCenter, which has these categories: general guides and location tools, education, business and commerce, communications, government, and electronic publications and publishers.

MCI Telecommunications

http://www.mci.com/

MCI has been a leader in elegant design and innovation on World Wide Web pages. Now that others have caught up, MCI has opted for speed rather than for the slow-loading graphics of the past. At this site, you can find out What's New and About MCI. You also can link to other resources at the For Home, For Work, and For the Net pages. If you'd like an overview of this site, click on map or index.

Two interesting links enable you to page someone with a networkMCI or SkyTel pager (click on networkMCI paging) or to get today's news or to shop (click on internetMCI).

Table 3.1 lists some major companies and their addresses on the Internet. Sites provide product and company information, and many furnish annual reports and employment services.

Computer Companies

It is not surprising that computer companies constitute a large segment of the businesses that have sites on the Internet. After all, developers of networking software, graphics adapters, sound cards, word processors, and so on have a gigantic head start over other companies. Managers and employees use computers daily and know that there are few limits.

This section concerns computer software and hardware companies. In the first part are companies that offer extras. For example, some companies provide detailed white papers and product descriptions for all their products. Other sites are loaded with links to other Internet resources and offer shareware or freeware to be downloaded or information about buying a personal computer. At the end of the section is a table of companies that have sites under construction or that have sites primarily for advertising purposes. However, check these sites from time to time; things are always changing on the Internet.

Amdahl

http://www.amdahl.com/

This site provides standard product and service information, press releases, employment listings, and many links to Internet sites and information.

It is well worth touring the Internet Exploration area, at which you can link to popular World Wide Web pages and servers, searchable indexes, technical information about the World Wide Web, HTML and HTTP documentation, current events, hot sites, new sites, and resources. Perhaps the best link of all is What's New; much thought has gone into compiling these entries.

Table 3.1: Major Corporations on the Internet

Corporation	Home Page URL	Product/Service
Allen-Bradley	http://www.ab.com/	manufacturer of industrial automation control products
Allied Signal, Inc.	http://www.as.kcp.com/home/ascorp.html	manufacturing: aerospace and automotive products, chemicals, fibers, etc.
American Airlines, Inc.	http://www.amrcorp.com/home.htm	air transportation
Andersen Consulting	http://www.ac.com	management consulting
AT&T	http://www.att.com/infocenter/toc.html	communications
AT&T Bell Laboratories	http://www.research.att.com/	communications research
Beckman Instruments, Inc.	http://www.beckman.com/bkmhome.htm	manufacturer of laboratory instruments
Bell Atlantic	http://www.bell-atl.com	communications
Bellcore	http://www.bellcore.com/	communications
BellSouth Telecommunications	http://www.bst.bls.com/	communications
Boeing Company	http://www.boeing.com/	aircraft manufacturing
Burlington Coat Factory Warehouse Corp.	http://www.coat.com/	apparel retailer
Canadian Airlines	http://www.cdnair.ca	transportation
CBS Inc.	http://www.cbs.com/	television and radio
Celestial Seasonings, Inc.	http://usa.net/celestial/seasonings.html	beverages
Chevron Corporation	http://www.chevron.com	oil and fuels
Chiat/Day, Inc.	http://www.chiatday.com	advertising
Chrysler Corporation	http://www.rossroy.com/chrysler.htm	automobiles and trucks
Citicorp	http://www.citicorp.com	banking
Club Med, Inc.	http://www.clubmed.com/	resorts
Coca-Cola Corporation, Inc.	http://www.cocacola.com/	beverages and food
Dialog Information Services	http://www.dialog.com/	online information
Dow Chemical Company	http://www.dow.com/	chemicals

Table 3.1: Major Corporations on the Internet (continued)

Corporation	Home Page URL	Product/Service
E.I. du Pont de Nemours	http://www.dupont.com/	chemicals
Eastman Kodak Company	http://www.kodak.com/	photography, printers, copiers
Electrolux	http://mmm.wwa.com/elux/index.html	household appliances
Electronic Data Systems Corp.	http://www.eds.com/	computer outsourcing
Eli Lilly and Company	http://www.lilly.com/	pharmaceuticals
Ernst & Young	http://www.ernsty.co.uk/ernsty/	accounting, auditing, taxes, consulting
Federal Express	http://www.fedex.com/	package delivery
FMC Corporation	http://fmcweb.ncsa.uiuc.edu/home.html	diversified manufacturing
Foote Cone & Belding Technology Group	http://www.fcb-tg.com/fcb-tg/	advertising
Ford Motor Company	http://www.ford.com/	automobiles and trucks
Frigidaire	http://www.frigidaire.com	household appliances
General Electric	http://www.ge.com/	manufacturing and communications
General Motors	http://www.gm.com/	automobiles and trucks
Goodyear Tire & Rubber Company	http://www.goodyear.com/	rubber products
Grumman Data Systems	http://axon.sora.org/	data-processing services
GTE Corporation	http://info.gte.com	telecommunications
HBO & Co.	http://www.hboc.com/	cable television and movie production
ITT Corporation	http://www.itthartford.com	telecommunications, insurance, etc.
JCPenney	http://www.jcpenney.com/	retailer
Jostens, Inc.	gopher://gopher.jostens.com:2071/	jewelry manufacturer
KPMG Online	http://www.kpmg.ca	accounting, auditing, taxes, consulting
Lockheed Martin	http://www.lmsc.lockheed.com/	aircraft manufacturing
Mail Boxes Etc.	http://www.mbe.com/	package delivery, office services
MassMutual Corp.	http://www.massmutual.com/	insurance
MCA/Universal	http://www.mca.com/	entertainment
McDonnell Douglas Aerospace	http://pat.mdc.com/	aircraft manufacturing
Mobil Corporation	http://www.mobil.com	oil

Table 3.1: Major Corporations on the Internet (continued)

Corporation	Home Page URL	Product/Service
Monsanto	http://www.monsanto.com/	chemicals
Motorola	http://www.mot.com	electronics
Mutual of New York (MONY)	http://www.mony.com/	insurance
Nationwide Insurance	http://www.nationwide.com/	insurance
Nippon Telephone and Telegraph California	http://www.nttam.com/	communications
Northern Telecom	http://www.nortel.com/	communications
Pacific Bell	http://www.pacbell.com/	communications
Pacific Telesis Group	http://www.pactel.com/	communications
Panasonic (Matsushita Electric)	http://www.mei.co.jp/index.html	electronics
Pizza Hut	http://www.pizzahut.com/	fast food
PolyGram NV	http://www.polygram.com/polygram/	entertainment
Price Waterhouse	http://www.pw.com/	accounting, auditing, taxes, consulting
Reebok	http://planetreebok.com/	sports apparel and shoes
Ricoh	http://www.crc.ricoh.com	office machines
Rockwell International	http://www.rockwell.com/	defense manufacturing
Rohm & Haas Co.	http://www.rohmhaas.com/	chemicals
Schlumberger	http://www.slb.com/	petroleum equipment
Scholastic Corp.	http://www.scholastic.com/	publishing
Sears Roebuck and Comp.	http://www.careermosaic.com/cm/sears/sears1.html	retailer
Service Merchandise Co.	http://www.svcmerch.com/service/svcmerch .html	retailer
Shell Oil Company	http://www.shellus.com/	oil
Silverado Mines Ltd.	http://www.silverado.com/gold/home.html	precious metals mining
Sony	http://www.sony.com/	electronics and entertainment
Southwest Airlines	http://www.iflyswa.com/	transportation
Southwestern Bell	http://www.sbc.com	communications

Table 3.1: Major Corporations on the Internet (continued)

Corporation	Home Page URL	Product/Service
Sprint	http://www.sprintlink.net/	entertainment
Texaco, Inc.	http://www.texaco.com/	oil
Time Warner, Inc.	http://www.timeinc.com/	publishing and communications
Toshiba Corporation	http://www.toshiba.co.jp/	electronics
U.S. Healthcare	http://www.ushc.com/	managed health care
Unilever United States	http://www.eat.com/	soap, food
United Parcel Service	http://www.ups.com/	package deliverer
Universal Studios	http://universtudios.com/	entertainment
US West Technologies	http://www.uswest.com/	communications
Volkswagen AG	http://volkswagen.com/	automobile manufacturing
Volvo AB	http://www.volvocars.com/	automobile manufacturing
Wal-Mart Stores, Inc.	http://sam.wal-mart.com	retailer
Warner Brothers/IUMA	http://iuma.com/IUMA/index_graphic.html	entertainment
Whirlpool Corporation	http://www.whirlpool.com	household appliances
Xerox	http://www.xerox.com/	office copiers and printers

Apple Computer Corporation

http://www.apple.com:80/

This commercial site can be useful to Apple hardware and software users. Here, you will find product support, developer information and services, white papers, many downloadable technical reports, user group information, and links to Apple-related sites, indexes, and software. You can download the *Information Alley* news magazine and read it using either Adobe Acrobat Reader or No Hands Common Ground, which you can download from this site.

Compaq

http://www-es.compaq.com/cgi-bin/present/table_of_contents.html

Compaq might have the most comprehensive product documentation on the Web. At this commercial site, you will find page after page of newsletters, product announcements, technical publications, and white papers.

You can download Acrobat Reader for Windows from this site.

Digital Equipment Corporation

http://www.digital.com/www-cgi-bin/textit/info/directory.html

Digital is one of the pioneers of World Wide Web pages. This text directory has links to a great deal of company and support information as well as to other Web servers.

To get customer information and Internet links, select Info Centers. The well-planned Reading Rooms section is like a virtual Internet link library, with an Education Reading Room, Research Reading Room, and Museums and Libraries Reading Room.

You can download Acrobat Reader for Windows from this site.

Chris Lopes on Internet Software Compatibility

How do you handle communications between computers that have incompatible operating systems?

If you're going to talk to machines out there on the Internet, obviously you need to have compatible software. For example, there are a lot of Unix machines, and there's a common protocol, sendmail, which is a mail program. Sometimes configuring sendmail can be extremely difficult. Very often people who have Unix machines have the biggest problem configuring sendmail so that they can actually talk to somebody out there. For transport protocol, you need to have compatible software on your computer and TCP/IP, which allows two computers to communicate. TCP/IP runs on anything from a small personal computer to large mainframes and supercomputers.

What happens when things don't work? It's not like when a company has its own company network. If things go wrong with a company network, the company can call a network control center. It doesn't work that way on the Internet; you have to do a lot of your own troubleshooting. When problems occur, somebody who

IBM Corporate Home Page

http://www.ibm.com/

This large, well-designed, primarily commercial site provides links to IBM locations worldwide, news, products, services and support, and technology and research. It is worth looking at the table of contents to see the extent of the information here.

IBM Index of Internet Resources

http://www.ibm.net/

This site provides one of the best and longest lists of Internet resources anywhere on the Net. An extra bonus is that there is almost no IBM advertising here. Categories include Worldwide Reference Library, Internet Search Tools, Lively Arts, Business District, Entertainment, Travel Center, News Rack, Shop the Net, Sports Scene, WWW Search Tools, FTP Sites, and Arcade. These pages warrant a good long look.

IBM PC Company

http://www.pc.ibm.com/

The IBM PC Company site is dedicated to personal computers. Here, you can obtain product information, news, support, and an extensive library of downloadable shareware for OS/2 and DOS.

You could actually run a small business using the shareware in the software library (look under File), which is updated every day. Programs, some of which are two or three years old, include a financial planner, an area code finder, a spreadsheet, a billing program, address books, checkbook managers, mailing lists, schedulers, and so on.

The pcweb central section includes what's new information (all IBM), an index of this site, and links to Internet resources—not updated regularly.

hasn't had a lot of experience can probably identify some of the more common problems, for example, some of the techniques that you can use to test connections.

Unix has been around for quite a while, and the software used to access the Internet (except for sendmail), such as TCP/IP, has been embedded in Unix for a number of years; the communications software is embedded right into the operating system. It's a thoroughly tested system; it has received more testing than most and also better support than most.

When you compare Unix with network servers, a lot of those servers were not really put together for this internetworking capability. They were more or less designed for small in-house PC networks. There have been modifications that allow them to internetwork, but it's been a painful process. What it means very often is embedding one protocol within another, which just adds another level of complexity; these servers are not really architected to do that. The actual transport mechanisms are a little more complicated. But as time goes on, the servers and the TCP/IP software are getting more robust and are now becoming a standard component of NetWare, Windows NT, and systems like that.

Intel

http://www.intel.com/

The Intel site is well designed with fast-loading graphics. You'll find a great deal of Intel information and advertising wherever you go.

If you plan to buy a new personal computer, check out Intel's valuable resources: Processors & PCs and Processor and System Performance. Select Processors & PCs to read *Selecting Your PC*, an entertaining, informative, and sometimes commercial, interactive manual. Visit this site before you buy.

Microsoft

http://www.microsoft.com/

This very large site furnishes users with product and technical information, press releases, articles, support bulletins, a searchable index, and a downloadable software library, primarily containing updated driver files and utilities.

The Microsoft Knowledge Base provides technical articles about problems and resolutions. If you have a problem with or a question about a Microsoft product, chances are that you will find your solution here.

Microsoft TV, which is part of this site, provides computer courses on cable television or on videotape. The cost of a videotape ranges from $19.95 to $25.00 plus $3.00 freight.

Siemens Nixdorf

http://www.sni.de/

This German site consists of product and service information and downloadable software. In some sections, the English is fractured but generally understandable.

Go to Goodies, from which you can download three clever and subtly commercial screen savers (see Figures 3.4, 3.5, and 3.6) and one demo program. Siemens expects to add more software to the Goodies section.

To install a screen saver, follow these steps:

1. Double-click on OFFWRLD.EXE, OFFWRLD2.EXE, or SCREENY.EXE in Windows Explorer or the My Computer window to decompress the file.

2. Double-click on SETUP.EXE.

3. In the first dialog box, click on the Installieren button.

4. In the second dialog box, click on OK. The set-up program places the screen saver (SCR file) in the WINDOWS folder.

5. Open the Display Properties dialog box. (Either right-click on the desktop; or click on the Start button, select Settings, choose Control Panel, and double-click on the Display icon.)

Figure 3.4 A scene from the OfficeWorld Adventures screen saver

6. Click on the Screen Saver tab.

7. Select OfficeWorld Adventures, OfficeWorld Adventures II, or Screeny Life! from the Screen Saver list box. (Click on Preview if you want to test the screen saver first.)

8. Click on OK.

Figure 3.5 An officer confronts a burglar, thanks to networked computers.

Sun Microsystems, Inc.

http://www.sun.com/

Sun, the sponsor of the SunSITE program at universities worldwide, provides a home page that is similar to a monthly magazine. At this site, you can read interviews with Internet personages (for example, the founders of the Yahoo Internet index), get company and product information, and access a hotlinked index of SunSITEs at universities worldwide.

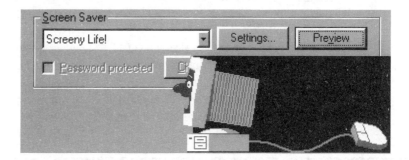

Figure 3.6 A half-eaten dialog box from the Screeny Life! screen saver

Sun provides a glossary of programming and computer terms and links to related terms. Go to http://www.xm.com/sunworld/glossary/glossary.html. Then click on a letter or Numbers.

At the SunSITE home page (http://www.sun.com/cgi-bin/show?/sunsite/index.html) are links to SunSITEs around the world.

HotJava (http://java.dnx.com) is a WWW browser that runs on several platforms.

Symantec

http://www.symantec.com/

At this site, Symantec provides company, service, and support information for products such as Norton Desktop, Norton Utilities, ACT! and Q&A. Here, Symantec furnishes links to the Anti-Virus Reference Center, other computer companies and Internet resources, and downloadable files.

The Fast Index (http://www.symantec.com/fastindx.html) provides text links. In the What's New section, you can volunteer to become a beta site for new software releases

Chris Lopes on Limiting Access to Files

On the World Wide Web, I've noticed that you cannot access some folders. How does a Web site mark private folders?

It's amazing that some machines on the Internet could be workstations sitting on somebody's desk. There can be different types of information on a machine; some of it may be for public consumption and some may not.

How do you identify that?

Let's say that you go to a machine and want to get some data using anonymous FTP. The person controlling that data could assign certain access rights to anonymous users. That would mean that you may not allow

and read product announcements. The Anti-Virus Reference Center links you to articles about viruses, What's Hot (see Figure 3.7), virus terminology and information, specific virus descriptions, and solutions using Norton Anti-Virus.

The link to Industry Vendors provides links to a long list of companies, Internet service providers, publications, commercial locations, and more.

Table 3.2 lists other computer companies. At the time of this writing, most sites were devoted to company, product, and service information.

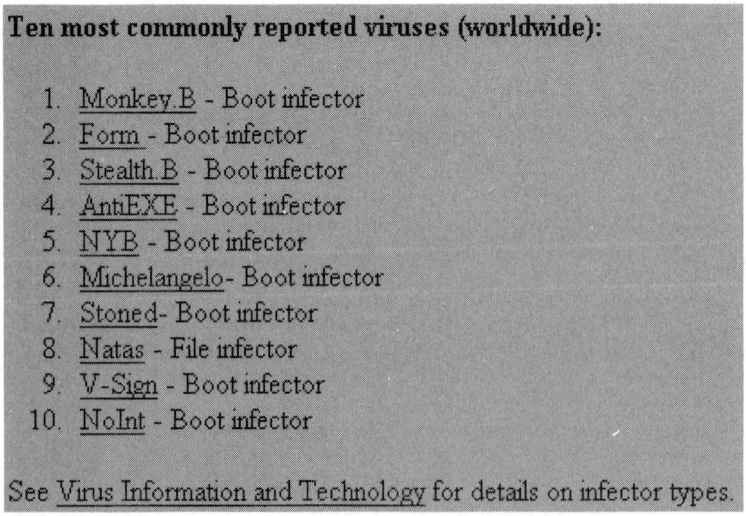

Company Directories

Company directories can range from thousands of international or country entries to a short list of companies in a small city. You can get good information from either type of directory. For example, if you are just starting a business in Austin, Texas, you can find suppliers, competitors, and even a restaurant review or two in the Austin Internet Yellow Pages. Or, if you market specialized electronic equipment to radio stations worldwide, you can compile a mailing list from the ITU Global Telecom Directory.

This section presents sites that list companies of all sizes and types.

Ten most commonly reported viruses (worldwide):

1. Monkey.B - Boot infector
2. Form - Boot infector
3. Stealth.B - Boot infector
4. AntiEXE - Boot infector
5. NYB - Boot infector
6. Michelangelo - Boot infector
7. Stoned - Boot infector
8. Natas - File infector
9. V-Sign - Boot infector
10. NoInt - Boot infector

See Virus Information and Technology for details on infector types.

Figure 3.7 The What's Hot list of "popular" viruses

ASM International® Materials Producers Directory

http://www.asm-intl.org/
www-asm/matprod/
matp_0.htm

ASM International, formerly the American Society for Metals, is an

visitors to see certain directories, or you may say it won't hurt if they see other directories. Even personal computers have at least some capability to protect the files. Most of the systems out there are multiuser systems; so they are a little more sophisticated than typical DOS.

[*Windows 95 allows users to assign file attributes: Read-only, Archive, Hidden, and System. Read-only files can be viewed, but cannot be edited or deleted. Archive files can be viewed, edited, or deleted. Hidden files are hidden so that outsiders do not even know that these files exist. System files are used to run Windows and should be hidden from visitors.*]

international organization of metallurgists and others working in materials sciences. The ASM International Materials Producers Directory claims to contain address and telephone information for more than 1,000 companies that produce and sell raw materials. To search the directory, click on a letter. The resulting pages are completely text; no Internet links are provided.

Audio Pro Resource Guide

http://www.cudenver.edu/
aes/audiopro/aproindex.html

The Audio Engineering Society (AES) presents a directory of audio and related companies on a long page. Links include National/International Professional Audio Companies, Product Components and Raw Materials, Audio Consulting Services, Localized Professional Audio Companies (worldwide),

and Additional Audio Related WWW Links. Each directory entry includes a link to its home page and usually a brief company description.

Austin Internet Yellow Pages

http://www.yp.com/

Austin Internet Store, Inc., furnishes lists of businesses and organizations based in Austin, Texas. Companies are arranged either alphabetically or by category. Also at this site is a restaurant guide (see Figure 3.8).

Figure 3.8 A graphic from the Austin Restaurants page of the Austin Internet Yellow Pages

Table 3.2: Selected Computer Companies on the Internet

Company	URL	Product/Service
3Com	http://www.3com.com/	networking hardware and software
Acorn Software, Inc.	http://www.acornsw.com/	storage-related software for Digital computers
Adaptec, Inc.	http://www.adaptec.com/	software, SCSI host adapters, network interface cards
Adobe Systems, Inc.	http://www.adobe.com/	software, including PostScript, typefaces, Adobe PageMaker, Adobe Photoshop, Adobe Illustrator, Adobe Persuasion, and Adobe Acrobat, which you can download from this site
Advanced Micro Devices, Inc.	http://www.amd.com/	integrated circuits: microprocessors, processors, memory
Advanced Storage Concepts	http://www.eden.com/~asc/	SCSI host adapter boards
Alta Technology	http://www.xmission.com/~altatech/	processors, interfaces, and software for parallel computing systems
Apple	http://www.apple.com/	Macintosh computers, Apple Newton, and software, such as QuickTime, Mac OS, Claris software products, eWorld online system
Asante Technologies, Inc.	http://www.asante.com/	Ethernet network adapters and hubs, network management software
askSam Systems	http://199.44.45.2/asKSam.htm	database software
Attachmate Corporation	http://www.atm.com/	client/server software
Bachman Information Systems	http://www.novalink.com/bachman/index.html	software: client/server development, process management, business modeling
Bentley Systems	http://www.bentley.com/	CAD software
Berkeley Software Design, Inc.	http://www.bsdi.com/	BSD/OS operating system
Bolt Beranek and Newman Inc.	http://www.bbn.com/	contract research and development services for computer, communications, and acoustics technologies
Borland International, Inc.	http://www.borland.com/	software: Turbo Pascal, Turbo C++, dBASE, Paradox, and client/server programs

Table 3.2: Selected Computer Companies on the Internet (continued)

Company	URL	Product/Service
Cambridge Scientific	http://www.camsci.com/	software for chemists and engineers
Carnegie Group, Inc.	http://www.cgi.com/CGI/	knowledge-based software for business
CheckPoint Software Technologies	http://www.checkpoint.com/	Internet security software
Cheyenne Software, Inc.	http://www.chey.com/	backup, fax, storage management, virus protection software
Cisco Systems	http://www.cisco.com/	internetworking operating system and management software and hardware
Claris Corporation	http://www.claris.com/	software for the Macintosh
Comptons New Media	http://www.comptons.com/	interactive multimedia software
CompuGraph International	http://www.compugraph.com/	hardware and software sales online
CompuServe	http://www.compuserve.com/	online service
Computer Associates International, Inc.	http://www.cai.com/	mainframe, midrange, PC, and Macintosh software
Computervision, Inc.	http://cvinfo.cv.com/	engineering data and life-cycle management software and services
Connectsoft	http://www.connectsoft.com/	e-mail and communications software; clip art and fonts
Convex Computer Corporation	http://www.convex.com/	supercomputers
Core Systems	http://www.corsys.com/	buyers and sellers of Unix hardware and software
Corel	http://www.corel.ca/	CorelDRAW, Ventura Publisher, PhotoPAINT
Cray Research, Inc.	http://www.cray.com/	supercomputers
Creative Labs	http://www.creaf.com/	sound cards
Data General Corp.	http://www.dg.com/	servers, storage products, and services
Dell Computer	http://www.dell.com	retail seller of computers, peripherals, and software
Delphi Internet	http://www.delphi.com/	online service
DeLorme Mapping	http://www.delorme.com/	map software

Table 3.2: Selected Computer Companies on the Internet (continued)

Company	URL	Product/Service
Delrina Corporation	http://www.delrina.com/	software for fax, voice, data communications, and electronic forms processing
Diamond Multimedia Systems, Inc.	http://www.diamondmm.com/	graphics and video cards
Diskovery Educational Systems	http://www.diskovery.com/Diskovery/	education software dealers
Electronic Arts	http://www.ea.com/80/	entertainment software for game systems, interactive CD-ROM players, and computers
Encore Computer Corporation	http://www.encore.com/	open, massively parallel, scalable computer and storage systems
Enterprise Integration Technologies (EIT)	http://www.eit.com/	information technology consulting company
Epic MegaGames	http://www.epicgames.com/	entertainment software for game systems, interactive CD-ROM players, and computers
Expersoft Corporation	http://www.expersoft.com/	software and services for the distributed object management field
Farallon Computing, Inc.	http://www.farallon.com/	Ethernet software
Frame Technology, Inc.	http://www.frame.com/	FrameMaker and other writing and publishing software
FTP Software, Inc.	http://www.ftp.com/	network software
Fujitsu	http://www.fujitsu.co.jp/index-e.html	computers, communications systems, and electronic devices
FutureSoft Engineering, Inc.	http://www.fse.com/	communications software
General Magic	http://www.genmagic.com/	communications software creation and hardware design
Groupe Bull	http://www.bull.com/	servers, personal computers, software, and services
Gupta Corporation	http://www.gupta.com/	client/server software
Harris Computer Systems	http://www.csd.harris.com/	computers, operating systems, and security software
Hayes Microcomputer Products	gopher://gopher.almac.co.uk/11/business/comms/hayes	modems
Hercules Computer Technology	http://www.hercules.com/	graphics boards and multimedia boards
Hewlett-Packard	http://www.hp.com/	personal computers, printers, software

Table 3.2: Selected Computer Companies on the Internet (continued)

Company	URL	Product/Service
Hitachi, Ltd.	http://www.hitachi.co.jp:80/	computers, semiconductors, and other non computer products
Id Software, Inc.	http://www.idsoftware.com/	Doom and other game software
Informix Software, Inc.	http://www.informix.com/	database and application development software
Interleaf, Inc.	http://www.ileaf.com/	publishing software
IONA Technologies	http://www.iona.ie/	software development kit
ISDN Systems Corporation	http://www.infoanalytic.com/isc/	LAN connectivity software
James River Group	http://www.jriver.com/	software for connecting PCs to Unix systems
Kaleida Labs	http://www.kaleida.com/	multimedia software, some of which you can download
Lexmark International	http://www.lexmark.com/	printers and printer drivers
Lotus Development Corporation	http://www.lotus.com/	Notes, Lotus 1-2-3, Lotus Approach, Lotus Word Pro, Lotus Freelance Graphics, Lotus Organizer, and other software
Lynx Real-Time Systems, Inc.	http://www.lynx.com/	real-time operating system
Mathsoft	http://www.mathsoft.com/	calculation, browser, and other software
MathWorks	http://www.mathworks.com/	scientific and engineering software
Media Vision, Inc.	http://www.mediavis.com/	sound cards
Micro Focus	http://www.mfltd.co.uk/	host and client/server software
MIPS Technologies, Inc.	http://www.mips.com/	microprocessors
Motorola PowerPC	http://www.mot.com/PowerPC/	personal computers
Nanao	http://www.traveller.com/nanao/	high-resolution monitors
NaviSoft	http://www.navisoft.com/	networking publishing software for the World Wide Web
NetManage, Inc.	http://www.netmanage.com/	Internet software
Netscape Communications Corporation	http://www.netscape.com/	Internet browser software
NeXT Computer	http://www.next.com/	NEXTSTEP and other software
Novell, Inc.	http://www.novell.com/	networking hardware and software

Table 3.2: Selected Computer Companies on the Internet (continued)

Company	URL	Product/Service
Olivetti North America	http://www.spk.olivetti.com/	client-server software; PCs; terminals; and printers
Oracle Corporation	http://www.oracle.com/	database, connectivity, client/server, and multimedia software
ORIGIN Systems, Inc.	http://www.ea.com/origin.html	games for game systems and computers
ParaSoft	http://www.parasoft.com/	tools for software development
Persoft	http://town.hall.org/sponsors/persoft.html	wireless bridge that connects sites
Philips Semiconductors North America Corp.	http://www.semiconductors.philips.com/ps/	semiconductors, products for communications
Pick Systems	http://www.picksys.com/	database software
Proteon, Inc.	http://www.proteon.com/	internetworking software
QMS	http://www.qms.com/	monochrome and color printers
Qualcomm	http://www.qualcomm.com/	enterprise software, such as Eudora electronic mail
Quantum Software Systems, Ltd.	http://www.qnx.com/	real-time operating system
Racal-Datacom	http://www.racal.com/	digital access and LAN products
Radius, Inc.	http://www.radius.com/	software and digital video
Rocket Science	http://rocketsci.com/	games for all CD-ROM platforms
Santa Cruz Operation, Inc. (SCO)	http://www.sco.com/	client/server software
SAS Institute	http://www.sas.com/	information delivery software
Seagate Technology	http://www.seagate.com/	hard drives
Sega of America	http://www.segaoa.com/	games for computers and game systems
Sequent Computer Systems, Inc.	http://www.sequent.com/	computers and software
Shiva Corporation	http://www.shiva.com/	remote access software
Silicon Graphics Incorporated	http://www.sgi.com/	hardware and software
Sleepless Software	http://www.xmission.com/~nosleep/	game software
Spyglass, Inc.	http://www.spyglass.com/	enhanced Mosaic and visual data analysis software

Table 3.2: Selected Computer Companies on the Internet (continued)

Company	URL	Product/Service
Standard Microsystems Corporation	http://www.smc.com/	chips, networking, LAN and Ethernet hardware
Sterling Software	http://www.sterling.com/	banking and network software
Sybase	http://www.sybase.com/	client/server software
Systems & Computer Technology Corp.	http://www.sctcorp.com	information management software for higher education, government, and utilities
Taligent, Inc.	http://www.taligent.com/	application development software
Tektronix	http://www.tek.com/	color printers, video systems, and network displays
Telebit	http://www.telebit.com/	routers, modems, and network hardware
Tera Computer	http://204.118.137.100/	high-performance computers
Thinking Machines Corporation	http://www.think.com/	supercomputers
Tippecanoe Systems, Inc.	http://www.tippecanoe.com/	information indexing and retrieval software
Unisys	http://www.unisys.com/	workstations, printers, servers, retail terminals, software
U.S. Robotics	http://www.primenet.com/usr/	modems
Virtual Entertainment	http://www.cts.com/~vman/	virtual reality games
Visionware	http://www.visionware.co.uk/	server, networking, and terminal emulation software
WAIS, Inc.	http://www.wais.com/	online publishing systems and services
Western Digital Corporation	http://www.wdc.com/	hard drives and graphics and video cards
Wolfram Research, Inc.	http://www.wri.com/	Mathematica software
The Wollongong Group	http://www.twg.com/	network operating systems, protocols
Xircom	http://www.organic.com:80/Commercial/Xircom	adapters and modems for mobile networking
XOR Network Engineering, Inc.	http://plaza.xor.com/xor/	networking engineering and support services; Internet services

BAM Online 100

http://www.sirius.com/~bam/list.html

This is an alphabetically arranged list of companies rated by the quality of their World Wide Web sites. Originally, the list was supposed to be released monthly. At the time of this writing, a new list had not appeared for several months.

Click on Wave Rating to see how the rating system works. Then click on The List to look at the list and optionally link to the companies on the list.

Bay Area Aerospace Database

http://www.lmsc.lockheed.com/aiaa/sf/db/dbhome.html

At this site, you can access a text list of aerospace companies in the San Francisco Bay area. Click on one of the 83 links to enter the database; you can scroll through all the entries. Each entry consists of fields with company name, address, telephone numbers, e-mail address or URL, SIC numbers, and other details.

Biomedical Companies

http://fairway.ecn.purdue.edu/~ieeeembs/companies.html

At this site, you can access biomedical companies by clicking on All companies in database or on Companies categorized by product/service. At the time of this writing, each of the 119 entries in the All companies list was composed of name and address; few links were provided. Product/service categories are Biotechnology, Laboratory Equipment, Medical Equipment, Pharmaceuticals, Prosthetics, and Surgical Equipment—a much shorter list.

BizWeb

http://www.bizweb.com/

The people at BizWeb state that they "scour the Internet for company and product information so you won't have to." At this company

directory/shopping site, you can either look for companies using a keyword search index or browse through a list of categories. If you are a first-time visitor, browsing is probably the way to go. To look for a company, click on a category link. On the resulting page, click on a link to "visit" the company. Some entries are preceded by small icons: The New icon indicates that the entry has been added within the last 30 days; the Updated icon indicates that the entry has been edited within the last 30 days; $ORDER$ indicates that the company will accept online orders.

The BLUE Directory of Food & Beverage Businesses

http://www.pvo.com/

This comprehensive site, provided by ProVisions Online, is a large list of food and beverage sites on the Internet. Major links include Allied Services (such as Internet cooking sites, kitchen equipment, food and beverage software, other directories, and so on); Associations and Organizations; Cool Sites of the Months for this and previous months; Educational Centers; Food Sciences, Research and Development; Manufacturers—General Product Information; Publications, Recipes, and References; Restaurants; Retailers (with links under Beverage and Foods headings); Specialty Gifts; and Wholesalers.

Canadian Internet Business Directory

http://cibd.com/cibd/

You can search this index of Canadian business, government, education, and organization sites by company name, province, or type. Because of an above-average graphic size (50 kilobytes), it takes some time to load.

To search, click on Company Name, Province, or Type. If you select Company Name, the companies, government departments, educational institutions, and organizations are arranged alphabetically. Click on a link to display a page of information.

Chandlerman's Corporate Page

http://naftalab.bus.utexas.edu/~chandler/corporate.html

This unique site (its buttons are certainly different) consists of corporate graphical links, with short descriptions. At the bottom of the page is a drop-down list box, from which you can choose other pages. Interesting pages are Wild Things and Useful Stuff.

Links at the Wild Things page go to electronic magazines, shopping, and entertainment pages. Choose Useful Stuff to go to Internet and computer-related sites: tutorials, indexes, jargon, and security. Take Us Home returns you to the home page.

Commercial Services on the Net

http://www.directory.net/

This well-designed site offers lists of business and commercial establishments (particularly those that provide Internet services to other companies), government departments, membership and professional organizations, nonprofit organizations, and more. At this site you can see what's new (updated daily), view the alphabetic listings, and search an index.

To search, type one or two keywords in the text box (see Figure 3.9) following the instructions immediately above it; then click on the Search button. To refine a two-keyword search, click on the AND or OR option button. Selecting AND finds listings that contain both keywords; selecting OR finds listings that contain at least one of the keywords. The results of a search are links that also show all the keywords for the entry.

Commercial WWW Servers

http://www.eit.com/web/www.servers/commercial.html

From Enterprise Integration Technologies (EIT), this site consists of a long, hot-linked, alphabetically arranged list of businesses. To search, either click on a letter or scroll down the list until you find the desired company. You'll find other resources at this address.

Companies on the Web

http://www.scescape.com/worldlibrary/business/companies/index.html

Companies on the Web is a comprehensive site providing lists of links for companies, large and small. To look for a company, scroll down the home page and click on a business type (from Advertising to Travel Agents) under the heading Companies on the Web. You'll see either a page of subcategories from which you can select or links for specific companies.

Computer and Communications Companies Directory

http://www.cmpcmm.com/cc/companies.html

At this site you can access lists of computer and communications companies through: an index, a full-text 250 kilobytes list of about 2,000 companies, a compressed version, links to almost 100 other company directories or company home pages that

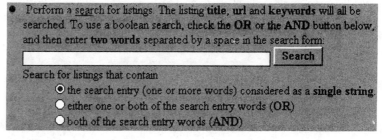

Figure 3.9 The directory search area of the Commercial Services on the Net page

Chris Lopes on Internet Addressing

Most machines have a name that's kind of user-friendly so that users can refer to a machine by a name (that is, username @organization-name.domain). The Internet address is made up of 4-byte fields of 32 bits. Each machine has different combinations of bits; so when you're talking about an Internet address, you're talking about the actual numeric address. There are mechanisms that allow you to map from this numeric to something that's more user-friendly.

Addresses aren't free, and they're very difficult to get. As a matter of fact, certain classes of addresses are not available, and even when they were, they were very expensive. But TCP/IP is being modified to extend the addressing capabilities within the Internet. From what I understand, it's being tested now. So this address constraint problem may be relieved in the very near future.

When the Internet was beginning—you know it started out as a military thing and the universities were using it. Some companies also had access, but it was kind of like an unwritten agreement that you would not use it for profit making; obviously all that has changed. Because the Internet is growing, the question is, Who's paying for all this? The money that companies pay for these addresses is one source of revenue.

There are different types of addresses. There are, for example, some environments that may have a lot of internal networks and not many machines on each network. Then, there are some companies that may have one or two networks, but they may have lots of machines on those networks; so you can map different types of addresses to get particular configurations. So you'll hear the terms Class A, B, and C addresses. Class A addresses are normally used by the biggest companies. Class B will be used by large companies—smaller than Class A—and Class C is for small companies. For example, I work for a small division; there's about 250 of us. I think we have three Class C addresses.

There's a technique called subnetting that further extends your address range. So, you can actually make one Class C address function like more than one if you need to. But that's a technique that you normally use internally. You have to coordinate the components that sit between your company and the Internet, but it's something that visitors who are coming into your system don't know about.

Computer ESP (Electronic Search Page)

http://www.uvision.com/

This impressive site provides comprehensive information about thousands of computer companies. To search for entries for a particular company or product, use the search index; type a company or product name in the text box at the top of the page and click on the Search button. You also can browse products—using either a full list or by detailed categories and subcategories.

Computer Hardware and Software Vendor List

http://sunsite.ust.hk/homepage/vendors.html

This nongraphical page of hundreds of links enables you to visit computer companies worldwide. Click on a typical link and go to the company home page for product information, customer support, press releases, and employment information.

contain company information, or an alphabetic version (simply click on a letter or on Non-alphabetic). Click on Overview to access related pages: conference listings, media, organizations, programs and projects, standards, and Usenet groups and FAQs.

The Dutch Yellow Pages

http://www.markt.nl/dyp/index-en.html

From the Twente University of Technology, this site consists of a searchable index of companies in the Netherlands, arranged alphabetically by category. To search the index, click on a category, a subcategory, and a company name. Each entry consists of the company name, a World Wide Web link, address, telephone number, fax number, and e-mail address.

Electronics Manufacturers on the Net

http://www.webscope.com/elx/homepage.html

This site lists manufacturers of electronic hardware. You can access this directory by product (Product Index) or by company (Alphabetical List of Companies). To search for a product, click on a category on one page, and then click on a company name on the next. To search for a company, click on a letter at the top of the page, which "jumps" to the part of the page on which that letter starts.

Global Commerce Link Business Directory

http://www.commerce.com:80/net2/bin/companies.cgi

At this page is a small searchable directory of alphabetically arranged companies and several libraries of various resources. Click on a letter to jump to the location of the desired company.

The Gray Pages™

http://www.trinet.com/tgp/

From *Triangle On-line*, an interactive magazine, comes a list of businesses in Charlotte and the Research Triangle Park area in North Carolina. Directory entries are organized under business

type, from Advertising to Writers. Click on a business type to go to a text page of names, street and city addresses, telephone numbers, and e-mail addresses.

The Insider: Public Companies

http://networth.galt.com/www/home/info/insider

The Insider provides a long and comprehensive list of World Wide Web sites of publicly held companies. To find a company, either click on a letter of the alphabet, or scroll down the list until you find the desired entry. A typical entry (see Figure 3.10) includes the stock exchange on which the company is traded, its symbol, and a word or phrase describing what the company produces.

To jump to the company's location on the list, click on a letter of the alphabet. You can also scroll through the list to make a selection.

Interactive Age Hot 1000

http://techweb.cmp.com/techweb/ia/hot1000/hot1.html

This site provides tables listing the top 1,000 North American companies by U.S. sales. (Click on *Click here* at the top of the home page if your browser does not support tables.) Each entry in the table

- Western Digital Corp. (NYSE: WDC) - disk drives
- Western Micro Technology Inc. (NASDAQ: WSTM) - electronic component supplies and testing
- Whirlpool Corp. (NYSE: WHR) - appliances
- The Williams Cos., Inc. (NYSE: WMB)
- Wind River Systems Inc. (NASDAQ: WIND)
- Wyman Gordon (NASDAQ: WYMN)

X:
- Xerox Corp. (NYSE: XRX)
- Xicor Inc. (NYSE: XICO) - memory device semiconductors
- Xilinx Inc. (NASDAQ: XLNX) - programmable logic semiconductors and software
- Xircom Inc. (NASDAQ: XIRC) - wireless computer network hardware
- Xylogics Inc. (NASDAQ: XLGX)

Y:

Figure 3.10 Part of the Insider list of publicly held companies

shows the company name, its sales, and telephone number. If the company has a site on the World Wide Web, click on a link to go to its home page.

Internet Business Pages

http://www.ibp.com/pit/index.html

From Pittsburgh, Pennsylvania, this site is composed of a list of links to small companies and organizations in the area. What's New shows the new listings, advertisers' specials, and news. Yellow Pages lists businesses and organizations and, sometimes, addresses, in alphabetic order by category.

Internet Digipages

http://www.milfac.co.uk/milfac/

Millennium Facilities Ltd. has produced files listing thousands of United Kingdom companies, in these categories: UK Companies Alphabetical Listing, UK Companies by Product/Service Category, Acquisition Register of UK Companies, and the Business Opportunities Database.

At the time of this writing, the best way to obtain company information was by selecting the Alphabetical Listing or the Product/Service Category; the Acquisition Register was where companies register, and the Business Opportunities Database was under construction.

ITU Global Telecom Directory

gopher://info.itu.ch:70/11/.1/ITU-Databases/.1/GlobalDir

This directory lists telecommunications companies, organizations, and government agencies worldwide. The directory contains names, titles, mailing addresses, and telephone and fax numbers for contacts within all ITU member organizations. Entries include radio, television, commissions, telecommunications, and satellite companies. Figure 3.11 shows a typical directory entry.

For information on how to search, click on the How to Search the ITU Global Telecom Directory icon.

Japanese Corporate Sites and R&D Laboratories

http://fuji.stanford.edu/japan_information/corporate_list.html

Mike Bayle and Burton Lee at Stanford University have compiled a list of the server sites of Japanese companies, offices of international companies, and research and development laboratories. Click on a link to go to its home page.

```
MCI Telecommunications Corporation, (United States)
-----------------------------------------------------------------
MCI Telecommunications Corporation
8283 Greenboro Drive, 1136/625
MCLEAN, VA 221026

Telephone      +1 703 442-6262

ITU-T Member: Yes ITU-R Member: Yes ITU-D Member: No

Mr. Peter P. Guggina,  MCI Telecommunications Corporation

Date of last modification : 31-January-95
```

Figure 3.11 An entry in the ITU Global Telecom Directory

Louisiana State Vendors

gopher://VM.CC.LATECH
.EDU:70/11/lascmain/vendors

At this site, you'll find the vendors that sell to the state of Louisiana. The list is sorted in two ways: by vendor identification number and alphabetically. Each entry consists of the name, address, and telephone number.

Milwaukee Marketplace

http://www.mixcom.com/

This page not only provides a list of companies in the Milwaukee area but also includes Milwaukee information: events, sports, places to visit, calendar of events, and classified ads.

The company list is alphabetically arranged by category. Click on a category to see a list of subcategories and links to companies. Click on the company name to see a page of information and sometimes links to other information.

Pan's List of Corporations

http://www.cs.utexas.edu/users/
paris/corporate.html

This is a gigantic page (millions of bytes) of graphical links (see Figure 3.12) to more than 100 alphabetically arranged corporate home pages, primarily for corporations in the computer and communications fields. Because of all the little graphics, this long list takes a long time to load. (The author should consider developing a

Chris Lopes on Telephone Lines and Internet Access Speed

Would you suggest that someone setting up a server use a special phone line?

It depends really on what your requirements are in terms of how much access you really intend on having. It's a rule of thumb that if you're going to access any system—connect to it more than three hours a day—you're actually better off having a dedicated link for yourself.

And that would be a higher speed?

Well, dedicated links normally run at higher speeds than lines that are connected by dial-up or something like that. That doesn't necessarily have to be the case. But you'd have to take a look at what your real needs are, and then you can make that decision accordingly. There are point-to-point links that run pretty slow. Basically, when it comes to paying for them, what is critical is the distance involved. And if it is a dial connection, is the point of provider a local call? Is there 800 service? There are a number of things that you have to look at. Basically, there's a wide range of connectivity, but what is important is

that you manage the traffic going in and out of your site; so it depends on whether you have many people or just a single individual using the line. If multiple people are using the line, normally there will be a router at the company site; and the router will be connected to the provider.

What about a high-speed line?

Graphics are made up of a lot more bits than text data; so depending on how long you want to wait, obviously a faster line will come back quicker.

And a faster computer?

The computer has to process this incoming stream. So you'll need components that are going to be able to handle that speed. Otherwise, you're defeating your purpose of having a high-speed line. You want to try to match your components with the speed of the line. But you don't want to get any more than you need. You want to have room for growth, and you don't want to be running at maximum when it comes to link capacity. But remember that high-speed links cost more money.

text version.) While you are waiting for the page to load, watch the changing graphic at the top of the page.

This site also includes links to Wall Street firms; this page was under construction and not working at the time of this writing. The link to the ZJ Hi-tech Park in China is slow to load; the largest graphic file is more than 113 kilobytes in size.

QuoteCom, Inc.

http://www.quote.com/

QuoteCom offers a searchable database of more than 1,200 U.S. and international companies and more than 200 industry profiles from the Reference Press. For a basic $9.95 membership, you can retrieve as many as 25 profiles a day; a non-member can download a single company profile for $2.95 or an industry profile for 95 cents.

Seanet Yellow Web Pages
http://www.seanet.com/yellow/

At this site is a small list of Seattle area businesses, arranged by type of business. A random check found few or no entries in certain categories.

Singapore On-Line Business Directory

http://www.asia-directory.com/~bruno/forms/1srch.htm

The first in Bruno Internet Information's planned Asian business directories covers Singapore companies and government business development agencies. Also included are links to Asian resources.

To search the directory, select a product/service category, and click on a letter or browse for a notebook document.

Software Publishers Association (SPA) Members

http://www.spa.org/members.htm

The SPA is a trade organization of more than 1,150 international members from the personal computer software industry: publishers, developers, distributors, retailers, consultants, and other companies. At this site, you can link to members of the organization, by using the letters at the top of the page or by scrolling down the list. If you are an SPA member, you can add your World Wide Web home page to the directory.

Figure 3.12 A section of graphical links from Pan's List of Corporations

The TechConnect Directory

http://www.butterfly.net/baltimore/techdirectory/techindex.html

From the Greater Baltimore Committee Technology Council comes a large searchable index of companies located in or near Baltimore, Maryland. Click on a company name to see an online text page for the company; there are no links.

The Texas 500

gopher://gopher.texas-one.org:500/11/tx500

The Reference Press, which compiles the Hoover guides, has produced a searchable index of Texas' top 500 companies.

One way of searching is to click from folder to folder until you see the links to companies. The top-level folders are arranged by type of industry. Click on an industry to see a list of subcategories. Then click on a subcategory to get a page of links.

You also can search the index by keyword. The typical entry contains name, address, telephone number, company officers, number of employees, sales in dollars, type of ownership (for example, corporation or partnership), description of the industry, and the source of the company profile.

Thomas Register of American Manufacturers

http://www.thomasregister.com/home.html

This commercial site provides information about the Thomas Publishing Company and its publications. At this home page, you'll find several links: Thomas Register Supplier Finder (an index of product and service suppliers for which you must register but do not have to pay), How to Buy It (25 articles on how to buy software and computer services), Free

Files! (the Windows version of the Thomas Register on CD-ROM demo software), About Thomas Register of American Manufacturers and About Thomas Register on CD-ROM (sales information), Thomas Corporate Home Page (corporate information on a very slow-loading page), and Your Listing in Thomas Register (how to register your company).

Tucson Area Directories

gopher://econ.tucson.az.us:70/11/biz/.tucsondir/tucsonbusmfg

At this site are three directories: aerospace and related companies, optics businesses (a very small list), and manufacturing firms.

You can search the aerospace directory (gopher://econ.tucson.az.us:70/11/biz/.tucsondir/tucsonaero) by keyword, or you can browse a text file.

The Manufacturer's Directory (gopher://econ.tucson.az.us:70/11/biz/.tucsondir/tucsonbusmfg) is composed of eight folders—seven alphabetic entries, and one a listing by SIC code. You can also search the directory by keyword.

U.S. Federal Subcontractor Directory

gopher://www.sbaonline.sba.gov:70/11/Government-Contracting/Subcontracting-Directory

This site could be a gold mine to small businesses searching for government contracts. Here, you can look through a directory of prime contractors, arranged by state and the District of Columbia, and sometimes by subcontractor. Directory information includes company name, address, contact name, and telephone number. In a column at the right side of the page is the type of business.

To look up a prime contractor, open a folder. The contents of the file are text. Information includes name, address, contact name, and telephone number.

World Wide Web Corporation Sites

http://www.yahoo.com/Business/Corporations/

This very large site might be the best place to start the search for a corporate home page. Corporations, mostly small ones, are arranged under a long list of categories, from Advertising to Weather Information. At the end of the list is a link to 20 indexes with business links.

World Wide Yellow Pages

http://www.yellow.com/

The World Wide Yellow Pages manages a searchable index of businesses all over the world. To look up a business, click on the search page. On the search page, select a business type, a name, or location. The businesses listed are almost all small ones, although companies such as Apple, MCI, and Microsoft are in the index.

To be included in the World Wide Yellow Pages, you can fill out an online form and select the type of listing. The basic listing—business name, address, telephone and fax numbers, e-mail address, URL, five business headings, keywords, and a 25-word description—costs $100 a year.

WWW Business Yellow Pages

http://www.cba.uh.edu/ylowpges/ylowpges.html

The Information Technology Department at the University of Houston College of Business Administration compiles lists of companies arranged alphabetically by business type. Special categories include Ability Impaired, The Black Experience: WWW Businesses and Organizations, College Student Resource Guide, and For Women on the Web. To add your company to the list, click on Submitting an Entry. Then fill in the form and submit it.

Chapter Four

Coming Attractions

- ◆ General Resources
- ◆ Economics Tables
- ◆ Economics Resources

Economics and Statistics

W hether you are writing a business plan or deciding whether to open a new business or division, the Internet has a great deal of up-to-date information that will be of value to you. For example, you can predict the growth or decline of a region by looking at U.S. Census demographics or Federal Reserve Bank economic indicators. Or you can illustrate a report with charts of stock market and mutual fund performance for your industry. Or you can decide whether to relocate or open a new facility in a particular area by looking at Bureau of Labor Statistics data on employment, unemployment, compensation, and productivity. You can download much of this information, which is handy for creating spreadsheets and charts.

This chapter supplies sources of economic indicators, demographic data, and other statistics. Additionally, many of these sites have links to other economic and business resources.

General Resources

Many statistics-related sites offer pages and pages of indicators, demographics, and indexes; some report on a particular industry or government segment, while others furnish a wide range of material. For example, you can get population information from the U.S. Census Bureau, and you can get all sorts of farm-related information from the U.S. Department of Agriculture. On the other hand, STAT-USA supplies business, trade, and economic information, and the Penn World Tables compare variables from many countries over more than 40 years.

Bureau of Labor Statistics (BLS)

http://stats.bls.gov/blshome.html

The BLS compiles economics and statistics data, known as LABSTAT. The BLS home page has links to news releases and to pages of data on employment and unemployment, prices and living conditions, compensation and working conditions, productivity and technology, and so on. Some of these files are huge (the data in one file started at 1941) and complex.

Each page at this site is accompanied by a graphic (10K), which is slow to load.

Tip
Before deciding to download a huge file that appears to be related to your interest, look at a similar small file to see if the information you want is available there.

To search LABSTAT (at http://stats.bls.gov/labstat.htm), read the introduction, and then follow these steps:

1. Click on Here to go to a Gopher menu.

2. Click on LABSTAT Overview to obtain the two-character code of the database you want to search.

3. Click on Time Series to display a list of files.

4. Select a file.

5. From the Gopher menu, choose a document. Note that its approximate size is within brackets.

6. To make sense of the data, you may have to select additional files. Figure 4.1 shows all the components that make up the Employment Cost Index.

CERN/ANU—Demography and Population Studies

http://coombs.anu.edu.au/ResFacilities/DemographyPage.html

Part of the WWW Virtual Library, this site from the Australian National University (ANU) contains 139 links to demographic information from all over the world. Resources include worldwide census information, a master list of U.S. demographic resources, and addresses for academic institutions, the United Nations, and population research and studies.

EconData

http://info.umd.edu:86/Educational_Resources/Academic ResourcesByTopic/EconomicsResources/EconData/.www/contents.html

http://www.inform.umd.edu:8080/EdRes/Topic/Economics/EconData/

gopher://pip.shsu.edu:70/11/ftp/economics/EconData

Inforum, at the Economics Department of the University of Maryland, has compiled a variety of economic time series. A time series is a set of data for specific dates or times. Statisticians use time series to predict future behavior based on trends in the data. At this site, time series are in downloadable, zipped (ZIP) files that contain files with DOC, HBK, HIN, and STB extensions. To find and download a file, first read the instructions on the home page, and then click on Contents. In the table of contents, click on a filename to download it to your computer. Although the downloaded file is zipped, it is very large (the average is more than 1 million bytes).

For more information about the EconData service and databases and how to use them, go to http://www.inform.umd.edu:8080/EdRes/Topic/Economics/EconData/Instructions/guide.

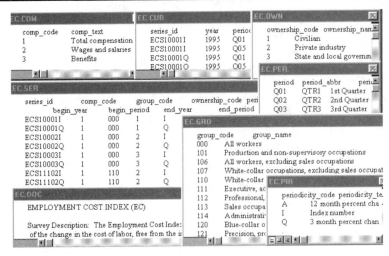

Figure 4.1 The components of the Employment Cost Index

Economic Bulletin Board (EBB)

gopher://una.hh.lib.umich.edu:70/11/ebb/

The EBB from the Graduate Library of the University of Michigan has economic data of almost every description: agricultural; exchange rates and monetary information, both current and historic; bond rates; Federal Reserve Bank credit and monetary statistics; public debt; savings bonds rates, sales, and values; employment and unemployment rates and costs; collective bargaining; payrolls; pollution and energy; housing and construction; business cycle indicators (BCI) and other economic indicators and indexes; import and export; manufacturing and industrial inventories, shipments, sales, and orders; and markets. A comprehensive table of contents for the EBB is at gopher://una.hh.lib.umich.edu:70/00/ebb/general/bull12.txt.

Tip

To manage the time series data in the U.S. Department of Commerce Business Cycle Indicators (BCI) and Current Business Statistics (BSDE) data files, download the BCI Manager, a Windows 3.1 program, from gopher://csf.Colorado.edu:70/00/econ/bci/ftp_info.

Economic Indicators and Data

gopher://infolib.lib.berkeley.edu:70/11/resdbs/busi/econindic

This page has links to Gopher sites that contain data from the Bureau of Labor Statistics (LABSTAT), Economic Bulletin Board (EBB), Gross State Product Tables, and U.S. Department of Agriculture. At the time of this writing, the Business & Economics List of Statistics Available, Federal Reserve Board Data (IMS Server), and Regional Statistics folders were not available.

Economics Index

http://csclub.uwaterloo.ca:80/u/nckwan/fin/econ.html

This index of economics resources includes bulletin boards; World Wide Web, Gopher,

and Telnet sites; and economics discussion groups. A nice feature is that each link is accompanied by a description of the site and, if appropriate, a description of problems in accessing the site.

Economics Worldwide Resources

http://www.einet.net/galaxy/Social-Sciences/Economics.html

http://galaxy.einet.net/galaxy/Social-Sciences/Economics.html

Galaxy is a multiple-subject index. With a couple of exceptions (a link to the *National Review* magazine and one to the University of Connecticut's Arctic Circle server), its economics section consists of economics, finance, and related resources: documents, guides, software, collections, periodicals, directories, organizations, academic organizations, commercial organizations, and a searchable index of all the topics covered by Galaxy.

Woodrow: Federal Reserve Bank of Minneapolis Information Service

http://woodrow.mpls.frb.fed.us/

Woodrow, named for Woodrow Wilson, the president who signed the act that started the Federal Reserve Bank (FRB) system, is a user-friendly site. Here you can find information about the FRB, online and print publications, and links to other Federal Reserve Banks as well as other economics resources. A very important feature at this site is Tracking the Economy, links to various economics indicators. The five links on the Tracking the Economy page are:

◆ The Beige Book is a commentary on current economic conditions in each Federal Reserve Bank region.

◆ Interest and Exchange Rate Charts provides charts on short-term and other interest rates and the trade-weighted value of the dollar.

◆ <u>U.S. Treasury Auction Results</u> links to the Treasury Auction Results page at gopher://una.hh.lib.umich.edu:70/11/ebb/treasury.

◆ <u>Federal Reserve Board Statistical Releases</u> provides links to 11 types of statistics, including industrial production, consumer installment credit, foreign exchange rates, interest rates, and so on.

◆ <u>National Economic Data</u> provides these categories of U.S. statistics: <u>General Data</u>, <u>Consumers</u>, <u>Housing</u>, <u>Business</u>, <u>Foreign</u>, <u>Government</u>, <u>Prices and Wages</u>, and <u>Financial/Money Supply Data</u>.

FINWeb—A Financial Economics Server

http://www.finweb.com

This index of financial economics resources includes links to online journals and an index (the search is free; the cost of an article is $8.50 plus a royalty fee) to periodicals (http://www.carl.org/uncover/unchome.html). You'll find other links to University of Texas at Austin working papers, National Bureau of Economic Research (NBER), NetEc (with more than 35,000 papers), both EDGAR sites (at NYU and at Internet Multicasting Service), EconData, the Experimental Stock Market Page from MIT and other stock pages, and other finance and economics sites on the World Wide Web as well as financial, law, and Internet indexes.

Gross State Product Data Tables

gopher://una.hh.lib.umich.edu:70/11/gsp

The University of Michigan has compiled gross state product tables by region in these categories: all the U.S., Far West, Great Lakes, Mideast, New England, Pacific, Plains, Rocky Mountain, Southeast, and Southwest.

Guide to Foreign Statistics, Economic Trends, and International Management

gopher://zeus.nijenrode.nl:70/11/Business/Statistics

This text file, arranged by world region, is a comprehensive master list of economics-related Internet sites, many outside the United States. Each entry contains a title or a topic, codes indicating the type of entry, and the Internet address. Many entries also contain a description and cross-references to other sites. The addresses are not limited to economics, but also include treaties, times around the world, and German mailing codes.

Nijenrode Economics

gopher://zeus.nijenrode.nl:70/11/Business/Economics

This site, from Nijenrode University, has links to most of the top economics sites. Here, you will find links to <u>Bill Goffe's Resources for Economists on the Internet</u>, economic data from around the world (for example, EconData, Business Cycle Indicators data and software, and the Economic Bulletin Board), Virginia economic databases (in WK1 format), <u>Hal Varian's Economics on the Internet</u>, and others.

Note
The link to the <u>National Trade Data Bank</u>, part of STAT-USA, which is now a subscriber service, is no longer available.

Resources for Economists on the Internet

http://netec.mcc.ac.uk/~adnetec/EconFAQ/EconFAQ.html

From Bill Goffe, Department of Economics and International Business, University of Southern Mississippi, this well-designed and well-organized site is one of the most gigantic lists on the

World Wide Web. (The downloadable ASCII version is more than 250 kilobytes.)

If you are a first-time visitor, click on <u>Table of Contents</u> to reveal a long list of links, including data links, Internet papers, online publications of all types, working papers, economic societies and organizations, links to many educational institutions and departments, Gophers and World Wide Web servers, libraries and educational services, and contacts for and information about the economics profession. Experienced visitors can click on <u>Shortcut Section</u> to access a shorter, concise list of the resources in the table of contents without descriptions and without e-mail resources included.

STAT-USA

http://www.stat-usa.gov/

An arm of the U.S. Department of Commerce, STAT-USA is a valuable subscription service that publishes business, trade, and economic information from more than 50 U.S. government agencies. STAT-USA is the gateway to the National Trade Data Bank (NTDB), the National Economic, Social and Environmental Data Bank (NESE-DB), the Economic Bulletin Board (EBB), and the Global Business Opportunities Service (GLOBUS), which includes the *Commerce Business Daily* and the Bureau of Economic Analysis (BEA).

The price for three months is $50 and for a full year is $150. To subscribe, call 202-482-1986 or 202-482-1526 Monday through Friday from 8:30 AM to 5:30 PM Eastern Time, send a message to stat-usa@doc.gov, or print the order form (http://www.stat-usa.gov/BEN/storder .html) and fax it to 202-482-2164.

To try a limited version of STAT-USA before signing up, go to http://www.stat-usa.gov/inqsample.html. To search the sample database, click on the Search button, enter a query in the text box, and click on the Run Query button. If you need help with search syntax, click on Here (immediately above the Run Query button). Then you can review sample queries and learn about the operators with which you can refine a search.

U.S. Census Bureau

http://gopher.census.gov:70/0/Bureau/

The U.S. Census Bureau provides demographic information to public and private agencies. Information at the home page includes county, state, U.S., and world data—from business, school, and news organizations. This site provides links to <u>County Business Patterns</u>, the <u>County and City Data Book</u>, the <u>Statistical Abstract of the United States</u>, <u>U.S. International Trade Statistics</u>, and so on and to other census servers on the World Wide Web.

This fast-loading and well-designed site is an example of good page design (see Figure 4.2).

Figure 4.2 The U.S. Census Bureau home page graphic

U.S. Census—1994 Statistical Abstract

http://www.census.gov:80/stat_abstract

The 1994 Statistical Abstract contains more than 1,400 tables and graphs on social, economic, and international subjects. Also at this site, you will find links to frequently requested tables, state rankings, and state and county profiles.

A searchable index of the Statistical Abstract is under construction; if your search is successful, the result is a very large (140K) text index, perhaps of the entire abstract.

An important part of this site is the monthly economic indicators (http://gopher.census.gov:70/1s/ Bureau/ Stat-Abstract/Economic-Indicators). The Monthly Time Series include economic indicators for retail, wholesale, and foreign trade; consumer installment credit; building permits and housing starts; new home construction, sales and mortgage rates; manufacturing; a variety of indexes; money supply (M1); interest rates; and civilian labor force and unemployment, personal income (see Figure 4.3), and gross domestic product.

Personal Income ($Billions)					
	1991	1992	1993	1994	1995
January	4,786	4,985	5,232	5,484	5,932
February	4,794	5,042	5,252	5,576	5,961
March	4,812	5,070	5,283	5,608	5,996
April	4,823	5,089	5,358	5,639	
May	4,838	5,102	5,374	5,665	
June	4,860	5,115	5,361	5,675	
July	4,852	5,137	5,356	5,704	
August	4,865	5,126	5,415	5,731	
September	4,890	5,181	5,416	5,768	
October	4,911	5,244	5,454	5,845	
November	4,912	5,246	5,483	5,842	
December	4,980	5,515	5,517	5,884	

Figure 4.3 Monthly personal income from 1991 through March 1995, formatted as part of a report

Searching Effectively

Searching the Internet requires really only one thing: patience. You can search in two ways: by using a search tool and by simply looking at individual sites for information. Search tools are powerful aids for finding specific information. But, just as in searching a conventional library, you are limited by your own knowledge in thinking up keywords on which to search. Finding information can be a daunting task, given the number of potential sites. Here are a few shortcuts that can speed up the process.

◆ First, find a good master list (megalist). Two good examples are SUNY-Oneonta, Inter-Links, and the Rome Laboratory (U.S. Air Force). Remember that each of these lists reflects more on the interests of the people who put them together than the information on the Internet. These lists, and the Internet in general, are highly redundant. You can get where you want to go in many ways.

U.S. Census—State and County Profiles

http://www.census.gov/stat_abstract/profile.html

The U.S. Census also provides a map (see Figure 4.4) on which you can click to gather demographic information by county or state. The report, in PRN (print) format, on a selected location includes data on population, vital statistics and health, education, crime rates, federal funds and social insurance, labor force, income, business, and some miscellaneous topics (energy expenses, motor vehicle statistics, farmland, and hazardous waste sites).

U.S. Census Bureau—Financial Data for State and Local Governments and Schools

http://www.census.gov/govs/mainpage.html

The U.S. Census Bureau provides a manual that classifies statistical data, summarizes descriptions of local government, and presents demographic data using four categories: the largest 50 cities and counties, school, state, and estimates by type of government by state.

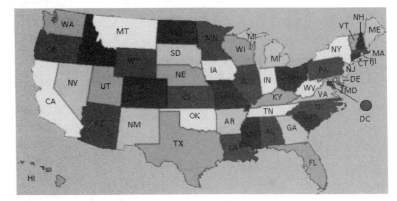

Figure 4.4 The map of the United States on which you can click to get state or county information

◆ Before starting a search, think about where you would expect to find the information that you want. For example, you are likely to find business and economics information at a business school site, and you can probably find information about Latin America at a site sponsored by in the Spanish department of a university. Don't discount geography when searching for information. For example, the University of Texas will have more information about Mexico than the University of Maine will.

◆ When searching through state university sites, remember what is economically important to each state.

◆ Lastly, it is easier to find information in a well-organized server. Of course, this does not help if the information itself is poorly organized.

Much of the information covers 1989–91. Although it is not up to date, you can compare some of the data with other more current demographic data in order to spot trends.

U.S. Department of Agriculture

gopher://usda.mannlib.cornell.edu:70/11/

Cornell University seems to be the epicenter of U.S. agricultural data from the Economic Research Service of the U.S. Department of Agriculture. You can download these files (see Table 4.1 in the following section), which are in the Lotus 1-2-3 WK1 format.

Economics Tables

In this part of the book, you'll find tables of economic indicators and statistical information resources. Rather than explain each entry in detail, this information is presented in tables to crowd in as much information as possible for the business people, students, and faculty who might benefit from it. The tables cover these subjects: Agriculture and Food; Currency and Money; Demographics; Education; Employment, Unemployment, and Labor; Energy and the Environment; Gross Domestic Product and Gross State Product; Housing and Construction; U.S. Government Indicators and Indexes; Manufacturing and Production; Miscellaneous; Income, Earnings, and Pay; Price and Productivity; Sales; and Trade.

Note

If, during an Internet session, you plan to access several of the files at sites listed in the following tables, go to the home page (for example, gopher://una.hh.lib.umich.edu:70/11/ebb/) or to a main starting point (for example, gopher://usda.mannlib.cornell.edu/, and click on <u>USDA Economics and Statistics Systems DATA SETS</u>). Next, click on a folder link, and then click on a particular file icon. After viewing the contents of the file, click on the Back button, then click on the next folder and file icons, and so on. Also be sure to explore these sites for files that are not documented in this book. Most Internet sites, including these, seem to be constantly under construction; so it is likely that you'll find new sources of information most times you visit.

Agriculture and Food

If you are a farmer, a supermarket or grocery store operator, a restaurateur, or an agriculture professor or economist, the information in Table 4.1 will be of interest. For example, you can look at the Agricultural Commodity Output, Changes in Food Consumption and Expenditures, and Crops Progress and Condition tables before you decide on the crops to plant. Or before starting a new restaurant, you can decide on the menu by evaluating Food, Food Consumption, General Interest, Inputs, International Agriculture, or Specialty Agriculture. Table 4.1 lists agricultural and food data, the URL of the site that contains the data, and the source of the site.

Table 4.1: Agriculture and Food Data

Data	URL	Source
1977, 1982 & 1987 Census of Agricultural Data (county & zip code)	gopher://usda.mannlib.cornell.edu:70/11/data-sets/general/93015/C	USDA/Cornell
1980 Population & Demographic Data (county & zip code)	gopher://usda.mannlib.cornell.edu:70/11/data-sets/general/93015/A	USDA/Cornell
1990 Census (county & zip code) STF3B ZIP & FIPS code data	gopher://usda.mannlib.cornell.edu:70/11/data-sets/general/93015/D	USDA/Cornell
Agricultural Baseline Project Tables	gopher://usda.mannlib.cornell.edu:70/11/data-sets/farm/94005	USDA/Cornell
Agricultural Commodity Output	gopher://usda.mannlib.cornell.edu:70/11/data-sets/farm/91008	USDA/Cornell
Agricultural Outlook Yearbook, 1960–91	gopher://usda.mannlib.cornell.edu:70/11/data-sets/general/87011	USDA/Cornell
Agworld International Ag Situation Reports	gopher://una.hh.lib.umich.edu:70/11/ebb/agworld	EBB
Americans and Food (a computer quiz)	gopher://usda.mannlib.cornell.edu:70/11/data-sets/food/91002	USDA/Cornell
Business: Value of Farmland, Manufacturing, Hourly Earnings, Exports (by state)	http://gopher.census.gov:70/1s/Bureau/Stat-Abstract/State-Rankings/busb.prn	US Census
Changes in Food Consumption and Expenditures	gopher://usda.mannlib.cornell.edu:70/11/data-sets/food/93004	USDA/Cornell
Cold Storage Holdings of Shrimp	gopher://una.hh.lib.umich.edu:70/00/ebb/misfiles/shrimp.noa	EBB
Costs of Production, 1980–91	gopher://usda.mannlib.cornell.edu:70/11/data-sets/farm/94010	USDA/Cornell
Cotton and Wool Yearbook	gopher://usda.mannlib.cornell.edu:70/11/data-sets/crops/89004	USDA/Cornell
Crops	gopher://usda.mannlib.cornell.edu:70/11/data-sets/crops	USDA/Cornell
Crops by State	gopher://usda.mannlib.cornell.edu:70/11/data-sets/crops/95111	USDA/Cornell
Crops County Data, 1972–92	gopher://usda.mannlib.cornell.edu:70/11/data-sets/crops/93100	USDA/Cornell
Crops County Data, 1992–93	gopher://usda.mannlib.cornell.edu:70/11/data-sets/crops/94101	USDA/Cornell

Table 4.1: Agriculture and Food Data (continued)

Data	URL	Source
Crops Progress and Condition, 1985–92	gopher://usda.mannlib.cornell.edu:70/11/data-sets/crops95101	USDA/Cornell
ERS Publications Database	gopher://usda.mannlib.cornell.edu:70/11/data-sets/general/93017	USDA/Cornell
Farm Business Balance Sheet	gopher://usda.mannlib.cornell.edu:70/11/data-sets/farm/93013	USDA/Cornell
Farm Credit System Operating Statistics	gopher://usda.mannlib.cornell.edu:70/11/data-sets/farm/94011	USDA/Cornell
Farm Operating and Financial Characteristics, 1990	gopher://usda.mannlib.cornell.edu:70/11/data-sets/farm/93016	USDA/Cornell
Farm Sector Balance Sheet	gopher://usda.mannlib.cornell.edu:70/11/data-sets/farm/93013	USDA/Cornell
Farm Sector Balance Sheet by Sales Class	gopher://usda.mannlib.cornell.edu:70/11/data-sets/farm/92003	USDA/Cornell
Farm Sector Financial Ratios, 1960–91	gopher://usda.mannlib.cornell.edu:70/11/data-sets/farm/93012	USDA/Cornell
Feed Grain Data by States, 1949–86	gopher://usda.mannlib.cornell.edu:70/11/data-sets/crops/87013	USDA/Cornell
Feed Grain Yearbook	gopher://usda.mannlib.cornell.edu:70/11/data-sets/crops/88007	USDA/Cornell
Feed Manufacturing	gopher://usda.mannlib.cornell.edu:70/11/data-sets/crops/89005	USDA/Cornell
Field Crops, Final Estimates	gopher://usda.mannlib.cornell.edu:70/11/data-sets/crops/94096	USDA/Cornell
Food, Beverages, and Tobacco Expenditures, 1970–88	gopher://usda.mannlib.cornell.edu:70/11/data-sets/food/96014	USDA/Cornell
Food	gopher://usda.mannlib.cornell.edu:70/11/data-sets/food	USDA/Cornell
Food Consumption	gopher://usda.mannlib.cornell.edu:70/11/data-sets/food/89015	USDA/Cornell
Food Spending in American Households, 1980–88	gopher://usda.mannlib.cornell.edu:70/11/data-sets/food/90005	USDA/Cornell
Frozen Fish Products	gopher://una.lib.umich.edu:70/00/ebb/mrsfiles/cldfish.noa	EBB

Table 4.1: Agriculture and Food Data (continued)

Data	URL	Source
General Interest (agricultural data)	gopher://usda.mannlib.cornell.edu:70/11/data-sets/general	USDA/Cornell
Historical State Farm Income Accounts	gopher://usda.mannlib.cornell.edu:70/11/data-sets/farm/93007	USDA/Cornell
Inputs (agricultural chemical usage, field crops summary, cropping practices, farm employment and wage rates, farm machinery statistics, fertilizer use and price statistics)	gopher://usda.mannlib.cornell.edu:70/11/data-sets/inputs	USDA/Cornell
International Agriculture	gopher://usda.mannlib.cornell.edu:70/11/data-sets/international	USDA/Cornell
Livestock, Dairy, and Poultry	gopher://usda.mannlib.cornell.edu:70/11/data-sets/livestock	USDA/Cornell
Oil Crops Yearbook	gopher://usda.mannlib.cornell.edu:70/11/data-sets/crops/89002	USDA/Cornell
Prices Received and Paid Indexes	gopher://usda.mannlib.cornell.edu:70/11/data-sets/crops/95917	USDA/Cornell
Prices Received by Farmers for Field Crops, 1984–92	gopher://usda.mannlib.cornell.edu:70/11/data-sets/crops/92151	USDA/Cornell
Prices Received by Farmers: Historic Prices & Indexes, 1908–92	gopher://usda.mannlib.cornell.edu:70/11/data-sets/crops/92152	USDA/Cornell
Rankings, 1993	gopher://usda.mannlib.cornell.edu:70/11/data-sets/crops/93180	USDA/Cornell
Referendum CVM Programs	gopher://usda.mannlib.cornell.edu:70/11/data-sets/general/93010	USDA/Cornell
Rice Stocks, Final Estimates	gopher://usda.mannlib.cornell.edu:70/11/data-sets/crops/94898	USDA/Cornell
Rice Yearbook	gopher://usda.mannlib.cornell.edu:70/11/data-sets/crops/89001	USDA/Cornell
Rural Affairs	gopher://usda.mannlib.cornell.edu:70/11/data-sets/rural	USDA/Cornell
Soybeans: Costs of Production, 1990	gopher://usda.mannlib.cornell.edu:70/11/data-sets/crops/94009	USDA/Cornell
Specialty Agriculture	gopher://usda.mannlib.cornell.edu:70/11/data-sets/specialty	USDA/Cornell
State-Level Costs of Production	gopher://usda.mannlib.cornell.edu:70/11/data-sets/farm/92013	USDA/Cornell
State-Level Wheat Statistics	gopher://usda.mannlib.cornell.edu:70/11/data-sets/crops/89016	USDA/Cornell
Stocks of Grains, Oilseeds, and Hay, 1988–93	gopher://usda.mannlib.cornell.edu:70/11/data-sets/crops/94897	USDA/Cornell
Structural Change in U.S. Agriculture, 1969–82	gopher://usda.mannlib.cornell.edu:70/11/data-sets/farm/90023	USDA/Cornell

Table 4.1: Agriculture and Food Data (continued)

Data	URL	Source
U.S. Corn and Soybean Weather/Production Models	gopher://usda.mannlib.cornell.edu:70/11/data-sets/crops/92001	USDA/Cornell
U.S. Farm Income	gopher://usda.mannlib.cornell.edu:70/11/data-sets/farm/90022	USDA/Cornell
U.S. Food Expenditures	gopher://usda.mannlib.cornell.edu:70/11/data-sets/food/91003	USDA/Cornell
U.S. Rice Industry Basebook Data	gopher://usda.mannlib.cornell.edu:70/11/data-sets/crops/94020	USDA/Cornell
USDA Agricultural Leads	gopher://una.hh.lib.umich.edu:70/11/ebb/usda	EBB
WASDE Crop Estimates	gopher://usda.mannlib.cornell.edu:70/11/data-sets/crops/95501	USDA/Cornell
Weather in U.S. Agriculture	gopher://usda.mannlib.cornell.edu:70/11/data-sets/general/92008	USDA/Cornell
Wheat Yearbook	gopher://usda.mannlib.cornell.edu:70/11/data-sets/crops/88008	USDA/Cornell
World Red Meat and Poultry Consumption, 1975–91	gopher://usda.mannlib.cornell.edu:70/11/data-sets/food/91004	USDA/Cornell
ZIPFIP Program and Database	gopher://usda.mannlib.cornell.edu:70/11/data-sets/general/93014	USDA/Cornell

An Interview with Bob O'Keefe

Bob O'Keefe (okeefe@rpi.edu and http://www.rpi.edu/~okeefe) is an associate professor in the Lally School of Management & Technology at Rensselaer Polytechnic Institute, Troy, New York. At present, his research and teaching are both focused on the use of the Internet (and particularly the Web) as channels for electronic commerce. In 1995 he taught one of the first MBA electives on Internet-related commerce, creating a virtual course in which students, projects sponsors, and the professor were all geographically dispersed. He has consulted with a number of organizations on Web strategy, edits a forum for Web strategy called Net.Value (http://www.owi.com/netvalue), and was a board member for the 1995 Tenagra Awards for Internet Marketing Excellence. He is one of the founders and associate editors of ISWorld Net (http://www.isworld.org). He is also struggling to maintain the Lally school's Web pages.

You're probably best known for the Interesting Business Sites page. When and how did it start? Any surprises along the way?

I started it last summer, probably in May or June 1994, as a teaching device for myself. In the spring of '94, I had put students in a number of my classes on the Web, let them surf, and found out that a lot of them just thrashed around.

It doesn't take too long to get up to speed though.

But we're a business school, and some of our students are executives who work during the week and don't have a great deal of extra time.

You want to very quickly show them what businesses are doing [on the Internet]; so I put together a list of things that I thought were interesting.

How did you find the sites for the list?

Mainly through my surfing. At first, I surfed for hours and hours, concentrating on reading newsgroups. So I would put all the effort in so that I could say here are 40 or 50 really interesting sites. Then I announced it to the world, and I didn't realize how rapidly somebody can be an information provider. The next thing I knew I was getting inundated with e-mail from people wanting to get on the list.

The list is really just random—ad hoc.

What don't you choose for the list?

Probably sites that are similar to those already on the list. For example, in the summer of 1994 all the computer companies came out with very good Web sites. And the first one or two were interesting. For example, Novell was in very early and put all its manuals online. Novell also distributed the e-mail addresses of its technical people so that users could e-mail those who put its products together. Then, of course, all the other computer companies came out with similar things.

Now and again, we come across something that is unusual and innovative. A thing that I really like, because it's so left field, is the Speak to Me catalog (http://clickshop.com/speak/), which is a catalog of toys that make sounds. You can browse through the catalog, play the sounds, and download them, which is very, very innovative.

I started to get e-mail from people I had put on the site, saying how many of the people who had visited their site had come through mine. One company, Software Net (http://software.net), which sells software and can deliver a lot of it over the network, told me that in the month or so after they went on the list about one in three people who were visiting their site came from my site.

I've been trying to think of a way to turn this into a commercial venture. I teamed up with a start-up company in our area here. The Interesting Business Sites will continue, but we will put together a commercial version of yellow pages.

How do you do that? Will you collect money using electronic cash?

The yellow pages will be free to anybody who visits. A company will have to pay to get on the list, as it would to get in the phone book yellow pages. But I've become convinced that what companies want out of this type of venture is the ability to put in 20 or 30 words and maybe a little graphic explaining who they are. People want some information before they click on the link. If you look at a company name, you have no idea what it does. So I think there's a real commercial need for better-designed, better-marketed, focused yellow pages. I think you need to give people some content. If you go to the telephone yellow pages, you get those little blocks of information. It seems to me that's necessary.

Currency and Money

If you are planning a business trip, checking exchange rates (for example, the 10 AM EST or 12 noon EST foreign exchange rates and the implied volatility rates for foreign exchange options data) helps you to decide when to trade your dollars for your traveling money, the countries to visit, and even how long to stay or the countries with which to deal. An importer or exporter must have the same information.

A stocks and bonds investor should know the current rates (see the Daily Treasury State and Local Government Bond Rates and the Federal Reserve Board Daily Treasury Quotes tables). Retailers can decide how much and the type of inventory to have on hand by checking the Consumer Installment Credit Outstanding and the Federal Reserve Board Consumer Credit tables (and then checking county and city demographics to decide on the product mix). Table 4.2 lists currency and other money data, the URL of the site that contains the data, and the source of the site.

Interesting Sites

NASA has one of the best sites on the Internet. For example, go to the Welcome to the Planets page at http://stardust.jpl.nasa.gov/planets/ to see some of the best graphics on the Net. Figure 4.5 shows the opening graphic.

Demographics

Looking at demographics before you move your operations to a different state or change the services that you provide is an important part of designing your business plan. For example, look at the Population: Living in Metro Areas and Elderly table before you decide where to start up a landscaping business in an area of older people. Table 4.3 lists demographic data, the URL of the site that contains the data, and the source of the site.

Education

Business owners and managers should check demographics before deciding on a marketing campaign. For example, a catalog seller targeting college students should identify the areas in which students are found. Looking at the Education: College Enrollment (1992, by state) table could be a first step in finding a market. Table 4.4 lists education statistics, the URL of the site that contains the statistics, and the source of the site.

Employment, Unemployment, and Labor

The human resources department of a business wanting to plan a benefits package for its employees could find out what other companies in the area are doing. Some sources of information are the Employee Benefits Survey, the Employment Cost Index, and the Negotiated Wage and Benefit Changes table. A guidance counselor could present students with a chart based on Employment Projections by Industry, Industry Employment Projections, or the Occupational Outlook tables. Table 4.5 lists employment, unemployment, and labor data, the site that contains the data, and the source of the site.

Welcome to the Planets

Figure 4.5 The nine planets on NASA's Welcome to the Planets page

Table 4.2: Currency and Money Data

Data	URL	Source
10 AM EST Foreign Exchange Rates	gopher://una.hh.lib.umich.edu:70/00/ebb/monetary/tenfx.frb	EBB
12 Noon EST Foreign Exchange Rates	gopher://una.hh.lib.umich.edu:70/00/ebb/monetary/noonfx.frb	EBB
Aggregate Reserves	gopher://una.hh.lib.umich.edu:70/00/ebb/monetary/resrv.frb	EBB
Business Investment and Plans 1993 to 1995	gopher://una.hh.lib.umich.edu:70/00/ebb/indicators/ips.cen	EBB
Commercial industrial Lines	http://woodrow.mpls.frb.fed.us/economy/natdata/finance.htm	Woodrow
Daily Treasury State and Local Government Bond Rates	gopher://una.hh.lib.umich.edu:70/00/ebb/monetary/bonds.slg	EBB
Factors Affecting Reserve Balances of Depository Institutions	gopher://una.hh.lib.umich.edu:70/00/ebb/monetary/far.frb	EBB
Flow of Fund Accounts (levels, quarterly)	http://www.inform.umd.edu:8080/EdRes/Topic/Economics/EconData/Data/USNational/Accounts/; then select fofllev.zip	EconData USNational Files
Flow of Fund Accounts (not seasonally adjusted)	http://www.inform.umd.edu:8080/EdRes/Topic/Economics/EconData/Data/USNational/Accounts/; then select fofnsa.zip	EconData USNational Files
Flow of Fund Accounts (seasonally adjusted)	http://www.inform.umd.edu:8080/EdRes/Topic/Economics/EconData/Data/USNational/Accounts/; then select fofsa.zip	EconData USNational Files
Flow of Funds	gopher://una.hh.lib.umich.edu:70/00/ebb/monetary/z7.frb	EBB
FRB-Atlanta Monthly US$ Index	gopher://una.hh.lib.umich.edu:70/00/ebb/monetary/frbindx.atl	EBB
FRB Bank Credit (H.8) Historical Data (bcdetail.exe)	gopher://una.hh.lib.umich.edu:70/00/ebb/monetary/bcdetail	EBB
FRB Consumer Credit	gopher://una.hh.lib.umich.edu:70/00/ebb/monetary/cncr.frb	EBB
FRB Daily Treasury Quotes (with CUSIP numbers)	gopher://una.hh.lib.umich.edu:70/00/ebb/monetary/quotes.txt	EBB
FRB Foreign Exchange Rates	gopher://una.hh.lib.umich.edu:70/00/ebb/monetary/exchange.frb	EBB
FRB Historical Money Stock Rev. Annual Benchmark & Seasonal Factors Review	gopher://una.hh.lib.umich.edu:70/00/ebb/monetary/h6detail	EBB
FRB Money Stock Data	gopher://una.hh.lib.umich.edu:70/00/ebb/monetary/money.frb	EBB
FRB Selected Interest Rates	gopher://una.hh.lib.umich.edu:70/00/ebb/monetary/interest.frb	EBB
Historical Money Stock Data	gopher://una.hh.lib.umich.edu:70/00/ebb/monetary/h6hist.frb	EBB
Implied Volatility Rates for Foreign Exchange Options	gopher://una.hh.lib.umich.edu:70/00/ebb/monetary/vrates.frb	EBB
Interest Rates on 3-Month T-Bills	http://woodrow.mpls.frb.fed.us/economy/natdata/p57.txt	Woodrow
Interest Rates Table for Calculating Subsidies, Etc.	gopher://una.hh.lib.umich.edu:70/00/ebb/monetary/cr-rates.tre	EBB

Table 4.2: Currency and Money Data (continued)

Data	URL	Source
International Balance of Payments (with permission from the International Monetary Fund)	http://info.umd.edu:86/Educational_Resources/AcademicResourcesByTopic/EconomicsResources/EconData/.www/econdata.html; then select IBOP.ZIP	EconData International Files
International Financial Statistics, quarterly (with permission from the International Monetary Fund)	http://info.umd.edu:86/Educational_Resources/AcademicResourcesByTopic/EconomicsResources/EconData/.www/econdata.html; then select IFSQ.ZIP	EconData International Files
International Financial Statistics, annual (with permission from the International Monetary Fund)	http://info.umd.edu:86/Educational_Resources/AcademicResourcesByTopic/EconomicsResources/EconData/.www/econdata.html; then select IFSA.ZIP	EconData International Files
International Monetary Fund	http://info.umd.edu:86/Educational_Resources/AcademicResourcesByTopic/EconomicsResources/EconData/.www/econdata.html; then select GFS.ZIP	EconData International Files (Note: Releasing this document requires explicit authorization from the IMF.)
Monetary Statistics	gopher://una.hh.lib.umich.edu:70/11/ebb/monetary	EBB
Money Supply (M1)	http://woodrow.mpls.frb.fed.us/economy/natdata/p46.txt	Woodrow
Monthly Foreign Exchange Rates	gopher://una.hh.lib.umich.edu:70/00/ebb/monetaryfxratesm.frb	EBB
Monthly Statement of Public Debt	gopher://una.hh.lib.umich.edu:70/00/ebb/monetary/mspd.txt	EBB
Monthly Treasury Statement	gopher://una.hh.lib.umich.edu:70/00/ebb/monetary/mts.txt	EBB
Savings Bonds Current Redemption Values (crvinfo.exe)	gopher://una.hh.lib.umich.edu:70/00/ebb/monetary/crvinfo	EBB
Savings Bond Rates (May–Oct 1989)	gopher://una.hh.lib.umich.edu:70/00/ebb/monetary/sbrate.tre	EBB
Treasury Savings Bond Sales	gopher://una.hh.lib.umich.edu:70/00/ebb/monetary/sbsales.tre	EBB
U.S. Treasury Auction Results	gopher://una.hh.lib.umich.edu:70/11/ebb/treasury	EBB

Table 4.3: Demographic Data

Data	URL	Source
Frequently Requested Population Tables	http://gopher.census.gov:70/1s/Bureau/Stat-Abstract/freq/pop	US Census
Population and Land Area—Countries	http://gopher.census.gov:70/0/Bureau/State-Abstract/freq/ 94s1351.prn	US Census
Population: 1993 and 2000 (by state)	http://gopher.census.gov:70/1s/Bureau/Stat-Abstract/State-Rankings/popa.prn	US Census
Population: Living in Metro Areas and Elderly (by state)	http://gopher.census.gov:70/1s/Bureau/Stat-Abstract/State-Rankings/popb.prn	US Census
Vital Statistics (1991; by state)	http://gopher.census.gov:70/1s/Bureau/Stat-Abstract/State-Rankings/vital.prn	US Census

Bob O'Keefe on Online Courses

Is Business Uses of the Internet your first online course?

Yes. It's going to be an experiment with students at R.P.I. and with a university I'm associated with in England. And I'm going to have each of them doing projects that are going to be provided by Internet companies. So students in multinational teams will work on a project.

So it's probably too early to ask what other courses you're planning.

A lot of universities are trying to make better use of the Internet in how we teach. For example, here at R.P.I. many of us have found that local newsgroups are just wonderful for courses. You can put copies of course material on the newsgroup. I've been doing that for about a year now, and there's a tremendous volume. Students can post anything they want, and you reply to what they post. Also, I tell my students that if they e-mail me, I'll reply to any email by the end of the evening. It doesn't matter where I am. I can be in England for a week or so, and I will reply to any comments.

Do you think there will be a time when a student will be able to get a degree or certificate without ever seeing the professor or visiting the campus?

Well, you can do that now. You can give 50 bucks to one of these companies out in California.

No, I'm talking about an accredited place.

I don't think so. I think there is an element of coming together and being in a common culture, which you get at a university. You learn as much from the other students as from the professors and the environment.

And even if you're exchanging e-mail or participating in part of a newsgroup is, it's not the same thing?

I think you can't completely replace traditional mediums. You can certainly augment them. But I can't see it myself.

What if you're a busy executive trying to get an MBA on the side and living in an area that doesn't have a good MBA school?

Then I think you can. I think what we'll see down the road are programs in whichwhere some element is done over the network and some element is done residentially. For example, we have satellite video programs, which have done very well. We got an award last year for being the best satellite program in the country. Students typically do courses over the video, and [professors] confer with students by e-mail and phone. Some students actually come for a semester, although less so now. And one can imagine large elements of the satellite component being replaced with Web-based materials, newsgroups, discussion groups, and so on.

There might always be an element that will be done over video, but ten years from now, we won't need satellites, we won't need specialized equipment to do video. Video conferencing will be done over the Internet. You can do it now; it's just incredibly slow. But when I can sit in my office and have a camera on my computer and arrange with a dozen students around the country to turn their computer and cameras on at the same time, you can have remote seminars.

Table 4.4: Education Statistics

Data	URL	Source
Education: College Enrollment (1992; by state)	http://gopher.census.gov:70/1s/Bureau/Stat-Abstract/State-Rankings/edub.prn	US Census
Education: Educational Attainment (1990; by state)	http://gopher.census.gov:70/1s/Bureau/Stat-Abstract/State-Rankings/educ.prn	US Census
Education: Public K-12 Enrollment, Teachers' Salaries (1993; by state)	http://gopher.census.gov:70/1s/Bureau/Stat-Abstract/State-Rankings/edua.prn	US Census
Educational Attainment—Race and Ethnicity	http://gopher.census.gov:70/0/Bureau/Stat-Abstract/freq/94s0232.prn	US Census

Table 4.5: Labor Statistics

Data	URL	Source
Civilian Labor Force	http://woodrow.mpls.frb.fed.us/economy/natdata.p21.txt	US Census/Bureau of Labor Statistics
Civilian Labor Force and Unemployment by State	gopher://una.hh.lib.umich.edu:70/00/ebb/employment/laus-1.bls	EBB
Collective Bargaining—Private Sector (BP)	gopher://stats.bls.gov:70/00haplitp.dev/doc/bp.doc	LABSTAT
Collective Bargaining—State & Local Government (BG)	gopher://stats.hls.gov:70/00haplitp.dev/doc/bg.doc	LABSTAT
Occupational Compensation Survey	http://stats.bls.gov/ocshome.htm	Bureau of Labor Statistics
Covered Employment and Wages (ES-202)	http://stats.bls.gov/cewhome.htm	Bureau of Labor Statistics
CPI Urban Wage Earners by Area	gopher://una.hh.lib.umich.edu:70/00/ebb/price/cpi-6.bls	EBB
CPI Urban Wage Earners by Commodity	gopher://una.hh.lib.umich.edu:70/00/ebb/price/cpi-4.bls	EBB
CPI Urban Wage Earners by Commodity (seasonally adjusted)	gopher://una.hh.lib.umich.edu:70/00/ebb/price/cpi-5.bls	EBB
Employee Benefits Survey (EB)	http://stats.bls.gov/ebhome.htm	LABSTAT
Employees on Nonagriculture Payrolls by State	gopher://una.hh.lib.umich.edu:70/00/ebb/employment/laus-2.bls	EBB
Employment Cost Index, Tables Only	gopher://una.hh.lib.umich.edu:70/00/ebb/employment/eci-tab.bls	EBB
Employment Cost Index, Text Only	gopher://una.hh.lib.umich.edu:70/00/ebb/employmenteci-txt.bls	EBB
Employment Cost Index (EE)	gopher://hapi.bls.gov:70/00hapiftp.dev/doc/ec.doc	LABSTAT
Employment Projections by Industry (EP)	gopher://hapi.bls.gov:70/00hapiftp.dev/doc/ep.doc	LABSTAT
Employment Situation, Text Only	gopher://una.hh.lib.umich.edu:70/00/ebb/employment/emp-txt.bls	EBB

Table 4.5: Labor Statistics (continued)

Data	URL	Source
Employment Situation Historical Data	gopher://una.hh.lib.umich.edu:70/00/ebb/employment/historical	EBB
Employment Situation: Complete Release (emp.exe)	gopher://una.hh.lib.umich.edu:70/00/ebb/employment/emp.bls	EBB
Employment Statistics	gopher://una.hh.lib.umich.edu:70/11/ebb/employment	EBB
Employment-Unemployment Statistics by State (saus.exe)	gopher://una.hh.lib.umich.edu:70/00/ebb/employment/saus.bls	EBB
Employment-Unemployment Statistics by State (tables)	gopher://una.hh.lib.umich.edu:70/00/ebb/employment/saus-tab.bls	EBB
Employment-Unemployment Statistics by State (text)	gopher://una.hh.lib.umich.edu:70/00/ebb/employment/saus-txt.bls	EBB
Employment: Participation Rates and Unemployment (199; by state)	http://gopher.census.gov:70/1s/Bureau/Stat-Abstract/State-Rankings/employa.prn	US Census
Employment: Services and Manufacturing (1993; by state)	http://gopher.census.gov:70/1s/Bureau/Stat-Abstract/State-Rankings/employh.prn	US Census
Establishments, Employees, and Payroll	http://gopher.census.gov:70/10/Bureau/Stat-Abstract/freq/cgp	US Census
FDI Employment, 1987	gopher://una.hh.lib.umich.edu:70/00/ebb/indicators/fdi-t2.txt	EBB
FDI Employment by State 1987	gopher://una.hh.lib.umich.edu:70/00/ebb/indicators/fdi-t3.txt	EBB
FDI Employment by State, 1987 (percentages)	gopher://una.hh.lib.umich.edu:70/00/ebb/indicators/fdi-t4.txt	EBB
Household Employment Statistics—A Tables	gopher://una.hh.lib.umich.edu:70/00/ebb/employment/emp-a.bls	EBB
Household Employment Statistics—B Tables	gopher://una.hh.lib.umich.edu:70/00/ebb/employment/emp-b.bls	EBB
Industry Employment Projections	http://stats.bls.gov/emproj.htm	Bureau of Labor Statistics
International Labor Statistics (IN)	gopher://stats.bls.gov:70/00hopiftp.dev/doc/in.doc	LABSTAT
Labor Force, Unemployment, etc. (from household survey)	http://info.umd.edu:86/Educational_Resources/AcademicResourcesByTopic/EconomicsResources/EconData/.www/contents.html; then select unlfc.zip	EconData StateLocal Files
Labor Force Statistics from the Current Population Survey	http://stats.bls.gov/labforce.htm	Bureau of Labor Statistics
Local Area Employment and Unemployment (tables only)	gopher://una.hh.lib.umich.edu:70/00/ebb/employment/laus-tab.bls	EBB
Local Area Employment and Unemployment (Text Only)	gopher://una.hh.lib.umich.edu:70/00/ebb/employment/laus-txt.bls	EBB
Local Area Employment and Unemployment Statistics	http://stats.bls.gov/locarea.htm	Bureau of Labor Statistics
Local Area Unemployment Statistics: Complete Release (laus.exe)	gopher://una.hh.lib.umich.edu:70/00/ebb/employment/laus.bls	EBB

Table 4.5: Labor Statistics (continued)

Data	URL	Source
Local Area Unemployment Statistics (LA)	gopher://stats.bls.gov:70/00hopitp.dev/doc/la.doc	LABSTAT
Major Collective Bargaining Settlement (average wage and compensation tables)	gopher://una.hh.lib.umich.edu:70/00/ebb/employment/cbar-tab.bls	EBB
Major Collective Bargaining Settlement (text only)	gopher://una.hh.lib.umich.edu:70/00/ebb/employment/cbar-txt.bls	EBB
Major Collective Bargaining Settlement: Complete Release (cbar.exe)	gopher://una.hh.lib.umich.edu:70/00/ebb/employment/cbar.bls	EBB
Money Supply (M1)	http://woodrow.mpls.frb.fed.us/economy/natdata/p46.txt	Woodrow
Monthly National Employment, Hours, Earnings and Diffusion Indices (not seasonally adjusted)	http://info.umd.edu:86/Educational_Resources/AcademicResourcesByTopic/EconomicsResources/EconData/.www/contents.html; then select ehensa.zip	EconData USNational Files
Monthly National Employment, Hours, Earnings and Diffusion Indices (seasonally adjusted)	http://info.umd.edu:86/Educational_Resources/AcademicResourcesByTopic/EconomicsResources/EconData/.www/contents.html; then select ehesa.zip	EconData USNational Files
Occupational Employment Statistics	http://stats.bls.gov/oeshome.htm	Bureau of Labor Statistics
Occupational Outlook	http://stats.bls.gov/ocohome.htm	Bureau of Labor Statistics
Revised Payroll Survey Employment Estimates to 3/91 Benchmarks	gopher://una.hh.lib.umich.edu:70/00/ebb/employment/pay-rev.bls	EBB
Revised Seasonally Adjusted Average Hourly/Weekly Earnings	gopher://una.hh.lib.umich.edu:70/00/ebb/indicators/real-3.bls	EBB
Safety & Health Statistics	http://stats.bls.gov/oshhome.htm	Bureau of Labor Statistics
State & Area Employment, Hours, & Earnings (SA)	gopher://stats.bls.gov:70/00hopitp.dev/doc/sa.doc	LABSTAT
State and Area Employment, Hours, and Earnings for AL, MS, TN, KY, AR, LA, OK, TX	http://info.umd.edu:86/Educational_Resources/AcademicResourcesByTopic/EconomicsResources/EconData/.www/contents.html; then select sc.zip	EconData StateLocal Files
State and Area Employment, Hours, and Earnings for DE, MD, VA, WV, NC, SC, GA, FL, DC, VI, PR	http://info.umd.edu:86/Educational_Resources/AcademicResourcesByTopic/EconomicsResources/EconData/.www/contents.html; then select satl.zip	EconData StateLocal Files

Table 4.5: Labor Statistics (continued)

Data	URL	Source
State and Area Employment, Hours, and Earnings for IL, WI, MN, IA, MO, ND, SD, NE, KS	http://info.umd.edu:86/Educational_Resources/AcademicResourcesByTopic/EconomicsResources/EconData/.www/contents.html; then select wnc.zip	EconData StateLocal Files
State and Area Employment, Hours, and Earnings for MT, ID, WY, CO, NM, AZ, UT, NV	http://info.umd.edu:86/Educational_Resources/AcademicResourcesByTopic/EconomicsResources/EconData/.www/contents.html; then select mount.zip	EconData StateLocal Files
State and Area Employment, Hours, and Earnings for NY, ME, NH, VT, MA, RI CT	http://info.umd.edu:86/Educational_Resources/AcademicResourcesByTopic/EconomicsResources/EconData/.www/contents.html; then select nyne.zip	EconData StateLocal Files
State and Area Employment, Hours, and Earnings for OH, IN, MI	http://info.umd.edu:86/Educational_Resources/AcademicResourcesByTopic/EconomicsResources/EconData/.www/contents.html; then select enc.zip	EconData StateLocal Files
State and Area Employment, Hours, and Earnings for PA And NJ	http://info.umd.edu:86/Educational_Resources/AcademicResourcesByTopic/EconomicsResources/EconData/.www/contents.html; then select matl.zip	EconData StateLocal Files
State and Area Employment, Hours, and Earnings for WA, OR, CA, AK & HI	http://info.umd.edu:86/Educational_Resources/AcademicResourcesByTopic/EconomicsResources/EconData/.www/contents.html; then select pac.zip	EconData StateLocal Files
Summary of Employment Cost Index 1st Q 1993	gopher://una.hh.lib.umich.edu:70/00/ebb/summaries/eci	EBB
Summary of the Employment Situation 12/1993	gopher://una.hh.lib.umich.edu:70/00/ebb/summaries/employ	EBB
Technology, Economic Growth, and Employment: Charts and Tables	gopher://una.hh.lib.umich.edu:70/00/ebb/summaries/esa001.wk1	EBB
Technology, Economic Growth, and Employment: Dept. of Commerce New Research Index 1st	gopher://una.hh.lib.umich.edu:70/00/ebb/summaries/esa001.txt	EBB
Unemployment Rates by State and Selected Industry Divisions	gopher://una.hh.lib.umich.edu:70/00/ebb/employment/laus-3.bls	EBB
Unemployment Rates by State and Selected Metro Areas (not seasonally adjusted)	gopher://una.hh.lib.umich.edu:70/00/ebb/employment/laus-4.bls	EBB
Unemployment Rates by State and Selected Metropolitan Areas	gopher://una.hh.lib.umich.edu:70/00/ebb/employment/laus-4.bls	EBB
Developments in Labor-Management Relations	http://stats.bls.gov/lmrhome.htm	
Work Stoppage Data (WS)	gopher://stats.bls.gov:70/00hopiftp.dev/doc/ws.doc	Bureau of Labor Statistics

Bob O'Keefe on Doing Business on the Internet

What advice would you give to a small company such as Nine Lives Clothing Store [a case that he has written] getting ready to use the Web, maybe investigating, trying to decide which hardware, which software to buy and so on?

Small companies increasingly have lots of options. The Nine Lives (http://chezhal.slip.netcom.com/) case is unusual because of good technical skills; they obtained all the software, did all the Web pages themselves, and actually did some programming. Most small companies can't do that.

Increasingly, companies go to an Internet provider or a Web consultant, who will host your Web page for a fee or design your Web page. Or if you want to spend more money, you can join one of the virtual malls. We did some work with a small company that translates high-tech materials; it pays a consultant to do local package work and look after a local area network. The consultant found a net provider for the company, and set up Internet access so that the company got e-mail. The provider hosts Web pages; so the consultant learned HTML and put together some Web pages for the company. The company probably pays $56 a month to have e-mail through the Internet provider and have its Web pages up.

Energy and the Environment

Utilities determining their fuel needs can chart the numbers in the Kilowatt Hours, Seasonally Adjusted file over a period of years to spot trends and spread out their expenditures over several months. Lobbyists for or against spending on the environment can analyze Pollution Abatement and Control data over several years to plan their action. Table 4.6 lists energy and environmental data, the URL of the site that contains the data, and the source of the site.

Gross Domestic Product and Gross State Product

A company planning a move to another state can look at the Income: Gross State Product and Disposable Personal Income (by state) data and interpret it in a couple of ways: If the disposable personal income for a particular state is higher than that of another state, product sales could be concentrated in the higher-income state, or a plant could be set up in the lower-income state to take advantage of lower wages. Table 4.7 lists gross domestic product and gross state product statistics, the URL of the site that contains the statistics, and the source of the site.

Housing and Construction

New house construction is sensitive to economic conditions, and economists use construction starts (for example, Housing Starts data, Housing Starts and Building Permits data, and New Privately Owned Housing Units Started data), in part, to predict future results. Many businesses (for example, banks, lumber companies, and retailers) respond to positive or negative house construction. When planning developments, builders want to construct houses that will sell. Studying the Characteristics of New Privately Owned 1-Family Houses data might mean the difference between success and failure. Table 4.8 lists housing and construction statistics, the URL of the site that contains the statistics, and the source of the site.

I noticed that in the Nine Lives case that they dial in to the provider, and it seemed as though they were on all day long. Do they have a dedicated line?

No, although the line is always open. The provider only needs to send them stuff when there's stuff to send. Internet providers are at the upper level of telecommunications. They have high bandwidth connections, which they can use for multiple phone lines. They can keep open, reopen, switch between them. There's not a great difference between some Internet providers and your local phone-switching center, which has a maximum number of lines that can go in and out and so on.

If a provider hosts Web pages for you, you can't do any of the sophisticated things: You can't put a catalog there, you can't do any of the programming necessary to have forms, and so on. But there are Web consultants who'll charge you money for doing that. There's a whole range. There are people paying $20 a month to have one page saying here we are and here's our phone number, all the way to companies that are investing six figures into putting up lots of materials and being able to deliver things over the network, and everything in between.

Web consulting must be a growing business.

It is a booming business.

Table 4.6: Energy and Environmental Data

Data	URL	Source
1990 Pollution Abatement and Control	gopher://una.hh.lib.umich.edu:70/00/ebb/indicators/polu-abt.bea	EBB
1992 Pollution Abatement and Control	gopher://una.hh.lib.umich.edu:70/00/ebb/indicators/pol-abt.bea	EBB
Acid Rain in the Northeastern United States	gopher://usda.mannlib.cornell.edu:70/11/data-sets/general/92017	USDA/Cornell
Energy Expenditures and Hazardous Waste Sites (by state)	http://gopher.census.gov:70/1s/Bureau/Stat-Abstract/State-Rankings/ misc.prn	US Census
Energy Statistics	gopher://una.hh.lib.umich.edu:70/11/ebb/energy	EBB
Energy Supply and Disposition	http://gopher.census.gov:70/0/Bureau/Stat-Abstract/freq/ 94s0290.prn	US Census
Kilowatt Hours (seasonally adjusted)	http://www.inform.umd.edu:8080/EdRes/Topic/Economics/EconData/Data/ USNational/BusInd/; then select kwhsa.zip	EconData USNational Files
Kilowatt Hours (not seasonally adjusted)	http://www.inform.umd.edu:8080/EdRes/Topic/Economics/EconData/Data/ USNational/BusInd/; then select kwhnsa.zip	EconData USNational Files
Kilowatt Hours, Updates	http://www.inform.umd.edu:8080/EdRes/Topic/Economics/EconData/Data/ USNational/BusInd/; then select kwhnew.zip	EconData USNational Files
Land, Water, and Conservation	gopher://usda.mannlib.cornell.edu:70/11/data-sets/land	USDA/Cornell
Natural Resources Inventory data (county only)	gopher://usda.mannlib.cornell.edu:70/11/data-sets/general/93015/B	USDA/Cornell
Ozone in the Northeastern United States	gopher://usda.mannlib.cornell.edu:70/11/data-sets/general/92018	USDA/Cornell

Table 4.7: Gross Domestic Product and Gross State Product Statistics

Data	URL	Source
All US States (Gross State Product by state and years)	gopher://una.hh.lib.umich.edu:70/11/gsp/allstates	GSP/UMich
Far West (Gross State Product by region and by state)	gopher://una.hh.lib.umich.edu:70/11/gsp/fw	GSP/UMich
Great Lakes (Gross State Product by region and by state)	gopher://una.hh.lib.umich.edu:70/11/gsp/gl	GSP/UMich
Gross Domestic Product—Nominal/Real	http://woodrow.mpls.frb.fed.us/econqmy/natdata/p16.txt	Woodrow
Gross Domestic Product, Personal Income, and Expenditures	http://gopher.census.gov:70/0/Bureau/Stat-Abstract/freq/94s0691.prn	US Census
Gross Domestic Product, Personal Consumption Expenditures, and Gross Private Domestic Investment	http://gopher.census.gov/70/0/Bureau/Stat-Abstract/freq/94s0691.prn	Bureau of Economic Analysis
Gross State Product	http://gopher.census.gov:70/0/Bureau/Stat-Abstract/freq/94s0688.prn	US Census
Gross State Product	http://info.umd.edu:06/Educational_Resources/AcademicResourcesByTopic/EconomicsResources/EconData/www/contents.html; then select gsp.zip	EconData StateLocal Files
Income: Gross State Product and Disposable Personal Income (by state)	http://gopher.census.gov:70/1s/Bureau/Stat-Abstract/State-Rankings/income.prn	US Census
Industry Codes and Titles, Gross State Product, Bureau of Economic Analysis	gopher:/una.hh.lib.umich.edu:70/00/gsp/induscodes	GSP/UMich
Mideast (Gross State Product by region and by state)	gopher:/una.hh.lib.umich.edu:70/11/gsp/me	GSP/UMich
New England (Gross State Product by region and by state)	gopher:/una.hh.lib.umich.edu:70/11/gsp/ne	GSP/UMich
Pacific (Gross State Product by region and by state)	gopher:/una.hh.lib.umich.edu:70/11/gsp/ah	GSP/UMich
Plains (Gross State Product by region and by state)	gopher:/una.hh.lib.umich.edu:70/11/gsp/pl	GSP/UMich
Rocky Mountain (Gross State Product by region and by state)	gopher:/una.hh.lib.umich.edu:70/11/gsp/rm	GSP/UMich
Southeast (Gross State Product by region and by state)	gopher://una.hh.lib.umich.edu:70/11/gsp/se	GSP/UMich
Southwest (Gross State Product by region and by state)	gopher://una.hh.lib.umich.edu:70/11/gsp/sw	GSP/UMich
Summary of Revised GDP and Corporate Profits (3rd Q 1993)	gopher://una.hh.lib.umich.edu:70/00/ebb/summaries/gdp-sum	EBB
United States Totals (Gross State Product by industry)	gopher://una.hh.lib.umich.edu:70/11/gsp/us	GSP - UMich
US Regional Totals (Gross State Product by Region)	gopher://una.hh.lib.umich.edu:70/11/gsp/regionals	GSP - UMich

Table 4.8: Housing and Construction Statistics

Data	URL	Source
Business: Failures and Housing (1993; by state)	http://gopher.census.gov:70/1s/Bureau/Stat-Abstract/State-Rankings/busa.prn	US Census
Census Construction Review Tables	gopher://una.hh.lib.umich.edu:70/00/ebb/indicators/revtables	EBB
Characteristics of New Privately Owned One-Family Houses	http://gopher.census.gov:70/0/Bureau/Stat-Abstract/freq/94s1204.prn	US Census
Housing Starts	gopher://una.hh.lib.umich.edu:70/00/ebb/indicators/house.cen	EBB
Housing Units Completed	gopher://una.hh.lib.umich.edu:70/00/ebb/indicators/hous-cmp.cen	EBB
Housing Vacancies	gopher://una.hh.lib.umich.edu:70/00/ebb/indicators/hous-vac.cen	EBB
Information on Construction Permits File	gopher://una.hh.lib.umich.edu:70/00/ebb/indicators/permits.doc	EBB
New Construction	gopher://una.hh.lib.umich.edu:70/00/ebb/indicators/const.cen	EBB
New Home Sales	gopher://una.hh.lib.umich.edu:70/00/ebb/indicators/	EBB
New Home Sales	http://gopher.census.gov:70/1s/Bureau/Stat-Abstract/Economic_Indicators/homesale.prn	US Census
New Privately Owned Housing Units Started	http://gopher.census.gov:70/0/Bureau/Stat-Abstract/freq/94s1202.prn	US Census
New Privately Owned Housing Units Started—Selected Characteristics	http://gopher.census.gov:70/0/Bureau/Stat-Abstract/freq/94s1202.htm	US Census
Summary of Construction (1993)	gopher://una.hh.lib.umich.edu:70/00/ebb/summaries/const	EBB
Summary of Housing Starts (1993)	gopher://una.hh.lib.umich.edu:70/00/ebb/summaries/house	EBB
Summary of Single-Family Home Sales (1993)	gopher://una.hh.lib.umich.edu:70/00/ebb/summaries/home-s1	EBB

Income, Earnings, and Pay

Trends in income are major factors as a company plans its future. If income drops in an area, the result is bound to be less spending on goods and services, especially those not considered necessities. Therefore, analysis of the Personal Income and Its Disposal, Personal Income and Outlays, State Personal Income, and Summary of Personal Income tables can help an outdoor furniture manufacturer or luxury car dealer determine the pattern of growth. Table 4.9 lists information about income, earnings, and pay, the URL of the site that contains the information, and the source of the site.

Manufacturing and Production

Whether they are planning new factories or the products to manufacture, plant owners and operators can use data from Manufacturing—Shipments, New Orders, and Unfilled Orders for Durable Goods; Shipments, Inventories, and Inventories/Shipments Ratios for Total Goods and from Manufacturing and Trade Inventories and Sales, in combination with data in other tables to plan spending on machinery, inventory, employees, and construction. Table 4.10 lists manufacturing and production data, the URL of the site that contains the data, and the source of the site.

Bob O'Keefe on Internet Culture

One of your students has worked on something called Barriers for Entry to the Internet as an intern for AT&T. What have you found?

The phone companies really see the Internet as the big boom in selling bandwidth in the future. You don't make a lot of money out of putting another phone line in a residence these days. You can have a company sending video images, which take up dozens of megabytes, over your phone lines and make good money out of it. The student really saw that the culture is changing quickly. For example, when she started working on this in September 1994, we and AT&T people thought one of the big barriers to entry would be cultural: that businesses don't understand the Internet culture, the language, the way things happen. I think by the end of last year, that just completely went out the window.

For example, a cultural thing is there's a way of writing e-mail, with the smiley faces, which was a bit off-putting. I think as a barrier, this has completely disappeared. The student collected material that showed how particular sites, Web sites, for example, had very rapidly changed and become far more mainstream and business-like. Six months ago, sites were using Internet words to describe themselves; six months later they were sounding like regular marketing stuff.

Another cultural thing is that you have to give something to the 'Net as well as take something away. A couple of companies have been frequently blasted in various articles for not conforming to the Internet culture,

Table 4.9: Income, Earnings, and Pay Data

Data	URL	Source
Annual National Income and Product Accounts (NIPA)	http://www.inform.umd.edu:8080/EdRes/Topic/Economics/ EconData/Data/ USNational/Accounts/; then select nipaa.zip	EconData USNational Files
Covered Employment and Wages (ES-202)	http://stats.bls.gov/coveremp.htm	Bureau of Labor Statistics
Disposable Personal Income	http://gopher.census.gov:70/0/Bureau/Stat-Abstract/freq/ 94s0697.prn	US Census
Earnings of Production Nonagricultural Workers	gopher://una.hh.lib.umich.edu:70/00/ebb/indicatorsreal-2.bls	EBB
Earnings of Production Workers	gopher://una.hh.lib.umich.edu:70/00/ebb/indicators/real-1.bls	EBB
Monthly National Income and Product Accounts	http://www.inform.umd.edu:8080/EdRes/Topic/Economics/ EconData/Data/ USNational/Accounts/; then select nipam.zip	EconData USNational Files
National Income and Products Accounts	gopher://una.hh.lib.umich.edu:70/11/ebb/nipa	EBB
Nonfarm Payroll Statistics from the Current Employment Statistics Survey	http://stats.bls.gov/payroll.htm	Bureau of Labor Statistics
Personal Income & Outlays Release (3/94) Changes	gopher://una.hh.lib.umich.edu:70/00/ebb/indicators/ changees.txt	EBB
Personal Income and Its Disposal	gopher://una.hh.lib.umich.edu:70/00/ebb/indicators/pi.prn	EBB
Personal Income and Outlays	gopher://una.hh.lib.umich.edu:70/00/ebb/indicators/pi.bea	EBB

for example, for not allowing staff to post to newsgroups. So there was the idea that companies were coming onto the Internet and they were reading newsgroups, they were taking information away but they weren't giving anything back. For example, in a business newsgroup, there might be information that is useful to you and your company, but if you don't share your information... I tried to persuade a company that I did some work for to give something back. I think it's nice to have a Web page that has at least a few links to other pages. They could not understand the value of doing that. All they wanted to do was to put up marketing and advertising information.

If a company provides the information or even information that is not related to itself, that's really an attraction.

I think it is. But I think there are a lot of small businesses that really view it as an inexpensive advertising mechanism.

It wouldn't take more than a day to find the links.

I know, but they don't see it like that; it's a cultural thing. They're saying, why would I give a link to a competitor? Well, maybe you wouldn't give a link to a competitor, but you might give a link to public domain information about what you do.

Table 4.9: Income, Earnings, and Pay Data (continued)

Data	URL	Source
Quarterly National Income and Product Accounts	http://www.inform.umd.edu:8080/EdRes/Topic/Economics/EconData/Data/ USNational/Accounts/; then select nipaq.zip	EconData USNational Files
Quarterly National Income and Product Accounts (NIPA) Update	http://www.inform.umd.edu:8080/EdRes/Topic/Economics/EconData/Data/USNational/Accounts/; then select newnip.zip	EconData USNational Files
State Personal Income	http://info.umd.edu:86/Educational_Resources/AcademicResourcesByTopic/EconomicsResources/EconData/.www/contents.html; then select spi.zip	EconData StateLocal Files
Summary of Personal Income 7/1993	gopher://una.hh.lib.umich.edu:70/00/ebb/summaries/perinc	EBB

Miscellaneous

The number of individuals or businesses filing for bankruptcy over a period of time is one indicator of a healthy or weak economy. Economists, bankers, and educators can use the data in the Bankruptcy tables to determine present conditions and predict future conditions for the entire country. Members of the press can research their stories about foreign officials who are friends or foes by studying the Foreign Assets Control Program. Table 4.11 lists miscellaneous data, the URL of the site that contains the data, and the source of the site.

Bob O'Keefe on Internet Page Design

Do you have any particular favorite Internet business pages that you go to or that you recommend to your students?

If I had to pick one, it would probably be the Real Beer page (http://realbeer.com/rbp/). That's in part because I like beer. But it's very well designed. The graphics are good; it's very fast. If your page is on a server that has high bandwidth access, and it comes through to people quickly, that's a big plus because people don't want to wait to see the images.

So many of the business schools show their buildings, and they seem to take forever.

That's right; you sit there and you wait ten minutes or so for the picture to come through. Graphics have to add value. It doesn't matter which medium you're working in; and at the moment, there are too many icons and

graphics that add no value whatsoever to the information. They are there because people can do it.

A site that sticks in my mind is a company called Master McNeil (http://www .naming.com/naming.html). It does a lot of work for Asian companies who want to sell things in America and need a product name. There are two aspects to its work: one is coming up with a good marketing name; another is making sure you can copyright it if you want to. And I like this company's site because it has good descriptions of work previously done and links to companies for which it has worked. For example, it has done a lot of work for Apple (http://www.apple .com/). At its site are descriptions of this work and pointers to the pages at Apple, describing the product it named. It's a very clever way to quickly put together something that's very useful for prospective customers.

Table 4.10: Manufacturing and Production Data

Data	URL	Source
Benchmark Revision-Monthly Manuf Shipments, Invent, Orders (82-92)	gopher://una.hh.lib.umich.edu:70/00/ebb/indicators/siorev.cen	EBB
Benchmark Revisions: Manufacturers' Shipments, Inventories, Orders	gopher://una.hh.lib.umich.edu:70/00/ebb/indicators/revsio.cen	EBB
Business: Value of Farmland, Manufacturing, Hourly Earnings, Exports (by state)	http://gopher.census.gov:70/1s/Bureau/Stat-Abstract/State-Rankings/busb.prn	US Census
Industrial Sector Analysis Reports (ISA)	gopher://una.hh.lib.umich.edu:70/11/ebb/isa	EBB
Industry Codes and Titles, Gross State Product, Bureau of Economic Analysis	gopher://una.hh.lib.umich.edu:70/00/gsp/induscodes	GSP/UMich
Manufacturing and Trade Inventories and Sales	gopher://una.hh.lib.umich.edu:70/00/ebb/indicators/inv-sale.cen	EBB
Plant and Equipment Expenditures	gopher://una.hh.lib.umich.edu:70/00/ebb/indicators/pe.cen	EBB
Shipments, Inventories, and Orders (s-i-o.exe)	gopher://una.hh.lib.umich.edu:70/00/ebb/indicators/s-l-o.cen	EBB
Summary of Durable Goods Orders (1993)	gopher://una.hh.lib.umich.edu:70/00/ebb/summaries/durgd	EBB
Summary of Industrial Prod and Capacity Utilitization (11/1993)	gopher://una.hh.lib.umich.edu:70/00/ebb/summaries/prod-ind	EBB

Table 4.10: Manufacturing and Production Data (continued)

Data	URL	Source
Summary of Plant and Equipment Spending 1994 Projections	gopher://una.hh.lib.umich.edu:70/00/ebb/summaries/pe	EBB
Summary of Shipments, Inventories, and Orders (1993)	gopher://una.hh.lib.umich.edu:70/00/ebb/summaries/s-i-o	EBB
Total Manufacturing & Trade Inventories	http://woodrow.mpls.frb.fed.us/economy/natdata/p56.txt	Woodrow

Table 4.11: Miscellaneous Statistics

Data	URL	Source
Annual NIPA Supplementary Tables	http://www.inform.umd.edu:8080/EdRes/Topic/Economics/EconData/Data/USNational/Accounts/; then select nipas.zip	EconData USNational Files
Bankruptcy Cases—Chapter	http://gopher.census.gov:70/0/Bureau/Stat-Abstract/freq/94s0850.prn	US Census
Bankruptcy Cases—States	http://gupher.census.gov:70/0/Bureau/Stat-Abstract/freq/94s0849.prn	US Census
BEA, BLS, and Census Joint Release Text	gopher://una.hh.lib.umich.edu:70/00/ebb/indicators/fdi-pr.txt	EBB
Best Markets Reports	gopher://una.hh.lib.umich.edu:70/11/ebb/bmr	EBB
Blue Pages of the Survey of Current Business	http://www.inform.umd.edu:8080/EdRes/Topic/Economics/EconData/Data/USNational/BusInd/; then select scb.zip	EconData USNational Files
Blue Pages Updates	http://www.inform.umd.edu:8080/EdRes/Topic/Economics/EconData/Data/USNational/BusInd/; then select newblue.zip	EconData USNational Files
Business: Failures and Housing (1993; by state)	http://gopher.census.gov:70/1s/Bureau/Stat-Abstract/State-Rankings/busa.prn	US Census
CPI Urban Consumers by Area	gopher://una.hh.lib.umich.edu:70/00/ebb/price/cpi-3.bls	EBB
CPI Urban Consumers by Commodity (seasonally adjusted)	gopher://una.hh.lib.umich.edu:70/00/ebb/price/cpi-2.bls	EBB
Crime (1992; by state)	http://gopher.census.gov:70/1s/Bureau/Stat-Abstract/State-Rankings/ crime.prn	US Census
Current Business Statistics	gopher://una.hh.lib.umich.edu:70/11/ebb/cbs	EBB
Defense Conversion Subcommittee (DCS) Information	gopher://una.hh.lib.umich.edu:11/ebb/defense	EBB
Durable Goods Shipments and Orders	gopher://una.hh.lib.umich.edu:70/00/ebb/indicators/durgd.cen	EBB
FDI by Industry (1987)	gopher://una.hh.lib.umich.edu:70/00/ebb/indicators/fdi-t1.txt	EBB
FDI Release and Tables (1987)	gopher://una.hh.lib.umich.edu:70/00/ebb/indicators/fdi	EBB
Federal Funds (that is, grants to each state)	http://gopher.census.gov:70/1s/Bureau/Stat-Abstract/State-Rankings/fed.prn	US Census
Foreign Assets Control Program	gopher://una.hh.lib.umich.edu:70/11/ebb/fac	EBB
Foreign Direct Investment in the U.S.	http://www.inform.umd.edu:8080/EdRes/Topic/Economics/EconData/Data/USNational/Accounts/; then select fdi.zip	EconData USNational Files

Table 4.11: Miscellaneous Statistics (continued)

Data	URL	Source
General Information Files	gopher://una.hh.lib.umich.edu:70/11/ebb/general	EBB
Geographic Profile (GP)	gopher://stats.bls.gov:70/00hopiftp.dev/doc/gp.doc	LABSTAT
Large Retailers' Profits, Advance Data, Third Quarter, 1993	http://gopher.census.gov:70/1s/Bureau/Stat-Abstract/State-Rankings/health.prn	US Census
	gopher://una.hh.lib.umich.edu:70/00/ebb/indicators/qfrret.cen	EBB
Miscellaneous Economic Files	gopher://una.hh.lib.umich.edu:70/11/ebb/misecon	EBB
Miscellaneous Files	gopher://una.hh.lib.umich.edu:70/11/ebb/misfiles	EBB
Motor Vehicle Registrations—States	http://gopher.census.gov:70/0/Bureau/Stat-Abstract/freq/94s1006.prn	US Census
Motor Vehicles (1992; by state)	http://gopher.census.gov:70/1s/Bureau/Stat-Abstract/State-Rankings/motor.prn	US Census
Occupational Injury and Illness Rates (HS)	gopher://stats.bls.gov:70/00hopiftp.dev/doc/hs.doc	LABSTAT
Occupational Injury and Illness Rates (SH)	gopher://stats.bls.gov:70/00hopiftp.dev/doc/sh.doc	LABSTAT
Regional Economic Information System (REIS)	gopher://ecix.doc.gcv:70/11/ecix/ecdef/econdata/regional	STAT-USA
Regional Economic Statistics	gopher://una.hh.lib.umich.edu:70/11/ebb/regional	EBB
Social Security and Public Aid (1992; by state)	http://gopher.census.gov:70/1s/Bureau/Stat-Abstract/State-Rankings/aid.prn	US Census
Software International Articles	gopher://una.hh.lib.umich.edu:70/11/ebb/soft	EBB
Special Studies and Reports	gopher://una.hh.lib.umich.edu:70/11/ebb/special	EBB
Summaries of Current Economic Conditions	gopher://una.hh.lib.umich.edu:70/11/ebb/summaries	EBB
Summary of Revisions and Changes in Business Cycle Indicators (BCI) Series	gopher://una.hh.lib.umich.edu:70/00/ebb/indicators/bci-rev.txt	EBB
Summary of the Current Account 3rd Q 1993	gopher://una.hh.lib.umich.edu:70/00/ebb/summaries/current	EBB
USA Statistics in Brief: Part 1 (population, law enforcement, education, communications and transportation, and housing, for 1980, 1990, and 1993)	http://www.census.gov/stat_abstract/brief.html	US Census
USA Statistics in Brief: Part 2 (health, social welfare, government, employment, income, prices, energy, agriculture, business, finance, and foreign commerce)	http://www.census.gov/stat_abstract/brief.html	US Census

Price and Productivity

Is production of a certain item increasing or declining? Will investing in plant construction, machinery, and employee training be profitable? The Index of Industrial Production Based on 1987 can help in making a decision. Table 4.12 lists price and productivity data, the URL of the site that contains the data, and the source of the site.

Sales

The last two months of every year are the biggest and most critical for nearly all retailers. Data such as Retail Sales, by Kind of Business, Retail Inventory, and the Inventory/Sales Ratio, and Revised Monthly Retail Sales (revret.exe) can not only document past sales but predict future sales. Table 4.13 lists sales statistics, the URL of the site that contains the statistics, and the source of the site.

Trade

There is no doubt that we are moving toward a world economy. The information in Eastern European Trade Leads can help an electronics exporter or publisher make inroads into new regions. A manufacturer can help make the decision about location and salaries by analyzing the International Labor Statistics data. Table 4.14 lists trade statistics, the URL of the site that contains the statistics, and the source of the site.

Napa Valley Wine Train

"A day without wine is a day without sunshine." --French Proverb

Figure 4.6 The train graphic from the Napa Valley Virtual Visit site

U.S. Government Indicators and Indexes

Many politicians these days want to distance themselves from the government. By using the Federal Government Productivity Index, they might be able to spot trends and use them to their advantage. Exporters and importers can use Summary of Import and Export Price

Table 4.12: Price and Productivity Data

Data	URL	Source
Average Price Data (AP)	gopher://stats.bls.gov:70/00hopiftp.dev/doc/ap.doc	LABSTAT
Consumer and Producer Price Indexes—by Major Groups	http://gopher.census.gov:70/1s/Bureau/Stat-Abstract/freq/945o747.prn	Bureau of Labor Statistics
Consumer Price Index (tables only)	gopher://una.hh.lib.umich.edu:70/00/ebb/price/cpi-tab.bls	EBB
Consumer Price Index (urban consumers by commodity)	gopher://una.hh.lib.umich.edu:70/00/ebb/price/cpi-1.bls	EBB
Consumer Price Index—All Urban Consumers (CU)	gopher://stats.bls.gov:70/00hopiftp.dev/doc/cu.doc	LABSTAT
Consumer Price Index—Urban Wage Earners and Clerical Workers (CW)	gopher://stats.bls.gov:70/00hopiftp.dev/doc/cw.doc	LABSTAT
Consumer Price Index Full Release (cpi.exe)	gopher://una.hh.lib.umich.edu:70/00/ebb/price/cpi.bls	EBB
Consumer Price Index (text only; current month)	gopher://una.hh.lib.umich.edu:70/00/ebb/price/cpi-txt.bls	EBB
Consumer Price Indexes	http://info.umd.edu:86/Educational_Resources/AcademicResourcesByTopic/EconomicsResources/EconData/www/contents.html; then select cpi.zip	EconData USNational Files
Consumer Price Indexes—Major Groups	http://gopher.census.gov:70/0/Bureau/Stat-Abstract/freq/945o747.prn	US Census
Consumer Price Indexes—Selected Items	http://gopher.census.gov:70/0/Bureau/Stat-Abstract/freq/945o748.prn	US Census
Government Productivity Measurement	http://stats.bls.gov/govprod.htm	Bureau of Labor Statistics
Industrial Production and Capacity Utilization (text format)	http://woodrow.mpls.frb.fed.us/economy/natdata/w-indpro.txt	Woodrow
Industrial Production Index—Total	http://woodrow.mpls.frb.fed.us/economy/natdata/p18.txt	Woodrow
Industrial Production Indexes (seasonally adjusted)	http://www.inform.umd.edu:8080/EdRes/Topic/Economics/EconData/USNational/BusInd/; then select ipsa.zip	EconData USNational Files
Industrial Production Indexes (not seasonally adjusted)	http://www.inform.umd.edu:8080/EdRes/Topic/Economics/EconData/USNational/BusInd/; then select ipnsa.zip	EconData USNational Files
Industrial Production Indexes, Updates	http://www.inform.umd.edu:8080/EdRes/Topic/Economics/EconData/USNational/BusInd/; then select ipnew.zip	EconData USNational Files
Industry Labor Productivity Index (PI)	gopher://stats.bls.gov:70/00hopiftp.dev/doc/pi.doc	LABSTAT
Industry Productivity Measures	http://stats.bls.gov/indprod.htm	Bureau of Labor Statistics
International Price Index (EI)	gopher://stats.bls.gov:70/00hopiftp.dev/doc/ei.doc	LABSTAT
Labor Productivity Measures	http://stats.bls.gov/labprod.htm	Bureau of Labor Statistics
Major Sector Multifactor Productivity Index (MP)	gopher://stats.bls.gov:70/00hopiftp.dev/doc/mp.doc	LABSTAT
Major Sector Productivity & Costs Index (PR)	gopher://stats.bls.gov:70/00hopiftp.dev/doc/pr.doc	LABSTAT

Table 4.12: Price and Productivity Data (continued)

Data	URL	Source
Multifactor Productivity Measures	http://stats.bls.gov/mutprod.htm	Bureau of Labor Statistics
Price and Productivity Statistics	gopher://una.hh.lib.umich.edu:70/11/ebb/price	EBB
Producer Price Index (tables only)	gopher://una.hh.lib.umich.edu:70/00/ebb/price/ppi-tab.bls	EBB
Producer Price Index (text only)	gopher://una.hh.lib.umich.edu:70/00/ebb/price/ppi-txt.bls	EBB
Producer Price Index (WP)	gopher://stats.bls.gov:70/00hopiftp.dev/doc/wp.doc	LABSTAT
Producer Price Index Full Release (ppi.exe)	gopher://una.hh.lib.umich.edu:70/00/ebb/price/ppi.bls	EBB
Producer Price Index Revision—Current Series (PE)	gopher://stats.bls.gov:70/00hopiftp.dev/doc/pc.doc	LABSTAT
Producer Price Index Revision—Discontinued Series (PD)	gopher://stats.bls.gov:70/00hopiftp.dev/doc/pd.doc	LABSTAT
Producer Price Indexes, Revised	http://info.umd.edu:86/Educational_Resources/AcademicResourcesByTopic/EconomicsResources/EconData/www/contents.html; then select ppir.zip	EconData USNational Files
Producer Price Indexes	http://info.umd.edu:86/Educational_Resources/AcademicResourcesByTopic/EconomicsResources/EconData/www/contents.html; then select ppi.zip	EconData USNational Files
Productivity & Cost (tables only)	gopher://una.hh.lib.umich.edu:70/00/ebb/price/prod-tab.bls	EBB
Productivity & Cost (text only)	gopher://una.hh.lib.umich.edu:70/00/ebb/price/prod-txt.bls	EBB
Productivity & Cost Full Release (prod.exe)	gopher://una.hh.lib.umich.edu:70/00/ebb/price/prod.bls	EBB
Summary of Productivity (3rd Quarter 1993)	gopher://una.hh.lib.umich.edu:70/00/ebb/summaries/prod	EBB

Table 4.13: Sales Statistics

Data	URL	Source
Advance Retail Sales	gopher://una.hh.lib.umich.edu:70/00/ebb/indicators/retail.cen	EBB
Business: Retail Sales (1992; by state)	http://gopher.census.gov:70/1s/Bureau/Stat-Abstract/State-Rankings/busc.prn	US Census
Inventory/Sales Ratio—Total	http://woodrow.mpls.frb.fed.us/economy/natdata/p52txt.txt	Woodrow
Monthly Retail Sales Summary, August 1995	gopher://una.hh.lib.umich.edu:70/00/ebb/indicators/rsum9508.cen	EBB
Monthly Retail Sales Summary, February 1995	gopher://una.hh.lib.umich.edu:70/00/ebb/indicators/rsum9502.cen	EBB
Monthly Retail Sales Summary, January 1995	gopher://una.hh.lib.umich.edu:70/00/ebb/indicators/rsum9501.cen	EBB
Monthly Retail Sales Summary, March 1995	gopher://una.hh.lib.umich.edu:70/00/ebb/indicators/rsum9503.cen	EBB
Monthly Retail Sales Summary, May 1995	gopher://una.hh.lib.umich.edu:70/00/ebb/indicators/rsum9505.cen	EBB

Table 4.13: Sales Statistics (continued)

Data	URL	Source
Monthly Wholesale Sales	gopher://una.hh.lib.umich.edu:70/00/ebb/indicators/whsale.cen	EBB
Retail Sales, by Kind of Business	http://gopher.census.gov:70/0/Bureau/Stat-Abstract/freq/94s1281.prn	US Census
Revised Monthly Retail Sales (revret.exe)	gopher://una.hh.lib.umich.edu:70/00/ebb/indicators/revret.cen	EBB
Summary of Advance Report of Retail Sales 1993	gopher://una.hh.lib.umich.edu:70/00/ebb/summaries/retail	EBB
Summary of Business Sales and Inventories 1993	gopher://una.hh.lib.umich.edu:70/00/ebb/summaries/inv-sale	EBB

Table 4.14: Trade Statistics

Data	URL	Source
U.S.-Mexico Trade	http://www.inform.umd.edu:8080/EdRes/Topic/Economics/EconData/Data/International/; then select usmextrd.zip	EconData International
Benchmark Revisions to Wholesale Trade Data	gopher://una.hh.lib.umich.edu:70/11/ebb/indicators	EBB
Direction of Trade Data (with permission from the International Monetary Fund)	http://info.umd.edu:86/Educational_Resources/AcademicResourcesByTopic/EconomicsResources/EconData/.www/contents.html; then select D0I.ZIP	EconData International Files
Eastern European Trade Leads	gopher://una.hh.lib.umich.edu:70/11/ebb/europe	EBB
Export Price Indexes and Percent Change (Table 2)	gopher://una.hh.lib.umich.edu:70/00/ebb/price/exim-2.bls	EBB
Export Price Indexes and Percent Change (Table 4)	gopher://una.hh.lib.umich.edu:70/00/ebb/price/exim-4.bls	EBB
Export/Import Price Indexes	http://info.umd.edu:86/Educational_Resources/AcademicResourcesByTopic/EconomicsResources/EconData/.www/contents.html; then select ximpi.zip	EconData USNational Files
Export/Import Price Indexes (monthly)	gopher://una.hh.lib.umich.edu:70/00/ebb/price/xm-m.bls	EBB
Foreign Trade	gopher://una.hh.lib.umich.edu:70/11/ebb/foreign	EBB
Import & Export Price Indexes & Tables (exim.exe)	gopher://una.hh.lib.umich.edu:70/00/ebb/price/exim.bls	EBB
Import and Export Price Indexes (tables only)	gopher://una.hh.lib.umich.edu:70/00/ebb/price/exim-tab.bls	EBB
Import and Export Price Indexes (text only)	gopher://una.hh.lib.umich.edu:70/00/ebb/price/exim-txt.bls	EBB
Import Price Indexes and Percent Change (Table 1)	gopher://una.hh.lib.umich.edu:70/00/ebb/price/exim-1.bls	EBB

Table 4.14: Trade Statistics (continued)

Data	URL	Source
Import Price Indexes and Percent Change (Table 3)	gopher://una.hh.lib.umich.edu:70/00/ebb/price/exim-3.bls	EBB
International Comparisons	http://stats.bls.gov/intlcomp.htm	Bureau of Labor Statistics
International Labor Statistics (IN)	gopher://stats.bls.gov:70/00hoplftp.dev/doc/in.doc	LABSTAT
International Market Insight (IMI) Reports	gopher://una.hh.lib.umich.edu:70/11/ebb/imi	EBB
Miscellaneous Trade Files	gopher://una.hh.lib.umich.edu:70/11/ebb/mistrade	EBB
National Export Strategy Files	gopher://una.hh.lib.umich.edu:70/11/ebb/nes	EBB
Penn World Tables	http://www.inform.umd.edu:8080/EdRes/Topic/Economics/EconData/Data/International/; then select pwt.zip	EconData International Files
Special Export Comparison Index	gopher://stats.bls.gov	LABSTAT
State by State Export Resource Listings	gopher://una.hh.lib.umich.edu:70/11/ebb/statex	EBB
Summary of Merchandise Trade (10/1993)	gopher://una.hh.lib.umich.edu:70/00/ebb/summaries/trade	EBB
Trade	gopher://usda.mannlib.cornell.edu:70/11/data-sets/trade	USDA/Cornell
Trade Opportunity Program (TOP)	gopher://una.hh.lib.umich.edu:70/11/ebb/top	EBB
U.S. Balance of Payments	http://www.inform.umd.edu:8080/EdRes/Topic/Economics/EconData/Data/USNational/Accounts/; then select bop.zip	EconData USNational Files
U.S. Exports and General Imports—Selected SITC Commodities	http://gopher.census.gov:70/0/Bureau/Stat-Abstract/freq/94s1330.prn	US Census
U.S. Exports and Imports of Merchandise	http://gopher.census.gov:70/0/Bureau/Stat-Abstract/freq/94s1323.prn	US Census
World Debt Tables (with permission from the World Bank)	http://info.umd.edu:86/Educational_Resources/AcademicResourcesByTopic/EconomicsResources/EconData/www/contents.html; then select WDT.ZIP	EconData International Files
World Tables of Social & Economic Indicators (with permission from the World Bank)	http://info.umd.edu:86/Educational_Resources/AcademicResourcesByTopic/EconomicsResources/EconData/www/contents.html; then select WTB.ZIP	EconData International Files

Bob O'Keefe on the Future of the Internet

Certainly, the Web browser tools are becoming all-in-one tools. For example, you can maintain your subscriptions through Netscape and read and write to newsgroups. Some tools enable you to do e-mail. And of course the way the Web protocol works, you can go off to a Gopher site through a Web browser. So, from a user point of view, we're very rapidly heading to a situation in which everyone will have an Internet package on his or her workstation or PC, and everything will seem fairly seamless to them.

Now, from the other end, in terms of providers, I can't see how anyone will set up a Gopher site; you'd do it as a Web page. There's always going to be a need for FTP. One of the things a lot of companies are doing with the Web is providing documents and materials that you can download, and some of them are going to be files in a particular format. If you're a manufacturing company, you might have CAD drawings in a particular format, which the Web will never ever be able to show. So people will need to download them and, then look at them or print them. So FTP's always going to be around. Now, if you do e-mail, newsgroups, the Web, and FTP, you've got just about everything covered.

Indexes data to help decide where and what to buy or sell. And, of course, bankers and economists use all the indexes in formulating predictions. Table 4.15 lists government indicators and indexes, the URL of the site that contains the indicators and indexes, and the source of the site.

Economics Resources

In contrast to the General Resources section, which consists of sites with economic information and many links to

Table 4.15: U.S. Government Indicators and Indexes

Data	URL	Source
2-Year Data for All Business Cycle Indicators (BCI) Series	gopher://una.hh.lib.umich.edu:70/00/ebb/indicators/bci2all	EBB
2-Year Data for All Business Cycle Indicators (BCI) Series (DOS Compressed Version)	gopher://una.hh.lib.umich.edu:70/00/ebb/indicators/bci2-all.dat	EBB
4-Year Data for All Business Cycle Indicators (BCI) Series	gopher://una.hh.lib.umich.edu:70/00/ebb/indicators/bcic-all.dat	EBB
BLS Employment Cost Index, Complete Release (eci.exe)	gopher://una.hh.lib.umich.edu:70/00/ebb/employment/eci.bls	EBB
Business Conditions Indicators	http://info.umd.edu:86/Educational_Resources/AcademicResources ByTopic/EconomicsResources/EconData/.www/contents.html; then select bci.zip	EconData USNational Files
Business Cycle Indicators (BCI) 2-Year Data (bci-2yr.exe)	gopher://una.hh.lib.umich.edu:70/00/ebb/indicators/bci-2yr.dat	EBB
Business Cycle Indicators (BCI) 4-Year Data	gopher://una.hh.lib.umich.edu:70/00/ebb/indicators/bci-4yr.dat	EBB
Business Cycle Indicators (BCI) 4-Year Data (in NTDB format)	gopher://una.hh.lib.umich.edu:70/00/ebb/indicators/bci-nt4y.dat	EBB
Business Cycle Indicators (BCI) Current data	gopher://una.hh.lib.umich.edu:70/00/ebb/indicators/BCIC	EBB
Business Cycle Indicators (BCI) Data Diskette	gopher://una.hh.lib.umich.edu:70/00/ebb/indicators/bciread.me	EBB

Table 4.15: U.S. Government Indicators and Indexes (continued)

Data	URL	Source
Business Cycle Indicators (BCI) Data Products	gopher://una.hh.lib.umich.edu:70/00/ebb/indicators/bciprod.doc	EBB
Business Cycle Indicators (BCI) Historical Data	gopher://una.hh.lib.umich.edu:70/00/ebb/indicators/BCIH	EBB
Bureau of Labor Statistics (BLS) Real earning—Tables 1-3	gopher://una.hh.lib.umich.edu:70/00/ebb/indicators/real-tab.bls	EBB
Bureau of Labor Statistics (BLS) Real earnings—Full Release	gopher://una.hh.lib.umich.edu:70/00/ebb/indicators/real.bls	EBB
Bureau of Labor Statistics (BLS) Real earnings—Text and Table A Only	gopher://una.hh.lib.umich.edu:70/00/ebb/indicators/real-txt.bls	EBB
Business Cycle Indicators (BCI) Series Titles and Series Numbers	gopher://una.hh.lib.umich.edu:70/00/ebb/indicators/bcititle.txt	EBB
Business Cycle Indicators (BCI) Series With Revisions Over 4 Years	gopher://una.hh.lib.umich.edu:70/00/ebb/indicators/bci-lrev.dat	EBB
Business Cycle Indicators (BCI) Series With Revisions Over 4 Years (Different Printing Format)	gopher://una.hh.lib.umich.edu:70/00/ebb/indicators/bci-lrev.prt	EBB
Comp Indexes of Leading, Coincident, and Lagging Indicators	gopher://una.hh.lib.umich.edu:70/00/ebb/summaries/index.bea	EBB
COMPINDX for Computing Composite Index Using Business Cycle Indicators (BCI) Data Files	gopher://una.hh.lib.umich.edu:70/00/ebb/indicators/compindx.exe	EBB
Composite Index of 11 Leading Indicators 1984–93	gopher://una.hh.lib.umich.edu:70/00/ebb/summaries/index.dat	EBB
Composite Index of Leading Indicators	gopher://una.hh.lib.umich.edu:70/00/ebb/indicators/index.lst	EBB
Department Store Inventory Price Index (LI)	gopher://stats.bls.gov:70/00hopiftp.dev/doc/li.doc	LABSTAT
Documentation for Current Business Cycle Indicators (BCI) Data	gopher://una.hh.lib.umich.edu:70/00/ebb/indicators/creadme.doc	EBB
Economic Indicators	gopher://una.hh.lib.umich.edu:70/11/ebb/indicators	EBB
Economic Indicators (Lotus 1-2-3 worksheet)	gopher://una.hh.lib.umich.edu:70/00/ebb/indicatorsei.wks	EBB
Economic Indicators Text Format	gopher://una.hh.lib.umich.edu:70/00/ebb/indicators/ei.prn	EBB
Federal Government Productivity Index (PF)	gopher://stats.bls.gov:70/00hopiftp.dev/doc/pf.doc	LABSTAT
Industry Statistics	gopher://una.hh.lib.umich.edu:70/11/ebb/industry	EBB
International Price Index (EI)	gopher://hopi.bls.gov:70/00hopftp.dev/doc/ei.doc	LABSTAT
Leading, Lagging & Coincident Indexes and Their Components	gopher://una.hh.lib.umich.edu:70/00/ebb/indicators/bci-c4yr.dat	EBB
Listing All Business Cycle Indicators (BCI) Series (by number)	gopher://una.hh.lib.umich.edu:70/00/ebb/indicators/bcinum.lst	EBB
Listing All Business Cycle Indicators (BCI) Series (by topic)	gopher://una.hh.lib.umich.edu:70/00/ebb/indicators/bcipub.lst	EBB

Table 4.15: U.S. Government Indicators and Indexes (continued)		
Data	*URL*	*Source*
Listing All Business Cycle Indicators (BCI) Series (IDs and titles)	gopher://una.hh.lib.umich.edu:70/00/ebb/indicators/bcilist	EBB
Revised Composite Indexes & Components	gopher://una.hh.lib.umich.edu:70/00/ebb/indicators/indexrev.dat	EBB
Revised Composite Indexes & Components: IDs & Titles	gopher://una.hh.lib.umich.edu:70/00/ebb/indicators/revlist	EBB
Revised Composite Indexes & Components: Text & Tables	gopher://una.hh.lib.umich.edu:70/00/ebb/indicators/indexrev.txt	EBB
Revisions and Changes in Business Cycle Indicators (BCI) Series	gopher://una.hh.lib.umich.edu:70/00/ebb/indicators/bci-lrev.txt	EBB
Summary of Consumer Price Index (1993)	gopher://una.hh.lib.umich.edu:70/00/ebb/summaries/cpi	EBB
Summary of Import and Export Price Indexes (1993)	gopher://una.hh.lib.umich.edu:70/00/ebb/summaries/exim	EBB
Summary of Leading, Lagging, Coincident Indicators (11/1993)	gopher://una.hh.lib.umich.edu:70/00/ebb/summaries/index	EBB
Summary Text File for Economic Indicators	gopher://una.hh.lib.umich.edu:70/00/ebb/indicators/ei.txt	EBB

other Internet resources, this section contains specific economics-related sites—although some offer a few noneconomic links.

In this section, you will find economics-related articles, journals, and working papers; data showing economic conditions around the world for more than 40 years; regional demographics that you can compile yourself; demographic data based on interviews; information about applying economics to the Internet; Gopher servers for college and university economics departments; and financial economics sites.

ECONbase

http://www.elsevier.nl/econbase/Menu.html

Elsevier/North-Holland, a publisher of economic materials, provides a searchable database of articles published after January 1, 1994. Each year about 2,000 articles are added to the database. To get abstracts and articles, you must be an economist, and you must subscribe to this service.

However, a nonsubscriber can see tables of contents for published journals. This means that you can go to an academic library and request specific issues. To see a table of contents, click on Contents of published issues.

Economics and the Internet

http://gopher.econ.lsa.umich.edu/EconInternet.html

From Hal Varian, a University of Michigan professor, this site is structured like a long article with many hot links. This is one of the few sites that provides information about the changing role of the National Science Foundation (NSF). Some of the more interesting subjects covered here are the history and background of the Internet, how to measure Internet traffic, the future of the Internet, links to companies, pricing information on the Internet, digital cash, why your company should hook up, Internet culture, network security, and much more. This site is not well organized, but it is packed with information.

You can view the entire file as a whole or broken into chapterlike files, or you can search using keywords and logical operators. For help in searching, look at http://www.cis.ohio-state.edu/htbin/info/info/perl.info.

Economics Working Papers Archive

gopher://econwpa.wustl.edu:70/1

This site contains economics working papers and publications in 22 subject areas and links to other economics servers. To search for a working paper, click on a subject. Then click on the index icon, browse the listings, or search by month. When you find a paper, click on it to start the download; you usually have the choice of downloading it in either PostScript or Acrobat (PDF) format.

Economics-Oriented Gopher Servers

gopher://Niord.SHSU.edu:70/11gopher_root%3A%5B_DATA.ECONOMICS.%5D

Sam Houston State University probably provides the biggest list of Gopher sites (about 60 of them) with economics-related information. Heavily represented are finance, business, and economics departments at universities and colleges and government links from around the world. Apparently, the links are verified regularly; all the links in a random check worked.

Bob O'Keefe on Regulating the Internet

The whole regulation thing is just going to be enormous. Because I'm originally English, I tend to think of things internationally. For example, in today's mail, a package with a disk with some simple software on it—Pascal programs that about two months ago, was returned from Cairo. The package had been opened, sealed up again, and sent back. The Egyptians are funny about importing software. If they find a disk, it's almost like a sealed border. But if somebody's on the Web, and they're in Cairo, that personthey can download the stuff, and the authorities will never know.

Another thing that will happen is taxation. Australia is seriously considering taxing Internet traffic. So a provider has to pay something like 50 cents for every 10 megabytes. Why not? Cars flow on the highway. We charge people tolls to pay for the highway. The view of the Australian government is that public funds have built the telecommunications infrastructure, and we should charge tolls should be charged for information flying across the wires. America is about the only deregulated phone system in the world. In America, it's very complicated because all long- distance providers are public companies.

Here's another example. In England, a lot of PC software is very expensive, mainly because of distribution channels. There are a few big distributors who don't have a great deal of competition. Plus, there's an 8eight per cent import tax plus, even if tax has been paid in America, local value-added tax, which is 17 1/2 per cent. The result is a program in England is about twice the cost it is in America. So what do you do if you want to buy a software product? You can get on the Web, and go somewhere like Software.net, give them a credit card number, they download the softwareit to your machine, and another border falls. The software has been imported, but the government doesn't know. Now presumably, you're breaking the law. To be within the law, you probably have to fill in a form and pay tax.

Financial Economics Network (FEN)

http://www.ssep.com/ssep/ssephome.html

From Social Science Electronic Publishing, Inc. (SSEP), this is the home page for the *Journal of Financial Abstracts*, a link to other financial sites, and to social sciences, accounting, economics, financial economics research, and legal scholarship networks. This site is under construction and is sparsely "populated." However, over a two-month period, the site has grown a great deal. Currently, you can get subscription information about the *Journal of Financial Abstracts*, go to an electronic placement forum, and read press releases and information about SSEP. Select Other Financial Webs to go to other finance and economic pages (for example, stock brokers and banks), and select Marr/Kirwood Official Guide to Business School Webs, to get ratings of business school sites worldwide.

Penn World Tables

gopher://nber.harvard.edu:70/11/.pwt56

The Penn World Tables (version 5.6) compare economic data from countries around the world for the years 1950 to 1992. To get started, click on the Description icon to display information about the tables and the list of 16 variables. Click on either Data (pwt56.asc, which is more than 1.5 million bytes) or Investment Data (pwtinves.prn, which is 123 kilobytes) to download files. Figure 4.7 shows part of a formatted version of PWTINVES.PRN. For an explanation of this version of the Penn World Tables, download and review the PWTREADM.DOC file.

Note

Because of the size of PWT56.ASC, downloading takes a long time, and the file may be too large for some programs (for example, Word for Windows 6 or Lotus 1-2-3 Version 5) to open.

Regional Economic Information System (REIS), 1969–92

http://www.lib.virginia.edu/socsci/reis/reis1.html

This searchable database contains local area economic data for U.S. states, counties, and metropolitan areas for 1969 to 1992. You can search for personal income by source, by per-capita personal income, by earnings, and by full- and part-time employment by industry and compile a custom table of the results.

Note

Some browsers (for example, Netscape) support this site; others (for example, Lynx and Mosaic) do not.

To search for information, follow these steps:

1. Select one or more city or metropolitan areas by clicking on your selection(s).

2. Choose variables from the Total Personal Income and Earnings Variables, or click on the checkbox above the list box to choose all the variables.

Country	Category	1950	1951	1952	1953	1954	1955	1956
ARGENTINA	Machinery	480	703	599	641	617	694	651
ARGENTINA	Business Construction	1403	2057	1752	1876	1806	2031	1904
ARGENTINA	Other Construction	590	866	737	790	760	855	802
ARGENTINA	Residential Construction	894	1311	1116	1195	1151	1294	1213
ARGENTINA	Transportation Equipment	208	304	259	278	267	301	282
AUSTRALIA	Machinery	2820	3337	1999	2643	3155	3307	2960
AUSTRALIA	Business Construction	2219	2626	1573	2080	2482	2603	2329
AUSTRALIA	Other Construction	1444	1709	1024	1353	1615	1694	1516
AUSTRALIA	Residential Construction	2239	2650	1587	2099	2505	2627	2351
AUSTRALIA	Transportation Equipment	1655	1959	1173	1552	1852	1942	1738
AUSTRIA	Machinery	537	688	712	595	785	1049	990
AUSTRIA	Business Construction	187	282	222	191	237	333	328
AUSTRIA	Other Construction	499	594	480	372	495	689	626
AUSTRIA	Residential Construction	567	431	520	516	595	662	681
AUSTRIA	Transportation Equipment	558	714	739	618	816	1090	1028
BELGIUM	Machinery	1926	1921	1946	2024	2163	2320	2546
BELGIUM	Business Construction	942	939	952	990	1058	1137	1250
BELGIUM	Other Construction	1002	1000	1013	1054	1187	1178	1340

Figure 4.7 Part of the pwtinves.prn, Investment Data, file

3. Choose employment variables, or check the checkbox to choose all the variables.

4. Select a range of years.

5. Click on Submit. Then wait for about 30 seconds for the data report to be compiled. Figure 4.8 shows the data from a report.

REIS Data Report						
VARIABLE	MSA	1969	1970	1971	1972	1973
TOTAL PERSONAL INCOME	PHILADELPHIA	20280282	21672910	22966325	24855398	26966747
POPULATION (1000s)	PHILADELPHIA	48291	48907	49127	48999	48603
PER CAPITA PERSONAL INCOME ($)	PHILADELPHIA	4200	4431	4675	5073	5548
TOTAL EMPLOYMENT	PHILADELPHIA	22280382	20856121	74866219	97632232	088
VARIABLE	MSA	1974	1975	1976	1977	1978
TOTAL PERSONAL INCOME	PHILADELPHIA	29426848	31575910	34566005	37628205	41504005
POPULATION (100s)	PHILADELPHIA	48375	48273	48203	48040	47854
PER CAPITA PERSONAL INCOME ($)	PHILADELPHIA	6083	6541	7171	7833	8673
TOTAL EMPLOYMENT	PHILADELPHIA	22223272	15262921	7114	22191065	2249315

Figure 4.8 A REIS data report for the years 1969 to 1973

Social Security Interview Statistics

http://www.ssa.gov:80/statistics/ors_home.html

The Office of Research and Statistics (ORS) of the Social Security Administration provides statistical data and research analyses of the old-age, survivors, and disability (OASDI) and Supplemental Security Income (SSI) programs based on interviews of new recipients. Businesses that provide goods and services to older Americans and those that would consider employing disabled workers can use this information.

To start a search of files that you can download (in WordPerfect 5.1/5.2 format, zipped), click on the word *Here* on the home page. Then choose from three subsequent pages.

Note
Because of the size of the files, downloading takes a long time, and files may be too large for some programs (for example, Word for Windows 6 or Lotus 1-2-3 Version 5) to open.

Chapter Five

Coming Attractions

- ◆ Business Schools
- ◆ Business School Lists
- ◆ Colleges and Universities
- ◆ Virtual Colleges
- ◆ Online Courses
- ◆ Writing Courses and Resources
- ◆ Hypertext Tutorials and Manuals
- ◆ Conferences

Education and Training

C olleges and universities have been on the Internet since its inception and are a rich source of information. This part of *The Business-to-Business Internet Directory* covers business schools, colleges and universities throughout the world, online educational institutions, and online business-related courses, course materials, seminars, and tutorials.

Whether you are a professor, student, researcher, or professional or amateur writer, you'll find the Internet invaluable. For example, if you want to learn about marketing and your schedule or location prohibits attending classes, you can take an online course or even design your own self-study program with online materials. Then, as you're preparing a report, rather than haul out that unabridged dictionary or dog-eared thesaurus, you can get on the Net and look up the word—in an up-to-date, perhaps even interactive, dictionary.

Business Schools

Whether you are a prospective MBA student, a manager who wants to research a topic in-depth, or a business owner who needs to consult with an academic expert, you will find what you are looking for in this part. Almost every university worldwide has at least one address on the Internet; business schools and departments are no exception. This section consists of lists from which you can look up business schools at colleges and universities in the U.S. and abroad. Also included are rankings of business schools and their home pages as well as a student survival guide.

Business Education Sites

http://www.mgmt.purdue.edu/HTML/bused.html

This list of business schools, some with multiple sites, on the World Wide Web is split into two sections: United States Business Education Schools and Foreign Business Schools. The emphasis is on the U.S. section. Many entries are Executive MBA programs from schools that you might not know offer MBAs, and some sites show more than one server. The list of schools outside the U.S. is short.

Note
The sponsor of this list, the Krannert Graduate School of Management at Purdue University, offers a home page (http://www2.mgmt.purdue.edu/) with excellent links to business and Internet resources in these categories: business and commercial, government, entertainment and travel, information technology, reference, and indexes and search engines.

Business School Gopher Servers

gopher://gopher.babson.edu

Surprisingly enough, the World Wide Web has been booming for just a couple of years. Before there was the Web, there was Gopher, and Babson is the primary source of Gopher-based business information. This very busy page lists many Gopher sites at business schools worldwide.

Business Schools and Other Internet Resources Worldwide

http://www.dartmouth.edu/pages/tuck/bschools.html

This very thorough and up-to-date list of World Wide Web sites at the most prestigious business schools in the U.S. and abroad also includes links to four comprehensive business school indexes.

Other places of interest include the Advertising Law Internet Site, FTC Advertising Guidelines, the White House, Federal Information Exchange, the Small

Interview with Wayne Marr

Wayne Marr, Vice President and Co-Founder (with Professor Michael C. Jensen of the Harvard Business School) of the Financial Economics Network (FEN) and Social Science Electronic Publishing (SSEP), is the author of numerous professional and trade articles. Professor Marr is a Founding and Managing Editor of the print journal, The Journal of Corporate Finance, *and is Associate Editor of various business journals and publications. Professor Marr has won several prizes for best papers in the financial economics field and was the 1986 GTE Emerging Scholar in Finance. In his spare time, he enjoys backpacking with his family and coaching his son Eric's Little League baseball team, the Pflugerville Braves.*

What is your personal background in computing and on the Internet?

I have worked with computers since college (now about 15 years), mostly with mainframes and minicomputers. When the PC came out and was widely available, I became what some would call a "hacker." I do not have any formal experience in computer programming, either from work or school; for the most part, I learned on my own.

I have worked on the Internet for about two years and came to an early conclusion that it would revolutionize the world, which I think it's doing.

How, when, and why did the Financial Economics Network start?

I started FEN in December 1994. Michael Jensen of Harvard (a Macintosh user with an avid interest in computers) joined me in January 1995. Since that time, Mike and I have stayed together. (Our personalities are very compatible, and we both are very curious people.)

Business Administration, and the United Kingdom Government Center for Information Services.

Business Schools Worldwide

http://www.yahoo.com/Business/Business_Schools/

This site presents an alphabetically arranged list of World Wide Web sites for business schools worldwide—some with brief descriptions. Sorted into the list are other entries (for example, Management Science and Publications).

Most sites in this section list just one URL—usually that for the home page—for each school. In contrast, this site lists multiple URLs for some schools. If a school has multiple URLs, its name is in **boldface**, and the number of URLs is in parentheses.

Most graduate school lists are sorted by the name of the business school, followed by its university or college. This list is arranged in reverse; you can look up the educational institution and then obtain the name of the business school.

Graduate School Rankings

http://www-cgi.cs.cmu.edu/afs/cs.cmu.edu/user/landay/pub/www/school-rankings.txt

Each year, the *U.S. News & World Report* ranks graduate schools in these categories: law, business, medical, engineering, and fine arts. This site presents the rankings and accompanying articles from the March 1994 issue.

I started FEN because of what I saw happening in the physical sciences and because I am impatient person. I simply don't enjoy waiting a week to get a letter. In fact, now I rarely write a "snail letter" and typically "curse" when forced; for the most part, these types of letters are out-dated. Therefore, I thought it was time to get the economics community online; so as the Nike commercial says, "Just do it." Well, I did it.

Initially, I started on a university computer, but found it too restrictive (FEN had to pay for itself); so we (Mike and I and two other partners, Gene Fama at the University of Chicago and Paul Hopper, a private businessman) put our own money into FEN and moved it to a private server.

How will FEN evolve?

I really do not know; the Internet is so unpredictable. When I started FEN, the World Wide Web wasn't really used. Now we use it all the time. However, one must remember that about two-thirds of our subscribers from more than 60 countries around the world *do not* have access to the Web. But I think it is coming.

Can you provide some details about the development of FEN?

I founded FEN, and then I found that Michael Jensen was very interested in electronic communication; so we set up a partnership with another academic. It didn't work out and ended poorly. Mike and I stayed together and began experimenting. Some things worked; some didn't.

Many of the "givens" in the academic world *do not* hold in the electronic academic community. Charging and pricing are different, and we are still studying this issue, some legal issues, and our basic corporate strategy. So today, I would say FEN is the most important and successful business network in the world, but I am truly amazed we (primarily Mike and I) were able to hold it all together. It was never what I envisioned.

Installing the Adobe Acrobat Reader

When you download documents from the Internet, often you will need to install a reader—either PostScript (*.PS) or Acrobat (*.PDF). You can find the Acrobat reader at a number of sites, including the Internal Revenue Service home page (http://www.ustreas.gov/treasury/bureaus/irs/taxforms.html) and at Adobe (ftp.adobe.com in the directory \pub\adobe\Acrobat\Applications\). If you download from the IRS page, do not follow the instructions. Although you can use them as a guide, a newer version of Acrobat automates many of the installation procedures.

To install Acrobat, follow these steps:

1. Download Acrobat.

2. Execute the ACROREAD.EXE file, which "uncompresses" files. The installation program displays a license agreement.

3. After reading the agreement, click on Accept. The installation program shows you the available disk space on the default drive and suggests a target drive and folder, C:\ACROREAD.

4. Either change the name and location of the target drive or accept it by clicking on Install. The installation program prompts you to fill out a registration card.

5. Click on OK.

6. Type your name and organization in the text boxes. Then click on OK. The installation program installs files to the selected drive and folder and informs you that Windows will be restarted.

If you have any questions about the Acrobat Reader, view and/or print README_R.TXT in the \HELP subfolder in the \ACROREAD folder, or use the "On-line Guide" help system.

Note

If you have a CompuServe account, you can obtain rankings that are more up to date. Click on Magazines at the main window, select U.S. News & World Report Online, click on Table of Contents, and select Graduate School Guide.

school lists. Because of one small GIF file, this page is somewhat slow to load.

The second URL, at the University of Canterbury in New Zealand, is not an exact mirror, but a smaller version of the Cranfield list.

Management Resources and Business Schools Worldwide

http://www.cranfield.ac.uk:80/som/cclt/links.html
http://www.mang.canterbury.ac.nz:80/links.html

The Cranfield Institute of Technology's alphabetically arranged list of business schools worldwide also contains many links to World Wide Web–based management and business resources and other business

Marr/Kirkwood Official Guide to Business School Webs

http://journal.com/ssep/bus.html

Wayne Marr and Hal Kirkwood examine business school home pages throughout the world and present a light-hearted but extensive five-star (the top rating) to no-star evaluation. This site, which gets better with every visit, is valuable not only for the potential b-school student but also for those who want to keep their business bookmark list up to date. Also included are links to many business schools arranged in a tabular format. The table column headings, which generally display Yes or No (for the presence or absence of a feature), are Business School (the name), Electronic Admission (Yes means that you can apply by sending an electronic admission form), Student Pages, Faculty Pages, Working Papers, Teaching Pages (course information), Alumni or Job Pages, Excellent Links (fun, business, or miscellaneous links), Overall Rating (up to five stars), and Last Look (the date of the last evaluation or visit).

Even if you are not interested in business schools, you can learn about the dos and don'ts of creating home pages from reading the ratings and visiting the sites.

The MBA Page

http://www.cob.ohio-state.edu/dept/fin/mba.htm

The MBA Page from the Fisher College of Business at Ohio State is a resource for business students, for those thinking about a master's degree in Business Administration, and for business people in general. A variety of links is provided, such as MBA Survival guides, MBA newspapers and online magazines, conferences, online classes, pages of student organizations, connections to the business world, books and book reviews, student home pages and resumés, placement

statistics and salaries, hints about applying to grad school, and miscellaneous fun sites. At this site you'll find Internet resources not available elsewhere.

A couple of links require Acrobat to read downloaded files in the PDF format.

World Wide Web Servers at Departments of Economics

http://sol.uvic.ca/1/econ/depts.html#Goup

From David Giles and Lief Bluck, in the Department of Economics at the University of Victoria, comes a fast-loading graphically enhanced list of economics departments worldwide. Good planning went into its business-related links; the authors have linked to super pages, for example, to Bill Goffe's Resources for Economists on the Internet (http://econwpa.wustl.edu/other_www/EconFAQ/EconFAQ.html), Lauri Saarinen's Economics WWW Page at the University of Helsinki (http://www.helsinki.fi/~lsaarine/econ.html), and Useful Information for Economists (http://soluvic.ca/1/econ/info.html). They provide links to World Wide Web information, economics resources, software, journals, Nobel laureates, and even jokes (see Figure 5.1) about economists and economics (http://www.etla.fi/pkm/joke.html), which even non-economists can enjoy.

Jokes about economists and economics

I believe that even   Adam Smith would enjoy these jokes...

Figure 5.1 An illustration from the Jokes about Economists and Economics home page

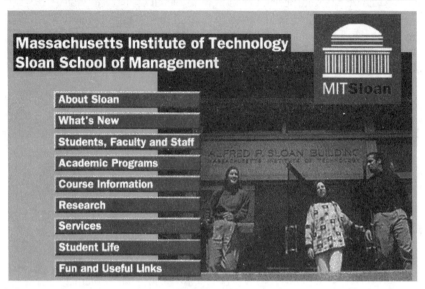

Figure 5.2 From MIT, the Sloan School of Management home page provides links on a good-looking graphic.

Figure 5.3 The Haas School of Business home page provides links on a small bar at the top of the page.

Business School Lists

If you know the name of the business school for which you are looking, this section may provide you with a shortcut. Rather than scrolling through the lists in the preceding section, you may find the address right in this section.

The U.S. business schools listed in Table 1.1 and the non-U.S. schools listed in Table 1.2 are a mere fraction of the hundreds of business schools and the thousands of colleges and universities on the Net. In addition to course and faculty listings, many of these sites provide Internet links and information, valuable business resources, and even local travel and weather information.

Colleges and universities are dynamic institutions, and links seem to change quite often; classes change and students graduate. In addition, many of these sites are always under construction and/or are moving from Gopher to World Wide Web sites.

Note
When the business school does not have a unique address, the URL is the main home page of the college or university from which you can view information about the business school.

Some business schools not only provide sites with excellent links to other schools and resources but also have some of the best-looking home pages on the World Wide Web. Figures 5.2 and 5.3 are two examples of outstanding home page graphics.

Table 5.1: Selected U.S. Business Schools

School	*Home Page URL*
Andrews University—School of Business	http://www.andrews.edu/SBA/
Babson College	gopher://gopher.babson.edu or http://www.babson.edu/
Baylor University—Hankamer School of Business	http://hsb.baylor.edu/
Boise State University—College of Business	http://www.idbsu.edu/business/cobhome.html
Bowling Green State University—College of Business Administration	http://www-cba.bgsu.edu/
Brigham Young University—Marriott School of Management	http://byu.edu
California Polytechnic at San Luis Obispo—Graduate Management Programs	http://www.calpoly.edu/~mgt/gmp/index.html
California State University Fullerton—School of Business and Economics	http://www.fullerton.edu:80/SBAE/default.html
Carnegie Mellon University	http://www.gsia.cmu.edu/
Case Western Reserve University—Weatherhead School of Management	http://litwww.cwru.edu/CWRU/wsom.html
Clark University—Graduate School of Management	http://www.clarku.edu/
Clemson University	http://www.clemson.edu/home.html
Cleveland State University—James J. Nance College of Business	http://cis.csuohio.edu/cba.html
College of William and Mary, Department of Computer Science	http://www.cs.wm.edu/
Columbia University	http://www.columbia.edu/cu/business/
Cornell University—Johnson Graduate School of Management	http://www.gsm.cornell.edu/ gopher://gopher.gsm.cornell.edu/
Dartmouth College—Amos Tuck School of Business	http://www.dartmouth.edu/pages/tuck/tuckhome.html
Defense Business Management University	http://sm.nps.navy.mil/DBMU/tom.html
DePaul University—Charles H. Kellstadt Graduate School of Business	http://www.depaul.edu/
Duke University—Fuqua School of Business	http://www.duke.edu:80/

Table 5.1: Selected U.S. Business Schools (continued)

School	*Home Page URL*
Emory University—Roberto C. Goizueta Business School	http://www.cc.emory.edu:80/BUS/homepage.html
Florida State University—College of Business	http://cob.fsu.edu
George Mason University—School of Business	http://www.ido.gmu.edu/~sba/Welcome.html
Georgetown University	http://www.georgetown.edu:80/guhome.html
Georgia State University	http://www.gsu.edu:80/dept/academic/./COBA/home.html
Harvard University—Harvard Business School	http://rigel.hbs.harvard.edu:80/
Indiana University	http://www.indiana.edu/~rugs/grdschl/grdblt/bus.html
Kent State University—College of Business	http://business.kent.edu/
Lehigh University	http://www.lehigh.edu/~www/academic-research/grad/business.html
Massachusetts Institute of Technology—Sloan School of Management	http://web.mit.edu/sloan/www
Michigan State University—Eli Broad College of Business	http://www.bus.msu.edu:80/
Mississippi State University—Academy of Management	http://www.msstate.edu:80/
National Technological University	http://www.ntu.edu:80/
New York University—Stern Business School	http://www.stern.nyu.edu/
Northwestern University—Kellogg Business School	gopher://skew.kellogg.nwu.edu/
Ohio State University—The Max M. Fisher College of Business	http://www.cob.ohio-state.edu:80/
Oregon State University—College of Business	http://www.bus.orst.edu:80/
Pennsylvania State University—Smeal College of Business Administration	http://www.psu.edu:80/academic/bluebook/Business_Administration/College_of_Business_Administration.html
Purdue University—Krannert School of Management	http://raider.mgmt.purdue.edu:80/
Rensselaer Polytechnic Institute—School of Management	http://www.rpi.edu/dept/mgmt/SOM.pages/SOM_home.html
Rice University	http://www.rice.edu:80/

Table 5.1: Selected U.S. Business Schools (continued)

School	Home Page URL
Southern Methodist University—Edwin L. Cox School of Business	http://www.cox.smu.edu:80/
Stanford University—Stanford Graduate School of Business	http://gsb-www.stanford.edu:80/
	http://www.tamu.edu
Texas Christian University—The M. J. Neeley School of Business	http://www.neeley.tcu.edu/
Tulane University—Freeman School of Business	http://freeman.sob.tulane.edu:80/
University of Alabama at Huntsville—College of Administrative Science	http://info.uah.edu:80/adminscidata.html
University of Arizona	http://www.arizona.edu:80/
University of California at Berkeley—Walter A. Haas School of Business	http://haas.berkeley.edu:80/
University of California at Irvine—Graduate School of Management	http://www.gsm/uci/edu/~gsm/
University of California at Los Angeles	http://www.ucla.edu/
University of Central Arkansas—College of Business Administration	http://wwwbusiness.uca.edu:80/
University of Chicago—Graduate School of Business	www-gsb.uchicago.edu/
University of Cincinnati—College of Business Administration	http://www.cba.uc.edu:80/
University of Delaware—College of Business and Economics	http://www.udel.edu/raker/
University of Georgia—The Terry College of Business	http://www.cba.uga.edu/
University of Houston—College of Business Administration	http://www.cba.uh.edu:80/
University of Illinois at Urbana-Champaign—College of Commerce and Business Administration	http://www.cba.uiuc.edu:80
University of Iowa—School of Management (or College of Business Administration)	http://www.biz.uiowa.edu:80/
University of Maryland—The Maryland Business School	http://www.bmgt.umd.edu:80/
University of Michigan—School of Business Administration	http://www.bus.umich.edu:80/
University of Minnesota—Carlson School of Management	http://www.csom.umn.edu/
University of Minnesota—Duluth—Management Studies	http://www.d.umn.edu:80/
University of Missouri—College of Business and Public Administration	http://tiger.bpa.missouri.edu/
University of Nebraska at Omaha—College of Business Administration	http://unicron.unomaha.edu:80/home.htm

Table 5.1: Selected U.S. Business Schools (continued)

School	Home Page URL
University of Nevada Las Vegas—College of Business and Economics	http://www.nscee.edu:80/
University of New Mexico—Robert O. Anderson Schools of Management	http://asm.unm.edu/
University of North Carolina—Kenan-Flagler Business School	cyclops.bschool.unc.edu/
University of Northern Iowa—College of Business Administration	http://www.cba.uni.edu:80/
University of Pennsylvania—Wharton School	http://www.wharton.upenn.edu:80/
University of Rochester—William E. Simon School of Management	http://www.history.rochester.edu/
University of South Carolina	http://www.csd.scarolina.edu:80/
University of Southern California—School of Business Administration	http://www.usc.edu:80/dept/sba/
University of Southern Indiana School of Business	http://www.usi.edu/business/
University of Tennessee at Knoxville	http://www.utk.edu
University of Texas at Austin—Graduate School of Business	http://kiwiclub.bus.utexas.edu:80/
University of Utah—David Eccles School of Business	http://www.business.utah.edu/
University of Vermont—Division of Engineering, Mathematics, and Business Administration	http://www.bsad.emba.uvm.edu/
University of Virginia	http://www.virginia.edu:80/
University of Washington School of Business Administration	http://http://weber.u.washington.edu/~bapub/
University of Wisconsin at Madison	http://www.wiscinfo.wisc.edu:80/
Vanderbilt—Owen Graduate School of Management	http://www.vanderbilt.edu:80/Owen/
Wake Forest University—Babcock Graduate School of Management	http://www.mba.wfu.edu:80/mba.html
Washington State University—College of Business and Economics	http://www.cbe.wsu.edu/
Willamette University—Atkinson Graduate School of Management	http://www.willamette.edu:80/agsm/
Yale School of Management	http://www.yale.edu/som/

Table 5.2: Selected Business Schools Outside the U.S.

School	Location	Home Page URL
Australian Graduate School of Management	Australia	http://www.agsm.unsw.edu.au:80/
Copenhagen Business School	Denmark	http://www.cbs.dk:80/
Cranfield School of Management	United Kingdom	http://www.cranfield.ac.uk:80/som/
Dalhousie University—Faculty of Management	Canada	http://quasar.sba.dal.ca:2000/
European Business Management School	United Kingdom	http://www.swan.ac.uk/ebms/home.html and http://msr61.swan.ac.uk/
Fraunhofer-Institut IAO	Germany	http://www.iao.fhg.de/
Hebrew University—Jerusalem School of Business Administration (JSBA)	Israel	http://shum.huji.ac.il/jcmc/jbsa.html
London Business School	United Kingdom	http://www.lbs.lon.ac.uk/
London School of Economics	United Kingdom	http://www.blpes.lse.ac.uk/
Macquarie University—Graduate School of Management	Australia	http://www.gsm.mq.edu.au/
Manchester School of Management	United Kingdom	http://info.mcc.ac.uk/SOM_Econ_G/msmindex.html
McGill University—Management	Canada	http://www.management.mcgill.ca
McMaster University—Michael G. DeGroote School of Business	Canada	http://www.mcmaster.ca/busdocs/sob.html
Nijenrode University	The Netherlands	http://www.nijenrode.nl
Royal Melbourne Institute of Technology (RMIT)—Business Faculty	Australia	http://www.bf.rmit.edu.au:80/
Simon Fraser University—Faculty of Business Administration	Canada	http://www.bus.sfu.ca:80/
Theseus Institute	France	http://www.theseus.fr:80/
University of Canterbury—Department of Management	New Zealand	http://www.mang.canterbury.ac.nz:80/
University of Plymouth—Plymouth Business School	United Kingdom	http://orac.pbs.plym.ac.uk:80/
University of St. Gallen—Institute for Information Management	Switzerland	http://www-iwi.unisg.ch:80/index.html
University of Tasmania—Department of Management	Australia	http://www.its.newnham.utas.edu.au/dept/comlaw/mgmt/
University of Waikato—School of Management Studies	New Zealand	http://tu.mngt.waikato.ac.nz:80/
University of Western Ontario—Western Business School	Canada	http://www.business.uwo.ca:80/

Wayne Marr on Home Pages

Professor Wayne Marr also is the originator of the Marr/Kirkwood Official Guide to Business School Webs, in which he rates the World Wide Web pages of business schools throughout the world.

When you rate home pages, what do you look for? What do you hope not to see?

1. Graphics are overstated. At first, most think graphics are the neatest thing on the Net. But after a few visits (especially with a slow connection), one begins to turn off the graphics. Therefore, large graphics (unless a text route is out) is a major no-no.

2. Is the structure of the Web easy to follow? If not, it is not rated well.

3. Is informational content available besides the traditional b-school (business school) "boilerplate"? This is critical. If this is the purpose of a Web, I don't return often. I like to see material to which I would otherwise not have access.

4. Are faculty taking an active role in the development of the Web? I know a lot of faculty from around the world and can usually tell when the faculty is involved. If it clearly looks like a student effort, it's not rated that well. This is not negative toward students. In fact, in my class, we had a contest to build the best Web page. But faculty need to be involved.

What are the primary differences between a five-star page and a four-star page?

Innovations...movies, Web classes, interactive forms, especially good links for students. Understand that most business students will use their college or b-school page as a starting point. Therefore, the richer the external links, the better...and this is because of my experience at Clemson. Clemson's b-school just came online (I will rate it as under construction). But guess where most business students should start? At the Marr/Kirkwood Official Guide to Business School Webs because of its rich set of links.

Colleges and Universities

Whether an educational institution has a nationally ranked business school, a small executive MBA program, or no business department at all, it can be an important resource—for both business and personal research. Colleges and universities of every size and description compile masses of material—on creating home pages or building houses, getting around the Internet or the city in which the institution is located, or finding Web servers or your family history. The list is endless.

For example, Washington University in St. Louis is the site of Huang's Futures Report and an economics working papers archive. Carnegie-Mellon not only presents English sites but also brokerage ratings. Kent State University offers a comprehensive online guide to business resources, and Sam Houston State University, the University of Maryland, and the University of Michigan present economic data.

This section provides lists of colleges and universities with Internet sites. Surf on!

Alternative Colleges Network

http://hampshire
.edu/~gip/ACN.html

This small site lists links to alternative colleges, online colleges, and distance learning centers. After the list of links is information about the Alternative Colleges Network and its members.

American Universities on the World Wide Web

http://www.clas.ufl.edu/CLAS/
american-universities.html

If you want to research only U.S. colleges and universities granting bachelors', masters', or doctors' degrees, this alphabetically arranged and nongraphical list of World Wide Web sites from Mike Conlon at the University of Florida is the site to visit. If an educational institution does not have its own campuswide Web site, the author provides a departmental home page. If you want to visit all sizes of educational institutions, from Abilene Christian to Youngstown State with stops at the University of the Virgin Islands and the Institute of Paper Science and Technology, this site is for you.

Saving Money on Your Internet Provider

Choosing the appropriate Internet provider can save you both money and frustration. Here are some ways that you can save money by selecting the right Internet provider.

◆ Get a list of all Internet providers in your area and chart and compare their rates—both peak and off-peak.

◆ Does the provider use standard voice telephone lines or special data lines?

◆ If a provider offers free introductory hours, use them to find out whether the service works for you. Is its telephone line stable or does it disconnect often? Are its connection and graphics software compatible with your computer system?

◆ Does the provider offer an attractive annual rate? If you have checked the service thoroughly and are sure that you will stay for at least one year, consider signing up.

◆ Two providers might give you the best combination of rates and service. For example, a provider without World Wide Web service might be cheaper for services such as e-mail.

◆ Every few months, prepare a new list of providers within your area code. Is a new provider offering a low introductory rate? Do any providers offer a better rate than the one you have?

◆ If you qualify, a college or university can be the best Internet provider of all: Its connection to the Internet is probably over high-speed, high-quality data lines, and the service is probably free.

◆ If you plan on using the Internet many hours each month, consider setting up a satellite office in an area in which your telephone connection would be a local call.

◆ If you have the technical knowledge, consider becoming a provider yourself.

◆ Once you select the provider that most closely matches your planned Internet usage, display a chart of its peak and off-peak rates near your computer, and try to match your hours of use with its best rates.

◆ You can save money on a provider that offers a few hours per month at a very attractive rate and additional hours at an extremely high rate. With this type of provider, it is critical to count the hours and even minutes of use.

Wayne Marr on Business on the Internet

What advice would you give to a small-business owner setting up an Internet site? What are the pitfalls?

1. Know your market and your products. It sounds trite, but it is very true.

2. Expect and know that the unexpected will happen; be flexible. If I had to read a story today on the development of FEN, I would not believe it. I will say it again. The most important skill or ability is to be flexible in what you do and how you react to changing situations. And the Internet is that—a system constantly in flux. So you must be willing to change at a moment's notice.

California State University Servers

http://www.sdsu.edu/csuservers.html

Maintained at San Diego State University, the California State University system site has links to World Wide Web and Gopher servers at 15 locations: CSU Bakersfield, CSU Chico, CSU Dominguez Hills, CSU Fresno, CSU Hayward, CSU Humboldt, CSU Long Beach, CSU Northridge, Cal Poly Pomona, CSU Sacramento, San Francisco State University, San Jose State University, CSU San Marcos, CSU Sonoma, and CSU Stanislaus. This site is graphics-free and fast-loading.

Campuswide Information Systems

http://www.rpi.edu/dept/library/html/cwis/cwis.html

This relatively short list of campuswide information systems around the world links you to campus servers primarily on the World Wide Web, but also to Telnet and Gopher servers. Sites are listed by region: Middle East and Africa, Europe and Russia, the Americas, with a separate listing for the United States and Australia. Curiously enough, there are no links to Asia and the Pacific.

The author, Polly-Alida Farrington at Rensselaer Polytechnic Institute, also has provided links to the master list of World Wide Web servers from CERN and the University of Minnesota's Gopher sites (in other words, nearly every Gopher site in the world).

College and University Home Pages Worldwide

http://www.mit.edu:8001/people/cdemello/univ.html

Christina DeMello has developed the best and most thorough site for college and university links. The author provides three ways to get to World Wide Web sites at educational institutions worldwide: You can view an alphabetically arranged file of all the colleges and universities; you can browse through multiple files, one for each letter of the alphabet; or you can download a single file.

Also at this site is a link to Mike Conlon's list of American universities and hot links to mirror sites; so if you cannot get the information at the main site, you can try elsewhere. One of the mirror sites provides this list arranged by geographical region. Only institutions with World Wide Web links are included, and there are no graphics to slow loading.

Colleges, Universities, and Other Educational Resources

http://www.nosc.mil:80/planet_earth/uni.html

Richard P. Bocker, the originator of the Planet Earth home page virtual library, provides "rooms" containing a variety of resources and a scattering of graphics, sound, and video. The Education Room contains not only alphabetically arranged links to college and university servers, but also other types of education-related links: two telephone directories (see the following entry), faculty and student body home pages, the U.S. Department of Education, information about scholarships, jobs, and careers, and more (from primary school to grad school rankings from *U.S. News & World Report*, community colleges, and vocational colleges).

Comprehensive List of Academic Servers

http://www.netgen.com/
cgi/comprehensive

Managed by Matthew Grey at Net Genesis, this index is invaluable for those who want a list of every World Wide Web site at an educational institution. For example, if you have an old URL that is no longer valid, compile a complete list of servers, and test the address on some of the servers.

To obtain the very long list of all the edu servers in this index, select edu from the list box, and click on the Submit button.

The Internet at Large: Educational Resources

http://rosebud.sdsc.edu/1/
SDSC/Geninfo/Internet/
education

From the San Diego Super-computer Center at the University of California, San Diego, comes a long list of educational resources: links to colleges and universities, interactive and distance learning, Internet resources, human languages and dictionaries, instructional development and technology, and even the Internet Poetry Archive.

Internet Servers at Historically Black Colleges and Universities (HBCU)

http://199.125.205.20/WebPages/dll/HBCUGateway/
allhbcu.htm

At this site, you will find links to 32 historically black colleges and universities (HBCU), in a tabular format (see Figure 5.4). Each entry includes a name and one or more links (Web, Gopher, or FTP). Also included at this site are links to Georgia Tech's Universal Black Pages and the University of the Western Cape, in Capetown, South Africa.

Minority Institution Information

http://web.fie.com/web/mol/sql/molis.htm

Part of MOLIS/FEDIX (Minority On-Line Information Service/Federal Information Exchange, Inc.), this page provides a list of minority

Internet Servers at ... *HBCU's*			
1	Alabama A&M University, AL	Web	
2	Alabama State University, AL	Web	
3	Bennett College, NC	Web	
4	Bowie State University, MD	Web	Gopher
5	Clark Atlanta University, GA	Web1	Web2
6	Dillard University, LA	Web	
7	Elizabeth City State University, NC	Web	
8	Fayetteville State University, NC	Web	Gopher
9	Fisk University, TN	Web	ftp
10	Florida Agricultural & Mechanical University, FL	Web1	Web2
11	Florida Memorial College, FL	Web	
12	Grambling State University, LA	Gopher	telnet**
13	Hampton University, VA	Web	

Figure 5.4 Click on a link in this table to go to the home page of an HBCU.

educational institutions in the U.S. You can look at a map of the U.S. (states in red have minority institutions), a list of institutions by name or state and name, a list of HBCU (Historically Black Colleges and Universities) institutions by name or state and name, or a list of HSI (Hispanic Serving Institutions) institutions by name or state and name. When you display a list of institutions, each entry provides a link, the name of the president, and a telephone number.

Peterson's Education Center

http://www.petersons.com:8080/home.html

Although this site is primarily an advertisement for *Peterson's Guides*, books about education, you can get summary information in these categories: Undergraduate Colleges, Financial Aid, Private Schools, Vocational-Technical Schools, Testing, Graduate and Professional Study/Faculty, Public Schools K-12, Distance Learning Opportunities, Careers and Jobs, Postgraduate Executive Education, Summer Programs for kids and teenagers, Continuing Education, and Learning for Fun and Enrichment—accessible from a large, graphical, and clickable menu, which loads somewhat slowly.

A typical entry is less than one page and directs you to a related *Peterson Guide* that you can buy. This page is a good starting point, but you'll have to go elsewhere to complete your research about an educational institution.

The Princeton Review

http://www.review.com:80/

The Princeton Review makes its bread and butter by preparing high school juniors and seniors and those who plan to attend graduate school for standardized tests, such as the PSAT, SAT, GRE, GMAT, LSAT, and so on.

This well-designed site starts with a large illustration (see Figure 5.5) on which you click to go to pages full of information about colleges; specific advanced degree programs in law, medicine, and business; general advanced degree programs; careers; and links to other educational resources arranged by category.

A typical module provides school rankings and, of course, information about the test that you must take for admission. For example, in the Business School area, you learn about the admission process, the GMAT, GMAT Prep, TOEFL, and TOEFl Prep. You'll also learn how to finance business school. Most modules allow you to search for a specific school by name or the region or state in which it is located. You can narrow a search by using logical operators: AND, OR, and NOT.

Figure 5.5 Click on a building or other object to go to a *Princeton Review* resource.

Schools and Education

http://www.speakeasy.org/~dbrick/Hot/schools.html

For a wider variety of links—from universities and colleges down to kindergartens, libraries, university courses, treatises and articles—go to this address. In addition, you'll find some commercial links to consulting services and advertisements for courses (some under the guise of information).

The two most valuable parts of this site are the comprehensive links to education-related lists and indexes and the links to multiple servers at some colleges and universities. Another advantage of using this site is that it is fast-loading despite its size; there are no graphics.

Universities Arranged by Country

http://www.yahoo.com/Education/Universities/

From David Filo and Jerry Yang at Yahoo, this site provides hot links to universities and colleges listed under the countries in which they are located. The numbers to the right of the countries don't necessarily represent educational institutions; they can indicate an index or a list. For example, select the United States, and you'll not only be able to view a complete listing (more than 40 kilobytes at the time of this writing) of colleges and universities, but you can search six indexes of colleges and universities too.

University of California Servers

http://www.ucop.edu/ucophome/ucservers.html

This UCLA site provides links to home pages at nine colleges in the University of California system plus institutions such as the Lawrence Berkeley Laboratory, Lawrence Livermore National Laboratory, Los Alamos National Laboratory, San Diego Supercomputer Center, and the University of California Hastings College of the Law. Hot links to both World Wide Web and Gopher addresses are provided.

University Phone Directory Index

http://fiaker.ncsa.uiuc.edu:8080/cgi-bin/phfd

This online telephone directory, from the University of Illinois at Champaign-Urbana, is a searchable index of names, addresses, and other information at more than 250 colleges and universities around the world. To search the index, select a college from the drop-down list, select the fields to be returned (Name, Phone, Email, Address, and Other), select the field on which to sort, and whether you want to use an ascending (A-Z) or descending (Z-A) sort. Click on the Submit button and hope for the best, because if your search is unsuccessful, you may not be able to return to the main index page.

A similar site, which can be difficult to link to, is at gopher://gopher.nd.edu/11/Non-Notre%20Dame%20Information%20Sources/Phone%20Books—Other%20Institutions/ts. When these sites work, they are very useful.

U.S. Universities and the World Lecture Hall

http://wwwhost.cc.utexas.edu/world/univ.html

From Team Web at the University of Texas at Austin, this site provides several valuable resources: an alphabetically arranged list of World Wide Web sites at U.S. colleges and universities; links to U.S. Community Colleges; K-12 education sites; links to the big three lists: Christina DeMello's, Mike Conlon's, and Yahoo's; and a link to the extensive course information at the World Lecture Hall.

The World Lecture Hall (http://wwwhost.cc.utexas.edu/world/instruction) is an alphabetically arranged list of 46 course categories, from which you can see how faculty members at many colleges and universities are using the World Wide Web to distribute course information, assignments, lecture notes, examinations, schedules, and online textbooks. Some categories may have only one course, and others contain several. It's interesting to tour some of the sites to see some excellent graphics, links to Web and Gopher servers and to other Internet sites, and even laboratory slides and tests. This is a good site for teachers and professors designing new courses. Business entries on the World Lecture Hall include Accounting, Communication, Computer Science, Economics, English and Technical Writing, Finance, Journalism, Management, Management Information Systems, Marketing, and Statistics.

The Virtual University

http://wwwcsif.cs.ucdavis.edu/virt-university/welcome-text.html

Elaine Lazarte and Vik Varma, at the University of California at Davis, present the Virtual University, which has lists of colleges, universities, departments, and organizations arranged under subjects of study, including Business and Economics. Each hot link is accompanied by a small college seal.

Perhaps the best part of this site is a virtual town,

which comes in two flavors: text and graphics (more than 200 kilobytes in size). From the town square (http://wwwcsif .cs.ucdavis.edu/virt-town/town-graphic.html), go to other places in town (see Figure 5.6). For

example, the business district (http://www.cs.ucdavis.edu/virt-town/finance.html) contains links to stock market information, stock quotes, EDGAR, commodities and futures information, the Koblas Currency Converter (however, it's an old URL), investment newsletters, banks, the Federal Reserve, stock markets, the Internal Revenue Service, and more.

Virtual Colleges

Virtual colleges and universities are some of the most exciting and new developments on the Internet. Be aware that some of these institutions have been founded recently and are not accredited. The future looks bright, however; some of the most prestigious universities, such as MIT, are sponsors.

This section lists online colleges and universities, which may or may not exist physically, and lists of training resources.

The Apple Virtual Campus

http://hed.info.apple.com/home.html

Apple provides online documents and links to resources in learning technologies for everyone, but especially for educators and trainers. Included are sections on distance learning, working together, information access, workflow, and mobility—with articles and hints for educators and trainers. The information access is probably the most valuable, with articles on how, when, and where to get academic solutions.

Although this is a commercial site, the pitch for Apple products almost always remains in the background. This site is

Figure 5.6 The Virtual Town's town square

graphically enhanced, but is designed so that pages load very quickly.

The Globewide Network Academy

http://uu-gna.mit.edu:8001/uu-gna/

The Globewide Network Academy is a consortium of colleges, universities, and other educational institutions that either provide online courses or serve institutions providing online courses. The GNA Consortium Members page provides hot links to the institutions that are members of the consortium. At the time of this writing, some new institutions were not accredited.

The online courses include several business, computer, and writing courses. Sample business courses include Introduction to Marketing, Problems of Development, Geographic Information Systems, and Strategic Planning.

One of the strengths of the GNA is its online documentation about its technical systems. Although this information is for GNA personnel, you can adapt it for your own use. Included is information about HTML (the basics, a style guide, and how to use editors), Perl, and NCSA HTTP tutorials.

Wayne Marr on Business Resources and Online Courses

What Internet business resources do you use most often, recommend to your students, or both?

The Marr/Kirkwood Official Guide to Business School Webs, Bill Goffe's Guide to Internet Resources for Economists on the Internet (http://econwpa.wustl.edu/other_www/EconFAQ/EconFAQ.html), and FEN (http://journal.com/ssep/bus.html). However, understand that Mike Jensen and I are creating this, and we haven't had a lot of time to devote. And there are some others, but most can be found on the Marr/Kirkwood Official Guide to Business School Webs.

What nonbusiness sites are your personal favorites?

I don't have much extra time to do much on the Net that is not work-related. For example, I get about three requests a day to rate something in the Marr/Kirkwood Official Guide to Business School Webs. But I would say Ken Griffey Jr.'s home page (http://www.mariners.org/ken.jr/ken.jr.home.html) because my son plays baseball, I am a coach of baseball, and I love baseball. So any time I see something related to baseball, I will check it out, and it will usually end up on my Hot list.

What are the characteristics of an effective online course or tutorial?

I don't think that what I call "deep thought" courses can be taught on the Net *yet*! These are the courses in which the Socratic method is extremely important (law school courses, for example). However, I think most of the courses in a business school can be taught via a combination of the Web, e-mail, and possibly some interactivity like IRC (Internet Relay Chat) or MOO (MUD, Object-Oriented). Any type of course that is rote memory is a candidate to be placed on the Net, and I think from a cost perspective, it will be. My colleagues don't like to hear this, but higher education in this country will not look the same in 10 years because of the Internet.

What is the role and future of the online course? Will a telecommuting student ever be able to get a degree or certificate with only online courses?

It has a very healthy future. We are making our first attempts at organizing it with FEN's virtual business school. It may take 10 years, but it will happen. NYU is already offering 16 hours (of for-credit courses) entirely through the Internet. And, yes, you will have degrees, certifications, and so on.

Saving Money on Your Telephone Connection

The telephone charges for using the Internet can be even more expensive than your provider bills. Here are some ways that you can save money on your telephone bill.

- If a provider offers a flat-rate 800 number, compare it with your local and long-distance service.

- If your provider's telephone number is a local call, see how many units the telephone company allows you each month. Contact your telephone company and investigate changing to another method of calculating local calls.

- If your provider's telephone number is not in your local dialing area, does your local telephone allow you to define the telephone exchange as a local call?

- If your provider's telephone number is a long-distance call within your area code, compare both your local telephone company and your long-distance company rates. (Your long-distance company has a prefix for long-distance calls within your area code.) Factor in the stability of the local and long-distance lines.

- If your provider's telephone number is considered a long-distance call within your area code, make a chart of hourly rates for peak and off-peak telephone charges and display it near your computer.

- If your telephone bill has jumped to hundreds of dollars per month, investigate a flat monthly rate provider.

- Look into getting a high-speed data line and matching it with a computer with a higher-speed processor and a faster modem.

information, an index to instructional technology connections, training companies, computer classes, and training resources.

If you want to arrange an Internet seminar or computer training at your company headquarters, this is probably the place at which you should start your search.

Online Courses

You can study course materials informally or take formal for-credit courses on the Internet. For example, you can learn a great deal about antitrust by browsing through the Antitrust Policy Hypertext Journal or find out how to market your company on the Internet by reviewing the Research Program on Marketing in Computer-Mediated Marketing Environments and Interactive Marketing course. If you are a government worker, you can order an 80-hour management statistics correspondence course from the Defense Business Management University.

This section lists and describes online business courses, tutorials, correspondence courses, papers, and online manuals.

Training Companies and Instructional Technology

http://www.yahoo.com/Business/Corporations/Computers/Training

http://www.yahoo.com/Education/Instructional_Technology_and_Training/

These lists of links include a variety of education sites, commercial sites, journals, articles, Internet

Antitrust Policy Hypertext Journal

http://www.vanderbilt.edu/Owen/froeb/antitrust/antitrust.html

From Professor Luke Froeb at Vanderbilt University, this online journal with hypertext links and plenty of footnotes is valuable for those studying antitrust policy, specific cases (for example, Microsoft), economics, law, and policy. Topics include horizontal mergers, price fixing and bid rigging, and vertical restraints.

Many of the articles are long (50–75K); so if your browser, modem, and/or computer are slow, you may have to wait a few minutes for articles to load. This site includes both text-based and graphics-based pages.

Business Courses at Penn State

gopher://gopher.ce.psu.edu:70/
1D-1%3A7288%3ASmeal%20Business%20College

For a long time, Penn State has been known as a good source of correspondence courses. The word is that Ben and Jerry learned how to make ice cream by taking a Penn State correspondence course.

At this site, you can explore for-credit distance courses in accounting, business administration, business law, business logistics, finance, management, marketing, and quantitative analysis.

Defense Business Management University

http://sm.nps.navy.mil/DBMU/catalog/correspond/
correspond.html
http://sm.nps.navy.mil/DBMU/catalog/interact/interact.html

These two sites from the Defense Business Management University provide correspondence and interactive business courses, primarily designed for military personnel and usually restricted to the military and U.S. government employees.

Courses include appropriation and cost accounting, disbursing operations management, financial management, management statistics, personal finance, and resource management. A typical course takes 4 to 80 hours to complete.

Dun & Bradstreet Information Services

http://www.dbisna.com:80

Dun & Bradstreet provides a free (for now) commercial site with seven short online business tutorials: Market Your Business Globally, Strategic Business Planning, Predicting Slow Payers, Research Effectively, Finding a Job, Tactical Marketing, and How to Manage Vendors.

A typical tutorial contains three sections: Trends, Tips, and Solutions (a bulleted list that tells how D&B can help you solve the problem). For example, in the Predicting Slow Payers tutorial, the Trends section contains four charts showing slow payment rates and the default rate by industry segment and by the age of the business. The Tips section describes how to make better credit decisions by applying the four Cs of Credit, using financial ratio analysis, tracking trends, and comparing with a peer group.

Economics of Businesses, Consumers, and Markets

http://www.vanderbilt.edu:80/Owen/froeb/mgt322/
mgt322.html

Professor Luke Froeb at Vanderbilt University provides this online course, which includes a syllabus, lecture notes, and problem sets. This course is tailored for classroom students; so expected grade distribution is provided. The reading list includes recommended reading—articles and books (even a murder mystery).

Small-business people and department heads who want to keep up to date with both current corporate strategies and international business can study these topics: wealth creation, auctions and bargaining, demand and supply of foreign exchange, production and cost, pricing, insurance, modern theory of the firm, strategy and managing quality, vertical integration, and contracts.

Innovation Guide to Management and Technology

http://www.euro.net/innovation/Indextext.html

Information Innovation provides an amazing number of business resources: an interactive management guide, a dictionary, software, a Web bibliography, and links to other places on the World Wide Web. Beware that the site design is both complex and convoluted, and there are some rough spots here and there. Information Innovation, a commercial site for subscribers, provides many pages for visitors too.

The centerpiece is the Innovation Guide to Management and Technology (http://www.euro.net:80/innovation/Management_Base/Man_Guide_Rel_1.0B1/MainTopics.html), a detailed interactive guide. Main topics range from artificial intelligence to visualization and include economics, finance, manufacturing, marketing, and strategy.

The Management and Technology Dictionary is arranged by the letters of the alphabet and numbers and symbols. Entries consist of technology and management terms; books, magazines, and articles; databases; and conferences and exhibitions. A typical entry may include any of the following: the name of author; cross-references to other areas; a term description; an illustration, a chart, or a diagram; and room for you to add comments next to each term.

Other resources are the Delphi Oracle, new management philosophies, Management Software (Web and Internet software), the Web Word, Web Bibliography (with bibliographic information about books, magazines, and articles), and useful sites on the Web.

KiwiClubWeb Server

http://kiwiclub.bus.utexas.edu/finance/kiwiserver/kiwiserver.html

Professor Richard MacMinn's KiwiClub at the University of Texas provides hot links to finance, Internet, and computer classes on the Internet as well as an extensive list of other Internet links: financial information, news, online references, archives, and more.

At this low-graphics site, you'll also find links to Internet resource guides and search tools; computer and technical information; banks in the U.S., England, Canada, and New Zealand; four Federal Reserve Banks; corporations; the Economic Bulletin Board and other economics resources; stock exchanges around the world and stock market information and ratings; personal finance and investment, bank rates, EDGAR, currency converters; S&P ratings, investment resources; U.S. government servers; news sources; and reference books.

Research Program on Marketing in Computer-Mediated Marketing Environments and Interactive Marketing on the Internet

http://www2000.ogsm.vanderbilt.edu/

Professors Donna L. Hoffman and Thomas P. Novak at Vanderbilt University are experts on marketing on the Internet, especially on the World Wide Web. Included at this site are links to other Hoffman and Novak marketing and advertising materials (http://www2000.ogsm.vanderbilt.edu/links.cgi) and lists of business schools, marketing departments, professional organizations, conferences, journals, marketing links, market-ing research, and marketing resources.

The design of this site is unique. It is well worth visiting, even if you are not particularly interested in marketing. When a page first appears, it contains what looks like a bulleted list. If you click on a bullet, however, it expands to a list of sublinks (see Figure 5.7).

Various Subject Matter Guides

gopher://una.hh.lib.umich
.edu/11/inetdirsstacks

This site at the University of Michigan provides a long list of all types of online texts on a variety of topics: business, writing, distance learning, computing, and the Internet.

▸ **Internet/Web Size and Demographics**
▸ **Measuring the "Clickstream" or "What's a `Hit'?"**
▸ **Directories of Commercial Web sites**

▾ *Doing Business on the Net*

● CommerceNet home page

● EINet Galaxy's Marketing and Sales page: A study of technologies, techniques, data, and regulations; with subheadings on: advertising, distribution, marketing, policy and regulation, product development, and sales

● How to Publish an ad on the World Wide Web

● Internet Media Services How to get a Web Page for your company

Figure 5.7 A Research Program on Marketing page showing an unexpanded portion at the top and an expanded part with links at the bottom

Writing Courses and Resources

Whether you are writing a short memorandum or a 100-page report, spelling, punctuation, and the way you put down the words can make the difference between success and failure. Using the resources in this section, you can check the placement of commas and semicolons, write a super resumé, read grammar columns, or find an online dictionary or thesaurus.

This section lists and describes Internet-based writing courses, laboratories, tutorials, and megalists that point the way to other writing resources. Also included are Table 5.3, a list of business and technical glossaries with which you can enhance your reports and technical documents and increase your knowledge of the Internet, and Table 5.4, a list of dictionaries and thesauruses for technical, business, and creative writing.

On-Line Writing Lab

http://owl.trc.purdue.edu/prose.html

From the On-Line Writing Lab (OWL) at Purdue University, this site contains articles on writing skills and links to many other writing

Interesting Site

Since Esperanto, the international language, was invented in 1887 by Dr. Ludwik L. Zamenhof, activists have been promoting it. You can learn more about Esperanto by visiting its World Wide Web site at http://wwwtios.cs.utwente.nl/esperanto/hypercourse.

sources. Categories under which you will find articles are Parts of Speech, Punctuation, Sentences, The Spelling Center, English as a Second Language, General Writing Concerns, Writing a Research Paper and Citing Sources, Resume and Cover Letter Guidance Center, and Business Writing Guidance Center. You also can find a list of almost 100 document titles, not arranged in any order, at http://owl.trc.purdue.edu/by-topic-alternate.html.

The main address for OWL, http://owl.trc.purdue.edu:80/our-writing-lab.html, slowly (because several photographs must load) reveals links to other writing labs and research sources on the Internet.

Saving Money and Time on the Internet

Here are some ways in which you can save time and money when connected to the Internet.

- Go directly to the site where you want to research, complete your work, and then sign off. Don't be side-tracked by hot links to other sites.

- Keep a diary of your sessions—when you logged on and off and the sites that you visited.

- Use a nongraphical browser or turn off graphics if you can. (Loading large graphic files takes a great deal of time.)

- If a site offers a choice between graphical and text pages, choose text.

- Use a megalist as a jumping-off point. For example, if you keep a database of businesses that have Internet sites, every few days, go to a "what's new" megalist with hot links. Then visit a site and add it to your database, go back to the megalist in order to jump to the next site,

and repeat until you have reached the end of the megalist.

- Find a site from which you can get the desired information and which provides reliable connections (that is, you can almost always connect to its server). Some colleges and universities (some examples are MIT, Clark University, Purdue University, and the Wharton School at the University of Pennsylvania) not only provide campus information but also have links to megalists and business resources.

- If your browser allows you to set up Hot lists, do so. Then at the start of each session, you can use the Hot list to resume your research, or each week you can visit hot sites to accumulate information.

- For new searches, find and learn one or two search indexes. Be sure that you know how it uses keywords.

- Thoroughly learn your browser software and its shortcuts. Read the manuals and view the help system.

The Online Writery

http://www.missouri.edu/
~wleric/writery.html

The Online Writery from the University of Missouri contains almost everything about writing: links to Internet search tools, writing guides and tutorials, a writing lab, and the Word and Image Gallery, in which you can publish your own works. The Skim & Dive site provides links to music, education, and zines.

A primary feature of this site is communications; you can chat with other writers, through e-mail or in real time.

The Undergraduate Writing Center

http://www.utexas.edu/depts/
uwc/.html/ main.html

From the University of Texas at Austin is a site with an online newsletter and links to writing resources on the Internet.

The newsletter combines articles about the writing center, columns about writing (for example, The Tangled Web of Jargon, a column about wordiness by Miss Grammars), and handouts, which are articles on a variety of topics (for example, apostrophes, brainstorming, documenting sources, nonsexist language, and reading literature).

The links include a list of about 20 dictionaries of every flavor: English dictionaries, thesauruses, computer dictionaries, foreign language-English dictionaries, a hacker's dictionary, and a hypertext Webster interface.

Table 5.3: Glossaries and Dictionaries of Business and Technical Terms, Abbreviations, and Acronyms

Name	URL	Description
Acronyms and Glossaries	http://atmos.es.mq.edu.au/acronyms.html	Links to various glossaries: Environmental and Environment-related Acronyms; a searchable Acronym Dictionary; the Earth Observing System (EOS) Glossary, Acronyms, and Abbreviations; the Pacific Marine Environmental Laboratory (PMEL) Acronym List, Radar Meteorology Glossary, NASA Thesaurus, BABEL: A Glossary of Computer Related Abbreviations and Acronyms, three weather guides, Global Change Acronyms and Abbreviations, Hacker's Jargon computer dictionary, and four sets of acronyms
Auto Lending and Leasing Terms	http://www.financenter.com/resources/autoloan/glossary.htm	A comprehensive glossary of auto lending and leasing terms followed by an index of links to the terms
BABEL—A Glossary of Computer Oriented Abbreviations and Acronyms	http://www.access.digex.net/~ikind/babel96a.html	A popular, large (139 kilobytes), and interactive glossary of computer-related abbreviations and terms of all types: "personal computing, multimedia, communications, programming, networking, etc."
Bellcore Glossary	http://www.bellcore.com/demotoo/glossary/index.html	Internet acronyms and abbreviations and a search index
The Biggest, Dumbest Glossary	http://www.joeboxer.com/glossary.html	A short glossary of Internet terms, not arranged in any particular order but with very thorough descriptions
Black Box Glossary of Data Communication Terms	http://www.blackbox.com/bb/refer/glossary.html/rigb0b0	A large glossary of telecommunications, computing, and Internet terms
Computing Oriented Abbreviations and Acronyms	http://crl.nmsu.edu/lists/Babel.html	A searchable index of the Babel Computing Oriented Abbreviation and Acronyms database
Credit Card Terms and Processes	http://www.financenter.com/resources/credit/credglos.htm	A glossary of credit card terms along with an index of links to the terms
DesignSphere Online Glossary	http://www.dsphere.net/glossary_ah.html	A printing, publishing, and design glossary and links to Henry Budgett's Typesetting and Publishing Glossary and the Glossary of Internet Terms
Direct Marketing Glossary	http://www.phoenix.ca/bmr/glossary/glossary.html	A glossary of direct marketing, statistics, and business terms
Export Glossary	gopher://gopher.umsl.edu:70/00/library/subjects/business/expguide/eg_app1	A comprehensive glossary of export terms

Table 5.3: Glossaries and Dictionaries of Business and Technical Terms, Abbreviations, and Acronyms (continued)

Name	URL	Description
Financial Aid Glossary	http://www.cs.cmu.edu/afs/cs.cmu.edu/user/mkant/Public/FinAid/html/glossary.html	Glossary of student financial-aid terms
Free On-Line Dictionary of Computing	http://wombat.doc.ic.ac.uk/foldoc/contents.html	An extremely large dictionary of computing terms that has been built with contributions from readers. You can access the dictionary as entire file (3.3 megabytes), zipped (1.3 megabytes), headings, by the letter of the alphabet, or with a search index.
Glossary of Aerodynamic Terms	gopher://venus.hyperk.com:2102/	A searchable or browsable glossary of aerodynamic terms
Glossary of Closing Costs	http://www.financenter.com/resources/homeloan/closing.htm	A list of closing costs terms followed by a table of links to those terms
Glossary of Export Terms	http://www.ihc-inc.com/glosintl.htm	A glossary of export terms (some must be filled in)
Glossary of Insurance and Financial Planning Terms	http://www.bus.orst.edu/faculty/nielson/glossary/glos_idx.htm	A detailed glossary of primarily insurance terms
Glossary of Internet Terms	http://iasw.com/glossary.html	A long page of links to descriptions of Internet and telecommunications terms
Glossary of Internet Terms	http://www.vfs.com/glossary.html	A short glossary of Internet terms—mostly technical
Glossary of Mortgage Terms	http://www.financenter.com/resources/homeloan/glossary.htm	A glossary of mortgage-lending terms followed by an index of links to those terms
Glossary of Technical Terms	http://www.precisionimages.com/gloss.htm	A glossary of mathematical, computing, telecommunications definitions and acronyms
Glossary of U.S. Government Terms	http://www.itsi.disa.mil/cfs/glossary.html	Definitions and acronyms for federal workers and those dealing with U.S. government agencies
Glossary of World Wide Web Terms and Acronyms	http://www.ncsa.uiuc.edu/SDG/Software/Mosaic/Glossary/index.html	A relatively short glossary of Internet terms in two formats: a table and a definition list
Guide to Web Terminology	http://www.euro.net/innovation/Web_Word_Base/Dictionary.html	A page of Internet and computing acronyms and terms
High Performance Computing and Communications Glossary	http://www.npac.syr.edu/nsc/hpccgloss/	A very large glossary of terms for those involved in computing (both hardware and software), the Internet, and telecommunications. Some definitions include links to other definitions. The entire glossary loads when you click on a letter of the alphabet.

Table 5.3: Glossaries and Dictionaries of Business and Technical Terms, Abbreviations, and Acronyms (continued)

Name	URL	Description
HTML Glossary	http://www.csci.csush.edu/dick/samples/comp.html glossary.html	A very short glossary of HTML terms
Hypertext Terms	http://www.w3.org/hypertext/WWW/Terms.html	An insider's look at hypertext terms used by the developers of the World Wide Web. Many definitions include links to other definitions.
ILC Glossary of Internet Terms	http://www.matisse.net/files/glossary.html	A list of Internet terms with easy-to-understand definitions
Internet Users' Glossary	http://www.cis.ohio-state.edu/htbin/rfc/rfc1392.html	Request for Comments (RFC1392), a comprehensive list of Internet terms and definitions along with some links to related RFCs
Management and Technology Dictionary	http://www.euro.net/innovation/Management_Base/ Mantec.Dictionary.html	A slow-loading, comprehensive, and interactive glossary of business, computing, and Internet terms. You have the opportunity to comment on each term.
The NCF (National Captial FreeNet) Glossary	http://www.ncf.carleton.ca/freeport/help/dictionary/menu	Links to several glossaries: of conventions, acronyms, English to French, terms, Smilies, and "other stuff" (links to a page of all these glossaries: quotes, abbreviations, medical definitions, ASCII Control Codes, and the "Off the Wall" Glossary)
The New Hacker's Dictionary	http://eps.mcgill.ca/jargon/jargon.htm	A "comprehensive compendium of hacker slang"; a hypertext version of the popular *Hacker's Dictionary*
On-Line Glossary of Technical Notation	http://www.mathpro.com/math/notation/notation.html	"Symbols, mathematical functions, and abbreviations used in technical documents." Click on a symbol or character to go to a page of related definitions.
Sun Microsystems Glossary	http://www.rec.uniba.sk/web/sg/GLOSSARY.HTML	Computing, electronics, Internet, and technology terms and acronyms
Telecommunications Glossary	http://www.wiltel.com/glossary/glossary.html	A glossary of telecommunications and other terms to which you can add. Many definitions contain links to other definitions.

Hypertext Tutorials and Manuals

The main difference between simple text documents and computer-based documents is hypertext, the links that allow you to jump to other pages. A reader of a text document usually looks at the document in blocks of successive pages. In contrast, a reader of a hypertext document jumps around using the hot-linked words.

This section lists hypertext resources, primarily those that demonstrate the use of hypertext—for technical manuals or for fiction. To learn more about creating hypertext documents and the technical background, refer to the HTML section of Appendix A.

Computer Writing and Research Lab

http://www.en.utexas.edu/

This valuable site introduces hypertext basics and provides many hot links to hypertext tutorials and texts. Here, you will find many good links to other hypertext resources, including an introduction to hypertext, which includes many links arranged by date, hypertext essays and fiction, and the Hypertext Hotel's What Is Hypertext.

Hypertext at Brown

http://swansong.stg.brown.edu/projects/hypertext/ hypertextov.html

This home page describes the history of hypertext at Brown University and provides hot links to hypertext documents and biographies of hypertext

Name	URL	Description
Table 5.4: Dictionaries, Thesauruses, and Other Desk References		
ANSI: Catalog Acronyms	http://www.ansi.org/cat_d.html	A list of acronyms for organizations, committees, councils, and associations
Bartlett's Familiar Quotations	http://www.cc.columbia.edu/acis/bartleby/ bartlett/	A slow-loading and large online version of the popular book. Included are a search index, author index, list of authors, sources of their quotations, and a section on the Bible.
Biographical Dictionary	http://www.mit.edu:8001/afs/athena/user/g/a/galileo/ Public/WWW/galileo .html	More than 15,000 biographies, covering people from ancient times to the current day, constantly updated
NASA Thesaurus	http://www.sti.nasa.gov/nasa-thesaurus .html	A comprehensive thesaurus of space, aeronautics, and other terms. Click on a letter and go to a page of links to broader terms or narrower terms and related terms.
Roget's Thesaurus	gopher://odie.niaid.nih.gov/77/.thesaurus/index	A search index in which you can type a word and get a document containing many related words
Webster's Dictionary	http://c.gp.cs.cmu.edu:5103/prog/webster?	A search index to various online Webster's dictionaries. Type a word, and click on the Look Up Definition button. The resulting word list and short definitions are links to the dictionaries in which they were found.

pioneers. You can learn about the editors HES and FRESS. Click on Hypertext at Brown to read poetry and early hypertext books and essays (with a tilt toward fiction and art). At the bottom of the page, you can go to the Hypertext Hotel MOO (a multi-participant object-oriented page) to write your own section.

What Is HyperText?

http://www.w3.org/hypertext/WWW/WhatIs.html

This popular site is deceptively short. However, the lists of links that you reach from the page are extensive and much longer. Topics covered at this site and links to other sites include a short page on the history of hypertext, descriptions of hypertext and Internet terms, hypertext basics, hypertext resources and standards, conferences, and commercial and academic products.

Conferences

Whether you are planning to attend a conference or give one, the pages in this section will provide you with the right resources. If you want to go to a show, you can view lists of conferences, expositions, and trade shows by name, location, or date. If you are organizing a show or presenting a session in a few weeks or months, you can get travel information (of course, be sure to look at the *Travel* chapter of this book for more information), arrange for speakers, book facilities, and rent slide projectors and other equipment.

Academic Conferences

http://info.desy.de/library/conf.txt

At this site, you will find a very large (440+ kilobytes) text file of academic conferences, particularly for physics, starting at 1988 and ending in 1997. Individual entries contain dates the conference is held, its name, and contact name, street address, and sometimes Internet address.

Interesting Sites

Thanks to the Internet, you don't have to lug those dictionaries and thesauruses around any more—not to mention turning on your radio to get the current time after a thunderbolt has brought your power to a halt. From a single page, you can look up words and technical terms, get the current date and time, and get a zip code or area code. Take your choice from the best virtual desktop reference pages: Books, Libraries, and References (at http://www.whittier.edu/www/html/books_libs.html), DeskTop References (at http://www.ll.mit.edu/ComLinks/deskref.html), General Electric Reference Sources (at http://www.mbl.edu/html/LIBRARY/LIBFILES/ready-ref.html), Martindale's Reference Desk (at http://www-sci.lib.uci.edu/HSG/Ref.html), My Virtual Reference Desk (at http://www.refdesk.com/), On-Line Dictionaries and Glossaries (at http://www.rahul.net/lai/glossaries.html), Virtual Reference Desk (at http://thorplus.lib.purdue.edu/reference/index.html), and VT's Reference Page (at http://www.hsv.com/reference/index.htm).

Conference Service Providers

http://www.netins.net/showcase/message/csp_home.html

This site appears to be under construction. The links are few for now, but the organization looks quite promising.

From this page, you can get a list of conferences—primarily in California—and conference resources: facilities, logistics management, software, travel providers (Airline 800 Numbers link), and miscellaneous services (graphics, recording services, documentation services, experts, and speakers and talent).

Digital Consulting, Inc. Conferences

http://www.dciexpo.com

Digital Consulting, a sponsor of computer- and Internet-related conferences, provides links to each of its events, seminars, and executive services. At this site, you'll find online registration

Wayne Marr on the Future of the Internet

What major changes do you predict for the Internet over the next few years?

I really don't know. However, being a professor I will answer. I think many things will "cease" being free, especially as the NSF (National Science Foundation) stops its funding. And I think it's a good thing. With no property rights, one tends to get things of little value on the Net using bandwidth. With property rights (that is, charging), only the most valued goods will be there. So I think one of the next steps is the slow establishment of property rights to "cyberspace."

What effect will electronic cash have on the Internet?

Simple, it *is* the shopping mall of the future for many, not all. My wife, for instance, is not going to buy perfume across the Net. But I understand that there is now a "smell board" being sold by some company. So the possibilities are endless. My son and I shop on the Net, and he loves it. I do too.

What effect will the popularity of the World Wide Web have on other utilities or tools?

I think the Web will eliminate them. The only other utilities I personally now use are e-mail (Eudora) and FTP. Sometimes I use Telnet, but that can be built into a Web. So, yes, I do believe the Web is the killer application people talk about.

How will the government's role change over time? Do you see more or less regulation?

Less, simply because no one government can control it, especially as we move to "microwave" communications. I personally do not like governments, and I think their influence is declining now with the advent of the Internet. I am not suggesting anarchy. I would suggest that if the Internet were around during the Vietnam War, the U.S. would have never entered the war.

You can search an alphabetically arranged list of shows—from well-known to obscure—by name, date, location (a clickable map), or keyword. The result of a search is a page with the conference name, city, state, country, and telephone number, followed by keywords.

When searching by keyword, the results are linked names of shows in no particular order. The list of keywords should be expanded and maintained. For example, you can use the keyword *Computer* to find one group of conferences, and *Computers* to find an entirely different group.

IAO Conference Announcements

http://www.iao.fhg.de/
Library/conferences/

This comprehensive and impressive site includes links to many conferences throughout the world. You can submit conference information, retrieve conference information from the news.announce.conferences newsgroup, read frequently asked questions, read archive statistics, or look at conferences by subject. The table of 35 subjects, from art to tourism and from business to psychology, starts more than halfway down the page. Click on a link to go to a page of sublinks. Then click on a sublink to reveal the list of links to conferences for the desired subject. Under the table of subjects, you'll find other links with which you can access events, mailing lists, and other conference-related Internet links. Also provided is a list of calls for papers.

brochures for trade shows and conferences such as Mobile World, Web World, Internet Expo, and Managing Enterprise Networks.

EXPOguide

http://www.expoguide.com

EXPOguide presents comprehensive listings of trade shows, conferences, and expositions: exhibitions, conference and meeting halls, show services, and other resources.

Internet Conference Calendar

http://www.automatrix.com/conferences/

This commercial page presents Internet-related conferences and symposia, expositions, calls for papers, courses and tutorials (some online), miscellaneous gatherings, a conference calendar organized geographically, and other conference listings. An index is planned.

Under Conferences and Symposia, you will find a list of events arranged by date. Click on a link to get detailed information about the event. Note that links for conferences that are currently taking place may no longer be in effect.

Click on Courses and Tutorials not only to see training events but also to link to courses, tutorials, and talks. The phrase *Any Time* next to a link often indicates an online resource. The links in this section are not always up to date.

NetExpo/Internet Business Conferences

http://www.cts.com/browse/netexpo/

NetExpo presents Internet business conferences, primarily in California. You can register online, find out about upcoming conferences, or get information about previous conferences. For example, you can read transcripts of presentations, which is an excellent, and hopefully expanding, part of this site.

Networking and Other Conferences

http://www.epm.ornl.gov/~batsell/conf.html

On this short page, you'll find 11 links to networking, computing, communications, Internet, and other conferences. Most sites are related to professional organizations; the others are related to Internet conference lists.

Reed Exhibition Companies

http://silkroute.com/silkroute/reed/reed.html

Reed Exhibition companies run conferences and exhibitions in Asia, Europe, and North America for 40 specific industry sectors, including computers and communications. Click on world-wide exhibition and conference schedule to access an alphabetically arranged list of events. Note that many of them have already taken place in 1994 and 1995, but many future events are listed as well.

At this site, you can look up and read about conferences by industry, region and date, or country; and you can register to be an exhibitor.

Robotics and Control-Related Conferences

http://www.cee.hw.ac.uk/~acc/conf-list.html

This text-only page provides links to many conferences, symposia, and conference-related Internet resures for those interested or working in robotics and other technical fields. At the top of the page are links to lists of upcoming conferences. Next are lists of links to specific conferences sorted by date. Calls for papers are also included for most entries. Some of

Interesting Site

One of the exciting things about being a regular user of the Internet is the certainty of finding at least one important or well-designed site with every session. A Business Researcher's Interests (at http://www.pitt.edu/~malhotra/interest.html) is a great site—both comprehensive and good-looking. This page provides a table of links for both business professionals and students. Click on a link to reveal a very long page of links to articles, reports, and other information about the desired topic as well as links to related resources.

the conferences listed here are robotics and other intelligent machines, neural networks, fuzzy systems, electronic imaging, virtual reality, motion control, automation, and much more.

Softbank Exposition and Conference Company

http://www.sbexpos.com/
http://www.zdexpos.com/

The Softbank Exposition and Conference Company (Softbank Expos) runs high-tech conferences and meetings, including Seybold Seminars, NetWorld+Interop, Windows Solutions, Digital World, ComputerMania, N+I Online, and Help Desk Institute. Simply click on a link to find out more about a particular conference or to register. Also at this site are links to publications that you can order, industry associations, and information about Softbank Expositions.

Speakers On-Line

http://speakers.starbolt.com/pub/speakers/web/
speakers.html

This Internet catalog provides a list of speakers and entertainers accessible by subject, budget, agent, or country. Also included is a search index, what's new, and help.

The best way to use this resource is by clicking on Subject, Budget, Agents, or Country. This enables you to access many more speakers than if you use the index. To use the index, click on Search. Then click on a category (Civil/Human Rights, Communication Skills, Inspiration, Journalists, Leisure & Recreation, The Environment, and Women's Rights), select a price range, and select a speaker.

Tech Expo: Technical Conference Information Center

http://www.techexpo.com/events/evnts-p1.html

The Tech Expo site assumes that you know something about the upcoming conference in which you are interested. On the home page, you can click on the Search button to look for conferences by name, topic, sponsoring organization, or location. Or you can click on a date to browse a list of conferences arranged chronologically. Listed here are a variety of technical, engineering, and computing conferences worldwide. At the bottom of the home page are four links to other conference-related sites.

Chapter Six

Engineering and Manufacturing

Engineering and Manufacturing

Engineering Resources

Whether or not you are an engineer, you'll want to take a look at the sites in this section. Many of the links will take you to areas that provide solutions to everyday problems. For example, need a diagram for enhancing your stereo system? You'll find it here. And if you're interested in general engineering problems and solutions or a particular field—such as aerospace, chemical engineering, or electrical engineering—you'll find that here too.

Because of college and university as well as government resources, there are many engineering and manufacturing resources on the Internet. During recent U.S. history, we lost many manufacturing jobs due to lack of research and development as well as our failure to keep up with the latest technologies, among other factors. Why set up your own research and development department when you can use the Internet? You can find out about new manufacturing processes, the best materials, efficient design methods, and quality programs that can help your business produce high-quality goods and services and even win awards. The resources in this chapter can help you learn more about how your engineers design your products by studying some of the same cases on which engineering students work. Or you can even read the diagrams that will help you to properly wire that home entertainment center or burglar alarm system.

Aerospace Engineering Resources

http://www.wpi.edu/~ching/aerohome.html

This site has many links to aerospace resources and more—especially to NASA. Categories include <u>This day, week, and year</u> (news), <u>NASA Resources</u> (eight of them), <u>Spacecraft</u>, <u>The Aerospace Industry</u> (jobs and companies), <u>Professional Tools</u> (calculations, equations, acronyms, resources, organizations, and publications),  <u>Technical Reports and Journals</u> (from NASA), <u>Research and Technology</u> (corporate and academic), <u>International Sources</u> (other space programs), <u>Software</u> (just one, EGADS for the Mac), and <u>Pictures</u>.

Interesting Site

The Growth of the World Wide Web site at http://www.netgen .com/info/growth.html provides text, graphics, and statistics about the short history of the World Wide Web, which began in 1990 and started growing rapidly in 1994. According to the information on this page, in December 1993, there were 623 sites and as of December 1994, the number had grown to 11,576. From this site, you can link to Matthew Gray's Comprehensive List of Sites (http://www.netgen.com/cgi/comprehensive), which attempts to keep up with the Web's growth, or you can add a host to the List.

Catalog of the Engineering Case Library

http://www.civeng.carleton.ca/ECL/

This site provides relatively nontechnical papers on very interesting engineering cases. You can link to What's New, a paper about writing engineering cases, Engineering Cases in the Classroom, a note on engineering cases, and The Case Catalog, which contains more than 250 cases (either abstracts or the entire case). You can search the catalog by subject or for the 32 reports that you can view online. Each entry in the catalog consists of a code, title, authors, abstract, number of pages, keywords, and electronic availability.

Chemical Engineering Faculty Directory

http://bevo.che.wisc.edu/che-faculty/index.html

The Chemical Engineering Faculty Directory provides an index with which you can search for a particular faculty member. You also can search for educational institutions worldwide or in the U.S. Worldwide institutions are alphabetically arranged by country, and U.S. institutions are alphabetically arranged by state. Countries, states, and institutions are aligned with the left margin of the page, making reading somewhat difficult.

Chemical Engineering Sites All Over the World

http://www.ciw.uni-karlsruhe.de/siteworl.html

This long and complete page lists chemical engineering departments at academic institutions all over the world. You can search by country or the U.S., in an alphabetically arranged list or in an alphabetically arranged annotated list. Some links go to the World-Wide Web Virtual Library: Chemical Engineering (at http://www.che.ufl.edu:80/WWW-CHE/).

Circuit Cookbook Archive

http://www.ee.ualberta.ca/HTML/cookbook.html

ftp://nyquist.ee.ualberta.ca/pub/cookbook

This site is the repository for circuit schematics (see Figure 6.1) and other files, arranged by subject (see the bottom of the home page for the list). Downloadable files are compressed using several utilities, all briefly described in the README file, which you should peruse first. To see an index of the entire archive, click on Contents; to access a particular category of file, click on a link under Breakdown of Files by Subject. Whether you are an engineer, a student, or someone who wants to build an electrical device, this site is an excellent resource.

CircuitWorld

http://www.halcyon.com/
rbormann/cirworld.htm

CircuitWorld has links to a variety of Internet resources related to printed circuits and semiconductors. Here you can access manufacturers, suppliers, organizations, associations, consultants, assemblers, designers, publications, and other Internet resources.

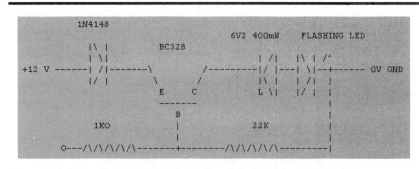

Figure 6.1 A simple circuit diagram from the Circuit Cookbook archive

E2W3: Electrical Engineering on the World Wide Web

http://www.e2w3.com/

This comprehensive site has links to a variety of electrical engineering and computer resources on the Internet. Here you can link to vendors of software, hardware, semiconductors, and peripherals; distributors and dealers; design and manufacturing services; manufacturing, assembly, and test equipment vendors; periodicals and publishers; conferences; courses; professional associations; Usenet news archives; FAQs; and Internet directories of all types.

The Electrical Engineering Circuits Archive

http://weber.u.washington.edu/~pfloyd/ee/index.html

This circuits database is for both engineering students and professionals. To get to the heart of this site, click on Circuit Diagrams and Application Notes, Component Data Sheets and Spice Models, EE Related Computer Programs, or Text Files of EE Information. In addition, you can submit a circuit design or component, link to an electronics newsgroup, or access many popular electrical engineering sites.

Engineering Educational Resources

http://www-sci.lib.uci.edu/SEP/engineer.html

This site, an accumulation of World Wide Web resources for teachers and students of engineering and science of all levels, is useful for both education and online research. Here you can get information about common weights and measures, laws and rules of physics, the periodic table, and chemical compounds; link to lessons on invention and writing; read about being a scientist; get help in solving a mathematical problem; visit a virtual wind tunnel; look at a glossary of aerodynamic terms; and much more.

The Engineering Electronics (EE) Shop

http://engr-www.unl.edu/ee/eeshop/eeshop.html

The EE Shop, from the University of Nebraska-Lincoln (UN-L), provides many electrical engineering links in these categories: Internet E.E. Information Sources (an impressive page of links), E.E. Labs and Shop Information (primarily UN-L-related), Software (software and software publishers), Miscellaneous Project Stuff (everything from electrical and an ASCII/decimal/octal/hex chart to acronyms to how to make playdough and how to build an FM [wireless microphone]), and the UN-L Repetitive Strain Injury Page.

Engineering Internet Resource Page

http://www.cera.com/engineer.htm

This site provides links to many engineering sites in a straightforward way with a minimum of graphics. Topics under which links are listed are Information Sources: Publications, Technical Reports, Archives, etc.; Hot Lists; Institutes, Institutions, Organizations, Universities; Miscellaneous; and Standards. A typical entry includes the name of the site, its URL, and a brief description. At the bottom of the list are links to some useful commercial sites.

The Engineering Pointers Page

http://marg.ntu.ac.uk/resources.html

Nottingham Trent University presents the Engineering Pointers Page, engineering resources on the Internet. Major topics under which links are arranged are New and Recent Additions, General, Manufacturing, Materials, Mechanical, Industrial, and Control. General and Manufacturing have the most entries, and the other categories have one or two.

Engineering-Related Mailing and Discussion Lists

http://marg.ntu.ac.uk/resources/mailbase.html

This site is a gateway to engineering-related mailing and discussion lists. Links to lists are categorized by mailbase, Listserv, and other. You can either join a specific list or view a list. At this site, you can learn about new lists and find out how to join, leave, or post questions to a list.

Enterprise Connection

http://enconn.com/

At this site, you will find "brochures and catalogs of companies who supply products and services to other engineering and manufacturing companies." You will also find links to companies that have products and services on the Enterprise Connection, the Unigraphics user group, links to other engineering and manufacturing sites, and the Match Maker (a brief list of listings of providers of products or services).

ICE: Internet Connections for Engineering

http://www.englib.cornell.edu/ice/ice-index.html

This gigantic index has links to chemistry, engineering, math, physics, and many other science pages. Entries on this long page are arranged alphabetically by topic. Click on a letter at the top of the page to jump to that letter of the alphabet.

Links not only include the expected engineering, science, and technology resources, but also museums, libraries, and commercial servers—some seemingly not related to engineering. This is a site to add to your Bookmarks list.

International Civil Engineering Resources

http://www.cage.curtin.edu.au/civil/links/links.html

The School of Civil Engineering at the Curtin University of Technology provides a well-organized and long list of civil engineering resources from around the world. Categories include Civil Engineering Pages on Larger Web Databases, University Web Servers, Other Civil Related Web Servers, Gopher Servers, FTP Sites, Mailing Lists, Bulletin Boards, Newsgroups, and Australian Web Sites.

Links to Engineering and IT Related Services

http://www.iee.org.uk/Misc/otherwww.htm

This site has a long and comprehensive list of engineering, Internet, and other links. Categories include Indexes, both Engineering Specific and General; Search Tools (Internet); Government and Official Organisations, primarily European; Standards Organisations; Institutions and Societies; Software Libraries; and Other Sites (reference works, a calendar of events, and miscellaneous sites).

Microelectronics in Canada (MIC)

http://www.cmc.ca/michp.html

Not just for Canadians, this site provides information about microelectronics, using integrated circuits. With both English and French pages, here you can find information about microelectronics: the history leading up to this technology and how microchips are created. To get to a particular page at this site, either click on the graphic or a text link. Topics include What is Microelectronics, Who is Involved in Canadian Microelectronics (corporate, academic, laboratory, and organization sites), National Initiatives, and Upcoming Events/Jobs.

Mark Williams on Programming for the Internet

Mark Williams is co-owner of Internet Presence and Publishing Services (IPPS), an Internet consulting and presence company. After acquiring a Cognitive Science/Computer Science degree from the University of California at San Diego, he spent four year as a scientific programmer and three years as a Unix administrator at the Salk Institute and Titan Client/Server Technologies. As a Unix administrator, Mark managed and developed companies' Internet connections. In early 1995, Mark went on to create IPPS (at http://www.ipps.com/).

What is CGI programming?

CGI (Common Gateway Interface) programming is essentially a way to incorporate search and online processing through a World Wide Web connection. For example, with CGI you can search through online databases, periodically post stock market information on a Web site, and request a server computer to process a set of calculations.

What is Java?

Java is a programming language created by Sun Microsystems to solve a number of modern programming problems. It was developed to be compact, robust, portable, and dynamic—ideal for the World Wide Web.

Basically, an *applet*, a program on the server side of the connection, is created. A browser able to run a Java program can connect to that server and execute the applet. The server can be contacted over the Internet or over a local network. The applet, unlike current CGI programming and scripts, has the ability to send information to the client when it deems necessary. This means that browsers can stay linked to a Web site and constantly receive updated information. This is a whole new avenue for client-server technology. Imagine, connecting to a stock market server and seeing a particular stock change in real time as the market changes—immediate knowledge of what is happening with your stock.

MIT ME: Resource List

http://me.mit.edu/resources/

The comprehensive MIT Mechanical Engineering Resource List enables you to do research on the Internet—mechanical engineering and other information. You can either search the list or click on a category: Web searching, Phone, Postal, Reference, Guides, Literature, Standards, Regulations, Patents, Copyrights/trademarks, Company information, Materials and supplies, Mechanical components, Electronical components, and Machine shops. If you are a mechanical engineer or use the Internet for any type of research, be sure to add this site to your Bookmarks list.

NASA Far West Regional Technology Transfer Center (RTTC)

http://cwis.usc.edu:80/dept/NASA/

The RTTC is a "technology brokerage, providing and facilitating information and business partnerships between the 700+ federal labs and the private sector." At this site, you can learn more about RTTC and its offerings. Categories include Technologies Available, Technology Opportunities, Affiliate Network, Links to T2 Resources, and a calendar of events.

Professional Organizations and Government Labs for Electrical Engineers

http://www.ee.umr.edu/orgs/

This site is a mix of professional organizations, institutes, government departments and agencies, and engineering resources. In addition, here you can link to electrical engineering departments, corporations, and computer science departments.

Semiconductor Subway

http://goesser.mit.edu/semisubway.html

The Semiconductor Subway is an imaginatively designed and fast-loading site. Click on any of the subway "stations" to go to engineering and manufacturing links (see Figure 6.2). The multicolored routes on which the stations are located reprsent categories: VLSI, MEMS, Fabrication, Manufacturing Research, CIM, Groups, and TCAD.

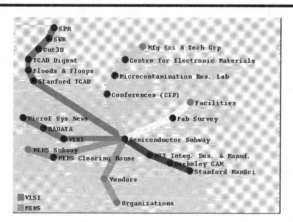

Figure 6.2   Click on a subway station to go to an engineering or a manufacturing site.

SHARE

http://cdr.stanford.edu/SHARE/

http://gummo.stanford.edu/html/SHARE/

SHARE is a research project that investigates product development involving teams of people from several organizations working over networks. The SHARE site is sponsored by Enterprise Integration Technologies (EIT; at http://www.eit.com/) and Stanford University's Center for Design

Research (CDR; at http://cdr.stanford.edu/) and Stanford Integrated Manufacturing Association (SIMA; at http://www-sima.stanford.edu/SIMA/). Here you can view information about projects, visit DesignNet (a directory of design and engineering services), and learn more about SHARE.

Unofficial Chemical Engineering Home Page

http://metro.turnpike.net/eng40705/

This long page provides many links to chemical engineering resources and directories, National University of Singapore chemical engineering students and staff, and other chemistry links. Chemical engineering and chemistry resources lists include the World-Wide Web Virtual Library: Chemical Engineering, a URL directory, and links to the EINet Galaxy index, the Yahoo index, and The World™ Guide to Engineering.

U.S. Army Corps of Engineers

http://www.usace.army.mil/

The U.S. Army Corps of Engineers "manages and executes engineering, construction, and real estate programs for the U.S. Army and Air Force, other federal agencies, and foreign governments as assigned" and responds to national emergencies. At this comprehensive site, you can learn about the corps' history, programs, and organization and can link to resources both inside and outside the corps.

VHDL International Users' Forum (VIUF)

http://vhdl.org/

At this site, you can learn more about the Very High Speed Integrated Circuit (VHSIC) Hardware Description Language (VHDL) and its standards and practices. Also at this site are links to an event

Interesting Site

Programmers often use fractals for screen savers and other graphics. You'll find a gallery of fractals at the Having Fun with Hydra site (at http://reality.sgi.com/employees/rck/hydra/) from Robert Keller at Silicon Graphics. Click on either <u>Cool Examples</u> or <u>Image Gallery</u> to see fractal images. Or click on <u>Interactive Archive</u> to

reveal a very large (174,413 bytes) but fast-loading page. Click on an image to change the fractal on the home page. Then scroll down so that both the fractal and option buttons are on screen (you may have to turn off tool bars and buttons to do so). Then click on option buttons and click on the picture, following the directions below the option buttons.

calendar, related servers, the VHDL Gopher server, and VHDL groups.

World-Wide Web Virtual Library: Aerospace

http://macwww.db.erau.edu/www_virtual_lib/aerospace.htm

This site, maintained by Embry-Riddle Aeronautical University, probably is the most thorough aerospace resource on the Internet. Here you can link to digitized aerospace images, manufacturers and businesses, museums, all NASA Internet sites, publications, and research resources from corporations, government, the Internet, and academia. In addition, you can link to rocketry and aviation resources, software engineering sites, and more.

World-Wide Web Virtual Library: Chemical Engineering

http://www.che.ufl.edu/WWW-CHE/index.html

This important and very large site for chemical and process engineering offers links under these topics: Meeting Announcements (and symposia), Sub-Fields, Organizations, Relevant Information Resources, Information Broker, Submitting Items to be Included, What Chemical and Process Engineering Includes, and a Call for Domain Administrators. Unlike most World-Wide Web Virtual Library engineering sites, the Chemical Engineering site consists of several pages.

World-Wide Web Virtual Library: Civil Engineering

http://www.ce.gatech.edu/WWW-CE/home.html

This engineering site, all on one page, provides links to many civil engineering departments at universities around the world.

World-Wide Web Virtual Library: Control Engineering

http://avalon.caltech.edu/extras/Virtual_Library/Control_VL.html

http://www-control.eng.cam.ac.uk/extras/Virtual_Library/Control_VL.html

At this primary site for control engineering, you can find links arranged under these categories: What's New, Systems and Control Information, Control Groups around the World (many of them), Professional Societies, Journals and Publishers, Control Information Services (a forum, e-mail list, database, and so on), Commercial Organisations (corporate sites), and Other Information (abstracts and tables of contents for books, downloadable software, bibliographies, and so on).

World-Wide Web Virtual Library: Electrical Engineering

http://arioch.gsfc.nasa.gov/wwwvl/ee.html

This long page is the primary electrical engineering source on the World Wide Web. Here you will find a table of contents of links: announcements of conferences, what's new (new links to companies and resources), information resources (links to important electrical engineering programs, organizations, and agencies), standards, products and services, academic and research institutions, and getting listed in the WWWVL/EE.

World-Wide Web Virtual Library: Engineering

http://arioch.gsfc.nasa.gov/wwwvl/engineering.html

This is the master engineering resource on the Internet and an ideal place to start searching for engineering pages. At this site, you can link to engineering virtual libraries for more than 20 specialties (http://arioch.gsfc.nasa.gov/wwwvl/engineering.html#spec), many other engineering-related resources (http://arioch.gsfc.nasa.gov/wwwvl/engineering.html#across_domains), standards, products and services, and academic and research institutions. You can also find out how to get listed. This site is on one long page; so just scroll down to see all its contents.

World-Wide Web Virtual Library: Industrial Engineering

http://isye.gatech.edu/www-ie/

This small site has links to academic programs, operations research, professional societies, and commercial pages related to industrial engineering. In addition, here you can access other World Wide Web virtual libraries for electrical engineering, human computer interaction, mathematics, mechanical engineering, and statistics.

World-Wide Web Virtual Library: Materials Engineering

http://m_struct.mie.clarkson.edu/VLmae.html

This site lists many materials engineering sites, most of them academic. Many sites simply provide information about a college or university department; however, others (for example, Cornell, Drexel, Los Alamos, University of Rochester, UMIST, Edison Welding Institute, and MIT, to name a few) offer worthwhile materials engineering information and links.

Note

The University of Michigan link is incorrect; the address should be http://www.engin.umich .edu/ dept/mse/.

World-Wide Web Virtual Library: Mechanical Engineering

http://cdr.stanford.edu:80/WWW-ME/home.html

This important mechanical engineering site provides a variety of resources: announcements (of conferences, calls for papers, and news), university departments, mechanical engineering institutes and societies (primarily academic), and vendor pages. Also included are online catalogs, networks, and information resources for corporate, governmental, and academic researchers.

World-Wide Web Virtual Library: Nuclear Engineering

http://neutrino.nuc.berkeley.edu/NEadm.html

This long page of nuclear-related links is arranged by topic: What's New; Nuclear Engineering Resources and Information; Nuclear Data and Related Information; Nuclear Energy Production and Radioactive Waste Management; Health Physics, Radiation Protection, Shielding, Standards; Radiation Applications; Related Information (primarily physics-related); Nuclear Engineering Department Web Servers; National Lab Web Servers (USA); and Related Professional Societies.

Yahoo Engineering Index

http://www.yahoo.com/Science/Engineering/

As always, Yahoo is an excellent resource, this time for engineering sites on the Internet. At this site, you can find links to various engineering specialties as well as to engineering ethics, ergonomics, events, libraries, organizations, and indexes.

Research and Development

The commercial and academic sites in this section point you to new technologies or enhancements of current technologies. Here you can read or order papers, learn about processes that are new to you, see demonstrations, and find out about projects currently under study.

GE Manufacturing Technology Laboratory (MTL)

http://ce-toolkit.crd.ge.com/

MTL "performs research and development in a wide range of manufacturing and engineering design technologies." Here are links to topics such as computer-aided manufacturing, concurrent engineering, chemical management information system (CMIS), CRD rapid protyping, overviews, an order form for listed papers (some are available online), Tcl and Tk freeware, and so on.

Mark Williams on Doing Business on the World Wide Web

Why would a business want to be on the World Wide Web?

Businesses should have a presence on the World Wide Web for four main reasons.

First, the World Wide Web serves as an important arena in which businesses can capture the explosive growth of consumerism on the Net. Millions of people use the Web to gather information about companies' products and services.

Second, the World Wide Web is an inexpensive medium in which to market your business, and with it you get the ability to change your information relatively easily and quickly. Some companies receive as many as 100,000 connections to their Web site every day. If a marketing department sent out that many brochures, disks, or letters every day, the accounting department would flip. The work hours alone would be astronomical, not to mention the materials and postage.

Third, the World Wide Web is interactive. Customers can send feedback to a company through form pages. Online, customers can complete registration forms, send e-mail, fill out surveys, and search through databases.

Finally, simply competition. There are thousands of World Wide Web sites on the Internet. Already, a large customer base does a significant amount of shopping and decision-making on the World Wide Web. If a company is not on the World Wide Web, not only is it viewed as behind the times, but the company will miss out on customer sales.

The How Things Work Project

http://www-ksl.stanford.edu/htw/htw-overview.html

The How Things Work (HTW) Project provides knowledge-based technology that will allow the successful manufacture of engineered devices. The knowledge base includes the basics of physics and engineering as well as models of devices. At this site, you can read a detailed project description with a table of links, links to papers, and diagrams (at http://ksl.stanford.edu/htw/htw-long-overview.html) and see HTW demonstrations (at http://www-ksl.stanford.edu/htw/htw-demos.html). At the time of this writing, the HTW Demonstrations page was composed of Device Modeling Environment (DME) and other links arranged under these categories: Guided Tours, Simulation Scenarios, Model Fragment Libraries, and Overviews.

Microelectro-mechanical Systems in Japan

http://itri.loyola.edu/MEMS/TOC.HTM

This online document reports on microelectromechanical systems (MEMS) in Japan, sponsored by U.S. government agencies and the Japanese Technology Evaluation Center (JTEC). When you reach this site, click on Executive Summary for an overview. Then scroll down the table of links until you find a topic that you'd like to read. Included at this site are links to the sites studied, an article on the history of microelectromechanical systems, and a glossary of terms.

Shock and Vibration Information Analysis Center (SAVIAC)

http://saviac.usae.bah.com/

SAVIAC is "sponsored by and operated for the Government structural dynamics community." When you arrive at this site, you see a large, fast-loading graphic. Click on Click Here at the bottom of the page to arrive at a table of contents page (http://saviac.usae.bah.com/contents.html). Click on About SAVIAC to read an overview. Other links at this site include What's New, News Groups, Symposium Info, Grab Bag (shareware, book reviews, who's who, software abstracts, and jobs), a journal and newsletters, the High

Strain Rate Material Properties Database, papers, and demo software and links to other servers.

Washington Technology Center (WTC)

http://www.wtc.washington.edu/

The WTC provides technical assistance and funding for companies in the state of Washington. This site, which was under construction at the time of this writing, contains several empty pages (About the WTC and Questions & Answers). Click on WTC Brochure to get an overview of WTC. Click on one of the seven technology development links to read an overview and find out about projects. At this site, you also can see what's new and view a Hot list of other Internet resources.

Information and Services

This short section provides information about two sites at which you can get technical assistance for your company as well as learn about new technologies.

Houston Advanced Research Center (HARC) Technology Transfer (HTT)

http://harc.edu/hti.html

Houston Advanced Research Center (HARC) Technology Transfer (HTT) "fosters alliances between HARC and the business community" and "provides financial, legal and marketing support to facilitate the commercialization of HARC products." At this site, you can investigate six technologies to be licensed and contact a liaison at HARC for further information.

Philadelphia IEEE Consultants' Network

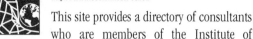

http://www.ece.vill.edu/conet/

This site provides a directory of consultants who are members of the Institute of Electrical and Electronics Engineers (IEEE) in the Philadelphia area. If you send specific requirements to this site (at conet.phila@ieee.org), you can get a free day of services in the Philadelphia area. To access the directory, click on Directory of Consultants. A typical entry provides the consultant's name, address, telephone numbers, e-mail addresses, areas of expertise, and a brief description of experience. At the bottom of this page are links to the Washington, D.C., area IEEE Consultant Networks and Electronics Distributors and Manufacturers.

Manufacturing Resources

You can find information as well as products to order on the Internet of the '90s. In this section, you can learn how your peers are working and which resources they are using: vendors from which they are buying, sources of materials, schools and publications, and other Internet sites.

The ArtMetal Resource to Metalworking

http://wuarchive.wustl.edu/edu/arts/metal/AM_res.html#Non Ferrous Metals

This long page is primarily for artists working with metal. However, those who want to learn more about metalworking, materials, processes, finishes, and design tools and processes can learn from these resources. Also at this site are links to literary resources, book reviews, metalsmith suppliers, blacksmith schools, and other Internet metalworking resources. At the time of this writing, this page seemed to be under construction; although the page was fully outlined, there were few links.

Avnet Industrial

http://cybermart.com/avind/

According to the information at this commercial site, Avnet Industrial sells more than 30,000 products—electronics, parts, and supplies. This site, featuring a very large graphic with no alternative text page, lists categories of products. Click on the graphic to access pages on Quality (Avnet's ISO-9002 rating), Product Lines (list of products), Manufacturers (a blank page), Value-Added Services (order and company information), Catalog Request (a form), and On Sale (featured products). (See Figure 6.3.)

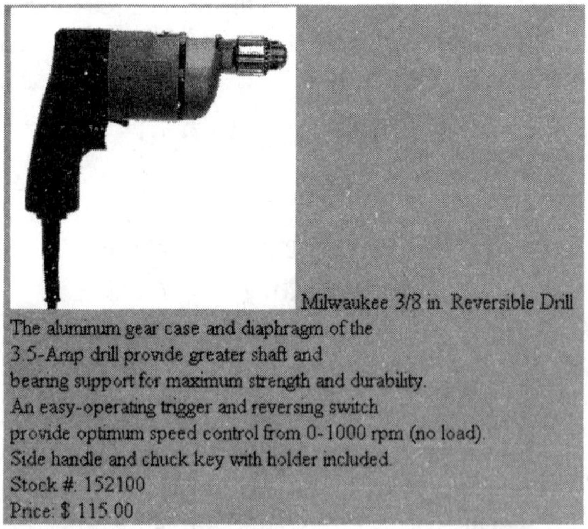

Milwaukee 3/8 in. Reversible Drill
The aluminum gear case and diaphragm of the
3.5-Amp drill provide greater shaft and
bearing support for maximum strength and durability.
An easy-operating trigger and reversing switch
provide optimum speed control from 0-1000 rpm (no load).
Side handle and chuck key with holder included.
Stock #: 152100
Price: $ 115.00

Figure 6.3   Before ordering, look at an illustration and read about a product.

EINet Manufacturing and Processing List

http://www.einet.net/galaxy/Engineering-and-Technology/
Manufacturing-and-Processing.html

This very large page lists manufacturing and processing Internet sites. You can find lists of links under Topics, New Items, Documents, Events, Product and Service Descriptions, Collections, Discussion Groups, Directories, Organizations, Academic Organizations, and Government Organizations.

GE Corporate Research and Development Manufacturing Technology Lab

http://camnet.ge.com/

The GE Corporate Research & Development (CRD) Manufacturing Technology Laboratory (MTL) researches "manufacturing and engineering design technologies such as CAD geometry, industrial lasers, NC-machine simulation, high strength composite manufacturing, non-destructive evaluation, and engineering software integration for GE businesses, the U.S. government, and various industrial and university partners."

At this site, you can link to CAMnet, for computer-aided manufacturing information; to CE-Toolkit, for concurrent engineering information; to CMIS, for chemical management resources (with Lockheed-Martin); and to RPTEC, the CRD Rapid Prototyping, Tooling, and Evaluation Center. You can also obtain papers and software.

Manufacturers Information Network

http://mfginfo.com/home.htm

http://mfginfo.com/

The Manufacturers Information Network is correct when it says that it is "a complete source of information for industry and those services related to manufacturing." Categories include What Is New (at the time of this writing, a list of corporate sites), Classified Ads (employment, used equipment, and goods & services), Industry Resources (general business sites, industrial sites, and other business resources), Manufacturing Articles, and Online News Discussion Groups. If you have any interest in manufacturing, this is a good starting point. And if you want to see an example of the newest Netscape technology—a home page with three separate windows—be sure to stop by.

Manufacturing Engineering Lab (MEL)

http://www.nist.gov/mel/melhome.html

The MEL site, from the National Institute of Standards and Technology (NIST), "helps U.S. industry turn technological opportunity into competitive advantage." MEL "develops and applies technology, measurement, and standards."

This site has articles about current manufacturing, MEL's role,

and the help that you can get from MEL. Articles include Basic Resource for Manufacturers, Pushing the Limits, Emphasis on Performance and Control, Information-Driven Manufacturing, Tapping the Resource, and Practical Assistance for Manufacturers. In the Tapping the Resource article are links to names and addresses of

---

MEL resources. Click on Offices and Divisions within MEL to view a list of names and addresses of divisions as well as links to additional information about the divisions.

Manufacturing Extension Partnership (MEP) Source

http://www.mep.nist.gov/

MEP, sponsored by the National Institute of Science and Technology (NIST), provides help to small U.S. manufacturers. MEP coordinates governmental support at local centers.

At this site, you can find the center near you, find out about events and services, learn about MEP and its programs, access NIST technical and standards resources, and link to many other resources and a Hot list.

Manufacturing Links

http://www.cranfield.ac.uk/public/mn/mr940715/links.htm

This site has links to some of the most popular manufacturing sites on the Internet: academic, organizations, Internet indexes, and so on. At the bottom of the list is a link to other Assorted

Manufacturing Web sites. Except for a very large (167,540 bytes) slow-loading graphic at the bottom of the page, this site is graphic-free.

Manufacturing Subject Guide and Directory

http://www.warwick.ac.uk/~esrjf/manufact.html

This comprehensive site links to pages that are "relevant to the manufacturing community." Links are arranged under these categories: New Events, Subject Areas (five products, manufacturing, education, and professional links), Online Manufacturing Exhibitions and Shows, Other Sources of Manufacturing Information on the Internet (Internet indexes, the sci.engr.manufacturing newsgroup, manufacturing research abstracts, and Mailbase on Manufacturing), and Manufacturing Related Commerce (books, a vendors catalog, service providers, and the Enterprise Connection, which is a company directory).

Manufacturing Systems Integration Division (MSID)

http://elib.cme.nist.gov/

The Manufacturing Systems Integration Division (MSID) of the National Institute of Standards and Technology (NIST) "contributes to the research and development of standards and technologies leading to the implementation of virtual manufacturing enterprises." At this site, you can read about the MSID mission, projects, and organization, get information about manufacturing and engineering, and go to manufacturing and engineering sites.

METAL Machining and Fabrication

http://www.mmf.com/metal/

This site is a center for metal-related Internet resources. Here you can link to manufacturers; material, equipment, and tool suppliers; design and engineering services; manufacturing hardware and software; consultants; shows and seminars; employment opportunities; advertisements; shop tips (shortcuts and hints for machining and fabrication); and manufacturing educational Web resources (trade, manufacturing, commercial, and government).

National Materials Exchange Network (NMEN): A Free Recycling Marketplace

http://www.earthcycle.com/nmen/index.html

NMEN is a busy "marketplace for trading and recycling used and surplus materials and goods." At the time of this writing, there were more than 11,800 listings from all over the world. The 30 categories of goods and materials ranged from acids to inorganic chemicals, plastic and rubber to textile and leather, construction material to container and pallet, aerospace to automotive.

To access the Exchange, you must create an account, which is activated immediately at no charge. Then access the Exchange, type search specifications, and click on the GO! button.

National Product Data Exchange Resource Center

http://elib.cme.nist.gov:80/pub/nipde/

The National Product Data Exchange Resource Center of the U.S. Product Data Association (US PRO) is part of the National Institute of

Standards and Technology (NIST). The research at the Resource Center will enable manufacturers and designers to enter product and design information online so that others—such as customers, vendors, and manufacturers—can order, place bids, or comment on a product.

At this site, which has both graphical and text versions, you can read FAQs and news about the system, learn about standards and protocols, follow projects, and link to other product data exchange resources.

government, and energy/environment policies; economic conditions and forecasts; manufacturing technologies; product developments; and international trade. The Manufacturing Functions topic is more closely related to manufacturing: process, material, machines, quality control, production planning and control, scheduling (empty at the time of this writing), and much more.

This site provides a wealth of information not only for manufacturers but also for all types of business people.

NC Manufacturing Extensions Partnership (NCMEP) Special Resources

http://www.ies.ncsu.edu/programs/mep/resourcs.htm

This site has a list of links to manufacturing-related and other Internet sites. Topics under which links are listed are Partnerships with NCMEP, Industry & Engineering Information Links (academic, topical, government, manufacturing and processing, and business), Web Searching Tools, and News.

Network for Excellence in Manufacturing Online

http://web.miep.org/miep/mainmenu.html

The Network for Excellence in Manufacturing (NEM), formerly the Michigan Industrial Extension Partnership, links "medium and small manufacturing companies with industrial extension agents and specialist resources in Michigan." Click on NEM Online Resources by Category to see a list of Internet resources, links, and descriptions for Manufacturing Environment and Manufacturing Functions. Manufacturing Environment primarily provides general business information: business practices (empty at the time of this writing); legal, labor,

PartNet

http://part.net

PartNet provides an online catalog of parts from which customers, such as engineers, purchasing agents, and sales and marketing departments, can order. Vendors also can place their components on PartNet using the PartNet Starter Kit. Before you start your search, click on Fact Sheet, which provides an overview, or FAQ Page, which can answer questions about searching the catalog, names of vendors, and so on.

Product Data Management Information Center (PDMIC)

http://www.ideal.com/pdmic/

Product Data Management (PDM) enables you to efficiently organize, control, and distribute design and manufacturing data. At this long page, you can learn more about PDM by reading about these topics:

- ◆ What Is Data Management?

- ◆ What Is Process Management?

- ◆ What Are the Benefits?

Mark Williams on the Future of the World Wide Web

How do you see the World Wide Web five years in the future?

The growth will still be explosive. By that time, the number of online consumers will be massive. The Web will also become more interactive. With the growth of programming languages such as Java, World Wide Web users will have complete interaction with companies around the world: real- time inventory control with suppliers, immediate stock quotes from NASDAQ and the Tokyo (Nikkei 225), complete malls to purchase your goods by keyboard, and more.

WOODWEB

http://www.woodweb.com/

WOODWEB is "the Information Resource for the Woodworking Industry." At this site, you can find out what's new, read articles, visit the Woodworker's Clinic, view two magazines, and access an Industry Index. The Industry Index is made up of several categories: Alphabetical List (all entries arranged alphabetically), Events Calendar, WOODWEB (returns to the home page), and "sublists": Associations, Business, Cabinets, Computer-Software, Electronics, Finishing, Hardware, Lumber-Plywood, Machines, Suppliers, and Tooling.

The World of Materials

http://tantalum.mit.edu/struc_mater/material_structures.html

This illustrated online article, written for new students, explains classes of materials—metals, ceramics, semiconductors, polymers—and describes their structures. Also included are a bibliography and links to more detailed pages.

Manufacturing Processes

To keep up, especially in the global economy, manufacturers must learn new techniques, operate "lean and mean," and constantly keep up to date. In this section, you'll find sites with which you can learn about new manufacturing processes and technologies.

Advanced Manufacturing Technology for Polymer Composite Structures in Japan

http://itri.loyola.edu/Polymers/TOC.htm

This online document evaluates manufacturing of polymer composite structures in the United States and Japan. Before reading the article, click on Executive Summary to get an illustrated overview. The document covers applications of composites in several industries, lists participants in the study, provides a questionnaire for Japanese companies, and includes a glossary.

National Excellence in Materials Joining (NEMJ)

http://ewi.ewi.org/nemj/home.html

NEMJ, managed by the Edison Welding Institute (EWI), offers advice and training in materials joining. At this site, you can learn about new technology and improve your current materials-joining processes. Click on PrimeNet, JoinNet, and NEMJ Education & Training to learn more about specific programs that are offered throughout the U.S. NEMJ also publishes an online newsletter, *Outreach*.

The Thermal Connection

http://www.csn.net/~takinfo/

At this commercial site, K&K Associates provides information about the Thermal

Analysis Kit (TAK) III, a thermal analyzer program that allows users to "do a complete thermal design, analysis, and presentation task."

The primary value of this site is its very useful links to thermal-related pages (a comprehensive list of thermal data files or databases that you can download) and guest articles (including thermal term definitions). You can submit a guest article using the guidelines provided here.

WeldNet

http://www.ewi.org/

This site is sponsored by Edison Welding Institute (EWI), a "non-profit industrial consortium dedicated to the development and dissemination of materials joining technologies to its member companies." Here you can learn about the EWI and link to the Navy Joining Center, National Excellence in Materials Joining (NEMJ), Precision Laser Machining, Special Services and Locations, Upcoming Events, the EWI Database Area, and What's New. In the Database Area, you can access two public databases: the EWI Research Report Database and EWI CRP Report abstracts. To search a database, you can enter the title, author, code, keyword, and so on.

CAD/CAM

If you are reading this book, you already know how valuable computers are—not just for spreadsheets, databases, word processing, and scheduling your time but also for design and manufacture. The sites in this section provide information about Computer-Aided Design (CAD), Computer-Aided Manufacturing (CAM), and other design and manufacturing techniques.

Agile and Advanced Manufacturing on the World Wide Web

http://www.sandia.gov/agil/home_page.html

This page has links to many manufacturing, engineering, and product development sites on the World Wide Web. Main categories under which links are arranged are Home, Directories, Tools, News & Pubs, and What's New. Clicking on a category just moves you down the page; so you can scroll up and down the page if you want to see the list of entries.

CAD Centre Publications

http://www.cad.strath.ac.uk/Publications.html

At this site are links to design and manufacturing papers and/or abstracts. Click on 1995, 1994, 1993, or Technical Reports, or scroll down the list until you see a paper to which you'd like to link. You can download some of these files in PostScript format. A typical entry contains a link with the size of the downloadable file and a link to author information.

CADLAB On-Line Documents

http://cadlab.www.ecn.purdue.edu/cadlab/Documents.html

At this site, from the Purdue University Computer Aided Design and Graphics Laboratory (CADLAB), you will find three documents: "Feature-Based Design for Mill-Turn and 3-Axis Machining," which must be downloaded; the very long *TWIN Solid Modeling Package Reference Manual*; and *GRAFIC Manual*, which documents routines for programming interactive graphics applications.

I_CARVE Lab

http://smartcad.me.wisc.edu/

In the Integrated Computer-Aided Research on Virtual Engineering Design and

Prototyping (I-CARVE) Lab at the University of Wisconsin, research "centers on Virtual Design and Virtual Prototyping to support Computer-Aided Concurrent Design." At this site, you can click on a graphic to read papers and view figures about components: Virtual Shape Synthesis, Neutral Shape Design, Abstractions, Features, Manufacturing, Disassembly, and Analysis.

At this site, you also can view lists of reports and publications. (For copies of articles, contact the authors.) At the bottom of the page is a link to related sites, primarily at academic institutions.

ICARIS—CIC Research Network

http://www.fagg.uni-lj.si/ICARIS/

This site is the comprehensive and very busy (that is, slow to respond) home page for integrated CAD in civil engineering and architecture. Here you can link to education resources and

networks for civil engineers, access a calendar of events, visit the library (which appears to be under construction), and use a subject index and a full-text keyword-based index of this site.

Subject indexes are civil engineering portions of standard Internet indexes (such as the Whole Internet Catalog, EINet Galaxy, and Planet Earth).

Interesting Site

The Wrecked Humor Collection at http://www.infi.net/~cashman/ humor is a great-looking, well-designed, and comprehensive humor site (with a background of jelly beans). At this site, you can find links to jokes, canonical lists, songs and parodies, and other Internet humor sites. You can also get lists of jokes about current news events, misread and misheard terms, science jokes, oxymorons, Barney, and, of course, lawyers.

LSI CAD FAQ

http://www.ece.ucdavis.edu/sscrl/clcfaq/faq/

This site comprises postings of frequently asked questions (FAQs) from the comp.lsi.cad and comp.lsi newsgroups. At the time of this writing, the table of contents included links to 66 topics. Some topics include links to downloadable files and CAD tools; others provide information about commercial products and other resources.

National Engineering Education Delivery System (NEEDS)

http://bishop.berkeley.edu/NEEDS_Home_Page.html

At this multimedia engineering site, you can obtain a great deal of educational material. Search the NEEDS courseware databases by title, author, or keyword. You also can view online courseware and online textbooks. To get an idea of the available courseware, primarily multimedia case studies, click on View Online Courseware.

Automation and Robotics

Automating manufacturing processes not only saves money on personnel but also enables a company to make a product using the finest measurements and tolerances. These sites, both commercial and academic, provide information about automation and robotics or demonstrate their use in the real world.

The Automation List

http://www.control.com/alist/alist.html

This moderated mailing list "provides a non-commercial forum for the discussion of automation topics." Here, you can access the frequently asked questions (FAQs); messages, arranged either by thread or chronologically; and World Wide Web addresses of participants. In the past, the discussions have included PLC languages, communications protocols, and standards.

AutomationNET

http://www.AutomationNET.com/

The AutomationNET site is devoted to automation—manufacturing, integration, education, and commercial needs. This promising site was either new or undergoing changes at the time of this writing. Either click on the image map (see Figure 6.4) or on a text item to go to one of several categories: Product Tree (links to equipment that you might need), Companies by Region (U.S. companies providing products and/or services), Products A-Z (under construction), Companies A-Z (alphabetically arranged U.S. companies), Consultants (under construction), Integrators (under construction), Conferences, Cool Web Sites (engineering and robotics sites), Feedback, and Register. At the bottom of the home page, you will find other engineering and manufacturing links.

Bucknell Engineering Animatronic Systems Technology (BEAST) Project

http://www.eg.bucknell.edu/~beast95/

The Bucknell Engineering Animatronics System Technology project will create an animated figure (similar to the presidents at Disney parks) to be displayed at the university's engineering building. This site provides links to research and design papers and diagrams of the four major sections of an animatronic system: master controller, animatronics, sensors, and microcontroller (see Figure 6.5). In addition,

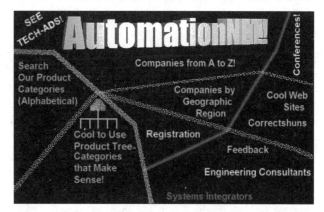

Figure 6.4   Click on part of the graphic to go to a category of links.

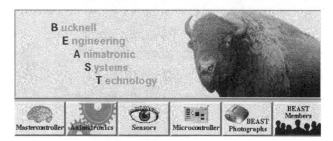

Figure 6.5   Click on one of the six buttons under the buffalo picture to learn about a particular part of the BEAST.

you can click on Sources (under the Resources topic) to see a text list of parts suppliers.

Eurobots Mobile ROBOTS Archive

http://cswww.essex.ac.uk/Eurobots/

This very large robotics site, directed at European mobile robot or Intelligent Autonomous Vehicles (IAVs) developers, is useful for anyone interested or working in robotics. To use the archive, click on Active Index, which is arranged by category: from Artificial Intelligence to Vision and including ArtificialLife, Communications, Navigation, Parts, and RobotPictures. Other categories on this page include competitions, conferences, FAQs, simulators, RobotGallery, and parts.

Institute for Robotics and Intelligent Systems

gopher://cwis.usc.edu:70/11/University_Information/ Academic_Departments/School_of_Engineering/ Research_and_Technology_Centers/IRIS

The Institute for Robotics and Intelligent Systems (IRIS) produces technical reports that you can order for $3 or download. Downloadable reports having an FTP number are in PostScript format and are at an anonymous FTP site (ftp://128.125.51.19 in the directory pub/Tech_rept/ Iris/1993/*). To look at the report abstracts, click on Technical Reports and then choose a year: 92 (18 reports), 93 (17 reports), or 94 (3 reports).

Internet Robotics Sources

http://www.cs.indiana.edu/robotics/world.html

This comprehensive robotics site, which was under construction at the time of this writing, provides links to FAQs; World Wide Web–accessible

robots; business, government, academic (very long), and miscellaneous World Wide Web pages; other indexes; newsgroups; FTP and Gopher sites; and software.

Laboratories at CMSR

http://hitech.technion.ac.il/CMSR_labs.html

This short page from the Jack W. Ullmann Center for Manufacturing Systems and Robotics (CMSR) is composed of links to laboratories in which manufacturing is studied. The subjects include automation, robotics, computer-integrated manufacturing, material processing, metal forming, and so on.

The Laboratory for Perceptual Robotics (LPR)

http://piglet.cs.umass.edu:4321/lpr.html

The Laboratory for Perceptual Robotics (LPR) site at the University of Massachusetts provides information about robotics, including research, facilities, publications (a long list of papers and technical reports that you can view), personnel, demos, announcements, and bibliographic information. At this site, you can watch movies or tour the lab. One of the best links is the Robotics Internet Resources Page (at http://piglet.cs.umass.edu:4321/robotics.html), which provides links to robotics by category and region, by type of Internet resource, interesting sites and indexes, and conferences.

MicroMechanics (MEMS) Server

http://mems.isi.edu/mems

This site is devoted to microelectromechanical systems (MEMS). Included here are links to a moderated discussion group, a newsletter, information about 16 MEMS fabrication facilities (primarily academic sites), and the archives of the MEMS clearinghouse. Click on <u>Archives of the MEMS Clearinghouse</u> to go to the most important page (http:// mems.isi.edu:80/archives/) at this site: links to <u>What's New</u>, <u>Fabrication Capabilities</u>, bibliographies, abstracts of dissertations, newsgroup articles, user files, the newsletter, assocations, industry pages, tools, and other information services.

NASA Space Telerobotics Program

http://ranier.oact.hq.nasa.gov/telerobotics_page/telerobotics.html

This site describes the research on space telerobotics for "remote mobility and manipulation." This program merges "robotics and teleoperations and creates new telerobotics technologies." Here you'll find diagrams and illustrations as well as links to additional information about the program: program description, program plan, and robot development tools. At the bottom of the home page are many links to other robotics labs, Internet robotics resources, and robotics projects. (See Figure 6.6.)

Robotics FAQ

http://www.frc.ri.cmu.edu/robotics-faq/

This site provides the frequently asked questions (FAQs) for the newsgroup comp.robotics. Topics include an overview of robotics, Internet resources, organizations, periodicals and publications, conferences and competitions, university programs, the robot industry, commercial sites, architecture, products, and more. Typically, answers include links to additional information or sites.

Technical Reports Archive Server

http://www.rdt.monash.edu.au/

This site, from the Monash University Department of Robotics and Digital Technology, provides downloadable technical reports, usually in PostScript format and compressed for faster file transfer. Each entry has a title, an author name, a link to an FTP directory and a filename, and an abstract. Many reports deal with telecommunications and the Internet.

Nanotechnology

Nanotechnology is manufacturing at the molecular level, with machines that you might find difficult to see without a microscope. Here you'll find a sampling of sites devoted to this popular topic.

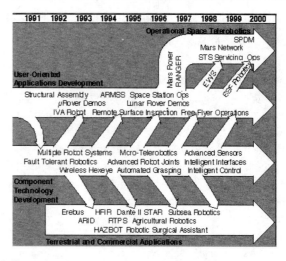

Figure 6.6 This illustration shows yearly development landmarks in the NASA Space Telerobotics Program.

NanoLink: Key Nanotechnology Sites on the Web

http://sunsite.nus.sg/MEMEX/nanolink.html

This site, sponsored by Memex Research Pte Ltd, Internet Research & Development Unit (IRDU), and SunSITE Singapore, provides a long and comprehensive list of links to nanotechnology sites all over the world, primarily from educational institutions. Also included are some links to molecular biology and physics sites.

NanoNet

http://snf.stanford.edu/NNUN

At the National Nanofabrication User Network, or NanoNet, users can experiment with nano and microfabrication design at the atomic level. Laboratories are located at Stanford, the University of California at Santa Barbara, Cornell, Penn State, and Howard. At this site, you can learn about NanoNet: its mission, organization, programs, and publications. In addition, you can fill in a form (if your browser is forms-capable) to submit a project.

Nanotechnology

ftp://ftp.parc.xerox.com/pub/nano/nano.html

This excell information, a bibliography, publications, prizes, articles and papers, and other nanotechnology sites.

Quality Assurance and Standards

Producing goods with a high degree of quality not only can bring in more business but also can save money: Doing it right the first time means that you don't have to repeat expensive processes, waste materials, and pay employees twice or more. This section provides links to quality and standards organizations and commercial and academic sites from which you can enhance a quality program, learn the proper techniques if you are just starting out, and even win awards.

CAD Framework Initiative, Inc. (CFI)

http://www.cfi.org/

CFI is "an international consortium whose mission is to improve product design and EDA (Electronic Design Automation) integration productivity

---

Mark Williams on Good World Wide Web Sites

What constitutes a quality World Wide Web site?

A good Web site is succinct, eye-catching, quick to download, and informative. Mediocre pages contain large graphics, which serve little or no purpose to the content of the site; this just causes the user to wait longer for the information to download. The home page, the first page of the site, should be quick to respond and not over-packed with information. I also believe that the URL to the site should be simple to remember. Better sites also contain indexes, database searches, and options for those who want only text displayed—not graphics.

Give me an example of what a good World Wide Web site can do for a business.

Web sites should provide a window both for customers and for employees to access company information. On the World Wide Web, businesses can host company brochures, show quarterly and annual reports, allow clients/customers to search through informative databases, collect information/statistics from employees in the field, host online registration pages, and more.

through open information, standards, and technology."
Working together, CFI members, from the U.S., Canada,
Europe, Japan, and Russia, identify existing standards
and develop new standards for design systems such as
ASCII data exchange formats, encapsulation, and integration of procedures. This home page provides information about CFI and its programs, a search index of
documents, demos, and issue tracking.

Computer and Communication Standards Documentation

http://www.cmpcmm.com/cc/standards.html

This extensive page provides links to a variety of standards: for computers, the Internet,
industry (both U.S. and worldwide), organizations that
write standards, telecommunications, multimedia, security, and much more. If you use standards for any of the
above, this is the first site to visit.

IEEE Standards

http://stdsbbs.ieee.org

At this site, you can learn all about IEEE
(Institute of Electrical and Electronics
Engineers, Inc.) standards, how to develop a standard,
standards committees and staff, and much more. Topics
included IEEE Standards FAQs (frequently asked questions), Announcements, Products and Publications
(and ordering information), Working Group Areas,
Standards Development Resources, Staff Information,
About the SPAsystem (Standards Process Automation
system), and Related WWW Sites.

ISO 9000 Forum

http://www.hike.te.chiba-u.ac.jp/ikeda/documentation/
iso9000/index.html

This forum provides facts about ISO 9000
standards. In addition, you can download public
domain and demo software in order to start ISO 9000
certification.

This page links to many other quality assurance sites,
including the TQM resources, college and university
pages (for example, Clemson College and Babson
College), and information about other quality sites and
archives.

ISO Easy

http://www.exit109.com/~leebee/

At this comprehensive International
Standards Organization (ISO) and quality
site, you can learn about the International Standards
for Quality Assurance systems (ISO 9000 and ISO 9001),
read frequently asked questions about ISO 9000 and
other standards, and link to articles. Here, you will also
find links to many ISO 9000 sites and four quality
resources, many commercial.

National Institute of Standards and Technology (NIST)

http://www.tecnet.org/nist-partnership.html

gopher://gopher-server.nist.gov:70/1

The National Institute of Standards and
Technology is the U.S. government department that researches and specifies quality standards.
The NIST Gopher is a large, convoluted site with many
folders, some of which are available from several
menus. Contents include newsletters, press releases,

department budget information, what's new, and conference schedules.

During your visit to this site, be sure to visit NIST News & General Information and NIST Industrial Impact–Brief Reports. The NIST News & General Information folder enables you to get to NIST UPDATE articles, the Guide to NIST, and NIST at a Glance. NIST Industrial Impact–Brief Reports contains a list of papers about specific corporations and organizations. So if you would like to see how a company in a particular industry deals with quality matters, look at this folder.

Standards by Organization

http://sneffels.its.bldrdoc.gov/out-d3.html/

This long page lists organizations, standard codes, and short descriptions of each code. Listed standards organizations include Assoc. Francaise de Normalisation, Association for Information and Image Management, American National Standards Institute (ANSI; by itself and jointly with other organizations), British Standards Institution, International Radio Consultative Comm., Code of Federal Regulations, European Computer Manufacturers' Assoc., Electronic Industries Association, International Alphabet, Institute of Electrical and Electronics Engineers, International Organization for Standardization (ISO), National Bureau of Standards, National Electrical Code, Standard Industrial Classification, the U.S. Naval Observatory, and others.

Note
You can find a master list of ISO Standards Codes at http://www.iso.ch/cate/cat.html.

Total Quality Management

gopher://nunic.nu.edu:70/11/somt/
Total%20Quality%20Management

This site is a central location of links to Babson College, Clemson College, the National Institute of Standards and Technology, and the University of Southern California. Also included here is the NYSERNet index, with which you can search for other Gopher sites.

Chapter Seven

Finance and Accounting

With both companies and individuals trying to get ahead in what often appears to be a hostile environment, it's no surprise that finance-related Internet sites—both business and personal—are so popular. In this part, you'll find out about finance and accounting sites that range between the extremes of investment and bankruptcy, from getting venture capital for a new business to getting a home mortgage.

General Resources

Many finance-related sites offer a small but important slice of information, such as the NASDAQ results for today or laws governing credit cards; other sites are the single sources for links that get you all types of financial help and information. From one site, you can check your investments and even trade online, read what the experts think about the direction of the markets worldwide, learn about investing before you spend your first dollar, look up insurance rates and company ratings,

and search for venture capital, real estate, mortgages, and loans.

This section presents the major sources of Internet-based accounting and financial information.

Accounting Resources on the Internet

http://www.rutgers.edu/Accounting/raw/internet/internet.htm

Rutgers University has furnished a well-designed and fast-loading site with a wide range of accounting-related topics for professionals, faculty, and students. Links are to organizations; journals; financial markets; U.S., Canadian, and Australian government agencies; taxation; SEC filings; international accounting; standards; university departments; information from accounting professors (none from Rutgers); professional information; publishers; and the CPA exam.

Bank.net

http://bank.net/

Bank.net provides a site at which you can find links to the best finance, economics, and business addresses on the Internet. You can access the information in three ways: Choose <u>Rich</u> to get full graphics, formats, and descriptions; choose <u>Text</u> to get descriptions but no graphics; and choose <u>Util</u> to get the fastest, uncluttered version.

Scott Yanoff on How He Started His Lists

Scott Yanoff compiles and publishes two popular Internet resource lists, the Internet Services List (at http://www.uwm.edu/ Mirror/inet.services.html or http://slacvx.slac.stanford .edu:80/misc/internet-services.html) and the Inter- Network Mail Guide (at ftp://ftp.csd.uwm.edu/ pub/internetwork-mail-guide). Yanoff began compiling Internet resource lists in September 1991 and is acknowledged as an expert on available information resources on the Internet. He is often referenced in books on the Internet, periodicals, and magazines. (See the June 1995 issue of Wired.*)*

Yanoff is currently attending the University of Wisconsin at Milwaukee, working on a master's degree in computer science and teaching Introduction to Computer Science programming. He is also employed full-time by SpectraCom, Inc., as a system administrator/Web developer, where he developed KidsCom (http://www.kidscom.com/), the popular Web site for kids. He writes bimonthly articles about the Internet's newest hot spots for the French Internet magazine Abplanete Internet.

Why did you start your list?

I started it as a list of six personal items and posted it to Usenet. As soon as I did, people began e-mailing me with suggestions. Next thing I knew, I was maintaining a list.

How did you select the first entries?

They were six popular items that I had read about on Usenet. I believe all six are still in the list. Two of them are CARL (at http://www.carl.org) and the Weather Underground (http://blueskies.sprl.umich.edu/).

How do you get the list on the Internet?

I just log in to my university account, go through my mail and Usenet, and edit the list.

How did your first readers find out about the list?

Most likely, through Usenet. I began posting the list and eventually put it into other formats.

loans; industry directories; data and statistics; company reports and research; and business and financial software.

FinanceNet Gopher Site

gopher://pula.financenet.gov

This Gopher site parallels FinanceNet's World Wide Web site (see the following entry) with one big exception: At this site, you can get specific information about government asset sales for the General Services Administration (GSA), Federal Deposit Insurance Corporation, the Commerce Business Daily Government Sales Listings, and State, Local, and International Sales. The Small Business Administration (SBA) address is not available, and the International entry is under construction.

FinanceNet World Wide Web Site

http://www.financenet.gov/

The FinanceNet World Wide Web site provides links to many indexes for finance professionals and interested individuals. Topics include accounting, auditing, finance, and economics; government pages; government and legislative resources; public administration resources; and human and general resources. At this site, you can get on a mailing list for government asset sales. Note that the FinanceNet Gopher site (see the previous entry) enables you to view government assets for sale.

Planning and maintaining a list of this size requires a great deal of organization. At this site, sometimes you'll find a link that doesn't seem to fit its category (for example, the Chicago Mercantile Exchange is listed under Think Tanks and Study Groups).

Bank.net has links to securities firms and related resources; economics research; think tanks and study groups; investing FAQs; law, insurance, and risk; international; venture capital; real estate, mortgages, and

This site is not particularly well organized, possibly because it seems to be new. When you are directed to a page at which you expect to find certain information, you may be disappointed. Also, the pages are difficult to read because of the heavy mix of italics, boldface, and underlines.

Gruntal and Company

http://www.gruntal.com/

Gruntal and Company's corporate site has plenty of good information presented in a straightforward manner. The home page is structured so that you can simply go to the subjects that interest you rather than having to go through company advertisements. Select the Weekly Market Summary Page to view a recent week's top-ten/bottom-ten groups, Dow Jones and other averages, money rates, new highs and lows, the current week's potential earnings reports, and gold and silver. Choose the Economic Pulse to get the unemployment rate and the inflation rate for the latest week and the previous week. Useful Pointers to Other Sites has links to Security APL, Holt's Market Report, QuoteCom Server, and New York University EDGAR Project.

Money Online from Money Magazine

http:/pathfinder.com/@@CJhBvSHFOgIAQJR3/money/moneyhome.html

The popular Money Personal Finance Center, from Time Warner's Pathfinder online service, offers links to articles, surveys, a list of savings institutions for specified cities, Money Daily (today's news), and a search of *Money* and other Time Warner magazines and features. Perhaps the best business feature is the 400 free company profiles from the Reference Press, a fee-based service at other sites.

An excellent feature at this site is the Money Quick Quote, which quickly displays a quote for a selected stock. Simply click on Quick Quotes, type a stock's symbol, and run the search. On the results page, you can click on a link to get another quote.

Tip

If you add a Quick Quote to your Bookmark list or Hot list, you can check the desired stock whenever you wish. Using this technique allows you to get the quote without typing the URL or the stock's symbol. To check multiple stocks, simply add multiple Quick Quote pages to your Bookmark list.

NETworth

http://networth.galt.com:80/www/home/networth.html

This commercial super site has all the investment information and finance links you would ever need. At the top of the home page, you'll find an up-to-date graph of the S&P 500 Index.

Links on this page are:

◆ The Mutual Fund Market Manager, from which you can search the NETworth Fund Profiles 500-fund database from Morningstar

◆ Meet the Experts, a forum with this week's expert from Montgomery Funds

◆ NETworth Secure, which uses Netscape's HTTP Secure protocol for secure communications

◆ NETworth Equities Center, which provides free stock quotes with a 15-minute delay

◆ What's New, which is information about this site—updated daily

◆ <u>NETworth Market Outlook</u>, a weekly market update

◆ <u>Internet Information Center</u>, which has links to newsletters, forums, and financial information

◆ <u>The Insider</u>, which furnishes links to many economic and financial resources

◆ <u>The Forum Reference Desk</u>, which is under construction

◆ <u>The Capitalist Newsletter</u>

Security APL

http://www.secapl.com:80/

This commercial site offers a variety of resources for investors, including PAWWS, an online financial management service company that provides accounting, brokerage services, quotes, news, reports, a portfolio management game, and more. Some PAWWS services are offered for a fee. Security APL also furnishes Quote Server, Sponsored WWW Sites, and The Podium (which provides links to two commercial pages for investment advisors).

Quote Server provides indexed searches of stock quotes, delayed by 15 minutes, and the Market Watch page, which tracks the Dow Jones averages, Standard and Poor's 500, NASDAQ, Canadian exchanges, and other indexes. To search the index, type the stock's ticker symbol in the text box, and click on Submit. Security APL also provides a chart (see Figure 7.1) of the NASDAQ Composite Index for the most recent active day.

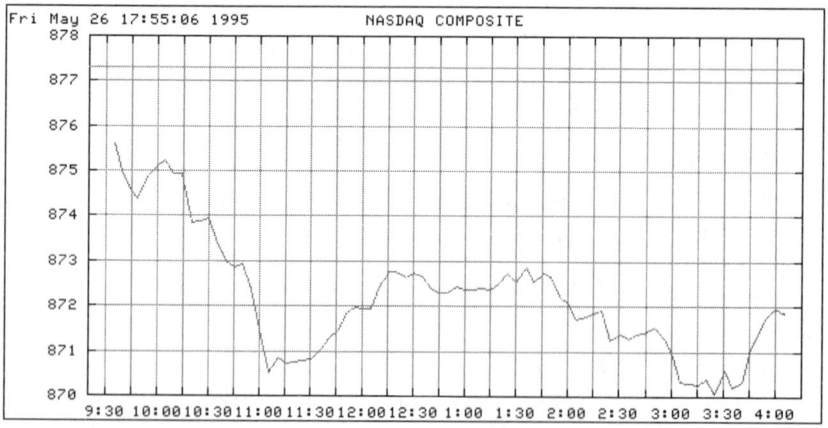

Summa Project

http://www.icaew.org.uk/welc-text.html

With an overseas perspective, this excellent list of accounting resources is worth adding to your Hot list. Here, you'll find most of the top accounting and finance addresses in the U.S. and new addresses from around the world, especially in the United Kingdom. Interesting links at this site include those to professional and standards bodies worldwide, World Wide Web tutorials and tools, the <u>Institute of Management Sciences Gopher</u>, the <u>Business Ethics Teaching Society (BETS)</u>, and the <u>International Association for Business and Society (IABS)</u>.

Wall Street Directory

http://www.cts.com/ ~wallst/index.html

Wall Street Directory provides a good-looking, well-organized graphical menu of links to a variety of business resources. The more than 20 headings range from brokerage services to statistics and data, and from education to downloadable software. The Main Index, consisting of about 60 entries, is the master list of links.

```
Fri May 26 17:55:06 1995          NASDAQ COMPOSITE
 878
 877
 876
 875
 874
 873
 872
 871
 870
      9:30 10:00 10:30 11:00 11:30 12:00 12:30 1:00 1:30 2:00 2:30 3:00 3:30 4:00
```

Figure 7.1 The NASDAQ Composite chart for a day of activity

One of the best categories at this site is Downloadable Software, which contains a long list of stock-charting, stock-tracking, and other finance software—demos, shareware, and freeware.

Wall Street Directory also furnishes two glossaries of investment and trading definitions and futures and options terms. Entries include a description, history, and sometimes the name of the person who created the term.

The World-Wide Web Virtual Library—Finance

http://www.w3.org/hypertext/DataSources/bySubject/Finance/Overview.html

The World-Wide Web Virtual Library for finance resources is as thorough as the other World-Wide Web virtual libraries. Finance-related links here include research departments and centers, indexes, journals, working papers for professionals and private investors, all the top finance sites, and a few new ones.

Money and Credit

You can use the Internet money sites to set a budget for a business trip or vacation anywhere in the world. Investigating exchange rates makes it possible to calculate the cost of your hotel, food, or rental vehicle and set a budget before you pack. Using money sites (and perhaps some of the information in the *Economics and Statistics* chapter), you can decide whether the trends say that it is economical to invest in a company in Moscow, Russia, or Moscow, Idaho. Or, if you have recently opened a small store, you can decide whether it is time to get a merchant account.

This section points to sites at which you can obtain today's exchange rates for currencies all over the world, learn about opening a merchant credit account, and find out about and sign up for electronic cash with which you can buy and sell on the Internet.

Cardservice International

http://www.icw.com/cardserv/crdsrv1.html

Cardservice International, an agent for four California banks, provides information on applying for merchant accounts (accounts that sellers establish with credit card companies so that buyers can purchase from the sellers with their credit cards) with major credit cards (Visa, MasterCard, American Express, Discover, Diners Club/Carte Blanche, and debit cards).

Currency Exchange

http://www.yahoo.com/Economy/Markets_and_Investments/Currency_Exchange

The Yahoo index presents up-to-date hot links to current foreign exchange rates from the Federal Reserve Bank of New York at 10 AM and 12 noon Eastern Standard Time. The 10 o'clock report covers the Canadian dollar, the Japanese yen, and 10 European currencies, and the noon report lists the exchange rates for 36 currencies. Other links at this site are to the exchange rates for the British pound, the Czech National Bank, Estonian Bank currency, the Koblas Currency Converter, and frequently asked questions about money abroad.

DigiCash

http://www.digicash.nl/

DigiCash is a pioneer in electronic cash and payment technology products that allow a buyer to provide secure information to a cyberspace seller. At this site, you can learn about DigiCash and electronic cash and download a free copy of its client software.

This site has links and a searchable index to shops that accept DigiCash. Currently, the list is small with very few recognizable names. However, DigiCash has agreements with Cybermalls, HotWired, NCSA, and Britannica; so we can expect to see this company all over the Net.

Scott Yanoff on the Internet Services List Today

Can you estimate how many readers visit your site during a given period?

I would guess 500,000 access my list per month. I have more than 3,000 on the mailing list, and our Web site at UWM services 180,000 requests per month for my list. Then the FTP server gets about another 100,000, and many hundreds of thousands access it through Usenet.

Where do you search for new entries?

I subscribe to HYTEL-L (at ftp://ftp.usask .ca/pub/hytelnet/pc), Internet Scout Report (at

http://rs.internic.net/scout_report-index), and Net Happenings (http://www.mid.net:80/NET/), and I scout the Usenet newsgroup.

What qualifies a site for your list?

(1) It must be free, (2) it must not be a commercial service just trying to sell something, and (3) it must be family oriented (that is, it cannot be sexually explicit or XXX-rated).

What site is your personal favorite?

YaZone (as http://www.spectracom.com/yazone/), a hangout for Gen-Xers.

GNN/Koblas Currency Converter

http://bin.gnn.com/cgi-bin/gnn/currency/

The popular and easy-to-use Koblas Currency Converter is found in lists and indexes all over the World Wide Web. To see how the currency of a particular country compares with each of more than 50 other currencies, simply click on the name of the country. For example, scroll down the list of countries and click on Japan. Then the list shows all 50+ currency rates compared with the yen.

Note

Another electronic cash provider is CyberCash, founded in 1994, at http://www .cybercash.com/.

FAQs for Money Abroad

http://www.inria.fr/robotvis/personnel/laveau/money-faq/money-abroad.html

This site provides in-depth information about money all over the world (North America, Europe, Asia, Oceania, Latin America, and Africa). Click on General Information to view the links to short essays about exchange rates, credit cards, travelers checks, and even the black market. Also included are links to current exchange rates.

Bankruptcy

No one wants to talk about it, but bankruptcy happens to thousands of companies and individuals every year. This section provides Internet resources for people on both sides of the issue: those who would like to invest in or check on troubled companies, and those who would like to learn about their choices.

Bankruptcy Information

gopher://info.psu.edu:70/00/psuinfo/University%20Life/Legal%20Rights%20and%20Safety%20Concerns/Bankruptcy

Penn State University provides online information, advice, and articles for its students and for those that find this address. This article explains how to deal with financial trouble and bankruptcy. Topics include tips about negotiating with creditors and obtaining counseling, two types of bankruptcy programs, and the rules and results of filing for bankruptcy.

Note
You can find other helpful articles by going to gopher://info.psu.edu:70/, clicking on Penn State Information, selecting University Life, and selecting a topic.

InterNet Bankruptcy Library

http://bankrupt.com/

This site, probably the principal bankruptcy-related site on the World Wide Web, presents bankruptcy information for companies and individuals contemplating bankruptcy and for those that might invest in or take over a bankrupt or near-bankrupt business.

Links include news reports from the U.S. and Canada, newsletters, conferences, organizations, a directory of professionals, consumer Chapter 7 and 13 issues, and publications. Also provided are links to the Bankruptcy Law Mailing List, Internet search tools, and other finance-related World Wide Web sites.

Taxes

How many times have you had to search at the last minute for an obscure tax form or study the code to figure out what an entry on a form actually means? In this section are sites from which you can download forms and read instructions—for the U.S., its states, and Canada.

Taxing Times

http://www.scubed.com/tax/index.html

At Taxing Times, you can download all federal tax forms (in PostScript and Acrobat PDF formats) and publications. Also included are links to state tax forms and instructions, Revenue Canada Taxation forms, the entire Tax Code, The Tax Digest, an Internet taxes newsgroup, the downloadable

Adobe Acrobat (PDF) Reader, and links to other tax information.

TaxSites

http://www.best.com/~ftmexpat/html/taxsites.html

TaxSites is probably the most complete tax site on the Internet. It has links to information about income and Social Security taxes, instructions, tax laws, tax-related newsgroups, U.S. and state tax publications, IRS and state forms, tax software, foreign income taxes, currency exchange, and much more.

This site provides direct links or instructions on getting to addresses from which you can download U.S. tax forms in Acrobat PDF, PostScript, SGML, PCL, and TIFF formats.

Note
IRS Publication 1167 provides guidelines for using downloaded tax forms.

Venture Capital

Whether you plan to search for venture capital or make it on your own, some of the sites in this section furnish good business-plan and business-planning information. For example, you can link to entrepreneurship sites, read the online articles, and find out how a venture capital firm evaluates potential clients and decides to invest. Using this information can help you set your company's direction for months and years ahead.

Accel Partners

http://www.accel.com/

Accel Partners invests in entrepreneurial companies. This site is almost entirely devoted to Accel and its strategy for success. Also included are business cards representing companies with which they have worked. A few cards provide links to home pages.

Accel has links to several entrepreneur-related Internet sites, such as Resources for Entrepreneurs, online articles on entrepreneurship, five articles from *Communications Week*, and a link to the *Communications Week* home page.

Venture Capital Firms on the Net

http://www.catalog.com:80/intersof/vc/vent_cap.html

This commercial site includes a fee-based search index of funding sources. All the other links appear to be free. Other resources at this site include articles on finding venture capitalists, consultants, and regional and state government venture capital organizations (including those for women and minorities). Other links include a free database of venture capital seekers and other venture capital sites.

Vista Growth Capital

http://www.gate.net/vista/menu.html

Vista Growth Capital invests primarily in foreign and domestic companies specializing in new technologies. No additional information or links are provided.

Banking and Banking Agencies

For the most part, banking on the Internet has not reached the stage of electronic transfer of funds. Most of the private banks in this section provide branch information (hours, products and services, and addresses). Selected sites, however, furnish information in a variety of media (newsletters, books, brochures, and videos), up-to-date economic analysis and reports, and even software that you can download.

This section starts with bank sites that offer interesting or important information: economic analysis; articles, and reports on the U.S., Canada, or regions; consumer guides; current financial news and economic indicators; and even downloadable software.

Bank of Montreal

http://www.bmo.com/

This large site is half advertisement for the Bank of Montreal and half useful information for businesses, investors, and citizens in Canada, the U.S., and Europe. Bank information includes a corporate profile, press releases, and speeches (most plug the bank, but some contain information and statistics that could help a Canadian business). Business information and links provide today's financial news, this week's economic indicators (consumer price indexes, industrial product price index, and new orders), predictions and market forecasts, and special one-page reports on topics such as employment, retail sales, consumer price index, housing, fiscal outlook, Budget 1995 (Canada), and trade.

Federal Deposit Insurance Corporation (FDIC)

http://fdic-serv.sura.net/index.html

gopher://gopher.fdic.gov/

The FDIC produces the Quarterly Banking Profile (QBP), which can be downloaded and which reports on the performance of commercial banks and savings institutions. Economists and others can use this report to analyze the national economy and the health of individual banks. This site has several links to other economics and finance resources, including the Corporate Library, which consists of online documents. The Gopher site provides many online documents; so be sure to visit.

Federal Reserve Bank—Atlanta

http://www.frbatlanta.org/

All Federal Reserve Bank sites on the Internet present excellent information. The Federal Reserve Bank of Atlanta is no exception; the site is rich with information. Some of the links you'll find here are: Banking Market Definitions (not the glossary that you might expect, but a definition of the areas within the regions covered by the bank), Community Affairs (from which you can download Partners, freeware that can help you calculate the home loan you can afford), Dollar Index (the trade-weighted dollar index of 18 major currencies), Manufacturers Survey (a survey and resulting indexes of manufacturers in the southeastern states), and Publications (economics reports, especially for the southeastern region).

Federal Reserve Bank—Boston

gopher://ftp.shsu.edu/11/
Economics/FRB-Boston

The Federal Reserve Bank in Boston provides print (PRN) files with banking, employment, hours and earnings, consumption and income, state taxes, construction, housing, and energy statistics for New England. Select the 00-INDEX folder to display an index of files, including a zipped archive for all the files.

Federal Reserve Bank—Chicago

gopher://gopher.great-lakes.net:2200/11/partners/ChicagoFed

The Federal Reserve Bank of Chicago maintains a site that is packed with information, economic indicators, publications, and video tapes. Here you can learn about the history of the Federal Reserve system, its regulations, and the locations of the Federal Reserve Banks. The bank provides guides, pamphlets, and books for consumers, educators, and students, and it provides videos that people in parts of Illinois, Indiana, Wisconsin, Michigan, and Iowa are encouraged to duplicate. Figure 7.2 shows a formatted version of a corporate business profits (PRN) print document.

For business people, perhaps the best resources at this site are glossaries of finance, banking, credit, and monetary policy (see Figure 7.3).

Gopher Menu

- Welcome to the Federal Reserve Bank of Chicago
- Background and Information
- Banking
- Economic Indicators
- Financial Markets
- General Publications
- Monetary Policy
- Papers and Texts
- Periodicals
- Speeches by Federal Reserve Officials

Figure 7.2 The list of folders at the Federal Reserve Bank of Chicago Gopher site

CERTIFICATE OF DEPOSIT (CD):   A form of time deposit at a bank or savings institution; a time deposit cannot be withdrawn before a specified maturity date without being subject to an interest penalty for early withdrawal. Small-denomination CDs are often purchased by individuals. Large CDs of $100,000 or more are often in negotiable form, meaning they can be sold or transferred among holders before maturity.

DEMAND DEPOSIT: A deposit payable on demand, or a time deposit with a maturity period or required notice period of less than 14 days, on which the depository institution does not reserve the right to require at least 14 days written notice of intended withdrawal. Commonly takes the form of a checking account.

DEPOSIT CEILING RATES OF INTEREST: Maximum interest rates that can be paid on savings and time deposits at federally insured commercial banks, mutual savings banks, savings and loan associations, and credit unions. Ceilings on credit union deposits are established by the National Credit Union Administration. Ceilings on deposits held by the other depository institutions are established by the Depository Institutions Deregulation Committee (DIDC). Under current law, deposit interest rate ceilings are being phased out over a six-year period, ending in 1986 under the oversight of the DIDC.

DISCOUNT RATE: The interest rate at which eligible depository institutions may borrow funds, usually for short periods, directly from the Federal Reserve Banks. The law requires the board of directors of each Reserve Bank to establish the discount rate every 14 days subject to the approval of the Board of Governors.

Figure 7.3   Terms in the glossary of monetary policy

Federal Reserve Bank—Chicago

http://www.frbchi.org/

This site, from the Federal Reserve Bank of Chicago, provides information under these links: Federal Reserve Information, Publications and Speeches, Economic Information, Consumer and Community Information, Bankers, Educators, and Media Professionals. Federal Reserve Information is mostly about the Federal Reserve Bank of Chicago, with links to other Federal Reserve Banks. Publications and Speeches contains many of the same publications and videos that you'll find at the Gopher site (see the prior entry). Click on Economic Information to a variety of links: Financial Markets Data, Economic Indicators Data, Labor Markets Data, Banking Data, Monetary

Policy, Regional Highlights, and Federal Reserve Board of Governors Statistics Releases.

Federal Reserve Bank—Cleveland

http://www.clev.frb.org/

The Federal Reserve Bank of Cleveland page provides information about the Fourth District (Ohio, western Pennsylvania, eastern Kentucky, and part of West Virginia) and economic resources. Links are arranged under these headings: General Information, Public Announcements (be sure to look at the list of press releases), Publications (many are applicable to both businesspersons and consumers and some contain economic trends), Data/Statistics (the Consumer Price Index [CPI] and selected interest rates), Functional Areas, Employment Opportunities, and Other Resources (a three-item list of banking links).

Federal Reserve Bank—Minneapolis (Woodrow)

http://woodrow.mpls.frb.fed.us/

Woodrow, named for Woodrow Wilson, the president who signed the Federal Reserve Act, provides information about the Federal Reserve, makes available the downloadable Partners mortgage loan qualification software, produces online and print publications, and has links to other Federal Reserve Banks and other resources. A very important feature is Tracking the Economy, a page of economic indicator links for the Ninth District and for the U.S. The five links on the Tracking the Economy page are:

◆ The Beige Book, a commentary on current economic conditions in each Federal Reserve Bank region

◆ Interest and Exchange Rate Charts, charts on short-term and other interest rates and the trade-weighted value of the dollar

◆ U.S. Treasury Auction Results, links to the Treasury Auction Results page at gopher://una .hh.lib.umich.edu:70/11/ebb/treasury

◆ Federal Reserve Board Statistical Releases, links to 11 statistics, including industrial production, consumer installment credit, foreign exchange rates, and interest rates

◆ National Economic Data, links to more than 50 categories of U.S. statistics: General Data, Consumers, Housing, Business, Foreign, Government, Prices and Wages, and Financial/Money Supply Data.

Federal Reserve Bank—New York

http://www.nhy.frb.org/

The Federal Reserve Bank of New York site is more colorful than other Federal Reserve Bank sites. On the home page, you'll find clickable graphics, a search index of the site, and a list of links, including one to a page of other Federal Reserve Bank sites. Major topics are Welcome, Market Rates, News Items, Publications, Research Publications, Savings Bonds, Treasury Direct, and What's New. Market Rates includes commercial paper rates, foreign exchange rates, a quote sheet (quotations for U.S. government securities), and selected interest rates (H. 15). Publications include the *Beige Book for the Second District* and those from other Federal Reserve Banks.

Click on Savings Bonds to get general information, use a redemption calculator, or learn about values, yields, and regulations. Perhaps the best feature is Treasury Direct, at which you can get basic information about treasury bills, notes, and bonds and establish an account under which you can purchase treasury securities.

Federal Reserve Bank— Philadelphia

http://www.libertynet.org/~fedresrv/fedpage.html

The Federal Reserve Bank of Philadelphia provides economic information about and publishes newsletters for the Pennsylvania-New Jersey-Delaware region and has links to general economic information.

Publications include the bimonthly *Business Review*, with articles on finance and business. The subjects of recent articles include derivatives, making money in the housing market, and how a little inflation can lead to a lot.

Federal Reserve Bank—St. Louis

http://www.stls.frb.org/

The Federal Reserve Bank of St. Louis serves the Eighth District, for all or parts of Arkansas, Missouri, Kentucky, Tennessee, Illinois, Indiana, and Mississippi. The major links at this site are: Federal Reserve System, FRB—St. Louis, FRED, Economic Research, Community Affairs, Mortgage Loan Qualification Software (Partners), Interesting WWW Sites (a comprehensive list), and Coming Soon to This Site. FRED (Federal Reserve Economic Data) is a large database of historical U.S. economic and financial data for both the Eighth District and the U.S. You can select from 12 categories of data, from Daily/Monthly U.S. Financial Data to Monthly Producer Price Indexes to Monthly Employment and Population Data. Most files can be downloaded; some are compressed.

Online Database Searches

If you are new to the Internet, finding specific information online can be difficult. You may be connected to the Net, but without directions it can take hours or days to reach your destination. Fortunately, the Internet hosts many online databases that index hundreds of thousands of Internet sites. With these databases, you can search for a topic of interest and receive a listing of Internet locations related to that topic.

Although these online databases contain huge numbers of listings from which to search, they vary in size. The smaller ones, of course, return search results quickly. Others, such as Lycos, contain an enormous number of resources and may take longer to respond to a request. Obviously, the larger databases often produce more search results.

Each database has its own features and flavor. Some of the more versatile databases, such as Lycos and WebCrawler, allow their users to use conjunctions (for example, AND and OR) to refine a search. For instance, a user can request a listing of Internet sites that contain information on SCUBA diving AND the PACIFIC Ocean. If you search for SCUBA alone, you may find out about scuba diving in the Indian Ocean or scuba equipment sold on the East Coast of the U.S. However, if you search for SCUBA AND PACIFIC, you are more likely to limit search results to your specific interest. Table 7.1 presents popular Internet databases. You'll find additional lists of Internet databases, search tools, and master lists on the inside front cover and inside back cover.

Federal Reserve Bank Publications

gopher://netec.mcc.ac.uk:70/11/NetEc/BibEc/fedu

At this address, you can find economic statistics and abstracts of articles (not the full text of the articles) published by the Federal Reserve Banks. Either click on the name of a bank to select from its publications, or search an index using keywords.

Federal Reserve Board Data

gopher://town.hall.org/1/other/fed

This site provides a variety of financial and economics data. Links include About the Federal Reserve Board Data, Flow of Funds Tables, Industrial Production and Capacity Utilitization (G.17), Industrial Production and Capacity Utilization (B.17 Historical), Reserves of Depository Institutions (H.3), Weekly Series on Assets and Liabilities of Large Commercial Banks (H.4.2), Selected Interest Rates (H.15 Series), Money Stock Measures and Components, and Other Federal Reserve Data Tables.

Highest FDIC Insured Bank Rates

http://gnn.com/gnn/meta/finance/res/mri.html

Using the information at this site, you can check a daily chart of the highest FDIC-insured bank rates for six months, one year, two years, and five years before buying an FDIC-insured certificate of deposit.

J. P. Morgan

http://www.jpmorgan.com/

J. P. Morgan provides a mix of company information and useful financial data and articles. Some of the best information at this site is in the Products and Services area. Here you will find research indexes, daily index returns, and a government bond index; a mortgage refinancing and applications for home purchases matrix; and data, articles, and reports that can be downloaded in PostScript or Acrobat PDF formats.

Royal Bank of Canada

http://www.royalbank.com/

The Royal Bank site provides bank information, a mortgage guide, and links to

Table 7.1: Internet Databases

Database	URL	Description
FTP search	http://ftpsearch.unit.no/ftpsearch	A search index of many FTP sites. Simply type a filename in the text box and expect the results within seconds.
GNA Meta Library Search	http://uu-gna.mit.edu:8001/cgi-bin/meta	A relatively small table with 4,000 rows and about 80,000 words. When you type a search string, a space between words represents an AND. The search is case-insensitive.
Gopher Jewels	gopher://cwis.usc.edu:70/11/Other_Gophers_and_Information_Resources/Gophers_by_Subject/Gopher_Jewels	An important list of Gopher resources (and a search index) arranged under a variety of topics.
InfoSeek Search	http://www.infoseek.com	A search index, which is case-sensitive. Punctuation identifies phrases: double quotes indicate the beginning and end of a phrase, a hyphen ties words together into a phrase, a plus sign indicates a required word or phrase, and a minus sign removes a word from a phrase. A maximum of 10 hits is returned.
Jumpstation I	http://www.stir.ac.uk/jsbin/js	A search index that uses a robot to find data in a document title or header. Jumpstation II will eventually replace Jumpstation I.
Jumpstation II	http://www.stir.ac.uk/jsbin/jsii	A search index that uses a robot to find data in a document title, header, or subject. You can scan servers; wildcards are accepted. Start a search by indicating whether the search is limited to title, header, or subject. Then type words in all or any of the text boxes. Finally, click on Submit.
Lycos	http://lycos.cs.cmu.edu	Lycos has various search databases from which to choose. Its largest database contains information on more than 750,000 sites and more than 3 million descriptions of links. The links are added automatically. During a search, Lycos evaluates the document title, headings, links, and keywords.
NCSA Internet Resources Meta-Index	http://www.ncsa.uiuc.edu/SDG/Software/Mosaic/MetaIndex.html	A meta-index of Internet directories and indexes. Click on a link to go to a site at which you can perform a search.
NIKOS	http://www.rns.com/cgi-bin/nomad	A keyword search index that supports multiple words. Type a series of words, and the search engine infers that each is separated with an AND. The developers plan to add OR and NOT and other improvements.

Table 7.1: Internet Databases (continued)

Database	URL	Description
Savvy Search	http://guaraldi.cs.colostate.edu:2000/	A search agent that simultaneously looks through 19 popular search indexes for the World Wide Web, Gopher, FTP, mailgroups, and more, ranks the results, and divides them into groups.
Wandex—the World Wide Web Wanderer	http://www.netgen.com/cgi/wandex	An automatically generated database with a simple search index. Type a keyword, and Wandex searches through all the Web servers in the database and returns a list of ranked results with a short description for each.
WebCrawler	http://webcrawler.com/	A search index with which you type keywords that are joined automatically as if you were typing an AND. You can turn off this automatic AND by clearing the checkbox below the text box in which you type the keywords. WebCrawler is now owned and operated by America Online.
W3 Search Engines	http://cuiwww.unige.ch/w3catalog	Searches for search indexes.
World Wide Web Worm	http://www.cs.colorado.edu/home/mcbryan/wwww.html	A very popular navigational aid. You can search for hypertext links or URLs by typing search specifications. Type one or more keywords, which have at least three characters and are either letters or numbers. You can use Unix syntax to build search strings. When filling in a specification, select search limits, a fast or slow seearch, and the number of matches. Then click on Start Search.
WWW Home Pages Broker	http://www.town.hall.org/brokers/www-home-pages/query.html	An automated system that finds home pages using Author, Keywords, Partial-Text, Title, URL, or URL-References. Searches of more than one word can be joined by AND. Strings can be enclosed within double quotes. To limit a search, you can start a search with Title, for example. If a period is within a search, precede it with a backslash.

information about Canadian and U.S. interest rates, exchange rates, Canadian employment, and the Canadian federal budget.

The mortgage guide is an online booklet, for Canadians but useful to U.S. residents, with some bank advertising and a mortgage calculator. *Trade Talk*, published quarterly, includes bank news and articles, such as "What Happened to the Mexican Peso?" "China's Economy," and Japan country information and graphs.

Toronto Dominion Bank

http://www.tdbank.ca/tdbank/

The Toronto Dominion Bank site has links to information about buying a house, freeware with which you can design and fill in your business plan, a newsletter, and financial and economic information about Canada and the U.S.

At this site, you can download the Business Planner, a freeware program that runs under Windows and DOS (at http://www.tdbank.ca/tdbank/Small-Business/ BUSPLANLIC.HTML). The Business Planner helps you create the forms that you would file with Toronto Dominion to apply for a business loan. If you live in the U.S., you can use it to create the skeleton of a very detailed business plan. Figure 7.4 shows a sample screen from the program.

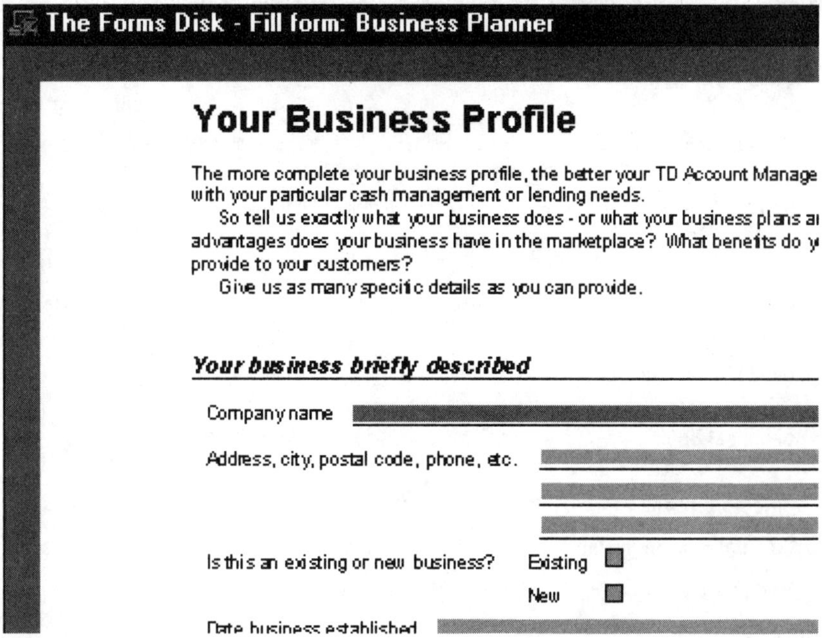

Wells Fargo Bank

http://www.wellsfargo.com/

This commercial site includes information about bank products and services, including online account balances. A new feature is a weekly article on California and worldwide economic conditions.

Perhaps the most unique aspect of this site is an online museum and a gallery of Old West art.

For the Internet addresses of some other banks on the Internet, see Table 7.2.

The Forms Disk - Fill form: Business Planner

Your Business Profile

The more complete your business profile, the better your TD Account Manage with your particular cash management or lending needs.

So tell us exactly what your business does - or what your business plans a advantages does your business have in the marketplace? What benefits do y provide to your customers?

Give us as many specific details as you can provide.

Your business briefly described

Company name

Address, city, postal code, phone, etc.

Is this an existing or new business?   Existing ☐

New ☐

Date business established

Figure 7.4 A sample screen from the Toronto Dominion Bank Business Planner program

---

Investments

According to some, money is the root of all evil, but perhaps Mark Twain was right when he stated, "The lack of money is the root of all evil." Researching potential ventures and tracking your investments carefully makes it more likely that your money will grow.

This section on investments is made up of two parts: Stocks, Bonds, and Other Markets and Mutual Funds.

Interesting Sites

HAPPINESS, n. An agreeable sensation arising from contemplating the misery of another. (Ambrose Bierce, *Devil's Dictionary*)

You can find works of writers such as Jane Austen, Ambrose Bierce, Emily Bronte, Willa Cather, Charles Dickens, Nathaniel Hawthorne, Washington Irving, William Shakespeare (complete works), and Mark Twain at http://www.notredame.ac.jp/ftplib/.

In addition, you can look up quotes using a searchable index, which you can set to scan all or some of the files at this site line by line.

Table 7.2: Selected Banks on the Internet

Bank	URL	Site Contents
Bank of America	http://www.bankamerica.com/	Addresses, ATM locations, online banking, link to IRS Tax Forms
Bank of Boston	http://www.llnl.gov/fstc/principals/ bank_of_boston .shtml	Products and services information
Bank of England	http://www.einet.net/hytelnet/FUL031.html	Directions for telnetting to search Bank of England Quarterly Bulletin Time Series data
Barclays Bank	http://www.barclays.co.uk/	Products and services information; link to the Barclay Square shopping mall
Chase Manhattan	http://www.llnl.gov/fstc/principals/chase_manhattan .shtml	Products and services information; annual report
Chemical Bank	http://www.llnl.gov/fstc/principals/chemical_bank .shtml	Half-page summary of its products and services
Citicorp/Citibank	http://www.tti.com/	Products and services information
Colonial Bancgroup, Inc.	http://www.traveller.com/colonial/	Products and services information
First Interstate Bank	http://www.hexadecimal.com/fi/	Products and services information; online report on the California economic recovery
First Union Corporation	http://www.firstunion.com/	Products and services information; Consumer Reference Library links to Online Career Center and Consumer's Guide
Huntington Bancshares, Inc.	http://www.huntington.com/	Products and services information; an article on retirement; more to come
Interfinance Limited	http://intergroup.com:80/interfinance/	Products and services information
La Jolla Bank	http://www.ljbank.com/dir007.htm	Products and services information

Stocks, Bonds, and Other Markets

On the Internet, you can find information about every form of investment—from brokers, from experts, and from fellow investors. In this section, you can get information about investments in general and about specific topics: brokerages, stocks, bonds, futures, options, and so on. In addition, you can obtain both today's prices and those for last week, last month, or the past several years.

Brokerage Ratings

http://www.cs.cmu.edu/afs/cs.cmu.edu/user/jdg/www/ invest_brokers.html

From the misc.invest newsgroup comes information about and ratings of brokerage firms. Topics include comparisons of full service and discount brokerages and a series of tables that compare some brokerages in price and service on $2,000, $8,000, and $32,000 trades and a table of ratings based on the trades. Also included are margin and call rates.

Chicago Mercantile Exchange (CME)

http://www.cme.com/cme/
index.html

The CME supplies information on futures and options, information about the exchange, and links to World Wide Web finance-related resources.

For potential and current investors, perhaps the most interesting part of this site is a 14-kilobyte glossary of futures-related terms (for example, arbitrage, bear, bear market, bull, bull market, call, margin, and put).

FAQ on Investments

http://www.cis.ohio-state.edu/
hypertext/faq/usenet/
investment -faq/general/
top.html

This seven-part archive contains frequently asked investment questions and answers from the general.misc.invest newsgroup. To find a topic, open Part 1, the table of contents. Topics include advice, analysis, bonds, exchanges, information sources, miscellaneous, regulation, retirement plan, stocks, software, tax code, trading, trivia, and warning.

Interesting Sites

On the World Wide Web, you can find information and images from museums and galleries in actual buildings or just on the Net. Here are some sites to visit:

ANU Art History Top Level Menu Page
(http://rubens.anu.edu.au/)

Welcome to the Computer Museum
(http://www.net.org/)

The Electric Gallery
(http://www.egallery.com/egallery/homepage.html)

Patch Stereogram Project
(http://192.253.114.31/Projects/stereograms/)

National Gallery of Australia
(http://www.ncsa.uiuc.edu/SDG/Experimental/
anu-art-history/nga.html)

National Arts Guide (http://www
.national-arts-guide.co.uk/uk/home.html)

A Random Collection of Arts
Information
(http://www.cco.caltech.edu/~rbasu.arts.html)

DC Art Calendar
(http://www.dc202.com/artcal.html)

NYC Museums
(http://astor.mediabridge.com/nyc/museums/)

The Homepage—Guy:Museums and
Museum Resources
(http://ivory.lm.com/~markt/Webmuseums.html)

Rooms for Researchers
(http://www.hike.te.chiba-u.ac.jp/rooms4res/)

Figure 7.5 shows a painting from the National Gallery of Australia, converted to a graphic image at the NCSA.

Figure 7.5 Part of a Rembrandt painting from the National Gallery of Australia

Holt's Stock Market Reports

http://metro.turnpike.net/holt/index.html

gopher://wuecon.wustl.edu:671/11/holt

George Holt produces same-day reports on the markets. A typical report includes links to indexes; averages; foreign markets; issues traded; new highs, lows; currency; gold; interest rates; most active (NYSE, NASDAQ, AMEX); stocks and optionable stocks with today's volume up more than 50%; stocks and optionable stocks that have reached a new high; and stocks and optionable stocks that have reached a new low.

The tables are not aligned; hence, they are somewhat difficult to read. But this service is free, you don't have to subscribe, and you don't have to read any advertising. On the other hand, the daily chart at the Web site is detailed and well designed.

Note
For a list of economic indicator resources, see the *Economic Conditions and Indicators* section in the *Economics and Statistics* chapter.

Hong Kong Stocks Reports

http://silkroute.com:80/silkroute/news/ITTI/index.html

This page presents an abridged version of the daily Hong Kong Market Summary. At this site, you'll find Hong Kong market news and trends and two articles: "Hong Kong Stock Market in a Nutshell" and "Hong Kong Hang Seng Index Shares P/E Ratios and Asian Markets Compared."

Huang's Weekly Futures Report

gopher://wuecon.wustl.edu:671/11/holt/weekfut

Paul C. Y. Huang presents detailed reports almost weekly on a recent week's futures,

their profits or losses, and comments. In addition to futures, a recent report showed changes in precious metals, currencies, stock indexes, the S&P 500, U.S. Treasury bonds and notes, and seven commodities. Comments covered new historical records, the yen/dollar exchange rate, the S&P 500 stock index, strength in cotton, the new Taiwan dollar, and the Taiwan equity market.

To subscribe to this service, send a message to pcyhuang @tpts1.seed.net.tw. In the message, include your name, profession, how you found out about the report, and why you are interested. To unsubscribe, return the complete header of a report in a message to the author.

The Investor Channel

http://www.wimsey.com/Magnet/mc/index5.html

Previously known as the Mining Channel, the Investor Channel (see Figure 7.6) provides free, up-to-date information, including company profiles, news releases, and stock quotes, particularly for Canadian mining companies. Select Featured Public Companies to view and optionally request company information: a snapshot (one-page) report, a full report, and news releases. Click on Corporate Information to see information about company officers, capitalization, share prices, registrations, and so on.

PC Quote/Spacecom Systems Stock Quote Server

http://www.spacecom.com:8001/Participants/pcquote/qmaster.html

Without subscription requirements or commercial messages, this site simply provides stock quotes with a 15-minute delay. Type the ticker symbol or the company name; then click on Submit.

This site is very busy and sometimes unavailable.

QuoteCom

http://www.quote.com/

QuoteCom furnishes stock and commodity quotes and analysis from U.S., Canadian, and European exchanges. This is a fee-based service primarily; however, non-paying users can get a maximum of five quotes in low traffic times (8 PM to 9 AM EST), can search the index using ticker symbols, and access some of the files.

If you are a paying customer and depending on service that you buy, you can get custom price charts, stock price alerts sent to your computer, Hoover company profiles, market analysis and news, an S&P stock guide and S&P news, Business Wire News, press releases from the PR Newswire, and more. Subscription plans range from $9.95 (basic) to $24.95 (for balance sheet data for more than 5000 U.S. stocks).

Figure 7.6   The home page graphic for the Investor Channel

Robert's Online Option Pricer

http://www.intrepid.com/~robertl/option-pricer.html

If you are into option buying and research, you can learn some terminology and how to price options at this site. Fill in the form to automatically price options on stocks, warrants, futures, long bonds, and currencies based on six variables.

To use the option pricer, fill in the stock price (in dollars and cents), the strike price (in dollars and cents), the dividend yield (in percent per year), interest rate (in percent per year), volatility (in percent per year), and the time left until expiration, and then click on the days, months, or years option button. Click on the Call option, Put option, American option, or European option. Finally, click on the Price It button. The result is the value, delta, gamma, and theta.

If you are a beginner, the form is daunting, and not all the terms are explained.

Russian Securities Market News

http://www.fe.msk.ru/infomarket/ewelcome.html

This well-illustrated site provides information about the Russian Exchange (RE), the Russian market. Both Russian and English language versions of this page are available.

Scott Yanoff on the World Wide Web and HTML

Why did you move the Internet Services List to the World Wide Web?

It's just the way to go these days. The WWW is the killer application of the Internet.

Which HTML editor(s) do you use?

I just use VI, a standard text editor.

Do you have any advice for a novice HTML coder?

Practice coding a lot first, and explore the Web to understand the proper way to do things.

How often should links be verified?

They should be verified monthly, but mine are not verified as often. I heavily rely on the kind users of the Internet.

Three topics of interest are at this address: Russia Exchange, Results of Currency Futures on RE, and Annual Report. Select Russia Exchange to get information about and the history of the RE; select Results of Currency Futures on RE and then choose a date to display a table of results for that day. Select Annual Report to see (at this writing) a very detailed annual report for 1994, illustrated with charts (see Figure 7.7).

The Stockmaster

http://www.ai.mit.edu/stocks.html

The popular Stockmaster site supplies stock charts (updated daily), mutual fund charts, top stocks, stock quotes, the latest issue of an e-mail quote file, lists of companies sorted by symbol, lists of ticker symbols sorted by company, a directory of historical data files (the basis for the graphs), and links to 16 other finance-related sites.

Treasury and Bond Quotes

gopher://una.hh.lib.umich.edu/00/ebb/monetary/quotes.txt

The Economic Bulletin Board (EBB) provides up-to-date tables of U.S. Treasury notes, bonds, and bills. The U.S. Treasury Notes and Bonds table includes the issue ID (CUSIP#), bid, ask, change, and yield. The U.S. Treasury Bills table adds the issue date. Tables end with rates for certificates of deposit (1-, 3-, and 6-month), commercial paper (30-, 60-, and 90-day), and federal funds (the effective rate trading range).

Note

The Economic Bulletin Board provides more than the information here. For additional EBB data, see the *Economics and Statistics* chapter.

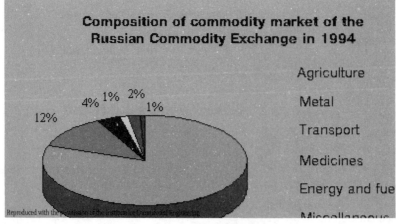

Figure 7.7   A chart from the Russian Exchange's annual report

Mutual Funds

A mutual fund is mix of stocks, bonds, and notes. On the Internet, you will find a great deal of information about mutual funds: how to get started investing in them, their performance over a particular time period, mutual fund filings, and articles. This section presents a collection of mutual fund resources.

FAQs on Mutual Funds

http://www.cis.ohio-state.edu/hypertext/faq/usenet/
investment-faq/mutual-funds/faq.html

Randy Marks presents frequently asked questions (FAQs) about mutual funds. At the top of the page is a table of contents of 24 questions linked to predominantly brief and understandable answers. For longer answers, the author changes to an outline format.

Note
Ohio State has a library of all types of FAQs from the Atlanta Olympic FAQ to Zyxel Modems. The list covers a wide variety of topics, including computing, sports, travel, UFOs and aliens, Tolkien, technical reports, and much more.

Fidelity Mutual Funds and Fund Prospectuses

http://www.fid-inv.com/img/index.html

Fidelity's site provides summary information for Fidelity mutual funds and fund prospectuses arranged by category— Money Market, Income, and Growth—and by subcategory. Click on a subcategory to display a list of funds. A typical page for a particular fund starts with identifying information and minimum requirements. Following that are a fund description; average annual total return over 1, 5, and 10 years; the name and information about the fund manager; performance

graphs (see Figure 7.8); an application; and a chance to order a prospectus.

The home page and pages on the next lower level load slowly because of some large graphics.

Mutual Fund Company Phone List

http://www.eunet.fi:80/gnn/ meta/finance/res/800.html

This utilitarian text page displays a list of 800 numbers for more than 300 alphabetically arranged mutual fund companies. There are no links or graphics.

Mutual Fund Reports

http://www.visions.com/netpages/mutuals/mutuals.html

This page provides both foreign and domestic mutual fund information. First, click on a fund category. Then click on a specific fund (funds are ranked by the most recent month's performance). A report on the fund, its type, volatility, and returns over periods as short as one month and as long as ten years appears. At the bottom of each report is the fund's mission statement.

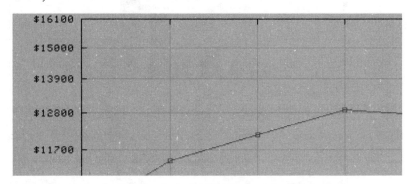

Figure 7.8   A chart showing the growth of a $10,000 investment in a Fidelity fund

Mutual Funds Activity Reports

http://edgar.stern.nyu.edu/mutual.html

At the Stern School at the New York University (NYU) EDGAR site you can research mutual fund SEC filings over time and create a list of links to the filings.

To produce a report, select a date range from the drop-down list. You can choose time periods ranging from the beginning of the project, January 1, 1994, to today, or you can choose to see just today's filings. Then select a form: ALL (which also includes other forms), 13G, 13D, or NSAR. Finally, select a mutual fund from the drop-down list, and click on the Submit Choices button. When the report appears, you can click on links to display the filing.

Nest Egg's Mutual Fund and Finance Information

http://nestegg.iddis.com/

IDD Publications, founded in 1935, publishes business magazines, directories, and newsletters. *Nest Egg Magazine*, an insert in selected suburban newspapers, is a financial tabloid for high-income and high net worth families.

At this address, you can check the performance of a selected mutual fund (see Figure 7.9) and read articles about investment. If you are using Netscape 2.0 (or later), be sure to stop by the home page to see the scrolling text banner at the bottom of the page.

Real Estate

If you plan to move to a new area or book a vacation rental, you don't even have to leave your house. Now, with the World Wide Web and a graphical browser, you can tour a house online; more and more real estate firms are marketing their properties online. Additionally, you can look into and fill out an application for a home loan using your Internet hookup.

In this section, you'll find real estate agencies, mortgage brokers and lenders, and several mortgage calculators with which you can estimate future payments, interest, and principal.

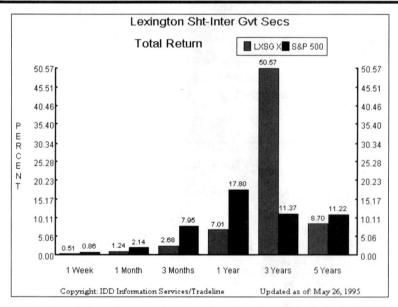

Figure 7.9 A chart comparing the performance of a selected mutual fund with the S&P 500 over six time periods

American Finance and Investment

http://www.dirs.com/mortgage/afi/

American Finance and Investment is a mortgage lender and broker that services all 50 states. Through this online service, you can check rates, view closing estimates, and apply online using the membership kit and your credit card.

Fair Oaks Financial

http://fofs.vip.best.com/

Located in Palo Alto, California, and for California buyers, Fair Oaks Financial Services brokers mortgage loans. (The lender pays the commission.) After you submit an online application and are approved, your loan will probably close within 21 days.

At this site, you will find much background information and the requirements (Inside a Loan File) as well as online resources: On-Line Rate Quote, On-Line Pre-qualification, On-Line Application, and On-Line Mortgage Calculator.

FractalNet WWW Real Estate Server

http://www.fractals.com/realestate.html

This very large and slow-loading site consists of an index of links to real estate resources all over the world, but primarily in California. Resources include real estate agencies, referral services, mortgage brokers, and some termite inspectors, structural engineers, and movers. Links also include current mortgage rates, Hugh Chou's mortgage payment calculator (see a following entry), and Usenet newsgroups.

Adding a Postscript Printer to Windows 95

If your printer is not defined as a PostScript printer, you may need to install a card in the printer.

1. Shut down as many applications as you can.

2. From the Control Panel, select the Printers icon.

3. In the Printers window, double-click on the Add Printer icon.

4. In the first Add Printer Wizard dialog box, click on Next.

5. In the Manufacturers list box, select the manufacturer of your printer.

6. In the Printers list box, select a PostScript option.

7. Click on Next.

8. Select the printer port and click on Next.

9. Optionally, give the printer a name and indicate whether it is the default printer. Then click on Next.

10. Indicate whether to print a test page. Then click on Finish.

11. Follow the onscreen instructions to insert a series of Windows setup disks.

HomeBuyer's Fair

http://www.homefair.com/

HomeBuyer's Fair presents new houses for sale in 23 cities; links to apartments for rent in the eastern United States, in Detroit, and in southern California; information about obtaining a mortgage; and links to other Internet real estate sites and other resources. Also included are relocation services and mortgage services, including several calculators (see Figure 7.10).

Mortgage Calculator

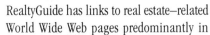

http://ibc.wustl.edu/mort.html

Hugh Chou's calculator (see Figure 7.11) is an amortization calculation form into which you type variables: the principal loan balance, annual interest rate, amortization length, and starting month. The result is a table of payments by interest and

principal. To use the calculator, your browser must support forms. Also included are links to an income tax calculator, a tax-deferred annuity calculator, and other real estate–related Internet sites.

RealtyGuide

http://www.xmission.com/~realtor1/relinks.html

RealtyGuide has links to real estate–related World Wide Web pages predominantly in North America, but also in Africa, Asia, Australia, and Europe. Also included are links to investment bankers, lenders, U.S. finance- and business-related departments, housing and architecture, and many other finance and business resources.

The top-level links are arranged by region of the world. Click on a region to reveal a list of links to a smaller region, then click to get to a city or metropolitan area, and finally click on an agency or a firm. The links can be very informative, with detailed listings and photographs and with online prompts for your address, to which will be sent a brochure.

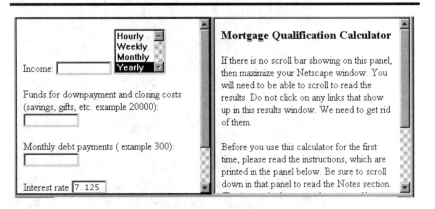

Figure 7.10 The Homebuyer's Mortgage Qualification Calculator, which is designed to work with the newest version of Netscape

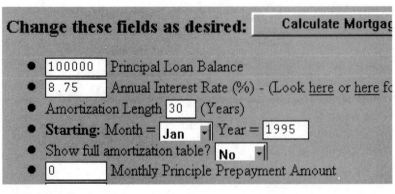

Figure 7.11 Hugh Chou's mortgage calculator

VA Oakland Regional Office

http://www.ccnet.com/services/va/welcome.html

If you are looking for a VA (Veteran's Administration) loan, you can get plenty of information at this well-designed site. Links include online articles about VA loans and the VA Lender's Handbook in two downloadable self-extracting files (in Word for Windows 2.0 format). Also included are a listing of VA-owned properties for sale in northern California and northern Nevada, links to real estate information sources, and the VA Benefits Manual.

Insurance and Risk Management

For any number of reasons, having the proper insurance coverage is essential; having insurance can keep you in business, and lack of insurance can mean ruin. If a power surge or lightning bolt blows out a computer, a customer slips on a wet floor, or an employee develops Carpal Tunnel Syndrome, insurance is critical.

In this section, you can find out about insurance—both business and personal. You can study insurance research papers and consumer-oriented articles, plan the proper amounts, review ratings of insurance companies, and compare prices of policies.

ARIAWeb

http://finweb.bus.utexas.edu/aria.html

The American Risk and Insurance Association (ARIA), a group of academics and insurance professionals, furnishes risk management and insurance research findings, news and announcements, and links to databases, working paper archives, and other Internet resources.

If you want to learn about risk management and insurance in depth or research before making an insurance decision, ARIA provides a searchable database of useful articles (for example, "The Complex Role of Age in Employer-Mandated Health Insurance," "Efficiency Comparisons between Mutual and Stock Life Insurance Companies," and "Risk Aversion, Prudence and Temperance: A Unified Approach"). A successful search results in titles of articles related to the keyword; the top rank is 1000 (an exact match). Click on a title to view an

abstract. Click on the word *here* at the bottom of the article to download a PostScript-format copy of the article.

Note
You must be a member of ARIA to use all their services. You can fill out an ARIA application form at this site.

The Insurance Information Institute's Internet Service

gopher://infx.infor.com:4200/1

This site, sponsored by the Insurance Information Institute (I.I.I.), presents insurance industry information from the industry's point of view. Although this is a commercial site, the advertising is minimal.

The online brochures are the equivalent of two or three printed pages. "Insuring Your Home Business" covers property and liability insurance, how much to buy and how to buy it, other types of business insurance, finding an agent, discounts, adjusting coverage as your company grows, and your state insurance department.

Insurance News Network (INN)

http://www.insure.com/

The INN presents information about automobile, home, and life insurance; links to INN state insurance sites; and Standard & Poor's ratings of insurance companies.

The home page links to the Quotesmith term life insurance price comparison service—a database of 160 insurers. If you complete the Quotesmith Price Comparison Request Form, Quotesmith will send price quotes for the 36 policies that come closest to meeting your requirements by first-class mail.

At this site, you can get insurance information (rates, insurers, and required coverage) for your state, county, city, or region.

RISKWeb

http://riskweb.bus.utexas.edu/riskweb.html

RISKWeb provides information on risk management and insurance, including annual meetings; mailing lists, working papers, and teaching archives; search engines for five databases; and announcements, job and resumé center, and RISKNet subscriber address information. Also included are many links to other risk management pages: ARIAWeb, other college and university home pages, organizations; finance links; Yahoo search facility; and a variety of others.

Personal Finance

Theoretically, personal finance is limited to planning and carrying out all nonbusiness monetary affairs: planning income and controlling expenses purely on a personal level. Realistically, all your finances—personal and business—overlap, sometimes in a very chaotic way. For example, you can use your automobile for business commuting and personal carpooling, sometimes on the same trip. And, if you operate a business out of your house, you have to decide whether to set aside part of your house as your office space.

This section deals with personal finance: personal finance general resources; credit and credit cards; and college scholarships, grants, and loans. Remember that you can get help on personal finance from almost every other section of this chapter.

Personal Finance General Resources

As in other parts of this book, many personal finance sites furnish all types of resources, and others provide information about a particular topic.

For example, the GNN Personal Finance Center not only furnishes links to personal finance sites but to investment, real estate, and tax pages; on the other hand, the FAQ on consumer credit and the Penn State articles on credit cover only consumer credit problems and solutions.

This section presents the major sources of Internet-based personal finance information.

FinanCenter

http://www.financenter.com/resources/

FinanCenter provides a wealth of valuable personal finance resources for consumers. The four main categories of topics are Financing a Home, Credit Card Applications, Financing an Automobile, and Current Rates. Click on a link to go to a page of calculations, rates, glossaries, and reports covering a particular topic. Under Credit Card Applications, you also will find a top-ten list of credit cards, and under Financing an Automobile is information about the yearly depreciation of sample cars. When you click on Current Rates, you can obtain information about loan rates for automobiles, boats, recreational vehicles (RVs), credit cards, and mortgages. Be sure to put this important site on your Bookmark list.

FTC Consumer Brochures

http://www.webcom.com/~lewrose/brochures.html

Lewis Rose has performed a valuable service by finding and creating links to 100 full-text consumer online brochures about topics ranging from art fraud to generic drugs.

Business-related titles include "Lost or Stolen: Credit and ATM Cards," "Getting Business Credit," "Cellular Telephone Lottery Update," "Cosigning a Loan," "Credit Practices Rule," "Facts for Business (Credit)," "Electronic Banking," "Fair Credit Billing," "Franchise and Business Opportunities," and "Investing in Wireless Cable TV." To view a brochure, simply click on its title. You also can join a mailing list by clicking at the bottom of an article.

LawTalk-Business Law and Personal Finance

http://www.law.indiana.edu/law/bizlaw.html
The Indiana University School of Law at Bloomington presents personal finance and business law information. At this site, you will find 20 articles that discuss bounced checks, living wills, arbitration, credit reporting, and so on.

Personal Finance Center

http://gnn.com/wic/wics/persfin.new.html
The Personal Finance Center from GNN (Global Network Navigator) is the premiere personal finance site on the World Wide Web. Click on All the Links to list all the personal finance sites on a variety of servers, newsgroups, e-mail resources, and Listservs, covering investment, credit cards, home finance, real estate, banking, financial planning, and taxes. Click on New Resources to see what's new.

Consumer Credit

Everyone seems to live by the credit card these days, and the credit card providers know that. Over the next month, it's quite likely that you will receive at least one or two credit card applications.

This section includes home pages that provide consumer credit information, international credit card resources, and FAQs about credit.

Credit Cards Information

gopher://info.psu.edu:70/00/psuinfo/University%20Life/
Legal%20Rights%20and%20Safety%20Concerns/
Credit%20Card%20Billing%20Problems
Penn State University provides online information, advice, and articles for its students and for those that find this address. This article explains how to use credit cards. Topics include credit card laws (particularly the Fair Credit Billing Act), your rights as a user, and advantages of using a credit card over cash.

Note
You can find other helpful articles by going to gopher://info.psu.edu:70/, clicking on Penn State Information, selecting University Life, and selecting a topic.

Credit History Information

gopher://info.psu.edu:70/00/psuinfo/University%20Life/
Legal%20Rights%20and%20Safety%20Concerns/
Your%20Credit%20History
Penn State University provides online information, advice, and articles for its students and for those that find this address. This article describes your rights as a credit card holder. Topics include how to obtain and correct a credit report.

FAQ on Consumer Credit

http://www.cis.ohio-state.edu/hypertext/faq/usenet/
consumer-credit-faq/top.html
This four-part archive contains frequently asked questions about consumer credit and answers

from the misc.consumers newsgroup. Part 1 lists the questions. The remaining parts have the answers, which are sometimes very detailed. Parts 2 and 3 cover credit cards, and Part 4 contains answers about credit reports.

MasterCard International Pointers

http://www.mastercard.com/

MasterCard International Pointers is one of the best-looking sites on the Web. This site is very commercial, however, and relatively new. At this page, you can find out what to do if you lose a card, read about the future of credit cards, search a very small index of ATM locations, and read very short, illustrated (see Figure 7.12) stories, fables, and folktales from around the world.

To find an ATM, choose a city (Brussels, Chicago, Hong Kong, London, Los Angeles, New York, Singapore, and Sydney), type all or part of a street name, click on an option button, and select the Show Me button. Figure 7.13 shows the form that you fill in to find a MasterCard ATM.

VISA Home Page

http://www.visa.com/visa/

From VISA International, this good-looking commercial site provides information about your VISA credit card and member services: what to do if you lose your card, financial tips for consumers, and an ATM locator guide that ends in your making a telephone call.

The result of making an ATM search is not an address on your screen but an 800 telephone number. To search for an ATM, select a region and a country from slow-loading pages. Finally, call the 800 number and get the ATM location.

Scholarships and Financial Aid

The expense of attending college controls the finances of many middle-aged parents and their student children—well beyond graduation. With colleges and universities so great a presence on the Internet, it isn't surprising that information about scholarships and financial aid is also appearing. In this section, you'll find sites with scholarship, grant, and financial aid information.

Figure 7.12 An illustration from a story at the MasterCard International site

The Ambitious Student's Guide to Financial Aid

http://www.infi.net/
collegemoney/toc1.html

Written by Robert and Anna Leider at Signet Bank, this comprehensive online book about financial aid and paying for college is composed of 25 chapters with many links, appendixes, and reference tables.

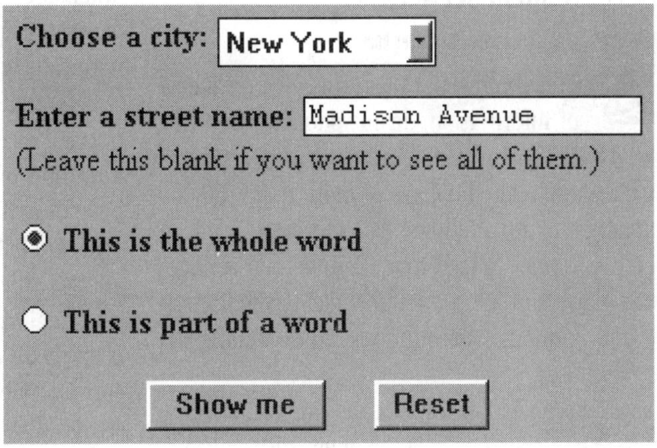

Chinook College Funding Service

http://www.chinook.com/
user/chinook2/

This commercial site from Chinook enables U.S. college students to search for scholarships. Also included is a brief description of the financial aid process, financial aid for non-U.S. citizens, major federal financial aid programs, state financial aid office addresses, background information about scholarships, how much, and Chinook company information. In addition, links to Internet indexes, lists, and information and other financial aid resources are provided.

Financial Aid Information

http://www.cs.cmu.edu/afs/cs/user/mkant/Public/
FinAid/finaid.html

From Mark Kantrowitz, an author of a book on scholarships and fellowships, these links thoroughly cover all areas of financial aid. Topics include frequently

Figure 7.13 Fill in this form to find a MasterCard ATM.

asked questions (FAQs), a glossary, grants, loans, exchange and out-of-state programs, U.S. government information, college and university financial aid offices, mailing lists, telephone numbers, publishers of financial aid books, financial aid consultants, and a short list of groups and subgroups of general education-related resources.

Loan Counselor

gopher://oasis.cc.purdue.edu:2525/11/student/cnslr

You can either search an index or browse Purdue University's comprehensive online document about getting and managing student loans. Select About Loan Counselor to get an overview of the articles: "Facts about Student Loans," "Managing Loan Indebtedness," and "List of Lenders."

Student Services

http://www.studentservices.com/

This commercial site furnishes a great deal of information: an introduction to a free money for college directory ($2 for shipping and handling), a searchable database of more than 180,000 scholarships, grants, fellowships, and loans, and an interactive Home College tour. Commercial services include a discount international student exchange ID card and campus subscriptions from Publishers Clearing House.

To start a scholarship search, type your major in the text box. Then click on Go. A list of awards, sponsors, and addresses appears. Click on More to go to the next part of this section. To get more information, fill in your name and address.

Before starting the Home College tour, fill in a registration form and click on Submit the Registration. Press Continue to continue with the tour (although you haven't really started). As of this writing, several colleges are listed in alphabetical order, by region, or by selected criteria (GPA or SAT requirements, yearly costs, size, region, setting [rural, small town, suburban, urban]), majors, financial aid, affiliation, school type (private, public, historically black, all female, all male) sports (division, men's sports, women's sports), Greek life, and housing.

Chapter Eight

Human Resources

Using the sites in this chapter, you can search for jobs using corporate, academic, and organization links and job services; learn how to deal with employers or those reporting to you; find out how to make your office or cubicle ergonomically correct and where to purchase ergonomic office furniture; and discover the occupational safety, health, and medical resources on the Internet as well as those that help you prevent illnesses and disabilities. In this chapter, you'll be able to obtain information about disabled employees and learn about programs and resources especially formulated for minorities and women. Finally, you'll find a list of online shopping malls and get addresses for sellers of office supplies and other merchandise.

Job Search

The Internet provides a wealth of information for those seeking jobs and career guidance. In this section, you'll just scratch the surface. In the first part, you'll find sources of employment opportunities, and then you'll learn about how to find online employment and career services.

Employment Opportunities

In this section, you'll find places at which jobs are posted. Here you will find jobs bulletin boards, corporate job and human resources pages, positions from and with professional organizations, jobs for those seeking particular types of employment, and sites that provide links to many other jobs pages. Table 8.1 is a list of corporate, organizational, and academic sites, their URLs, and a "snapshot" of the jobs offered on the day that I visited each site.

Note
If you don't find the job opportunity for which you are looking in this section, refer to two other sections of this book: Organizations and Associations in the *Business Management* chapter and Computer Companies and Major Companies on the Internet in the *Corporations and Industries* chapter. Many professional organizations and most companies provide human resources or jobs pages at their Internet sites.

Table 8.1: Selected Employment Opportunities on the Internet

Job Source	URL	Description	Selected Positions or Types
Academic Position Network	gopher://wcni.cis.umn.edu:11111/	Academic positions by U.S. state or country and educational institution or company	Vice President, User Services Manager, Network Engineer, RDBMS Specialist, Microcomputer-Network Consultant, Dean, Professor, Instructor, Directory of Computing Services
Advanced Micro Devices	http://www.careermosaic.com/cm/amd/amd3.html	Jobs for producer of micro-processor products, applications solutions products, and non-volatile memory and programmable logic in Sunnyvale, CA, and Austin, TX	Administrative, Engineering, Facilities, Finance, Human Resources, Info Systems, Legal, Manufacturing, Marketing, Production Control, Purchasing, Sales, Technical Support categories
Airline Employee Placement Service	http://205.164.229.4/aeps/aepshm.html	Airline jobs for registered users	Pilots, Flight Attendants, Mechanics
Altera Corporation	http://www.careermosaic.com/cm/altera/	Positions for producer of programmable logic devices and computer-aided engineering logic development chips in San Jose, CA	IC Design Engineers, Software Engineers, Product Engineers, Product Marketing Engineers, Field Applications Engineers, Applications Engineers, Test Engineers, CAD Engineers, CMOS IC Design Engineers, Layout Designers, Technical Writer
Amdahl Corporation	http://www.amdahl.com/doc/employment/	Jobs, for a California company, listed under 15 categories	Business Development, Compatible Systems, Customer Services, Electronic Manufacturing, Enterprise Storage Systems, Field Operations, Finance, Human Resources, Information Services, Information Technology Consulting, Marketing, Open Enterprise Systems, Administration, College Recruiting, Co-op/Internships

Table 8.1: Selected Employment Opportunities on the Internet (continued)

Job Source	URL	Description	Selected Positions or Types
American Management Systems	http://www.amsinc.com/greatplc/webjobs	Jobs in the U.S. and Canada listed by business area, desired skills, geographic location, and type of position	PowerBuilder Developers, SmallTalk Programmers, SmallTalk Team Leaders, Analysts/Designers, Lotus Notes Developers/Designers/Trainers, Object-Oriented Analysts/Designers/Developers
American Institute of Physics	http://aip.org/employ/openings.html	Current job openings at the American Institute of Physics	Computer Senior Staff Assistant; Manager, Editorial Operations; Marketing Manager, Journals & Electronic Products; Publishing Systems Specialist
Andersen Consulting	http://www.ac.com/recruit/map.htm	Jobs in international management and technology consultancy in the U.S., Canada, Latin America, and Europe	Assistant Consultant, Consultant, Manager
Argonne National Laboratory	http://www.anl.gov/HR/emplhome.html	Jobs for a government laboratory in Illinois	Chief of Operations, Senior Secretary, Environmental Engineer/Scientist, Battalion Chief, Applications Development, Chemistry, Computer Science, Janitor, Mechanical Engineering, Electrical/Electronic Engineering, Chief Technician, Technician
Association of Commonwealth Universities	http://www.niss.ac.uk/news/acu/acu.html	International academic openings	Professor, Lecturer, Chair, Vice-Chancellor, Purchasing Officer
AT&T	http://www.careermosaic.com/cm/att/att6.html	U.S. telecommunications jobs	Software Engineers, Staff Editor, Managing Editor, Art Director, Data Processing Associates, Software/Hardware Systems Developer, Mixed Signal CMOS Designer, Test Equipment Engineers, Test Equipment Technicians, Test Engineers, PC/LAN Software Technician, Data Network Sales, Sales Manager, Management Consultants

Table 8.1: Selected Employment Opportunities on the Internet (continued)

Job Source	URL	Description	Selected Positions or Types
Auspex Systems	http://www.auspex.com/Jobs.html	U.S. and International jobs for a network hardware manufacturer	A/P Administrator; Cost Analyst; Channels Executive; Public Relations Manager; Product Marketing Manager; Business Manager, Sales; Systems Engineer Manager; System Engineer; Sales Account Executive; Prepress/Publishing System Engineer; Manufacturing Specialist; Programmer/Analyst; Material Handler
Biotechnology Career Center	http://www.bio.com/hr/hr_index.html	Job Searches, Career Guides, and Search Firms	Scientist, Technical Writer, Manufacturing Engineer, Advanced Engineers, Manufacturing Prep Tech, Regulatory Affairs Specialist, Validation Engineer, QA Product Release Specialist, Process Development Associate, Biostatistics & Data Management, Medical & Regulatory Affairs at laboratories, pharmaceutical firms, research, and biomedical companies
BMEnet Jobs List	http://fairway.ecn.purdue.edu/bme/jobs	International bioengineering, computer, biomechanics, biomedical, and engineering positions, primarily in academia (difficult to reach)	Postdoctoral Research Associate, Biomedical Director, Engineering Manager, Chair, Biomechanical Engineer, Engineering Director
Bolt Beranek and Newman Inc.	http://www.bbn.com/jobs/jobs.html	Jobs with an Internet provider, software solutions developer	Software Engineer, Patent Counsel, Lotus Notes Admin/Leader, PC Project Leader, Unix System Administrator, Helpdesk Administrator, Telecom Analyst, Senior Secretary, Executive Secretary, Finance P & A Manager, Home Office Manager, Financial Systems Integrator, Senior Benefits Analyst

Table 8.1: Selected Employment Opportunities on the Internet (continued)

Job Source	URL	Description	Selected Positions or Types
Bristol Technology, Inc.	http://www.bristol.com/	Positions with a software company in Connecticut	Software Developer, Sales Associate
Brown University Job Listings	gopher://gopher.brown.edu:70/11/brown/departs/hum_res/jobinfo	Positions at Brown University, Providence, RI	Food Service Worker, Office Aide to Research Assistant, Computing Coordinator, Programmer/Analyst, Technical Writer, Biostatistician, Associate Director (Food Services)
BTG Incorporated	http://www.btg.com/jobs/jobmenu.html	A technology integration company with U.S. jobs	Internet Specialist, Software Engineer, Configuration Management Specialist, Systems Administrator, Technical Writer, Technical Leader, Software Engineers, Engineers, Architects, Imaging Engineer, Sales, Software Development Engineers, Configuration Management/Testing Specialist, Microsoft Windows NT Programmer
The California Job Bulletin Board	http://www.webcom.com/~career/job_board.html	A bulletin board with links to California jobs—primarily computer-related	Software Developers, Support Analysts, Product Managers, Independent Sales Representatives, Warehouse Manager, Product Support Representative, LAN Administrator, Programmer Analysts, Senior Purchasing Agent, Cold Drink Sales Representatives, Help Desk Technician, Macro Media Director PC/Mac Programmer
CambridgeSoft Corporation	http://www.camsci.com/abouthome.html	Positions for a developer of desktop applications for chemists and engineers in Cambridge, MA	Computational Chemist, Software Developer, Technical Support and Testing

Table 8.1: Selected Employment Opportunities on the Internet (continued)

Job Source	URL	Description	Selected Positions or Types
Chronicle of Higher Education	gopher://chronicle.merit.edu:70/11/.ads	Worldwide jobs in many categories: for corporations, museums, foundations, medical facilities, parks and recreational facilities, etc.	Faculty, research, administrative, executive, and positions outside academe
Cisco Employment Opportunities	http://cio.cisco.com/public/Employment.html	International jobs with Cisco, "the leading global supplier of internetworking products devices."	Software Engineer; Manager, Quality; Engineering Technician, Customer Service Associate, Service Account Manager, Information Technology Engineer, Project Manager, Human Resources Manager, Human Resources Trainer, Sales Program Manager
CRL Employment Opportunities	http://www.crl.com/emp_opps.html	Jobs in San Francisco for a company providing dial-up Internet access and dedicated connections	Account Executive, Sales and Customer Support Representative, Network Operations Center Engineer
Dartmouth College Job Flyer	gopher://gopher.dartmouth.EDU:70/11/Careers/Jobflyer	Jobs at Dartmouth College, Hanover, NH	Assistant Director—Grants & Contracts, Computer Support Consultant, Library Administrative Assistant, Medical Research Assistant, Senior Secretary, Administrative Assistant, Maintenance Worker
DigiCash	http://www.digicash.nl/news/jobs.html	Jobs at an Amsterdam, Netherlands, company that develops software for Internet payment technology products	Software Development/Design, Documentation, Support

Table 8.1: Selected Employment Opportunities on the Internet (continued)

Job Source	URL	Description	Selected Positions or Types
E-Shop	http://www.eshop.com/corp/jobs.html	Jobs for a company in San Mateo, CA, providing online shopping on the Internet	Windows Authoring Tools Engineer, Merchant Tools Manager, Interactive Information Designer and Writer, Network/System Administrator, Manager/Director of Operations, QA Test Lead/Engineer (Unix), Director of Creative Services, Graphic Designer and Illustrator, Multimedia Developer, Senior Management
EIT	http://www.eit.com/new/employment	Jobs for a software developer and service provider on the Internet	Ecommerce Applications Engineer, Quality Assurance Engineer, Software Engineer, Technical Support, Project Leader, Digital Artist, Technical Writer
Federal Jobs	gopher://caligari.dartmouth.edu:70/11/fedjobs	Job lists downloaded from U.S. government bulletin boards, state organizations; jobs available worldwide	Administrative Law Judge, Air Reserve Technician, Audiologist, Nurse, Social Worker, Environmental Engineer, Assistant Kitch Chief, Telephone Operator, Computer Industry Openings
Floathe Johnson	http://www.floathe.com:80/floathe_page/joblist.html	Job openings at a Kirkland, WA, advertising agency	Production Supervisor, Senior Copywriter, Senior Account Executive, Research Director, TechnoBranding Project Coordinator, Multimedia Producer
Graphics Industry Employment—Canada	http://degaulle.hil.unb.ca/UNB_G_Services/employment.html	Jobs in Canada's graphics industry	Flexographic Press Operator, Photocopy Operator, Press Operator, Bindery Person, Typesetter, Printer, Press Person

Table 8.1: Selected Employment Opportunities on the Internet (continued)

Job Source	URL	Description	Selected Positions or Types
Institute of Electrical and Electronics Engineers, Inc. (IEEE)	http://www.ieee.org/jobs.html	U.S. jobs by region from the Institute of Electrical and Electronics Engineers, Inc. (IEEE)	Software Engineer, Senior Engineer, Member of Technical Staff, Reliability/Component Engineer, MS Windows NT Software Developer, Unix Systems Administrator, Senior Systems Engineer, Electrical Design Engineer, Software Verification and Validation Engineer, Engineer, Electrical Engineer
Insurance Career Connection	http://www.onramp.net/icc	Jobs for the insurance and managed care industry	Underwriters, Loss Control Specialist, Workers Compensation Claims Specialist, Workers Compensation Claims Representative, Sales Representative, Underwriting Specialist, Commercial Producer, Regional Litigation Manager, Construction Claims Defect Manager, In-House Counsel, Underwriting Manager, Workers Compensation Marketing, Adjusters
Intel	http://www.intel.com/cm/intel/index.html	Jobs in the western U.S. for manufacturer of processors, networking and modem products, and so on	Senior Mechanical Design Engineer, Self-Sustaining Manufacturing Technician, Software Engineers, Technical Marketing Engineers, BIOS Engineers, Hardware Engineering Manager, Financial Analyst, Planning and Logistics Analyst, Accountant, Wide Area Network Support Specialist, Production Manager, Technical Supervisors, Senior Manufacturing Engineer, Information Services Analyst, Program Manager

Table 8.1: Selected Employment Opportunities on the Internet (continued)

Job Source	URL	Description	Selected Positions or Types
International Jobs List	http://www.timeshigher.newsint.co.uk/THES/INTERVIEW/INT/CURRENT/jobclass_menu.html	International academic jobs	Principals, Senior Managers, Deans, Heads of Department, Professors, Lecturers, Fellowship, Librarians
InterNIC Registration Services Job Openings	http://rs.internic.net/jobs.html	The organization that registers Intenet addresses	Software Engineer, Programmer Analyst
Intuit, Inc.	http://www.careermosaic.com/cm/intuit/intuit5.html	Jobs in California from the makers of financial and tax software	Product Marketing Managers, Software Development Engineers, Software Quality Assurance Engineers, Technical Writers, Seasonal Inbound Sales/Customer Support Representatives
J. Robert Scott Executive Search	http://www2.j-robert-scott.com/jrs/opportun.html	Executive search firm	Senior executive positions for entrepreneurs
The Job Board	http://www.io.org/~jwsmith/jobs.html/	Computer jobs in Canada (be sure to read the rules and suggestions for applying)	Systems Architects, Senior Developer, Developers, Windows Warrior, Visual Basic Wizard, Connectivity Geek
Job Openings for Economists (JOE)	gopher://vuinfo.vanderbilt.edu:70/11/employment/joe/	Worldwide jobs from the American Economic Association	Professor, Economist, Director, Research Economist, Research Fellow
Job-Search Bulletin Board	gopher://rodent.cis.umn.edu:1111g/	From the University of Minnesota College of Education, this site contains postings of U.S.-wide education positions	Administrative Assistant, Directory, Principal, Teacher, Superintendent, Building Administrator, Associate Alumni Director, Assistant Gymnastics Coach

Table 8.1: Selected Employment Opportunities on the Internet (continued)

Job Source	URL	Description	Selected Positions or Types
JobServe	http://www.jobserve.com/jobserve.html	"Contract & permanent vacancies from agencies throughout the UK, Europe, and World-Wide" sent via e-mail and viewable as database records	Technical Writer, Trainer, Access Analyst/Programmer, Access Security Consultant, Security Team Leader, Analyst, Developer, Operator, PC Support, Process Control Engineer
J. P. Morgan	http://careers.jpmorgan.com/CorpInfo/Careers/Home_Page.html	Pages with information about working at J. P. Morgan and lists of U.S. openings	Investment Banking, Equity Research, Municipal Finance, Markets, Private Client Services, Global Technology and Operations, Financial, Audit, Management Services, Human Resources
Manufacturing Jobs	http://mfginfo.com/htm/jobsview.htm	A text list of job opportunities, primarily for the U.S., but some international	Developers, Sales, Home-Based Employment, Distributor, CNC Mill Programmer/Operator, Manufacturing Software Specialist, Moldmaker, Manufacturer's Representative, Process Engineer
McKinley Job Openings	http://www.mckinley.com/mckinley-txt/jobs.html	Jobs at The McKinley Group, a start-up Internet company near San Francisco	Copyeditor, Account Executive—Advertising, Web Maestro, Staff Accountant, Public Relations Director"
Metal Machining and Fabrication Employment Opportunities	http://www.mmf.com/metal/employ/employ.htm	For-fee help wanted ads for metal machining and fabrication	Mechanical Inspector, Brake Operator

Table 8.1: Selected Employment Opportunities on the Internet (continued)

Job Source	URL	Description	Selected Positions or Types
Microelectronic Jobs	http://www.cmc.ca/Careers/jobs.html	Jobs in Canada for technological firms (not all up to date)	Program Managers, Engineers, Software Developers, Circuit Designer, Application Engineer, Test Engineers, Senior IC Design Engineers, Electronics Design Engineers
Microsoft	http://www.microsoft.com/Jobs/ms.htm	Large site with several job-related links	New Graduates and Internships, Developer Products, Product Support, International, User Education, Microsoft Consulting Services, Corporate Sales and Marketing, Networking and Operating Systems, Consumer Products, Desktop Products, Advanced Technology, Information Technology Group
Microsoft Campus Recruiting	http://www.microsoft.com/jobs/campus/default.htm	The campus recruiting site with corporate, job, and local information and more	Software Design Engineer, Program Manager, Software Design Engineer in Test Development, Software Test Engineer, Support Engineer, Developer Support Engineer
National Semiconductor Employment Opportunities	http://www.nsc.com/hr/jobindex.html	Jobs for communications, consumer, industrial, and personal systems in the U.S.	Principal Circuit Design Engineer, Principal Engineer, Senior Unix Systems Programmer, Digital Design Engineer, Senior Engineering Manager, Staff Engineer—Circuit Design, Engineering Project Manager, Marketing Manager, Sr. Communications Specialist, Senior Design Engineer, Patent Counsel, Business Marketing Manager, Senior Software Engineer
New Frontiers Information Corporation (NFIC)	http://www.nfic.com/nfic_positions.html	Jobs from a provider of Internet-based commercial applications located in Cambridge, MA	Unix Programmer, Windows Programmer, System Administrator

	Table 8.1: Selected Employment Opportunities on the Internet (continued)		
Job Source	*URL*	*Description*	*Selected Positions or Types*
National Institutes of Health (NIH)	gopher://gopher.nih.gov:70/11/campus/vacancies	NIH job vacancies organized by grade, organization, and occupational series	Associate Director, Director, Computer Specialist, Executive Officer, Program Analysis Officer, Program Analyst, Health Scientist Administrator, Medical Officer, Fire Chief, Medical Technologist, Psychologist, Pharmacist, Biologist, Chemist, Psychiatric Nurse, Secretary, Occupational Therapist, Physical Therapist
NISS Information Gateway	http://www.niss.ac.uk/news/jobs/disc.html	Academic job vacancies in various departments	Professor, Lecturer, Research Assistant, Librarian, Analyst/Programmer
North Carolina Community College System	http://bull.ncdcc.cc.nc.us/colleges/colljobs.htm/	Jobs at the 59 North Carolina community colleges	Early Childhood Instructor, Recruiter, Psychiatric/Mental Health Nursing Instructor, Computer Services Coordinator, Computer Instructor, Veteran's Assistance Counselor, Computer Support Technician, Morning Edition Host/Producer, Dean, Vice President of Academic Affairs, Library Technical Assistant
NYSERnet	http://nysernet.org/about/jobs.html	Internet Service Provider	Customer Support Representative, Dial Product Specialist, Systems Programmer, Network Provisioning Specialist

Table 8.1: Selected Employment Opportunities on the Internet (continued)

Job Source	URL	Description	Selected Positions or Types
Open Market, Inc.	http://www.openmarket.com/hiring	Software company for Internet commerce located in Cambridge, MA, and Palo Alto, CA	Customer Support Engineer, Internet Services Support Engineer, Infrastructure Development Engineer, Production System Administrator, Database Administrator, Database Applications Engineer, Technical Lead, Windows Application engineers, Software Test/Quality Engineer, Web Applications Engineer, Payment Operations Support, Technical Customer Support
Organic Jobs	http://www.organic.com/Home/Info/Jobs/index.html	Jobs with a San Francisco advertising agency	Design Director, Production Manager, Production Assistant, Tool Developer/Scripter
PeopleBank	http://www.peoplebank.co.uk/ten/candvac.htm	Jobs in Europe and the United Kingdom	Marketing Director, Network Consultant, Network Design and Implementation Engineer, Contract Computer Positions
Precision Digital Images (PDI) Employment Opportunities	http://www.precisionimages.com/emply_op.htm	Imaging hardware and software	Marketing/WWW Specialist, Sales Engineer, Marketing Manager, Hardware Engineer, Windows Software Engineer, Application Engineer
Read-Rite	http://www.careermosaic.com:80/cm/readrite/rr11.html	International jobs for supplier of thin film recording heads for the disk drive industry	Investor/Public Relations, Senior Facilities Engineer, Staff Engineer, Manufacturing System Analyst, R&D Engineer

Table 8.1: Selected Employment Opportunities on the Internet (continued)

Job Source	URL	Description	Selected Positions or Types
Risk Management and Insurance Job and Resume Center	http://www.riskweb.com/careers.html	"Job opportunities for and resumes of terminally qualified Risk Management and Insurance professionals and academicians"	Academic positions, consultants, and risk management professionals
Roadway Employment Opportunities	http://www.roadway.com/rit/employ.htm	Transportation services	Mainframe Programmer, Technical Programmer/Analyst, Technical Analyst, Technologist, PC Support Representative, Technical Writer
San Francisco City & County	http://www.well.com/user/ctywatch/joblstng.html	Permanent employment opportunities with the city and county of San Francisco	Chief Surveyor, Building Inspector, Electrical Line Worker, Medical Transcriber Typist, Psychiatric Technician, Licensed Vocational Nurse, Registered Nurse, Head Nurse, Nurse Practitioner, Anesthetist, Pharmacist, Paramedic, Occupational Therapist, Physical Therapist
Science Applications International Corporation	http://www.saic.com:80/empopp/index.html/	U.S jobs for a high-technology research and engineering company	Accounts Receivable Supervisor, Administrative Assistant, Administrator, Technical Information Specialist, Financial Management Training Specialist, Senior Risk Management Analyst, RFP Coordinator, Executive Specialist, Contracts Manager, Financial Controller, Subcontracts/Purchasing Agent, System Engineer, Senior Project Control Specialist, Project Manager, Program Manager, Librarian, Senior Graphics Specialist, Logistics Analyst, Software Engineer, Programmer, Project Manager

Table 8.1: Selected Employment Opportunities on the Internet (continued)

Job Source	URL	Description	Selected Positions or Types
Science Global Career Network	http://www.edoc.com/sgcn/ or gopher://gopher.aaas.org.71/11/.classify	International classified ads from *Science* magazine: text ads and image ads for faculty, postdoctoral, and scientists	Professor, Researcher, Chair, Director
The Scientist	http://www.hiss.ac.uk/news/sci_jobs/scijobs.html	International academic jobs (not up-to-date)	Research Chemist, Postdoctoral Research Associate, Professor, Pediatric Physician Scientist
Seagate	http://www.careermosaic.com/cm/seagate	International jobs for a company that "provides products for storing, managing, and accessing digital information"	Senior Industrial Engineer, Vacuum Process Engineer, Bar Lap Software Engineer, Process Engineer, Probe Test Engineer, Mechanical Integration Engineer, System Analyst/Programmer, Senior PCB Designer, Head Integration Engineer, Test Programmer
Standard Microsystems Corporation	http://www.smc.com/hr/joblist.html	New York, California, and Massachusetts jobs in data communications technologies	Quality Manager, Director—Design Automation, Manager—Product Marketing, Electronic Programs Manager, Public Relations Manager, Senior Process Engineer, Manufacturing Engineer, Product Test Engineer, Project Hardware Engineer, Senior Production Test Engineer, Principal Design Engineer, Design Automation Engineer, Senior Field Applications Engineer, Quality Engineer, Lotus Notes Programmer/Analyst, Network Systems Analyst

Table 8.1: Selected Employment Opportunities on the Internet (continued)

Job Source	URL	Description	Selected Positions or Types
Sun Microsystems	http://www.careermosaic.com/cm/sun/sun5.html	U.S. jobs at Sun Microsystems, producers of workstations and software	Systems Engineering, Networking Solutions Consulting, Software Development, Hardware Engineering, Technical Phone Support/Customer Service, Engineering/Internal Systems Support, Marketing, Technical Pre-Sales Support, Sales/Account Management, Software Engineer, Diagnostics Software Engineer, Competitive Analyst, Marketing Programs Specialist, Database Engineer, Unix System Software Engineer, Staff Engineer, Product Engineer
Symantec	http://www.careermosaic.com/cm/symantec	California-, and Massachusetts-based jobs with a major software company	Software Engineer, Manager, SQA Engineering; Product Manager; SQA Analyst; Administrative Assistant; Senior Manager, Development; Administrative Specialist; Senior Manager, Product Marketing; Manager, Channel Marketing; Corporate Account Representative; Technical Writer Specialist; Manager, Business Relations; Product Specialist
Tandem Computers, Inc.	http://www.careermosaic.com/cm/tandem/tm3.html	Jobs from a producer of hardware and software	In the Marketing area: Account Executive, Pre Sales Systems Analyst, Territory Sales Representative. In the MIS area: Data Warehouse Administrators, DSS Client/Server Tool Experts, Data Migration/Warehouse Experts, Solution Architects, Project Managers, Practice Managers

Table 8.1: Selected Employment Opportunities on the Internet (continued)

Job Source	URL	Description	Selected Positions or Types
Tektronix	http://www.tek.com/Tektronix/Careers/welcome.html	Career opportunities, college recruitment with a company that produces measurement devices, color printing and imaging, and video and networking systems	Software Engineers, Mechanical Engineers, Video Hardware/Software Engineers, Media Engineers, Manufacturing Engineers, Information Systems, Procurement/Commodity Specialists, Accounting and Finance, Human Resources, Technical Marketing, Technicians, Administrative Support
Thinking Machines Corporation	http://cmns-sparc.think.com:80/tmhtml/TMC/jobpostings.html	Positions at corporate headquarters and at some customer sites	Program Manager, Commercial Applications Research/Developer, Software Developer, Language/Compiler Developer, Test Engineer, Sales Order Administration Coordinator, Course Developer/Instructor, System Support Engineer
Union Bank	http://www.careermosaic.com/cm/union_bank/ub6.html	Jobs with a San Francisco bank	Financial Services Officer, Business Relationship Officers, Credit Officers, Priority Banking Officers, Defined Contribution Administrators, Financial Analysts, Accounting Officers, Middle Market Commercial Lenders, Lower Middle Market Portfolio Managers, Lower Middle Market Business Development Officers

Table 8.1: Selected Employment Opportunities on the Internet (continued)

Job Source	URL	Description	Selected Positions or Types
US West	http://www.careermosaic.com/cm/uswest/usw7.html	Jobs from a frame relay service provider and advanced data networking solutions	Technical Consultant, Product Marketing Manager, Product Marketing Engineer, Senior Engineer
UUNET Career Opportunities	http://www.alter.net/jobs.html	Major Internet service provider	Capacity Planning/Performance Engineer, Database Architect, Internet Services Engineer, Network Engineer, NT System Administrator, Installation/Testing Engineer, Lab Technician, Security Engineer, Software Engineer, Systems Engineer
WWW Virtual Library: Statistics: Job Announcements	http://www.stat.ufl.edu/users/carol/JobAnnouncements.html	International statistics-related jobs	Director, Professor, Numerate Biologist/Statistician, Physician/Statistician, Biostatistician, Research Scientist, Coordinator Statistical research, Data Analyst

AMI WWW Employment Opportunities & Resumé Postings

http://www.mountain.net/Pinnacle/amiwww/emppage.html

On this single page, you can find links to many of the most popular jobs pages: CareerMosaic (at http://www.careermosaic.com/cm/), Employment Opportunities and Job Resources on the Internet (http://www.wpi.edu/~mfriley/jobguide.html), Interactive Employment Network (http://www.espan.com/), The Job Board (http://www.io.org/~jwsmith/jobs.html), Job Hunting (http://www.virginia.edu), The Monster Board (http://www.monster.com/), and Organizations with in-house job listings (http://ageninfotamu.edu/jobs.html).

Biomedical Engineering Jobs

http://bme.www.ecn.purdue.edu/bme/jobpage.html

This site provides links to a variety of jobs—not just in biomedical engineering. Sites to which this page links are BMEnet listings (http://bme.www.ecn.purdue.edu/bme/jobs), Science Magazine Postings (gopher://gopher.aaas.org:71/11/.classify), and National Institutes of Health (NIH) Vacancies (gopher://gopher.nih.gov:70/11/campus/vacancies).

Interesting Site

The Microbrewery & Brewpub Guide (at http://www.mount.com/mww/mww.html/px/) contains a database of microbreweries and brewpubs throughout the U.S. To search the database, either click on Search the Guide Now or scroll down to the bottom of the page to a clickable U.S. map (see Figure 8.1). When you reach the page for your state, scroll down the alphabetically arranged page to see the entries, which include the name, address, telephone number, and list of products.

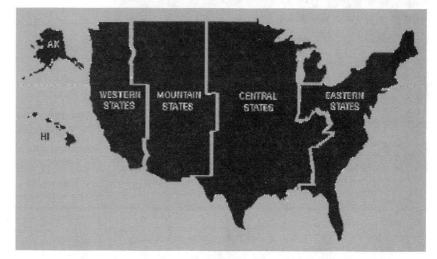

Figure 8.1   Click on a section of the country in which you want to search for a brewpub.

Careerpath.com

http://www.careerpath.com

Careerpath.com is a database of employment advertisements for the current week and the previous week from prominent newspapers: *Boston Globe, Chicago Tribune, Los Angeles Times, The New York Times, San Jose Mercury News,* and *The Washington Post.* To use the service, you must register. Simply click on Register, fill in the online form,

and click on the Register button. Once you have registered, click on Search to look through the want ads for selected newspapers, job types, and keywords. You must select at least one newspaper and a job type or keyword, following the instructions on the search page. To look for jobs in a particular field, select from the Job Categories scroll box. If you are looking for a particular job title, however, type a keyword in the Optional Keywords text box below the Search CareerPath.com button.

Job List

http://asae.org/jobs/

This site contains a list of more than 130 links to Internet job pages. Most links are to academic sites; however, you'll also find addresses for major Internet career services and agencies, commercial sites, government departments, and categories of jobs.

Jobs Listing

http://www.yahoo.com/Business/Employment/Jobs/

This comprehensive list is composed of links to a variety of employment sites: commercial, organizations, government, regional, employment agencies, publications, and job type resources—primarily for jobs in the U.S. Also included are links to career advice and job indexes. Consider making this one of your first stops when starting your job search.

Interesting Site

When you have a few minutes to spend on doing nothing and have a fast graphics browser, visit the Joe Boxer site (at http://www.joeboxer.com/normal/world.html/px/), which sells boxer shorts. You'll never see more imaginative backgrounds, and the artwork isn't too bad either. Figure 8.2 shows a page from our first visit.

This site not only subtly sells Joe Boxer underwear but also includes an excellent page (at http://www.joeboxer.com/utilities.html) of Web page development programs and utilities for viewing movies and graphics files and for listening to sound files for Windows and the Macintosh.

The News and Observer Classified Advertisements

gopher://merlin.nando.net/
11/nando/classads/

At this site, you can browse today's and last Sunday's classified advertisements from the North Carolina *News and Observer*. You can browse or search the listings. If you are browsing, click on 10 to see Administrative/Clerical positions. Other lists provide Lost Pets (1), Real Estate (102), and Office Furniture (103). To search, type a keyword in the text box and press Enter.

Figure 8.2   A typical imaginative page from the Joe Boxer site

The Riley Job Guide

http://www.wpi.edu/~mfriley/jobguide.html

This is probably the best job guide on the Internet. Here you will find what's new, a quick list of the files, a long list of the same files with descriptions, links to other sites, and further information about this guide. Clicking on the Quick List, Long List, or Reciprocal Links brings you to lower parts of the main page; so you can actually scroll down to an area that you want to see, thereby scanning other sites along the way. Margaret F. Riley, the author and coordinator of Networked Resources at Worcester Polytechnic Institute, and a group of experts have done a masterly job of putting this together. Also visit her home page to find some good links to other Internet resources.

Employment Services

This section is composed of Internet job and career services for those looking for a position in a particular field and those searching for generic jobs and help.

Academic Physician and Scientist

gopher://aps.acad-phy-sci.com/

At this site, you can search for positions in academic medicine. This online publication is mailed to physicians, scientists, senior residents, and fellows at medical schools and teaching hospitals. Folders at this site include About Academic Physician and Scientist, an overview; Contacts, names and addresses for the site; and Administrative Positions, Basic Science Positions, Clinical Science Positions, Food and Drug Administration (FDA) Opportunities, and NIH (National Institutes of Health) Opportunities.

America's Job Bank

http://www.ajb.dni.us/ajb/

America's Job Bank, which links 1,800 state Employment Service offices, claims to contain information about 250,000 job openings. To search for a job, click on Job Search on the home page. On the job search page, you can search a national database (Search Nationwide using America's Job Bank), link to a database for a particular state (Links to State Employment Service Web Sites), or look through Employer Maintained Job Listings.

If you don't know your military specialty or job code, click on Self Directed (the most likely choice for those of us without the *Dictionary of Occupational Titles* or knowledge of assigning occupation titles to particular jobs). Then fill in the first form by clicking on an option button and clicking on the Submit Query button. Continue clicking on option buttons and Submit Query buttons and going through pages of forms until you have narrowed the search to the desired job title. It's a good idea to write down the list of selections along the way. You may have to backtrack, using trial and error and changing option button selections until you get to the desired page. Consider saving the final page of a successful search as a bookmark so that you can check it from time to time without going through the network of pages. This site could benefit from a search index that would allow you to look for specific job titles.

Note
You can try to find a job code in the *Dictionary of Occupational Titles* at the Occupational Outlook Handbooks site (gopher://UMSLVMA.UMSL.EDU:70/11// LIBRARY/GOVDOCS/OOHA/OOHB). However, you have to be pretty sure about the exact job title to find the appropriate job code.

California Career & Employment Center

http://www.webcom.com/~career/

This site, which was under construction at the time of this writing, provides employment and other resources. Links include:

◆ Employer Resource Center

◆ Job Seek Resource Center

◆ Entrepreneur Resource Center

◆ Education Resource Center

◆ Worldwide Resumé/Talent Bank

◆ Help Wanted USA Job Database

◆ Post Your Job Openings On-Line

◆ Post Your Resume On-Line

◆ The Career Mall

◆ Other Useful Resources

◆ Hot Job Openings in California

◆ USENET Employment Newsgroups

◆ The Business Mall

Career Mosaic

http://www.careermosaic.com/cm/home.html

Career Mosaic is a gigantic site from Bernard Hodes Advertising, Inc. U.S. and worldwide job information is arranged under these categories (see Figure 8.3): CollegeConnection (information for those who will soon graduate), J.O.B.S. (a searchable database of jobs), information about specific employers, the Online Job Fair (for information systems, engineering, or telecommunications professionals), and much more.

A special feature is the link to a search index of the Usenet Jobs Offered newsgroups, which is updated once a day. To search the index, type a keyword (such as the job type and/or region in which you want to work) using the instructions at the top of the page. Most of the jobs in the search index are in computing, the Internet, and other technical pursuits.

Figure 8.3 Click on a home page link to obtain job information or to find out about this site.

FSG Online

http://www.gate.net/biotech-jobs/

FSG Online claims to be "the Internet's premiere staffing resource for the biotechnology, pharmaceutical, and medical industries." Here you can find a menu with links to a discussion group, jobs registry, salary survey results, and recruiters. In addition, job candidates can search listed jobs, and recruiters can search resumés, and both can obtain other services.

This site also has links to other employment-related pages: recruiting firms, job banks, and Internet indexes. FSG Online charges companies fees for obtaining employees.

Graduate Horizons

http://www.gold.net/arcadia/horizons/

This very large site, which contains career and job information for recent graduates in the United Kingdom, provides links under these categories: Graduate Employers, Careering Ahead, Dates for Your Diary, Careers Hotlist, and TalkBack.

Click on Graduate Employers to see a list of employers arranged under work categories: Accountants; IT & Telecommunications; and Science, Engineering & Manufacturing. Careering Ahead provides guides to careers and job applications: vacation work, writing resumés, and dealing with interviews—for U.K. and U.S. graduates. Dates for Your Diary lists dates for career fairs and other employment-related meetings and events. Careers Hotlist is composed of many employment links from the U.K. and the U.S.

HiTech Careers

http://www.cyberplex.com/hitech

This commercial site provides links to show guides for career fairs and information

about high-tech companies. Also included is a search index of show guides. Categories at this site include New, Events This Week, Upcoming Events, and Recent Events. Clicking on Employers shows you company information and career opportunities as of the last career fair in which the company participated. Clicking on Career Fairs simply shows you another list of upcoming and recent events.

Jobs, Employment, Placement Services, and Programs

gopher:/una.hh.lib.umich.edu:70/00/
inetdirsstacks/acadlist.jobs

From Diane K. Kovacs and The Directory Team, this site is part of the Directory of Scholarly Electronic Conferences, a very large library at the University of Michigan. Here you'll find lists of Internet addresses related to job postings, job-related events, and job-related discussion groups. Jobs are primarily in the academic, engineering, computing, and scientific areas.

Note
If you can't get directly to this address, use the gopher://una.hh.lib.umich.edu:70/11/inetdirsstacks URL and select Jobs, Employment, Placement Services from the list.

The Lendman Group

http://www.infi.net/~lendmnjd/

The Lendman Group runs career fairs, primarily for engineering, computing, and other technical professionals. This commercial site lists career fairs and hints for succeeding at fairs: The Power Resumé and The 11 Career Fair Tools. You can register at this site to forward your resumé to participating companies.

Medsearch America

http://www.medsearch.com/

Medsearch America is a job service for positions in the medical field all over the world. You can search its database by employer, industry, job category, location, title, or keyword. At the time of this writing, occupations ranged from physician to administrative assistant and even some nonmedical titles (buyer, C/C++ programmer, and business consultant) but did not include all health-care occupations (for example, paramedic and emergency medical technician).

NCS Career Magazine

http://www.careermag.com/careermag/

This site provides information about careers—employers as well as a career forum. In addition, you can search for jobs, post your resumé, or post messages and read about Job Search Issues, Workplace Issues, or General Discussion in the forum. Click on Job Openings on the home page to look through recently posted jobs or to look through Usenet newsgroups job postings. Career Links provides a list of many other job-related Internet resources.

Occupational Outlook Handbooks

gopher://UMSLVMA.UMSL.EDU:70/11//LIBRARY/
GOVDOCS/OOHA/OOHB

The gigantic Occupational Outlook Handbooks for 1994–95 and 1992–93 provide information about 333 specific jobs. Here you also can find out about career planning and training (for example, writing a resumé and interviewing techniques). If you are a student, you can read about jobs of the future, and if you are a human resources professional, you can explore the handbooks for detailed job descriptions and job codes. Click on Dictionary of Occupational Titles Coverage for a list of numbers, titles, and cross-references to the Occupational Outlook Handbooks.

The Online Career Center

http://occ.com/

The Online Career Center is a large nonprofit site sponsored by many large corporations and organizations. (See the Company Home Pages starting at http://www.occ.com/occ/Companies/A.html.) Although there is no charge for applicants, member companies and organizations pay a membership fee.

Categories (see Figure 8.4) at this site include Search Jobs (a page with many links that you can browse or search by job, state, or city; you can access company

Figure 8.4   The Online Career Center has many links to job and career resources as well as a search index.

home pages that are alphabetically arranged or arranged by industry), Search Resumés (look through the submitted resumés by keyword or by state), Recruiter's Office (submitting job ads, newsletters, advertising agencies, placement offices, and so on), Career Assistance (hints on finding a job and building your career), OCC "On Campus" (college recruiting, college and university lists, resumés, alumni associations, college placement offices, and so on), Cultural Diversity (links to women and minority pages), Career Fairs & Events (coming events and links to firms that run career expositions), Corporate Membership, How to Enter Resumés, How to Enter Jobs, and About OCC.

Job Search and Employment Opportunities: Best Bets from the Net

http://www.lib.umich.edu/chdocs/employment/

This site lists links to job search and employment opportunities resources on the Internet. The links are listed in a table of contents format so that it's easy to find a particular category. Click on a link to open a page with further information about specific resources, and then click on a link to use the resource. This is an excellent starting point for your first Internet job search.

Compensation and Benefits

Many companies are considering employee ownership for a variety of reasons. Two of the links in this section provide information about employee ownership.

BenefitsLink

http://www.magicnet.net:80/benefits/index.html

This one-page site provides all types of information for those who are interested in

retirement plans and pensions. Using the extensive links, you can read articles and newsletters; view the text of laws, regulations, and codes; subscribe to mailing lists; link to other benefits pages; and much more. Also included are benefits-related downloadable shareware; Potpourri, relevant resources of all types for benefits and human resources professionals and other interested individuals; and a glossary to which you can add terms and descriptions.

Employee Motivation and Empowerment

http://www.saic.org/fed/motivation/

This site, sponsored by the Foundation for Enterprise Development, a nonprofit organization that supports business development, comprises seven articles. Click on a link to read one of the following articles: Creating an Ownership Culture, Be Creative When Rewarding Employees, Build Intrinsic Motivation into Your Incentive Programs, Simple Gestures Count the Most, Evolution of a Cash Bonus System, Asset Appreciation Produces Best Returns, and Small Business Forum—Do Employee Rewards and Recognition Programs Work?

Interesting Site

The $401K Retirement Planner (at http://www.awa.com/softlock/tturner/401kplan.html) is downloadable shareware that you can use to manage your 401(k) plan. This shareware program has versions for Windows, Macintosh, and Powermacs. An Internet-based version is planned. The $401K Retirement Planner analyzes your balance and sets a retirement income using variables such as the rate of inflation, number of years before retirement, and the current contributions.

Foundation for Enterprise Development

http://www.saic.com/fed/

The Foundation for Enterprise Development (FED) is a nonprofit organization that supports business development and employee ownership of businesses. The home page contains these topics: What's New (coming events, articles, and copies of the newsletter), Newsletter, Calendar (either a clickable map or text page of events sponsored by FED and other organizations), Survey, FAQs (a few questions and answers about FED and equity compensationion), the Business Resource Library (very useful articles, primarily dealing with employee ownership and compensation), and the Entrepreneur's Guide to Equity Compensation (an overview and guide to equity-based compensation and options).

Newsletters on Compensation and Retirement Plans

http://www.insworld.com/Newsletter/

This commercial site provides links to 1994 and 1995 *Benefit Insights* newsletters, "a non-technical publication for decision makers." These publications, which seem to be designed for human resources managers and small business principals, include *Keeping Records of Plan Participants*, *Five Reasons to Sponsor a Qualified Plan*, and *Participation Requirements for Qualified Plans*. Scattered throughout these online documents are links to commercial sites and benefits tables.

Salary Guides

http://www.espan.com/salary/salary.html

What salary should you make for your computer-related job? At this site, you can read a salary survey compiled by Source EDP, a national recruiting firm. Other information at this site includes Trends in Computing (Source's predictions for computing

in the next few years), Position Responsibilities (brief job descriptions and links to other pages at this site), and other career-planning information.

Labor Relations

This section presents information about labor relations, primarily from the employee's point of view. Here you'll find resources on labor management, labor laws, links to government agencies, discussion groups, research, and educational resources.

Agricultural Labor Information

gopher://caticsuf.csufresno.edu:70/11/atinet/labor

This comprehensive site is dedicated to agricultural labor, including employment, labor management and training, the Agricultural Labor Relations Board, the Agricultural Personnel Management Program, a wage and benefit survey, the California Economics Database System, the California Labor Commissioner, California Posting Requirements, Federal child labor laws, Farm Labor Contractor Lists for the U.S. and for California, the Migrant & Seasonal Agricultural Protection Act, and information about the Targeted Industries Partnership Program (TIPP).

LaborNet

http://www.igc.apc.org/labornet/

gopher://gopher.igc.apc.org:70/11/labor

LaborNet is made up of labor unions, activists, and organizations. Both the World Wide Web and Gopher sites provide information about unions and organizations, a calendar of events, and publications and news. The Gopher site adds LaborNet's Guide to Internet Resources on Labor (at which some resources are relatively old), and the Web site has links to PeaceNet, EcoNet, ConflictNet, and WomensNet—all of which contain interesting information and links.

Labor Issues

gopher://garnet.berkeley.edu:1250/11/.labor

Part of the Electronic Democracy Information Network (EDIN) Gopher, this section contains folders dealing with labor issues: unions; the U.S. Department of Labor; labor discussion groups, research, and education resources; women (mostly inactive links), gays, and race (the folder icon represents a good link) and the workplace; and other labor-related Gopher sites, mostly with a sympathetic point of view.

Ergonomics

With people working longer and longer hours, comfort in the office has become more and more important. Not only should you use an ergonomically correct chair but the lighting and surroundings are major factors in

performance. This section has links to ergonomic research and resources, articles and papers, checklists and questionnaires, furniture sources, and even office plans.

Cornell Theory Center

http://www.tc.cornell.edu:80/~hedge

This page provides links to a study on preventing carpal tunnel syndrome. (For details of the study, go to http://www.tc.cornell.edu/Research/MetaScience/Articles/CIE/IRI/Hedge/hedge.html.) Also included are articles that cover topics such as posture and back

injuries, carpet emissions, indoor air quality, and office lighting. You need MPEG-playing software and Netscape for optimal viewing.

ErgoWeb

http://www.ergoweb.com

This deceptively small but understandably popular home page provides many ergonomic links. One of the main attractions is an online working draft of the Occupational Safety and Health Administration's (OSHA's) Proposed Ergonomics Protection Standard (307 pages with tables and figures).

A quick way to get an overall view of ErgoWeb's contents and documents is to select Index. Or choose Information Resources for links to periodicals, books, data, standards and guidelines, and a keyword search index.

The ToolBox area displays links to checklists that help to identify hazards and guide you to the right analytical

questionnaire. Questionnaires are detailed and written in "academese," making them difficult to understand. However, if you can translate and answer all the questions, a good analysis is likely.

Public case studies describe solutions to ergonomic problems. Because of confidentiality concerns, private case studies are not available to the general public.

Guidelines for Designing Effective and Healthy Learning Environments

http://wwwetb.nlm.nih.gov/monograp/ergo/index.html

This online document discusses the ergonomics and hazards of the workplace and, most important, gives detailed specifications and measurements for the monitor, seating, acoustics,

Interesting Site

Who says you can't get something for nothing or at least almost nothing? Visit the Freebie Update (at http://www.winternet.com/~julie/freebie.html). Julie Pederson, who compiles the list weekly, finds giveaways primarily from companies promoting their products. On the day I visited, the available goodies included a map of farmers markets, a parent resource guide, a recipe booklet, a packet of jack-o-lantern seeds (for $1), pogs, a health and fitness video, a greeting card from the White House (for a 50th anniversary or 80th birthday), a rock-collecting catalog, and a free pattern for a dog or cat collar.

lighting, and general environment related to the individual occupying a workspace. Additional topics are multiple group learning workstations and training and exercise.

Industrial Ergonomics

http://www.ludd.luth.se/~anthony/ergo/ergo.html

This very small page describes ergonomics in a three-paragraph article and provides links to six good ergonomic sites.

North Carolina Ergonomics Resource Center

http://www2.ncsu.edu/ncsu/CIL/NCERC/index.html

The North Carolina Ergonomics Resource Center, sponsored by the North Carolina Department of Labor and North Carolina State University, "seeks to improve productivity, safety, and well-being of the people of North Carolina, in all sectors of business and industry." At this site, you can learn about programs and services, get information about the center, and link to other ergonomics resources (More Ergonomic Info). When you click on More Ergonomic

Info, the top of the page is composed of three links, and the rest of the page shows the results of WebCrawler, NIKOS, Galaxy, and Gopher searches for ergonomics.

Typing Posture, Ergonomics, Prevention, Treatment

gopher://gopher.mit.edu:3714/0D%20marathon.mit.edu%209000%2027198%20css-tps

This short article covers relaxation, exercises, and treatment for posture problems while typing. Also included is information about adjusting your chair and using the appropriate keyboard.

Occupational Safety

When trying to protect yourself, fellow employees, and subordinates from injury, the best and most up to date safety information is imperative. The excellent sites in this section not only provide occupational safety resources but also give you information about how to maintain safety at home.

Center for Safety in the Arts

http://www.tmn.com/1/Artswire/csa/

This well-designed, nongraphical, and comprehensive site not only provides information about hazards in the arts (such as visual arts, performing arts, and so on), but also contains lists of links on general safety resources. Here you'll find links to health hazard articles and other Internet resources: art hazards, general hazards, precautions (preventives), laws and regulations, resources (links to government agencies, suppliers, a bibliography, and other Internet resources), and other health and safety Gophers and Web sites. Note that next to each link to an article is its size, in kilobytes.

Index of Occupational Safety and Health Resources

http://turva.me.tut.fi/~tuusital/oshlinkstext.html

This well-designed site has links to occupational safety, ergonomics, and emergency management pages as well as links to professional organizations, human-computer interaction, commercial resources, international government agencies, universities and institutes, and other occupational safety and health Internet resources. In most cases, after clicking on a link on the home page, you will find a new page loaded with links.

Safety and Health Sites on the Internet

http://www.osha.gov/safelinks.html

Provided by the Occupational Safety and Health Administration (OSHA), this site contains valuable links to ergonomics, occupational and environmental medicine, U.S. and international government agencies, and other health, safety, and disease control sites.

Safety Information Resources on the Internet

gopher://siri.uvm.edu:70/

From the University of Vermont, this site provides a great deal of information about safety and environmental health. Clicking on the Read Me link displays a page with information about changes to the site. The Index of SIRI File Names is searchable, but if you don't know specific keywords, it's difficult to use. Clicking on SAFETY list information produces a page filled with safety-related resources: organizations, fact sheets, health, and risk and insurance information. Some of the links here are outdated. The News folder is primarily a collection of miscellaneous links. The SIRI file library contains a variety of files (be sure to read the Read Me file first).

Safety Technology Institute

http://willow.sti.jrc.it/

The Safety Technology Institute researches nuclear energy, safeguards, nondestructive analysis, nuclear waste, and so on. It also studies

industrial hazards, earthquake engineering, indoor working environment, and natural environment. Most links on the home page point to articles (with links to other Internet resources) on the institute's research. Both folders at the Gopher site (click on the picture of the gopher) contain additional information about safety.

Near the bottom of the page are links to the World-Wide Web Virtual Library and other useful World Wide Web sites.

Swedish National Institute for Working Life

http://www.nioh.se/nioh.htm

This site, with a few Swedish language pages, provides links to safety and health sites on the Internet, conferences and coming events, and resources for the institute staff. Clicking on Ongoing Projects or Arbline Catalogue opens a search index into which you can type keywords. One of the best links at this site is the KIBIC List of Biomedical Resources - by Subject (at http://www.mic.ki.se/Other.html), a great site that provides a comprehensive list of links to biomedical and medical resources on the Internet.

Swedish Working Life Fund— Case Studies

http://www.nioh.se/alf/alfeng/alfengr.htm

At this site is a list of 15 very interesting case studies from the Swedish Working Life Fund. Topics include healthier workplaces and working environments, retraining, job rotation, and teamwork.

Medical and Health Resources

The sites in this section provide information about health, prevention, and maladies as well as papers, case studies, and links to other health sites. Some resources in this section are the most comprehensive and impressive in the entire book. Not only are the resources in this section worthwhile for businesses, they are quite valuable for family use.

Agency for Toxic Substances and Disease Registry (ATSDR) Science Corner

http://atsdr1.atsdr.cdc.gov:8080/cx.html

At this very large site, you can search for environmental health information on the World Wide Web. You can link to a list of the most popular documents or use a search index. (Click on Examples to see how to construct a search.) Also included are links to long and short documents, press releases, case studies, and miscellaneous toxic substance and public health sites. In addition, this site provides links to Internet tutorials and papers, government agencies, organizations, and a great deal more. This site is not as well organized as it could be. Its managers should consider breaking it up into pages of related links.

KIBIC Biomedical Information Resources & Services

http://www.mic.ki.se/Other.html

From the Karolinska Institute, this site provides a comprehensive list of international links to biomedical and medical topics such as chemistry, biophysics, radiology, several biology fields, pathology, diseases (this page is very thorough), pharmacology, toxicology, occupational safety and health, medical and scientific ethics, telemedicine, animals and plants, and related organizations. Click on any link on the home page to reveal a page containing many more links. For those interested in medicine, science, and related fields as well as those who work in those areas, this outstanding site is well worth exploring.

Center for Injury Research and Control

http://www.pitt.edu/~hweiss/injury.htm/

This long page of Internet resources is directed at health-care professionals and others who are interested in injury research and control. The Main Index lists many injury-related resources—both auxiliary sites and injury-specific—and other Internet sites. Injuries covered at this site are related to fire safety and burns, transportation, poisonings, violence, firearms, safety and occupational safety, rural safety, and others. To go to a site, either click on a category button (see Figure 8.5) or scroll down the page.

Health Services/Technology Assessment Text

http://text.nlm.nih.gov/

From the U.S. National Institutes of Health's (NIH) National Library of Medicine, this site provides access to six databases: AHCPR Supported Guidelines, ATIS (HIV/AIDS Technical Information), NIH Warren G. Magnuson Clinical Research Studies, NIH Conferences and Workshops, PHS Guide to Clinical Preventive Services, and SAMHSA/CSAT Treatment Improvement Protocol (TIP).

When you select a database and click on the Submit button, a query screen appears. Type a diagnosis, sign, or symptom, and then click on the Start Search button.

From the results screen (see Figure 8.6), click on a link to reveal a list of articles (see Figure 8.7).

HospitalWeb

http://dem0nmac.mgh
.harvard.edu/hospitalweb.html

This site, from John Lester at the Massachusetts General Hospital, is a list of hospitals that have World Wide Web sites. Links are listed under states (in the U.S.) or countries. At the time of this writing, this growing list included 117 U.S. hospitals and 53 hospitals outside the U.S. At the bottom of this single page are links to medical school lists, lists of medical resources, and medical companies or organizations.

Martindale's Health Science Guide

http://www-sci.lib.uci
.edu/HSG/HSGuide.html

This gigantic site, created by Jim Martindale, an inventor, scientist, and politician, contains links to a great deal of medical information that laypersons, students, and medical professionals can use. The author claims that the site contains more than 12,300 teaching files, more than 19,300 medical cases, 273 courses/textbooks, thousands of graphic displays, and more than 3,400 MPEG movies.

Figure 8.5   Click on a button to go to a particular injury-related or safety page.

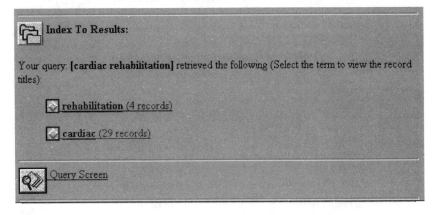

Figure 8.6   Click on a link resulting from the search to see a list of papers related to your query.

On the home page, you'll find links to medical, dental, veterinary, pharmacy, nursing, public health, nutrition, and allied health centers. (This site is so all-encompassing that at the bottom of the page, you'll even find links to a reference desk, international services,

- 95-H-0051: Evaluation and Therapy of Heart Disease in Patients not Participating in Research (Teaching Protocol)

- 95-H-0048: Tomographic Myocardial Wall Motion Analysis in Patients with Myocardial Ischemia and in Normal Subjects

- 95-H-0047: Training Protocol: Evaluation of Patients with Heart Disease Not Eligible for Research Protocols

- 94-N-0186: Positron Emission Tomographic (PET) Scanning of Sympathetic Innervation and Function in Patients with Neurocardiologic Disorders

Figure 8.7   Click on a link to read a paper about your query.

a law center, and a science center.) Categories within the medical center are anatomy & histology, anesthesiology & surgery, clinical—primary care, medical imaging, medical law, pathology & virology, pediatrics & gynecology, radiology, and international support services centers.

Medical/Educational Internet Sites

http://www.med.ucalgary.ca:70/1/servers

This long list of medical sites, from the University of Calgary, provides links to a variety of resources: from organizations such as the American Heart Association and the Canadian Medical Association to information about specific maladies and medical specialties. Also included are links to standards, tutorials, newsletters, educational institutions, and laboratories. Simply scroll down the alphabetically arranged list until you find the link that you want.

Medical Education Information Center (MEDIC)

http://hyrax.med.uth.tmc.edu/home.htm

The multimedia medical information service from the Department of Pathology and Laboratory Medicine at the Houston Medical School

provides a variety of medical information. Categories on the home page are Introduction, Education Programs (courses and schedules at the medical school), Health Care Professional, Medical Informatics, Pathology and Laboratory Medicine, Health Explorer, MI-WAY: Medical Information Super Highway, and What's New in Medicine. The most valuable link for the layperson is Health Explorer, which provides articles on healthy living, diseases and illnesses, and other medical topics.

Medical Education Page

http://www.primenet.com/~gwa/med.ed/

This well-designed site is managed by Gregory Allen, a medical student, and is designed for medical and premedical students. Laypersons can benefit from visiting this site, which provides many links in these categories: News, FAQs & FTP Sites; Medical Indices; Medical Specialties Page; Interview Feedback Page; Medical Reference; Medical Courses Page; Medical Schools on the Net; and Miscellaneous Links.

Medical Matrix: A Guide to Internet Medical Resources

http://www.kumc.edu:80/mmatrix/

The Medical Matrix is a comprehensive list of clinical medical resources directed to medical professionals but useable by the layperson. On the home page, you will find a table of 24 categories of links. Click on a link to open a page of related links and information. One asset of this site is the description that accompanies each of the links below the home page table of links.

Note

Medical Matrix also has a Gopher site at gopher://una.hh.lib.umich.edu:70/00/inetdirsstacks/ medclin:malet.

Multilingual Glossary of Technical and Popular Medical Terms

http://allserv.rug.ac.be/~rvdstich/eugloss/welcome.html

This project, commissioned by the European Commission, is a database that you can browse by language (Danish, Dutch, English, French, German, Italian, Portuguese, and Spanish) and view brief descriptions of medical terms. To search for a term or browse the database, click on Browse by language, choose a language, click on a letter of the alphabet, and browse the resulting list. Each term consists of the popular term and its technical equivalent. There are two ways to use the list: viewing part of the database or viewing the entire glossary.

To access the glossary entry for a particular term, click on the letter with which it starts or click on the L icon preceding the letter. Then click on a G icon to view the glossary entry for the term. To view the multiligual lemma collection (a term's translation in all the languages supported at this site), click on the M icon.

To access the entire glossary (more than 20 kilobytes), click on Browse in the glossary. Then scroll down the list, clicking on the L icon to see a description.

Note

You can also find a list of medical terminology and abbreviations at http://www.fishnet.net/~bctr/ m_terms.html.

Multimedia Medical Reference Library

http://www.tiac.net/users/jtward/index.html

From Jonathan Tward, an MD/Ph.D student at Tufts University, this site, available in a graphical and a text version, provides a variety of medical information—especially for medical students. The main categories are Comprehensive Medical Information (the best link at this site, an alphabetically arranged list of diseases and specialties), Medical School Curriculum, Medical Images and Movies, Medical On-Line Audio Recordings, Medical Software for Download, Medical School Homepages, Research Journals (one journal), Hospitals from HospitalWeb, Other Medical Indices, and Search the Internet.

OncoLink

http://cancer.med.upenn.edu/

Presented by the University of Pennsylvania, OncoLink is one of the most complete oncological sites on the Internet. At the top of the home page are buttons that point to What's New, Cancer News, Meetings, Journals, Search, and Statistics. On the main menu, you'll find eight links: Disease Oriented Menus; Medical Specialty Oriented Menus (for both people and animals); Psychosocial Support and Personal Experiences; Cancer Causes, Screening, and Prevention; Clinical Trials; Global Resources for Cancer Information; Frequently Asked Questions (FAQ) about Cancer; and Financial Issues for Patients. Each item on the menu leads to a list of cancer-related links.

The Physician's Guide to the Internet

http://www.webcom.com/pgi

This site provides links for physicians who are making their first trips on the Internet. Major categories include Physician Lifestyle, Clinical

Practice, Postgraduate Education, FunStuff, New Physician, Other Medical Internet Gateways, and Internet Tips and Tutorials. Others also can benefit from using this site; physicians aren't the only people who must attend to personal finance and family life, travel, restaurants, wine, and buying a house.

Poisons Information Database

http://biomed.nus.sg/PID/PID.html

The valuable but incomplete Poisons Information Database, from the National University of Singapore, provides links to information about plant, snake, and animal toxins and to directories of antivenoms, toxicologists, and 226 poison-control centers worldwide. If the author added a search index, this site would be much more worthwhile.

The Virtual Hospital

http://indy.radiology.uiowa.edu/VirtualHospital.html

This very popular and comprehensive site provides information for patients, health-care providers, and other interested visitors. You can find links and information under four categories: Welcome (information about the site, the College of Medicine and University of Iowa Hospitals and Clinics, and what's new), For Patients (health and hospital staff information), For Healthcare Providers (teaching tools, clinical guidelines, and publications), and Beyond the Virtual Hospital (links to other University of Iowa resources and other health resources on the Internet).

Also included at this site is a searchable index and an outline, which shows you all the links at this site, presented in three levels. The outline might be the fastest way to get to the information that you desire.

World Health Organization (WHO)

http://www.who.ch/

The World Health Organization (WHO) is an international organization that came into existence in 1948. WHO directs international health work, assists governments in strengthening their health services, and promotes the prevention and control of diseases through research and improving housing, nutrition, and so on.

At this site, you can learn about WHO's programs; read the World Health Report, press releases, and newsletters; access the WHO Statistical Information System (WHOSIS); get vaccination requirements and health advice for international travel; and link to the WHO Gopher server and other health-related Internet resources.

World-Wide Web Virtual Library: Biosciences—Medicine

http://golgi.harvard.edu/biopages/medicine.html

This site provides links to medical and bio-medical Internet resources as well as indexes and catalogs with which you can start your own search. Most of this long page consists of links to academic institutions all over the world. In addition, you can find information on particular diseases and injuries, health issues, government and commercial sites, links to journals, and a variety of medical resources, including veterinary medicine, pharmacology, dentistry, death, dermatology, eye research, and so on.

Yahoo's Health Resources

http://www.yahoo.com/Health/

Yahoo, one of the premiere sources of information on the Internet, presents a health page loaded with a variety of health-related links. Categories include alternative medicine, commercial health products, companies, conferences, death and dying, dentistry, disabilities, diseases and conditions, education, emergency services, EMF health issues, employment, environmental health, fitness, general health, geriatrics and aging, health administration, health care, institutes, insurance, magazines, medicine, mental health, news, nursing, nutrition, occupational safety and health, pharmacology, policy, public health and safety, sexuality, support groups, travel, weight issues, women's health, and workplace.

Health Care

In this section, you'll find out how to take care of your health and deal with health problems. Using these resources, you'll learn how to find health providers as well as informative articles about diet, nutrition, childcare, and specific health issues.

Agency for Health Policy and Research Guidelines (AHCPR) Consumer Guides

http://text.nlm.nih.gov/ahcpr/guidesp.html

This site presents links to 17 guidebooks about various health issues primarily directed at consumers. To view a guidebook, click on the link, and then click on an icon next to Table of Contents to jump to a document onscreen. All the documents are actually on one long page, however; so when you save or print, you can do so from any part of the document.

HEALTHLINE

http://healthline.umt.edu:700

Sponsored by the University of Montana Student Health Services, HEALTHLINE is loaded with links to a variety of health resources from diet to sleep, from labeling of food and health products to dealing with a natural disaster. The top part of the page is an article containing many links, and the bottom part consists of a list of links. Much of the information is related to the University of Montana, but a great deal is important for anyone researching a particular health issue.

Iowa Health Book

http://vh.radiology.uiowa.edu/

From the Virtual Hospital at the University of Iowa, this site presents links to articles by title, organs and/or systems of the body (breast, cardiovascular, genitourinary, hematologic, immunologic, musculoskeletal, neurological/psychiatric, and pulmonary), or hospital department. Accessing articles by title is probably the fastest method of finding the appropriate subject matter.

North Jersey Health Care Guide

http://www.bergen.com/health95/

The North Jersey Health Care Guide comprises articles about health topics. Although it's directed at residents of northern New Jersey, there is plenty here for anyone. The most important links are Index (a list of links to articles), Health Tips (a page of information about nutrition, kids, cancer, and stress), Look It Up (with an index to the documents at this site and SavvySearch, another tool that searches the Internet), and Other Health and Medical Links.

Maladies

This section provides links for those with particular illnesses and health problems or caregivers. Using these resources, you can learn more about a particular malady, how to prevent it, or how to live with it.

AIDS Education Training Project (AETP)

http://www.ach.uams.edu/~bnd/aids/

At this site, developed by the Arkansas Children's Hospital and the University of Arkansas, you'll find information about the AIDS Education Training Project (AETP) as well as links to 6 papers about HIV/AIDS and to 10 other AIDS World Wide Web sites: indexes, international programs, the Centers for Disease Control (CDC) AIDS Clearinghouse, and information for caregivers. You'll also find a link to the misc.health.aids newsgroup.

Attention Deficit Disorder (ADD) Page

http://www-leland.stanford.edu/group/dss/
Information.by.disability/Attention.Deficit.Disorder

This short text-only page provides links to Internet resources for Attention Deficit Disorder (ADD) and Attention Deficit Hyperactivity Disorder (ADHD). Among the links here are Web sites, newsgroup archives, the home page of the Children and Adults with Attention Deficit Disorder (CHADD) organization, several FAQs, medications, and a checklist for adults who think that they may have ADD. Also included is a link to Project PURSUIT (at http://pursuit.rehab.uiuc.edu/), a site formed to "help students with disabilities pursue careers in science, engineering, and mathematics."

Centers for Disease Control and Prevention AIDS Clearinghouse

gopher://cdcnac.aspensys.com:72/11/

The Centers for Disease Control (CDC) National AIDS Clearinghouse is packed with information about HIV/AIDS geared toward those who work in prevention, treatment, and support. Included is a daily summary, articles, statistics, news from involved U.S. agencies, information about the disease, workplace issues, prevention, testing, counseling, and treatment. Also included are information about resources, hotlines, and links to other AIDS-related Gopher servers.

Chronic Fatigue Syndrome/Myalgic Encephalomyelitis

http://metro.turnpike.net/C/cfs-news/

This long page provides a variety of links mixed with information about Chronic Fatigue Syndrome/Myalgic Encephalomyelitis (CFS/ME). The headings under which links are arranged are News, Information, Discussion, Other CFS-Related Pages, Dutch Resources, and Canadian Resources. At the top of the page is a link to a quick index. If you click on the link, a page with a short list of CFS/ME links and no other information appears.

Computer-Related Repetitive Strain Injury

http://engr-www.unl.edu/ee/eeshop/rsi.html

This illustrated article, written by Paul Marxhausen, who has repetitive strain injury himself, is an introduction to the malady. Topics include What's RSI? Symptoms, Prevention, What If?

Learn More, Network Sites, and FindADoc (miscellaneous resources, including lists of clinics and Internet indexes). Also included are excellent links to ergonomics and health sites.

The Epilepsy Web Page

http://www.swcp.com/~djf/epilepsy/index.html

This long and comprehensive page provides a variety of information about epilepsy. Links are arranged under these categories: Epilepsy Specific, Clinical Trials (one link at the time of this writing), Neuroscience and Neurobiology, Pharmaceutical Information (one link to the Pharmaceutical Information Network at http://pharminfo.com/), Disability Resources, and Related WEB Pages. Either click on a link to go to that category or scroll down the page until you reach the category.

Instant Access Treasure Chest

http://128.172.170.24/ld/ld.html

The Instant Access Treasure Chest, the Guide to Learning Disabilities (LD) and Foreign Language Learning, is a long education-related page of Internet resources for Attention Deficit Disorder, Attention Deficit Hyperactivity Disorder, Dyslexia, Auditory Deficits, Visual Deficits, and so on. Clicking on a link moves down the page to the appropriate heading. Under the heading are links to Internet resources: papers, centers, organizations, corporate sites, and government agencies. Whether or not you are an educator, you can find useful information here.

One A.D.D. Place—Attention Deficit Disorder

http://www.iquest.net/greatconnect/oneaddplace/

This graphical site provides a variety of information about Attention Deficit Disorder (ADD). On this long page, links are arranged under these categories: Welcome to One ADD Place, What's NEW, General Adult ADD Symptom Checklist, Scattered Thoughts (Famous People with ADD, Multiple Intelligences, Values and Lifestyles Questionnaire, and Are You an Adrenaline Junkie?), the Children and Adults with Attention Deficit Disorders (C.H.A.D.D.) organization, and Other ADD-Related Resources on the Internet. In addition, you can click on Library to access a short page of papers, articles, and references.

A Patient's Guide to Carpal Tunnel Syndrome

http://www.cyberport.net/mmg/cts/ctsintro.html

A Patient's Guide to Carpal Tunnel Syndrome, created by the Medical Multimedia Group (MMG), consists of a home page of links to documents on anatomy, diagnosis, and treatment and to

the MMG home page. At the bottom of the page is a link to the Carpal Tunnel Syndrome frequently asked questions (CTSFAQ). Clicking on a link reveals a page with illustrations and links to other illustrations. This site is well designed and attractive.

Note

The Medical Multimedia Group also provides patient's guides to knee problems (at http://www.cyberport.net/mmg/knee/knees.html) **and low back pain** (at http://www.cyberport.net/ mmg/back/backpain.html).

Repetitive Stress Injuries

http://hoohana.aloha.net/~billpeay/TECHT08.html

This site presents an eight-article series by Bill Peay. Written for laypersons, these articles describe the anatomy and treatment of repetitive stress injuries (RSI). Also included are links to other RSI pages.

Exercise and Prevention

Exercise and diet are important ways of preventing illness. The sites in this section provide questions and answers, articles, specific exercise routines, and diets.

The Abdominal Training FAQ

http://www.dstc.edu.au/RDU/staff/nigel-ward/abfaq/abdominal-training.html

This site, devoted to training the abdominal area, provides versions of archived newsgroup messages from misc.fitness.misc, misc.fitness.weights, misc.fitness.aerobics, misc.answers, and news.answers. You can use the information at this site in two ways: You can go to a single large page, or you can go to multiple small documents with links to the other documents.

Exercise Questions and Answers

http://www.hoptechno.com/exercise.htm

This online article, written by Joanne Larsen, a dietitian, answers questions about exercise and diet. Also included are the reasons that some programs work and why you feel the way you do during and after exercise.

Fitness Gopher Site

gopher://gopher.uiuc.edu/11/UI/CSF/health/heainfo/Fitness

This site contains four links: a short article on Body Composition; nine articles on various Exercise—Guidelines, Programs, and Resources; a Fitness Resources page (just for the Champaign-Urbana, IL, area); and nine articles on injuries.

N.E.W. Start Guidelines

http://www.wid.com/user/new-start/exer.html

This site provides information about an exercise and diet plan developed by Howard Widensky. The author underwent open heart surgery at an early age and is a prophet for a no-fat diet and a solid exercise program. At this site, you will find valuable and easy-to-understand information on both diet and exercise.

The Workout from Hell

http://www.dtek.chalmers.se/Climbing/Training/TWFH.html

This article, by John Long, details the routines for those serious about successfully participating in sports and/or keeping "superfit." After an introduction, the author writes about the rules governing this workout and phases of the program. This is for serious athletes only.

Americans with Disabilities

Those empowered to hire for a business should know the laws dealing with the disabled as well as the resources that provide information about laws, education, and specific disabilities. The sites in this section can help you learn about hiring the disabled and helping them to become useful and happy employees.

Deaf World Wide Web Server

http://web.cal.msu.edu/deaf/deafintro.html

This comprehensive site at Michigan State University (MSU) provides deafness information and resources for students at MSU and for others—in Michigan and outside. On the home page are six links: Educational Deaf Resources, Electronic Deaf Resources, MSU Deaf Information, Michigan Deaf

Resources, General Deaf Information, and Deaf Alert (student projects). Clicking on a link brings you to a page with a link to MSU's Deaf Gopher. Also included are links to Deaf World Wide Web servers and the Deaf Gopher.

Disabled Students of Stanford (DSS)

http://www-leland.stanford.edu/group/dss/

This site, managed by the Disabled Students of Stanford University (DSS), provides excellent information and links to other disability sites. For example, click on General Information to go to a page of links to university disability sites, laboratories, programs, and more. Or click on Information by Disability to access pages for Attention Deficit Disorder, Blind, Deaf, Learning Disabilities, and Polio. At the time of this writing, parts of the site seemed to be under construction.

DO-IT Server

gopher://hawking.u.washington.edu:70/11/

The DO-IT (Disabilities, Opportunities, Internetworking, and Technology) site, funded by the National Science Foundation and administered by the University of Washington, provides information for disabled people desiring to participate in science, engineering, and mathematics education and careers. At this site are links to Internet, science, engineering, mathematics, education, and college programs for the disabled. Also included are many other links to other disability-related resources.

Electronic Rehabilitation Resource Centre

gopher://sjuvm.stjohns.edu/11/disabled

This large site, from St. John's University, not only contains disability and medical information but also provides links to related resources: organizations, publications (a very long list of links), laws, and government agencies. Included at this site are links to a dyslexia database, adaptive and assistive devices, the national clearing house for rehabilitation training materials, an autism archive, repetitive strain injury, chronic fatigue syndrome information, and more.

Internet Disability Resources and Links

gopher://lib-gopher.lib.indiana.edu/11/disability/internet-lspd

This site from the University of Indiana-Bloomington provides four links to Internet disability resources: LISTSERVs concerning Persons with Disabilities (a long text file of Listservs and instructions for subscribing), Services to the Blind and Physically Handicapped (from the Library of Congress Marvel system), Cornucopia of Disability Information (CODI; many resources and statistics from SUNY Buffalo), and the Americans with Disabilities Act (the text from the University of California at Santa Cruz).

University of Minnesota Disability Gopher

gopher://disserv.stu.umn.edu:70/1

This Gopher server is designed to provide services for the disabled at the University of Minnesota. In addition to local resources, this site contains links to Project LEEDS—Leadership Education to Empower Disabled Students, a national program, and Other Disability Resources on the Internet, a comprehensive directory of disability sites including these categories: Career Development Resources; Disability-Specific Gophers; Documents, Periodicals & Other Resources; General Disability Organizations and Resources; Health & Rehabilitation Resources; and Technology & Disability Resources.

Contacting the Outside World

The importance of the impression you make on the people with whom you communicate cannot be stressed enough. A letter with an inaccurate address can stop prospective clients before they even read your pitch. Until lately, finding a zip code involved going to the local post office, buying two large volumes, or making a telephone call to a coworker, postal worker, or even the person to whom you are addressing a mailing. When making a large mailing, multiply that scenario by 10 or 20. This section provides Internet sites that you can use to find an area code, zip+4 code, country code, or even the latitude and longitude of a particular town or city.

What if you are new to an area and want to find an office supplies vendor or computer repair business quickly? Some sites in this section can help you find your new resources in just a few minutes.

555-1212.COM

http://www.555-1212.com/ACLOOKUP.HTML

At this easy-to-use site, you can look up a business in a particular area. The first step of the search provides the area code for a city or town. If that's all the information you want, you can stop right there.

To start the search, type at least three letters of the city name and click on the Click This button. When the results appear and if you want to find a particular company, click on the link to the area code. Then you can click on a letter to look for a business category starting with that letter, view all the business categories (the best choice since this site is under construction), or type the name of the business for which you are looking.

AmeriCom Long Distance Area Decoder

http://www.xmission.com/~americom-aclookup

AmeriCom, a long-distance provider in Utah, offers a very useful search index of area codes and country codes worldwide. Type the name of a city (required for the search to work) and state and/or country in the text boxes, and click on the Submit button. The results, at the bottom of the page, show the city, state, country, area code (if the city is in the U.S.), country code, and AmeriCom's rates per minute.

AT&T Internet Toll-Free 800 Directory

http://www.tollfree.att.net/textonly.html

http://www.tollfree.att.net/

The AT&T Internet Toll-Free 800 Directory lists toll-free telephone numbers for many businesses. Telephone numbers are listed under letters of the alphabet. So, for instance, to look up office supplies, click on O, wait for a long page to load, scroll down the page, and click on Office Supplies. The next page to appear either provides a list of links so that you can narrow your search or a text-only page of telephone numbers and company names.

Country Codes

gopher://info.mcc.ac.uk:70/00/miscellany/country_codes

This text-only page lists International Organization for Standardization (ISO) 3166 country codes and two- and three-letter abbreviations. For example, using this list the United States is US, USA, or 840.

Geographic Nameserver

http://www.mit.edu:8001/geo

At this site from MIT, you can look up zip codes for cities and towns using a database from the University of Michigan. Either type the city or town name or the name along with its state (city and state must be separated by a comma and a space) and press Enter. The resulting information can include the city or town name, the county in which it is located, the state or province, the country, latitude, longitude, population elevation, and zip code.

NYNEX Interactive Yellow Pages

http://www.niyp.com/

This well-designed commercial site not only provides telephone numbers of companies advertising in the NYNEX (New York–New England) yellow pages but also includes listings for companies across the U.S. NYNEX claims to list 16.5 million businesses. You can search by Business Name or Business Type. Select the type of search, select the states in which you want to look, scroll down the page, type a name or business type, and click on the Search button. When the results appear, you can either narrow your search further (by city/town, street, zip code, or area code) or view a few listings at a time. The results include only the name and telephone number. To see a list of addresses for a group of businesses, click on Click here for detailed address information under a group of entries. NYNEX provides a link with which you can get more information.

Other links include Hot Sites, Your World (links to many Web sites), Message Center and Link Me (with which you can communicate with NYNEX and request a link to your Web site), and Stuff (strictly NYNEX company information and plans for the future).

Also included is a link to the Directory Store from which you can get information about ordering telephone books (Interactive, Specialty, International, Domestic, and Canada) from around the world. Unfortunately, you still have to make a telephone call to place your order.

U.S. Geography Names Database

gopher://gopher.stanford.edu:4320/7geo%20search

gopher://gopher.bucknell.edu:4320/7geo%20search

This is a good site with which to get interesting information about a city or town. Type the name of the town or its zip code in the text box and press Enter. The resulting page lists all the towns or cities with that name. Click on the desired town and state link to see a document that lists some or all of the following information: City, State/Province, Nation, Feature Code, Latitude, Longitude, 1980 Population, Elevation, ZIP Codes, and Counties. Note that if you type a popular name, the connection might "time out" (that is, log you off without completing the search). In that case, find its zip code using another site in this section, and try this site again using the zip code instead of the name.

U.S. Telephone Area Codes

gopher://gopher.stanford.edu:4320/7areacode

gopher://odie.niaid.nih.gov:70/77/deskref/.areacode/index

These identical search indexes provide area codes for many cities and regions in the U.S. Just type the name of a city and press Enter. You'll either get specific information or a list of regions from which you can choose to refine your search. When the results appear, don't bother to click on Search Results in a file. The file contains the same information that you see on your screen.

ZIP+4 Code Directory

http://www.usps.gov/ncsc/

At this site, you can type an address, a city, and a state and get a zip+4 code or type a zip code and get the city and state. You'll have better luck if you are searching for a medium- or large-sized business rather than a small one.

Also included at this site is a link to documents listing official postal service abbreviations for states and street suffixes (surprisingly, this is very long), information about addressing your mailings properly, and a link to the U.S. Postal Service home page. You also can find U.S. Postal Service abbreviations at gopher://gopher .Princeton.EDU:70/00/.files/university/postal.

Minorities in Business

Minorities in business can find valuable resources when surfing the Net. Using the sites in this section, you can find government programs and resources, discussions and messages, links to minority businesses, and colleges and universities that have predominantly minority students.

AFFAM-L: Affirmative Action News and Updates

gopher://garnet.berkeley.edu:1250/11/.race/.affam

This extremely busy site contains the archives for the AFFAM-L listserv. At the time of this writing, links included messages for dates ranging from March to October 1995. Here you'll find many affirmative action topics—from equality for women in country clubs to texts of speeches.

ARC Race File

gopher://garnet.berkeley.edu:1250/11/.race/

Part of the Electronic Democracy Information Network (EDIN) Gopher, this busy site is devoted to studying economic and sociological information related to race. Folders include information about trends in communities of color, race Gophers on the Internet (these links are old and no longer viable), African-Americans, Asian-Americans, Latinos, Native Americans, Fourth World, Affirmative Action, Environmental Racism & Ecojustice, and Immigration Issues. Although very little information, other than Affirmative Action, applies to business topics, this site provides a good background.

FEDIX/MOLIS

http://web.fie.com/

The Federal Information Exchange (FIE), sponsored by the U.S. Department of Energy, started the Minority On-Line Information Service (MOLIS) in 1990. MOLIS provides research information to Historically Black Colleges and Universities (HBCUs) and Hispanic Serving Institutions (HSIs).

At this important site, you'll find links to Federal Opportunities (opportunities and information from U.S. government agencies for minority and other businesses), Minority Colleges & Universities (links to educational institutions), Used Equipment (free or leased equipment from U.S. government departments for academic institutions), Electronic Research Administration (a demonstration program of automated processing of university research applications to the Department of Energy and information about Electronic Data Interchange [EDI]), and Association Web Pages & Traditional BBS Systems. Also included are announcements of upcoming events and new features at this site.

Minority Business Development Administration (MBDA)

http://www.doc.gov/resources/MBDA_info.html

A division of the Department of Commerce, the MBDA supports minority-owned businesses. Click on What is the Minority Business Development Agency to learn about its services, the groups that it serves, and its mission. To find an MBDA office near you, click on Regional Minority Business Development Centers. Click on MBDA Public Affairs Division to subscribe to the MBDA electronic bulletin.

Minority Business and Professional Directory (MBPD)

http://www.commerce.net:80/directories/companies/minority.business/

This site is "a magazine style directory/yellow pages of the minority/woman-owned business community. The publication consists of classified advertisements of minority-owned businesses and professional services—plus advertisements by major corporations and government agencies."

You can search this site in two ways: by entering keywords in a search index or by browsing the directory. There is enough content here so that either type of search works well. Random searches of the directory showed that most vendors were located in northern California.

To add your business to the MBPD, get the address information at http://www.minbizdir.com/.

Resources for Diversity

http://www.nova.edu/Inter-Links/diversity.html

This site is composed of 16 links to minority and women Internet resources. Here you can link to African Studies, Chicago-LatinoNet, Disability Information, Feminism Resources, Gay and Lesbian Resources, Native American, and Latin resources.

The Universal Black Pages

http://www.gatech.edu/bgsa/blackpages.html

The home page of this site is composed of a table of contents with 17 links, from Life to Entertainment, and from Businesses to Engineering, Science, and Technology. Almost every link on the home page leads to a long list of valuable Internet resources for African-American men and women.

Women in Business

The sites in this section provide career information for women—especially for those interested in traditionally male occupations—as well as surveys, links to other Internet resources for women, and helpful hints that any businessperson will find useful.

Exploring Your Future in Math and Science

http://www.cs.wisc.edu/~karavan/afl/home.html

This attractive and informative page, a project by Andrew Frank-Loron, Jennifer Handrich, and Chia-Chen Wu, is composed of a short paper on the reasons women are "less likely to enter professions in math and science" and links to related Internet resources, including How Much Money Is in This for Me? (a salary survey from the January 1995 issue of *Working Woman*), Huge List of Other WWW Resources for Women in Science (actually, it's not that huge), and Even Bigger List of Internet Listservers.

Interesting Site

The NetWatch Top Ten Links (at http://www.pulver.com/netwatch/topten/topten.htm) provides an interesting mix of excellent links organized as follows: <u>Art</u>, <u>Brainfood</u>, <u>Broadcasting</u>, <u>Cyberdrinks</u>, <u>Education</u>, <u>Electronic Music</u>, <u>Family</u>, <u>Gay Interest</u>, <u>Intelligent Agents/Information Agents</u>, <u>Interesting Devices on the Net</u>, <u>Marketing</u>, <u>Media on the Net</u>, <u>Music Performance</u>, <u>Net Access for Disabled</u>, <u>Net Tools</u>, <u>Printing Resources on the Internet</u>, <u>Real Estate</u>, <u>Science</u>, <u>Science Fiction</u>, <u>Senior Issues</u>, <u>Software Development</u>, <u>Telecommunications</u>, <u>Voice/Video on the Net</u>, <u>VRML</u>, and <u>Women's Issues</u>.

Click on Women's Issues to go to a page of links accompanied by brief descriptions. On this page, you can find valuable business links, information about women on the Internet, and other women-related sites. Or click on Net Access for Disabled to access a list of both academic and commercial disability sites. Be sure to visit this site, and be prepared to spend some time here.

Gender Issues Directory

http://cpsr.org/cpsr/gender/gender.html

gopher://gopher.cpsr.org:70/11/cpsr//gender

The World Wide Web site for the Computer Professionals for Social Responsibility (CPSR) organization provides links to articles about gender issues, many related to women in computing. Other links deal with feminism, communication differences between men and women, and minority information.

CPSR's Gopher site has links to articles and information about gender and job status (especially computer science) issues. Included are links to articles, bibliographies, Internet resources, and newsgroups. Note that the two links with dates refer to 1994 events.

Gender Issues in Technology

gopher://porpoise.oise.on.ca:70/11/resources/IRes4Ed/resources/gender/Gender%20Issues%20in%20Technology

This small site tackles gender issues in technology: Gender Issues in Computing, Gender Issues in Design and Technology, and Gender Issues in Networking. Click on <u>About Gender Issues in Technology</u> for an overview of the contents of this site. Click on other links to display presentations, discussions, and papers. Note that the contents of this site are uneven; some links lead to empty pages and others have moved, but most working links provide excellent information.

What Every Woman Student Needs to Know about the Engineering Workplace

http://www.webfoot.com/advice/women.in.eng.html

This long article by Kaitlin Duck Sherwood describes the pitfalls and rewards of women working in a formerly male field—engineering. Regardless of your occupation or gender, reading this article can help you get along in the workplace. Also included here are links to other work-related Internet resources.

The Women's Page

http://www.mit.edu:8001/people/sorokin/women/index.html

This long page of links is a generic women's resource with many links that might help a businesswoman or someone planning a career. Business-related categories include <u>Women in Computer Science and Engineering</u>, <u>Women in Academia and Industry</u>, and <u>Information Clearinghouses and References</u>.

Women's Web

http://www.sfgate.com/new/examiner/womensweb.html

This page, from the *San Francisco Chronicle* and the *San Francisco Examiner*, provides stories about women in the news as well as a list of Internet resources that provide information for women. The links include news, guides to the Internet, organizations, and other women's Internet pages. At the time of this writing, this site was under construction; some of the Internet links were no longer viable.

Online Shopping

This last section provides shopping resources—for work and play. In the first part, you'll find some of the many Internet malls. On the last pages are tables of shops that sell everything from office supplies to flowers to toys. *Caveat emptor!*

All-Internet Shopping Directory

http://www.webcom/com/~tbrown/

This very large site includes links to Malls & Such, Computer & Internet, Automotive, Consumer Electronics, Sporting Goods, Arts & Entertainment, Flowers & Gifts, Lifestyle, Services, Travel, Health & Fitness, Hobbies, and Bargain Bonanza. It's rather difficult to find your way around this site. A simple table of contents would be very useful. In the meantime, you can take a fast automated tour of the pages; click on Autopilot Tour at the bottom of the home page. Before doing so, remove as many of the tool bars as you can from your computer screen in order to have a better view of each page.

Auctions of Unclaimed Items

http://www.usps.gov/consumer/auctions.htm

You can get information about sales of unclaimed loose-in-the-mails items held at the U.S. Postal Service Mail Recovery Centers. This site provides the addresses of the Mail Recovery Centers in Atlanta, Philadelphia, St. Paul, and San Francisco. You can have yourself added to a mailing list by writing to one of the Purchasing Service Centers listed on this page.

The Branch Mall

http://branch.com/

http://branch.com:1080/

The Branch Mall is a very large site with both retail (that is, consumer or home) and business center

shopping. Its business center contains links to computer hardware and furniture, computer software and services, electronics and electrical, communications, printing, business/legal/financial, business opportunities and franchises, and real estate—investments, management and construction.

CatalogLink

http://cataloglink.com/

This site lists and describes major-league catalogs that you can order. On the home page, you'll find these links: Electronics, Gifts,

Recreation/Hobbies, Office/Computer, Home/Family, and Apparel. Click on a link to go to a page that lists catalogs for the selected category. Then click on the name of the catalog that you want to order, and click on the Send Free Catalog button.

Internet Voyager

Almost every resource documented in *The Internet Business-to-Business Directory* is an online one. *The Internet Voyager* is one of the exceptions: It is printed on paper and sent via "snail mail" each month. As most Internet sites have done, this newsletter has grown and gotten better looking. At this point, *The Internet Voyager* provides 16 pages of information: Access Tools (browsers, e-mail programs, and other Internet applications), Net Stops (reviews of several types of Internet sites, including Business & Finance), and two Departments. For more information, contact Internet Voyager at Blue Dolphin Communications, Inc., 83 Boston Post Road, Sudbury, MA 01776 or at 508-443-6363.

Catalog Mart

http://catalog.savvy.com/

This slow-loading site with a large opening graphic claims to have links to more than 10,000 free catalogs. To obtain information about this site, click on Information on the home page. After reading the information page, you can look at the catalog subjects by clicking on Click Here. At the top of the following page, you are prompted to register (giving your name, address, telephone number, and e-mail address). If you don't want to register, simply scroll down the page to see the list of subjects. Business subjects include books, business cards, cabinets, computer software, computers, copiers and fax machines, laboratory and science equipment, microscopes, office and business supplies, pens and pencils, and much more.

Defense Reutilization and Marketing Service (DRMS)

http://131.87.1.51/

At this site, you can find surplus U.S. Department of Defense property. Articles available range from computers to vehicles, from furniture to clothing, and so on. People can buy at Zone, International, or Retail sales. Some pages at this site contain large photographs and are slow-loading. Click on a link under Public Sales to find out about DRMS sale items. You can download a catalog or view a dynamic catalog. Click on Searchable Public Asset Database to access the index in which you can search four different ways. Because of the size of the database, try to narrow the search as much as you can by selecting as many options as you can.

Digimall

http://digimall.com/

Digimall (see Figure 8.8) showcases online stores and runs an order system. Click on Store Listings to see a list of the vendors at the mall, and click on Free Catalogs to reveal a page on which you can order catalogs from well-known catalog houses. At the time of this writing, the only business-related vendor at the mall was DigiCore, a computer reseller.

eShop Inc.

http://www.eshop.com/

This small electronic mall, which requires registration, not only offers shopping at Tower Records, 1-800-FLOWERS, Insight, and Spiegel, but provides coupons and other promotional items. This site provides links to personal services, fast graphics, and indexes to available merchandise at each store. To shop at this site, you must download free software.

Good Cheap Stuff

http://www.onramp.net/
goodstuf/

At this site, you can have an agent find manufacturers' closeouts at below wholesale prices. On the home page, check one of 24 checkboxes to explore. Then scroll down the page to type a special request (if you wish). Type your e-mail address in the next text box. Then scroll down and click on the Click Here to Create Your Agent button. The agent will search the Internet and return the results to your e-mail address.

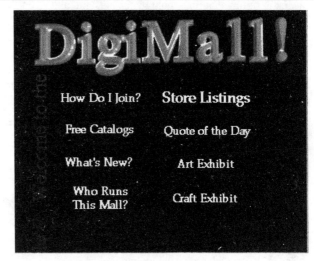

Figure 8.8 Click on a link to learn more about this site or to shop.

After you enter a search, you can click on a link to browse an illustrated page (at http://www.onramp.net/goodstuff/prodindex.html), as shown in Figure 8.9. Products include electronics, clothing, collectibles, and more. The link to the order form is at the bottom of the page.

Hall of Malls

http://nsns.com/
MouseTracks/HallofMalls.html

This plain site, a good place to start a search for shopping sites on the Internet, provides links to more than 100 malls on the Internet. Most are

shopping sites, but a few are lists of links to business services or other information.

The Internet Mall

http://www.internet-mall.com/

This well-designed and gigantic supermall from Dave Taylor has been around for a long time (at least in Internet time). On the home page, you will find links to eight categories: Food and Beverages; Clothes and Sporting Goods; Computer Hardware and Software; Books, Magazines, and Other

1940's Gas Pump Telephone with Night Light. Contains a modern push button phone inside!

Retail: $100 GSC price: $46.87

Figure 8.9 See an illustration of a clearance item and read about it before ordering.

Media; Furniture and Household Items; Personal and Professional Services; Personal Items and Gifts; and Automotive and Related. Clicking on a category brings you to a page of subcategories. Finally, click on a subcategory to reveal a page of many links to the desired online store and/or e-mail address.

Internet Shopping Network

http://shop.internet.net/

The well-designed Internet Shopping Network provides links to many well-known companies, such as Hammacher Schlemmer, FTD, and Omaha Steaks. Many

other links at this mall are related to computer software and hardware home electronics. Other categories include Home & Office, Food, and Flowers.

Mad Mats

http://www.earthlink.net/~madmats/

You can buy unique mouse pads and wrist rests (see Figure 8.10) from this site by either clicking on a link to an e-mail address or calling

Figure 8.10   This illustration from the Mad Mats site shows some mouse pads and wrist rests.

on the telephone to request a catalog (which arrives thanks to the U.S. Postal Service "snail mail").

The MegaMall

http://infotique.lm.com/megamall.html

The MegaMall, with attractive but slow-to-load graphics, contains 49 departments and 140 stores. You can shop by category or by accessing an alphabetically arranged list of stores. The mall merchants not only sell goods but also services.

NECX Direct

http://necxdirect.necx.com:8002/?

NECX Direct claims to sell more than 20,000 computer products. Founded in 1980, NECX is located near Boston. Click on Info Center to view a page of information about the company and the products it sells. To shop NECX Direct, you can be a Buyer's Club member for a membership fee or a regular. Categories at this site include Super Deals, Power Search, Membership Office, Order Center, Windows '95 Showcase, Notebooks and PCMCIA, Cards and Boards, Multimedia Hardware, Drives and Storage, Ram and CPU Upgrades, Desktop Computers, Modems, Monitors, Printers, Software, Edutainment, Mac HQ, Networking, Accessories, Scanners, and NECX Direct. When you click on a category, a page of products and prices appears. Click on a link to get more information about products and/or manufacturers.

Shopping 2000

http://shopping2000.com/

Shopping 2000 sells products and services from merchants listed under these categories: Music, Books, Video & Art; Wear It; OfficeWare & Electronics; Sports Center; @ Home & On the Road, Flowers & Gifts; Kids & Games; and Food & Wine, as shown in Figure 8.11. You can window shop, but you must register to buy from this site.

Virtually Everything

http://www.mbnet.mb.ca/flatland/mall/

This Winnipeg electronic mall includes a clickable map (see Figure 8.12), which actually looks as though it came from a mall and even includes a parking lot. Click on an area of the map, and go to the related home page. At the time of this writing, there were 31 stores, including several under construction and spaces for many more.

White Rabbit Toys

http://toystore.com/

This site shows what an online store should look like—good design, few graphics, and a straightforward,

Figure 8.11   Click on a button to select a shopping category.

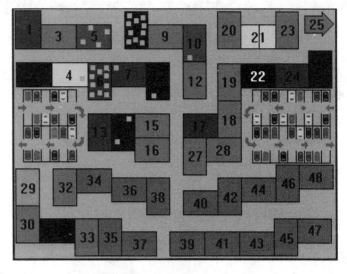

Figure 8.12   The Virtually Everything home page contains a map very similar to those you find at shopping malls.

nonjarring presentation. In order to see illustrations of the toys (which saves loading time on pictures that you don't want to see), you must click on a link.

Among the brands sold here are Brio, Creativity for Kids, Gund, Primetime Playthings, and Ravensburger.

Selected Retailers on the Net

Many companies, from small retailers to popular catalogs, are jumping onto the Net. A start-up business can reach plenty of new customers across the U.S. or around the world with an attractive site. Or a major company can generate sales from the most sophisticated people —those who regularly visit the Internet. Tables 8.2 to 8.18 present a small selection of the retailers—from those selling arts and crafts to office supplies and gifts and flowers to computer software online.

Table 8.2: Selected Internet Shops—Art and Crafts

Shop	URL
Art Wolfe, Inc.—The Art of Photographing Nature	http://branch.com/wolfe/wolfe.htm
Gallery of American Artisans	http://www.usa.net/gallery/
Pieces of Nature	http://www.csn.net/~lisaneif

Table 8:3: Selected Internet Shops—Books

Shop	URL	Description
ACC Bookstore	http://www.on-the-net.com/acc-corp	Linux books and programs
Amazon.com Books	http://www.amazon.com/	
Antiquarian Booksellers' Association of America (ABAA)	http://www.clark.net/pub/rmharris/catalogs/ungercat/	A list of more than 100 booksellers, online catalogs, and other book-related links
Atomic Books	http://www.clark.net/pub/atomicbk/home.html	Alternative fiction and low-brow books, crime and punishment, cult film & video, Literary Finds for Mutated Minds
Book Stacks Unlimited	http://www.books.com/	More than 400,000 books and other resources for book buyers
Book Stores	http://www.cis.ohio-state.edu/hypertext/faq/usenet/books/stores/top.html	Lists of bookstores in Asia, Europe, North America, and by mail
Bookzone	http://ttx.com/bookzone	Fiction and nonfiction books, audio books (well-designed search form)
Computer Literacy Bookshops, Inc.	http://www.clbooks.com/	Computer books and many other types of books
CPIC Technical and Professional Bookstore	http://web.idirect.com/~cpic	Remainders and books for business and technical professionals
The Dragon and the Unicorn Bookstore	http://infoweb.net/books/index.html	Science fiction and fantasy

Shop	URL	Description
Future Fantasy Bookstore	http://futfan/home.html	Science fiction, fantasy, and mysteries (nice illustration)
Golden Quill Bookshop	http://www.aescon.com/quill/index.htm	Fiction and nonfiction books
Internet Road Map to Books	http://www.bookport.com/htbin/welcome/misc	A page of links to bookstores, bestseller lists, publishers' Web pages, online books, and those in the book industry
JF Lehmanns Fachbuchhandlung	http://www.germany.EU.net/shop/JFL/Welcome.e.html	Books, journals, CD-ROMs with English language and German language pages
Laissez-Faire Books	http://www.lfb.org/	Books listed under these categories: Economics, Children and the Family, Culture, Education, Environmentalism, Feminism, Fiction & Entertainment, and so on
Linköping Science Fiction & Fantasy Archive	http://www.lysator.liu.se:7500/sf_archive/sf_main.html	Science fiction and fantasy books
Meyer Boswell Books, Inc.	http://www.toc.com/meyerbos/	Rare and scholarly books on the law
Midnight Special Bookstore's Independent Bookstore Link	http://www.cinenet.net/msbooks/freeevents.html	Links to bookstores, primarily in California but also in the U.S. and worldwide, and links to other book resources
Midnight Special Bookstore	http://www.cinenet.net/msbooks/homepage.html	Books and videos: bestsellers, poetry, biography, and more
The Nando.net Bookstore	http://www.nando.net/bookstore/bookmain.html	Books, posters, News & Observer reprints
PolyEster Records and Books	http://www.glasswings.com.au/PolyEster/index.html	Australian books and CDs
Powell's Technical Books	http://www.technical.powells.portland.or.us/	Technical books in architecture, chemistry, computing, communications, and more
Read USA	http://branch.com/readusa/readusa.html	General interest, computer, audio tapes, and CD-ROM at a discount
Reiter's Books	http://www.awa.com/reiters/index.html	Many nonfiction books in many categories
Softpro Books	http://storefront.xor.com/softpro/index.html	Computing and programming books
University of California Irvine Bookstore	http://www.book.uci.edu/	Books, music clothing, gifts
University Press Books/Berkeley	http://www.fractals.com/upb/html/upb_intro.html	A variety of books by university presses

Table 8:3: Selected Internet Shops—Books (continued)

Table 8.4: Selected Internet Shops—Clothing and Accessories

Shop	URL
1 World Apparel	http://www2.clever.net/1world/home.html
Alert and Oriented Uniform Superstore	http://www.amsquare.com/uniform/index.html
America's T-Shirt Catalog	http://www.a1.com/shirt/t-shirt.html
Bikini Factory	http://www.robust.com/bikini
Boston Slicker Company Ltd.	http://www.webcom.com/~dml/slicker/slicker.html
Cashmere at CocoKane	http://www.demon.co.uk/cocokane/
Charm Woven Labels	http://www.charmwoven.com/~charm
The Commuter CoverUp™	http://branch.com/sami/sami.html
Computer T-Shirts from Elswear	http://branch.com/shirts/shirts.html
CyberShoes	http://www.awa.com/cybershoes/
Cyberspace Navigator Hat	http://branch.com/giftconn/cybernav/cybernav.htm
Golden Gate—Rebecca Raggs	http://www.best.com/~ggate/golden-gate.cgi?downtown
Lands' End	http://www.landsend.com/
L'eggs Online Store!	http://www.pantyhose.com/access.html
Lingerie, Roses, and More...	http://www.amsquare.com/lingerie/index.html
MARCOART Tee Shirts	http://www.awa.com/marcoart/
Net Sweats & Tees	http://amsquare.com/netsweat/netsweat.html
Netgear	http://branch.com/netgear/netgear.htm
Netsurfer—Internet T-Shirts	http://branch.com/netsurfer/netsurfr.html
The Official Bubba Bulmash Collection	http://www.com/bubba
Sobels	http://www.tricon.net/Comm/sobel/index.html
Warehouse—The Elegant Tuxedos	http://branch.com/tuxedo/tuxedo.html
Wild Ties	http://branch.com/wildties/
Worldwide Flag Wear	http://www.amsquare.com/flagwear/index.html

Table 8.5: Selected Internet Shops—Computing

Shop	URL
ActionCall	http://awa.com/ac/
ADP Autonet—Wide Area Data Communications Network	http://branch.com/adp/home.htm
Anchiano Computer Eyewear—Protection Against Computer Eyestrain	http://branch.com/eyewear/eyewear.html
CCI World—An Interactive Marketplace for Computer Products and Internet Services	http://cciworld.com
CD-Labs	http://branch.com/cdlabs/cdlabs.htm
COMCOM Systems	http://www.intbc.com/comcom/
CompUSA	http://www.compUSA.com/
CrazyBob's® CD's and Diskettes	http://www.crazybob.com/
Creative Computers	http://www.pc-mall.com/
CyberSave, The Online Wholesale Club	http://cybersave.com
DAKCO PC Products Division	http://dakco.lm.com/fdawa.html
Digital Dynamics—CD ROM Services	http://branch.com/dd/dd.html
Digital Print Services	http://awa.com/digprint/digprint.html
Disk-O-Tape	http://disk-o-tape.com/
Edge Publishing Inc.	http://www.imt.net/~edgepub/index.html
Hartford Computer Group	http://awa.com/hartford/hartford.html
Iconation	http://www.cin.net/cinusers/photoicn/photoicn.html
Marcus Associates—We Purchase Used Computer and Communications Equipment	http://branch.com/marcus/marcus.html
Compfort Home Page	http://www.netaxs.com/~iris/cts/compfort.html
Micro Star Software Club	http://awa.com/microstar/
MicroWarehouse Inc.	http://www.warehouse.com/
Network Express—ISDN Networking Solutions	http://branch.com/netexpress/index.html
Rhythm, It's Easy—Duets with Your Computer	http://branch.com/rhythm/rhythm.htm
SoftLock Services	http://awa.com/softlock/slhome.html
Software Spectrum, Inc.	http://www.swspectrum.com/
Superchargers	http://register.com/quick/schome.htm
Walnut Creek CDROM and Software	http://hobbes.cdrom.com/

Table 8.6: Selected Internet Shops—Food and Drink

Shop	URL
American Homebrewers Association	http://branch.com/zymurgy/zymurgy.htm
American Pacific Tea and Spice Co.	http://www.amsquare.com/teashop/index.html
Aroma Borealis	http://www.supernet.ab.ca/Mall/Business/coffee.html
Chocolate Strawberries by Sophisticated Chocolates	http://branch.com/sophisticated/sophist.html
The Coffee Shop	http://www.amsquare.com/coffee/homepage.html
Food by Phone!	http://branch.com/phonfood/phonfood.htm
Forest Hill Vineyard	http://branch.com/wine/wine.html
Godiva Chocolates	http://www.godiva.com/
Goodies from Goodman—Food Gifts and Flowers by Mail!	http://branch.com/goodies/goodies.html
Hawaii's Best Espresso Company	http://hoohana.aloha.net/~bec/
Hyman Smith Coffee	http://www.awa.com/coffee/
Indian River Fruit	http://www.awa.com/fruit/
Kibco Gourmet Sauces	http://www.flinet.com/~dmw/kibco.html
Liqueurs OnLine	http://www.gpkg.com/liqueurs
Lobster Direct (from Nova Scotia)	http://novaweb.com/lobster/
Lobsternet (from Maine)	http://branch.com/lobster/lobster.htm
Maverick Ranch Meats	http://cybermart.com/maverick/
Orfila Vineyards	http://branch.com/orfila/orfila.html
P&W Seafood of Florida	http://www.pwseafood.com
Phoenician Olive Oil	http://www.oliveoil.com/oliveoil/
Salsa Express	http://www.stw.com/se/se.htm
Sandy Bay Saffron	http://www.virtumall.com/sandybay/home.html
SeaBear Seafoods	http://www.amsquare.com/seabear/index.html
Sunnyland Farms	http://www.amsquare.com/sunny/sunny.html
Todd & Holland—Tea Merchants	http://www.branch.com/teas/teas.html
Toucan Chocolates—Fine Chocolates	http://branch.com/toucan/toucan.html
Virtual Vineyards	http://www.virtualvin.com/infoseek/
Zaro's Bread Basket (bagels)	http://www.nybagels.com/

Table 8.7: Selected Internet Shops—Furniture and Accessories

Shop	URL
Ergonomic Technologies—Safe Workstations	http://branch.com/ergonomic/ergonmc.html
Marrakesh Express	http://www.uslink.net/ddavis/
Simply Stated Affordable Furnishings	http://haven.ios.com/~nouri/
United Computer Group, Inc.—Ergonomic Computer Furniture	http://branch.com/ucg/ucg.htm

Table 8.8: Selected Internet Shops—Gifts and Flowers

Shop	URL
Bonsai Boy of New York	http://branch.com/bonsai/bonsai.html
Bonsai Etcetera	http://www.shore.net/~adfx/2636.html
Downtown Anywhere Souvenir Shop	http://www.awa.com/souven/
Exotic Flowers of Hawaii	http://branch.com/hawaii/hawaii.html
Fabulous Flags from Ember'Glo Gifts and Flowers	http://branch.com/ember/ember.html
Flower Link	http://go.flowerlink.com/html/menu1.html
Flowers...For Me?	http://www.awa.com/flower/f0.html
Flowerstop—Your Online Fresh Flower Market	http://www.flowerstop.com/fstop/fstopmain.html
FTD—INTERNET	http://www.novator.com/FTD-Catalog
Gift Connection—Corporate and Personal Gifts and Flowers	http://branch.com/frames/frames.html
Giftworld—High Quality Handmade Gifts and Flowers	http://giftworld.com/

Table 8.8: Selected Internet Shops—Gifts and Flowers (continued)

Shop	URL
The Golden Rose by Silvercraft	http://branch.com/silvercraft/rosa.htm
Grant's Flowers	http://branch.com/flowers/flowers.html
Hawaii Orchids	http://www.ilhawaii.net/pt/hiorchid.html
Tropical Flowers by Charles	http://hoohana.aloha.net/~charles/
High Quality Hand-Made Gift Baskets	http://branch.com/basket/basket.htm
Mayflower Gifts and Flowers	http://branch.com/mayflower/mayflow.htm
Miniature Wine Grapevines of California	http://branch.com/dutch/dutch.htm
Nature's Blooms	http://cybermart.com/nb/
The Rubber Stamp Queen	http://www.dol.com/queen/
The Upscale Wholesale Shop	http://www.upscale.com
VaporWare 0.0	http://www.infohaus.com/access/by-seller/NOVELTY_SPACE
A White Dove On-line Flower and Gift Shop	http://branch.com/flower-shop/whtdove.html

Table 8.9: Selected Internet Shops—Health and Beauty

Shop	URL
Avalon Skin Care Products	http://www.dash.com/netro/sho/avalon/avalon.html
DFH Discount Supplements	http://branch.com/vitamin/vitamin.html
Formulas for Health	http://branch.com/health/health.html
The Fragrance Source	http://branch.com/fragrance/menu.html
Health Source	http://branch.com/hsource/home.htm
L de L Retinol Vitamin A Formulations	http://branch.com/retinol/retinol.htm
Lens Direct	http://www.pclens.com/
Lifestyle Hearing Inc.	http://biz.rtd.com/lifestyle_hearing
Louise Bianco Skin Care, Inc.	http://branch.com/bianco/bianco.htm
Morr-View InterOptical Shoppe	http://branch.com/morrview/intro.htm
Nature's Wealth	http://branch.com/nature/wealth.htm
The Sunglass Connection	http://branch.com/sunglass/sunglass.htm
Verify, LTD	http://branch.com/verify/verify.html

Table 8.10: Selected Internet Shops—Household and Safety

Shop	URL
Allergen Clean Vacuum Cleaners from Miele	http://branch.com/sweeps/miele.htm
Amish Country	http://www.awa.com/amish/
Belson Manufacturing Company (barbeque grills, picnic tables, etc.)	http://webmart.freedom.net/belson/home.html
Cohasset Birdhouses Gift Shop	http://www.xensei.com:80/users/kevinpr/
Cornell's True Value Hardware (Eastchester, NY)	http://206.67.47.2/Cornells.htm
Crime Prevention Manual: BUG OFF!	http://branch.com/crime/crime.html
Fuller Brush Products	http://branch.com/fuller/fuller.html
Nicor 1—Home, Garden & Entertainment Products	http://www.netnet.net/nicor1/
Oreck Vacuum Center	http://cybermart.com/oreck/
Rains and Pours	http://www.shops.net/shops/rains/
Safe at Home	http://branch.com/safety/safety.htm
S.O.S. Pool Alarm	http://branch.com/pool/pool.html
Seat Handler	http://ngwwmall.com/shops/seat_handler
Specialty Eyewear	http://www.eyewear.com/excel/
Unique Mexican Stoneware	http://www.awa.com/tp/

Table 8.11: Selected Internet Shops—Jewelry

Shop	URL
Amethyst Galleries (rock shop and gemstones)	http://mineral.galleries.com/default.htm
Gem Hut	http://zeus.javanet.com/gemhut/
Gold Fantasy	http://www.robust.com/gold
KCS Imports	http://branch.com/kcs/kcs1.htm
Milne Jewelry Company	http://branch.com/milne/Milne01.html
Robert L. Straight Solid Gold Custom Jewelry	http://www.stw.com/rls/rls.htm
ZIMCOM—Computer Jewelry	http://branch.com/zimcom/computr.html

Table 8.12: Selected Internet Shops—Miscellaneous Merchandise	
Shop	*URL*
The Five and Dime	http://www.awa.com/five/
Good Stuff Cheap	http://www.onramp.net/goodstuf
Hawaii General Store	http://204.182.49.10/Store.html
Speak To Me Catalog	http://clickshop.com/speak/
Spiegel	http://www.spiegel.com/spiegel/
The Starshire Stores	http://www.awa.com/starshire/
Sundance Catalog	http://cybermart.com/sundance/
Visi-Tech	http://www.tiac.net/users/visitech/home.html

Table 8.13: Selected Internet Shops—Music and Video	
Shop	*URL*
CD ROM Boating	http://emporium.turnpike.net/~megamall/cd_compo.htm
CDnow! The Internet Music Store	http://cdnow.com/
Complete Internet Training Bundle	http://awa.com/dde/
Corinth Video	http://awa.com/video/
Discount Music Connection	http://branch.com/dmc/dmc.htm
Dynamic Recordings Indie Label	http://www.dynrec.com
Internet Videos, Inc.	http://www.webcom.com/~ivi/DA.html
King's Keyboard House	/http://branch.com/kings/kings.html
The Melody Shop	http://branch.com/melody.com/
The Minor Chord	http://www.ultranet.com/~minchord/
Music Boulevard	http://www.musicblvd.com
The Music Express Etc.	http://branch.com/cdexpress/cdexprs.html
NOVA Videos from WGBH	http://branch.com/nova/nova.html
Pinconning Electronics	http://branch.com/rshack/rshack.htm
Radio Partner Custom Earsets	http://branch.com/rp/rp.htm
Sharper Image	http://www.sharperimage.com/tsi/
Weightlifting 101—Instructional Videotape	http://branch.com/zand/zand.htm
WholeARTS Music Mall	http://www.wholarts.com/music

Table 8.14: Selected Internet Shops—Office Supplies

Shop	URL
Anchor Box Company	http://www.issb.com/directory/a/anchor/index.html
Current®	http://www.currentinc.com/current/
fontsOnline™	http://www.dol.com/fontsOnline/
Forms Solutions	http://www.imageserve.com/FSHome.html
Micro Format Specialty Paper Products	http://www.sendit.com/mformat/home.html
The Paperia	http://www.libertynet.org/~paperia
Productivity Plus Catalog	http://www.timemanagement.com/tmgt/
Staples	http://www.staples.com/
WebStampers	http://www.webstamp.com/~stamps

Table 8.15: Selected Internet Shops—Pet Supplies

Shop	URL
Aquatic Technology	http://www.actwin.com/AquaticTech/
Austin Wholesale Petshop Supplies	http://webcom.com/~pets/austins/welcome.html
Creative Bird Accessories	http://www.webscope.com/cba/
Pet Supplies On-Line	http://www.awa.com/pets/
ProRein & Lead	http://www.iu.net/prorein
Reed Enterprises Fish Hobbyist Goods	http://www.io.com/~kslandry/Reed_Enterprises.html
Unique Concepts—Treat of the Month Club for Cats and Dogs	http://branch.com/treats/treats.html

Table 8.16: Selected Internet Shops—Sports and Outdoor Recreation

Shop	URL
Blue Ridge Mountain Sports	http://www.brms.com/brms.html
Capt'n Mikes Tackle Towne	http://www.awa.com/cm/
D & P Enterprises	http://www.worldprofit.com/madpent.htm
The Great All Outdoors Trading Company	http://www.nt.net/allout/itcom.htm
L. L. Bean	http://www.llbean.com/
LogOn Sports	http://www.logonsports.com/
New Image International Inc.	http://branch.com/newim/newim.htm
Rocky Mountain Outfitters	http://www.packs.com/rmo
Tennis Dynamite	http://branch.com/tendyn/tendyn.htm

Table 8.17: Selected Internet Shops—Telecommunications

Shop	URL
Credi-Call	http://branch.com/cc/cc.htm
FREE PAGERS	http://branch.com/pagers/pagers.html
TeleChoice Telecommunication	http://www.awa.com/tc/
Telephone Calling Cards—Maxim	http://branch.com/maxim/maxim.html

Table 8.18: Selected Internet Shops—Toys and Games

Shop	URL
1950's Fun—The Original Burp Gun	http://branch.com/burpco/burpco.html
Gamelink CD-ROM Catalog	http://laonline.com/cdrom
Halloween Mart	http://www.accessnv.com/halloween/
Quorum Direct™ Discovery Toys™	http://www.the-wire.com/woburn/quorum.html
Renaissance 2000	http://www.ren2k.com
The Toy Box	http://branch.com/toybox/toybox.htm

Chapter Nine

Coming Attractions

- ◆ General Legal Resources
- ◆ Corporate Law
- ◆ Patents and Trademarks
- ◆ Copyrights and Intellectual Rights
- ◆ Federal Laws and Regulations
- ◆ NAFTA
- ◆ GATT
- ◆ International Law
- ◆ International Government Resources
- ◆ General U.S. Government Resources
- ◆ U.S. Government Directory
- ◆ State Government

Law and Government

Law and
Governme

T he sites in this chapter provide information about law and government. Using the legal sites, you can access Internet-based law libraries, find information about legal specialties and criminal justice, and obtain resources for both lawyers and laypersons. You can read about the impact of the Internet on practicing law. You can even use a resource to find an attorney in your community or nearby.

In the government section of this chapter, you can access full-text versions of regulations and laws; learn all about copyrights, intellectual property rights, patents, and trademarks; and look up 20 years of patents in a database. In addition, you can visit federal law libraries, NAFTA- and GATT-related sites, international law and government pages, and general and specific U.S. government resources on the Internet.

General Legal Resources

The Internet provides a wealth of legal resources—from online academic law libraries to advice for attorneys using the Net for the first time. In this section, you can visit massive law libraries, get business information, find business forms, review up-to-date criminal justice resources and same-day U.S. Supreme Court decisions, and much more.

'Lectric Law Library™

http://www.inter-law.com/

This site provides law-related information, products, and services as well as information for those starting businesses. Although most of the resources are free, some are provided on floppy disks for a fee. If you are a first-time visitor to this site and can stand a little lame humor, go on the guided tour, which includes a useful map of the site. Otherwise, you can go to the Rotunda, the centerpiece of the Library. Categories include The Inner Sanctum (information about the Library), The Study of Law Study (primarily for students), The Reference Room (statutes, rules, case law, and an encyclopedia of terms and topics), The

News Room, The Law for Business Lounge (download-able documents and links for business people), The Laypeople's Law Lounge, The Legal Professional's Lounge, The Periodical Reading Room, The Rubber Room (humor and the bizarre), The Forms Room (downloadable or printable business forms), and The Bookstore (software and files that you can order).

Cecil Greek's Criminal Justice Page

http://www.stpt.usf.edu/~greek/cj.html

Dr. Cecil Greek, an associate professor of criminology at the University of South Florida, has gathered a gigantic list of law and criminal justice links (see Figure 9.1). Some of the categories are Searchable Law Sites; Federal Criminal Justice Agencies; International Criminal Justice Resources; Police Agencies & Resources; Crime-Related Web Sites; Juvenile Delinquency Sites (where else would you find a link to Sabina's Bodyart Pages?); Drug and Alcohol Pages; Prisons and the Death Penalty; Criminal Justice in the Media; and Civil Liberties, Due Process, and the Courts (which includes Internet security and public interest topics). While you're visiting, take a look at his wonderful home page (with links to Bruce Springsteen,

Vincent Van Gogh, and the cartoon characters Beany & Cecil, among others). Be aware that occasionally it's difficult to read the dark text against the dark background.

Criminal Enforcement Bulletin
http://www.haledorr.com/criminal_news.html

This article, dated December 1994, provides information about internal investigations and how they can aid corporate management in exploring and remedying potential misconduct—even as a preemptive strike before a civil suit or government investigation. Headings include When to Consider an Internal Investigation, Who Should Conduct the Internal Investigation, Structuring the Investigation, Conducting the Investigation, Documentation and Disclosure of Findings, and Impact of Federal Sentencing Guidelines.

Emory Law Library Electronic Reference Desk

http://law.emory.edu/LAW/refdesk/toc.html

This deceptively small home page with a search index to nine categories of links is a super site. Select a category and click on the Go to Topic button. Main categories include Computer and Internet Information (some law resources), Employment and Education Information, Federal Agencies and Organizations (a comprehensive list of links), Federal Materials (cases, codes, and laws), Finding Aids (legal indexes, legal directories, and Internet search tools), Foreign Materials (law and nonlaw resources arranged by country),

Figure 9.1 A photograph of Alcatraz introduces you to Cecil Greek's Criminal Justice page.

International Materials (a list of various links), Law Firms and Individual Lawyers (law firms, lawyers, and legal directories), and Law Schools (U.S. law schools).

Global LawNet

http://www.lawnet.net/

Global LawNet, Inc. (GLN), a commercial company owned and operated by lawyers, provides Internet services to lawyers. At this well-designed site, you can find law links, federal information, and state information. Click on Law Links to go to a very long page of links to law resources arranged under eight categories: Legal Resource Sites, Legal Resources Outside the United States, Sites on Specific Legal Areas, Organizations and Publishers, Legal Services, Law Libraries (some online), Law-Related Journals, and Law-Related Newsgroups and Mailing Lists.

Clicking on Federal Information provides government sites, United States statutes, federal court decisions, and federal search indexes. In addition, you can use a clickable map to get lists of Global LawNet subscribers, law firms, bar associations, services, state law online, law schools, and law libraries for each state. Note that many state pages do not provide links under every one of the categories but usually provide links to state laws.

Hale and Dorr

http://www.haledorr.com/

Hale and Dorr are counselors at law located in Boston, in Manchester, New Hampshire, and in Washington, D.C. At this site, you can find information about the firm, legal newsletters and publications, and a page of other legal resources, including the Federal Register, the Library of Congress Legislative History database, Massachusetts Access to Government Information Service, and U.S. courts and government departments. Also included is the Special Focus page,

which has additional information about the firm, an SEC EDGAR guide, and a thorough report on the Bankruptcy Reform Act of 1994.

Indiana University School of Law–Bloomington

http://www.law.indiana.edu/law/

The Indiana University School of Law–Bloomington provides a variety of legal links—to information about the law school itself, online versions of legal journals, other legal servers (including Cornell Law School and the World-Wide Web Virtual Library), Indiana state legal materials, environmental law resources, sound files, and specific cases particularly related to legal matters involving the Internet.

Internet Resources for Women's Legal and Public Policy Information

http://asa.ugl.lib.umich.edu:80/chdocs/womenpolicy/womenlawpolicy.html

This site has links to Internet resources that provide information on legal and public policy issues both at home and at work. Business-related topics are sexual harassment, women and development, women in the military, women of color, women with disabilities, and work issues. Many links appear on multiple pages. A typical entry includes the link, the author, and a one-paragraph description. You can access an alphabetically arranged list of the same resources without descriptions at http://asa.ugl.lib.umich.edu:80/chdocs/womenpolicy/alphalist.html.

Lawyering on the Internet

http://www.ncl.ac.uk/~nlawwww/articles1/widdis1.html

This long (48 kilobytes) and informative article, by Robin Widdison, the Director of the Centre for Law and Computing at the University of Durham, in the UK, discusses the impact of the Internet on the law professional. He discusses the lasting nature of the Internet, what the Internet allows its users to do, and how the Internet will impact legal practice and education. You can download a copy of the article by clicking on Download This File near the top of the page.

The Legal Domain Network

http://www.law.vill.edu:2000/
A joint creation of the Center for Information Law and Policy at the Villanova University School of Law and the Center for Law and Computers at Chicago-Kent College of Law, the Legal Domain Network serves as a clearinghouse to law-related Usenet Listservs without your having to subscribe. It also serves as a forum for law-related organizations. At this site, an individual who is not a member of an organization subscribing to the Legal Domain Network can search archives of legal Listservs for certain discussions.

LEGAL dot NET™

http://www.legal.net/
LEGAL dot NET™ is a commercial site that provides a registry of attorneys and law firms primarily in the U.S., as well as resources for attorneys and laypersons. You can search for attorneys and law firms by area of practice and by country, name, or state. Only those registered at LEGAL dot NET appear in this directory. Two types of listings are available: free and premium service, for those wanting listings with graphics, photographs, sound, and links to other sites.

Clicking on Topics for Attorneys reveals a page of links to LEGAL dot NET commercial services; surveys; an online forum with classified ads; a commercial directory of legal services; an extensive page of articles, columns, notes, and press releases; and links to bar associations. Clicking on Nonattorneys provides links to

many of the links for attorneys. In addition, you can obtain information (and optionally order forms and software) about California child and spousal support and California divorces.

The Legal Information Institute (LII)

http://www.law.cornell.edu/
Sponsored by the Cornell Law School, the Legal Information Institute (LII) is a popular site containing many legal links, including same-day Supreme Court decisions, decisions of the New York Court of Appeals, the full U.S. Code and other legal documents, and a list of names and e-mail addresses of U.S. law school faculty members. Scroll down the home page to see the contents of the site: Items of Current Interest, Main Menus, About This Site and the LII, and Other Sites to Visit If You Don't Find It Here.

The Legal Pad

http://www.pond.com/~pinky/legal.pad/legalpad.htm
The Legal Pad, designed and maintained by a law student at Seton Hall University, provides more than 600 legal links, including the journal of a first-year law student, a page of law firms on the Web, a long and impressive page of legal resources, and a list of law schools worldwide. Some of the pages at this site are difficult to read; the dark background doesn't provide enough contrast for the text.

Legal Research Tools

http://www.fplc.edu/toolbox.htm
The Franklin Pierce Law Center provides a page of legal links to many of the most popular legal resources on the Internet. Here you can find other pages of legal links, directories, commercial pages, newsgroups, and so on.

Legal Resources on the Net

http://jcomm.uoregon.edu/~tgleason/Law_j202.html

This long nongraphical page contains links to a variety of legal sources arranged under categories: General Reference and Law Libraries, Courts, Federal Communication Commission (FCC), Telecommunication, Policy Organizations, Computer Law (including Speech on the Internet), Intellectual Property, Communication Lawyers and Law Firms on the Net, and Journals. This site is an excellent starting point for those looking for legal resources, especially those related to telecommunications.

Legal Standard for Inventorship

http://biotechlaw.ari.net/mbinvent.html

This article, by Melvin Blecher, Ph.D., who is Of Counsel to a Washington, D.C., law firm and a professor emeritus at Georgetown University, describes the concept of legal inventorship for research scientists. Included in the article is the definition of legal inventor and the legal standards used to categorize an inventor versus a research assistant, financial backer, or supplier of materials.

LEGI-SLATE Gopher Service

gopher://gopher.legislate.com:70/1

LEGI-SLATE is a combination free and fee-based service that provides information about congressional and regulatory resources. Here you can find out about all bills and resolutions brought before the U.S. Congress since 1993. The public has free access to the title, status, cosponsors, and locations of text versions of bills, committee reports, and counterpart or companion bills. Subscribers pay at least $750 a year for unrestricted access to the database.

Interesting Site

If you have a dog or a cat or are looking into getting one, Cyber-Pet (at http://cyberpet.com/) can be a big help. Click on *Cyber-Dog* or *Cyber-Cat* (under construction at the time of this writing) to find a pet from a breeder or a rescue club, to learn about specific breeds, to discover sources of pet products and services, or to link to other pet-related sites.

Lex Mundi's Hieros Gamos

http://www.hg.org/

Hieros Gamos provides legal information in English, German, Spanish, French, and Italian. Established by Lex Mundi, an international association of 125 law firms, this comprehensive site provides links to bar associations, legal associations, law schools, publishers, associated services, vendors, government sites, law firms, alternative dispute resolution (ADR), legal education, online services, and law sites. Also provided are links to a newstand, a law library, employment resources, and a meetings calendar. Hieros Gamos claims to provide more than 6,000 listings with more than 5,000 links. To use this site, click on a link on the home page, which usually displays a page of regional links. Click on the region you want to explore to reveal a page of links—some commercial.

Martindale's Virtual Medical Law Center

http://www-sci.lib.uci.edu/HSG/Legal.html

This very large site is a subset of Martindale's very impressive medical site (at http://www-sci.lib.uci.edu/HSG/HSGuide.html). Here you can link to a reference desk, what's new section, support services (which include travel information; language fonts, software, and dictionaries; mail and package delivery services; and news); search indexes of law and legislation from the U.S. and Canada, and law material under these categories: Copyright & Patents, International & National Law, and World Law Resources. If you visit, be prepared to stay for a while.

Meta-Index for Legal Research

http://www.gsu.edu/~lawadmn/lawform.html

This site at the Georgia State University College of Law provides access to 19 legal search indexes. Indexes are arranged by Judicial Opinions (from the U.S. Supreme Court and the Federal Circuit courts), Legislation (from the U.S. Congress), Federal Regulation, Other Legal Sources (three indexes), and People in Law (the Directory of Legal Academia and West's Legal Directory). To run a search, simply type a keyword and click on the Search button.

REFLAW: The Virtual Law Library Reference Desk

http://law.wuacc.edu/washlaw/reflaw/reflaw.html

The Washburn University School of Law Library Reference Department presents REFLAW: The Virtual Law Library Reference Desk. Here you can search the Internet for legal and many other resources. Categories include Professor's Choice (a variety of legal and nonlegal resources), Books/Publishers, Business, Courts, Elections & Politics, General Reference, Government, International, Internet, Kansas Web, Legal Research, Legislation, Librarian's Choice, Library Circ., Listservs, Local Government, Media, Misc, New NEWS, and NII (National Information Infrastructure).

The Seamless Web

http://seamless.com/

This popular and well-designed site, for both attorneys and laypersons, is very easy to use. The home page presents four main sections: The Chambers (what's new), The Commons (papers about law-related topics), The Shingle (home pages of lawyers and other legal service businesses), and The Crossroads (with links to many law sites organized under eight categories). Also included is a job listing service, interactive bulletin board, listing of expert witnesses, and a chat line.

University of Southern California (USC) Law Library

http://www.usc.edu/dept/law-lib/index.html

This well-designed master site provides links to nine types of legal resources on the Internet. On one long page, you'll find links to legal resources, a law school directory, practice-oriented resources, government resources, law/pre-law student information, legal computing information, legal journals, career services, and virtual law libraries. When you click on a link on the home page, you remain at USC; however, the resulting links bring you to legal resources all over the world.

VCILP—The Legal Web

http://ming.law.vill.edu/vcilp/legalweb.html

From the Villanova Center for Information Law and Policy (VCILP) comes The Legal Web, which provides links to Internet sites of many law schools and law firms worldwide. Also included is a very impressive list of links to law journals and law-related publications. Although these links are not original to this site, Ken Mortensen at Villanova has provided excellent resources—at a single address.

West's Legal Directory

http://www.westpub.com/htbin/wld

gopher://odin.indstate.edu:70/11/ref.dir/info.dir/west.dir

West Publishing, a legal and educational publisher, provides news, business, and financial information. Using West's Legal Directory, you can search for individual attorneys, law firms, courts, government agencies, and so on in the U.S. and Canada. Simply type a keyword, such as a last name or city, and click on Search. For those whose browsers do not support forms, West provides a Gopher-based directory.

World-Wide Web Virtual Library— Law

http://www.law.indiana.edu:80/law/lawindex.html

This comprehensive site is an excellent place to start a search for Internet-based legal resources. Here you can find links to law sections of Internet indexes, lists of legal links, law schools, law firms, government servers, law journals and publications, and categories of laws—throughout the world. Other categories are constitutions, law FAQs, information technology related to law, electronic law, forensics, GATT, legal aspects of using software, and much much more.

Yahoo Law Resources

http://www.yahoo.com/Government/Law/

Yahoo provides a wealth of information about many topics, including the law. Here you'll find 29 legal indexes and 33 categories of links: from antitrust to Usenet. Business-related topics include arbitration and mediation, commercial, consumer, employment law, environmental, immigration, intellectual property, international, legal research, property, and tax.

Corporate Law

The sites in this section present legal information from a business point of view. You can visit advertising, corporate, and securities law sites; and you can read the full text of the Bankruptcy Reform Act of 1994, general provisions of the Uniform Commercial Code, the Securities Act of 1933, and the Securities Exchange Act of 1934.

Advertising Law Internet Site

http://www.webcom.com/~lewrose/home.html

This site, maintained by Lewis Rose, an advertising and marketing law partner with the law firm Arent Fox Kintner Plotkin & Kahn, provides a page of links to advertising and marketing law sites categorized as follows: United States Advertising Law, Links to Other Internet Advertising/Marketing/ Consumer Law Sites, Join in the Discussion, and Advertising Law Internet Site Administrivia. Interesting links include how to choose a business name; Federal

Trade Commission (FTC) rules, business compliance manuals, and consumer brochures; the Better Business Bureau On-line Complaint Form, and the European Commission Advertising/Consumer Law server.

Bankruptcy Reform Act of 1994

http://www.haledorr.com/bankref94.html

Hale & Dorr, a law firm with a large site on the World Wide Web, presents an analysis of the Bankruptcy Reform Act of 1994. At the top of this long page is a table of links. Click on a link to move to the selected topic, or scroll down the page until you find it. Subjects covered in this analysis are security interests, contracts, return of goods, compensation of trustees, and the National Bankruptcy Review Commission.

The Center for Corporate Law

http://www.law.uc.edu/CCL/index.html

This small page from the Center for Corporate Law at the University of Cincinnati College of Law provides electronic data related to corporate and securities law. At this site, you'll find the full text of the Securities Act of 1933, the Securities Exchange Act of 1934, and rules and regulations related to those acts.

Uniform Commercial Code, Articles 1-9 General Provisions

http://www.law.cornell.edu/ucc/ucc.table.html

This hypertext document provides Articles 1 to 9 of the Uniform Commercial Code (U.C.C.) as well as a link to the U.C.C.-based state commercial codes.

The Articles are:

◆ Article 1: General Provisions

◆ Article 2: Sales

◆ Article 2A: Leases

◆ Article 3: Negotiable Instruments

◆ Article 4: Bank Deposits and Collections

◆ Article 4A: Funds Transfers

◆ Article 5: Letters of Credit

◆ Article 6: Bulk Transfers

◆ Article 7: Warehouse Receipts, Bills of Lading and Other Documents of Title

◆ Article 8: Investment Securities

◆ Article 9: Secured Transactions: Sales of Accounts and Chattel Paper

Patents and Trademarks

In the course of business, many people must learn about trademarks and patents. In this section, you will find out how to register a trademark, how to get to the appropriate resources, read the full-text of U.S. patent law, discover U.S. adjustments to international patent law, and search 20 years of U.S. patents.

Note

Be sure to visit the related section, *Copyrights and Intellectual Rights*, immediately following this section.

Basic Facts About Registering a Trademark

http://www.uspto.gov/web/trad_reg_info/toc.html

If you produce goods, you may need to register trademarks to protect your products. This online article, which can be ordered or downloaded in several formats, deals with trademarks: how to register one, requirements, and U.S. Patent and

Trademark Office resources. You also can download application forms from this site.

GATT-Related Changes in the U.S. Patent System, Part 1

http://biotechlaw.ari.net/provis.html

Because of GATT (General Agreement on Tarrifs and Trade), the U.S. has had to amend its patent laws to change the length of a patent term, to file a provisional application, and to enact the "first inventor" principle for inventions outside the U.S. This online article, by Stephen A. Bent of the Foley & Lardner law firm, discusses U.S. provisional applications: characteristics, uses and misuses, and the procedure.

General Information Concerning Patents

http://www.uspto.gov/web/patinfo/toc.html

On this page, from the U.S. Patent and Trademark Office, is a table of links to general information about patents. This is a full-text version of a document (Stock Ordering Number: 003-004-00661-7) that you can order from the Superintendent of Documents. The document includes information about the U.S. Patent and Trademark Office, what can be patented, patent laws, conditions for getting a patent, filing fees, applications, and much more.

Index to Manual of Classification of Patents

http://sunsite.unc.edu/patents/

This very large site provides the Manual of Classification of Patents in a searchable index. Click on a link on the home page to access the index, or scroll down the page to view the list in order to determine the class to which an invention is assigned. The first part of your search produces a preliminary class or subclass for your invention. Then you can continue the search to verify your selection.

Overview of United States Patent Law

http://biotechlaw.ari.net/patentov.html

This online article, by Phillip B. C. Jones, discusses U.S. patents and their background and gives an interpretation of the U.S. patent law. Here you can read about the law and its effects.

Patent Law Web Server

http://www.patents.com/index.htm

This comprehensive site from Oppedahl & Larson, a law firm, provides information about these categories: patents, copyrights, trademarks, trade secrets, computer law, intellectual property, and how to contact offices and organizations from which you can get help. Clicking on a link typically provides a page of very useful links to U.S. and international resources. Also included is information about Oppedahl & Larson.

Patent Sources

http://www.ohiou.edu/ictto/patents.html

This small page contains links to 11 patent-related international Internet sites that deal with search indexes, laws, government agencies, and library connections.

U.S. Patent Act

http://www.law.cornell.edu/usc/35/i_iv/overview.html

This site, from the Legal Information Institute at Cornell University, provides a full-text version and a searchable index of the U.S. Patent Act, as Amended (1994), in 4 parts and 37 chapters.

U.S. Patent Links

http://town.hall.org/patent/patent.html

This short page provides a variety of links to patent and trademark resources on the Internet. Included are announcements, links to the U.S.

Patent and Trademark Office, the Copyright Office, the AIDS patent database, articles, acts, a search index, and a patent law server.

U.S. Patents at CNIDR

http://patents.cnidr.org:4242/

The Center for Networked Information Discovery and Retrieval (CNIDR), in cooperation with the National Science Foundation (NSF) and the U.S. Patent and Trademark Office, has provided free patent information since November 1995. You can search a database of more than 20 years of patent bibliographic text data. To search, click on Access the Patent Database and then click on Simple Search Page, Boolean Search Page, or Advanced Command-Line Search Page. Then submit a query (for example, the type of invention, the inventor or an inventor cited in the application, the company holding the patent), click on the Submit Query button, and wait for the results (see Figure 9.2). Then click on a link to find out more information about the selected patent.

Copyrights and Intellectual Rights

Copyrights and intellectual property rights information for all types of media—from books to multimedia presentations—seems to change from day to day. New technologies and the world economy force constant adjustments. In this section, you can learn the current copyright law and plans for the future—for the U.S. and internationally.

Note
Be sure to visit the related section, *Patents and Trademarks*, immediately preceding this section.

Creative Incentive Coalition

http://www.podesta.com/cic/index.html

The Creative Incentive Coalition provides intellectual rights information for copyright owners and users of publications, music and sound recordings, art works, reference materials, films and television, video games, and multimedia works. Also included at this site are links to the Copyright Office (gopher://marvel.loc.gov/11/copyright), the Information Infrastructure Task Force Working Group on Intellectual Property (http://www.uspto.gov), and the National Information Infrastructure Virtual Library (http://nii.nist.gov).

Note

The link **Information Infrastructure Task Force Working Group on Intellectual Property** is mislabeled. That link actually goes to the home page of the U.S. Patent Office (http://www.uspto.gov).

Intellectual Property and the NII

http://www.uspto.gov/niiip.html

The Information Infrastructure Task Force (IITF), formed in 1993, addresses the future of the National Information Infrastructure (NII). The Working Group on Intellectual Property Rights prepared this Preliminary Draft, a very large (more than 200 kilobytes) but fast-loading document. The Preliminary Draft presents the current results of an examination and analysis of intellectual property law, especially copyright law.

Score	Title
(100)	(5,440,237) Electronic force sensing with sensor normalization
(098)	(5,439,304) Keyboard
(096)	(361,030) *Ergonomic* handle
(094)	(5,435,066) Cutting device and assembly
(091)	(5,432,510) Ambidextrous single hand chordic data management device
(089)	(5,427,359) *Ergonomic* handrail/bumper
(087)	(5,426,449) Pyramid shaped *ergonomic* keyboard
(085)	(359,508) *Ergonomic* pen
(082)	(5,423,813) Resectoscope and electrode assembly
(080)	(5,423,531) Hockey stick handle
(078)	(5,423,098) Bed lounge

Figure 9.2   The results of a search in the patents database at the Center for Networked Information Discovery and Retrieval (CNIDR)

Intellectual Property Law Primer for Multimedia Developers

http://www.eff.org/pub/CAF/law/ip-primer

This copyrighted article, written by J. Dianne Brinson and Mark F. Radcliffe, provides information on creating and distributing multimedia works and obtaining a copyright. Here you can get an overview of the intellectual property laws, including copyright, patent, trademark, and trade secret laws. The last section of the article deals with works on which you can get a copyright.

Intellectual Property Rights Laws

http://www.ladas.com/index.html

This home page for the Ladas & Parry law firm presents information about the protection of intellectual property rights worldwide. Here you can find links to information about patents worldwide, provisional patent applications, and trademarks. You can link to a list of Recent Developments in the World of Intellectual Property and two versions of a table of contents: a list and an excellent abstracted version (at http://www.ladas.com/abstract.html). Clicking on a typical link displays a very informative article. Although this is a commercial site, Ladas & Parry presents itself in a very low-key way.

Intellectual Property Sites

http://www.einet.net/galaxy/Law/Intellectual-Property.html

EINet Galaxy is a very useful index of Internet sites of every type. On its Intellectual Property page, you can find links to intellectual property sites, articles, announcements, collections (copyright, patent, trade secrets, and trademark links), periodicals, directories, and organizations.

Software International Articles

gopher://una.hh.lib.umich.edu:70/11/ebb/soft

The Economics Bulletin Board (EBB) provides trade information, economic statistics, and links to U.S. government agencies and international business leads. In this folder, you can find articles about sales of computer software and hardware worldwide, upcoming events, and information copyright protection of software throughout the world.

U.S. Copyright Office

gopher://marvel.loc.gov/11/copyright

The U.S. Copyright Office, which is a department of the Library of Congress, provides this site to introduce you to its services and to acquaint you with other copyright resources on the Internet. Click on Copyright Basics (Circular 1) for an overview of copyrights. This circular and 24 others are available if you click on Copyright Information Circulars. Many of the other links lead you to the same list of circulars.

To search the Library of Congress copyright online files (you must be able to Telnet), click on Research in Copyright Office Files. Then click on Search Copyright Online Files at LC.

Federal Laws and Regulations

To run a business today, you must be knowledgeable in many fields: business management, scheduling, accounting, computing, and law, among others. In this section, you can put on your legal hat and read the full text of several federal laws, regulations, and documents such as the U.S. Constitution and Declaration of Independence; keep up to date with recent decisions; and learn how to abide by particular federal laws and regulations.

Americans with Disabilities Act of 1990

gopher://val-dor.cc.buffalo.edu:70/11/.legislation/

This important site not only presents the full text of the Americans with Disabilities Act but also provides links to resources for the disabled, including other acts. At this site, you'll find information about voting accessibility, a document center, the Pocket Guide to Federal Help, and the Social Security Administration's disability benefits.

Black Lung Law Library

http://www.asacon.com/oalj/libbla.htm

This site, from the Office of Administrative Law Judges in the U.S. Department of Labor, provides a short list of links to newsletters, the Black Lung Benefits Act, the Black Lung Desk Book (from 1991), recent U.S. Supreme Court decisions, and statutory and regulatory materials.

Board of Contract Appeals Rules

http://www.asacon.com/oalj/public/bca/refrnc/41c60.htm

This site, from the Office of Administrative Law Judges in the U.S. Department of Labor, provides a very long list of sections of subparts of Part 29-60—Procedures for Settling Contract Dispute Appeals. At the top of this page is a note that these regulations are no longer printed in the Code of Federal Regulations, but are still in effect.

Citizens Guide on Using the Freedom of Information Act

gopher://csf.Colorado.EDU:70/00/eforum/comm/
Freedom-of-Info-Act

The Government Printing Office (GPO) has sold almost 50,000 copies of *The Citizens Guide on Using the Freedom of Information Act and the Privacy Act of 1974 to Request Government Records*. The complete text is now online on a single long page. Sections include How to Use This Guide, Which Act to Use, The Freedom of Information Act, and The Privacy Act of 1974.

Civil Rights Law Library

http://www.asacon.com/oalj/libofccp.htm

This site, from the Office of Administrative Law Judges in the U.S. Department of Labor, provides a short list of links to cases relating to enforcement actions of the Office of Federal Contract Compliance Programs (OFCCP). At this site, you can access a comprehensive case list; the Office of Civil Rights, Section 503 Digest; a newsletter; and statutory and regulatory materials and other related materials.

Code of Federal Regulations (CFR)—Pension and Welfare Benefits

http://www.dol.gov/dol/allcfr/29cfr/
toc_Part2500-2599/Part2500-2599_toc.htm

This part of the CFR presents Parts 2500-2599, Chapter XXV—Pension and Welfare Benefits Administration (PWBA), USDOL. Subchapters include parts about the Employee Retirement Income Security Act of 1974 (ERISA), definitions of terms, and rules and regulations for reporting and disclosure, minimum standards for employee pension benefit plans, fiduciary responsibility, administration and enforcement, and so on.

Code of Federal Regulations (CFR)

http://www.dol.gov/dol/oaw/public/regs/cfr/main.htm

"The CFR contains all the general and permanent rules published in the Federal Register" for the following: Labor-Management Reporting and Disclosure Act, Urban Mass Transportation Act, and Airline Employee Protection Act. Under each link is a short description, which includes the name of the office administering the act.

Cosmetics Handbook

http://vm.cfsan.fda.gov/~lrd/cos-hdbk.txt

This long (74,252 bytes) text document describes the Federal Drug Administration's requirements and policies on producing and labeling cosmetics. The Cosmetics Handbook, dated 1992, is composed of five parts: Regulatory Requirements for Marketing, Cosmetic Good Manufacturing Practice Guidelines, Costmetic Product-Related Regulatory Requirements and Health Hazard Issues, Permanently

& Provisionally Listed Color Additives, and How to Obtain FDA Cosmetic Regulations.

Federal Communications Commission Notices/Rules

gopher://fcc.gov:70/11//Daily_Releases

This site from the Federal Communications Commission (FCC) contains links to Daily Business, which provides daily summaries of FCC activities and orders, and to Daily Digest, which contains daily news releases, such as coming events and filings.

Immigration Law Library

http://www.asacon.com/oalj/libina.htm

This site, from the Office of Administrative Law Judges in the U.S. Department of Labor, provides a short list of links to a newsletter, the BALCA (Board of Alien Labor Certification Appeals) Benchbook 2nd Edition (covering overviews of appeals from 1987 to April 1994), BALCA Benchbook Supplement (from April 1994 to now), and an index of labor-related immigration statutes and regulations.

Internet Law Library

http://www.pls.com:8001/

This nongraphical page provides links to U.S. federal, state, and territorial laws as well as laws of other nations, treaties and international law, laws arranged by subject, law school law library

catalogs and services, attorney and legal profession directories, and review of law books. Developed by the U.S. Congress House Information Resources (H.I.R.), this is a demonstration project containing more than 1,600 links. Here you can find multiple copies of the U.S. Constitution, the Declaration of

Independence, the Articles of Confederation, the Equal Rights Amendment, Federalist Papers, and much more.

Job Training Partnership Act 1992

http://www.ttrc.doleta.gov/html/jtpahome.html

This site, from the Employment and Training Administration of the U.S. Department of Labor, not only includes the full text of the Job Training Partnership Act of 1992 but also provides information about specific programs for these categories: Adults, Disabled, Dislocated Workers, Homeless, Older Workers, Indian and Native American, Summer Youth, Year-Round Youth, summaries of research for adults and youth in basic skills, general education development, job search, job skills, literacy, and on-the-job training. Also included are links to Demonstration Projects, Adult Dislocated Workers, Labor Market Information, Private Sector, Program Evaluation, and other resources.

JTPA/CETA Law Library

http://www.asacon.com/oalj/libjtp.htm

This site, from the Office of Administrative Law Judges in the U.S. Department of Labor, provides a short list of links to decisions under the Job Training Partnership Act (JTPA) and Comprehensive Employment & Training Act (CEA). Here you also will find a newsletter and case list.

Library of Wage Appeals Board and Service Contract Act Decisions

http://www.asacon.com/oalj/libdba.htm

This site, from the Office of Administrative Law Judges in the U.S. Department of Labor, provides a short list of links to a newsletter, a case list of Wage Appeals Board decisions, a case list of decisions concerning the Service Contract Act and related acts, and statutory and regulatory materials.

Longshore Law Library

http://www.asacon.com/oalj/liblhc.htm

This site, from the Office of Administrative Law Judges in the U.S. Department of Labor, provides a short list of links for the Longshore and Harbor Workers' Compensation Act: newsletters, the text of the act, recent U.S. Supreme Court decisions, and statutory and regulatory materials and other related materials.

Miscellaneous Traditional Law Library

http://www.asacon.com/oalj/libtrad.htm

This site, from the Office of Administrative Law Judges in the U.S. Department of Labor, provides a short list of links to miscellaneous cases: child labor, Program Fraud Civil Remedies Act, Employee Polygraph Protection Act, ERISA, Fair Labor Standard Act, and Trade Act. At this site, you can access a newsletter (at the time of this writing, the link did not work), a case list, and statutory and regulatory materials and other related materials.

Occupational Safety and Health Act of 1970 (as amended 1990)

http://www.osha-slc.gov/
OshAct_toc/OshAct_toc_by_sect.html

gopher://gabby.osha-slc.gov/

The Occupational Safety and Health Act "assures safe and healthful working conditions for working men and women." This site contains the full text of this act.

OSHA Computerized Information System (OCIS)

http://www.osha-slc.gov//p/

This site provides links and search indexes to information about OSHA's programs, offices, regulations, documents, technical information, and training as well as links to other OSHA and

U.S. government servers. When you run a search, you can specify a search in OSHA Regulations, OSHA Notices in the Federal Register, OSHA Act of 1970, Standard Interpretations, or all the above. Simply type a word or phrase in the text box and click on Submit.

Social Security Administration Legislative Information

http://www.ssa.gov/legislation/legis_intro.html

This Social Security Administration page provides information about and links to recent legislation affecting benefits and programs. Here, you can link to Thomas (at http://thomas.loc.gov/), the source of legislative information for the U.S. Congress, and read summaries of congressional activities.

Whistleblower Law Library

http://www.asacon.com/oalj/libwhist.htm

This site, from the Office of Administrative Law Judges in the U.S. Department of Labor, provides a short list of links to newsletters, decisions, statutory and regulatory materials, and a caselist and citator for whistleblower cases. This is a supplement to the Whistleblower Library CD-ROM, which also includes older decisions.

NAFTA

The North American Free Trade Agreement (NAFTA) changes the way in which the U.S., Canada, and Mexico do business. In fact, the entire Western hemisphere is affected by this agreement. Using the resources in this section, you can read the full text of NAFTA, link to NAFTA-related pages, and visit business and other sites all over the world.

The NAFTA Resource Center

http://www.tpusa.com/nafta/nafta.html

The NAFTA Resource Center provides links to the full text of NAFTA, the U.S. Department of Commerce NAFTA desk, a summary and analysis of NAFTA from a law firm, and the NAFTA Customs Guide.

A valuable part of this site is the page from the NAFTA desk; this lists NAFTA-related documents that you can

order and many that you can read online. Also on this page are two other sets of online documents: Doing Business in Canada and Doing Business in Mexico.

NaftaLab

http://naftalab.bus.utexas.edu/

This home page provides links to all types of information about the North American Free Trade Agreement (NAFTA), with an emphasis on the U.S. and Mexico. Not only can you access full text versions of NAFTA agreements, but you also can access regional resources, including links to telecommunications and information, economic development, educational development, medical and health resources, information infrastructures, and international trade information. This nongraphical page presents the background of NaftaLab and a table of links to which you can jump.

NAFTANet

http://www.nafta.net/

This site with both English and Spanish language pages not only includes the text of NAFTA and GATT (see the following section) but also provides links to information about doing business in

Mexico and other countries throughout the world. Other links include news from U.S. and Mexican newspapers, business calendars, financial markets, weather, travel, and home pages for some Latin American, Caribbean, and South American countries as well as Canada, Mexico, the U.S., and the state of Texas.

GATT

The General Agreement on Tariffs and Trade (GATT) impacts international trade. In this section, you can read the full text of GATT as well as documents leading up to the final agreement. In addition, you can learn how U.S. business must adjust to GATT with changes to patent laws, trademark protection, copyright law, and other intellectual property rights.

General Agreement on Tariffs and Trade (GATT) Texts

gopher://cyfer.esusda.gov:70/11/ace/policy/gatt/

This site provides full text versions of the General Agreement on Tariffs and Trade (GATT) from the Uruguay round of multilateral trade negotiations. Text of understandings, agreements, declarations, and decisions are also included. At the bottom of the page are links to downloadable documents in WordPerfect 5.1 and zipped formats. You also can find the text of GATT at http://heiwww.unige.ch/gatt/final_act/.

Intellectual Property Provisions of GATT

http://www.ladas.com/gatt.html

This long page, from the Ladas & Parry law firm, explores the way in which GATT addresses intellectual property: patent laws, trademark protection, copyright law, and other intellectual property issues. Either click on a link at the top of the page, or scroll down the page until you get to the desired section, which includes an analysis and the provisions of GATT. Information here is not presented in a technical way; it's written for the layperson.

International Law

In this world economy, the businessperson who ignores international law is operating at a distinct disadvantage. In the 1990s, knowledge is truly power. In this section, you can view international laws, agreements, constitutions, and historical documents and visit world organizations. You can visit an international trade library with full text of laws, links to organizations and agencies, and downloadable documents.

Foreign & International Law Documents

gopher://gopher.law.cornell
.edu:70/11/foreign

This site is composed of folders containing files of information about international sites. Countries and regions with documents here include Australia, Canada, Eastern Europe, Germany, and North America. Also here are some documents from the United Nations.

You also can find world constitutions, links to the World Health Organization (WHO), multilateral treaties, and historical documents: from the Laws of William the Conquerer to the Communist Manifesto.

International Trade Law Project (ITLP)

http://ananse.irv.uit.no/trade_law/

The International Trade Law Project (ITLP) was started in 1993 under the auspices of the Law Faculty of the University of Tromso, in Norway. At this good-looking site, click on a button (see Figure 9.3) to find a trade law library, which consists of Internet links to many law and Internet resources: treaties (GATT, Maastricht, NAFTA), conventions, model laws, trade-related organizations, agencies, dispute settlement, intellectual property, electronic data interchange, enforcement, leasing, free trade, insurance, and the United Nations Commission on International Trade Law (UNCITRAL). Many UNCITRAL documents are downloadable in Adobe Acrobat (PDF) format.

Maastricht Treaty of European Union

gopher://wiretap.Spies.COM:70/11/Gov/Maast

The Maastricht Treaty, or the Treaty on European Union, signed at Maastricht in 1992, establishes the European Community (EC). This

Figure 9.3   Click on a button to link to a page of trade law resources.

site provides the complete text of the treaty. Before viewing the files, click on README to learn about the files, including Common Provisions, View to Establishing the EC, Coal and Steel Community, Atomic Energy Community, Common Foreign & Security Policy, Justice & Home Affairs, and Final Provisions.

United Nations Convention on Contracts for the International Sale of Goods

gopher://gopher.law.cornell.edu:70/00/
foreign/fletcher/KAV2420.txt

This site presents a full-text version of the United Nations Convention on Contracts for the International Sale of Goods. This convention, signed in 1980, establishes uniform rules governing contracts for the sale of goods between member states of the United Nations.

International Government Resources

When doing business on an international scale, learning about government resources can be an important contribution to success. In this section, you will find links to government departments and agencies worldwide. In addition, you can learn more about particular countries by reading some of the U.S. government-furnished and other documents here: treaties and agreements, United Nations programs, international affairs documents, constitutions of several countries and the European Commission, and much more.

Australia Department of Finance

http://www.nla.gov.au/finance/home.html

The Department of Finance for the Commonwealth of Australia provides links to the Commonwealth Budget, speeches, statements, forecasts, and statistics.

Also included are budget statements from past years, publications, links to its divisions, other financial resources at government agencies (United Kingdom, the U.S., Canada, and New Zealand), and other Australian government agencies.

British Columbia Archives and Records Service (BCARS)

http://www.bcars.gs.gov.bc.ca/bcars.html

This large slow-loading site provides links to records and archives for the Ministry of Government Services, Province of British Columbia. Topics include the Photo-Imaging Database, Cartographic Records Pilot Project, Research Library (with 10,000 publications), Overview of Textual Records, the Finding Aid Databases, and the Virtual Reference Room. You can also find network exhibitions: paintings, photographs, and prints (see Figure 9.4) exhibited online.

British Columbia, Ministry of Environment, Lands, and Parks

http://www.env.gov.bc.ca/

The Ministry of Environment, Lands, and Parks protects, conserves, and restores "the full range of biological and physical diversity native to British Columbia." At this site, you can view ministry

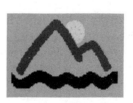

documents, learn about the departments within the ministry, link to forums, and learn about upcoming conferences. In addition, you can link to ministry reports, studies, and the Integrated Pest Management Information System (IPMIS) (at http://pupux1.env.gov.bc.ca/~ipmis/ipmis.html), a searchable index of information about pest (insects and animals) management.

Canadian Department of Foreign Affairs and International Trade (DFAIT)

http://www.dfait-maeci.gc.ca/ english/menu.htm

This site, in both English and in French, provides links to six pages: Introduction, What's New, Gopher Site, Information by Subject, Information by Geographic Areas, and Other Sources of Information. You can read about this site by going to http://www .dfaitmaeci.gc.ca/english/infoweb/infoweb.htm or by clicking on Introduction and then clicking on About the DFAIT Web. A good way to move around this site is to click on Information by Subject, which reveals six links: Foreign Policy, International Trade, International Cultural Relations, Canada and the Provinces, Investing and Doing Business in Canada, and Consular Services.

Figure 9.4   Victoria, British Columbia, in 1889

CCTA Government Information Service

http://www.open.gov.uk/

At first glance, the official United Kingdom government information site looks very small. The home page contains links to what's new, two experimental search indexes, four Government On-Line links, and information about the server and usage statistics. If you know the name of the organization that you want to visit, click on Index by Organisation. This reveals a clickable list of letters of the alphabet. Click to display a list of links to a variety of government and other resources (including government departments, museums, hospitals, laboratories, and so on). Click on Index by Function to view lists organized by functions, such as awards, benefits, careers, data protection, and so on.

CopNet Police Resource List

http://police.sas.ab.ca/prl/index.html

This well-designed and comprehensive list of international links contains a variety of resources—from local police departments to international agencies. At the top of this long page is an index: International Agencies; Canadian Agencies; European Sites; U.S. Federal Agencies; U.S. State/Municipal/ County Policy Agencies; Military Police; Native Police; University Police Agencies; Police Associations, Unions, Organizations; List Servers; Seminars; and Training, Fitness, and Standards.

Documents from Countries around the World

gopher://garnet.berkeley.edu:1250/11/.gov/.othergov/

At this very busy site, you can link to folders about world laws, law documents, and information about countries worldwide. Folders include World Constitutions, Background Notes (from the U.S. Department of State), Country Information & State Department Travel Advisories, Asia, Australian Law Documents, Canadian Documents, Europe, Israel Information Service, Latin America, Mexico, and Soviet Archives. Click on a link to find more folders or documents.

Government of British Columbia

http://www.gov.bc.ca/

This well-designed and good-looking site provides many links to information about the government of British Columbia as well as tourist information, business opportunities, and an overview of environment matters. To go to a particular page, click on the large graphic (see Figure 9.5) or click on a directory link. If you don't want to load the large graphic, you can choose small graphics (at http://www.gov.bc.ca/bchomesmall.html) or text-only (at http://www.gov.bc.ca/bchometext.html).

Her Majesty's Treasury

http://www.hm-treasury.gov.uk/index.html

This slow-loading home page presents links to her majesty's treasury in the United Kingdom, with news, press releases, the text of speeches, minutes of meetings, reports, and many other links to government finance in the UK. Also provided are links to CCTA's Government Information Service (at http://www.open.gov.uk/) and Other Government Departments Press Releases (at http://www.ws.pipex.com/coi).

International, U.S., State, and Local Government Servers

http://www.eff.org/govt.html

The Electronic Frontier Foundation (EFF), a nonprofit civil liberties organization dedicated to online interests, presents a nongraphical and comprehensive list of international, U.S., state, and local government links. The list is arranged in this hierarchical order: international, continent, country, state/province/region, county/parish/township/metropolis, and city/town/village/neighborhood.

Figure 9.5 Click on a button to get government, business, or tourist information about British Columbia.

The United States section is arranged by branches of government, U.S. miscellaneous and meta-indexes, government-related, political organizations, meta-indexes for state and local government, state maps, and state/regional/local. You can access this information in hierarchical segments or in a single-page format, which is about 170 kilobytes in length. This site not only contains many government pages but also many travel resources.

International Government Information

http://www.lib.uwaterloo.ca/discipline/Government

This comprehensive site provides information about governments worldwide, with an emphasis on Canada. Here is a center point of a great deal of government information: treaties and agreements, United Nations programs, international affairs documents, constitutions of several countries and the European Commission. Note that the United States section, which provides links to many government departments and agencies, also includes links to state government resources.

New Zealand Government Web Pages

http://www.govt.nz/

At this site, you can find a variety of links to information about New Zealand: its government, politics, ministries and departments, legislation, and national history. Also included are current topics: letters, papers, Budget 95, and what's new.

South African Government

gopher://gopher.ru.ac.za/11/politics

This site provides links to information about South Africa—its government, ruling political party, constitution, news, and newsgroups.

Clicking on a folder icon usually reveals a long page of links to documents, speeches, newsgroup archives, and so on. A bonus of visiting this site is the Weekly Mail and Guardian Public Domain folder, which contains links to up-to-date news stories.

Yahoo Countries Links

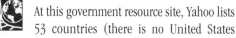

http://www.yahoo.com/Government/Countries

At this government resource site, Yahoo lists 53 countries (there is no United States entry). Click on a country name to reveal a page with

Interesting Site

Although you won't find any partisan politics in this book (mainly because I'd have to publicize the side that I don't like), the perennial presidental candidate, Pat Paulsen, is worth a mention. At the Pat Paulsen for President site (at http://www.amdest.com/Pat/pat.html), you can find pictures of the candidate as well as links to his political poll, a downloadable "animated, audio, interactive, presidential trivia file" (approximately 1.3 megabites [sic]), press releases and platform positions, political documents with Pat's slant, a plea for volunteers, and great holiday gifts.

links to documents, embassies and consulates, law, and research labs, and so on and other miscellaneous government information.

General U.S. Government Resources

The U.S. government provides many valuable resources for both business and personal life. Using the resources in this section, you can start discovering what the U.S. has to offer. Here you can find lists of links to specialized resources—such as aerospace—and general information, not only at U.S. sites but also at some international, state, and local pages.

Aerospace Business Development Center

http://arganet.tenagra.com/Tenagra/aero_bd.html

This valuable commercial site provides links (most from NASA) related to business development and procurement in the aerospace industry. Categories include Procurement Centers, U.S. Department of Defense sites, News and Press Releases of Interest, Procurements Related Information Sources (government-based sites, guides, and directories), and Other Links of Interest (many related to aerospace and aviation).

Askew School's Government Guide

http://www.fsu.edu:80/~spap/research/govern.html

This well-designed site at Florida State University provides government-related links to many general survey guides (Internet sites providing lists of government links); to federal, state (especially Florida), and international government agency information servers; and to popular government and political servers.

The Brookings Institution

http://www.brook.edu/

The Brookings Institution is a private, independent, and nonprofit think tank that does research in economics, government, and foreign policy. At this site, you can learn about its history, programs, and scholars; read publications and press releases; and visit its online library. The Brookings Institution Library provides links to news summaries; political stories and reports; Internet tools and resources; and resources of particular interest to Brookings scholars. These valuable links are categorized as follows: Economics, International Relations, Law, Politics and Government, Reference, Research Centers and Think Tanks, and Washington Resources.

Catalog of Federal Domestic Assistance

gopher://solar.rtd.utk.edu:70/11/Federal/CFDA

The comprehensive Catalog of Federal Domestic Assistance provides information about U.S. government programs, projects, services, and activities. In this index, you can search for "grants, loans, loan guarantees, scholarships, mortgage loans, insurance, and other types of financial assistance." You also can search for technical assistance, counseling, statistical, and other expert information. To search, type one or more keywords and press Enter. After a few seconds, links to the search results appear. Then click on a link to view a text document, which provides a summary of the resource.

Federal Acquisition Jumpstation

http://procure.msfc.nasa.gov/fedproc/home.html/bd

This large and very useful site, sponsored by the Office of Federal Procurement Policy, the National Aeronautics and Space Administration, and the Federal Aviation Administration, provides links to U.S. government procurement pages and to home pages for U.S. government departments and agencies. From this page, you can "retrieve acquisition forecasts, announcements of upcoming and current acquisitions, solicitations, small business assistance information, plus federal acquisition regulations." Categories are arranged under these major headings: Departments of the Executive Branch, Independent Agencies of the Executive Branch, Federal Acquisition Regulations and Related Information, Small Business Assistance, Electronic Commerce in the Federal Arena, Streamlining Federal Acquisitions, and Links to Other Federal Government Destinations.

Federal Government Agencies on the WWW

http://www.lib.lsu.edu/gov/fedgov.html

This well-organized and easy-to-use page presents U.S. federal government resources under six major categories on which you can click to jump down the page. You also can scroll down the page to find a link under Executive Branch, Executive Agencies, Judicial Branch, Legislative Branch, Independent Agencies, Quasi-Official Agencies, and Other Government Indexes. The author, David Wuolu, has entered resources with links (in blue text) and without current links (black text).

Federal Information Exchange (FIE)

http://web.fie.com/

With the support of the U.S. Department of Energy and nine other government departments or agencies, the Federal Information Exchange (FIE) provides federal information for the education and research communities. Here, you can find federal opportunities by agency, subject, or audience. Click on a

link to reveal a page of opportunities arranged by agency, subject, or audience. Links include:

- FEDIX (federal opportunities, the centerpiece of this site)

- MOLIS (Minority Colleges & Universities)

- EQUIPMENT (federal equipment grants to eligible educational institutions and laboratories)

- ERA (Electronic Research Administration, a demonstration project that automates the grants process)

- RAMS (a collection of sources for research administrators at educational institutions)

FedWorld

http://www.fedworld.gov/

This gigantic site, from the National Technical Information Service (NTIS), provides links to a wide variety of U.S. government  resources through the World Wide Web and Telnet. Here you can read abstracts of government reports and order catalogs from all government agencies, especially from the U.S. Department of Commerce; link to other FedWorld sites in order to access business (at http://www.fedworld.gov/bus.htm), health and safety (http://www.fedworld.gov/hlthftp.htm), and environment (at http://www.fedworld.gov/envir.htm) files. On this long page, you also can link to resources by alphabetically arranged subject.

FinanceNet

http://www.financenet.gov/

This impressive site, sponsored in part by the National Performance Review (NPR), provides links to federal, state, and local government resources and to other sites arranged under these categories: Government Sales (at http://pula.financenet.gov:80/sales.htm) for the public and government employees, State & Local, Library, Mailing Lists, Resources, What's New, Newsgroups, Event Calendars, and Best of the 'Net. Also included are two search indexes: for FinanceNet documents and related Web sites and the Internet.

Government Information INFOMINE

http://lib-www.ucr.edu/govpub/

This comprehensive site, provided by the University of California Regents, contains many links to U.S., state, and local government resources. Primary categories at this site are Search (a Keywords, Subjects, and/or Title search with a list of keywords thoughtfully provided), What's New (the links didn't work), Table of Contents, Subject, Keyword, Title, and Author (this seems to be arranged by government agency).

GPO Gate

http://ssdc.ucsd.edu/gpo/

This important site, from the University of California at San Diego, provides a searchable index of these full-text databases: Congressional Bills, Congressional Record Index, GAO Reports, Public Laws, Congressional Directory, Congressional Reports, Government Manual, Senate Calendars, Congressional Documents, Economic Indicators, History of Bills, Unified Agenda, Congressional Record, Federal Register,

House Calendars, United States Code, and other full-text sources. Also included at this site are links to the university, government documents, and more. To search, type one or more keywords and click on the Run Search button. After a few seconds, the results appear on your screen (see Figure 9.6). You can download some files from this site in ASCII or Acrobat PDF formats.

Johnson Space Center (JSC) Procurement Home Page

http://www.jsc.nasa.gov/bd2/

This useful site provides links to procurement and business opportunities pages at NASA and at other U.S. government departments

and agencies. In addition, you can find links to small business resources on the Internet. Particular links include Business Opportunities, Search NASA Synopses, Procurement Reference Documents, Other NASA Procurement Home Pages, Federal Acquisition Jumpstation, Johnson Space Center Acquisition Forecast FY 96, and the NF533 Reporting Process for Contracts (a downloadable Windows-based tutorial).

Political Scientist's Guide to the Internet

http://www.trincoll.edu/pols/home.html

This good-looking online guide provides links to U.S. government, state government, and international sites. On the home page, click on Federal to reveal links to the three branches of U.S. government and other indexes of U.S. government links. The State page presents links under alphabetically arranged state headings. Clicking on the International Affairs link opens the World-Wide Web Virtual Library International Affairs page (at http://www.pitt.edu/~ian/ianres.html), which is described in the *Trade and Markets* chapter.

U.S. Government Gopher Site

gopher://garnet.berkeley.edu:1250/11/.gov/.nat

This very busy site provides links to Gopher sites for all branches of the U.S. government, many government servers, documents, and other Gophers that provide information about the U.S. government. Also included is a folder for Politics & Elections.

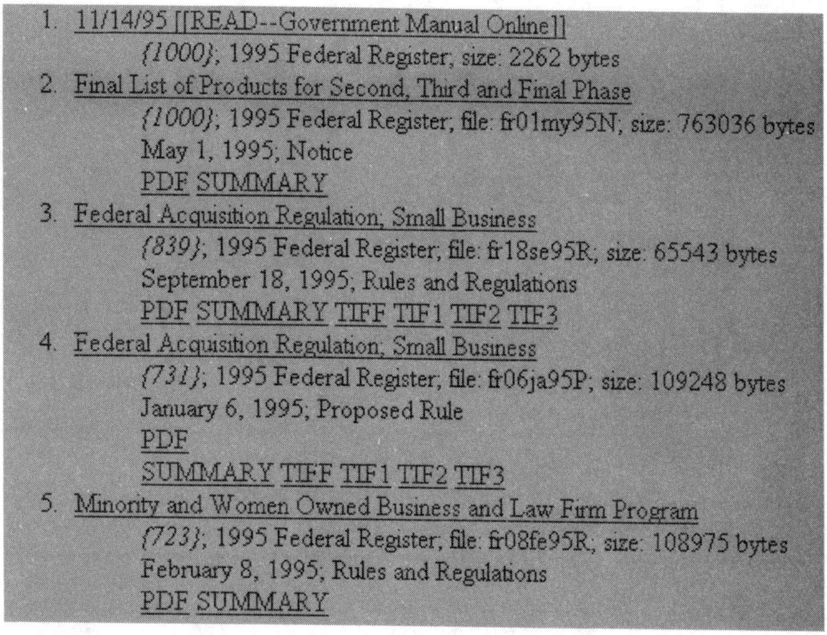

1. 11/14/95 [[READ--Government Manual Online]]
   {1000}; 1995 Federal Register; size: 2262 bytes
2. Final List of Products for Second, Third and Final Phase
   {1000}; 1995 Federal Register; file: fr01my95N; size: 763036 bytes
   May 1, 1995; Notice
   PDF SUMMARY
3. Federal Acquisition Regulation; Small Business
   {839}; 1995 Federal Register; file: fr18se95R; size: 65543 bytes
   September 18, 1995; Rules and Regulations
   PDF SUMMARY TIFF TIF1 TIF2 TIF3
4. Federal Acquisition Regulation; Small Business
   {731}; 1995 Federal Register; file: fr06ja95P; size: 109248 bytes
   January 6, 1995; Proposed Rule
   PDF
   SUMMARY TIFF TIF1 TIF2 TIF3
5. Minority and Women Owned Business and Law Firm Program
   {723}; 1995 Federal Register; file: fr08fe95R; size: 108975 bytes
   February 8, 1995; Rules and Regulations
   PDF SUMMARY

Figure 9.6 The results of a GPO Gate keyword search

U.S. Supreme Court Justices Directory

http://www.law.cornell.edu/supct/directory/overview.html

The Legal Information Institute, at Cornell University, presents a list of justices of the U.S. Supreme Court and the highest courts in each state. The list originates from Your Nation's Courts Series from WANT Publishing Company. The list is updated every January. To peruse the list, either click on the U.S. Supreme Court or a letter of the alphabet. You also can scroll down the page and click on a state. State information includes the chief justice and his or her mailing address and telephone number and a list of justices. Also included are names, addresses, and telephone numbers for clerks of the court.

U.S. Supreme Court Decisions

http://www.law.cornell.edu/supct/supct.table.html

The Legal Information Institute of Cornell University provides decisions of the U.S. Supreme Court for 1990 to the current year. You can search an index by topic, by keyword, or by first party and second party names. More detailed information (for example, using e-mail to contact the court and other miscellaneous information) is provided for the current term and the previous term.

World-Wide Web Virtual Library: U.S. Government Information Sources

http://iridium.nttc.edu/gov_res.html

This list of more than 750 links to U.S. government resources provides links arranged

Figure 9.7   The GSA home page provides a graphically pleasing set of buttons on which to click to go to other pages.

Figure 9.8   NTIA provides a superhighway image on which you can click to reveal pages.

under these categories: Federal Branches (that is, executive, judicial, and legislative), Executive Departments (including subdepartments), Independent Agencies (government agencies not under departments), Other Related Government Resources (miscellaneous U.S. government links), and Search for a Government Resource (a search index).

U.S. Government Directory

The population of U.S. government sites on the Internet grows day by day. Many sites are not the drab government issue that you might expect. In fact, some (see Figures 9.7 and 9.8) present their information in a very imaginative and even award-winning way. In this section, you will find a very large table (see Table 9.1) with pages and pages of links to U.S. government departments, agencies, and offices.

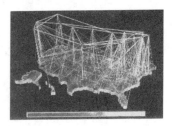

Table 9.1: Government Agency Internet Sites

Agency	URL	Description	Major Topics
Adult Training Programs	http://www.doleta.gov/programs/adtrain.htm	Links from the Employment and Training Administration (ETA), an office of the U.S. Department of Labor	Job Training Partnership Act (JTPA), Apprenticeship Training, Base Closing Assistance
Asia-Pacific Technology Program	http://www.doc.gov/aptp.html	Carries out the mandates of the Japanese Technical Literature Act of 1986 and the U.S.-Japan Science and Technology Agreement of 1988; a program of the Technology Administration of the U.S. Department of Commerce	What Is the Asia-Pacific Technology Program, Where Is the Asia-Pacific Technology Program, Who Is the Asia-Pacific Technology Program, Special Functions, Other Japanese Technology Information, Flash Announcements, United States Government (links to other programs monitoring Japanese technology)
Bureau of Economic Analysis	http://www.bea.doc.gov	The U.S. accountant, provides information on economic growth, regional development, and the U.S. position in the world economy; an agency of the U.S. Department of Commerce	About BEA, What's New, User's Guide to BEA Information, News Releases, BEA Publications (both online and for sale through the BEA or the U.S. Government Printing Office), Information and Data Files (a link to STAT-USA, a fee-based system)
Bureau of International Labor Affairs (ILAB)	http://www.dol.gov/dol/ilab/	Assists in formulating international economic, trade, and immigration policies affecting American workers; a bureau of the U.S. Department of Labor	Mission Statement, Organizational Components (Office of International Economic Affairs, Office of International Organizations, Office of Foreign Relations, National Administrative Office, Child Labor Group), Key Personnel and Phone Numbers

Table 9.1: Government Agency Internet Sites (continued)

Agency	URL	Description	Major Topics
Bureau of Justice Statistics (BJS)	http://ncjrs.aspensys.com:81/1/new2/aboutbjs.html	The primary source for criminal justice statistics; part of the U.S. Department of Justice	Search the Bureau of Justice Statistics Publications and Releases, Press Releases, Publications, Publications Catalog, Telephone Contacts, Bulletin Board List; archives at http://ncjrs.umich.edu/resources.html
Bureau of Labor Statistics (BLS)	http://stats.bls.gov/blshome.html	The principal fact-finding agency for the U.S. government in the field of labor economics and statistics; an agency of the U.S. Department of Labor	Data (Most Requested Series, Selective Access, News Releases, Series Report, Gopher, Economy at a Glance), Economy at a Glance, Keyword Search of BLS Web Pages, Surveys & Programs (Employment & Unemployment, Prices & Living Conditions, Compensation & Working Conditions, Productivity & Technology, Employment Projections, International Programs, Other Surveys), Publications (Occupational Outlook Handbook, News Releases, Information), Regional Information (data and information about 10 regions of the U.S.), BLS Information, Research Papers (papers by BLS authors)
CapWeb	http://policy.net/capweb/congress.html	A guide to the U.S. Congress	What's New on CapWeb (with many links); The Senate; The House of Representatives; The Library of Congress; E-mail, Bills, Votes, Laws & Other Stuff; Congressional Support Agencies; Capitol Hill and Washington, D.C.; Other Related Resources

Table 9.1: Government Agency Internet Sites (continued)

Agency	URL	Description	Major Topics
Census Bureau Home Page	http://www.census.gov/	Collects data about the people and economy of the U.S.; a division of the U.S. Department of Commerce	Greetings, Population and Housing, Economy, Geography, Data Access Tools, Search, About the Census Bureau, Latest News, Ask the Experts, Market Place, Pop Clocks, Data Maps, Genealogy, Radio Broadcasts, Other Topics, Archive, HTTP Files, FTP Files, BBS, Excellent Sites, Employment Opportunities
Centers for Disease Control (CDC)	http://www.cdc.gov/	Prevents and controls disease, injury, and disability; an agency of the Public Health Service, under the Department of Health and Human Services	About the Centers for Disease Control and Prevention (CDC); What's New; Diseases' Health Risks; Prevention Guidelines and Strategies; Travelers' Health; Publications, Products, and Subscription Services; Scientific Data, Surveillance, and Health Statistics; Funding Opportunities; Training and Employment Opportunities; and Information Networks and Other Information Sources
Central Intelligence Agency	http://www.odci.gov/cia	Collects and analyzes information on developments in foreign countries for the president, Congress, and other leaders	What's New, About the CIA, Publications (the World Factbook, Factbook on Intelligence, CIA Maps and Publications, Chiefs of State and Cabinet Members of Foreign Governments, Intelligence Literature), Public Affairs (speeches, press releases, and FAQs), Other Intelligence Community Links
Child Labor Group	http://www.dol.gov/dol/ilab/public/aboutilab/org/child.htm	Reports on international child labor; within Bureau of International Labor Affairs (ILAB), a bureau of the U.S. Department of Labor	Text page

Table 9.1: Government Agency Internet Sites (continued)

Agency	URL	Description	Major Topics
CLIO—U.S. National Archives and Records Administration	http://www.nara.gov/ and gopher://gopher.nara.gov/	An information system that combines information from the National Archives and Records Administration (NARA) with Internet resources	Strategic Directions for the National Archives, What Is CLIO, About the National Archives and Records Administration, Information about NARA Holdings, Online Exhibit Hall, Genealogy, Information for Archivists and Records Managers, The Federal Register, National Historical Publications and Records Commission, Other Gopher Servers and Internet Resources, The NARA Library, Letters to CLIO, CLIO Recently Added or Updated Items
Commerce Information Locator Service (CILS)	http://www.doc.gov/cgi-bin/enter_query/public/cils	A search index for the collection of explanatory information on more than 300 services of the U.S. Department	A search index
Congressional Black Caucus	http://drum.ncsc.org/~carter/CBC.html	African-American members of the U.S. House of Representatives	Congressional Black Caucus Legislative Agenda, The 93-94 CBC Guide, Members' Reports, CBC Statement on Haiti (9/29/94), Rep. Melvin Watt 12th District, North Carolina, Congressional E-Mail Address Listing (a partial list), News Media E-Mail Address Listing (at the time of this writing, a blank page)
Defense Logistics Service Center	http://www.dlsc.dla.mil/	A supply management and catalog system of the U.S. Department of Defense (this site is somewhat slow-loading because of a very large graphic)	Customer Support, Products & Services, Database Maintenance, DLSC FIIG Library, and Electronic Commercial Catalogs

Table 9.1: Government Agency Internet Sites (continued)

Agency	URL	Description	Major Topics
Defense Technical Information Center (DTIC) Gopher	gopher://asc.dtic.dla.mil/	A research arm of the U.S. Department of Defense	Cooperative Programs for Reinvestment (CPR), Federal Information (the U.S. Budget for 1994 and many other links), Information Analysis Centers (IAC), U.S. Government Gopher Servers (from NSF), Small Business Innovation Research Program (SBIR), and Technology Transfer
Defense Technical Information Center (DTIC) Web Page	http://www.dtic.dla.mil/dtiw/ or http://asc.dtic.dla.mil/	Part of the Scientific and Technical Information Program, U.S. Department of Defense	About DTIC, What's New, DTIW, Gopher, Anon.ftp, DTIC Organization (you must register for some DTIC services)
Dislocated Worker Programs	http://www.doleta.gov/programs/disloc.htm	Links from the Employment and Training Administration (ETA), an office of the U.S. Department of Labor	Base Closing Assistance, Economic Dislocation and Worker Adjustment Assistance, NAFTA Transitional Adjustment Assistance, Enterprise Council (Enterprise, Pioneers), One-Stop Career Centers, Trade Adjustment Assistance, Worker Adjustment and Retraining Notification (WARN), Plant Closing Assistance
Economic Development Administration	http://www.doc.gov/resources/EDA_info.html	Provides grants to nonprofit and local governments for projects that alleviate unemployment and underemployment in economically distressed areas; part of the U.S. Department of Commerce	What Is the Economic Development Administration, Economic Conversion Information Exchange

Table 9.1: Government Agency Internet Sites (continued)

Agency	URL	Description	Major Topics
Economics and Statistics Administration (ESA)	http://www.doc.gov/resources/ESA_info.html	Provides much of the statistical, economic, and demographic information collected by the U.S. government; a division of the U.S. Department of Commerce	Bureau of the Census, STAT-USA, Bureau of Economic Analysis (BEA)
Employment and Training Administration (ETA)	http://www.doleta.gov/	Ensures that American workers, employers, students, and those seeking work can obtain information, employment services, and training; part of the U.S. Department of Labor	Information about the Assistant Secretary, Information about the Employment and Training Administration, What's New, Media Releases, Regulatory and Statutory Information (including circulars on cost principles for state, local, and Indian tribal governments and for nonprofit organizations), Information on ETA's Programs and Services (nine links to training and employment programs), Other ETA Related Sites
Employment Services	http://www.doleta.gov/programs/empserv.htm	Links from the Employment and Training Administration (ETA), an office of the U.S. Department of Labor	America's Job Bank, Foreign Labor Certification, Occupational Information Network, One-Stop Career Centers
Employment Standards Administration (ESA)	http://www.dol.gov/dol/esa/	Enforces and administers numerous federal labor standards through the Office of Federal Contract Compliance Programs (OFCCP), the Office of Workers' Compensation Programs (OWCP), and the Wage and Hour Division (WHD); a bureau of the U.S. Department of Labor	Information about the Assistant Secretary, Information about ESA, What's New, Media Releases, Statutory and Regulatory Information (Statutes and Executive Orders, Unified Agenda of Federal Regulations, Code of Federal Regulations [CFRs], Notices of Proposed Rulemaking, Compliance Assistance Information), Information about ESA's Programs and Activities, Grant and Contract Information

Table 9.1: Government Agency Internet Sites (continued)

Agency	URL	Description	Major Topics
FDA Center for Veterinary Medicine (CVM)	http://www.cvm.fda.gov/	Regulates the manufacture and distribution of food additives and drugs that will be given to animals	Offices, Further Information, Other Links, What's New
Federal Aviation Administration	http://www.faa.gov/	Regulates civil aviation, an arm of the U.S. Department of Transportation	News & Information, Other FAA Internet Sites, Aviation Internet Sites, Federal Government Sites (for WWW and Gopher), Products & Programs, FAA Gopher, FAA Bulletin Boards
Federal Bureau of Investigation (FBI)	http://www.fbi.gov/	Criminal investigation division of the U.S. Department of Justice	What's New, Overview, Investigations, Office of Public and Congressional Affairs, and General Information
Federal Bureau of Prisons	http://gopher.usdoj.gov/bureaus/bop.html	Protects society by confining offenders in prisons and community-based facilities	Long text page
Federal Communications Commission (FCC)	http://www.fcc.gov/	Regulates U.S. interstate and international communications by radio, television, wire, satellite, and cable	Daily Digest, Commission Agenda, Current Rulemaking, Auctions, Speeches, Getting Information, Common Carrier Bureau, Wireless Bureau, Mass Media Bureau, Cable Bureau, International Bureau, Engineering & Technology Bureau, Compliance & Information Bureau, Other Offices

Table 9.1: Government Agency Internet Sites (continued)

Agency	URL	Description	Major Topics
Federal Railroad Administration (FRA)	http://www.dot.gov/dotinfo/fra/welcome.html	The railroad-administering arm of the U.S. Department of Transportation	FRA—Who We Are and What We Do, FRA's Mission and Vision, Biographical Summary of the Administrator, Biographical Summary of the Deputy Administrator, Office of Public Affairs, Office of Safety, Office of Policy, Gage Restraint Measurement System (a track strength evaluation program)
Federal Supply Service (FSS)	http://www.gsa.gov/fss.htm	An organization that procures goods and services for U.S. government agencies; a division of the GSA	Federal Supply Service Electronic Mall; Federal Supply Schedules; Stock Program; Consolidated Purchase Contracts; Contracts for Travel, Transportation, and Other Services; Electronic Data Interchange; FSS Commodity Centers
Federal Trade Commission	http://www.ftc.gov/	The department that regulates advertising and marketing.	Consumer Alert! Online Scams; FTC News Releases; Notices of Hearings, Transcripts, and Requests for Public Comment; FTC ConsumerLine; FTC Telemarketing Sales Rule
General Accounting Office (GAO)	http://www.gao.gov/	The investigative arm of the U.S. Congress	GAO Daybook, Recently Issued Reports, Reports and Testimony, Most Frequently Requested Reports, About GAO, Frequently Asked Questions, GAO Policy and Guidance Materials, Bid Protests at GAO: A Descriptive Guide (downloadable in PDF format), Government Auditing Standards: 1994 Revision (downloadable in PDF format), Questionnaire Programing Language (QPL), Search GAO Reports

Table 9.1: Government Agency Internet Sites (continued)

Agency	URL	Description	Major Topics
General Services Administration (GSA)	http://www.gsa.gov/	Provides guidance on issues relating to the procurement of goods and services used by federal agencies (both graphical and text versions)	What's New, Federal Travel, Real & Misc Property, Commerce, About GSA, Search GSA, Top Ten, Consumer Information, GSA Advantage, Regional Offices, Federal Information, Government Wide Policy, Publications, Education & Training
Government Printing Office (GPO)	http://www.access.gpo.gov/	Prints, binds, and distributes the publications of the U.S. Congress as well as the executive departments and establishments of the federal government	About the Government Printing Office, Free Access to Federal Government Publications, Online Databases Available via Subscriptions, Services Available to Federal Agencies, Business and Contracting Opportunities, Navigation Aids
GrantsNet	http://www.os.dhhs.gov/progorg/grantsnet/	A tool for finding and exchanging information about federal grant programs	GrantsNet Services, What's New, How to Subscribe and/or Query Our Electronic Mailing List, Post Grant Resource Information, Where Do I Start, Grant Profiles and Announcements, Governmentwide Rules, Agency-Specific Rules, Dispute Resolution, Who's Who, Publications/Newsletters/Associations, HHS Organization and Employee Locator, Calendar of Events, Grants Process Reinvention and Streamlining Activities, FinanceNet, Other Grants-Related Electronic NETworks

Table 9.1: Government Agency Internet Sites (continued)

Agency	URL	Description	Major Topics
High Performance Computing and Communications (HPCC)— National Coordination Office (NCO)	http://www.hpcc.gov/ or gopher://gopher.hpcc.gov/1/	Provides focus for high-performance computing and communications	Fiscal Year 1996 Blue Book; HPCC FY 1996 Implementation Plan; American in the Age of Information: A Forum; Committee on Information and Communications (CIC) Strategic Implementation Plan; HPCC FY 1995 Implementation Plan; FY 1995 Blue Book; FY 1994 Blue Book; NCO Fact Sheets; Reports, Periodicals, and Announcements; Grants and Research Contracts; HPCC Agency Information Servers; White House Statements/Policy Papers; Legislation and Testimony; Related Information; Glossary of Acronyms; Address and Directions to NCO; NCO Director; What's New
Information Infrastructure Task Force (IITF)	http://iitf.doc.gov/	A division of the White House, helps formulate administration positions on key telecommunications issues	Categories: Information about the IITF, Other WWW Servers
Institute for Telecommunications Sciences	http://www.its.bldrdoc.gov/Home.html	The research and engineeering branch of the National Telecommunications and Information Administration (NTIA), which in turn is part of the U.S. Department of Commerce	ITS Research, Engineering, and Standards Development; ITS Organization; The National Telecommunications and Informaiton Administration; NII: The National Information Infrastructure; GII: The Global Information Infrastructure (under construction); the ITS Anonymous FTP Server (at ftp://ftp.its.bldrdoc.gov); A Visitor's Guide; What's New

Table 9.1: Government Agency Internet Sites (continued)

Agency	URL	Description	Major Topics
Internal Revenue Service (IRS)	http://www.irs.ustreas.gov/	Collects tax revenue; a bureau of the U.S. Department of the Treasury	Tax Stats, Tax Info for You, Tax Info for Business, Electronic Services, Taxpayer Help and Ed, Tax Regs in English, IRS Newstand, Forms & Pubs, What's Hot, Meet the Commissioner, Comments & Help, Site Tree (slow-loading site)
International Trade Administration (ITA)	http://www.ita.doc.gov/	Helps U.S. companies sell products and services abroad; part of the U.S. Department of Commerce	About the International Trade Administration, Hot Issues and Announcements, FAQs—Frequently Asked Exporting Questions, ITA's Customer Standards, Trade Information Center, The Exporter Advocacy Program, Big Emerging Markets, ABC Program, US-China Management Education and Training Initiative, United Aid, Export Trading Company Affairs, and Information and Services
Justice Information Technology Network (JUSTNET)	http://nletc.aspensys.com:83/nletchome.html	The research and development component of the U.S. Department of Justice	Office of Science and Technology, Regional Technology Centers Service, News and Hot Topics, NLECTC (National Law Enforcement and Corrections Technology Center) Reports Data Base, NLECTC Publications, Standards and Testing Information, Other Law Enforcement Information Resources

Table 9.1: Government Agency Internet Sites (continued)

Agency	URL	Description	Major Topics
Library of Congress	http://lcweb.loc.gov/ or http://www.loc.gov/	The nation's library	About the Library and the World Wide Web, Exhibits and Events, Services and Publications, Digital Library Collections, LC Online Systems, Congress and Government, Library of Congress Indexes to Other World Wide Web Services
Library of Congress Marvel System	gopher://marvel.loc.gov/11	Machine-Assisted Realization of the Virtual Electronic Library (MARVEL), the Nation's library	About LC MARVEL; Events, Facilities, Publications, and Services; Research and Reference; Libraries and Publishers; Copyright; Library of Congress Online Systems; Employee Information; U.S. Congress; Government Information; Global Electronic Library; Internet Resources; What's New on LC MARVEL; Search LC MARVEL Menus
Lyndon B. Johnson Space Center (JSC)	http://www.jsc.nasa.gov/	Division of NASA	JSC Services, a search index and NASA Services. Under JSC Services, you can find Organizations on the Internet, Services by Subject, What's New, Business Opportunities, Contractors, Site Map, Office of Inspector General, and Internal JSC Home Page
The Maritime Administration (MARAD)	http://marad.dot.gov/	Oversees domestic and international movement of people and cargo on the sea; part of the U.S. Department of Transportation (very large initial graphic)	About the Maritime Administration, Key Personnel Areas of Interest, Resource and Education Center, FAQs, Bulletin Board (Marlinspike), Other Home Pages to Visit, DOT Telephone Book

Table 9.1: Government Agency Internet Sites (continued)

Agency	URL	Description	Major Topics
Mine Safety and Health Administration (MSHA)	http://199.115.12.200/	Administers the provisions of the Federal Mine Safety and Health Act of 1977; a bureau of the U.S. Department of Labor	Information about MSHA; Information about the Assistant Secretary; What's New; News Releases, Speeches, Special Reports, and Congressional Testimony; Statutory and Regulatory Information; Safety and Health Information; Mining Accident and Injury Information; Miscellaneous Federal Register Notices; Other Internet Sites
National Aeronautics and Space Administration (NASA)	http://www.gsfc.nasa.gov/NASA_homepage.html	Conducts aeronautical and space activities and creates a science program	Welcome, Today@NASA, Organization, Q&A, NASA Centers, Go To, Gallery, Aeronautics, Space Science, Mission to Planet Earth, Technology Development, Human Space Flight
National Center for Toxicological Research	http://www.fda.gov/opacom/hptoxic.html/ or gopher://gopher.nctr.fda.gov/	Investigates the biological effects of widely used chemicals, a division of the FDA	A text page with a link to a very small Gopher site
National Criminal Justice Reference Service (NCJRS)	http://ncjrs.aspensys.com:81/1/new2/homepage.html	An extensive source of information on criminal and juvenile justice; a division of the National Institute of Justice, the research and development agency of the U.S. Department of Justice	U.S. Department of Justice, Office of Justice Programs, National Institute of Justice, Office of Juvenile Justice and Delinquency Prevention, Bureau of Justice Statistics, Bureau of Justice Assistance, Office for Victims of Crime, Office of National Drug Control Policy, Sourcebook of Criminal Justice Statistics, Juvenile Offenders and Victims: A National Report, National Institute of Justice Journal, Universal Hiring Program, National Drug Control Strategy, Criminal Justice Information by Topic (nine links), Internet Directories and Search Engines

Table 9.1: Government Agency Internet Sites (continued)

Agency	URL	Description	Major Topics
National Institutes of Health	http://www.nih.gov/	A biomedical research center and federal focal point for biomedical research in the U.S.	What's New, News & Events, Health Information, Grants and Contracts, Scientific Resources, Institutes & Offices
National Oceanic and Atmospheric Administration (NOAA)	http://www.noaa.gov/	Promotes global environmental stewardship in order to conserve the U.S. marine and coastal resources	NOAA in the News, Rebuild Fisheries, Seasonal and Interannual Forecasts, Protected Species, Coastal Ecosystems Health, Long Term Global Change, Warnings and Forecasts, Navigation and Positioning, Satellites, Fleet, Environmental Information Services, High Performance Computing and Communications, Access to NOAA Information and Data Services, Line and Program Offices
National Park Service	http://www.nps.gov/	369 national parks, monuments, battlefields, military parks, historical parks, historic sites, lakeshores, seashores, recreation areas, scenic rivers and trails, and the White House	Where in the World, Visit Your National Parks, Preserving America's Heritage, Electronic Visitor Center, Caring for the American Legacy, Working with Partners, Parks, NPS News, Hot Topics

Table 9.1: Government Agency Internet Sites (continued)

Agency	URL	Description	Major Topics
National Performance Review	http://www.npr.gov/ or http://www.npr.gov/index.html	A White House group	Highlights, NPR Reports, NPR News Room, NPR Library (performance agreements and executive orders), NPR Links to Other World Wide Web Services
National Science Foundation (NSF)	http://www.nsf.gov/	An independent agency that promotes the progress of science and engineering	NSF Focus Areas, News of Interest (including statistical reports on U.S. science and engineering), NSF World of Science & Engineering, Overview, Org & Staff, Program Deadlines, Grants & Program Areas (including guides and manuals), Info & Pubs (with a database of downloadable publications), and FastLane
National Security Agency (NSA)	http://www.nsa.gov:8080/	Signals intelligence and communications security activities, information systems security for national security systems, operations security training mission; a combat support agency within the U.S. Department of Defense	NSA's Mission Statement, About NSA, The Director's Page, National Cryptologic Museum, Documents and Papers (e.g., VENONA)
National Technical Information Service (NTIS)	http://www.fedworld.gov/ntis/ntishome.html	Gathers and markets scientific, technical, and business-related information; division of U.S. Department of Commerce	FedWorld, NTIS Bibliographic Database, NTIS Alerts, Federal Research in Progress (FEDRIP), Freebies (newsletters and catalogs), Foreign Broadcast Information Service (FBIS) Daily Reports, World News Connection (WNC; under construction), NTIS FAX Direct (many documents that you can order using your touch-tone telephone), NTIS Published Searches, American Technology Preeminence Act (ATPA), Japan Information

Table 9.1: Government Agency Internet Sites (continued)

Agency	URL	Description	Major Topics
National Telecommunications and Information Administration (NTIA)	http://www.ntia.doc.gov/ or gopher://gopher.ntia.doc.gov/11/	U.S. Department of Commerce organization that advises on telecommunications policy	Web site: Spectrum Management, Research & Technology, IITF, New, Public Safety, Grants and Assistance, Minority Telecommunications Development Program Resource Center, NII Superhighway, International Policy, Domestic Policy. Gopher site: New Items, Who Is NTIA (link doesn't work), FCC Filings, Policy Papers, Congressional Testimony and Statements, NTIA Notices and Hearings, NTIA Speaks, NTIA Openness Program, Office of Spectrum Management, International Activities, NTIA Grant Programs—TIIAP, PTFP, and NECET, etc.
Occupational Safety and Health Administration	http://www.osha.gov/	The part of the U.S. Department of Labor that enforces safety and health on the job	What's New, Media Releases, Publications, OSHA Information, Standards, Statistics, Compliance Assistance
Office of Administrative Law Judges (OALJ)	http://www.asacon.com/oalj/	The administrative law bureau of the U.S. Department of Labor	Information about the Chief Judge, Information about the Office of Administrative Law Judges (OALJ), What's New, Statutory and Regulatory Information (parts of the Administrative Procedure Act); Black Lung: rules for Board of Contract Appeals; Immigration; Longshore; Miscellaneous "Traditional"; OFCCP Disputes; Rules of Practice and Procedure; Whistleblower; Titles 20, 29, 30, 41, and 48 of the Code of Federal Regulations; Information on Programs and Activities

Table 9.1: Government Agency Internet Sites (continued)

Agency	URL	Description	Major Topics
Office of Air & Space Commercialization	http://www.doc.gov/oasc.html	Helps to formulate policies that foster the growth and international competitiveness of the U.S. commercial space sector; part of the U.S. Department of Commerce	OASC Mission, Commercial Remote Sensing, Space Transportation Policy, Launch Trade Agreements, Emerging Markets, Current Space Market Trends (under construction at the time of this writing)
Office of Business Liaison	http://www.doc.gov/osec/obl.html	The primary point for contact between the U.S. Department of Commerce and the business community	Objectives of the Office
Office of Economic Conversion Information Exchange (OECI)	http://ecix.doc.gov/ecix/ecixhomepage.html	Serves the information needs of communities, businesses, and individuals in adjusting to the effects of defense downsizing and other changing economic conditions; a service of the Economic Development Administration of the U.S. Department of Commerce	About OECI, Search the OECI System, General Information and Background, Programs of the Economic Development Administration (EDA), PARCELS Information System, Cooperative Programs for Reinvestment, Adjustment Programs and Laws, Economic and Defense Data, Information Sources, Who to Contact, Technology Development and Application, Office of Worker and Community Transition (from the Department of Energy), OECI Link Page
Office of Federal Contract Compliance Program (OFCCP)	http://www.dol.gov/dol/esa/public/aboutesa/org/ofcp_org/ofcp_org.htm	Ensures that companies that do business with the government promote affirmative action and equal employment opportunity; an office of the U.S. Department of Labor	Information about the Deputy Assistant Secretary, Information about the Office of Federal Contract Compliance Programs (OFCCP), Organization Chart, Mission Statement, Vision Statement, Key Personnel and Phone Numbers

Table 9.1: Government Agency Internet Sites (continued)

Agency	URL	Description	Major Topics
Office of Foreign Relations	http://www.dol.gov/dol/ilab/public/aboutilab/org/ofr.htm	Carries out a program of technical assistance to developing countries and former-Communist countries; within the Bureau of International Labor Affairs (ILAB), a bureau of the U.S. Department of Labor	A text page
Office of International Economic Affairs (OIEA)	http://www.dol.gov/dol/ilab/public/aboutilab/org/oiea.htm	Responsible for assuring that full consideration is given to the impacts of trade, investment, and immigration policies on domestic employment and U.S. workers' welfare; within Bureau of International Labor Affairs (ILAB), a bureau of the U.S. Department of Labor	A text page
Office of Research and Statistics	http://www.ssa.gov/statistics/ors_home.html	The data-gathering office of the Social Security Administration	Fast Facts & Figures About Social Security (English and Spanish versions), Social Security Programs Throughout the World, Income of the Aged Chartbook (1992), SSI Recipients by State and County, Tables from the Annual Statistical Supplement, Social Security Bulletin Abstracts, Tables of Current Operating Statistics, Research & Statistics Publications
Office of Science and Technology Policy	http://www.whitehouse.gov/OSTP.html	A White House office that provides expert advice to the president in all areas of science and technology	What Is OSTP and What Does It Do, What's New, OSTP Publications and Testimony, White House Publications: Science and Technology Documents, Significant Accomplishments in Science and Technology Policy, Links to Science and Technology Resources

Table 9.1: Government Agency Internet Sites (continued)

Agency	URL	Description	Major Topics
Office of Small and Disadvantaged Business Utilization	http://www.dot.gov/dotinfo/ost/osdbu/welcome.html	Created to assist minority-, disadvantaged-, and women-owned businesses wanting to receive financing for transportation-related projects; part of the U.S. Department of Transportation	Overview, Browse OSDBU information via the DOT Gopher, Read OSDBU's Transportation Link Newsletters
Office of Small Business and Minority Affairs (OSBMA)	http://www.dol.gov/dol/oshma/	Gives small, disadvantaged, and women-owned businesses maximum opportunity to participate in government contracting and grant activities for supplies and services; a bureau of the U.S. Department of Labor	Information about the Director, Information about OSBMA, Media Releases, Information on OSBMA's Programs and Activities, Grant and Contract Information (no information at the time of this writing), and Available Publications
Office of Technology Assessment (OTA)	http://www.ota.gov/	Analyzes emerging, difficult, and often highly technical issues for congressional committees	About OTA, OTA Publications, Work in Progress, Contacting OTA, Online Access, Congressional Resources
Office of the American Workplace (OAW)	http://www.dol.gov/dol/oaw/	Encourages business competitiveness and the skills, involvement, and commitment of front-line workers, while promoting more effective worker-management relations; a bureau of the U.S. Department of Labor	Information on the Assistant Secretary, Information about the Office of the American Workplace, What's New, Statutory and Regulatory Programs and Assistance, and Programs and Initiatives

Table 9.1: Government Agency Internet Sites (continued)

Agency	URL	Description	Major Topics
Office of Workers' Compensation Programs (OWCP)	http://www.dol.gov/dol/esa/public/aboutesa/org/owcp_org/owcp_org.htm	An office of the U.S. Department of Labor	Information about the Deputy Assistant Secretary, Key Personnel and Phone Numbers (site under construction at the time of this writing)
Partnerships for a Competitive Economy (PACE)	http://www.doc.gov/pace/pacepge.html	Enhances the overall climate for innovation by identifying, exploring, and advocating policy reforms to assure America's economic future; a program of the Office of Technology Policy of the U.S. Department of Commerce	Links to events and a text page
Peace Corps	http://www.clark.net/pub/peace/PeaceCorps.html	Promotes world peace and friendship by providing qualified volunteers to interested countries in need of trained human resources	How to Volunteer, Agency Information, Domestic Programs, What's New
Pension and Welfare Benefits Administration (PWBA)	http://www.dol.gov/dol/pwba/	Protects the integrity of pensions, health plans, and other employee benefits for more than 200 million people; a bureau of the U.S. Department of Labor	Information about the Assistant Secretary, Information about PWBA, What's New, Media Releases, Statutory and Regulatory Information, and Information about PWBA's Programs and Activities
Social Security Administration	http://www.ssa.gov/	A social insurance program that pays retired workers a continuing income after retirement and that pays disabled people benefits	60th Anniversary, Disability Process Redesign, Policy Forum, Guide for Employers, Teachers Kit (for secondary school teachers), Rulings, Research and Statistics, Search, Benefit Information, En Espanol, Legislation, FAQs, Forms, Public Information Resources, International, Other Servers of Interest

Table 9.1: Government Agency Internet Sites (continued)

Agency	URL	Description	Major Topics
Special Population Programs	http://www.doleta.gov/programs/specpop.htm	Links from the Employment and Training Administration (ETA), an office of the U.S. Department of Labor	Indian and Native American Training Program, Migrant and Seasonal Farmworker Training Program, Senior Community Service Employment Program
STAT-USA	http://www.stat-usa.gov/	Provides comprehensive economic, business, and social-environmental program data produced by more than 50 U.S. government sources; a fee-based service of the U.S. Department of Commerce	About STAT-USA; Order Form; What's New; Free Test Drive; National Trade Data Bank; Economic Bulletin/LE; GLOBUS—Procurement Opportunities; Nat'l Economic, Social, and Env. DB; Bureau of Economic Analysis
Thomas: Legislative Information on the Internet	http://thomas.loc.gov/	Provides full text versions of legislation, the Congressional Record, and more; a service of the U.S. Congress through the Library of Congress	Full Text of Legislation, Full Text of the Congressional Record, Bill Summary and Status, Hot Legislation, The Constitution of the United States (a search index), U.S. House of Representatives, U.S. Senate, C-SPAN, Library of Congress, LOCIS, LC MARVEL
U.S. Business Advisor	http://www.far.npr.gov/VOOB/index.html	Division of National Performance Review: a one-stop site for government-provided business services and information—graphical and text pages	News, Regulatory Assistance, Guided Tour

Table 9.1: Government Agency Internet Sites (continued)

Agency	URL	Description	Major Topics
U.S. Department of Agriculture	http://www.usda.gov/	The Cabinet-level department responsible for agriculture-related government programs and policies	What's New, Message from the Secretary, 1995 Farm Bill, USDA Visitor Information Center, USDA Program Missions, USDA Agencies and Programs, USDA's News and Current Information, Government Information Locator Service (GILS), A Topical Guide to Agricultural Programs, USDA: A Historical Note, The Internet
U.S. Department of Commerce	http://www.doc.gov/	Promotes American businesses and trade in many ways, through the development of new technologies, providing statistical data, granting patents, and promoting entrepreneurship	Messages and Information from the Secretary, What's New, U.S. Department of Commerce Agencies (which includes a link to the Budget of the United States, Fiscal Year 1996), Commerce Information Locator Service (CILS), On-Line Information Services, Connect to the White House WWW Server
U.S. Department of Defense	http://www.dtic.dla.mil/defenselink/	The Cabinet-level department responsible for the defense of the U.S. and the military branches	Office of the Secretary, Joint Chiefs of Staff, Army, Navy, Air Force, Marine Corps, Coast Guard, Reserve, National Guard, Unified Commands, Other Components, Contents, Finding Information (a search index)
U.S. Department of Defense Acquisition Workforce	http://www.dtic.dla.mil/acqed2/acqed.html	Information for those in the acquisition community at the U.S. Department of Defense	FAQs; Legislation; Regulations; Critical Acquisition Positions; Acquisition Education, Training, and Career Development; Defense Acquisition University; Defense Technical Information Web; Defense Technical Information Center

Table 9.1: Government Agency Internet Sites (continued)

Agency	URL	Description	Major Topics
U.S. Department of Education	http://www.ed.gov/	The Cabinet-level department responsible for federal education programs	Welcome, Secretary's Initiatives, Programs & Services, Publications & Products (including publications for parents), People & Offices, News, Guides, Money Matters, Other Sites, Search
U.S. Department of Energy	http://www.doe.gov/	The Cabinet-level department responsible for federal energy programs	About the Department of Energy; Information Services; Department of Energy News and Hot Topics (including Technology Partnership Opportunities); What's New on the Department's Network; OPENNET; People, Places, and Organizations; and Electronic Exchange Initiative
U.S. Department of Health and Human Resources	http://www.os.dhhs.gov/	The principal agency for protecting the health of all Americans and providing essential human services, especially for those who are least able to help themselves	About HHS, HHS Agencies on the Internet, News & Public Affairs, Consumer Information, What's New, GrantsNet, Research/Date, Policy, Topic Index
U.S. Department of Housing and Urban Development (HUD) Gopher Site	gopher://gopher.hud.gov/	The federal department responsible for public housing and enhancing cities and urban areas	Programs, Assets Sales, Research Information Service, the Inspector General, HUD-CLIPS (six months of handbooks, Letters, Notices, Federal Register Announcements, etc.)
U.S. Department of Housing and Urban Development (HUD) Web Site	http://www.hud.gov/	The federal department responsible for public housing and enhancing cities and urban areas	What's New; Cities, Communities, and Neighborhoods; Places to Live; Doing Business with HUD; Research; Tool Kit (downloadable documents, directories, Catalog of Federal Domestic Assistance); About HUD; Frequently Asked Questions

Table 9.1: Government Agency Internet Sites (continued)

Agency	URL	Description	Major Topics
U.S. Department of Justice	http://justice2.usdoj.gov/ or http://www.usdoj.gov/	The criminal justice department at the Cabinet level	Justice Department Organizations, Justice Department Issues, Other Justice Department Information Sources, Other Federal Government Information Sources, Other Criminal Justice Information Sources
U.S. Department of Justice Gopher	gopher://justice2.usdoj.gov:70/11/	The criminal justice department at the Cabinet level	Office of the Attorney General, Civil Rights Division, Crime Bill Information, the Environment and Natural Resources Division, Federal Bureau of Investigation, Federal Bureau of Prisons, Immigration and Naturalization Service, Career Opportunities, and News and Press Releases from the United States Attorneys, IGNet
U.S. Department of Justice, Antitrust Division	http://gopher.usdoj.gov/atr/atr.htm	Enforces antitrust laws and regulations, part of the U.S. Department of Justice	U.S. vs. Microsoft; U.S. vs. Pilkington, Competitive Impact Statement; Intellectual Property in the Clinton Administration; The Role of Antitrust in International Trade; Report from the Antitrust Division (dated 1994); Innovation and Antitrust; Antitrust Policy Towards Telecommuniation Alliances; Antitrust Draft Guidelines for International Policy; Antitrust Gopher Information

Table 9.1: Government Agency Internet Sites (continued)

Agency	URL	Description	Major Topics
U.S. Department of Labor	http://www.dol.gov/ or gopher://marvel.loc.gov/11/federal/fedinfo/byagency/executive/labor	Charged with preparing the American workforce for new and better jobs and ensuring the adequacy of America's workplaces	Department Agencies, America's Job Bank, Information about the Secretary, Information about the Department of Labor, What's New, Media Releases, Statutory and Regulatory Information, Information on the Department's Programs and Activities, Labor-Related Data, Grant and Contract Information, Information Sources Outside DOL, Status & Plans for DOL on the Internet
U.S. Department of Transportation	http://www.dot.gov/ or gopher://gopher.dot.gov/	Air, water, rail, and road transportation matters at the Cabinet level	What's New, Browse the DOT Administrations, DOT News and Information, General Information, Useful Internet Sites, DOT Talk
U.S. Department of Treasury	http://www.ustreas.gov/ or http://www.ustreas.gov/treasury/homepage.html	The Cabinet-level department overseeing the control of currency and the collection of taxes	Who's Who, Treasury Bureaus, Treasury Services, What's New, Treasury Electronic Library, Short Cut to IRS Taxforms (http://www.ustreas.gov/treasury/bureaus/irs/taxforms.html), Treasury Reinvention/GITS
U.S. Department of Veterans Affairs	http://www.va.gov/	Provides federal benefits to veterans and their dependents	What's New, Veterans Day, U.S. Veterans and Data on Veterans, History of Support for Veterans, What Are My VA Benefits (Summary of Services for Veterans and Veterans Benefits Manual—1995 Edition), VA Facilities, Announcements for Veterans, Department of Veterans Affairs, Information for Veterans on Other Servers, Medical Automation, Informatic Standards, VHA Reorganization Documents, WWW Directory of Resources

Table 9.1: Government Agency Internet Sites (continued)

Agency	URL	Description	Major Topics
U.S. Food and Drug Administration (FDA)	http://www.fda.gov/fdahomepage.html	Regulates food, cosmetics, medicines, medical devices, radiation-emitting products, feed and drugs for pets and farm animals	FDA News, Animal Drugs, Biologics, Cosmetics, Human Drugs, Foods, Toxicology, Medical Devices and Radiological Health, Inspections and Imports, and More Choices (general FDA information)
U.S. Geological Survey's Earth Resources Observation Systems (EROS) Data Center (EDC)	http://edcwww.cr.usgs.gov/eros-home.html	A data management, systems development, and research field center that processes data from NASA Landsat satellites; part of the U.S. Department of the Interior	What's New, Products (data and photographs), Services, Research Projects, EDC Affiliates, General Information
U.S. House of Representatives Gopher Site	gopher://gopher.house.gov	One of the two federal legislative bodies	Directories, e-mail addresses, educational resources, and congressional legislative resources
U.S. House of Representatives Web Site	http://www.house.gov/	One of the two federal legislative bodies	What's New; The Legislative Process (current bills and resolutions); Schedules; Who's Who and How to Contact Them (directories of members and committees—names, addresses, and telephone numbers—at http://www.house.gov/mbr_dir/membr_dir.html); Organization and Operations; Member, Committee, and House Organizations' Published Information (links to other House Internet servers); Laws (the U.S. Code and the Internet Law Library); Visitor Information; Educational Resources; Empowering the Citizen; Listing of All Information; and Other Government Information Resources (links to many resources)

Table 9.1: Government Agency Internet Sites (continued)

Agency	URL	Description	Major Topics
U.S. Information Agency (USIA)	http://www.usia.gov/	An independent foreign affairs agency that explains and supports U.S. foreign policy and promotes U.S. national interests through a wide range of overseas information programs	What's New, Fast Facts, And More Information on Selected Programs (About the U.S. Information Agency, Education and Cultural Exchanges, U.S. International Broadcasting, USIA Research and Overseas Media Reaction, USIA Foreign Press Centers)
U.S. Nuclear Regulatory Commission (USNRC)	http://www.nrc.gov/	Ensures adequate protection of the public health and safety, common defense and security, and the environment in the use of nuclear materials in the U.S.	Welcome, Mission and Organization, NRC's Principal Offices, Nuclear Reactors, Nuclear Material, Radioactive Waste Disposal, News and Information
U.S. Patent and Trademark Office	http://www.uspto.gov/	Administers patents and trademarks; under the U.S. Department of Commerce	Welcome to the U.S. Patent and Trademark Office, General Patent and Trademark Information, What's New, U.S. Patent and Trademark Office Services and Information, Other Internet Resources, Search U.S. Patent Bibliographic Data Base (from the Center for Networked Information Discovery and Retrieval [CNIDR]), Search the AIDS Patent Data Base (the Patent Bibliographic Data Base includes more than 20 years of patent bibliographic text data)
U.S. Postal Service	http://www.usps.gov/	The U.S. mail delivery service, now a semiprivate organization	Today's Features, Your Post Office (get zip codes, postal rates, consumer information, other U.S. postal sites), The Business Section (products and services, business forms and publications), Postal Business Center addresses, F.Y.I (including the Postal Information Locator Service), 1996 Stamps Program

Table 9.1: Government Agency Internet Sites (continued)

Agency	URL	Description	Major Topics
U.S. Travel and Tourism Administration	http://www.doc.gov/resources/ustta.html	The U.S. official National Tourism Office, used to attract international tourists to the United States; part of the U.S. Department of Commerce	Information from the Under Secretary, USTTA at a Glance, Calendar of Events, Ordering Publications (fee-based subscriptions and free publications), State Tourism Offices and State WWW Sites
Unemployment Benefits	http://www.doleta.gov/programs/uibene.htm	Links from the Employment and Training Administration (ETA), an office of the U.S. Department of Labor	Disaster Unemployment Assistance, Extended Benefits, Trade Readjustment Allowances, Unemployment Compensation, Unemployment Compensation for Federal Employees, Unemployment Compensation for Ex-Servicemembers (Note: All these links lead to the Unemployment Insurance Web Site at http://www.itsc.state.md.us/.)
Unemployment Insurance Information	http://www.doleta.gov/programs/uiinfo.htm	Links from the Employment and Training Administration (ETA), an office of the U.S. Department of Labor	Worker Profiling, Benefits Information, Tax Contributions Information, Statistics (Note: All these links lead to the Unemployment Insurance Web Site at http://www.itsc.state.md.us/.)
United States Geological Survey (USGS)	http://info.er.usgs.gov/USGSHome.html	The largest U.S. earth science research and information agency	What's New, USGS Fact Sheets, General Information, Educational Resources, USGS Information Releases, Environmental Research, Publications and Data Products, Internet Resources
The United States Senate Gopher Site	gopher://ftp.senate.gov/	One of the two federal legislative bodies	Senate directory, documents from individual members and from committees, a search index, and a link to the Library of Congress Gopher server

Table 9.1: Government Agency Internet Sites (continued)

Agency	URL	Description	Major Topics
The United States Senate Web Site	http://www.senate.gov/	One of the two federal legislative bodies	Senators, Senate committees, a history, tourist information, and links to other Senate and government sites
Veterans' Employment and Training Service (VETS)	http://www.dol.gov/dol/vets/	Helps veterans, reservists, and National Guard members in securing employment and the rights and benefits associated with such; a bureau of the U.S. Department of Labor	Information about the Assistant Secretary, Information about VETS, Media Releases, Statutory and Regulatory Information, Information about VETS Programs and Activities, Grants and Contract Awards Information
Wage and Hour Division (WHD)	http://www.dol.gov/dol/esa/public/aboutesa/org/whd_org/whd_org.htm	Enforces administrative and educational programs to protect U.S. workers using the Fair Labor Standards Act and other acts; an office of the U.S. Department of Labor	Information about the Wage and Hour Administrator, Mission Statement, Vision Statement, Key Personnel and Phone Numbers, History of Wage and Hour, WHD Chronology, Media Releases/Fact Sheets, Statutory and Regulatory Information
White House	http://www.whitehouse.gov/	The office and home of the president of the U.S. This page is available in graphical or text versions.	Executive Branch (Executive Office of the President, The President's Cabinet, Independence Federal Agencies and Commissions, Find Information about Other Branches of Government), First Family, Tours, What's New, Publications, President's Welcome Message, Guest Book, Vice President's Welcome Message

Table 9.1: Government Agency Internet Sites (continued)

Agency	URL	Description	Major Topics
White House Files	http://english-server.hss.cmu.edu/WhiteHouse.html	This site, from Carnegie Mellon University, provides a link to the White House (at http://www.whitehouse.gov/) and enables you to search some White House archives at Texas A&M.	Election information, appointments and nominations, domestic and international affairs, press briefings and conferences, memoranda, and many other documents from 1992, 1993, and 1994
Women's Bureau (WB)	http://www.dol.gov/dol/wb/	Serves and promotes the interests of working women; a bureau of the U.S. Department of Labor	Information about the Director, Information about the Women's Bureau, What's New, Media Releases, Information on the Women's Bureau's Programs and Activities, Labor-Related Data, and Publications Available from the Women's Bureau (including the post series)
Youth Training Programs	http://www.doleta.gov/programs/youthtrn.htm	Links from the Employment and Training Administration (ETA), an office of the U.S. Department of Labor	Apprenticeship Training, Job Corps, School to Work, JTPA Summer Youth Employment, JTPA Year-Round Youth Training, One-Stop Career Centers, Youth Fair Chance

State Government

At the time of this writing, U.S. state governments were somewhat behind the federal government in Internet site development; you'll find many more Gopher sites than World Wide Web pages. However, given the growth of the Net, this is bound to change. In this section, you will find indexes that provide state links and a large table of state government sites (see Table 9.2).

Note
When searching for state pages, be sure to go to the large International, U.S., State, and Local Government Servers site at htt;://www.elf.org/govt.html. **You can read more about this impressive site in the** *International Government Resources* **section.**

World-Wide Web Virtual Library: Law: State Government Servers

http://www.law.indiana.edu/law/states.html

The typical World-Wide Web Virtual Library page, including this site, is full of valuable resources. This page presents state resources of all types arranged under an alphabetically organized list of states. Obviously, each state's content depends on its activity on the Internet. You will find small entries such as Arkansas with its public schools and Delaware with its public library. On the other hand, California provides the most links—not surprising, considering its population of high-technology companies.

Yahoo List of State Government Servers

http://www.yahoo.com/Government/States

On the first page of this State Government section, you will find links to individual states and to state government indexes (four at the time of this writing). When you click on a state, you will go to a page with a variety of links—to government departments, books, associations, and libraries.

Table 9.2: Selected State Government Resources

Resource	URL	Links
Alabama (Library of Congress Gopher)	gopher://marvel.loc.gov:70/11/federal/state.local/al/	Alabama Cooperative Extension System Gopher, Mobile Area Free-Net (Telnet connection)
Alabama (Library of Congress Web)	http://lcweb.loc.gov/global/state/al-govt.html	Information Services of the State of Alabama, Alabama Secretary of State, Alabama State and Local Government
Alaska Court of Appeals Decisions	http://www.touchngo.com/ap/ap.htm	Touch N' Go™, The Electronic In and Out Board, Touch N' Go Systems, Inc., Law Offices of James B. Gottstein, Series of Appeals Organized by Date, Supreme Court Opinions (Alaska), The Alaska Legal Resource Center
Alaska Government & Non-Profit Home Pages	http://www.alaska.net/gov.html	Many links to government and non-profit organizations
Alaska (Information about Alaska)	gopher://info.alaska.edu:70/11s/Alaska	About Alaska, Alaska Justice Resource Center, Alaska Constitution, Alaska Politics, Alaska Public Radio, Alaska's Neighbors, Alaska Weather, Historical Documents, Literature, Other Alaska Servers, Search Alaska Place Names, Sports and Recreation, Topics and Links of Interest to Alaska, TV—Northern Exposure, Usenet News—alt.culture.alaska

Table 9.2: Selected State Government Resources (continued)

Resource	URL	Links
The Alaska Legal Resource Center	http://www.touchngo.com/lglcntr/lglcntr.htm	Touch N' Go™, The Electronic In and Out Board, Touch N' Go Systems, Inc., Law Offices of James B. Gottstein, Alaska Supreme Court Opinions, Alaska Court of Appeals Opinions, U.S. Supreme Court Opinions, Cornell's Legal Information Institute, Alaska Constitution, Alaska Statutes, Alaska Administrative Code, U.S. District Court Local Rules, Special Interest Items, Alaska Attorneys, Accounts, Legal Support Services, Real Estate Appraisers, Federal Legal Resources, List of Legal Lists, State of Alaska Home Page, Web Search Engines and Directories
Alaska (Library of Congress Gopher)	gopher://marvel.loc.gov:70/11/federal/state.local/ak	Alaska Legislative Information (Univ. of Alaska), Statewide Library Electronic Doorway (SLED Telnet connection)
Alaska (Library of Congress Web)	http://lcweb.loc.gov/global/state/ak-gov.html	State of Alaska World Wide Web Server; Alaska's Top Elected Officals; Governor's Home Page; Alaska Information Server; Alaska Justice Resource Center; Alaska 2001; Alaska Public Radio; Alaska Supreme Court Opinions (General Appeals); Alaska Court of Appeals Opinions (Criminal Appeals); Alaska Court of Appeals Memorandum Opinion and Judgments (MOJ); Alaska Constitution; Past Governors of the State of Alaska; Alaska Statehood Act; Alaska City Link; Alaska's Cities, Town, and Villages; Juneau Web; Alaska Government; State of Alaska
Alaska (State of Alaska Home Page)	http://www.state.ak.us/	Agency Directory, Frequently Asked Questions, What's New, Top 10 List, Keyword Search, Feedback
Alaska Supreme Court Cases	http://www.touchngo.com/sp/sp.html	Touch N' Go™, The Electronic In and Out Board, Touch N' Go Systems, Inc., Law Offices of James B. Gottstein, Subject Index to Alaska Supreme Court Opinions, 1996 Alaska Supreme Court Opinions (Chronological), 1995 Alaska Supreme Court Opinions (Chronological), 1994 Alaska Supreme Court Opinions (Chronological), 1993 Alaska Supreme Court Opinions (Chronological), 1992 Alaska Supreme Court Opinions (Chronological), 1991 Alaska Supreme Court Opinions (Chronological), a series of opinions
Arizona (Library of Congress Web)	http://lcweb.loc.gov/global/state/az-gov.html	Arizona, General Information; Governor's Arizona Science and Technology Council; Governor's Strategic Partnership for Economic Development (GSPED); Public Communication Technology Project; Arizona Government
Arkansas (Library of Congress Gopher)	gopher://marvel.loc.gov:70/11/federal/state.local/ar/	Arkansas Public School Computer Network

Table 9.2: Selected State Government Resources (continued)

Resource	URL	Links
Arkansas (Library of Congress Web)	http://lcweb.loc.gov/global/state/ar-gov.html	Arkansas State Government, Arkansas State and Local Government
California (Berkeley)	gopher://garnet.berkeley.edu:1250/11/.gov/.states/.cal	1994 Election Information, California Department of Education, California Emergency Services Index, Legislative Information, Local Government, Information Access to Government, Local Governments
California (Cyberspace Today Government Information)	http://www.cybertoday.com/ct/gov/	Office of the President of the United States, The United States Senate, The United States House of Representatives, Office of the Governor of California, The California State Senate, The California Assembly, City of Berkeley, City of Palo Alto, City and County of San Francisco
California Government Agency and Commission List	http://www.svpal.org/~rav/agencies.html	Most Important Points of Entry (California State Senate, Assembly, Code, Government Network), Other Agencies and Commissions (very long list of links and nonlinks)
California Government Information from CPSR	gopher://gopher.cpsr.org:70/11/cpsr/states/california	1994.elections.html, 19940401.cal_gov_info_FAQ, 19941101.cal_gov_info_FAQ, 19950401.cal_gov_info_FAQ, 19950801.cegi.txt, 19951015.cegi.txt, CEGI.form.html, CEGI Images, asbly roster, several GIF pages, cal_gov_info_FAQ.html, califother.html, califpols.html, cegi.html, cegi.txt, cegi_questionnaire, contents.html, govaccess, header.html, ldc, leginfo, municipal.html, new.html, otherstates.html, proposed.html, regional.html, research.html, rosters, senate_roster, state.html, sunnyvale_online_report, toc.html, top.html, wishlist.html (Computer Professionals for Social Responsibility)
California Legislation	gopher://sen.ca.gov/	Access Options for the California State Legislature; What's New; About the California Legislature Gopher; Penal Code Section 502; State Senate (Offices and Floor Action); State Assembly (Miscellany); Legislature (Join Senate/Assembly) Topics; Access bill text, analyses, codes, etc.; Other California Agencies, Gophers, and Information; and other Internet resources
California (Library of Congress Gopher)	gopher://marvel.loc.gov:70/11/federal/state.local/ca/	California Government: General Resources, California State Government, California County/Area Agoverments, California City Governments

Table 9.2: Selected State Government Resources (continued)

Resource	URL	Links
California (Library of Congress Web)	http://lcweb.loc.gov/global/state/ca-gov.html	California Legislative Counsel's Office Legislative WWW Site; California State Code; California State Assembly; California State Senate; California Hemp Initiative; California State Government Network (CSGNet); California Home Page; California Electronic Government Information; Governor's Office of Emergency Services; Department of Conservation; Department of Fish and Game Natural Heritage Division; Department of Forestry & Fire Protection; Department of General Services; Department of Industrial Relations; Department of Transportation; Department of Water Resources; Department of Water Resources, Division of Planning; California Water Page; Department of Water Resources, Snow Survey; Division of State Architect; California Energy Commission; Environmental Resources Evaluation System (CERES); Public Utilities Commission; State Lands Commission; California Geographical Survey; California Electronic Map Library; California Census Data Archive; Digital Map Database: TIGER/Line Files for All of California's Counties; Association of Bay Area Governments (ABAG); Alameda County; Santa Cruz County; Sonoma and Marin Counties; South Orange County Municipal Court; Los Angeles; City of West Hollywood; San Francisco Unified School District; California State and Local Government
California State Assembly	http://www.assembly.ca.gov/	Members of the Assembly, Television Schedule, Committee Hearings, Daily Files, Legislative Calendar, Bill Information, Assembly Committees, Tour of State Capitol, Assembly Resources, Selected Resources, Links to Other Government Agencies
California State Home Page	http://www.ca.gov/	California State Information & Services (a variety of resources); Indexes, What's New, and State Servers
California State Senate	http://www.sen.ca.gov/	Welcome to the California State Senate; New/Changed/Enhanced Features; User's Guide and Tutorial (How to Find Legislative Info); Senate Members, Committees, and Offices; Legislation: Bills, Codes, Schedules, TV Coverage; Assembly and State Government information; Senate Internet Services; Selected WWW Search Engines; Miscellaneous Government Information; Other California and Misc. Information
California (Your Government: A Guide to California Officials, Agencies, and Laws)	http://agency.resource.ca.gov/gov/official	Elected Officials, Judiciary, California State Laws & Proposed Legislation, State Agencies & Departments, Local Government, Other Sources for California Government Information
Colorado (Library of Congress Gopher)	gopher://marvel.loc.gov:70/11/federal/state.local/co/	Colorado Legislative Information, Colorado Springs Community News Service

Table 9.2: Selected State Government Resources (continued)

Resource	URL	Links
Colorado (Library of Congress Web)	http://lcweb.loc.gov/global/state/co-gov.html	Colorado State Government, Colorado State Legislative Information (CLISC), Colorado State and Local Government
Connecticut (Library of Congress Web)	http://lcweb.loc.gov/global/state/ct-gov.html	Connecticut Home Page; Connecticut Law and Government; Connecticut State Democratic Legislators; Connecticut State Library; Connecticut Cities, Town, and Boroughs
Delaware (Library of Congress Gopher)	gopher://marvel.loc.gov:70/11/federal/state.local/de/	Delaware Public Library Gopher
Delaware (Library of Congress Web)	http://lcweb.loc.gov/global/state/de-gov.html	State of Delaware, Delaware State and Local Government
Florida (Library of Congress Gopher)	gopher://marvel.loc.gov:70/11/federal/state.local/fl/	Florida Government Information Locator (Florida State Library), Florida Department of Environmental Protection, Florida Information Resources Network (FIRN), Alachua County Free-Net (Telnet connection), Tallahassee Free-Net (Telnet connection), Tampa Bay Library Consortium (SUNLINE) (Telnet connection)
Florida (Library of Congress Web)	http://lcweb.loc.gov/global/state/fl-gov.html	Florida Legislative Page; Florida State Government; Florida Government Location Information Service; Florida Department of State, Division of Library and Information Services; Florida Attorney General's Office; State Labor Information; Alachua Freenet; City of Melbourne; Florida State Government
Georgia (Library of Congress Gopher)	gopher://marvel.loc.gov:70/11/federal/state.local/ga/	State of Georgia Gopher (Gonet—Georgia Online), Georgia: Legislative Acts, Georgia Department of Technical and Adult Education, Computer Systems Protection Act of Georgia
Georgia (Library of Congress Web)	http://lcweb.loc.gov/global/state/ga-gov.html	Georgia State Information, Georgia Law and Information, Central Savannah River Area 9CSRA) Regional Development Center, Taylor Road Middle School, Georgia State and Local Government
Georgia (State)	gopher://gopher.dnas.state.ga.us/ or gopher://PeachNet.EDU:70/11/State%20of%20Georgia	Legislative Acts; Merit System of Personnel Administration Job Information; Secretary of State, Department of Archives and History; State Micro-computer Contracts; State Microcomputer Peripherals Contracts; State Workstation Contracts
Hawaii Government Information from CPSR	gopher://gopher.cpsr.org:70/11/cpsr/states/hawaii	hb 2023 (Computer Professionals for Social Responsibility)
Hawaii (Library of Congress Gopher)	gopher://marvel.loc.gov:70/11/federal/state.local/hi/	Hawaii ACCESS: Legislative Information Service, State Legislature (Telnet connection); Hawaii Department of Education

Table 9.2: Selected State Government Resources (continued)

Resource	URL	Links
Hawaii (Library of Congress Web)	http://lcweb.loc.gov/global/state/hi-gov.html	Hawaii Home Page; State of Hawaii WWW; Hawaii, Inc.; Department of Education; Hawaiian Sovereignty; Hawaii State Government
Idaho (Library of Congress Web)	http://lcweb.loc.gov/global/state/id-gov.html	Idaho State Government
Illinois (Library of Congress Web)	http://lcweb.loc.gov/global/state/il-gov.html	State of Illinois Home Page, Chicago City Government, Illinois State and Local Government
Indiana (Library of Congress Gopher)	gopher://marvel.loc.gov:70/11/federal/state.local/in/	Indiana Department of Education, Indiana Higher Education Telecommunications System, Indiana State Library (Telnet connection)
Indiana (Library of Congress Web)	http://lcweb.loc.gov/global/state/in-gov.html	Access Indiana Indiana Legal Information, Indiana Code, Indiana Bills, Indiana Constitution, 1994 Indiana State Legislators, St. Joseph County Public Library, Michiana Freenet, Indiana State Government
Iowa (Library of Congress Web)	http://lcweb.loc.gov/global/state/ia-gov.html	State of Iowa Web Site, Speaker of the Iowa State House, Iowa FY96-97 Budget in Brief, IOWA Database, Iowa State Library, SILO (State of Iowa Libraries Online)
Kansas (Library of Congress Gopher)	gopher://marvel.loc.gov:70/11/federal/state.local/ks/	Information Network of Kansas (Telnet connection), Kansas City (Kansas) Public Library (Telnet connection), Kansas Schools Information
Kentucky (Library of Congress Gopher)	gopher://marvel.loc.gov:70/11/federal/state.local/ky/	Kentucky Department of Information Services
Kentucky (Library of Congress Web)	http://lcweb.loc.gov/global/state/ky-gov.html	Commonwealth of Kentucky, Kentucky State Government
Louisiana (Info Louisiana)	http://www.state.la.us/	Governor's Office, State Departments, Louisiana Profiles, Job Listings, Legislature, Education, Tourism, Search, Text Only
Louisiana (Library of Congress Gopher)	gopher://marvel.loc.gov:70/11/federal/state.local/la/	Louisiana Population Data Center (LSU)
Louisiana (Library of Congress Web)	http://lcweb.loc.gov/global/state/la-gov.html	Info Louisiana, Louisiana State Legislature, Louisiana State House of Representatives, Louisiana State Senate, State Library of Louisiana, LA Homepage: Government and Educational Institutions, Louisiana Population Data Center, GPGC (Governor's Program for Gifted Children) WWW Server, LEAP: The Louisiana Electronic Assistance Program, Louisiana Servers, City of New Orleans Government, The Chamber: New Orleans and the River Region, Louisiana State and Local Government
Maine (Library of Congress Web)	http://lcweb.loc.gov/global/state/me-gov.html	State of Maine

Table 9.2: Selected State Government Resources (continued)

Resource	URL	Links
Maryland (Library of Congress Gopher)	gopher://marvel.loc.gov:70/11/federal/state.local/md/	Sailor (State of Maryland Gopher), State of Maryland Telephone Directory (Telnet connection), Maryland State Agencies, Maryland State Documents List (from UMBC Library), Maryland City and County Agencies, Maryland Educational Organizations, Maryland Libraries, Chesapeake Freenet (Easton, MD), Baltimore County Public Library (Telnet connection), Prince George's County Memory Library System (Telnet connection)
Maryland (Library of Congress Web)	http://lcweb.loc.gov/global/state/md-gov.html	Maryland State and Local Government; State of Maryland Government; Maryland State Archives; Annapolis City Hall; Baltimore; Baltimore City Government/Agency Phone Numbers; Gaithersburg, Montgomery County, MD; Maryland State and Local Government
Maryland Sailor System	gopher://sailor.lib.md.us/	Using Sailor; Search Sailor; Go to a Library; Find Information by Topic; Community Information; Government Information; Sailing the Internet; What's New, Hon?; Feedback Please (Telnet connection)
Maryland State Archives	http://www.mdarchives.state.md.us/	All about the Maryland State Archives, Maryland and Its Government, Reference Services (schedules and services), Geographical Services, Education and Outreach, Preservation and Conservation, What's New
Massachusetts (Library of Congress Gopher)	gopher://marvel.loc.gov:70/11/federal/state.local/ma/	Massachusetts Department of Education, Massachusetts Education Computer Network, Massachusetts Library and Information Network, Merrimack Valley Library Consortium (Massachusetts) (Telnet connection), North of Boston Library Exchange
Massachusetts (Library of Congress Web)	http://lcweb.loc.gov/global/state/ma-gov.html	Commonwealth of Massachusetts; Massachusetts Access to Government Network (MAGNet); Cambridge, Massachusetts; Hanscom AFB School System; Massachusetts State and Local Government
Michigan Government	http://mlink.lib.umich.edu/MI-government/MI-government-index.html	Search, Home Page, MEL (Michigan Electronic Library) Main Menu, Back, About MEL, Send Comments, Help, Michigan Constitution, The Executive Office, Michigan's Legislature, Michigan's Congressional Delegation 1995/1996, Michigan 1994 General Election Office Results (Federal), Michigan 1994 General Election Office Results (State)
Michigan (Library of Congress Web)	http://lcweb.loc.gov/global/state/mi-gov.html	State of Michigan Web Server, Michigan Department of Education, Michigan Department of Natural Resources, Michigan Department of State, Michigan Rehabilitation Services, Michiana Freenet, Michigan State and Local Government
Minnesota Government Information from CPSR	gopher://gopher.cpsr.org:70/11/cpsr/states/minnesota	access minn upd2, access minnesota (Computer Professionals for Social Responsibility)

Table 9.2: Selected State Government Resources (continued)

Resource	URL	Links
Minnesota House and Senate Legislative Gopher Server	gopher://gopher.revisor.leg.state.mn.us	About the Minnesota House and Senate Legislative Gopher Service, What's New on the Minnesota House and Senate Legislative Gopher, About the Legislative Branch of Minnesota Government, Minnesota House of Representatives, Minnesota Senate, Capitol Area Information, Legislation and Bill Tracing, Minnesota Statutes and Minnesota Session Laws, Legislative Reference Library, Joint Legislative Departments and Commissions, Other Minnesota Government Information Services, Other Gopher and Information Servers, Yesterday's Gopher Usage Report, Current Session Schedules
Minnesota (Library of Congress Gopher)	gopher://marvel.loc.gov:70/11/federal/state.local/mn/	Access Minnesota (Electronic Government Information & Services); State of Minnesota Gopher Server; Minnesota Legislature Gopher; Minnesota State Information (via Berkeley); Minnesota State Government Directory; Department of Natural Resources, Minerals Division; Minnesota Extension Service Gopher; Minnesota Higher Education Coordinating Board; InfoMNs (K-12 Education Project); Minnesota Center for Arts Education; City of St. Paul, Minnesota; Mankato, Minnesota News Gopher
Minnesota (Library of Congress Web)	http://lcweb.loc.gov/global/state/mn-gov.html	Minnesota E-Democracy Project; Minnesota Government Information and Services; Minnesota Legislature; Department of Natural Resources, Minerals Division; Department of Transportation; InfoMNs: Internet for Minnesota Schools; Center for Arts Education; Minnesota Local Government; Minnesota Community Networks—Local Government Information; Minnesota Cities and Towns; Cities of Mankato and North Mankato; St. Paul (Minnesota) Government; Minnesota State and Local Government
Minnesota State Government Resources	gopher://gopher.state.mn.us/	North Star—Minnesota Government Information and Services, Minnesota Office of the Governor, Minnesota State Legislature, Minnesota Center for Arts Education, Minnesota Government Information Access Council, Minnesota Department of Health's Gopher Server, Minnesota Higher Education Coordinating Board, SNAP (Statewide Network Access Planning Users Group), Minnesota Department of Transportation's Gopher Server, University of Minnesota (Mother Gopher)
Mississippi (Library of Congress Gopher)	gopher://marvel.loc.gov:70/11/federal/state.local/ms/	Mississippi Central Data Processing Authority
Mississippi (Library of Congress Web)	http://lcweb.loc.gov/global/state/ms-gov.html	Maps, Mississippi Central Data Processing Authority, Project LEAP (Learn, Earn, and Prosper), Mississippi State and Local Government
Missouri Commission on Management & Productivity (COMAP)	gopher://services.more.net/11/StOfMoInfo/comap	About the MOREnet (Missouri Research and Education) Gopher, MOREnet Information, MOREnet & Member Resources, Other Information and Resources (Internet), State of Missouri Information
Missouri Education Programs & Activities	gopher://services.dese.state.mo.us/	About..., Missouri Elementary and Secondary Education Information, Missouri Higher Education Information, Educational Projects and Resources, Missouri Higher Education Information (CBHE Gopher)

Table 9.2: Selected State Government Resources (continued)

Resource	URL	Links
Missouri (Library of Congress Gopher)	gopher://marvel.loc.gov:70/11/federal/state local/mo/	Kansas City (Missouri) Public Library (Telnet connection); Missouri Census Information, 1990 (from U.Missouri); Missouri Coordinating Board for Higher Education; Missouri Department of Elementary and Secondary Education; Missouri Politics (U. Missouri; St. Louis); Missouri Research and Education Network; Missouri Weather; Rural Area Information Network (RAIN Missouri) (Telnet connection)
Missouri (Library of Congress Web)	http://lcweb.loc.gov/global/state/mo-gov.html	Missouri Office of the Secretary of State, Missouri Social and Economic Data, Missouri State and Local Government
Missouri State Government Information	gopher://services.more.net:70/11/StOfMoInfo	Missouri General Assembly House of Representatives, Archives for STATE GOVERNMENT-L, COMAP (Commission on Management and Productivity) Information, Missouri Rural Opportunities Council
Montana (Library of Congress Web)	http://lcweb.loc.gov/global/state/mt-gov.html	State of Montana Information Delivery System; Lincoln County, Montana
Nebraska (Library of Congress Web)	http://lcweb.loc.gov/global/state/ne-gov.html	Nebraska State Government, State of Nebraska Agency Services, Nebraska Courts and Other Legal Resources (Legal Net), Nebraska Libraries (Library Net), Nebraska State and Local Government
Nevada (Library of Congress Web)	http://lcweb.loc.gov/global/state/nv-gov.html	Clark County, Clark County Fire Department, City of Las Vegas, City of Reno
New York Capital Region Government	http://www.crisny.org/government/gov .capreg.html	Albany County & Communities, Rensselaer County & Communities, Saratoga County & Communities, Schenectady County & Communities, Communities Outside the Capital Region
New York (Government in New York State)	http://www.crisny.org/government/gov.ny.html	New York State, Executive Branch, Judicial Branch, Legislative Branch, Additional Resources (Grants and Programs, New York State Local Government Telcommunications Initiative, and Voting Information)
New York (Library of Congress Gopher)	gopher://marvel.loc.gov:70/11/federal/state local/ny/	New York State Assembly Gopher, New York State Senate Online Public Exchange Network (OPEN—Senate), New York State Government Information Locator (NYS Library), New York State Budget, Buffalo Freenet (Telnet connection), New York METRO Gopher (Reference and Research Library Cooperative), New York Office of Telecommunications Policy and Development, New York State Archives and Records Administration, New York State Court of Appeals (Telnet connection), New York State Department of Health, New York State Education Department, New York State Facts, New York State Library Gopher, New York State Local Government Telecommunications Initiative, New York State Office of General Services (Contracts Database), New York State and Federal Information via NYSERNET.

Table 9.2: Selected State Government Resources (continued)

Resource	URL	Links
New York (Library of Congress Web)	http://lcweb.loc.gov/global/state/ny-gov.html	New York State Government Locator Service, New York Office of General Services State Contracts Database, Capital Region Information Services, New York Court of Appeals, Cornell Municipal Information Exchange, Capital Region Information Services, New York State and Local Government
New York State Assembly	gopher://assembly.state.ny.us:70/1	Legislative Information System index, New York State Assembly Legislative Information System, Announcements, Economic and Revenue Report 1994-95 and 1995-96
New York Senate	gopher://gopher.senate.state.ny.us/	Gopher Status, January 1996; New York Senate Member Directory; New York Senate Legislative Schedule; New York Senate Rules; New York Senate Committee Membership and Schedule; New York Legislative Public Hearings; New York Senate Reports; New York State Government Information Locator Service; New York Legislative Bill Information
New York State Government Information Locator	gopher://unix2.nysed.gov/	What's New on the New York State Library Gopher, About the New York State Library Gopher, Search This Gopher (Jughead), What's New, The New York State Library—Facilities and Services, New York State Government Information Locator, Full Texts of Publications of the New York State Library, Search the New York State Library Catalog (OPAC) (Telnet connection), Full Texts of New York State Government Publications, Other Gopher and Information Servers, United States Government Information, search Other Library Catalogs, Search the Internet, FreeNets, New York State Government Agencies, New York State 1995 Budget, New York State 1996 Budget
New York State Senate	http://www.senate.state.ny.us	My Senator, Offices, Bills, Meet Committees, Hearings, Review (the law), Reports, Press Releases, Communicate, State Senator by Zip Code, Information about the Senate and Legislature, State and Federal Governing Bodies
North Carolina (Bill Status, Calendars, and Legislator Information System)	ftp://ftp.legislature.state.nc.us/	Documents and folders (Be sure to look at the REASSUME.TXT file first)
North Carolina Legislature Gopher Server	gopher://ftp.legislature.state.nc.us:70/1/	REASSUME, bill info, calendars, index, index.old, legislative offices reports, misc, people, vote history
North Carolina (Library of Congress Gopher)	gopher://marvel.loc.gov:70/11/federal/state.local/nc/	North Carolina State Government Gopher, North Carolina General Assembly, North Carolina State/Local Government Information (via Institute of Government), North Carolina Supreme Court Decisions (Experimental), North Carolina State Library, Central North Carolina Library Consortium (Telnet connection), Western North Carolina Library Network (Telnet connection), University of North Carolina Coast Library Consortium (Telnet connection), North Carolina Community College System, North Carolina Cooperative Extension Program, North Carolina Department of Public Instruction

Table 9.2: Selected State Government Resources (continued)

Resources	URL	Links
North Carolina (Library of Congress Web)	http://lcweb.loc.gov/global/state/nc-gov.html	North Carolina State Information, North Carolina State Library, North Carolina Department of Public Instruction, North Carolina State and Local Government Information
North Carolina State Government Gopher	gopher://gopher.sips.state.nc.us/	Welcome to the N.C. State Government Gopher Server, TCP/IP and the Internet, New Internet User's Top 10 Reading List, North Carolina Information Highway, North Carolina General Assembly, MCNC (Microelectronics, Computing, and Networking Center) Gopher Server and Other Sites Worldwide, United States Government Gophers
North Dakota Legislative Bill Information	gopher://gopher.isnet.is:70/11/hytelnet/sites2/oth000/oth068	Legislative Bills Information (Telnet connection)
North Dakota (Library of Congress Gopher)	gopher://marvel.loc.gov:70/11/federal/state.local/nd/	North Dakota Legislative Bills Information, North Dakota State Gopher
North Dakota State Legislative Information	gopher://VM1.NODAK.EDU:7020/	About the NDUS Legislative Gopher—READ FIRST, Bill Status and Actions, Daily Chamber Calendars, Committee Hearings Data
Ohio Legislative Directories	gopher://gopher.osc.edu:70/11/Ohio%20Legislative%20Information/Legislative%20Information%20%26%20Directories	About the Legislative Directory, Current Ohio State Government Directories, Ohio House of Rep (1994 information), Ohio Senate (1994 information), State Officials, U.S. House of Rep (1994 information), U.S. Senators (1994 information)
Ohio Legislative Information	gopher://gopher.osc.edu:70/11/Ohio%20Legislative%20Information/	Legislative Information & Directories, Ohio Extension Services Demo
Ohio (Library of Congress Web)	http://lcweb.loc.gov/global/state/oh-gov.html	State Library of Ohio, Ohio Online Export Directory Home Page, Ohio State and Local Government
Ohio State Government Information	gopher://gizmo.freenet.columbus.oh.us:70/11/governmentcenter/stateofohio	Franklin Soil and Water Conservation District, Office of Budget and Management, Office of the Secretary of State, Ohio Department of Commerce, Ohio Department of Development, Ohio Dispute Resolution Commission, Ohio Tuition Trust Authority, State Government Job Opportunities, State of Ohio Government Directories
Oklahoma (Library of Congress Gopher)	gopher://marvel.loc.gov:70/11/federal/state.local/ok/	Oklahoma Geological Survey Observatory, Oklahoma State Regents Higher Education Net, Tulsa County Sheriff's Office
Oklahoma (Library of Congress Web)	http://lcweb.loc.gov/global/state/ok-gov.html	Oklahoma State Government Information Server, Oklahoma State Regents for Higher Education (OSRHE), Oklahoma Department of Transportation, Tulsa County Sheriff's Office

Table 9.2: Selected State Government Resources (continued)

Resource	URL	Links
Oklahoma (Tulsa County Sheriff's Office (TCSO))	gopher://gopher.galstar.com:70/11/tcso	About the Tulsa County Sheriff's Office Gopher Site, Tulsa County's Most Wanted, Oklahoma's Most Wanted, Press Releases, Tulsa County Jail Statistics, Crime Statistics, D.A.R.E., Gangs Task Force, Safety Information, Other Information, Public Meetings, Bombing of the Federal Building in Oklahoma City, Tulsa Sheriff's Mission Statement
Oregon (Library of Congress Gopher)	gopher://marvel.loc.gov:70/11/federal/state.local/or/	Oregon Legislative Gopher, Oregon Legislative FTP Site, Oregon Legislative Information System (via Oregon State), Oregon Online Gopher (includes State Agency, State Jobs Info), Oregon State System for Higher Education (OSSHE) Gopher, Eugene Free-Net (Telnet connection), Chemeketa Cooperative Regional Library System (Telnet connection), Portland (Oregon) Public Schools (PPS)
Oregon (Library of Congress Web)	http://lcweb.loc.gov/global/state/or-gov.html	Oregon Online; Oregon State Library; State Archives Public Information Server; Department of Administrative Services, Printing Section; Department of Agriculture; Department of Fish and Wildlife; Department of Forestry; Information Resources Management Division; City of Eugene; Oregon State and Local Government
Oregon (OLIS)	gopher://gaia.ucs.orst.edu:70/11/osu-l+s/OLIS/	About OSSHE (Oregon State System of Higher Education) Legislative Information Directory, Academic Issues, Financial, Operations, Individual Campus Issues, Contacting Your Legislator, 1994 Ballot Measures, Bill Tracking Form, OSU Gateway to OSSHENET (Bill Tracking Matrix), OSU Gateway to Oregon Legislative Information Gopher, Priority Bills, Working Directory
Oregon On-Line (Gopher)	gopher://www.state.or.us:70/1/	News, Community Resources, Economy, Education, Telecommunication, Government, Research Material, Governor's Home Page
Oregon On-Line (Web)	http://www.state.or.us/	Government (Oregon State Government WEB Pages, Telecommunication Information, State E-Mail Directory Search, State of Oregon Telephone Directory, Oregon Online Gopher), Community (Oregon Community Home Pages, Other Resources, Natural Resources), Commerce (Oregon's Economy, Job Opportunities, Business Information, Oregon Tax Information, Other Tax Information), Education (Research Material, Educational Groups and Topics, Educational Institutions, Info)
Pennsylvania (Library of Congress Gopher)	gopher://marvel.loc.gov:70/11/federal/state.local/pa/	CHESConet (Chester County (PA) Information Network), Pennsylvania Information from PennInfo, State System of Higher Education Universities

Table 9.2: Selected State Government Resources (continued)

Resource	URL	Links
Pennsylvania (Library of Congress Web)	http://lcweb.loc.gov/global/state/pa-gov.html	Commonwealth of Pennsylvania WWW, Pennsylvania Legislative Information, Pennsylvania State Data Center, Pennsylvania State Government, Allegheny County and Pittsburgh, Pennsylvania State and Local Government
Rhode Island (Library of Congress Web)	http://lcweb.loc.gov/global/state/ri-gov.html	Rhode Island State Archives, The Governor's State of the State Address and Budget Message, City of Providence, Rhode Island State and Local Government
South Carolina (Library of Congress Gopher)	gopher://marvel.loc.gov:70/11/federal/state.local/sc/	MidNet: Community Access for Columbia and the Midlands (Telnet connection)
South Carolina (Library of Congress Web)	http://lcweb.loc.gov/global/state/sc-gov.html	South Carolina State Government Homepage, Department of Natural Resources, South Carolina Page, Strom Thurmond Institute, South Carolina State and Local Government
South Dakota (Library of Congress Gopher)	gopher://marvel.loc.gov:70/11/federal/state.local/sd/	South Dakota Library Network (Telnet connection), State of South Dakota Gopher
South Dakota (Library of Congress Web)	http://lcweb.loc.gov/global/state/sd-gov.html	State of South Dakota, South Dakota State and Local Government
State Government Gophers	gopher://cwis.usc.edu/11/Other_Gophers_and_Information_Resources/Gopher-Jewels/government/states	35 folders: Alaska, Arizona, California, Colorado, Florida, Georgia, Hawaii, Indiana, Maryland, Michigan, Minnesota, Missouri, Nebraska, New York, North Carolina, North Dakota, Ohio, Oregon, Texas, Utah, Virginia, Wisconsin, and Wyoming state government Gopher sites
State Governors	http://law.wuacc.edu/washlaw/rellaw/relgovern.html	State governors of the U.S., including the name of the state, its two-letter abbreviation, the name of the governor, and his or her party affiliation
Tennessee Education Network (TEN)	gopher://gopher.ten.k12.tn.us/1	Welcome to the Tennessee Education Network (TEN Gopher; Information about the TEN (Tennessee Education Network); TEN Notes; What's New; TEN Information Resources; TEN Conferences, Workshops, Training; On-Line Library Catalogs and Databases; Other Gopher Servers and Information Servers; Acceptable Use Policies; Security Policies
Tennessee (Library of Congress Gopher)	gopher://marvel.loc.gov:70/11/federal/state.local/tn/	Jackson Freenet (Telnet connection), Nashville Public Library (Telnet connection)

Table 9.2: Selected State Government Resources (continued)

Resource	URL	Links
Tennessee (Library of Congress Web)	http://lcweb.loc.gov/global/state/tn-gov.html	State of Tennessee Home Page, Tennessee Government Resources Index, Governor, Tennessee Executive Branch Departments, Tennessee Legislative Information, Tennessee Members of the U.S. House of Representatives, Tennessee Economic Development Center, Tennessee Small Business Development Center, Tennessee Counties: Demographic Information, Tennessee Cities, Lawrence County Home Page, Chattanooga, Knoxville, Metropolitan Government of Nashville and Davidson County, State of Tennessee, Tennessee State and Local Government
Texas Department of Commerce (TDOC)	gopher://gopher.tdoc.texas.gov/	Welcome to TDOC Gopher, Internet Sources Managed by Commerce, Texas Legislation Affecting Business, TDOC Program Information, Community Profiles, Texas County Demographics, About Gopher, Internet File Server (FTP) Sites, Other Gophers, Texas-One, USENET News (from Michigan State)
Texas Legislative Gopher	gopher://capitol.tlc.texas.gov/	Folders about Texas government: the Senate, House of Representatives, the Capitol, the Constitution; many links to other Texas resources, legislative information for 19 states, U.S. government resources, and so on
Texas (Library of Congress Gopher)	gopher://marvel.loc.gov:70/11/federal/state.local/tx/	Texas Information Highway, Texas Legislative Gopher, Texas Legislative Budget Board (BBS) (Telnet connection), Computer Crimes Statute, Hi_T.E.C. (Texas Employment Commission BBS) (Telnet connection), Texas Business Resources, Texas Department of Commerce, Texas Department of Health, Texas Department of Information Resources, Texas Documents Information Listserv, Texas Education Agency Gopher, Texas Education Network, Texas Guaranteed Student Loan Corp. Gopher (TGSLC), Texas Higher Education Coordinating Board Gopher, Texas Natural Resources Information System (FTP Site), Texas State Electronic Library, Texas State Employees' Retirement System, Texas State Library Catalog (Telnet connection), Texas State Technology Assessment Center, Window on State Government (Telnet connection)
Texas (Library of Congress Web)	http://lcweb.loc.gov/global/state/tx-gov.html	State of Texas Government Information, State of Texas Legislative Information, Texas Legislative Information, Texas Constitution, Comptroller of Public Accounts, Department of Health, General Services Commission, Secretary of State, State Employment Information, TeNet: Texas Education Network, TEXAS-ONE, Texas Rules of Civil Evidence, Texas Rules of Criminal Evidence, Texas Family Law Materials, Texas Family Code, Austin City Connection, Texas State and Local Government
Utah Legislation	gopher://gopher.cc.utah.edu/0if%20Campus%20Information/State%20of%20Utah	Constitution, Utah; Governor's Office of Planning and Budget; Governor's Speeches; Legislators; Office of Education: SLC (Salt Lake Valley) Environmental Resource Directory; SLCPD Crime Reports, UTA (Utah Transit Authority) Bus Routes; Utah Education Network; Utah Legislative Bills; Utah State Code; Utah Travel Council, Travel Guide

Table 9.2: Selected State Government Resources (continued)

Resource	URL	Links
Utah (Library of Congress Gopher)	gopher://marvel.loc.gov:70/11/federal/state.local/ut/	Utah Information, Utah Education Network, Salt Lake City
Utah (Library of Congress Web)	http://lcweb.loc.gov/global/state/ut-gov.html	Utah State WWW Server, Utah Automated Geographic Reference Center (AGRC), Utah State Archives and Records Service, Utah State and Local Government
Vermont (Library of Congress Web)	http://lcweb.loc.gov/global/state/vt-gov.html	Vermont State Government
Virginia Government	http://dit1.state.va.us/home/governmt.html	Governor, Lieutenant Governor, Citizen Services, Virginia State Government, Local Government Links of Interest, Other State Government Home Pages, Selected Federal Government Agency Linnks, Virginia General Assembly
Virginia Legislative Information	gopher://minerva.acc.virginia.edu:70/11/admin/govrel	Legislative updates by date (somewhat dated), Legislative Update, About This Gopher Hole, mfp-eforeword.html
Virginia (Library of Congress Gopher)	gopher://marvel.loc.gov:70/11/federal/state.local/va/	Central Virginia Free-Net (CeVaNet) (Telnet connection), Commonwealth of Virginia Information (via George Mason University), Library of Virginia (General and Archives Mss. Collections) (Telnet connection), Southeastern Virginia Regional Freenet (SEVAnet) (Telnet connection), Virginia Department of Information Technology, Virginia Department of Information Technology Procurement, Virginia Library and Information Network (VLIN)
Virginia (Library of Congress Web)	http://lcweb.loc.gov/global/state/va-gov.html	Virginia Government; Virginia General Assembly; Virginia Commonwealth NetServer; Virginia State Council of Higher Education for Virginia (SCHEV); Virginia Library and Information Network (VLIN); Virginia Department of Transportation; Virginia On-Line Atlas; Virginia County and City Census Data (1990 Census); CVaNet: Central Virginia FreeNet; Southeastern Virginia Regional Freenet (SEVAnet); Arlington County, Virginia, Information Server; Blacksburg Electornic Village (BEV); Virginia State and Local Government
Virginia (Welcome to Virginia)	http://dit1.state.va.us/	Visitor's Guide, Government, Education, Around the State, Virginia's Conditions, What's New
Washington Legislature	gopher://leginfo.leg.wa.gov/	Disclaimer Notice, Read this information first; What information is available; How information is organized in these directories; User support policies; Symbols in Bill Text; What is the Internet?; Glossary of terms for Internet resources; Access bills, calendars, RCW (Revised Code of Washington), etc.; How to perform Bill/RCW searches; Frequently Asked Questions
Washington (Library of Congress Web)	http://lcweb.loc.gov/global/state/wa-gov.html	Home Page Washington, Washington (State) Legislative Budget Committee, Department of Health, Seattle Area Traffic, Office of Superintendent of Public Instruction, King County Government, Seattle Government, Seattle Area Traffic, Washington State and Local Government

Table 9.2: Selected State Government Resources (continued)

Resource	URL	Links
West Virginia Legislative Information	gopher://WVWM.WVNET.EDU/	About MountainGopher, From the National Capitol, From the West Virginia State Capitol, West Virginia State Agencies, West Virginia State Colleges and Universities, West Virginia Private Enterprise, WVNET (statewide computer network), News and Weather, Libraries, Phonebooks, Distance Education, Internet Resources, Other Gopher and Information Servers
West Virginia (Library of Congress Gopher)	gopher://marvel.loc.gov:70/11/federal/state.local/wv/	Mountain Gopher, West Virginia Legislative Information
West Virginia (Library of Congress Web)	http://lcweb.loc.gov/global/state/wv-gov.html	U.S. Senator Jay Rockefeller (D-WV), West Virginia Network for Educational Telecomputing, West Virginia Network for Education Telecomputing Gopher, Office of the West Virginia Governor, West Virginia Library Commission, West Virginia K-12 Home Page, Division of Rehabilitation Services, Charleston, Seneca Rocks, Upshur County, West Virginia State and Local Government
Wisconsin Legislature	gopher://badger.state.wi.us:70/11/	Information about Badger, the State of Wisconsin Info Server; Search All Titles in Badger; General Statewide Information; Directories of People, Organizations, and Services; Discussion Groups; Calendars, Events, Schedules, Announcements; Libraries and Other Reference Sources; Wisconsin State Agencies, Departments, and Governmental Branches; University of Wisconsin Gopher Servers; Federal Agency Gopher Servers; Other Gopher and Information Servers
Wisconsin (Library of Congress Gopher)	gopher://marvel.loc.gov:70/11/federal/state.local/wi/	Badger: State of Wisconsin Gopher, State Agencies via Badger, Wisconsin Community Information Partnership
Wisconsin (Library of Congress Web)	http://lcweb.loc.gov/global/state/wi-gov.html	BADGER: State of Wisconsin Information Server; Wisconsin Elected Officials; Wisconsin State Agencies, Departments, and Governmental Branches; Wisconsin State and Local Government
Wyoming Legislature	gopher://ferret.state.wy.us:70/11/wgov/lb	Citizen's Guide to the Wyoming Legislature, Wyoming State Statutes, House and Senate Standing Committee Lists, Information about Wyoming's Legislators, Consensus Revenue Estimating Group, Program Evaluation Reports, Historical Information (about recent times in the Legislature), 1995 Interim Activities, Information about the 1996 Legislative Session
Wyoming (Library of Congress Gopher)	gopher://marvel.loc.gov:70/11/federal/state.local/wy/	State of Wyoming, Ferret Gopher; Wyoming State Library

Table 9.2: Selected State Government Resources (continued)

Resource	URL	Links
Wyoming State Government	gopher://ferret.state.wy.us/	Welcome Message from Wyoming Ferret, Miscellaneous Ferret Topics (including Help), What's New, Phone Numbers for Ferret Access, Helpful Search Engine for Ferret (Jughead), Help for Anet and Telnet Users, Tourism Information, Wyoming Job Bank, Wyoming State Government, Citizen Comment Forms, Wyoming State Statutes, 1996 Proposed Bills, Other State of Wyoming Gophers, Wyoming's Home Page
Yahoo List of State Government Servers	http://www.yahoo.com/Government/States	Links to states and state government indexes

Chapter Ten

News and Events

I f you're on the road in an unfamiliar place or if you want to check on a news story that is changing hourly, the Internet is a great source. In this chapter, you'll find out about resources that provide a variety of news sites and those that present a particular type of information. You'll also be able to find a radio or television channel and its schedule for the day.

This chapter also presents a variety of newspaper-related resources: comics and sports, in particular. For example, if you are addicted to Dilbert or if you miss seeing The Far Side or Calvin and Hobbes, you can visit them on the Web. Or if you want to see how Penn State or the Phillies did yesterday, you can find out here. In this chapter, you'll even learn where you can read the obituaries.

General Resources

In this section, we present news-related sites that contain a variety of resources—comprehensive sites containing all types of news and even opinions—and sources for journalists.

ClariNet

http://www.clarinet.com/

ClariNet Communications Corp., which claims to have more than 1,000,000 subscribers, sends "live news (including technology-related wire stories), timely computer industry news, syndicated columns and features, financial information, stock quotes, and more." Categories include Global and U.S. News, Business News, Techwire, Computer Industry, Internet/Online News, Sports, Syndicated Features, and Commerce Business Daily.

Even if you are not a subscriber, *ClariNet* provides ClariNet Tearsheets, which summarize the top ten stories in U.S. and General News, Business News, World News, and Computers and Technology and lists sample closings of computer and technology stocks. In addition, you can look at the sample newsgroup and an archive of eight comic strips.

Daily News—Free Internet Sources

http://www.helsinki.fi/~lsaarine/news.html

gopher://gopher.nstn.ca:70/11/Cybrary/News/news

This comprehensive and nongraphical catalog of news-related Internet sites originates from Sam Sternberg and has been converted to HTML by Lauri Saarinen at the University of Helsinki.

On the home page, you can link to Parts 1 and 2 of the catalog, read an introductory guide, or look at the table of contents. The Guide and Table of Contents are both good ways to start searching this site. News links in Part 1 are arranged globally, regionally, and then nationally. In Part 2, you'll find other news resources, including journalism, news associations, radio and television networks and stations, sources of alternative news, and commercial news online sites.

Also included on the home page are selected mirrors for this site and other news sources: a mailing list, other catalogs, two journalism resource lists, and CRAYON (at http://crayon.net/), an Internet site at which you can create your own newspaper.

The Daily News—Just the Links

http://www.cs.vu.nl/~gerben/news.html

This comprehensive Netherlands site provides links to many online newspapers and magazines covering news stories. Categories under which the links are arranged include Current Events, Europe, U.S.A., North and South America except the U.S.A., Asia and Africa, Oceania, the World, Old Current Events, Other Lists of News Sources, and European Weather.

Editor & Publisher Interactive

http://www.mediainfo.com/edpub/e-papers.home.page.html

This comprehensive site, a resource for the newspaper industry, tracks online activities of newspapers around the world. Resources include Site of the Week, FAQ (Frequently Asked Questions), Newspaper Services on Commercial Online Services, Newspaper Services on the Internet, Misc. Electronic Newspaper Services (a list of links to news, press, video, and pricing and other information), Newspapers Reported to Be Working on Online Projects, and Screen Shots of Online Newspaper Services on Various Platforms.

Other resources include a column, essays and papers, publications and research papers, consultants, free news services, press associations, wire services, and much much more.

Environmental News Network

http://www.enn.com/

The Environmental News Network (ENN) sponsors this large and award-winning site, which provides "a timely and accurate look at a variety of environmental topics." Main categories at this site include Today's News, Click on the graphic (see Figure 10.1) to access Features (feature stories), Calendar (coming events), Marketplace (advertisements and pages from U.S. government agencies, commercial firms, publications, and organizations), Forum, Library (abstracts, articles, papers, and stories), News Archive, Navigator (Environmental Links), About ENN, and Membership.

The Eric Friedheim Library and News Information Center

http://town.hall.org/
places/npc/newsroom.html

This promising site, which was under construction at the time of this writing, presents a variety of sites from Washington, D.C., and other locations. Resources at this site, which is sponsored by the National Press Club, include the Information Center Membership and Services Information (not available at the time of this writing); Internet Journalism Resources (General Reference, Resources for or by Journalists, News Media Online, and Internet Training Materials); Hot News (research sources, the 1996 campaign, press releases, text of speeches, and public relations links); and Announcements and Press Releases (under construction at the time of this writing); Order a Transcript or Tapes from National Press Club Luncheon Speeches (lists of speeches, ordering information, and sound files), and Access to News Media Online (many links to electronic journals, print sources online, and TV and radio online).

Film and Broadcasting Page

http://www.io.org/~proeser/

If you have any interest in film and broadcasting, this is the ultimate site for you. This long and comprehensive page provides links to film and broadcast media under the following categories: Broadcasters, Film Studios, Audio Resources, Manufacturers and Services, FAQs (Frequently Asked

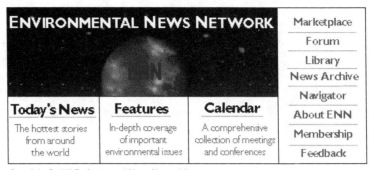

Copyright © 1995 Environmental News Network Inc.

Figure 10.1 Click on part of the graphic to access one of the pages at the Environmental News Network (ENN).

Questions), Regulations, Associations, Festivals, Newsgroups, Educational Programs, Conferences, Related Usenet Newsgroups, and more.

To use this site, either click on a category at the top of the page or scroll down the page until you get to the desired resource.

Financial Times

http://www.ft.com/

The *Financial Times*, founded in 1888, provides business and economic news to the international community. Based in London, it also presents the News in Brief and Today's Top Story.

Business news from the *Financial Times* includes stories from different regions, technology news, and world stock markets, delayed by 30 minutes.

Inter-Links News and Weather

http://www.nova.edu/Inter-Links/news_weather.html

This short list of news and weather items from Inter-Links at Nova University, provides links to today's news (The Daily Inc., CNN Interactive, Nando Times, NY TimesFax, Reuters News Summary, TIME Daily News, USA Today, National

Public Radio, which requires the RealAudio sound player), two links to Florida and National weather, and general weather (Weather Maps/Movies, Daily Planet, PSC Weather Center, WXP Weather Server, Weather Information Superhighway).

Note
You can find additional weather resources in the *Travel* chapter.

Internet CNN Newsroom

http://www.nmis.org/NewsInteractive/CNN/Newsroom/contents.html

If you have an MPEG video viewer to view news stories or you simply want to read the headlines, CNN provides news clips of yesterday's or previous news stories: worldwide, nationally, and locally. Find a story and either click on MPEG (for an MPEG newsclip) or CC (for the printed headlines). Categories include CNN News Room (the opening credits), News Broadcasts by Date (Newsroom Guide, Entire Broadcast, Top Stories, Feature Stories), and the Internet CNN Newsroom Library, a search index of the online news stories.

To search the library, type a name or a keyword in the text box and press Enter. When the search is complete, you can access the MPEG or text file, read a list of questions, use a student handout, and click on links associated with the subject of the story.

Internet Resources for Environmental Journalists

http://www.sej.org/

The Society of Environmental Journalists (SEJ) presents this site, which provides links to Internet environmental resources, SEJ and other organizations, announcements, the *SEJournal*, and other newsletters.

The environmental resources are organized in an impressive list of subjects from Agencies (U.S. government) to Wildlife, and including Biotechnology, Business and Industry, Federal Regulations and Related Documents, Recycling, and Water Pollution.

Launch Pad for Journalists

http://www.tribnet.com/journ.htm

This comprehensive site is an excellent source of research links on the Internet. Categories include Guide to 18,000+ Sites on the WWW (a link to Yahoo, the gigantic Internet search resource), Kevin's Internet Encyclopedia (many Internet links arranged by subject), Harvest Information Server (an integrated set of search tools), American Journalism Review, Army Corp of Engineers, Business & Finance, Computers & Technology, Courts & Law, Crime, Entertainment, Environment, Health, International Organizations (generally, peace groups), News, U.S. Government, Religion, Science, Sports, Transportation, Weather, United Nations, Libraries, and Federally Funded Research Database (links to agencies that provide research funds).

News Tribune TRIBweb

http://www.tribnet.com/

This Seattle, Washington, site, is divided into three categories: News Areas, Fun & Entertainment, and Informational Resources. Under News Areas, you will find news and sports from the last 10 days and Seattle weather. In the Fun & Entertainment category are "cool places on the net" and Internet shopping areas. The Informational Resources section has general information on travel and government sites.

NewsLink

http://www.newslink.org/

NewsLink says that it offers 2,266 free links; this claim seems to be true, and the numbers are growing. Before accessing the links, you can decide whether to register. Either fill in the form and click on the Sign Guest Register button, or click on the Skip Registration button. If you don't register, the server tracks you as you click on a button. When you move to the next page, you can click on links to go to hundreds of Newspaper, Broadcast, Magazine, and Special Links as well as Top 10 and Site of the Week lists. In addition, you can preview research on online publishing.

When you click on a link, you go to a page on which you click a subtopic. For example, if you click on Newspapers, the next page offers three categories: U.S. papers, non-U.S. newspapers in regions of the world, and campus newspapers.

PRESSline

http://www.pressline.com/

This promising site is composed of a search index that contains more than 20,000 press releases covering many topics. You can search the database by Categories, Company Name, Trade Shows, New Releases, Information, Key Word, German, and French. To start a search, click on a category, type in the text box, and click on Start the Search. When the search is completed, click on a link to read the text of the press release. If the list is long, you have to read press releases until you find the one that you want; most filenames do not even hint at the content of the document.

Performing a search using Categories might help to cut down on the number of documents to be reviewed.

SimbaNet

http://www.simbanet.com/

SimbaNet, a service of SIMBA Information, Inc., claims that it is the Web resource for media professionals. Headings at this site include Hot News, What's New from SIMBA, Cowles/SIMBA Media Daily (a daily media industry online update), Sources (newsletter samples), Events, Forums, Register Now (registration is free), and About SIMBA.

Today.Com

http://today.com/

http://today.com:80/

Virtual Office, Inc., presents a site that provides links to What's New Internet sites as well as to many other news sites: News Today, Politics Today, Weather Today, Business Today, Technology Today, Sports Today, Fun Today, Comics Today, and X of the Day (on this day...).

Trib.com News

http://www1.trib.com/NEWS

This site not only points to top news stories of the day but also provides links to sources of background information. One category at this site is Wire & News Services (which has some sound files). Also included are links to Weather, Associated Press, and Local News in the U.S., Canada, United Kingdom, Israel, Ireland, South Africa, and Russia.

Note

Some audio files at this site require a RealAudio player, which you can download by clicking on a link to Progressive Networks, the developer of RealAudio.

Interesting Sites

The Internet is loaded with multimedia sites at which you can listen to sounds or look at videos or movies. If your computer is not the latest state-of-the-art machine, how can you make sense of the formats and locate files to download to your PC? As you might have figured out, the Internet provides the answers.

At the Multimedia File Information site (at http://ac.dal.ca/~dong/table.htm), you can get an understandable guide that covers PC file formats on the Internet, has links to downloadable files, and then tells you how to use the files. Formats include text, compressed files, software, games, pictures, sound and music, foreign languages, and movies. This is an excellent starting point for an exploration of multimedia matters.

The Netscape Sound How-To page (http://burgoyne.com/vaudio/netsound.html) helps you download, install, and set up the programs that can play audio files while Netscape is running. You can choose from three audio players: GOLDWAVE (which plays WAV, VOC, IFF, AU, SND, and MAT audio formats), WPLANY (Windows Play Any File for VOC, AU, WAV, SND, and IFF formats), and WHAM (Waveform Hold and Modify for WAV, VOC, IFF, AU, and AIFF formats).

VDOnet Corp (at http://www.vdolive.com/vdos.htm) offers a video or movie player (that runs as a separate program) or a plug-in (that "attaches" to your browser). From this site, you also can download movies and videos to test the player or plug-in.

Finally, from the Joe Boxer's Bigger, Dumber Utility Library (at http://www.joeboxer.com/utilities.html), you can not only download sound (Xing, SoundApps, and WPLNY), graphics (LView), and movie/video (MPEG Play, Sparkle, Quicktime, and quicktimevcr3.6.hqx) players but also can get compression/decompression files and Web page development utilities for both Windows and the Macintosh.

USA Today

http://www.usatoday.com/

http://www.nova.edu/Inter-Links/usatoday.html

USA Today, which looks almost exactly the way it does on the newsstand, provides a well-designed mix of news and other features: Sports, Money, Life, Weather, Top News, Feedback, Opinion, Snapshot, Lottery Numbers, and Internet news. Just click on the front page (see Figure 10.2) to go to the type of news that you desire.

Its weather map shows today's temperatures. Simply click on the map to get forecasts for a particular region and optionally for a selected city.

Virtual Daily News

http://www.infi.net/~opfer/daily.htm

This well-organized commercial site, run by Steven E. Opfer of Norfolk State University,

Tribune Corporate Home Page

http://www.tribune.com/

The Tribune owns several newspapers and the Chicago Cubs, among other businesses. News resources at this site include Tribune News; Other Tribune Sites, which link to some of the Tribune's news-related businesses; and Swimming Pool, which lists many newspapers worldwide.

provides links to many popular news sites: CNN Interactive, USA Today, Mercury Center, internetMCI, and Time. Categories under which links are organized include Front Page Headlines, Briefs, and Stories; U.S.; World; Business, Urban, Regional, Weather, and Sports as well as The Arts, Technology, Modern Life, and Education. The business news links, in particular, are extensive.

Voice of America (VOA) and WORLDNET

gopher://gopher.voa.gov:70/1/

The Voice of America (VOA), in existence since the 1940s, provides up-to-date news, features, music, and other entertainment worldwide. WORLDNET is a similar service on television.

This site provides information about VOA, newswire stories for the past seven days, Chinese radio scripts, downloadable Internet audio files in AU and WAV formats, VOA programs and schedules, Talk to America radio call-in show, Worldnet television schedules, e-mail addresses, broadcasts to Cuba, and What's New.

WebOvision

http://www.webovision.com/cgibin/var/media/index.html

This gigantic site provides links to media and media-related resources under the following categories: World Television, USA Television, Television Shows, World Radio, USA Radio, San Diego Media, Publications, Journalism, News Links, Media Services, Film & Theatre, and Cool Web Links. When you click on a typical link, a page with alphabetical links and a search index appear. You also can scroll down the page until you find a link to explore. Other links reveal pages of resources.

Figure 10.2   Click on the *USA Today* front page to go to News, Sports, Money, Life, Weather, or Scores.

World Media On Line

http://www.worldmedia.fr/wm/

This experimental and growing service shows how journalism works online. *Sarajevo On Line* not only reports the news but also allows readers to communicate with residents. The *Russian Chronicles* traveled along the Trans-Siberian railway tracks (see Figure 10.3) and produced an

Figure 10.3   The map showing the Russian Chronicles trip

exhibit of photographs and documented the journey with interviews and maps. Other resources at this site are Planet Reporter (Investigative Hypermedia Service), Tour '95 (Sporting Events), and the upcoming World Media Weekly.

Yahoo Listings

http://www.spub.ksu.edu/other/journ.html

This short page is composed of links to Yahoo's University Publications, K-12 School Publications, Commercial Publications, Radio, Television, and Other Journalism Sites on the Internet.

Yahoo News Resources

http://www.yahoo.com/News/

What can you say about Yahoo that hasn't been said before? As always, this page is full of valuable resources and links to lists and indexes. This site provides links to journalism categories, such as Current Headlines, Business, Commercial, Daily, Government, Health, International, Internet Newsletters, Journalism, Legal, Magazines, Newswires, Politics, Sports, Technology, Unversity Newspapers, Usenet, Weekly, What's New, and much more.

Radio and Television

Imagine being in a lonely motel room in a place far from home. Rather than channel-surf, get on your computer and find some of the local radio and television stations in the area. Many provide links to their national network so that you can even check the evening's schedule.

In this section are resources that provide lists of stations, primarily in the U.S.

ABC Primetime

http://www.abctelevision.com/

This small ABC Television site is composed of links to several featured shows and to ABC RadioNet (http://www.abcradionet.com/).

RadioNet, a free membership service for which you must register, is testing a feed of national news stories, in RealAudio format, updated hourly or more often. Other features include local news, sports, weather, quotes, and commentaries. To use RadioNet, you must download the RealAudio audio player.

eye on the net@cbs

http://www.cbs.com/

CBS Television presents a commercial site that features some of its shows, including The Late Show with David Letterman, CBS Sports, CBS News (its overnight news show), and a FAQ List. Also included is a downloadable CBS screen saver. At the time of this writing, this site was under construction. At this point, the best page at the site, is the Reporters' Resource Page (http://uttm.com/reporter), which provides links to a variety of research sites arranged under various categories.

FOX Online

http://www.foxnetwork.com/home.html

The official Fox site, which is definitely aimed at its young demographic group, provides four links: Fox Kids Network, Fox Sports, Fox Entertainment, and What's New. Click on Fox Entertainment to go to another page of links: Chat Room, Fox Boards (discussion groups), Games (Famous Partners is an easy trivia game in which you match the names of very famous partners), This Week (this week's schedule), Fox Favorites, New Shows, Specials, Fox Rocks, and Cool Like Us.

GREAT! Television HOTLINKS

http://www.greattv.com/GREAT_TELEVISION_HOTLINKS.html

This may be the only television site you'll ever need. Here, you'll find links to official and unofficial home pages, the television pages for all the master lists (for example, Yahoo and the World-Wide Web Virtual Library), public relations sites, television listings worldwide, and other major television lists.

National Public Radio (NPR)

http://www.npr.org/

NPR presents a well-designed site that includes news stories, special features, programs, member stations, NPR overseas, transcripts, and more. Of special interest is NPR News and Cultural

Programs, at which you can get information (credits, addresses, schedules, and so on) about NPR programs. Also included are NPR stations with sites on the Internet.

NBC HTTV

http://www.nbc.com/

The good-looking but slow-loading NBC site is composed of these resources: 1996 Olympic Games, Shows (shows, stars, and specials), Your NBC Station (a clickable map with links to affiliates), Sports, Peacock Park (games, promotions, and a

free, downloadable screen saver), News (information about its shows—no current news), CNBC (information and schedules), NBC Production Facilities, and NBC News Intellicast Weather (nicely presented national and local weather).

Public Broadcasting Service (PBS) Online

http://www.pbs.org/

The well-designed PBS Online site provides links to several pages: What's On PBS, Inside PBS, PBS Learning Services, PBS Store, Your PBS Station (links to local public stations), and Online Newshour, with interviews and updated news. The PBS Program Navigator is an alphabetically arranged index of programs. A unique feature is a search index with a drop-down list of programs, the best presentation of programs of all the network sites.

Radio Stations on the Internet

http://wmbr.mit.edu/stations/list.html

Theodric Young, at MIT, has produced a comprehensive list of radio stations that have Internet links. You can access U.S. radio stations (either by call letters or by state); Canadian, Australian, European, and other international radio stations; and some radio networks.

The Satellite TV Page

http://itre.uncecs.edu/misc/sat.html

If you are outside the limits of your local cable systems or are planning to use one of today's high-technology satellite dishes, be sure to visit this site from Jay Novello at the Institute for Transportation Research and Education. If you are a novice, you will find the best links in the Gary Bourgois,

Programmers' Web Sites, Miscellaneous Satellite-Related Links, and Links People Have Asked Me to Add sections.

Ultimate TV List

http://tvnet.com/UTVL/utvl.html

TV Net is referred to as "your starting point for Television Hot-Spots in Cyberspace." It features more than 300 links to more than 550 shows, including almost 800 World Wide Web pages. It also has links to cable companies throughout the United States. Use the Search feature or look at the alphabetical or genre listings to find your favorite show. Also included at this site is a Listings by Resource section as well as What's New.

What's On Tonite!

http://tv1.com/wot/index.html

How many times have you been on the road and wanted to relax in front of the tube in a strange city? If you don't carry your *TV Guide* with you, this unique site has what you want. First, select a region of the U.S. Then select the way in which you want the listings formatted: in a grid, by time, by program type, or channel—either graphically or text-only. Obviously, taking the text-only route is the fastest. Listings include networks and many cable stations as well as links to additional information.

A new version of What's On Tonite! is in the testing phase. In addition to television listings, you'll be able to get news, link to cable companies, and buy merchandise. Registration will be free.

Yahoo Radio List

http://www.yahoo.com/entertainment/radio/stations/

Yahoo divides its radio station entries into Indices (there were 10 of them at the time of this writing), Commercial, Commercial Resources, and Public. When you click on Commercial, you'll find another index plus links to four subcategories. Clicking on Corporate Resources, you'll find a list of companies that make products or provide services for radio stations and listeners, especially those involved with amateur radio.

Yahoo Television List

http://www.yahoo.com/Entertainment/Television/

Yahoo presents television resources under 23 categories, from Actors and Actresses to Video. Of particular interest are Satellite, Schedules, Shows (both current and classics), and Stations.

Newspapers

Newspapers are hopping onto the Internet in droves. This section provides you with sites that keep track of the latest additions and a table containing newspapers from the U.S. So, if you are a businessperson, you can read the news of the city you're about to visit; if you're a parent, prospective student, or alumni, you can read campus news of a particular college or university. Be sure to look at the tables of newspapers.

Table 10.1 lists selected U.S. newspapers on the Internet, their URLs, and the main headings under which you can find news. Table 10.2 lists international newspapers found on the Internet.

Table 10.1: Selected U.S. Newspapers on the Internet

Name/Location	URL	Main Headings
Anchorage Daily News (Anchorage, AK)	http://www.adn.com/htmlpages/adn/home.html	Alaska Headlines, E-mail Edition, Archives, Alaska Voices, Early Warning (Upcoming Events), Daily News Contacts (Subscription Information, E-mail Addresses, Research, Alaska Cartoons, Just Doin It (Recreational Sports), Links
Anderson Independent-Mail (Upstate South Carolina, Northeast Georgia)	http://www.globalvision.net/ANDERSON/	Local News, National and World News, Newspapers on the WWW, Sports (Area Colleges, Major League Baseball, National Football League, Racing News, College and Pro Basketball, and More, Weather, Money (Stocks and Investing, Mortgage Calculator), Leisure Time Entertainment and Television, Comics and Humor, Travel and Leisure, About Us, and Anderson, S.C. (Information about Anderson, Things to Do and See
Arkansas Democrat Gazette (Arkansas)	http://www.ardemgaz.com/	NewsGeek Notebook (Technology News), Today's Top Stories, Classified Ads, Entertainment Guide, Adobe Acrobat Pages (Select Specific Pages), Photo Gallery, Previous Features, Email Our Newsroom, Democrat-Gazette Info, and Other Useful Links
Asbury Park Press*Net (Asbury Park, NJ)	http://www.injersery.com/Media/PressNet/doc/home.html/	About Press*Net, Current Edition, Classifieds, Feature Stories, Hoopla (Sports), Cyber News (Page Up-Weekly Electronic 'Zine), Good Causes, Enterprise (Investigative Reporting), Virtual Tour of Rutger's Sculpture, What's Going On, and Rutgers' Football
Aspen Times (Aspen, CO)	http://www.infosphere.com:80/aspenonline/directory/times/timesindex.html	Cover Story; General News; Arts & Entertainment; The Week's Sports, Events, Arts & Entertainment Listings; Business/Real Estate; Opinion, Editorials and Pizza Bones Cartoon; Society; and Previous Issues, Features & Profiles
Athens Messenger/Athens News/Marietta Times (OH)	gopher://seorf.ohiou.edu:2001/11/seorf.stuff/Med	Athens Media Access Center (Athens Center for Film and Video, Special Events), Athens Messenger (News and Opinion, Voters Guide), Athens News (Issues by Date), Marietta Times (Under Construction)
Atlanta Journal-Constitution (Atlanta, GA)	http://www.ajc.com/	Fastball (the Atlanta Braves Baseball), Olympics Report (Ticket Update, What's New, and Olympics Guide), Welcome to Atlanta (Visitor's Guide, Virtual Driving Tour, Georgia Web Sites, and Weather)

Table 10.1: Selected U.S. Newspapers on the Internet (continued)

Name/Location	URL	Main Headings
The Bakersfield Californian (Bakersfield, CA)	http://www.kern.com/tbc	Local News, Classified, National News, Weather, Eye StreetEntertainment, Family, Home & Garden, On the Go/Travel, Health & Fitness, Food, Money, Movies, TV, Music, Youth, and Technology), Sports, Business, Kern Life (Local News), Opinion, School Link, Cyberian (What's New), and Kern County's Ticket Connection
The Baltimore Sun (Baltimore, MD)	http://www.sunsource.com/sunsource/	Feature Stories, Merchandise
Beloit Daily News (Beloit, WI)	http://boss1.bossnt.com/bdn.html	Today's Top Local News Stories, Daily News Special Sections, Archives, Schedule of Local Government Meetings, Wheels Page Columns (Automobiles), Letter to the Editor, Your Favorite Comic Strips, Other Interesting WWW Sites, Career Opportunities, Subscription Information, National News, Sports, Reuters News Summary, Search the Web, and Miracle: A Chronology (Story of White Buffalo)
Birmingham Post-Herald (Birmingham, AL)	http://www.postherald.com/	Headlines, PHTODAY.ZIP, Previous Week, Digest, Metro, Features, Sports, Business, Commentary, Best Bets (Weekly Calendar), and Birmingham Post-Herald Information
The Boston Globe (Boston, MA)	http://www.globe.com/	Media, The Common, Arts/Diversions, Sports/Outdoors, Real Estate, Help Wanted, Highlights, Feature Stories, Feedback, Keyword Search, Help
Breakers (coastal North Carolina)	http://www.eastnc.coastalnet.com/cnmedia/jdnews/breaker1.htm	break'n NEWS (Entertainment News), FAST breaks (Sports), break AWAY (MAX Magazine–Concerts, Reviews, Places to Go, Local Drama, Gallery, Sports & Recreation, Festivals, For Kids), BEST breaks (Best Places in Eastern N.C.), BEYOND breakers (Computers, Games, and More), ABOUT breakers (Ads, Subscription Information), and Next on Breakers
Campus Press (University of Colorado, Boulder, CO)	http://bcn.boulder.co.us/campuspress/Presshome.html	News, Fun, Internet, Sports, Calendar, Services, Weather, Opinion, Mail
Cape Coral Pages (Cape Coral, FL)	http://www.capecoral.com/	Business, Classified Ads, Cool Web Sites, Florida Wildlife, Leisure, Real Estate Today, and About Cape Coral (Map, Facts & Information, History, Schools & Colleges)

Table 10.1: Selected U.S. Newspapers on the Internet (continued)

Name/Location	URL	Main Headings
Cape May Star and Wave (Cape May, NJ)	http://www.acy.digex.net/~cmwave/contents.html	Headlines, What's New, Weekly Local News, Highlights and Features (Internet and Computer News, News Links, Site of the Week, Weather, Picture Gallery, and More), More Info and Help, South Jersey Area Home Pages, and Link to The Sentinel Ledger of Ocean City
The Capital (Annapolis, MD)	http://www.infi.net/capital/	Top Stories, Navy News, Sources Say (People and Politics Behind the News), Top Ten Stories (Including Updates), Archives, Business, Entertainment, Sports, Hotlinks, Opinion, Market, Tour, and Lifestyle
The Capital Times (Dane County, WI)	http://www.infi.net/madison/news/tct.shtml	Favorite Films, Feature Story, Forum Section, Hot Topics, Savvy (Meet a Local Personality, Ask the Expert), Weather, News for Kids, U.S. News, TCT Links (Favorite Links), and About The Capital Times
Casco Bay Weekly (Portland, ME)	http://www.maine.com/cbw/	Cover Story, Casco Bay Weekly Current Issue, Portland Guide, Archive, Business District (Personals, Rentals, Help Wanted), Rotary (Internet Links)
Casper Star Tribune (Casper, WY)	http://www.trib.com/	Headline News, Headline News from CBS, News from Canadian Press, News Stories from the Montreal Gazette, Voice of America Stories, News, Sports, Money, Weather, Travel, Features, and Search The World Wide Web
Central Ohio SOURCE (Columbus, OH)	http://www.sddt.com/~columbus/	News, Technology, Small Business, Lifestyles, Real Estate, Public Notices, Library, About Us, Community, Special Reports, Legal Affairs, Finance, Government, Associations, Assistance, Index, What's New (Clickable Map, Courts, Central Ohio Stocks, Today's News from The Daily Reporter, Bar Briefs Magazine, Association Newsletters, Small Business Column, Business Professional Profiles, Weather), and Subscription Information
Chat Times (Chattanooga, TN)	http://www.chattimes.com/	Times Extra (Community Events), Cityscape (Times Almanac, Goodtimes, A World of Links), Classified, and Questions
Chicago Sun-Times (Chicago, IL)	http://www.suntimes.com/index.html	Connected (Internet Links), Traffic & Weather, Sports/Entertainment/Reviews, Don Crabb Q & A, Education, Sound Off/Letter, General Information, and Stock Quote Hotline

Table 10.1: Selected U.S. Newspapers on the Internet (continued)

Name/Location	URL	Main Headings
Chicago Tribune (Chicago, IL)	http://www.chicago.tribune.com/	Job Opportunities, Company Profiles, and Feature Articles
Christian Science Monitor (national news)	http://freerange.com/csmonitor/	Special Editions until the multimedia version is issued
The Chronicle Online (Duke University Community, Durham, NC)	http://www.chronicle.duke.edu	Today's News, Online Dateabank (Archives, Sports Stats, Special Features, and More), and Information (The Staff, Contact Information, and More
CITYPAPER ONLINE (Baltimore, MD)	http://www.citypaper.com/	No Cover (Local Bands, Short List–What's Happening), Baltimore's Weekly Picks (Music, Dance, Art, Books, Highlights), Classifieds, Cyberpunk (Baltimore Links), Film Clips, Personals, Sound Tracks, About City Paper, Television, and Syndicated Links
Columbus Dispatch (Central Ohio)	gopher://gopher.freenet.columbus.oh.us	Freenet Information, Local and National Libraries, Local Health Services, Area Governments, News, Weather, Calendar of Events, and Business Connection
Columbus Dispatch (Columbus, OH)	gopher://gizmo.freenet.columbus.oh.us:70/11/news-weather-calendar/dispatch	Connections to The Dispatch on the World Wide Web, Consumer Law, Contacting the Dispatch Staff, Government Information, Newspapers in Education, Updated News, Sports and Local Information, Weekender, and a Dining Guide
Cornell Chronicle (Cornell University, Ithaca, NY)	gopher://gopher.cit.cornell.edu:7070/11/.dirs/CHRON	News Stories, Calendar
Creative Loafing Online (Atlanta, GA)	http://www.cln.com/atl/CONTENTS.HTM	Feature Stories, Arts & Entertainment, The Big Picture (Television and Movies), Cuisine, News (Lead Stories, Features), Think Tank (Commentary), Vibes (Music), Etcetera, Happenings, Loafer's Exchange (Companions, Real Estate), Creative Loafing Information, and Archives
CumberLink (Carlisle, PA)	http://www1.trib.com/CUMBERLINK/	Software Sites (Shareware and Freeware Sites); The Sentinel (Today's News); Web Search; Cumberland County Information, Tours; Virtual Library Reference Area; Weather; Franklin County Infromation, Tours; Site for Teachers, Students, and Parents; Listings, TV Sites; Pennsylvania Information; Penn State Football Unofficial Home Page; epix System News; U.S. Government, National Politics; Sports World; Money; Local Events, Places to Go; World, National News; Fun Sites; and CumberLink Users' Page
Daily Illini (University of Illinois, Champaign, IL)	gopher://gopher.uiuc.edu:70/11/UI/DI	A time-delayed newspaper; News Articles

Table 10.1: Selected U.S. Newspapers on the Internet (continued)

Name/Location	URL	Main Headings
The Daily News Leader (Augusta County, Staunton, and Waynesboro, VA)	http://www.fqa.com:80/daily/	Publisher's Welcome, News and Information, Advertise on the Leader, History, Subscription Information, Leader Phonebook, Photo, Sports, Classified, Links, and Etc. (Arts and Entertainment)
The Daily Tar Heel Electronic Edition (University of North Carolina, Chapel Hill, NC)	http://www.unc.edu/pubs/dth/dth.html	Current Issue, and Browse the Archives
Daily Texan (University of Texas)	gopher://gopherhost.cc.utexas.edu:3003/1/microlib/info/texan	Table of Contents, News Stories, News Briefs, Viewpoint, Firing Line, Around Campus, State Briefs, Sound Bites, Calendar, Briefs, Standings, Sports (Collegiate and Professional)
The Daily Times Online (Salisbury, MD)	http://www.intercom.net/dailytimes/	Cover Story, Local & State, Lifestyle, Food & Style, Sports, Religion, Community Forum, Calendar of Events, Travel, Neighborhoods, The Daily Times Online, Staff, News-Related Links, and Archives
Dallas Morning News (Dallas, TX)	http://www.pic.net/tdmn/tdmn.html	Special News, and Opinions
DCI Online! (Delta County, CO)	http://www.dci-press.com/	News Briefs, Local Schools Home Page, News Links, Open Forum, News, Opinion, Regions, For Fun, Events, Sports, Issues, Mall, Arts, and What's Cooking
Democrat and Chronicle Times-Union Digital Edition (Rochester, NY)	http://www.RochesterandC.com/	About Us, Advertisers, Diversions (Drive, Eat and Drink, Get Reel, Go, Skiing, Wysiwyg-Current Computer Columns and Software Reviews), and Sports
Detroit Free Press (Detroit, MI)	http://gopher.det-freepress.com:9002/	About the Detroit Free Press Online, About This System, Contacting the Free Press, Phone Numbers, How to Get Back Copies and Articles, U.S. and Michigan Politics, Journalism Resources, Freedom of Information, Search the Internet, Weather, On-line Library Catalogs in Michigan, Privacy in the Digital Age, MichNet, and Gopher Sites
Detroit Free Press (Detroit, MI)	http://gopher.det-freepress.com:9002	Connections to Information about the Detroit Free Press, Local and National Politics, Weather, Search the Internet, On-line Library Catalogs in MI, MichNet, and other Gopher Information

Table 10.1: Selected U.S. Newspapers on the Internet (continued)

Name/Location	URL	Main Headings
The Digital Missourian (Missouri)	http://digmo.org/	Top News, Local & State, Nation & World, Sports, Weather, Business, Science & Health, Community Forum, Show Me Columbia, The Reference Desk, The Marketplace, and Kids' Stuff
DJC Online (Seattle, WA)	http://www.djc.com/	Headlines, Breaking News, Business, Construction, Real Estate, Architecture & Engineering, Auctions, Law, Environment, Technology, Machinery, Public Notices, Credit (Liens and Bankruptcy News), Index, Feedback, and Design 95 (Stories about Firms, Projects, and Trends in Northwest Architecture and Engineering); registration required for full access
The East Hampton Independent (East Hampton, NY)	http://www.peconic.net/independent/	Cover Story, Editorial, and Feature Articles
Electric Examiner (San Francisco, CA)	http://www.sfgate.com/examiner/index.html	News, Business, Sports, Style, Archives, Editorials, Examiner Magazine, Travel, Habitat, Epicure, Real Estate, Classifieds, Zippy the Pinhead Comic, Homearts, and Feature Stories
Evansville Courier (Evansville, IN)	http://www.evansville.net/newsweb/	Courier Feature Stories, Hometown Heroes, AP Daily News Stories, Local and National News, Sports, Business, and Entertainment
Family World	http://family.com/	Events Calendars, Feature Stories and Articles, Parents Forum, Internet Resources, Shoppertunities, School Articles, People and Information, About Family World
Fayetteville Online (Fayetteville, NC)	http://www.infi.net/FOTO/	News, Weather, Sports, Business, Military, Features, Things to Do, North Carolina Web Sites, Editorials, Discover Fayetteville, and Fayetteville Online Newsgroup
Gainesville Sun and University of Florida (Gainesville, FL)	http://news.jou.ufl.edu/	State & Region News, CyberAge (Features about the Internet), Scene Magazines, Issues, Archives, and News Extra
The Gate (San Francisco, CA)	http://www.sfgate.com/ or http://cyber.sfgate.com:80/examiner/	From the San Francisco Chronicle and The San Francisco Examiner, Cybersports, The Columnists, San Francisco Stories, The Silicon Valley Report (Computers, Industry News, Technology), Entertainment and the Arts, The Gate Digital Gallery, What's Up (Technical Developments), and Contests
The Gazette (Eastern Iowa)	http://www.infi.net/hyiowa/gazette/index.htm	Iowa Today, The Iowa Hawkeye Report, National News, Local News, Archive, Subscription Information, and Web Links

Table 10.1: Selected U.S. Newspapers on the Internet (continued)

Name/Location	URL	Main Headings
GT OnLine (Colorado Springs, CO)	http://www.usa.net/gazette/	Daily News, What's New (Fun Guide, Hot Links, React—Teen News), Weather, Top Story, World News, National News, Sports, Opinion, Go! (Entertainment), Business, Features, Gateway to Colorado (Guide to Recreation, Travel, and Tourism), Pikes Peak Almanac & Answer Book, Archives, A Walk Around Downtown Colorado Springs, and GT Internet Gateway to News and Services
Hartford Courant (Hartford, CT)	http://www.courant.com/news/thc-news.htm	Top News, Business, Trend/Outlook, Connecticut News, National News, International News, Opinion, and Special Features (Sport, Spirit and Splendor)
Hastings Tribune Internet Edition (Hastings, NE)	http://www.crweb.com/tribune/index.html	Feature Story, More News, Sports, Opinions, Local Links, Classified, Comics, and Nebraska Land Products, Cybermall
Hollis Brookline Journal (Hollis, NH)	http://www.jlc.net/HBJ/Home.html	News arranged by Date (Front Page, Hollis News, Brookline News, Sports News), Letters to the Editor, Town Information
The Home News & Tribune (New Jersey)	http://www.injersey.com/Media/HNT/Doc/	Regional News, New Jersey News, World & Nation News, Business News, Technology, Sports, Opinions, Entertainment, Living, Food, Calendars, News4Kids, Classified Ads, and Help & Info
Houston Chronicle (Houston, TX)	http://www.chron.com/ or http://chron.com/ or http://www1.chron.com/	Houston (Community-oriented Internet Sites), Chronicle (News), Headlines (News and Sports), and Marketplace
icon (Iowa City, IA)	http://www.jeonet.com/icon/	This Week (Opinion, News, Cover Story), Arts Around, Theater, On Stage, Across The River—Alternative Health Care, On Screen, and Stageside, Back Issues (By Month), and The Best of Iowa City (Food and Drink; Arts and Entertainment; Shopping; Necessities; Celebs and Media; Body, Health and Fitness; Choose Your Own; Campus Life; and City Living)
Idaho Mountain Express and Guide (Sun Valley, ID)	http://www.mtexpress.com/	Arts & Entertainment, Weekly Calendar, Classifieds, Subscriptions, What's New, Sun Valley Guide Online, General News, This Week's Editorial, This Week's Feature, and Other Stories This Week
The Indianapolis Register (Indianapolis, IN)	http://www.inetdirect.net/indianapolis-register/	The Indianapolis Register (Profiles, Opinions, Health, Business, Events, What's Happening), and About Indianapolis
The Inquirer and Mirror (Nantucket, MA)	http://www.Nantucket.net/inkym/	This Week's News, Sports Scoreboard, Columns, Horoscope, Calendar, Feature Story, Back Issues, Subscription Information, Nantucket Food, Nantucket Inns, and Nantucket Homes

Table 10.1: Selected U.S. Newspapers on the Internet (continued)

Name/Location	URL	Main Headings
Inside Illinois (University of Illinois, Champaign, IL)	gopher://gopher.uiuc.edu:70/11/UI/II	News Stories about University of Illinois departments, classes, and events; Calendar, Deaths, Energy Monitor, Inside Light, Job Market
Inside University of Virginia (University of Virginia, Charlottesville, VA)	gopher://minerva.acc.Virginia.EDU:70/11/pubs/InsideUVa	News Stories, Briefly Noted, Inside UVA Masthead, Inside UVA Deadline and Misc. Info
Internet Daily News (The Virtual Press, Hawaii)	http://tvp.com/idn.html	Business, Publishing, Entertainment, Resources, Letters to the Editor, and Index of Columnists (under construction)
ISTHMUS The Daily Page (Madison, WI)	http://www.thedailypage.com/	Chronicle (The Week to Come, Feature Story), Movies, Entertainment, Lifeline, Personals, Classifieds, Local News, Weather, Sports, Email, and Boulevard (Index of Alternative Newsweeklies and WWW Sites emphasizing Arts, Entertainment, Contemporary Culture, and Politics)
Journal and Courier Online (Lafayette and West Lafayette, IN)	http://www.mdn.com/jconline/	The Purdue Extra (Purdue's Online Newspaper), Today's Edition, Previous Editions, Calendars, Frequently Asked Questions, Lafayette Area Resources, and more
Journal Newspapers (MD, VA, and DC)	http://www.infi.net/journal	Local News, Features, and Opinions; Journal Community Guide; Discussion Groups and Feedback; Sports; Weather; Business; and Entertainment
The Knoxville News (Knoxville, TN)	http://www.knoxnews.com/	Classifieds, Feature Story, Vol Football, KnoxLink, Features, and East Tennessee
The Kokomo Herald (Kokomo, IN)	http://www.holli.com/herald/	Current Issue, Back Issues, Subscription Information, Letter to the Editor, Link to NewsLink
LA PRENSA de San Antonio (San Antonio, TX)	http://www.hispanic.com/LaPrensa/LaPrensa.html	Headlines, La Prensa Archives, and Meet the Staff
Lawrence Journal-World (Lawrence, KS)	http://www.ljworld.com	Welcome, Guestbook, Other Links, Back Issues, Local News, Sports, Entertainment, Classified, About Lawrence, Reader Reaction, Weather, Maps

Table 10.1: Selected U.S. Newspapers on the Internet (continued)

Name/Location	URL	Main Headings
The Leader OnLine (Port Townsend, WA)	http://www.olympus.net/biz/leader/leader.html	Hot off the Press (News Flash, Today's Events), OnLine Features (Publisher's Welcome, Business Index, Expert of the Week, Who's Who, Weather, Community Calendar, Arts Calendar, Classifieds), Newspaper Sections (Area News; Area Personalities; Home, Health & Family; Cops & Robbers & Courts; Arts & Entertainment; Sports & Recreation; Business & Economics; Letters to the Editor; Community Organizations; and Back Issues)
The Maui News (Maui, HI)	http://www.maui.net/~mauinews/news.html	News (Local, State, County, Sports, Classified, Weather), Of Special Interest (Letters, Editorial, Maui Net, Features, and Check It Out), Entertainment (Scene, Calendar, Music, Resorts, Events), Vacation Rentals, Photos, and Hot Links
Mercury Center Web (San Jose, CA)	http://www.sjmercury.com/	Mercury Mall (Advertisers), Frequently Asked Questions, What's New, Mercury News Job Openings, Community Connections, Getting Ahead, New Comics, Feature Stories, Breaking News, Today's Newspaper, Today's Classified, Comic Directory, and News Library
Miami Herald (Miami, FL)	http://herald.kri.com/	Under Construction
Middlesex News (Boston, MA high-tech suburbs)	gopher://ftp.std.com/11/periodicals/Middlesex-News	Today in the News, Movie Reviews, Restaurant Reviews, Selected Columns, Entertainment Information, Calendar of Events, MetroWest Organizations, Cyberspace, Week in Review, Middlesex News Auto Weekly, Lottery Results, Government, and History
Milford Cabinet and Wilton Journal (Milford and Wilton, NH)	http://www.ilc.net/Cabinet/Home.html or http://www.cabinet.com/Cabinet/Home.html	Front Page News, Hollis-Brookline Journal Link, Town Index, Other Topics (Business Directory, Peek at the Week, Classified, Editorials, Sports, Business, Religious Services), Milford Amherst Area Chamber of Commerce, and Weather Forecast
Missoulian ON LINE (Missoula, MT)	http://www.missoulian.com/	What's New, Photo Gallery, Grizzly Football, Montana Writers, Missoulian Products, Missoula Weather, Montana Movies, Montana Maps, Missoulian Cookbook, and About the Missoulian
Morning Star (Wilmington, NC)	http://starnews.wilmington.net/	Civic Affairs, Movie Reviews, Along the Cape Fear, Weather Information

Table 10.1: Selected U.S. Newspapers on the Internet (continued)

Name/Location	URL	Main Headings
Nando Times (Raleigh, NC)	http://www2.nando.net/nt/nando.cgi?lowtext	Top Story, Main Sections (World News, Nation News, Sports News, Politics News), Other Sections (Business, Info Tech, Health & Science, Voices, Entertainment, Something Else-Odd Stories, Sports Server, and In the Press Box)
Nebraska WEB (Nebraska)	http://newsone.com/	Searchable Classified Ads, News, Sports, Opinion, Life & Music, Photos, Cartoons, and About Us
New York Times Internet Edition (New York, NY)	http://nytimesfax.com/	Front Page Highlights; Foreign, National and Business News; Sports; Crossword Puzzle; Selected Editorials and Commentaries. Registration required.
The News-Times (Danbury, CT)	http://www.danbury.lib.ct.us/media/news/	Today's News (Local News, Regional News, Business, Kid's News), Television, Today's Weather, National, National Sports, Classified, Video, Local Sports, International, Automotive, Music, Books, Connecticut Lotto Results, Computer, Health, Movies, and The Comic Page, Features (Recipes, Neighbors Column, Weekly Events, School Lunches, Photo Stories), The Mortgage Marketplace, and Letters to the Editor
News Tribune (Tacoma, WA)	http://www.tribnet.com/	News Areas (News Stories, Sports Stories, Weather Report, Movie Reviews, Classsified Ads, and the Vladivostok News) Fun & Entertainment, Informational Resources (tourism, Internet links, Washington government)
Newtown Bee (Newtown, CT)	http://www.thebee.com/	Antiques and the Arts Weekly, Newtown Bee, and HORSES Monthly
NJBIZ.COM BUSINESS News (New Jersey)	http://www.injersey.com/Media/NjBiz/	Current Issue, Managing Smarter, Focus Section, Editorial Calendar, Calendar of Business Events, Business Services, Business Mailbox, N.J. Business Ombudsman, and Archive
The Nugget (Deschutes County, OR)	http://www.nuggetnews.com/	Front Page, Back Issues, Next Page, Previous Page, Sisters Oregon (Wall Phone Chat, Events Calendar, News Links and Political Views, The Great Outdoors, Classified, Lodging, Food, Vital Statistics, History, Emergency Directory, How to Get Here, Homepages), and Information
Observer & Eccentric On-Line (Southeastern MI)	http://www.oeonline.com/	News, What's New, Classifieds, Subscribers Home Pages, The Detroit Institute of Arts, What's Hot (Favorite Places on the Web), Entertainment, Personals, and Shopping
Oregon News Network (Douglas County, OR)	http://www.oregonnews.com/	News, Sports, Weather, Oregon Outdoors and Tourism, State and County Information, Internet Road Map (Web Sites), and Oregon Business Directory

Table 10.1: Selected U.S. Newspapers on the Internet (continued)

Name/Location	URL	Main Headings
OutNOW! (San Jose, CA)	http://www.outnow.com	The Internet's Gay Newspaper (Feature Article, Bay Area News, National News, Opinion, Arts, Guide, and Classified), and Archives
Palo Alto Weekly	http://www.service.com/PAW/home.html	New Features, Cover Story, Notes & Comments, Local News, Local Sports, Arts & Entertainment, Eating Out, Movies, Home & Real Estate, MarketPlace, and Back Issues
Philadelphia Inquirer and Philadelphia Daily News (Philadelphia, PA)	http://www.phillynews.com/	Search Index, Feature Stories, Archives, HeartNet, Planet Jobs, The Crossword, Cybernews, Today's Headlines, Table of Contents
Pilot Online (Southeastern VA)	http://www.infi.net/pilot/	Top Story, Features, Classifieds and Personals, Real Estate Web, Career Web, Auto Web, Index, News, Fun, Shopping, Talk, and Extra
Pittston Gazette (Pittston, PA)	http://www.microserve.net/Pittston/	Feature Story, Classified Ads, TV Listings, Local 5 Day Forecast, Headline News, Opinion Editorial, Cartoon, Town Notes, Sports, Church News, School News, Senior News, Obituaries, Late Breaking News, On-Line Personals, Information of Greater Pittson, Information on Pittston Area School District, Information on Wyoming Area School District
Portland Press Herald Maine Sunday Telegram (Portland, ME)	http://www.portland.net/ph/	News, Viewpoints, Business, Sports, Entertainment, Classified, Weather, Maine Marketplace, Appalachian Trail, Bay Net (News, Information, and Dialogue about Casco Bay), The Bridge (Construction Project), Investigative Reporting, See Maine, and Library (Fee-based Research System)
The Post-Star (Glens Falls, NY)	http://www.albany.globalone.net/poststar/psnews.html	National News, Local News, Sports Page, The Scene, Classifieds, Stock, and Subscription Information
Providence Business News (Providence, RI)	http://www.pbn.com/	Current Issue (Main News Stories, Rhode Island News Briefs, Business Notes, Business Formations, Calendar of Events, Corporate Profile, Editorials, Letters, Opinion, Small Business, Stockwatch Updates, Massachusetts News Briefs, Executive Poll), Past Issues, Search (by Subject), Rediscover Rhode Island
Public News (Houston, TX)	http://www.NeoSoft.com/publicnews/	Alternative Newsweekly (Politics, Performing Arts, Film, Literature, Music, Sports, and Reviews)
Quincy Herald-Whig (Quincy, IL)	http://www.cis.net/~whig/	Local News, Weather, Sports, Arts/Events, Quincy Herald Information, and Oakley/Lindsay Center (an Exhibition Hall/Theater/Office Complex)

Table 10.1: Selected U.S. Newspapers on the Internet (continued)

Name/Location	URL	Main Headings
The Record (Troy, NY)	http://www.albany.globalone.net/RECORD/	The Record (History), Today's Headlines, Sports, Community News, Classifieds, Steppin' Out, Movie Times & Reviews, Around Troy, and Great Deals
The Roanoke Times Online (Roanoke, VA)	http://www.infi.net/roatimes/	News and Information, The Roanoke Marketplace, Classifieds, News Archives, Subscription Information, Guide to the Roanoke Valley, Calendar of Events & Entertainment, Roanoke News Headlines, Roanoke Sports, Virginia Public School Rankings, New Century Council Report, Seniors' Internet Links, Kids' Links to the Internet, and What's New
Rochester Business Journal on the Web (Rochester, NY)	http://www.rbj.net/	Highlights, Picture of the Week, Bausch & Lomb CEO Daviel Gill's Remarks, Simon School Dean Charles Plosser's Annual Economic Outlook, Subscription Information, Advertising Information, Sample Issue, Local Companies and Organizations Web Sites, Business News and Data on the Net
The Roundtop Register (Round Top, TX)	http://www.rtis.com/reg/roundtop/	Feature Story, News, Arts, Internet, Editorial, Events, History, Merchants, Calendar, and Map
The Salt Lake Tribune UTAH ONLINE (Salt Lake City, UT)	http://www.sltrib.com/	Front Page, World, Utah, Sports, Opinion, Business, Outdoors, Weather, and Archive
San Diego Source (San Diego, CA)	http://www.sddt.com/	What's New, Breaking News, Technology, Special Reports, Education, Legal Affairs, Lifestyles, Finance, Real Estate, Government, Public Notices, The World, Library, Assistance, Source Sites
San Francisco Bay Guardian (San Francisco Bay, CA)	http://www.sfbayguardian.com/	Cover Story, Politics, Arts & Entertainment, San Francisco Guides, Epicenter (Feature Stories), Single (Personals), and Public Forum
San Mateo Times (San Mateo, CA)	http://www.baynet.com/smtimes/	Top News Stories, Featured Story, Main Section (Weekly Horoscope, Daily Stock Quotes, Weather, Comics), Marketplace (Real Estate, Real Estate Financing, BayNet Homes Service, Classified), Search the Archive
Santa Rosa Press Democrat (Santa Rosa, CA)	http://www.pressdemo.com/library/	Help for New Users, What's New, Library Reference, Newsroom Research, Redwood Empire on the Web
The Sentinel Ledger (Ocean City area, NJ)	http://www.acy.digex.net/~ocledger/contents.html	Headline News, What's New, Highlights and Features, More Info and Help, South Jersey Area Home Pages, Link to The Cape May Star and Wave

Table 10.1: Selected U.S. Newspapers on the Internet (continued)

Name/Location	URL	Main Headings
Shepherd Express (Milwaukee, WI)	http://www.shepherd-express.com/	Culture and Nightlife, Food and Drink, Local Flavor (Local Celebrities), Places (Favorite Places), Public Life (Entertainment), Goods and Services, Calendar of Events, Photo, Art for Art's Sake Column, Media Musings, Expresso (Week's News), Film Reviews, Art Kumbalek (Radio Personality), Disc Reviews, Talking Sports, Back Issues, and Links (Topics vary from week to week.)
SignOn San Diego (San Diego, CA)	http://www.uniontrib.com/	Homebuying Net, At Home in San Diego, Chargers Report, Communities, About the Union-Tribune, Night & Day (Entertainment), Special Reports, and The Trail to San Diego (GOP National Convention and Presidential Campaign Coverage)
Sioux City Journal Online (Sioux City, IA)	http://www1.trib.com/scjournal	Local News, Opinion, Business, Sports, Almanac, Living, What's Hot, Neighbors, Politics, Real Estate, Advertisers
Southern Maine Coastal Beacon (Saco, ME)	http://www.biddeford.com/~beacon/welcome.html	The Coastal Beacon (Selected Articles and Columns), The Maine Index (Maine Resources- Universities and Colleges, Commercial, Yellow Pages, Community, Cool Sites, Publications, Internet Related, State & Local Government)
The Spencer Butte Gazette (Eugene, OR)	http://www.efn.org/~sgazette/gazette.html	Feature Story, Weather, Sports, Business Pages, Gazette Classifieds, Global Newslink, Local Newslink, Letters to the Editor, and The Eugene Pages
sptimes.com (St. Petersburg, FL)	http://www.sptimes.com/	In the News (National News, Business News, Tampa Bay and State, Sports), Tampa Bay Sports, Features (Tampa Bay Area Guide, Florida Aquarium, Treasures of the Szars, Point of View),and In Search of a Job (100,000 Job Listings from over 40 U.S. Newspapers)
St. Paul Pioneer Press (St. Paul, MN)	http://www.skypoint.com/pioneerpress/	Feature Stories, Twin Cities Attractions
St. Petersburg Times (St. Petersburg, FL)	http://www.times.st-pete.fl.us/	In the News (News of the Day), Sports, Features, Job Listings, and Index

Table 10.1: Selected U.S. Newspapers on the Internet (continued)

Name/Location	URL	Main Headings
The Standard-Times (southeastern MA)	http://www.S-T.com/NewStandard/	Welcome, Subscription Information, Daily Digest (Top News), Headline Index (Today's Offerings or Look Back), AP Stories (General, Foreign, Finance, Washington, Politics, Sports), Daily Datea (Lotteries, Almanac, NOAA Forecast), Our Listings (Bits & Pieces, Clubs, Concerts, Dance, Galleries, Health, Kids, Learning, Movies, Museums, Nightlife, On Stage, Potluck, Sales, Support, Videos), Letters to the Editor, Tell It (Anonymous Feedback), Announcements (Community, Club, or Event), Comics, So What Else is New?, The Information Zone, Fore-site: Our Site of the Week, Last Week's Site, Other Webs Worth Wandering, AdLine (Area Companies), Other Media Online, and Software Starting Places (excellent site)
StarPhoenix (Canada)	http://www.wbm.ca/star	Today's Headlines, What's New, Features and Columns, Reading Rooms (The Newsroom, The Locker Room, The Weather Office, The Cultural Center, The Marketplace, The Boardroom, and The Theme Park), and Surfing the Net (News and Other Links)
Star Tribune (Minneapolis/St.Paul, MN)	http://www.startribune.com/	News Summary, Special Projects, Advertising\Links, Star Tribune Online, About Star Tribune, Star Tribune Merchandise
StarNet (Tucson, AZ)	http://www.azstarnet.com/	StarNet El Tour De Tucson (Bike Race), Daily Star Sample, Wire Services, El Mercado (Merchants), Insider Guides, Resource Center, What's New and What's Hot
SUN Center (Edmond, OK)	http://www.edmondsun.com/	Daily News, Real Estate Center, Classified Online, Entertainment, Food and More, Contact SUN Staff
SUN-LINK (Hanover, PA)	http://www.sun-link.com/	The Evening Sun On Line, School Zone, Area Visitor's Guide, About Sun-Link and Netrax, Hanover/Adams Information, and Hot Links
Sun.ONE (Gainesville, FL)	http://www.jou.ufl.edu/enews/sun/	News, Area, Info, Cool Links, and Staff
Syracuse New Times (Syracuse, NY)	http://www.rway.com/newtimes/	New Times Picks (Featured Events), Concerts, Clubs, Film, Exhibits, Stage, Dance, Literati, Learning, Outings, Sports, Specials, Self-Help and Support, Classified
Syracuse OnLine (Syracuse, NY)	http://www.syracuse.com/	Top Stories, News Sections (Sports, News, Leisure, Humor, Jobs), Guide to Syracuse, Favorite Places on the Internet, and Newspaper Links

Table 10.1: Selected U.S. Newspapers on the Internet (continued)

Name/Location	URL	Main Headings
The Tech (Massachusetts Institute of Technology)	http://the-tech.mit.edu/	Search the full-text archives, Browse the full-text archives, The Tech Indexing Project, Firehose Tavern archive, About this server, What's new on this server, About the Tech, News Bulletin Board, How to Advertise in The Tech, Other MIT Resources
Telluride Times-Journal (Telluride, CO)	http://www.adone.com/telluride/	Entertainment, Calendar, Columns, Editorial, Sports, Business, Browse, What to Do, Visitor Services, Restaurant and Lodging, Subscription Info, Staff, News, Classifieds, Telluride (Air Travel Information, Extended Calendar, Ski Season Information, Restaurant and Lodging Guide, Ski Area Map, Nursery Information)
The Times Higher Education Supplement (Essex, UK)	http://www.timeshigher.newsint.co.uk/	InterView (Jobs Worldwide), Research News, UK News, International News, Opinion, Perspective, Books, Multimedia, Synthesis (Universities and Industry), Noticeboard, and Research Opportunities
The Times Newspaper Group (San Jose, CA)	http://www.ipac.net/tng/tnghome.html	Times Film Forum, TimesStyle (Guide to Writing for the Times), Theophilus Forum (Interactive Religion and Ethics Net Sit, Times Features (Automotive, Business, Dining, Entertainment, Religion, Health, Travel, Pets), Community Calendar, Holiday Happenings, The Editor's Page), Links to Newspapers in the Times Group
Times Publishing Company (Erie, PA)	http://www.timesnews.com/	Today's Headlines, About Times Publishing Company, Advertising Information, Marketing Statistics & Maps, and Newspaper Products
Times-Mail (Bedford and Lawrence County, IN)	http://www.tmnews.com/	News, Bedford Public Library, Shareware Link, Times-Mail Information, Sports, Opinion, County Information Page, Indiana Media, Indiana Schools, and Indiana Government
TimesLink (Wichita Falls, North Texas, Southern OK)	http://www.wtt.com/	Local News, Business, Opinions, Weather, Sports, Search the Web, Fun Sites, Wichita Falls (Area School Numbers, Area City Hall Numbers, Hotline Numbers, State Parks and Area Lakes, Midwestern State University, Vernon Regional Junior College, Luknet-Internet Access Provider)
Town Crier Online (Palm Beach County, FL)	http://www.adone.com/crier/index.htm	Town-Crier Information, Town-Crier News & Editorials, Palms West Communities Calendar, Classsifieds, AdOne Classified Network (Nationwide Classifieds)

Table 10.1: Selected U.S. Newspapers on the Internet (continued)

Name/Location	URL	Main Headings
Triad Online (Greensboro, NC)	http://www.infi.net/nr/triad.html	News & Commentary, Business, Sports & Recreation (including UNCG Men's Basketball), Weather, Cybermail, Web Links (The Associated Press, Reuters, Cable News Network and others), Eating & Entertainment, Community & Government, and Forums & Feedback
Tribune (Charlottesville, VA)	http://www.fwnet.com/	Friends and Family, Pleasant Places in the Piedmont: A Guided Tour, Financial Services, What's New, and Other Services (Book Reviews, Selected Articles, Programming,
Tribune-Review TRIButaries (Pittsburgh, PA)	http://tribune-review.com/trib/	News, Weather, Sports, Business, Editorial, Letters to the Editor, Comments
Tucson Weekly Online (Tucson, AZ)	http://desert.net/tw/twhome.htm	Quick Map or Contents (Currents, City Week, Music, Review,Cinema, The Back Page), Indices (Music Bin, Film Vault, Chow Scans, and Back Issues)
University of Minnesota News (University of Minnesota)	gopher://joeboy.micro.umn.edu:70/11/providers/urel/News	Events & Lectures, Facts about the University, Medical & Science News, News Releases, and Publication Guide
Vacaville Reporter (Solano County, CA)	http://www.thereporter.com/	Local Columnists, Fishing Report, Special Reports, Special Events, and the Welcome Connection (Information on the Area)
Village Voice and LA Weekly (NY and CA)	http://www.villagevoice.com/	A combined effort by the *Village Voice* and the *LA Weekly*. It will include Listings and Personals. (under construction)
Wall Street Journal on Web (national)	http://www.wsj.com/	Money & Investing Update, The Wall Street Journal (Headlines, College Program Information, Directory of Products and Services, Subscription Information), Personal Journal (Customized Electronic Edition), Personal Technology, Classroom Edition, and Internet Directory
The Wasatch Wave...On Line! (Heber Valley, UT)	http://www.ditell.com/~tomnoff/	Wave Articles and Features, Calendar of Local Events, Classifieds, Subscription Information, and Internet Links

Table 10.1: Selected U.S. Newspapers on the Internet (continued)

Name/Location	URL	Main Headings
Washington Free Press (Seattle, WA)	http://www.speakeasy.org/wfp/idx/00.html	Activism, Book Reviews, Corporate Crime, Cultural Criticixm, Editorial, Environment, Film, Health, Human Rights, Humor & Satire, Interviews, Labor, Media, Music, Seattle City Politics, Transportation, Washington State Politics
Washington Times National Weekly (District of Columbia)	http://www.townhall.com/wash_times/	Top News Story, Inside the Beltway (Washington, D.C. News), Editorials, Feature Story, Politics, Letters to the Editor, Map, Town Hall (Internet Discussions on Issues within the Conservative Community), and Search
Western News On-Line (Northwest MT)	http://www.libby.org/WesternNews/	This Week's News, Spring and Summer in the Kootenai Valley, and Lincoln County Home Page
Wisconsin State Journal (Wisconsin)	http://www.infi.net/madison/news/wsj.shtml	News, Opinion, News Links, and Talk to Us
Women's Wire hot off the wire (national)	http://www.women.com/wwire/html/1.in.html	Women's News Topics, Women's Healthline, E-lineEntertainment), Horoscope, and Fashion Wire
The Woodinville WEEKLY online (Greater Woodinville, WA)	http://www.nwnews.com/ww.html	Current Issue, Affiliates, Back Issues, and Late Breaking News
ZEPHYR (Galesburg, IL)	http://www.misslink.net/zephyr/fronpg.htm	Calendar of Events, List of Public Meetings, News, Sports, Health, Religion, Movie Reviews, Commentary, Features, Weather, and Weather Map

Table 10.2: Selected International Newspapers on the Internet

Name/Location	URL	Main Headings
The Age (Melbourne, Australia)	http://www.theage.com.au/	News, Features, Classifieds, Technology, Links to The Sydney Morning Herald and Australian Financial News
The Asahi Shimbun (Japan)	http://www.asahi-net.or.jp/an-e/index.e.html	Information, Topics, Japanese
The Associated Newspapers of Ceylon Limited (Sri Lanka)	http://www.lanka.net/lakehouse/	Daily News Link (Today's Paper, Yesterday's Paper, This Week's Sunday Observer, Archives), Sunday Observer (This Week's Paper, Yesterday's Paper, Last Week's Paper, Archives)
Athens News (Athens, Greece)	http://www.dolnet.gr/Athnews/Athnews.htm	Greek News, Economy, Arts and Entertainment, Sports, Diplomacy, Weather, Classified Ads, Back Issues, About the Paper, Letters to the Editor, and Athens News Club
Barrie Advance (Barrie, Ontario, Canada)	http://www.barint.on.ca/advance/emessage.html	Editor's Note, Real Estate, Classified, Barrie Advance (News, Opinion, and Sports), Sincerely Yours Dateing Service, Psychic Page (a 900 number)
Bermuda Sun Limited (Bermuda)	http://www.bermudasun.org/	News Centre, Morgue (Past Issues), Archive (Full Text Speeches and Other Documents), Employment Centre, Advertising, Government Notices, Bermuda Surf (Information about Bermuda), and The Bermuda Connection (Information about Bermuda from Andrew Riker)
Business Day (Thailand)	http://www.asia1.com.sg/bizdaily/	General, Business, Financial, Features, Stock, Old Issues, Advertise, Job Openings, AsiaOne, Business Times, BT Stock-Watch, Computer Times, and Zaobao
The Cambodia Times (Cambodia)	http://www.jaring.my/at-asia/camb_at_asia/camb_times/ct_list.html	Shockwave Website, Current Issues, Back Issues, Reflections & Salutations, and @Asia (Country Profile, Economy, Sihanouk—Father of Cambodia, Hottest Site this side of Cyberspace with Links to Virtual Exhibition, Malaysia @ Asia, China @ Asia, and Cambodia @ Asia)
China Daily (China)	http://www.ihep.ac.cn/cdaily/cdai.html	Science and Culture Page, and Feature Stories (by Date
The Daily News Worldwide (Canada)	http://www.htxnews.com/media/daily/	News, Perspective, Matinee/Life, Business, Sports, Weather, and Letters to the Editor
Daily Record Sunday Mail (Glasgow, Scotland)	http://www.record-mail.co.uk/rm/	News, Sport, Features, Letters, Contests, The Mag, Photo Gallery, and Record Romance (24-Hour Telephone Dating Service)

Table 10.2: Selected International Newspapers on the Internet (continued)

Name/Location	URL	Main Headings
durhamnews (Durham Region, Ontario, Canada)	http://www.durhamnews.net/	Feature Story, News, Sports, Opinion, Arts, Real Estate, Classified, Advertisers, and Directory
Electronic Herald (Scotland)	http://web1.cims.co.uk/herald/	News, Sport, Business, Features, Feedback, and Images of Glasgow
The Electronic Mail & Guardian (Johannesburg, South Africa)	http://www.mg.co.za/mg/	News and Features, Book Excerpts, Past Issues, Entertainment, WEBFEET Guide, PCReview Online, Open Africa (African Travel), Mail and Guardian Television, and Work @za (Careers Center)
Estado de Minas (Brazil) (in Portuguese)	http://www.estaminas.com.br/	Internet, Software, Byte a Byte, Infotribo
Evening Times (Glasgow, Scotland)	http://web1.cims.co.uk/eveningtimes/	Feature Story, News, Sport, LifeTimes (Showbiz, Problems, Stars, Music, Scotty's Soap, Opinions, Crossword, Features, Backchat, Sam on the Net, and Funnies), Fighting for You (Scotland Against Drugs), Mick and Billy (Cartoon)
Folha de Sao Paulo (Sao Paulo, Brazil)	http://www.folha.com.br	Portuguese language newspaper
The Gazette (University of Waterloo, Canada)	http://www.adm.uwaterloo.ca/bulletin/	News Stories for the University
The Globe and Mail (Canada)	http://www.globeandmail.ca/	Report on Business, National Issues Forum, News, Archives, What's Coming This Week, and Marketplace
Halifax Herald (Halifax, Nova Scotia, Canada)	http://www.herald.ns.ca/	Newscentre (Today's Top Stories, Bruce MacKinnon's Cartoon, Web Links, Just 4 Kids), Daily Edition (The Chronicle-Herald), Services Offered (Advertising, Bulletin Board, Phone-in Information System, and Library Archive), About Us (The Halifax Herald Limited, Our Province, Tribute to Nova Scotia), and Tour of the Maritimes (Weather, Nova Scotia Towns, New Brunswick, and Prince Edward Island)
Herald Sun Info@ctive (Melbourne, Victoria, Australia)	http://www.aone.net.au/HWT/	Quicklinks, AFL Home Page, Get Wired (Internet Sites, Gadgets, Software, Music and Movies, Guide to Computer Games), You'll Love Every Piece of Victoria (Leisure Activities), and Delphi Australia (many interesting links to Fashion, News, Fortune-telling, TV, etc.)
The Hindu (India)	http://www.webpage.com/hindu/	About Us, Search Engine, The Week that Was, About The Hindu Online, Advertisements, Classifieds, Employment Opportunities, and The Hindu Online Business Directory, What's New, and Back Issues

Table 10.2: Selected International Newspapers on the Internet (continued)

Name/Location	URL	Main Headings
HongKong Standard TIGERNET (Hong Kong)	http://www.hkstandard.com/	News, Financial Review, JobMarket, PC Market, Archive, Information, Tourism, Personal Webs, Internet Links, Contact Information (Editorial, Classified, Marketing, Web Master, Job Market, Display Advertising, Circulation/Subscription, System Administration)
The Independent (New Zealand)	http://www.kete.co.nz/datex/independent/welcome.htm	Search the Independent, Search Hints
Independent Newspapers Ltd. (South Africa)	www.independent.co.za/news/	Headlines, Business, Politics, Entertainment, Leader, Interactive, Sport, Lifestyles, Columns, Hard News, Transport Column, Tavern of the Seas Column, Cape Town, and SA Times (London)
IndiaWorld (India)	http://www.indiaworld.com/	Preview, Subscribe, Today's Additions, Gifting, Headlines, India Daily, Business Quotes, Busybee, Laxman, India Today, Kalnirnay, Movies, Cricket, and Quiz (some areas require registration)
Irish News Global Edition (Northern Ireland)	http://www.irishnews.com/	Home Page, Today's Edition, Archive, News Flashes, Other Links, and E-mail
The Irish Times On the Web (Ireland)	http://www.irish-times.ie/	Front Page News, Home News, Sport, Opinion, Editorial & Letters, Foreign News, and Finance
Jam Jam (Japan)	http://www.mainichi.co.jp/index-e.html	Headline News, All That's Happening in Japan (Politics/Business, Domestic, Editorial), Photo Gallery, High-Tech Shower, Japan Deep-Down, and Sumo
Jerusalem Post (Jerusalem, Israel)	http://www.jpost.co.il/	Feature Story, News, Business, What's Happening, Opinion, People & Places, and Columns
The Kamloops Daily News (British Columbia, Canada)	http://www.netshop.net/dailynews/daily_news.html or http://www.netshop.bc.ca/dailynews/daily_news.html	News, Community Forum (Letters to the Editor, Columns, and Editorials), Business News, Sports News, and
Kyodo Cyber Express (Kyodo, Japan)	http://www.toppan.co.jp/kyodo/	Kyodo Visual News, The World Heritages (Sites Around the World), Top10 News
Lancashire Evening Telegraph (Lancashire, UK)	http://www.reednews.co.uk/let/	News, Sport, Archive, Index, Motors, Property, What's On, and Marketplace

Table 10.2: Selected International Newspapers on the Internet (continued)

Name/Location	URL	Main Headings
Lethbridge Herald (Lethbridge, Alberta, Canada)	http://www.lis.ab.ca/herald/	News (Local, National, World), Sports (Local, Alberta Winter Games, World), Features, Editorials, Commodities, Coming Events, Elected Officials), The Herald (About the Lethbridge Herald, Links), and Your Views
The London Free Press (Ontario, Canada)	http://www.lfpress.com	London & Region; Sports; Weather; Special Sections; Business; Our Times; Opinions; Buy, Sell & Tell; Subscription Information; and Media Links
The Montreal Gazette (Montreal, Canada)	http://www.vir.com/gazette/index.html	Current News (Background Reading), Opinions, and Aislin (Terry Mosher, Canadian Political Cartoonist)
National Business Review (New Zealand)	http://www.kate.co.nz/datex/nbr/welcome.htm	Search the National Business Review, Search Hints
The New South Polar Times (Antartica)	http://139.132.40.31/NSPT/NSPThomePage.html/	The GENII Project, About The New South Polar Times, Feature Story, Notes from Davis Station, Current Issue, Back Issues, Lessons and Ideas, Information and Data, Submitting Questions, Other Resources, The Climate Monitoring and Diagnostic Laboratory, Antartic Support Associates, The Blizzard, Antartic Exploration, and Radio Darts (under construction)
News Review (United Kingdom)	http://www.news-review.co.uk/	Summary of Economic, Financial, and Corporate News of 12 Newspapers (The Daily Express, The Daily Mail, The Daily Telegraph, The Guardian, The Independent, The Times, S.Express-Big Issue, The Independent on Sunday, The Mail on Sunday, The Observer, The Sunday Express, The Sunday Telegraph, and The Sunday Times), Back Issues
Ottawa Citizen (Ottawa, Ontario, Canada)	http://freenet.carleton.ca/freeport/newspaper/citizen/menu	Citizen Services; Comments/Suggestions; Letters to the Editor; Entertainment, Dining & Wine; Community Events; Pro Sports Schedules; and Often Asked Questions
The Post (Zambia)	http://www.zamnet.zm/zamnet/post/post.html	The Front Page, News, Business, Columns, Editorial Comment, Letters to the Editor, Life and Features, Special Report, Sports, Archives, and Zambian National WWW Server
The Press On-Line (New Zealand)	http://www.press.co.nz/1295/9512160l.htm	Feature Stories, Current Events, Editorials, Archives, What's On, Real Estate, and How to Reach The Press

Table 10.2: Selected International Newspapers on the Internet (continued)

Name/Location	URL	Main Headings
Reed Regional Newspapers Lancashire (Lancashire, England)	http://www.reednews.co.uk/	Market Place, Motors, Property, What's On Entertainment, Mobile Discos, Jumble Sales/Car Boot, Taxis/Transport, Dining Out, Take Away/Catering, Ents Services, Clubs, Pubs, Craft Antique Fairs, Cinemas, Theatres, Concerts, Dancing, Function Suites, Forthcoming Events, Outdoor Entertainment, Places to Visit, Shows, Special Events, Sports, Links to Newspaper Sites (Lancashire Evening Telegraph, Bolton Evening News, Blackburn Citizen, Blackpool Citizen, Leigh Journal, Burnley Citizen, Chorley Citizen, Preston Citizen, Bury Journal, Lancaster Citizen, St. Helens Star)
Romanian Press Review (Romania)	http://www.halcyon.com/rompr/	Current Issue, Cover Story, Subscription Information, Back Issues, and Featured Romania Link
Shepparton Internet (Shepparton, Australia)	http://www.sheppnews.com.au/	Read the News, New (New Sites & Stuff), Help (The Internet, Finding Stuff, Speed, Netscape, Making Homepages, Helpers & Utilities), Links (Aussie Links, Our Mates–Australian Providers, Hot Stuff, Surf of Die, Serious Stuff—Including the Visible Human Project, Virtual Tourism), Feature Story, Tools, News Pages, Kids Pages, Search Engines, and Breaking News
St. Petersburg Press (St. Petersburg, Russia)	http://www.spb.su:80/sppress/ or http://www.spb.su/sppress/	Current Issue, Archives, and Culture & Lifestyle Guide
La Stampa (Torino, Italy)(Italian language)	http://www.lastampa.it	La Stampa, Tuttoscienze, Dayfax, I Film (registration required)
The Star Online (Malaysia)	http://www.jaring.my/~start/	News, Business, Sports, Features, What's New, eXtra conomic Report, Selected Articles, Kuala Lumpur Stock Exchange, Currency Exchange Rates, KLSE News Updates, AudioFile & AV, Weather Forecast, The Funny Pages)
The StarPhoenix Online (Saskatoon, Saskatchewan, Canada)	http://www.wbm.ca/users/sphoenix/index.html	Today's Headlines, Features and Columns, YackBack Feedback (Comments, Suggestions, or Inquiries), Frequently Asked Questions, Customer Service Center, Reading Rooms (Newsroom, Locker Room, Weather Office, Cultural Center, Marketplace, Boardroom, Theme Park), and Surfing the Net
Sterling News ONLINE (Canada)	http:www.sterlingnews.com/	News from Ottawa, Victoria, and Vancouver; Columns; Sports; News from St. John, Dawson Creek, Cranbrook, Kimberley, Nelson, Trail, Prince Rupert, and Port Alberni; News from Niagara Falls and Collingwood; Classified Advertising Network; and Advertising

Table 10.2: Selected International Newspapers on the Internet (continued)

Name/Location	URL	Main Headings
The Straits Times (Singapore)	http://www.asia1.com.sg/straitstimes/	Singapore, Region, World, Cybernews, Sports, Perspective, Opinion, Lifestyle, Images, Comics, Marketplace, About Us, Top Story, Shopping
The TICO TIMES Online (San Jose, Costa Rica)	http://magi.com/calypso/times.html	Top Story, News Briefs, Business, Exploring Costa Rica, Central American Page, Tropical Conservation News Bureau, Subscription Information, Costa Rica's Academic Network, and Costa Rica's Home Page
The Times Colonist (Victoria, British Columbia, Canada)	http://www.interlink.bc.ca/timesc/index.html	Daily News, Local Webs, Special Interests, summaries of news stories
Tokyo KaleidoScoop (Tokyo, Japan)	http://www.smn.co.jp/	Headlines, Calendar, Information, Discussion, Features, Gallery, Bulletin, Directory, Library, Staff Page
Utusan MALAYSIA (Malaysia)	http://www.asiaconnect.com.my/utusan/	Bahasa Malaysia News Summary, Bahasa Malaysia Full Edition, English News Summary, French News Summary, German News Summary, Utusan Archive
Vannet (British Columbia, Canada)	http://www.vannet.com/	Links to The Vancouver Echo, The Delta Optimist, The Coquitlam Now, Good Health Magazine, Westcoast Families (Guide to Family Fun and Facts), The North Shore News, and Talking Personals
Winnipeg Free Press (Winnipeg, Manitoba, Canada)	http://www.freepress.mb.ca/freepress	Daily News Summary and Highlights, and Feature Stories
X-NET (Edmonton, Canada)	http://www.itv.ca/examiner/xnet.htm	Cover Story, Columnists, and Features
The Yomiuri Shimbun (Japan)	http://www.yomiuri.co.jp/	Today's Editorials & Hot News, Yomiuri (Monthly Magazine, What's New, Yomiuri Shimbun, Nippon Television Network Corporation, Yomiuri Telecasting Corporation, The Hochi Shimbun (Sports and Leisure), and Yomiuri Entertainment World

Campus Newspapers on the Internet

http://beacon-www.asa.utk.edu/resources/papers.html

This long page contains links to college newspapers and magazines on the Internet. Arranged by type of circulation (daily, weekly, and so on), each item on the list is preceded by a Web icon or a Gopher icon. Also included are experimental papers and other lists of college papers and journalism resources.

Interesting Site

Today's Horoscopes (at http://marilyn.metawire.com/stars/ and http://www.bubble.com/webstars/index.html), written by Jonathan Cainer of the UK *Daily Mail*, provides horoscopes for the day on which you visit. Simply scroll down this attractive page, click on your zodiac sign, and read the brief message. You also can order, for a fee, personal horoscopes and year-ahead horoscopes. Also included are links to other horoscopes, an introduction to astrology, and astrological links.

Weekly Cyber-Stars Horoscopes (at http://marilyn.metawire.com/stars/cyber/stars.html or http://www.bubble.com/cybstars/stars.html) presents a weekly horoscope (running from Monday to Sunday) for those who would prefer to look further into the future.

The Electronic Newstand

http://www.enews.com/

This popular site provides selections of articles and sometimes subscription information for the world's leading magazines, newsletters,

newspapers, and catalogs. Links are organized under New on the Newstand, Editor's Choice, the latest News and Sports, Gift Center, Business, Computers and Technology, Entertainment, Automotive, Health, Politics, Travel, Sports and Recreation, Renaissance Room, Books, News Services, Catalogs, Newspapers, and All Titles.

Nando.net

http://www.nando.net/

Nando.net, an online service of the *News & Observer* in North Carolina, contains many news links. Under News & Information, you can find The Nando Times (continuously updated world, U.S., business, and sports news), Nando News Network (a fee-based news and information service), and NandoNext (with work from high school students in the Research Triangle). The Sports Server provides the online "Fan's Guide to ACC Basketball," a teaser for a book that you can order here as well as links to many other sports resources. Also included are what's new page, entertainment links, North Carolina resources, online articles, and some *News & Observer* features—even an online novel.

Virtual Library of Hampton Roads

http://www.infi.net/~cwt/news.html

From Landmark Communications and Knight-Ridder, this site lists 39 news sources, many in Virginia. Non-Virginia links include CBS World News, Reuters World Headlines, Pathfinder, The Gate, National Public Radio, the Nando Times, The London Telegraph, St. Petersburg Press, The China News Digest, several California newspapers, Yahoo Current Events, the Web Newspaper List, and Spanish-language news from Mexico.

Sports

Sports are as popular as mom and apple pie. Sports sites on the Internet abound. In this section, you can find some major free sports sites.

Table 10.3 lists sports sites on the Internet, their URLs, and the categories under which you can find information.

Fun.Com

http://fun.com/

The Fun.Com site doesn't limit itself to sports. In fact, sports is a very small part of this site. Major topics include Music, Fourtune [sic] Telling, Interactive Games, and Sports. Under Music, you'll find the World Wide Web of Music (a super music site), Hyperreal, and Hip Hop Online.

Subcategories under Fourtune Telling are tarot readings and horoscopes. Interactive Games include

MUDs, Games Domain, and Info-Mac Archives (public-domain Macintosh software). Finally, getting to sports: under Sports, you will find ESPNet Sportszone (a major fee-based sports resource), AudioNet (audio sports files), and Nando Sports (a comprehensive sports site).

GNN Sports

http://gnn.com/gnn/meta/sports/

Kurt Hoyt, a reporter for STATS, Inc., edits this large Global Network Navigator site. Sports covered here include auto racing (six links to auto racing resources), baseball (articles, schedules, and news about major and minor league baseball), basketball, football, soccer, and hockey.

John Skilton's Baseball Links

http://ssnet.com/~skilton/baseball.html

http://users.aol.com/jsbaseball/baseball.html

John Skilton presents more than 500 baseball links on a background of pinstripes. Topics under which you will find links are Baseball Link of the Week; What's New; Scores, Stats & Schedules; Major League Team Info; Minor League Team Info; College Baseball; Amateur & Semi-Pro Baseball; Youth Baseball; International Baseball; News Servers, Archives & Miscellaneous; Baseball Merchandise; Cards and Collectibles; Stadiums; and Baseball Newsgroups.

Table 10.3: Selected Sports Sites on the Internet

Site	URL	Main Headings
Arizona Diamondbacks Baseball (Phoenix, AZ)	http://www.primenet.com/~pwb/dback.html	Arizona Diamondback Information (Stadium, Particulars), Baseball Links
Augusta Chronicle (Augusta, GA)	http://www.cris.com/~masters	Masters Golf Tournament Coverage (News & Analysis, Tour the Course, Leaderboard, Photo Gallery, History, Players, Trivia Challenge, Collectible Editions, WWW Links, and About Masters on-Line
Baltimore Orioles Baseball	http://pluto.njcc.com/~nieporen/oriole.html	Weekly Notes, The Ripken Page, Stadiums, Fan Mailing List, Schedule, Ticket Info, Broadcasting, Standings, Minor League Affiliates, Pictures, Rosters, Statistics, Usenet Newsgroups, Miscellaneous
Baseball Hall of Fame (Cooperstown, NY)	http://www.enews.com/bas_hall_fame/overview.html	Overview of the Baseball Hall of Fame, Features, Contest, Memories and Dreams, Library & Archive, Directions to Cooperstown, Admission and Hours, and Merchandise
Baseball Server (Nando.net)	http://www2.nando.net/SportServer/baseball/	World Series, Leading Off (News, Games, Box Scores, Previews), American League, National League, Statistics, Standings, Transactions, Farm Teams, and archives
Basketball Server (Nando.net)	http://www2.nando.net/SportServer/basketball/	Nando Sports Chat, PC Travel (Airline Reservations and Tickets), Professional Basketball, College Basketball (Division I), and Basketball Server Archives
Boston Red Sox Baseball	http://research.ftp.com/~solensky/bosox.html	Boston Red Sox Information (Archives, Schedule and Results, Ticket Ordering, Radio Stations), Baseball Links
Canadian Football League (Toronto, Canada)	http://www.cfl.ca/	What's New, Press Releases, This Week in the CFL, Player of the Week, Club Information, Game Results and League Standings, Statistics, Transactions, League Schedule and Television Broadcasters, The Grey Cup (the CFL ChampionshipTrophy), History of the CFL, Glossary of CFL Terms, Hall of Fame, and CFL Merchandise
Chicago Cubs Baseball	http://www.students.uiuc.edu/~k-jerbi/Cubs/	The Dugout, The Scoreboard, The Press Box, The Archives, The Ticket Office, The Bleachers (Quotes), and The Front Office
Cincinnati Reds Baseball	http://jinx.umsl.edu/~s895760/reds.html	Multimedia Page, Broadcast Sites, Fan Club Members, Major League Baseball Links
Cleveland Indians Baseball	http://www.apk.net/sports/Cle-web/Indians/	Cleveland Indians Final Statistics, Indians Headlines, Official Indians Page, Baseball Links, Schedules, Ticket Information, Merchandise, Archives, Standings, and Scores

Table 10.3: Selected Sports Sites on the Internet (continued)

Site	URL	Main Headings
College Football (Global Network Navigator)	http://gnn.com/gnn/meta/sports/football/ncaa/index.html	College Football News (Headline News, Live Scoreboard, Schedule, CNN/USA Today Top 25, and Sports Book), Division Standings and Schedules, and College Links
Colorado Rockies Baseball	http://www.rmii.com/rockies/	Ticket Exchange, Memorabilia, Headlines, Today's Coverage, Schedules, Updates and Boxscores, Clubhouse Information, Feature Articles, and Columns
ESPNet SportsZone (Starwave Corporation and ESPN Inc.) (fee-based)	http://web1.starwave.com	Sports Scores, Feature Articles, Columnists, Sports Talk, Daily Line, Industry Insider, Fantasy Football, Today's Best
Football Server (Nando.net)	http://www2.nando.net/SportServer/football/	Professional Football, College Football, and Archives
GNN Sports (Global Network Navigator)	http://gnn.com/gnn/meta/sports/basketball/ncaa/index.html	Auto Racing (Auto Racing Resources), Baseball (Articles, Schedules, and News about Major and Minor League Baseball), Basketball, Football, Soccer, and Hockey
Golf (Global Network Navigator)	http://gnn.com/gnn/meta/sports/other/golf.html	Professional Golf Association News (Headline News, Live Leaderboard, Rankings, and Schedule, Tours Links, Other Servers
GolfData Web	http://www.gdol.com	InterGolf, specializing in International Golf Vacations; NBC Golf Tour (Tournaments, Courses, Resorts, Schools, Publications, Pro Shop, Featured Courses, Travel, Associations & Clubs, Back Nine Magazine, Player Bios, and more
Green Bay Packers	http://www.inmarket.com/stew/packsked.htm	Season, Lambeau Field Facts, Draft Selections
Hockey (Global Network Navigator)	http://gnn.com/gnn/meta/sports/hockey/index.html	National Hockey Association News (Headline News, Live Scoreboard, Standings, Schedule, Team Pages), Features, Hockey Around the Net (Hockey Links, and NHL Team Pages)
Instant Baseball (Instant Sports, Inc.)	http://www.InstantSports.com/baseball.html	Today's Games (Play by Play), Yesterday's Games, Standings, Statistics, Schedules, and Box Scores
International Baseball Association	http://monviso2.alpcom.it/digesu/	Baseball (in America, Asia, Africa, Oceania, and Europe, and News (Baseball Challenges, Champions Cup, Tournaments, and more)

Table 10.3: Selected Sports Sites on the Internet (continued)

Site	URL	Main Headings
Internet Squash Federation	http://www.ncl.ac.uk/~npb/	Featured Games Online, Australian Institute of Sport, Clubs, Coaching and Training, Contacts, Hardware, Mail Order, Usenet News, Olympics 2000, Player Profiles, Publications, Rankings, Software, Tournaments, Travel, TV Coverage, Squash on Video, and more
Japanese Professional Baseball	http://www.inter.co.jp/Baseball/	Team Standings, Batting Leaders, Pitching Leaders, Player Register (Japanese and Others), and Leaders
Los Angeles Dodgers Baseball	http://deepthought.armory.com/~lew/sports/baseball/	Schedules, Standings, Statistics, Roster, Dodger Stadium Map and Photo, and Ticket Information
Major League Baseball @ Bat	http://www2.pcy.mci.net/mlb/index.html or http://www.internetMCI.com/mlb/	Game-by-Game Results, World Series (Facts, Statistics & History), Post Season, The Leagues, Scores & Stats, News & Notes, MLB Photo Gallery, MLB Clubhouse Shop
Minnesota Twins Baseball	http://www.winternet.com/~pdthomas/twins.html	News, Statistics, Minor League Information, Rosters, Schedules, Ticket Information, Scores, and Archives
Montreal Expos	http://www.islandnet.com/~mkp/Expos/Expos.html	Expos Schedule, Expos Statistics, Major League Baseball, ESP-NET SportsZone Expos Clubhouse, USA Today Expos Team Area, NandO.Net Baseball Server, alt.sports.baseball.montreal-expos, Montreal Expos Electronic Mailing List, Ticket Information, Articles, Olympic Stadium Layout, Photo, Ottawa Lynx Page
National Basketball Association	http://www.getnet.com/engrave/nba.html	Links to all National Basketball Teams
National Football League (Global Network Navigator)	http://gnn.com/gnn/meta/sports/football/nfl/index.html	National Football League News (Headline News, Live Scoreboard, Standings, Schedules, and Team Pages), The NFL Beat (Team Close Ups), Features (Training Camp Pranks, and NFL Calendar), NFL Sites, and Team Links
NBA Standings (ESPNet SportsZone) (fee-based)	http://web1.starwave.com/nba/sta/entry.html	NBA Standings
NFL Home Page	http://www.nflhome.com/	NFL Teams, NFL Newswire, NFL Library, NFL Kids, Team Talk, NFL Headlines, League Statistics, NFL Live Chat, NFL Rule Book, NFL Broadcast, Gameday Live
Oakland Raiders	http://www.cyberzine.com/raiders/	Ticket Orders, Schedule, Raiders Chat

Table 10.3: Selected Sports Sites on the Internet (continued)

Site	URL	Main Headings
Olympic Games Homepage (IBM)	http://www.atlanta.olympic.org/acog/d-newlook.html	Welcome to the Games, Sports & Venues, Official Program, Travel, Tickets, Official Products, Olympic Arts Festival, News, and The Fun Side
Olympics (Global Network Navigator)	http://gnn.com/gnn/meta/sports/other/olympics.html	Links to Olympic Information
Other Sports Servers (Global Network Navigator)	http://gnn.com/gnn/meta/sports/other/servers.html	Links to All Sports
Philadelphia Phillies Baseball	http://storm.cadcam.iupui.edu/phils/phils.html	Schedule, Statistics, and Standings
Pittsburgh Steelers	http://steelershome.com/steelers/	Steelers Merchandise Catalog, Steelers News, Team Pictures
Rec.Sports.Soccer-The Web Page (United Kingdom)	http://www.atm.ch.cam.ac.uk:80/sports/	Soccer Links, The English Premier League, FIFA Rules, Helpful Hints, Questions & Answers, Soccer Terminology, Computer Soccer Games, 1994 World Cup, and Current Standings
The Rest of the Story (Basketball) (Global Network Navigator)	http://gnn.com/gnn/meta/sports/basketball/rest/index.html	Continental Basketball Association Digest, and American Players in Greece
San Francisco Giants Virtual Dugout	http://www.sman.com/	San Francisco Giants Headlines (Player Information, Roster0. Virtual Dugout Lineup (Final Standings, Giants Fun Page, Special Events, Current Roster and Player Bios, Merchandise, Giants Hall of Fame, and Minor League Teams)
San Jose Sharks	http://www.sj-sharks.com/	Sharks News, Players, Team Records (Current and Historic), Management, Schedule, Ticket Info, The Game, Minor Leagues
Seattle Mariners Home Plate	http://www.mariners.org/	Mariner's Team Gear, What's New, Mariners Web Forum, Overview (Press Releases, Game Reports, Schedules, Ticket Information, Roster, Spring Training, Minor Leagues, and Archives)
Soccer (Global Network Navigator)	http://gnn.com/gnn/meta/sports/soccer/index.html	Headline News, and Soccer Links
Sport (Cambridge, England)	http://www.atm.ch.cam.ac.uk:80/sports/sports.html	Sport Site of the Week, Index (The Mother of All Sports-Soccer), America's Favourite Sports (American Football, Baseball, and Basketball), More Ball Sports, Wheel Sports, Water Sports, Out and About (Outdoor Sports), The Rest (Miscellaneous), Run Away (Other Sports Servers And Sports-related Newsgroups), Commercial Sites, and New Entries

Table 10.3: Selected Sports Sites on the Internet (continued)

Site	URL	Main Headings
The Sports Server (The News and Observer Publishing Co.)	http://www2.nando.net/SportServer/	Links to The Baseball Server, Hockey Server, Basketball Server, Football Server (Present Games, Past Games, Statistics, Player Profiles, and mor, The Sports Page and Sport Chat
SportsAccess (Sports Illustrated)	http://pathfinder.com/@@Y6ahz3HxfqMAZBtl/si/welcome.html	Latest Headlines; News, Scores, and Stats; SI's Classic Edition; SI's NFL Preview; SI's Guide to the Olympic Games; SI's College Football Preview; and Fantasy Leagues
Tennis (Global Network Navigator)	http://gnn.com/gnn/meta/sports/other/tennis.html	Tennis Links
Toronto Blue Jays Baseball (Author's Pick)	http://www.bluejays.ca/bluejays/	Player Biographies, Trivia Games, Ticket Information, Game Schedules, Press Releases, Surveys, E-Mail to Players, Team Photo, Blue Jays Fantasy Camp, Kid's Zone (Contests, Trivia, Baseball Math, Interviews), and Interview of the Month
Washington Bullets Newsgroup	news:alt.sports.basketball.nba.wash-bullets	New Articles, Catchup All Articles
Washington Capitals Newsgroup	news:alt.sports.hockey.nhl.wash-capitals	Current Hockey Articles
Washington Redskins (Nando.net)	http://www2.nando.net/SportServer/football/nfl/was.html	Game Day, Redskins' Signals, Statistics, Team History, and Information
Washington Redskins Newsgroup	news:alt.sports.football.pro.wash-redskins	New Articles
Washington Redskins	http://www.email.net/www/bkayton/skins.html	Current 1995 Season, Current Skins News, Current Editorials, General Information, Hall of Fame and Redskins History, Previous Season, ESPNET Sportszone, Inside the Redskins, Redskins Image Library, Other NFL Web Stuff, and Trivia
Women's Basketball (Global Network Navigator)	http://gnn.com/gnn/meta/sports/basketball/women/index.html	1994-95 Review, NCAA Women's Basketball Tournament, ACC Tournament Results, SEC Conference Updates and Awards, Big East Tournament Results, Feature Articles, Archives, and Women's Basketball Links
World Wide Web Tennis Server (The Tenagra Corporation)	http://www.tennisserver.com/	Higdon's New Game (Commentary), Tennis News, Player Tip of the Month, Mental Equipment Tip of the Month, Rules & Codes of Tennis, Player Pictures, Tournaments, Merchandise, Clubs, Links to other Tennis Information

Comic Strips

Almost every newspaper contains pages of comic strips or at least one or two political cartoons. You can find many of these on the Internet—a few you can find only on the Net. This section contains sites that list tons of cartoon links.

The BORDERLINE

http://www.cts.com/~bordenln/index.html#top

The Borderline is referred to as a "Humor Netazine." The cartoons are by Gabe Martin, and a new one appears daily. At this site you will find a list of the last 10 Borderline cartoons as well as a link to a complete Borderline Cartoon Archive.

Cartoons from around the World

http://www.eng.clemson.edu/~cshan/

Tony Shan provides links to 33 cartoons, comic strips, and other resources (see the bottom of the page). He claims to be the world's most complete cartoon source. Links include the most popular comic strip sites, the CartooNet European resource (with optional registration), and the Inkwell, a collection of editorial cartoons.

Comics 'n Stuff!

http://www.phlab.missouri.edu/~c617145/comix.html

This site is an impressive compilation of cartoons and comic strips from around the world. Categories include Index of Comics, Other Comic Links, Announcements, Frequently Asked Questions, New Stuff, The Comics 'n Stuff WebChat Room, Comics 'n Stuff Query Search, and, at the bottom of the page, an alphabetically arranged list of comics on the Internet.

Tip
The key next to the title, Comics on the Web, describes the icons to the left of the links.

Comix World

http://www.comix-world.com/

The first time you visit this site, you might think that it's for comic book dealers and nothing more. However, this site also includes links to comic strips and cartoons. Click on Best of COMIX.Web to go to links that COMIX WORLD thinks are worth a visit. Other links on the home page—Comix Shows, Comix Dictionary, Comix.Web, and Comix Dealers—are comic book-related.

The Doonesbury Electronic Town Hall

http://www.doonesbury.com/

Although this is the home page for Doonesbury Comics by Gary Trudeau, much more can be found here. Click on Daily Briefings, and you will find PoliticsUSA, "the leading Web site for political news, resources and involvement." Straw Poll, now under construction, will allow you to state your views on various issues and compare them with the views of others. Chat Hall, also under construction, will be an open forum. Go back in time by selecting Flashback. Select a year to see a vintage Doonesbury strip and read what was happening in the world the week it was published. Get Involved will let you "learn about organizations close to Doonesbury's heart." Finally, Sell Out will be your Doonesbury shopping headquarters.

The Looney Tunes Website

http://www.io.org/~rabrink/Overview.html

Created by Richard Brinklow, this site has ever-increasing sound samples of Looney Tune characters. You will also find links to other "Looney sites," including cartoon pictures in full color.

This Modern World

http://www.well.com/user/tomorrow/

This site is devoted to This Modern World, a topical cartoon strip created by Tom Tomorrow. Some cartoons are accompanied by the articles that inspired them. There is information on This Modern World books and clothing and past newsletters, articles, and discussions concerning political cartoons.

Yahoo! Daily Comics

http://www.yahoo.com/News/Daily/Comics/

This small page lists eight links to daily comics: Borderline Daily Cartoon, The Daily Feed, Dilbert, Kev's World, Today's Computer Cartoon, United Media Comic Strips, United Media— The Inkwell Editorial Cartoons, and Wild Life.

Government News

The U.S. government provides a great deal of information for journalists, businesspersons, and interested laypersons. In this section, you can find a few of the best government news sites.

Note
Most U.S. government agencies provide news at their home pages. To find more U.S. government sites, go to the *Law and Government* chapter.

AirForce Link News

http://www.dtic.dla.mil/airforcelink/pa/index.html

This site, from the Air Force News Agency, provides U.S. Air Force and U.S. Department of Defense News and Information, including Current and Previous Releases, DefenseLINK News, AFNS

Features, and a search index of previous releases. As you move down the page, you can view links to previous stories preceded by the date on which they were filed.

The Community, Air, and Space Report

http://www.newspace.com/publications/casr/home.html

This small and pleasant-looking page, from Keith Stein, provides satellite launch reports, aviation news, and Washington, D.C., news. Categories include The Latest Reports (a list of launches, a description, and the date of the story), Upcoming Launches (the estimated date and time, the name of the mission, the vehicle, and the agency), Downlink Frequencies (radio frequencies and other information), and From the Airwaves (news and WAV sound files from recent flights).

Federal News Service

http://www.fednews.com/

This commercial service provides many news services for paid subscribers. Other users, however, can obtain information about press conferences and daily schedules in Washington, D.C.; in Russia; and at the United Nations.

NASA NewsRoom

http://www.gsfc.nasa.gov/
hqpao/newsroom.html

NASA provides valuable online information on technology, space, astronomy, education, and much more. Keeping with its high standards, the NASA Newsroom (see Figure 10.4) provides a wealth of information as well as links to other NASA sites. Whether you're a journalist researching the shuttle program, a journalist writing about NASA's Internet presence, or a teacher preparing a lesson plan on astronomy, you'll find it here. You can even request a speaker from the NASA Speakers Bureau.

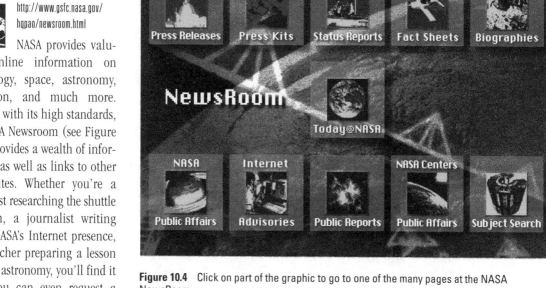

Figure 10.4 Click on part of the graphic to go to one of the many pages at the NASA NewsRoom.

Categories include Today @ NASA, Press Releases, Press Kits, Status Reports, Fact Sheets, Biographies, NASA Public Affairs, Public Reports, NASA Centers Public Affairs, Internet Advisories, and Subject Search (a search index).

these categories: News, Features, Columns, Bill Gates, Live Chat, and Discussion Groups. A valuable feature of this site is a search index with which you can find the full text of stories from previous issues.

Internet News

It's quite obvious that you'll find sites for obtaining both Internet and computer news. This section contains two excellent sites for obtaining Internet news.

Computer News Daily

http://nytsyn.com/cgi-bin/times/lead/go/

This online newspaper, from the *New York Times*, provides daily news organized under

Cowles SIMBA Media Daily

http://www.mecklerweb.com/netday/simba/internet.html

Another excellent source of Internet news is *SIMBA Media Daily*. At the top of the page are links to Mecklermedia's iWORLD and SIMBA Information's SIMBANet (at http://www.simbanet.com/). The rest of the page consists of a list of links to stories, with the most recent at the top. When you click on a link, the full text of the story, sometimes with links, appears.

Chapter Eleven

Science and Technology

Science and technology have been an active part of the Internet since its invention. For years, scientists, professors, and college students have been using the vast networks of connections to share and research scientific and technological information. In this chapter, we introduce valuable Internet sites that continue to keep science-related professionals and university students interested in cyberspace.

Many of the entries in this chapter consist of lists of science and technology sites, which are a good starting point for your exploration of specific topics.

General Resources

The sites in this section are generic or all-encompassing science and technology sites. Here, you will find basic science pages, educational resources, databases, the first of several NASA sites in this chapter, and much more.

Basic Science Research Resources

gopher://welchlink.welch.jhu.edu:70/11/
Basic%20science%20research%20resources

This Johns Hopkins site provides links to documents, databases, catalogs, online newsletters, and discussion groups dealing with basic science. Most links are to Gopher sites. Folders include Resource Guides and Locators; Databanks—Sequences, Structures, Gene Mapping, etc.; Literature Databases and Library Catalogs; Strains and Stocks, Culture Collections, Enzymes, and Reagents; Molecular Biology Software Archives; Electronic Publications and Newsgroups; Print Publications and Journal Tables of Contents; Funding Resources; Selected Other Bioscience Gophers; and Global Biological Information Servers (arranged alphabetically and by subject).

C&C's Earth Science Emporium

http://nlu.nl.edu/bthu/nlu/eight/es/Homepage.html

This site, intended for teachers and students at the elementary and secondary level, is worth visiting regardless of your age or occupation. On the home page, you can choose from General Earth Science, Astronomy, Geology, Meteorology, or Oceanography. Also included is a Meta-Index of Earth Science Resources, which includes indexes for the five categories. Figures 11.1 and 11.2 show NASA photographs found in the Astronomy section.

Figure 11.1 A photograph of the damaged Apollo 13 service module from the NASA Images site

Interesting Site

The NASA Images site (at http://images.jsc.nasa.gov/images/pao /) features photographs taken from space during the U.S. space program. Included are many pictures of the earth taken from the moon and from spacecraft and lunar modules.

Community of Science

http://cos.gdb.org/

The Community of Science comprises databases in which you can find researchers with particular interests and knowledge. Here, you also can find an inventory of inventions and research laboratories in the U.S. and Canada. While you're visiting,

you can add yourself to the database or edit your entry. Major categories at this site include the U.S. Patents Citation Database, Federally Funded Research in the U.S., Commerce Business Daily, the Federal Register, Search for Funding Opportunities, and the Canadian Community of Science Databases.

Holography

http://hmt.com/holography/index.html

Hypermedia Technologies presents a variety of information about holography. Holography is a type of photography in which many views are shot of an object, allowing you to see various views as you move from one side to another or move the object to which the hologram is attached. Major categories here include What's New, Commercial Holography, Artists, Galleries (the link to the Royal Holographic Art Gallery was not working at the time of this writing), Articles (good introductions to the technology), Holography Education (including a FAQ), Holography Publications, Miscellaneous, and Other Holography Related Sites.

Infomine

http://lib-www.ucr.edu/physci/

The University of California regents present INFOMINE, a "comprehensive physical sciences, engineering, computing and math Internet resource collection." The best way to search this site is to click on Table of Contents or Subject. If you are comfortable using search indexes, search the database using approved keywords (click on Keyword to see a list). This site presents a wide variety of resources—from Abbreviations to Z39.50 (a database protocol).

KSC Commercial-ization Home Page

http://technology.ksc.nasa.gov/

NASA owns more than 1,000 patents and patent applications that private businesses can license for a fee. NASA also offers technical assistance to licensees. This well-designed NASA site presents information about technology transfer and its programs. Major categories include What's New, What We Offer, TechTracS TechSearch (a search index), Partners Wanted, Let's Make a Deal, Successful Partnerships, Our Staff Will Help You, and Other NASA Resources.

To get information that might help you develop your own technologies, click on TechTracS TechSearch. You can search this system by clicking on Technology Categories (if you are a first-time visitor, this is the better choice) or Keywords (lists of keywords under letters of the alphabet). A typical document contains an abstract, the reporting date, information about the publication from which it comes, and the availability of a technical support package, patent, and licensing. At the bottom of each document is a link on which you can click to get more information about this technology.

Figure11.2 A photograph from space showing all of New York City and parts of Long Island, Connecticut, and New Jersey. Can you see Central Park?

to get more information. (This is the same as clicking on More Info on the home page.)

To search, type keywords and logical operators in the text box. Then click on Begin Search. When the search is complete, lists of documents are arranged under the databases that you have chosen.

NASA Technical Report Server (NTRS)

http://techreports.larc.nasa.gov/cgi-bin/NTRS

At this site, you can search through 14 NASA and other federal research servers for documents and abstracts of documents that you can order. To learn how this server works, click on Quick Start. On this page, you can click on Frequently Asked Questions

Planet Earth Science and Technology Page

http://white.nosc.mil/planet_earth/science.html

The Planet Earth site is a comprehensive online library of information and links. At its Science and Technology page, which has links to many education-related sites, you can find links categorized as follows: Who's Who in Science, Science Servers (including magazines, corporate and academic sites, and indexes), Science and Mathematics Education Resources (arranged under many science and technology categories of education), Science Disciplines (11 of them), Technology, and Other Science Topics.

Science and Technology Resources

http://gnn.com/gnn/wic/wics/sci.new.html

From the Global Network Navigator (GNN), this site provides links to science and technology pages arranged under these categories: Artificial Intelligence, Astronomy, Aviation and Aeronautics, Biology, Chemistry, Engineering, Environmental Studies, Geography, Geology, Mathematics, NASA & Space Exploration, Oceanography, Paleontology, Physics, and Weather & Meteorology.

A unique part of this site is a list of links to the week's ten most popular science and technology sites at GNN and the number of hits for each.

Scientific Web Resources

http://boris.qub.ac.uk/edward/

This very popular site, from Edward Smyth at Queens University in Belfast, has many links to scientific and other resources on the Internet. Be warned that many of these pages also include graphic images. Major categories under which you can find information are Campus-Wide Meta-Search, List of the World's Most Powerful Computing Sites, Company Meta-Pages (primarily computer but many others), Research Labs Meta-Pages (most from the U.S.), and University Meta-Pages (by country: Canada, Germany, Ireland, Japan, the U.S., and other).

To get started with the Campus-Wide Meta-Search, click on one of the links under the heading Recently Modified Documents. This will give you an idea of the

content of the index. You can search for keywords in titles, headings, metatags, links, by document type, author, schools and departments, academic services, or by topic.

Subject-Related Internet Catalog

gopher://infoserver.ciesin.org/11/catalog/

This large site has links to primarily science- and education-related Gopher sites worldwide. From the home page, you can link to documents, archives, government agencies, libraries, and much more. The headings under which you can find information include Computing, Education, Energy, Environment, Forestry, Government, Health, History, Humanities, Law, Politics, and Social.

Units Conversion

http://eardc.swt.edu/cgi-bin/ucon/ucon.pl

This imaginative site converts 17 types of measures from one value to another. To use the converter (see Figure 11.3), select a measure, type the "from value" in the top text box and select the unit of measure, and select the "to value's" unit of measure. Then click on Go.

World-Wide Web Virtual Library: History of Science, Technology, and Medicine

http://www.asap.unimelb.edu.au/hstm/hstm_ove.htm

This very interesting site provides links related to the history of science, technology, and medicine; you'll find many museums and electronic documents here. Categories under which you can find links are Overview, New, Lists (lists, collections, and bibliographies), Organisations (upcoming conferences, organizations, and departments), Specialised (lists of links under subject topics), Biographies (an illustrated biographical dictionary, which is growing and under construction), Institutions (academic and government), Museums (see Figure 11.4), E-Journals, and Email (lists and newsgroups).

World-Wide Web Virtual Library: Technology Transfer

http://iridium.nttc.edu/gov/other/tech.html

Technology transfer converts technologies developed by the U.S. government to commercial products. The National Technology Transfer Center's list of technical transfer information consists of five major categories: Tech Transfer Information, Government Links, University Links, Corporate Links, and Other Links. Each category provides several useful links. For example, under the heading Government Tech Transfer Links (reached by clicking on Government Links), you can find links to many federal laboratories and agencies as well as papers on technology transfer. Under University Tech Transfer Links are direct links to technology transfer departments at almost 20 U.S. and Canadian universities. If you are searching for a new product for your company, consider starting at this site.

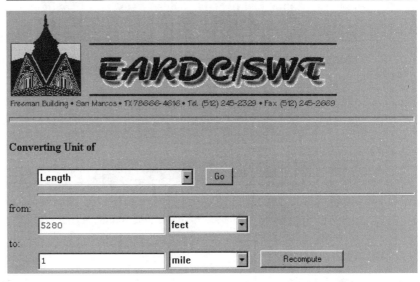

Figure 11.3 Type a value in the text box, select options, and click on Go to convert a unit of measure.

Figure 11.4 A photograph of Eniac, an early mainframe computer

Yahoo List of Science Resources

http://www.yahoo.com/Science/

Yahoo presents 43 categories of scientific links from Acoustics to Zoology. As always, you can find links at Yahoo that cannot be found elsewhere. If you want to find a comprehensive starting point for your scientific search, start here.

Agriculture

Farmers were among the first group of people to use the computer to run their businesses. In this section, you'll find some of the many agriculture resources—for both business and home.

Note

You'll find agriculture statistics and demographics in the *Economics and Statistics* chapter.

Agricultural Info, Family Issues, Food, Nutrition, and the Environment

http://www.cs.indiana.edu/internet/agri.html

This site provides links to a variety of Internet agricultural resources via Telnet (remember that Netscape does not support Telnet), FTP, Gopher, and the World Wide Web—at primarily academic sites. Here you can get information on subscribing to agriculture e-mail lists and services, home horticulture and gardening, and obtaining help from the Cooperative Extension Service for your state (click on USDA Extension Service Gopher and then Information Servers—Cooperative Extension System [CES]). Note that the links to Missouri Horticulture Guides and Texas A&M Master Gardener Project were not working at the time of this writing.

Botany-Related URLS

http://www.helsinki.fi/kmus/botany.html

This site, developed by Raino Lampinen, a botanist at the Botanical Museum, Finnish Museum of Natural History at the University of Helsinki, consists of approximately 1,000 botanical links. You can view the links on one long page (more than 200 kilobytes) or click on Main Menu (at http://www.helsinki.fi/kmus/ botmenu.html) to see a list of 17 topics ranging from Arboreta and Botanical Gardens to Vascular Plant Families.

Environmentally Friendly Agriculture

gopher://garnet.berkeley.edu:1250/11/.envi/.agric

This site presents a short list of folders and one document covering sustainable agriculture. Folders include the archive of the Worker Protection Standards (WPS) Forum (some downloadable files with the Z extension), the National Campaign for Pesticide Policy Reform (with the Summary of Pesticide Food Safety Act of 1994), Sustainable Agriculture (some useful farm and home agriculture links), and the U.S. Department of Agriculture Gopher site. Two links, IPMnet and Pesticide Action Network North America, were not working at the time of this writing.

Not Just Cows

http://www.lib.lsu.edu/sci/njc.html

This gigantic and comprehensive site, by Wilfred Drew of Morrisville College of Agriculture and Technology, provides all sorts of agricultural links—primarily academic. The top part of the page lists library catalogs with Telnet, Gopher, or World Wide Web connections. Under a typical entry, you will find the title, one or more links, and instructions for accessing the site. The next section provides Gopher sites from the U.S. Department of Agriculture Cooperative Extension Services, other government agencies worldwide, and subject collections. In the next sections, you will find agricultural bulletin board systems (BBS), World Wide Web sites, searchable databases, electronic magazines and newsletters, almanac servers (e-mail and Listservs), and Usenet newsgroups. At the bottom of this long page are links to excellent Internet tutorials and references.

You can find official mirror sites at http://www.lib.lsu.edu/ sci/njc.html, http://asa.ugl.lib.umich.edu/chdocs/agriculture.html, and http://www.bubl.bath.ac.uk/BUBL/Cows.html, among others.

U.S. Department of Agriculture Research Database

http://medoc.gdb.org/ best/stc/usda-best.html

The USDA Research Database contains the "information on ongoing and recently completed projects sponsored or conducted primarily within the USDA and State university research system. Some 30,000 project summaries, including the latest progress reports and lists of recent publications coming out of the research, are maintained in the file on an ongoing basis." At the time of this writing, this promising site for scientists and academics appeared to be under construction: Requested documents seem to be preceded and followed by parts of other documents.

Interesting Site

If you are a home gardener, you'll want to check out the excellent General Gardening Sites page (at http://www.btw.com/urls/garden.htm), which provides all sorts of Internet gardening links. Major categories include General Gardening Sites, General Gardening Catalogs and Supplies, Specialty Cultivation, Gardening Questions Answered, Botanical Gardens, Botany/Biology/ Environment, Landscape Architecture/Environmental Design, Insects/Entomology, Garden Arts and Letters, and Other Directories.

To search the database, either type keywords and operators in the text box at the bottom of the page or click on Search the USDA Research Database and fill in the text box on the resulting page. After completing a search, a page with results preceded by scores from 1 to 1000 appears, as shown in Figure 11.5. Click on a link to read part of the requested document.

Entries are preceded by a score. The score is scaled from 1 to 1000, and is a relative rating suggesting the appropriateness of each document with respect to the given query. The maximum number of results returned from a search is 100.

1. 95 MOLECULAR GENETICS AND CULTIVAR IMPROVEMENT OF GREENHOUSE CROPS

2. 74 CULTURAL AND PHYSIOLOGICAL STUDIES OF ORNAMENTAL CROPS

3. 71 EVALUATING THE PERFORMANCE OF ORNAMENTAL FLOWERING PLANTS AND VEGETAB LES

4. 68 MATHEMATICAL MODELING OF ORNAMENTAL CROPPING SYSTEMS

5. 67 EFFECTS OF CULTURAL FACTORS ON PRODUCTION AND POSTHARVEST QUALITY OF FOLIAGE AND FLOWERING PLANTS

6. 65 BIOCONTROL OF MULTIFLORA ROSE AND SELECTED WEEDS

7. 63 NITROGEN NUTRITION OF CONTAINER CROPS

Figure11.5 Partial results from a database search using the keyword *roses*

As with most search indexes on the Internet, a list of keywords is not provided; so you have to feel your way at first.

World-Wide Web Virtual Library: Agriculture

http://www.w3.org/hypertext/
DataSources/bySubject/Agriculture.html

This short page lists some of the best agriculture resources on the Internet. Links include academic sites from Indiana University, North Carolina State University, and Cornell, the National Agricultural Library of the U.S. Department of Agriculture, and the appropriately titled agricultural resource: Not Just Cows. The World-Wide Web Virtual Library: Agriculture is an excellent starting point for finding agriculture sites on the Internet.

Anthropology and Archeology

Although the local bookstore may have only a few books on anthropology or archeology, many Internet sites are devoted to the two sciences. Almost every university in the world has a site on the Internet. Of these, a large percentage have anthropology or archeology departments online with research and department information available to all. Those listed here demonstrate the quantity and quality of anthropology or archeology information on the Internet.

The Ancient City of Athens

http://www.indiana.edu/~kglowack/Athens/Athens.html

This site, presented by the Indiana University Department of Classical Studies, provides a photographic archive of ancient Greece. Online photographs focus on the archeological and architectural remains of Athens. If you are interested in the monumental structures of Athens, this site will provide hours of enjoyment—more than 200 scanned pictures are accompanied by brief descriptions.

ArchNet

http://spirit.lib.uconn.edu/ArchNet/ArchNet.html

ArchNet is an excellent resource for students and professional archeologists. This site from the University of Connecticut provides links to more than 1,000 valuable sites. With an attractive and well-designed Web page, users can easily find what they need to know about archeology: museums, maps, theories, sites by region, journals, e-mail directories, and more. If for some reason you cannot find a topic of interest, a search page is even provided for document titles and contents. (See Figure 11.6.)

Figure 11.6 Click on a button on the ArchNet home page to obtain valuable archeological information.

Architecture

The sciences and technologies that architects use to design a house incorporate not only design but also engineering, ecology, and energy. Whether you are working on an office building, a factory, or a house, you'll find excellent architecture resources in this section.

1NTERPRO-AEC Construction Products Manufacturers

http://www.ipr.com/interpro/pagestor/products/

This massive directory provides names, addresses, telephone numbers, and fax numbers or URLs of suppliers of almost everything to construct and furnish a building. To search this site, click on a division (the number within parentheses is the number of listings), a subdivision on the next page, and a manufacturer on the next page. If a manufacturer name appears in **boldface**, you will go to a home page; otherwise, a text page appears.

Architecture and Building

http://www.unlv.edu/library/ARCH/index.html

This comprehensive and downloadable (in WordPerfect 5.1 format) document, compiled by Jeanne M. Brown, Architecture Studies Librarian at the University of Nevada, Las Vegas, provides links to architecture, building, and construction sites. The document is divided into six sections: Web and Gopher Sites (by far the largest), Listservs, Newsgroups, Indexes, Library Catalogs, and FTP Sites.

Energy Efficient Housing in Canada

http://www.ualberta.ca/~amulder/house/

The Energy Efficient Housing in Canada site hosted by the University of Alberta provides information about developing homes and buildings that conserve energy. This site achieves its mission of educating the public about energy conservation in household management through informing the public

of the R-2000 house and the advance house program, providing links to other energy conservation resources, and supplying renovation suggestions for current housing. The R-2000 and advance house program are architectural techniques that effectively conserve more than 10 percent more energy than conventional houses.

HOME TEAM Intelligent Home Resources

http://www.hometeam.com/

For those planning to build or remodel a house or office, this valuable commercial site provides a variety of links to home automation resources. To use this page, scroll down to the Main Menu. Then access the links, which are arranged in a table of contents format. Major headings here include Description of Intelligent Homes; An Overview of Proposed Standards; Lighting Controls; Security Systems; Communications Systems; Entertainment

Interesting Site

At The Self-Sufficient Solar House (http://www.ise.fhg.de/Institute.Projects.SelfSuffSolHouse.english.html), learn how the Fraunhofer Institute for Solar Energy Systems is building a solar house in Freiburg, Germany. The house obtains its energy from thermal and photovoltaic solar energy. This page provides all the construction and architectural details.

Networks; Home Theaters; Energy Management; Windows, Doors & Gate Controls; Plumbing Controls; Outdoor Equipment Controls; Automation Controllers; List of Service Providers; Other Resources of Interest; Intelligent Home Classified Ads; News That Could Affect

the Industry; Articles of Interest to Intelligent Home Enthusiasts; Industry Survey; Join the HOME TEAM; and HOME TEAM Member List.

Synergetics

http://www.teleport.com/~pdx4d/synhome.html

This elegant site—dedicated to R. Buckminster Fuller, famous for the geodesic dome—provides information about synergetics, which "connect to the visual arts via Euler's Law." Categories at this site (see Figure 11.7) are Intro, Geodesic Dome, Fuller Projection (Fuller's method of creating projection maps), Design Science, and Links. (Clicking on A Growing List of Contributors at ftp://ftp .teleport.com/ pub/users/pdx4d/artindex.html provides many links.)

Tip
You can download a sample (UNFOLDS.ZIP, which is 381 kilobytes in size and results in the movie, UNFOLDS.MOV) of a Fuller projection by clicking on the illustration in the middle of the Fuller Projection page.

Interesting Site

The wonderful Design Science and Art Galleries site (at ftp://ftp.teleport.com/pub/users/pdx4d/artindex.html), from Kirby Urner, also the creator of the Synergetics site, provides links to artists working with synergetics and domes. Here, you can download constructions and computer programs, view designs and photographs, and go to Web pages covering the work of R. Buckminster Fuller. While you're here, be sure to scroll all the way down this page to go to Supporting Software (at http://www .teleport.com/~pdx4d/sw_gall.html) and Other Resources (at http:// www.teleport.com/~pdx4d/res_gall.html).

World-Wide Web Virtual Library: Architecture

http://www.clr.toronto .edu:1080/VIRTUALLIB/ arch.html

This deceptively small site is an excellent starting point for exploring architecture-related Internet resources. Links are presented in a tabular format; so major categories are aligned with the left margin, and subtopics appear in rows next to their headings. Categories include General, Groups, Indiv, Sources, Talk, and

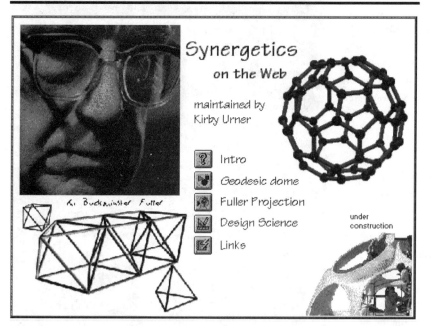

Figure 11.7 Click on any button to travel around the Synergetics site.

Other. Also included is a search index with which you can search this site.

Astronomy and Space

Astronomy and space are two exciting topics found in great quantity on the Internet. Because laboratories and government agencies around the world are submitting new data daily, the Internet is the only medium that can provide current information. Particularly through the World Wide Web, you will find millions of facts and awesome pictures from space. In this section are a few of the many astronomy sites on the Internet.

The Comet Observation Home Page

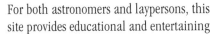

http://encke.jpl.nasa.gov/

For both astronomers and laypersons, this site provides educational and entertaining information on comets. Technical observations, light curve data and charts, and Ephemerides of all the visible comets provide professional astronomers with valuable information for their research. For everyone else, lists of currently visible comets, comet definitions, information on the Hale Bopp comet, and many spectacular pictures make this site entertaining. If you still need more information on comets, the Comet Observation Home Page contains links to other comet-related sites.

Comets and Meteor Showers

http://medicine.wustl.edu/~kronkg/index.html

This site provides valuable information about comets, meteor showers, and general astronomy for both professional and amateur astronomers. In the comet section, the author of this page, Gary Kronk, describes various comets in detail. Learn their origins and their current locations.

If meteor showers interest you, investigate meteor showers. Broken down by month, you can find out the best nights for watching the skies. For instance, the calendar might indicate that during the night of your birthday major activity in the skies will occur due to Lyrids meteor showers. If this is the case, click on Lyrids and receive a complete review of the showers: observer's synopsis and history. In addition, the general astronomy section provides links to many other astronomy sites focusing on stars, planets, and more.

Index Librorum Liberorum

http://www.fourmilab.ch/

John Walker, founder of Autodesk, provides astronomy, programming, politics, and other resources at this large and unique site. If you visit, be prepared to stay a long time and to revisit often. The astronomy resources include two screen savers, starship flight simulation, an earth viewer, an Excel catalog of the Palomar Observatory Sky Survey, Solar System Live, an Earth/Planetarium/Satellite, a new version terraformed planet every day, and a satellite tracker. Other resources include programming language kernels and macros, public domain electronic books, French tutorial tools, and much more.

The New Space Network

http://www.isso.org/ISSOhomePg.html

Many space professionals agree that the space program will be privatized eventually. The New Space Network "is an information clearinghouse for anyone interested in small and low-cost space programs." Major categories include Feature Attractions (a trivia game, "text tidbits" of a book that you can order, and coming events), Industry Listings, Publications, and What's New.

The Nine Planets

http://seds.lpl.arizona.edu/nineplanets/
nineplanets/nineplanets.html

This site is a great example of a well-organized and informative World Wide Web site. The author of this site, Bill Arnett, describes all the nine planets and their satellites with text, graphics, videos, and sounds. Each planet has its own page filled with facts to supercharge any term paper. Interested in the moon? At your disposal is a complete description of the satellite in multimedia form, from photographs of Buzz Aldrin on the moon to videos from the Galileo satellite. I found every page goes into great detail. If you or your child is curious about astronomy, be sure to visit this educational and enjoyable site.

Space Link

http://spacelink.msfc.nasa.gov/

If you are interested in aerospace technologies, you will enjoy visiting NASA's Space Link, which contains volumes of educational and entertaining information about the space programs and related issues. Exhilarating pages of information and images await visitors through several routes: About Spacelink, Educational Services, Instructional Materials, NASA Overview, NASA News, NASA Projects, SpaceLink Frequently Asked Questions, and Spacelink Hot Topics (see Figure 11.8). For example, this site provides the space shuttle launch schedules for several months into the future.

SPACE/MATH— Constants and Equations

http://www.ksc.nasa.gov/
facts/faq04.html

Forgot how to measure the radius of a black hole? Fortunately, NASA has a Web site that lists math/space equations and constants. From the mass of the moon to the acceleration equation of a rocket, you will find the needed space-related formula at this site. By the way, the radius of a black hole is $2GM/c^2$.

Figure 11.8 NASA's Spacelink home page: educational and entertaining information about space and the space programs

Views of the Solar System

http://bang.lanl.gov/solarsys/

With almost 1,000 high-resolution images, animation, and more than 200 densely filled pages of text and statistics, this U.S. government resource is bound to provide years of valuable education to the Internet public. In total, this site provides more than 840 megabytes of valuable information about our solar system.

This site supplies an in-depth description of the *Apollo 16* moon landing: the *Apollo 16* flight badge, the crew, the objective, a complete description of the mission, and more.

WDVL: Webstars

http://www.stars.com/WebStars/

This ambitious site goes far beyond astrophysics, astronomy resources, and related literature, newsgroups, and software. Other major categories include links to virtual reality sites, very useful style and reference guides for coding World Wide Web pages, and corporate pages. Note that two or three links were not active at the time of this writing.

World-Wide Web Virtual Library: Astronomy and Astrophysics

http://www.w3.org/hypertext/DataSources/
bySubject/astro/astro.html

This very large and comphrensive page, maintained by the AstroWeb Consortium of nine people at seven institutions, is composed of links arranged under these headings: Observations, Data, Publications, People, Organizations, Software, Research Areas of Astronomy, Various Lists of Astronomy, Astronomical Imagery, Education, History, and Miscellaneous. Also included are a Master Database and Announcements & Quality Control. Entries are tested three times a day and

updated once a day. This site is an excellent starting point for any type of search of astronomy resources on the Internet. (See Figure 11.9.)

Figure 11.9 An image of Saturn taken by the Hubble Space Telescope, from the UK HIST Support Facility Team

Biology

Biology is much more complex than dissecting frogs and identifying amoebas under a microscope. The science also concerns cell biology, microbiology, and biochemistry. To keep up with all the advances in biology, the Internet hosts a wealth of current research information accessible to all. In this section are a few biology sites to help you with your research.

Arachnology

http://dns.ufsia.ac.be/Arachnology/Arachnology.html

Interested in the study of arachnids: spiders, scorpions, ticks, and mites? If so, this is the site for you. Probably everything you want to know about those eight-legged critters is here. From numerous pictures to first-aid tips for poisonous bites, this site holds a wealth of information about all arachnids. Available to the arachnid hobbyist and professional are articles, courses, news reports, society information, pictures, movies, and publications. Special attention is given to poisons, bites, diseases, and phobias. This site is for professional and amateur biologists. It's an interesting and educational site for all to visit unless you suffer from arachanophobia (fear of these little creatures), which this site also covers.

Biology Databases

http://gc.bcm.tmc.edu:8088/bio/

With the huge amount of information and research findings in the world, finding the data you need for your biology studies or research can be laborious. Fortunately, there are sites like this one. This site, from the Baylor College of Medicine, assists you in searching for the biology information that you need. Here, you can find links to numerous online database search engines. If you are looking for specific information about DNA or gene features, you can find database search engines that specialize in that technology. Simply click on that link, and you are transported to another Web site containing the desired database. Although this site may not offer more than links to other sites, you will find it very useful when searching for answers to specific research problems.

BioMolecular Research Tools

http://www.public.iastate.edu/~pedro/research_tools.html

This excellent site helps academic and professional biologists locate the information they need from the millions of megabytes of online biology data. This Web page provides hundreds of links to biology sites, search indexes, guides, tutorials, journals, newsletters, and other research tools. Next to each link are brief review codes describing the usefulness of

the site and the connection type. Each code is represented by a color coded image. For instance, a red dot next to a link means that the site is an excellent reference. Visitors without a graphical browser can choose to see the codes as text.

Biotechnology Information Center

http://www.inform.umd.edu:8080/EdRes/Topic/AgrEnv/Biotech

As population growth increases exponentially, so does the world's demand for food. Every year, millions of people around the world go hungry or starve. Agricultural biotechnology is a study that may provide the means to deal with such issues. The Biotechnology Information Center (BIC) focuses on many aspects of agricultural biotechnology and shares its research with the online community. Through this site, BIC provides agricultural biotechnology publications, education resources, newsletters, description of patents, news releases and reports, and software. If you are looking for a specific topic, you can use BIC's keyword search form. Simply enter a keyword describing your interest and press Enter. The server then sifts through its archives to find files containing the text contents you specified.

The Brain Med Page

http://maui.net/~jms/brainuse.html

This site addresses chemical processes in the brain and the relationship of those processes to behavioral responses. Brain Med compiles medical research from various sites. Presented in a nonintimidating and understandable format, the information at this site seems to be geared toward educating the nonmedical professional. Brain Med focuses on important medical issues such as: migraines, drugs, psychological disorders, personality, perception, behaviors, and more. If the interaction between chemicals and the brain interest you, investigate this site.

Brain Map

http://ric.uthscsa.edu/services/

This site, from the Health Science Center at the University of Texas and intended for neurologists, offers information on human functional neuroanatomy. To help you find the information that you need, the creators have incorporated the information in a searchable relational database. To query the database, select multiple criteria from drop-down lists and fields in the following categories: reference, behavioral, location, and protocol. The results appear in a nicely formatted table, from which you can request further information by clicking on links.

Digital Anatomist Program

http://www1.biostr.washington.edu/DigitalAnatomist.html

This site, resulting from a collaboration between anatomists and computer scientists within the University of Washington Department of Biological Structure, provides anatomy information through the graphical medium of the World Wide Web. Here, you can view detailed three-dimensional images of the human anatomy. This site focuses on various projects: online interactive anatomic atlas, the human brain, 3-D anatomical reconstruction from medical images, medical image segmentation, symbolic knowledge base, and software development environments.

EMBL Protein & Peptide Group

http://www.mann.embl-heidelberg.de/

This site focuses on the Biochemical Instrumentation program at the European Molecular Biology Laboratory (EMBL) in Heidelberg, Germany. It concerns the development and optimization of new methods for sequence analysis and synthesis of DNA and proteins and the innovative design of biochemical instruments in this field. EMBL concentrates on the development of new sensitive methods for identifying and characterizing proteins and peptides.

This site provides information related to mass spectrometry; protein sequence databases; software developments for data acquisition; data analysis; and genomic sequence database searching using mass spectrometric data.

Human Genome Data Base

http://gdbwww.gdb.org/

This site, from the Johns Hopkins University School of Medicine, provides information on the Human Genome Project, a comprehensive catalog of human genes and genetic disorders with full-text annotations on current genetic research and clinical disorders. It provides the information through the use of the Genome Data Base GDB. This database supports biomedical research, clinical practice, and professional and scientific education by providing human gene mapping information. Since the database processes complex searches involving multiple variables, just about any request you submit will be fulfilled.

Magnetic Resonance Microscopy of Embryos

http://wwwcivm.mc.duke.edu/civmPeople/SmithBR/brs.html

If you're involved or interested in developmental biology, you'll want to check out the site provided by the Department of Radiology at Duke University Medical Center. Through this site, you can view vivid magnetic resonance microscope images of embryos at different periods of their developmental cycle. This site also describes how the images were acquired, other research projects, and the Center for In Vivo Microscopy.

Manual of Neuroanesthesia

http://mcan15.med.nyu.edu/neuroman/contents.html

This site, by Keith J Ruskin, M.D., and Robert Langer, M.D., supplies essential information about neuroanesthesia. Topics include disaster management, pre-operative evaluation, basic monitors, induction, positioning, maintenance, and so on. This site even has a neuroanesthesia checklist that you can print and use.

Molecular Biophysics

http://alfred.niehs.nih.gov/

The Laboratory of Molecular Biophysics, a department of The National Institute of Environmental Health Sciences, performs fundamental research into toxicological mechanisms. This important site addresses toxicology, the study of poisons, antidotes, and their effects. Those needing to know the antidote of a certain poison for a patient will find the contents of this site invaluable. This site contains a Spin Trap & Magnetic Resonance Database and a Human cDNA Functionality Database and provides information about reproductive and developmental toxicology.

Primer on Molecular Genetics

http://www.gdb.org/Dan/DOE/intro.html

This tutorial, from the U.S. Department of Energy, covers Molecular Genetics, offering various starting points for novice or experienced users. If you have never been exposed to this technology before, you can begin the tutorial with an introductory chapter, which describes the basics of genetics. If you are more experienced, you can jump to a chapter about sequencing or physical maps. Also provided are mapping and sequencing databases and a genetics glossary.

World-Wide Web Virtual Library: Biotechnology

http://www.cato.com/interweb/cato/biotech/

This short page provides links to biotechnology sites on the Internet. As explained here, biotechnology "covers pharmaceutical development, genetic engineering, medical device

development, pharmacology, and toxicology." The two categories here are Biotechnology (with several subcategories) and Other Virtual Library fields.

Chemistry

Research companies around the world are making amazing discoveries in chemistry today. You can wait weeks or months for the journal articles describing each discovery to come to the library. However, many of these discoveries are being published on the Internet immediately after being found. The Internet is an excellent medium to keep up with the quickly evolving science of chemistry.

Center for Microscopy and Microanalysis

http://www.uq.oz.au/nanoworld/nanohome.html

The Center for Microscopy and Microanalysis, at the University of Queensland, Australia, is a research facility specializing in analyzing the structure and composition of materials through the monitoring of interaction of electrons, X rays, photons, and ions. You can read about the center's involvement in superconductors, life cell processes, and microanalysis. If you are not a professional chemist but are interested in intriguing chemistry discoveries, look at the center's Image Gallery where you will find magnified images of bacteria, crystals, insects, and more. However, if you have nightmares of giant ants taking over the world, I recommend skipping this site.

Chemical Information on the Internet

http://hackberry.chem.niu.edu/

This home page of the Chemistry Department of Northern Illinois University provides links to eight chemistry-related pages:

- ◆ Chemistry Conferences

- ◆ Chemistry Department Graduate Programs (U.S. educational institutions)

- ◆ Chemists Email Address Database

- ◆ Chemical Company Stock Prices (weekly quotes from this week, last week, recent months, and recent years)

- ◆ Chemistry Software (for-fee, shareware, and freeware arranged under Ab Initio, Crystallography, Databases, Density Functional, Desktop Publishing and Molecular Modeling, Modeling, Molecular Dynamics, Nomenclature, Scientific Visualization, and Semiempirical)

- ◆ Chemistry Academic Employment Clearinghouse

- ◆ Journal Submission Guidelines (for 17 journals)

- ◆ Chemistry Information on the Internet (a very long list)

The Fisher Scientific Internet Catalog

http://www.fisher1.com/

This commercial site is composed of four interactive catalogs: The Fisher Catalog, Fisher Safety America, The Fisher Chemical Catalog, and Fisher What's New. Each catalog home page contains icons on which you can click to get help, look for an item using a search index, go to an order list, or go to the home page with its table of links.

To use a catalog, click on the link for the catalog, scroll down the resulting page, and then click on one of the chemicals, which are arranged by the accepted nomenclature. To get order information about a particular chemical, click on it.

Hazardous Chemical Database

http://odin.chemistry.uakron.edu/erd/

Are you wondering if that green boiling solution you just made is hazardous? If so, you might want to investigate this site hosted by Dr. James K. Hardy at the Department of Chemistry, of the University of Akron. This site provides a powerful database that lists more than 1,300 hazardous chemicals. Simply enter the name of the chemical of interest and click on Search. The search results is a list of hazardous chemical compounds that match or contain your requested chemical. Each listed compound is linked to a page that has the compound's complete description: names, synonyms, formula, physical data, NFPA ratings, DOT guides, and registry numbers.

Internet Chemistry Resources

http://www.rpi.edu/dept/chem/cheminfo/chemres.html

The Chemistry Department at Rensselaer Polytechnic Institute presents a selective but long list of chemistry and other Internet resources. The top part of this page lists 14 categories in which you can find links. Near the bottom of the page is a link to the ChemRes *Harvest* Broker, which searches this site and more than 700 others.

Molecular Structure Laboratory

http://sbchem.sunysb.edu/msl/homepage.html

The Molecular Structure Laboratory, from the State University of New York at Stony Brook, provides many links related to crystallography (see Figures 11.10 and 11.11). The top part of this page presents information about the department. Scroll down the page to view Crystallographic Resources on the Net, Molecular Graphics, Recent Results, and much more. Under the heading Recent Results, you'll find amazing illustrations of crystal structures of organic, inorganic, and organometallic compounds.

Figure 11.10 A sodium chloride crystal image from the custom molecular graphics program CHEM-RAY, developed by Prof. Joseph W. Lauher

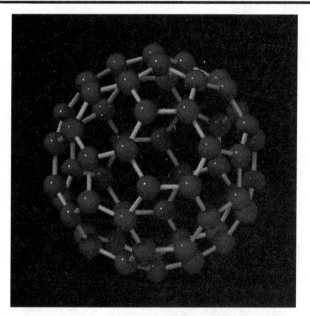

Figure 11.11 An image of buckminsterfullerene, C60 produced by CHEM-RAY, a product of Molecular Structure Corporation

Nuclear Decay Data in the MIRD Format

http://www.dne.bnl.gov/html/nndc/formmird.html

The National Nuclear Data Center, at the Brookhaven National Laboratory, provides this page on which you can enter a nuclide (using the AAAZZ or ZZ-AAA format), select an output device (PostScript, Tektronix, or HPGL), and submit. The results provide the proper medical internal radiation dose.

Periodic Table of the Elements

http://www-c8.lanl.gov/infosys/html/periodic/periodic.html

http://www-c8.lanl.gov/infosys/html/periodic/periodic-main.html

Probably one of the most essential references in chemistry (and one of the most popular chemistry sites provided on the Internet, as you will see in the next two entries) is the Periodic Table of the Elements. Robert Husted, formerly a graduate research assistant at Los Alamos National Laboratory, has provided an attractive and functional periodic table online (see Figure 11.12). With all the elements displayed in a well-designed periodic chart, it is easy to find information about the element you need. Unlike other online periodic table sites, this one provides a history of the elements' recognition in modern science. This site is ideal for students and non-chemists because the information is delivered using little technical jargon.

Note
Other Periodic Tables of the Elements are located at http://www.cs.ubc.ca/elements/tab/periodic-table **and** gopher://ucsbuxa.ucsb.edu:3001/11/.Sciences/.Chemistry/.periodic.table.

Periodic Table of the Elements

http://ripple.bu.edu/Gavin/PeriodicTable/table.html

This periodic table contains information for the professional chemist. The initial screen has a periodic chart from which you can select an element of interest. Selecting an element from the chart produces a page describing the element's technical properties: atomic weight, radii/pm, electronegativities, effective nuclear charge, bond enthalpies, and so on. If you have difficulties finding your element on the chart, you can also enter the name of the element in a search field.

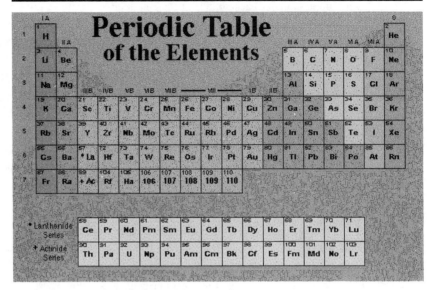

Figure 11.12 An interactive periodic table

Ecology and the Environment

Ecology is the study of living organisms and the environment in which they live. This section offers ecology and environment sites that answer many questions and address issues of concern, whether you are running a "green" business, planning a new division in another part of the world, or just interested in the health of this planet.

Consortium for International Earth Science Information Network (CIESIN)

gopher://gopher.ciesin.org/

The CIESIN is a nonprofit corporation formed to provide access to and enhance the use of environmental information worldwide. Through this comprehensive site, you can access the Human Dimensions Programme (HDP), Global Change Research Information Office (GCRIO), CIESIN Human Dimensions Kiosk, CIESIN Electronic Bookshelf, and the Environmental Internet Catalog (other environmental resources on the Internet).

HDP, started in 1990, deals with the way in which humans affect the environment and how changes in the environment affect humans. GCRIO answers worldwide requests for information about many aspects of global change.

The CIESIN Human Dimensions Kiosk contains information about its interactive electronic forum on sharing information about human dimensions of global environmental change. Through the CIESIN Electronic Bookshelf, you can research many documents and databases, including a glossary of terms and acronyms.

Consortium on Green Design and Manufacturing

http://www.me.berkeley.edu/green/

The Consortium on Green Design and Manufacturing is a partnership among industry, government, and the University of California at Berkeley. This site provides information about the consortium, sponsors, background, abstracts of publications, research overview, and faculty and students. Click on Related Sites in Green Design and Manufacturing at the bottom of the page to access a page of links to government, academic, and other "green" research sites.

EcoNet

http://www.igc.apc.org/econet

gopher://gopher.igc.apc.org/11/environment

EcoNet, part of the Institute for Global Communications, "serves organizations and individuals working for environmental preservation and sustainability." From this site, you can access EcoNet's Gopher server, New and Featured Items, EcoNet Issue Resource Center, and Organizations. The EcoNet Issue Resource Center, the centerpiece of this site, provides environmental links arranged under more than 20 headings. Clicking on most headings reveals a long list of subcategories or links. This site is a good starting point for a search of the Internet's environmental resources.

The EnviroLink Network

http://envirolink.org/

The EnviroLink Network is an international, nonprofit environmental information service founded by Josh Knauer, a student at Carnegie Mellon University. This well-designed site provides an environmental library, green marketplace, a forum, and a search index. The library links are arranged under nine headings: Activism, EnviroEvents, Environmental Education Network, Environmental E-Mail List Archives, Green Business and Product Information (a link to the marketplace), Government Resources (a long list of international and U.S. links), Issue Listings, Organization Directory, and Publications.

Environmental Resources Information Network (ERIN)

http://kaos.erin.gov.au/erin.html

This site, from the Australian Department of the Environment and other agencies, provides online articles about the environment: Air, Land and Water, Humans and the Environment, Life, Marine and Coasts, State of Environment Reporting, Integrating Environment and Development, and General Information. Of particular interest are articles about the greenhouse effect and cleaner production. Also included are Environmental Fact Sheets.

Gap Analysis

http://www.nr.usu.edu:80/gap/

The rapid loss of other living creatures—biodiversity—is a major problem in the world today. A proposed solution is Gap Analysis, which is "a rapid conservation evaluation method for assessing the current status of biodiversity at large spatial scales. This evaluation method provides a systematic approach for evaluating the protection afforded biodiversity in given areas." To learn more about Gap Analysis, access this site.

Rainforests

http://fig.cox.miami.edu/Faculty/NickCarter/rainforests.html

The rainforests of the world are being destroyed at an alarming rate. As citizens of the world, we need to be aware of the issues of our planet. This site, created by Nicholas B. Carter, focuses on salvaging our rainforests and describes what is happening to our environment. He includes chapters from books, articles, and links to other rainforest sites in an effort to help achieve the preservation of rainforests.

World Forum for Acoustic Ecology (WFAE)

http://interact.uoregon.edu/MediaLit/WFAEHomePage

The WFAE is a coalition of professionals and organizations whose mission is to protect the environment from harmful sounds. This involves studying living organisms and their relationship with their sonic environment. When an unhealthy balance is found, WFAE draws attention to the location. Environmentally conscious individuals can register, subscribe to the WFAE discussion group, and research using the documents and articles at this site.

Energy

In the last two decades, the U.S. government has contributed billions of dollars toward discovering and researching alternative forms of energy. With this sort of attention, you can be sure that the Internet has many sites pertaining to this science.

EIA Short-Term Energy Model

http://apollo.osti.gov/html/eia/stem/stem.html

This computer program for personal computers running Windows 3.1 or greater processes information used by the Energy Information Administration (EIA), part of the U.S. Department of Energy, to forecast and analyze energy usage. The program contains "up to two years of historical data and up to two years of forecast information for 270 energy and related economic and noneconomic variables." Included on this page are hardware and software requirements and ordering, downloading, and installation instructions.

Energy Efficiency and Renewable Energy Network

http://www.eren.doe.gov/

The Department of Energy hosts the Energy Efficiency and Renewable Energy Network, a Web site that locates and manages information about energy efficient technologies. Through this site, you can visit the Office of Energy Efficiency and Renewable Energy; read news, events, and hot topics; search the energy information through online databases; and visit the Energy Efficiency and Renewable Energy Clearinghouse (EREC). EREC offers information on various topics by providing publications, customized responses, and referrals to energy organizations.

The Oil and Gas Industry on the Web

http://www.lonestar.net:80/oil_gas.html

This site is simply a list of petroleum resources, including current petroleum prices, professional organizations, Internet links, government agencies, and major corporations. To access a page of links to aerospace (especially NASA), semiconductor, and scientific resources, and to use the CUI W3 Catalog search index, click on Dupont's Performance Lubricants World Wide Web.

Solstice: Center for Renewable Energy and Sustainable Technology

http://solstice.crest.org/

Solstice presents information about energy efficiency, renewable energy, and sustainable living. Under each category are lists of links, from Buildings to Case Studies and much more. Other topics are What's New, CREST Store, Subject Index, About

CREST, Mailing Lists, Keyword Search, Organizations on Solstice, Events Calendar, and Related Net Sites. If this is your first visit, click on Subject Index to reveal a page of links arranged by subject. If you are planning to build a house or want to take advantage of natural energy sources, tour this site.

World-Wide Web Virtual Library: Energy

http://solstice.crest.org/online/virtual-library/VLib-energy.html

This long page provides plenty of information about a variety of energy resources on the Internet. Links are arranged by Internet server type: WWW, Gopher, & FTP Sites (by far the largest); Usenet Groups; Mailing Lists; and Experts, which was empty at the time of this writing. The best way to search this site for the first time is to scroll from beginning to end.

Geography, Geology, and Geophysics

Geography, geology, and geophysics may not be evolving as quickly as chemistry or physics. However, the Internet is still an excellent resource for any questions in these fields. As the Internet continues to grow, so will its information about geography, geology, and geophysics.

Earth Science Site of the Week

http://agcwww.bio.ns.ca/misc/geores/sotw/sotw.html

Every week, the Geological Survey Commission (GSC) chooses an earth science Web site to highlight. The focus of the earth science study is anything earth-related, from oceanography to gravity. This site provides access to all past highlighted sites, arranged in both chronological and subject order.

Those involved in exciting earth science projects can submit an entry for GSC's attention. Simply complete the online form or e-mail moir@agc.bio.ns.ca.

National Geophysical Data Center (NGDC)

http://www.ngdc.noaa.gov/ngdc.html

This essential site for geography professionals contains extensive information in various geography studies:

- Solid Earth Geophysics is composed of many files focusing on global change, geomagnetism, seismology, natural hazards, gravity, topography, and other global phenomena.

- Solar Terrestrial Physics provides information on geomagnetic field magnifications, ionospheric data, solar and upper atmosphere, GOES satellite data, DMSP satellite data, and the Space Physics Interactive Data Resource (SPIDR).

- Marine Geology and Geophysics supplies databases for both coastal and open ocean areas.

- Paleoclimate Program offers information on climate modeling, ice-core researching, paleoceanographic and paleovegetation studies, and more.

- Defense Meteorological Satellite Program (DMSP) consists of two satellites orbiting over the earth's poles monitoring meteorological, oceanographic, and solar-terrestrial physics environments.

- The National Snow and Ice Data Center (NSIDC) supplies information for snow and ice processes, with concentrations in interactions among snow, ice, atmosphere, and ocean.

Physical Geography Resources

http://feature.geography.wisc.edu/phys.htm

Studies have indicated that in comparison with the population of other industrial nations, U.S. citizens are among the least educated in geography. This impressive site, which is made possible by a grant from the Instructional Technology Grant program of the University of Wisconsin-Madison, provides a database of online geography resources. Presented in a list format, this site supplies links to the worlds more useful geography-related sites: current weather images, maps and movies; current weather data; climate images and data; atmospheric composition (such as trace gases); solar; ocean data and images; earth topography; stream flow data; vegetation; soils; information servers; lists of information servers; and frequently asked questions files.

World-Wide Web Virtual Library: Geography

http://hpb1.hwc.ca:10002/WWW_VL_Geography.html

This medium-sized page contains links arranged under three headings: General Information, Information about Countries, and Information about Educational Institutions. This site comprises a variety of resources: map viewers, landscape ecology resources, educational institutions, geographic names for Canada and the U.S., the *CIA World Factbook* (1994), and travel information.

Mathematics and Statistics

Whether you are keeping the books, analyzing income, or estimating future expenses, every business person encounters math as part of operating a company or department. If you took a college statistics class because it was required—not because you wanted to—you may have some catching up to do. In this section, you'll find a variety of mathematics and statistics resources— some on a very basic level.

Guide to Available Mathematical Software

http://gams.nist.gov/

This well-designed site is "a cross-index and virtual repository of mathematical and statistical software components of use in computational science and engineering." You can learn more about this project by clicking on Project Summary or Repositories Indexed under Background Information. If you are new to this site, clicking on Problem Decision Tree provides you with a list of problems or topics for which there is available software or a software module. Continue to click on subtopics until you reach the desired software.

A Guide to Statistical Computing Resources on the Internet

http://asa.ugl.lib.umich.edu/chdocs/statistics/general.html

This very long page provides information and links to statistical resources on the Internet. Each entry on the list is composed of a title/link, a very informative one- or three-paragraph description, the URL and related information, and contact information. You can find the brief index to this site at the bottom of the page. Here, you'll find Web sites, Gopher sites, mailing lists, Listservs, and much more.

Mathematical Sites on the Internet

http://www.math.psu.edu/OtherMath.html

This very long and comprehensive page provides links to mathematical sites worldwide. At the top of the page is a table of contents with 11 headings: General, Related Topics, Mathematics Department Web Servers (a very large category), Societies and Associations, Institutes and Centers, Commercial Pages, Mathematics Journals, Mathematics Preprints, Subject Area Pages, Other Archived Material, and Mathematics Software. Scroll down the page to see the links under the headings.

Note
This site also provides another choice (at http://www.math.psu.edu/MathLists/Contents.html). This alternate page is broken into several files.

Mathematics Information Servers

http://www.coe.uncc.edu/cas/math_depts_www.html

This comprehensive page lists many mathematics resources from around the world. At the top of the page is a table of contents with these headings: General, Mathematics Department Web Servers, Other Organizations, Mathematics Journals, Mathematics Preprints, and Mathematics Software. Under General, you will find indexes and other mathematics lists of links—both World Wide Web and Gopher sites. Clicking on Other Organizations jumps to a group of links for organizations, laboratories, and commercial sites. Mathematics Journals are divided into electronic and printed publications.

Statistics and Statistical Graphics Resources

http://www.math.yorku.ca/SCS/StatResource.html

Many of the statistical sites on the Internet are long and detailed. This fast-growing academic-related site is not an exception: It provides links to general statistical resources, statistical associations, statistics departments at universities worldwide, information about popular statistical software, data visualization and statistical graphics, psychology and psychometrics, online courses, data, categorical data analysis, statistical packages, and Unix. If you are a first-time visitor to this site, simply scroll down the page to see its contents.

Statistics Servers and Other Links

http://www.isds.duke.edu/stats-sites.html

This long, plain but impressive page presents statistical-related links: Academic Departmental Servers by country; Archives (statistics, demographics, data sets, reports, and case studies); ASA (American Statistical Association); Bayesian Sites; Job Announcements; Journals and Preprints; Mathematics Servers (six links); Miscellaneous (links to probability sites, graduate programs, resampling, and more); Newsgroups; Societies, Groups, and Associations; Software (commercial sites, software resources, and programming information); Statistics Education; and StatLib (see the following entry).

StatLib

http://lib.stat.cmu.edu/

StatLib is a comprehensive "system for distributing statistical software, datasets, and information." At the top of this page is a quick index with 41 topics followed by links to short and long indexes. If you are a first-time visitor, clicking on one of the index links will help you understand the contents of this site. The short index provides brief explanations, and the long index is more descriptive.

World-Wide Web Virtual Library: Mathematics

http://euclid.math.fsu.edu/Science/math.html

The home page of this major mathematical site consists of headings on which you can click to go to pages of links. Categories at this site include Specialized Fields, Mathematics Department Web Servers, General Resources, Mathematical Software Index, Mathematics Gophers, Mathematics Newsgroups, Preprints, Electronic Journals, High School Servers, Addresses, Bibliographies, and TeX Archives.

Oceanography

Universities and government agencies seem to provide the bulk of public oceanography information. You will find many of these information archives through the Internet. Described in this section are a few sites that we found valuable for oceanography research.

Harbor Branch Oceanographic Institution

http://www.hboi.edu/

The third largest marine research facility in the United States, Harbor Branch Oceanographic Institution, Inc., (HOBI) provides online oceanograpy information. HOBI performs research and education in the marine sciences; biological, chemical, and environmental sciences; marine biomedical sciences; aquaculture; and ocean engineering. Through this well-designed site, you can learn about the facilities, programs, research, and marine science projects. Valuable marine information is provided in the newsletter, which you can find on the aquaculture division page.

National Marine Fisheries Service (NMFS)

http://kingfish.ssp.nmfs.gov/home-page.html

The National Marine Fisheries Service (NMFS) regulates programs designed to support the conservation and management of domestic and international living marine resources. At this site, you can access the National Oceanic and Atmospheric Administration (NOAA), its parent agency; publications; and technical reports. Also provided is the Our Living Oceans report, which discusses the past and current fisheries' relationship with the living ocean and provides information on marine species and ecology in relationship to harvesting operations.

National Oceanic and Atmospheric Administration (NOAA) Network Information Center

http://www.nnic.noaa.gov/

A valuable oceanography site is the U.S. National Oceanic and Atmospheric Administration's (NOAA) Network Information Center. Here, you can search through volumes of information on many online databases. From the home page, you can visit various sections: What's New, the Gopher site, Weather, the FTP section, Science and Technology, Oceans and Atmospheres, NOAA Search Router, NOAA Stats, Data Centers, Internet Resources, NOAA Personnel Locator, NOAA Regional Map, and NICWORLD. If you are searching for a particular topic, Science and Technologies and the Oceans and Atmospheres sections provide powerful database search tools.

NOAA also provides an online chat session using World Wide Web form abilities. This means that you don't have to own a chat program to communicate.

Scripps Institution of Oceanography

http://orpheus.ucsd.edu/sio/

Scripps Institution of Oceanography, founded about 90 years ago, is one of the "largest and most important centers for marine science research and graduate training in the world." At this site (see Figure 11.13), you can learn about Scripps and the University of California at San Diego, under which Scripps operates. This site provides a very long and impressive list (at http://orpheus.ucsd.edu/sio/inst/) of oceanography resources on the Internet, schedules and information about its research ships and marine facilities, oceanographic data, geological data, and a search index, which was under construction at the time of this writing.

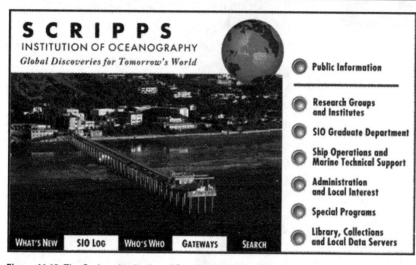

Figure 11.13 The Scripps Institution of Oceanography home page, with its featured topics

aspects of marine science and to the education of marine scientists."

At this site, you can access general information about Woods Hole, items of local interest to employees and visitors, a list of Woods Hole servers, a library (you'll find some good resources here), a calendar of events, education programs, and what's new. In addition, under Information Resources outside Woods Hole, be sure to check out Oceanographic Information, a long list of other oceanographic links.

Shark Attacks

http://www.io.org/~gwshark/sharks.html

Sharks are among the few creatures known to attack and eat humans. Sharks, however, are getting bad press: Drowning accounts for far more fatalities than shark attacks. Fewer than 10 percent of shark species have been known to attack humans, and they attack humans because of mistaken identity.

This site offers valuable information if you are researching the dangers of sharks but not if you want to know more about sharks, the animals.

Woods Hole Oceanographic Institution

http://www.whoi.edu/index.html

Woods Hole Oceanographic Institution "is the largest independent marine science research facility in the United States. Founded in 1930, the Institution is dedicated to the study of all

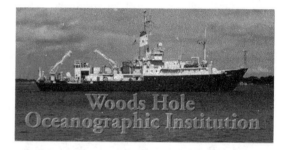

World-Wide Web Virtual Library: Oceanography

http://www.mth.uea.ac.uk/ocean/oceanography.html

This straightforward and comprehensive site presents lists of worldwide links related to oceanography. At the top of the page is a table of contents, which lists new entries, countries, server type, and subjects under which links are arranged. Among the sites you will find here are institutes and government agencies and laboratories, educational institutions, and businesses.

Physics

Physics is a dynamic science with research labs all over the world. Through the Internet, you have access to many of these resource pools of information. In this section, you will find a few sites that we believe can be research assets.

E-Print Archives

http://xxx.lanl.gov/

E-Print Archives is an online document retrieval system for physics and mathematics. It provides extensive information in its archives for your use. You can access information by traveling through directories within directories. Or you can complete a search request form. If you do choose to find your document through the search form, you will notice that the interface is not very intuitive and rather complicated. To be sure that you did actually search the archives completely, travel through the directory tree to find your papers.

The Einstein Papers Project

http://web.mit.edu/~redingtn/www/netadv/welcome.html/

The Net Advance of Physics is a composition of physics-related materials and links for scientists and graduate students. The information is presented in a list of categories containing subtopics. Each list item (category and subtopic) is a hyperlink connecting the user to a Web site specializing in the topic or to further lists narrowing down the topic of interest. The categories presented are as follows: general physics, astrophysics, condensed matter physics, electromagnetics, mathematical and theoretical physics, quantum physics and chemistry, and history and philosophy of physics.

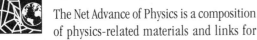

Interesting Site

If you own a pet, NetVet (at http://netvet.wustl.edu/vet.htm) is an excellent site to have in your Hot list. The creators, the Washington University Division of Comparative Medicine, supply extensive information on animals and animal-related resources. Subsites of information include what's new, searches, profession, virtual library, colleges, organizations, animals, references, laws/regulations, mailing lists, resources, Gopher sites, and electronic zoo. Almost anything you want to know about animals, particularly pets, can be found here. For example, this site contains a few references concerning first aid for your pets. Now, when your dog tips over the trash container and eats an aluminum can, you know what to do.

Another veterinary site at Cornell University provides interesting veterinary links including the Cornell Canine Page (at http://zoo.vet.cornell.edu/~dlm7/canine.html) and External Links from CU Vet (http://zoo.vet.cornell.edu/extlinks.html).

High Energy Physics Information Center

http://jean-luc.ncsa.uiuc.edu/

If you are familiar with the development of the Internet, you probably know about the contributions of the National Center for Supercomputing Applications (NCSA). You may not know, however, that NCSA conducts relativity research studies, which focus on the relationship of time, space, and matter as applied in Einstein's Theory of General Relativity. NCSA's Relativity Group uses supercomputers to study black holes (see Figure 11.14 and Figure 11.15), gravitational waves, and other phenomena predicted by Einstein's theory. Here, you can access technical papers discussing black holes, gravitational waves, self-gravitating scalar fields, numerical relativity, cosmology, hydrodynamics, and more. Also included are exhibits and movies that are truly amazing.

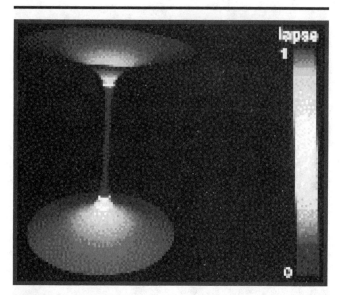

Figure 11.14 NCSA provides incredible computer-generated images of black holes and their effects on time, space, and matter.

Measurements and Weights

http://www.ic.gov/94fact/appendf/appendf.html

Need to know the conversion of a specific weight or measurement? You can find a large list of conversions at the Central Intelligence Agency (CIA). Supplied conversions include mathematical notation and metric interrelationships.

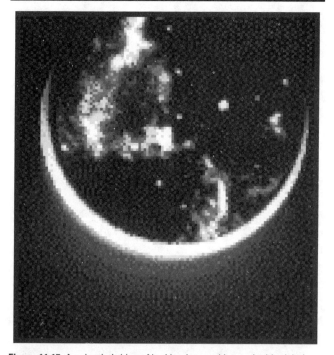

Figure 11.15 A scientist's idea of looking into and beyond a black hole

Chapter Twelve

Trade and Markets

International Business Resources

The sites in this large section usually provide links to many countries or provide general information about the world, its regions, and/or countries. Other entries in this section cover trade in general. If you are just deciding whether to expand into foreign markets, this is an ideal place to start.

B ecause of the steady movement toward an international economy, it's a good idea to explore the possibilities of trading with countries outside the United States. To get ready to expand your horizons, plan to do a great deal of research—not only into the business practices in a region or a particular country, but also into its history, culture, climate and geography, and political climate.

Many entries in this chapter are not country-specific but provide many links to country and region lists from which you can start your research.

Note
The *Law and Government* chapter provides links to specific information about and the text of NAFTA, GATT, and other international agreements and treaties. In that chapter, you'll also find links to international government organizations.

Army Area Handbooks

gopher://UMSLVMA.UMSL.EDU:70/11/LIBRARY//SUBJECTS/
BUSINESS/INTMKTG/ARMYAHBS

These Army Area Handbooks, written from 1988 to 1994, are online documents that you can study before deciding whether to do business in a particular country. Chapters cover the history, geography, and demographics and current business and cultural conditions. Areas documented are China, Egypt, Indonesia, Israel, Japan, Philippines, Singapore, Somalia, South Korea, and Yugoslavia.

These handbooks are good companion pieces for the following entry: "Background Notes—Dept. of State Country Information."

Background Notes—Dept. of State Country Information

gopher://UMSLVMA.UMSL.EDU:70/11/LIBRARY//SUBJECTS/
BUSINESS/INTMKTG/BNOTES

Prepared by the U.S. Department of State, "background notes provide brief, factual summaries concerning the people, history, government, economy, and foreign relations of about 170 countries (excluding the United States) and of selected international organizations." A typical document is two or three pages of information packed with brief notes and descriptions.

Berkeley Roundtable on the International Economy (BRIE)

http://server.berkeley.edu/BRIE/brochure.html

"The Berkeley Roundtable on the International Economy (BRIE) is an interdisciplinary research project that focuses on international economic competition and the development and application of advanced technologies. Founded by a group of faculty at the University of California at Berkeley in 1982, BRIE has quickly become one of the leading intellectual voices debating government policy and business strategy in America."

At this valuable site, you can learn about BRIE; get names and addresses of participants; peruse the full text of papers, notes, and online articles; and link to Selected Starting Points: international, U.S. government, Internet information, and academic sites.

Center for Global Trade Development

http://www.primenet.com/~cgtd/

The Center for Global Trade Development (CGTD) is "an independent global economic research organization, monitoring socio-economic events and trends of over 220 countries and geo-economic areas of the world—focusing on major issues related to economic development, industrial and trade growth, globalization and international trade with special emphasis on emerging market technologies."

This commercial site—with English, German, French, and Spanish language versions—primarily advertises CGTD's print directories. You can obtain some country information, however, by clicking on Analysis & Surveys, Smartest WWW Links, and World Currencies. All other links are commercial.

Country Commercial Guides

gopher://dosfan.lib.uic.edu:70/
1D-1%3A8210%3A4country%20commer

The U.S. Department of State presents comprehensive commercial guides for countries all over the world. Click on a country link to get a long page covering all or most of these major topics: Executive Summary, Economic Trends and Outlook, Political Environment, Marketing U.S. Products and Services, Leading Sectors for U.S. Exports and Investment, Trade Regulations and Standards, Investment Climate, Political Environment, Trade and Project Financing, Business Travel, and several appendixes.

Country Information—Trade, News, and Events

gopher://una.hh.lib.umich.edu/11/ebb/imi

This page of links provides news about projects, information about upcoming events, and warnings of dangerous conditions. Simply scroll down the page until you find the country or region in which you do business, want to visit, or want to learn about, click on a link, and read a text-only paper. At the time of this writing, this long page included links ranging from Africa to Yemen.

Country Reports on Economic Policy and Trade Practices

gopher://UMSLVMA.UMSL.EDU:70/11/LIBRARY//SUBJECTS/BUSINESS/INTMKTG/CRPT

Country reports, from the U.S. Department of State, are annual reports written to comply with the Omnibus Trade and Competitiveness Act of 1988. Each document is a "detailed report regarding the economic policy and trade practices of each country with which the United States has an economic or trade relationship." Be sure to read the Program Description to get an overview of the reports. A typical report covers key economic indicators, recent events, and the country's policies on exchange rate, trade, debt, and export subsidies. Also included are barriers to trade with the U.S., protection of U.S. intellectual property, and the country's treatment of workers. Note that many of these reports were written in the early 1990s.

Eastern Europe Trade Leads

gopher://una.hh.lib.umich.edu:70/11/ebb/europe

The four files in this folder provide documents on Eastern Europe Trade Leads and BISNIS (Business Information Service for the Newly Independent States) information for 1994 and 1995. The documents are prepared by the U.S. Department of Commerce.

Electronic Trading Opportunity System: ETO Newsweek Service

http://www.unicc.org/untpdc/eto/newsweek/overview.html

This site provides Electronic Trading Opportunities (ETO) in several categories and formats for those involved in international trade. You can go to this site regularly, or you can automatically receive ETOs via e-mail (simply click on register on the

home page). Also included at this site is the ETO Forum. Note that most links are connected to newsgroups.

The Embassy Page

http://www.globescope.com/web/gsis/embpage.html

The Embassy Page contains links to embassies and consulates in the United States and worldwide. Simply click on a button on the home page to reveal a page of links headed by the letters of the alphabet. Most embassy pages provide trade, business, and cultural links. Also included at this site are related resources—a short list of links to international business resources.

Foreign Trade

gopher://una.hh.lib.umich.edu:70/11/ebb/foreign

This site contains documents with information about merchandise trade, exchange rates, the U.S. international investment position, trade statistics, tables, and more. Some documents can be downloaded in ASCII or WK1 format. When using one of these documents, be sure to check the date; some are from the early 1990s.

InfoQuest! Information Services

http://www.teleport.com/~tbchad/

InfoQuest! Information Services "provides businesses with online database research for planning, competitive intelligence, and market research." The business is operated by Terry Brainerd Chadwick, a trade and Internet expert whose interview appears in this chapter. The top of the home page is composed of links to online course summaries, which can help you conduct research and market courses on the Internet. Each online document presents information for those doing business within and outside the U.S. The next section of the home page is devoted to library and nonlibrary resources. The end of the page consists of links to a variety of resources, for businesspersons, educators, and those interested in learning more about the Internet.

International Business Practices

gopher://UMSLVMA.UMSL.EDU:70/11/LIBRARY//SUBJECTS/BUSINESS/INTMKTG/IBPA

International Business Practices, from the International Trade Administration of the U.S. Department of Commerce, "is designed to provide U.S. firms with an overview of legal practices in 117 countries, and to provide up-to-date information on some of the nuances involved with operating in other countries." This document contains five chapters, with topics ranging from financing export transactions to international sales agent and distributor agreements. Following the chapters are links to five regions or the alternative, All Countries Covered Herein in One Big Menu.

A typical country report describes how a foreign business is allowed to operate in the country, including approved corporate structures, foreign investment, import duties and restrictions, intellectual property rights, corporate taxes and regulations, and contact information. Where possible, specific laws are cited. This document was written in 1993.

International Business Resources on the WWW

http://ciber.bus.msu.edu/busres.htm

This comprehensive master list provides a variety of links to international business resources arranged under 14 categories: publications, regional- or country-specific information, international trade, statistical data, company information or directories, government resources, international trade shows, utilities (such as currency converters, area code/country code search indexes, FedEx and UPS tracking forms, and so on), and other business indexes. This site is a required bookmark for international traders.

International Market Insight (IMI) Reports

gopher://una.hh.lib.umich.edu:70/11/ebb/imi

The many documents in this folder discuss market conditions and U.S.-partnered projects throughout the world. Each document describes one or more projects in a particular country or region. A sample document contains summary information (for example, title, post of origin, author, date of report, and so on), a subject, introduction, and list of projects (including project name, borrowing agency, loan

Terry Brainerd Chadwick on a Client's Internet Needs

Terry Brainerd Chadwick is president of InfoQuest! (at http://www.teleport.com/~tbchad), a company that offers services in using the Internet to meet particular business needs, including marketing, making contacts, finding opportunities, keeping current, and locating regulations and data. Chadwick has more than 14 years experience working in business information centers and more than 5 years of Internet experience. She operated the Trade Information Service at the International Trade Institute for five years, assisting businesses with international trade market research. She speaks at major information conferences, including the National Online Conference and Internet World; has written many articles on business information resources, computer networking, and online search techniques; and teaches seminars on these subjects.

amount, description, and so on). The best way to explore this site is to choose a country or region, click on the link, and find out whether the report is of any use.

contain much information. The General Information by Country link provides much more.

LEAD Guide to Information on International Trade

http://www.chiangmai.ac.th/LEADTrade.html

This long, text-only page provides international trade links arranged under these headings: Current News, Online Descriptive Guides, Online Directories, Online Document Collections, Major Data Servers, Conferences and Newsgroups, International Organizations, Utilities, and Other LEAD Guides. Many resources here are academic Gopher sites, and a few links are either old or inactive.

Market Potential Indicators for Emerging Markets

http://ciber.bus.msu.edu/publicat/mktptind.htm

This Michigan State University study, dated September 15, 1995, "ranks the market potential of 23 countries identified as 'Emerging Markets' by *The Economist*." Each market is ranked and indexed by market size, market growth rate, market intensity, market consumption capacity, commercial infrastructure, economic freedom, market receptivity, and overall market opportunity index. This wide document is formatted as a table.

Library of Congress Country Information

gopher://marvel.loc.gov/11/federal/foreign

The Library of Congress presents information for many countries. On the home page, you can click on General Information by Country to open a page of entry points for a great deal of country information, or you can select a specific country. In general, the country folders on the home page do not

Overseas Business Reports

gopher://UMSLVMA.UMSL.EDU:70/11/LIBRARY//
SUBJECTS/BUSINESS/INTMKTG/OBR

The International Trade Administration, part of the U.S. Department of Commerce, has prepared Overseas Business Reports (many of them quite extensive and large) for selected countries: Argentina, Austria, Bahamas, Bolivia, Brazil, Canada, Chile, Gabon, Germany (West), Greece, Iceland, Ireland, Italy,

---

What do you most often recommend for clients establishing a corporate presence on the Internet?

In general, I recommend that everybody have a Web presence, but it may not be the best overall choice for a particular client. For instance, I've been working with an educator who is trying to market to teachers worldwide. I've told her I think she ought to have a Web site as the image focus—one small page—but her documents probably ought to reside on a Gopher because more people will have access to them that way. Her other solution should probably be to set up her own Listserv because she has lesson plans and things that she wants to distribute and wants to be able to post answers to questions so that she doesn't have to reanswer them. In her case, I said, "Yes, you want a Web site so that you show up and have your image, but you're really going to want to do other things to reach your clients."

I basically recommend that everybody at least have a Web page. It is a company's image on the Net. But I'm not necessarily recommending that a company's major activity involves the Net.

Jamaica, Japan, Kenya, Madagascar, Malaysia, Netherlands, South Africa, Spain, Thailand, United Kingdom, Uruguay, and Zaire. These reports were written in 1992 or 1993; so current changes are not addressed. The structure of these reports differs country by country.

Trade Compass℠

http://www.tradecompass.com/

Trade Compass provides up-to-date information and a large library of documents for registered members and for guests. Both members and guests must sign in to use this service. Membership is free; simply fill in a form, select optional subscription services (for businesses in international trade), and click on the Send Registration button.

The advantage of using this site is that you can get the latest business information: international trade leads, including the *Commerce Business Daily*; credit reports; company and industry directories; logistics management; trade news; and much more.

A special feature is the search index, which is always at the bottom of the page (once you have signed on). Simply type a keyword, select a category, and click on the Search button.

The Trading Floor

http://trading.wmw.com/

This large and promising site, filled with trade links and information, looks as though it will eventually be a good starting point for those in international trade. Here you can jump to 16 topics under which links are listed. At the time of this writing, some of the topics had no links. "Populated" topics include Country-Specific Information, Export Information, Legal Aspects of Trade, Market Information, Statistical Information, and Trade Leads.

Virtual Library on International Development

http://www.synapse.net/~acdi03/indexg/welcome.htm

This comprehensive site from Canada, with English and French language pages, comprises many links helpful for those in international development. In addition to country and government information, many resources include social indicators and articles about human rights. Find country-specific information by clicking on that region on a map or scroll down the page of buttons. Major headings under which buttons are organized are Organizations, Thematique Resources, and Other Services. Other buttons and headings include Some Excellent Resources; Mandate for Canadian ODA (Official Development Assistance); and Making Choices, Paying the Price.

To get a complete picture of a country or region in which you want to do business, tour this important site.

WebEc—International Economics

http://www.helsinki.fi/WebEc/webecf.html

This long and thorough page of links from Lauri Saarinen can help you to get economic, business, and trade information about countries around the world. At the top of the page are links to the rest of the page. Major links here are International Affairs, International Trade, Collections, Data, News, Journals and Working Papers, Mailing Lists, International Finance, Foreign Exchange, International Organizations, Collections, Organizations, International Treaties, Treaties, WP (a search of the WoPEc Database index), RFE (a search of the EconFAQ index), and Search. Note that some of the links on this page are purely commercial sites.

World Factbook

http://www.odci.gov/cia/publications/95fact/index.html

The Central Intelligence Agency (CIA) annually publishes the very popular *World Factbook*, which reports on countries and regions worldwide. At this site, you can read the current *World Factbook*. At the top of the page are links to letters of the alphabet. To jump to information about a particular country or region, click on the letter that starts its name. On the resulting page, click on the country name. A typical page includes a map with major cities marked, a narrative about current activities in the country, Geography, People (including demographics, language, and literacy rate), Government (and the U.S. relationship to it), Economy, Transportation, Communications, and Defense Forces.

Export and Import Information

The Internet provides a great deal of information about exporting your goods to other countries and importing from other countries. This section provides excellent resources for those who are just starting out. Here, you'll find tutorials, basic but detailed guides, and checklists that will help you get started.

A Basic Guide to Exporting

gopher://UMSLVMA.UMSL.EDU:70/11/LIBRARY//
SUBJECTS/BUSINESS/INTMKTG/EXPGUIDE

This important and comprehensive document, prepared by the International Trade Administration of the U.S. Department of Commerce, provides detailed information about exporting from the U.S. Its 16 chapters cover topics from Export Strategy to Technology Licensing & Joint Ventures. The document

also includes an export glossary, a directory of federal export assistance, state and local sources of assistance, U.S. and overseas contacts, and a bibliography.

Best Market Reports

gopher://una.hh.lib.umich.edu:70/11/ebb/bmr

The Best Market Reports are compiled by 62 United States and Foreign Commercial (US&FCS) posts around the world. Each of these text documents provides an industry overview, key markets, and assessments of the best markets. The industries reported on are apparel, automotive parts and service equipment, building products, computer software, computers and peripherals, electrical power systems, laboratory scientific equipment, medical equipment, pollution control equipment, sporting goods and recreational equipment, and telecommunications equipment.

Breaking into the Trade Game: A Small Business Guide to Exporting

gopher://UMSLVMA.UMSL.EDU:70/11/LIBRARY//
SUBJECTS/BUSINESS/INTMKTG/EG_BREAK

This online document, created by the U.S. Small Business Administration (SBA) and AT&T, provides insights into exporting for small businesses. Its seven chapters guide you through the decision to export, identifying your markets, entering a foreign market, transacting and financing, transporting goods, and forming strategic alliances. Also included is a valuable International Business Plan workbook, which you can print and fill in as you read the chapters. Concluding the document are 10 sections (appendixes) that provide names and addresses of U.S. government contacts, foreign embassies in the U.S., chambers of commerce and trade organizations, publications, international calling codes, and a glossary of terms.

Export Procedures (1995)

http://vm.cfsan.fda.gov/~lrd/certific.txt

In this text-only document, the Food and Drug Administration (FDA) outlines the procedures for exporting foods and cosmetics, including obtaining Certificates of Export, the criteria that the FDA uses to allow an export, the forms that must be filed, and agency addresses.

Export Process Assistant

http://venture.cob.ohio-state.edu:1111/tutorial/openingscr.html

The Export Process Assistant, developed at the Center for Information Technologies in Management (CITM) Ohio State University, contains a tutorial/checklist and links to export information services. Be sure to read the Executive Summary, which describes current conditions and offers trade statistics; it points out the advantages of participating in the international marketplace. Click on the tutorial icon to reveal a six-part checklist: Statement of Objectives, Assessment of Resources, Product Analysis, Target Market Research and Analysis, Market Entry Strategy, and Implementation. Then scroll down the page, clicking on links to read related articles. Other resources at this site include a Product FAQ, Export FAQ, and directory of links—for trade and Internet resources.

ExporTutor

http://web.miep.org/tutor/index.html

This 10-step program, developed by the International Business Center at Michigan State University, is a guide to "Success in Foreign Markets." Using the tutorial, you can assess your company, plan for its expansion into international markets, and implement the plan. Also included at this site are

Terry Brainerd Chadwick on the Web and Other Internet Options

I don't use any of the Gopher programs anymore. I just get to Gopher sites through the Web. The real difference is that more people have access to Gophers, particularly if you're talking about educators who are still often running on dial lines and not on the Web. This is particularly true for the client that I'm talking about because I've been hired to help her build her own site. Now, with the Web, you have to code everything in HTML. But with Gopher, you just put some plain-text documents down; anybody can get them and anybody can read them. So, it's how the data is presented, the ease of presenting it, and again who's your target audience. If your target audience is people who use only the Web and are very visually oriented, it's OK to make that your sole presence, but if your target audience is people who may be operating off 286's around the world and who have very limited access to the Internet, Gopher might be a better choice than the Web.

Also, there are Listservs and FTP, and I don't want people to forget the whole idea of Telnetting into unique databases. The real problem I've found with a lot of the people who call themselves Web developers is that they're newcomers and they don't really even understand that there's more to the Internet.

What it comes down to is the Internet is all about communicating between people. The real power of the Internet is not in the flashy ads. It's in the communications and the relationships you build with people online. The business people who are most successful on the Web understand that and are active in discussion groups. They don't just put up flashy Web sites with pictures that the majority of people can't access.

You think that most people do not use the graphical browsers?

I haven't seen statistics that convince me that the majority of the people who have Internet access (and I'm counting even those who have e-mail access) have visual access yet.

the Quick Consultant (links to documents covering areas of business from accounting and taxation to value chain analysis) and References (links to publications and resources for specific countries or industries, and more).

Foreign Trade Division— U.S. Census

http://www.census.gov/ftp/pub/foreign-trade/www/

The U.S. Census Bureau presents a page of links to export information, including Schedule B (the Export Commodity Classification), the Top 10 International Trading Partners, news about the Automated Export System from the U.S. Customs Services and the U.S. Census, reports, press releases, and a Guide to Foreign Trade Statistics. Also included are links to Who's Who in Foreign Trade at the U.S. Census and a page of good international trade links.

Global Export Market Information (GEMS)

http://www.itaiep.doc.gov/

From the U.S. Department of Commerce, GEMS, "a service of the International Economic Policy group of the International Trade Administration," provides trade information. This site has links to international export pages: TransAtlantic Business Dialogue, NAFTA, Russia and the Newly Independent States, and the Big Emerging Markets home page. Also included are graphical and text links to Central and Eastern Europe Business Information Center Online (CEEBIC), BISNIS Online, SABIT (Special American Business Internship Training Program), and the Northern Ireland and the Border Counties of Ireland home page. After you click on a link, you'll find a page of links to documents about various international trade issues and events.

National Export Strategy Files

gopher://una.hh.lib.umich.edu:70/11/ebb/nes

This very interesting online document explores the way in which exports fit into the overall U.S. economy and how the U.S. must adjust to the world economy by being successful exporters. The document is composed of six chapters, six appendixes, a progress report, and two updates (the latest dated June 1, 1994). Chapter topics include resource allocation, export promotion services, export financing, regulatory obstacles to exports, and the future of the national export strategy.

State by State Export Resource Listings

gopher://una.hh.lib.umich.edu:70/11/ebb/statex

This folder provides state name, addresses, telephone numbers, and names of international trade contacts for every state. Click on the name of a state to open a text file with this important information. An extra bonus from these documents are contacts from whom you can get other business information: Small Business Administration (SBA), Small Business Development Centers (SBDC), and Minority Business Development Centers (MBDC).

U.S. Food and Drug Administration (FDA) Import Procedures

http://vm.cfsan.fda.gov/~lrd/import.txt

If you plan to import an FDA-regulated food into the U.S., read this text-only document. Information includes the forms that must accompany the import and step-by-step procedures that the FDA follows in allowing entry of the product.

U.S. Food and Drug Administration (FDA) ORA Import Alerts

http://www.fda.gov/ora/import/ora_import_program.html

The Food and Drug Administration (FDA) "enforces the Federal Food, Drug, and Cosmetic (FDC) Act and other laws which are designed to protect consumers' health, safety, and pocketbook. These laws apply equally to domestic and imported products."

This comprehensive site provides a detailed description of the FDA ORA Import Program, lists of current Import Alerts (by country, by industry, by the identifying number assigned to the alert, or using a search index of the entire FDA site), Import Detention Reports, and other Import related information.

African Resources

Some African countries, particularly South Africa, can be excellent sources of business. The resources in this section should help you research and prepare your entry into this large market.

African Studies World Wide Web Server

http://www.sas.upenn.edu/African_Studies/AS.html

The African Studies server at the University of Pennsylvania provides valuable information about African countries. Click on Country-Specific to go to a page of links to African Embassies & Diplomats in the U.S. (1994), General Map of Africa, National Holidays, and U.S. State Department Travel Warnings and Consular Information Sheets. Following that are links to 55 countries. A typical country page contains a link to a map, a U.S. State Department Travel Advisory, information about the country's embassy in the U.S., its CIA *World Factbook* entry, and a variety of other resources.

ExiNet

http://www.aztec.co.za/exinet/exinet.html

ExiNet provides a mix of local business links and information about exporting, travel, and tourism in South Africa. For example, click on South African Exporters to go to a page of manufacturers of goods for export. Click on a category to reveal a page of information about goods as well as links. Or click on The Cape Town City Council (http://www.ctcc.gov.za/ or the "graphics lite" page at http://www.ctcc.gov.za/ccclite.html) to obtain a variety of information about Capetown and South Africa.

Virtual Africa

http://www.africa.com/

This attractive commercial site provides extensive information about traveling to and doing business in South Africa. The best links at this site are South African Travel and Tourism and South African Business. Click on South African Travel and Tourism to visit tourist pages. The South African Business section presents a mix of businesses that can help you do business in South Africa. For example, if you click on The JSE and African Stock Exchange Overview, you can obtain a list of companies on the stock exchanges in Africa. Or click on Contacts SA to go to a page of commercial sites and the South Africa Chambers of Commerce.

Asian and Pacific Rim Resources

Asia and the Pacific Rim (including the Western United States) seem to be the fastest growing economic region of the world. The Internet reflects the dynamic growth of this area. This section presents a few of the many valuable links to the countries of Asia.

Asia in Cyberspace

http://silkroute.com/silkroute/asia/rsrc/asia.html

This attractive site provides information about Asia, Australia, and New Zealand. You can access the information by Country (see Figure 12.1) or Category. A typical country page provides a list of links organized by category. Click on Asia to access many resources, arranged under headings such as Business, Directory, Education, General Information, and News. For the business "surfer," country pages include such topics as Education, Government, Institutions, Library, and Publishing. Also included is a search index of th site.

Asia, Inc. Online

http://www.asia-inc.com/

Asia, Inc. Online is an online business magazine that presents current business news, feature reports on Japan, new products and technological advances, articles on Asians who operate successful businesses outside Asia, and features about finance—both corporate and personal. Major links on the home page include Today's Financial News, This Week's Special Items, Feature Stories, Departments, Conference Rooms, Past Issues, Registration, and Net Resources for Asia. For now, you can visit any page but Conference Rooms without

Figure 12.1 Click on a link to go to an Internet site associated with a country.

Terry Brainerd Chadwick on Graphical Browsers

New versions of graphical browsers offer some very fancy things. There's some controversy about that in terms of how pages developed for programs such as Netscape look when you use other viewers. For instance, now a developer has the ability to set in a background; so you can put a graphic in that will make your entire site. You can also specify colors. It's gotten very sophisticated, and there's still a lot of controversy over whether those elements will even be adopted as standards. So there's a lot of jockeying going on, and that's the other part of the Web design—making sure that you're designing things that everybody can see. If you've got a client that only wants to tap people at the very front edge, there are a lot of elements to think of.

That was something I hadn't even thought of.

A lot of people in the Web design business don't understand these things and quality control and testing. But clients don't always understand that; all they see is that price and this price. My price might be two or three times higher. Most people don't understand all the elements that go into designing and maintaining a good Web site.

registering (for no charge). This site is well worth exploring for those interested in learning about business in Asia.

Asia-Pacific Information Gopher Site

gopher://emailhost.ait.ac.th:70/11/AsiaInfo

This comprehensive list provides information about Asia-Pacific business practices and currency and has computer-related resources and links to other Internet resources in Asia. Click on Information by Country to access a variety of documents about countries in the region. You can get information about government agencies, human rights, labor trends, and travel, and you can link to other Internet resources for that country. Areas covered at this site are Bangladesh, Bhutan, Brunei, Burma (Myanmar), Cambodia, China, Hongkong, India, Indonesia, Korea, Laos, Macau, Malaysia, Mongolia, Nepal, Philippines, Singapore, Sri Lanka, Taiwan, Thailand, and Vietnam.

Asia-Pacific Information Web Site

http://SunSITE.sut.ac.jp/asia/asia.html

This long page is composed of links to Asian, Pacific, and other resources. At the top of the page are icons (see Figure 12.2) on which you can click to see a regional map or maps of countries in the region. The rest of the page lists links to variety of Asian and Pacific resources—both World Wide Web and Gopher.

Asian Development Bank (ADB)

http://www.asiandevbank.org/

The Asian Development Bank (ADB), "a development finance institution consisting of 56 members, is engaged in promoting the economic

and social progress of its developing member countries in the Asian and Pacific region." The ten links on the home page provide all sorts of information, from business opportunities to environmental impact assessments, from news releases and publications (generally ADB sales pitches) to links to other international organizations. Go to ADB Publications Catalog (http://www.asiandevbank.org/pubguidepub95.html) for a list of publications—some free and some for a price. Perhaps the most valuable page at this site is Asian Development Outlook 1995 & 1996 Publication Summary (http://www.asiandevbank.org/ado95/ado95.html).

International Export Connections Library

http://www.teleport.com/~iexportc/library.htm

International Export Connections is a commercial service that has specialized in Middle East trade since 1991. This site provides a minimum of corporate advertising and many resources for those interested in Middle East trade. The highlight of this site is the library, which contains many resources about the Arabian countries of the Middle East: Algeria, Bahrain, Jordan, Kuwait, Morocco, Oman, Qatar, Saudi Arabia, Syria, United Arab Emirates, Yemen, Egypt, and Sudan. All the links here are worthwhile. Be aware that when linking to Info Via Photo: Pictures from the Arabian Countries, you can elect to click on the small graphics to display full-screen and slow-loading photographs.

Japan External Trade Organization (JETRO)

http://www.jetro.go.jp/

The Japan External Trade Organization (JETRO) is a "nonprofit, Japanese

Figure 12.2 A bar on which you can click to go to a category of Internet links

government related organization dedicated to promoting mutually beneficial trade and economic relations between Japan and other nations." At this site, you can learn about Japanese government procurement and assistance programs, get facts and figures on Japan's trade and economy, view information about Business Japanese, find out about the JETRO support system, and much more. If you are interested in exporting products to Japan, be sure to explore this site.

Japan's Economy

gopher://gan1.ncc.go.jp/11/
JAPAN/Economy

This site contains general text-only information about Japan—mostly dating from the 1980s. Despite the age of the documents, you can use them to get a good background about Japan: postwar development and recovery and economic conditions (employment and labor, finance, fiscal policy, industry, and economic trends).

Japanese R&D Web Server Addresses

http://www.doc.gov/aptp/
web.html

For those interested in the latest Japanese technologies and research, this valuable page from the Asia-Pacific Technology Program provides links to a variety of Japanese resources. The list is arranged under these headings: Japanese Governmental Institutions, Special Corporations, Japanese Universities, Inter-University Research Institutes, and Private Sector.

South-East Asia Information

http://sunsite.nus.sg/asiasvc.html

The South-East Asia Information site provides information about Brunei, Burma, Cambodia, Indonesia, Laos, Malaysia, Philippines, Singapore, Thailand, and Vietnam. Either click on a link or on a country flag on the map (see Figure 12.3) to reveal a country page. A typical page is composed of links (culture, travel, business, and so on) to other sites related to the country and a short article about the country.

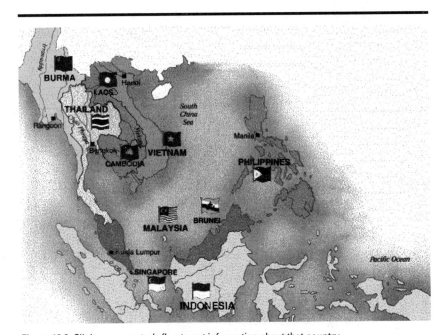

Figure 12.3 Click on a country's flag to get information about that country.

World-Wide Web Virtual Library: Asian Studies

http://coombs.anu.edu.au/WWWVL-AsianStudies.html

This massive site contains any information you'd ever want about Asia and its countries, Australia, New Zealand, and parts of Russia and its former satellites. At the top of the page is an index, which spreads both horizontally and vertically. Each link in the index is related to the entire region, part of the region, or a specific country. Click on a link to jump down the page to that category. The emphasis is on academic areas; however, you'll find plenty of other information here.

World-Wide Web Virtual Library: Middle East Studies

http://menic.utexas.edu/mes.html

This site, from the Center for Middle Eastern Studies at the University of Texas at Austin, provides links to information about countries in the Middle East. Here you can get information about Algeria, Bahrain, Egypt, Iran, Iraq, Israel, Jordan, Kuwait, Lebanon, Libya, Mauritania, Morocco, Oman, Palestine, Qatar, Saudi Arabia, Sudan, Syria, Tunisia, Turkey, United Arab Emirates, and Yemen. In addition, you can click on Other Useful Country Home Pages to display links to other Middle East sites and pages (primarily academic resources) for countries worldwide. Other resources at this site are organized under these headings: Information about the Middle East and General Information. You also can look for resources at this site by using the search index at the bottom of the page.

World-Wide Web Virtual Library: Pacific Studies

http://coombs.anu.edu.au/WWWVL-PacificStudies.html

This long page of Pacific Rim resources includes links to the Asia-Pacific area as a whole, the islands of the Pacific (including Hawaii), Australia, and New Zealand. To access a resource, either click on a link in the horizontally arranged index or scroll down the page. First-time visitors should scroll down the page to look at everything along the way. Resources include history, academic studies, culture, travel, fishing, and individual country pages. As you

might imagine, some of the smaller countries have very few links. This is a good site to get background information for a country in which you want to do business or travel.

Oceanian Resources

Australia and New Zealand are important participants in the economics of the Pacific Rim. In addition, having the same English language background adds to the positive feelings that many Americans have about the residents of Oceania. This section provides excellent country guides and master lists of Oceania resources on the Internet.

Australian Economic Views

http://www.norwich.com.au/monrep/curmon.htm

This short monthly report, from Norwich Investment Management Limited, presents the Australian Economic Outlook, International Economic Outlook, Australian Financial Markets, and International Financial Markets. The information is presented on one page; so you can either scroll down the page or click on a link to jump to a particular subject. At the bottom of the page, the best link is Today's News, which covers the overseas markets, including reports from stock markets worldwide, and the Australian market with results for the major movers—both rising and falling.

Australian Embassy, Washington, DC

http://www.aust.emb.nw.dc.us/

The Australian Embassy in the U.S. provides all types of information about the country: travel information, a clickable map, and frequently asked questions (FAQs). Also included are Visas and Immigration, Customs, Economy, International Trade, Geography and Climate, Flora and Fauna, People,

History, Government, Culture, Tourist Tips, and links to other Australian sites.

A Comprehensive Index to Information on Australia

http://www.telstra.com.au/meta/australia.html

This long and comprehensive page provides many Australia Internet links, from its Internet resources to travel and events. After a large map of Australia (not clickable, just an illustration) is a table of these links: Comprehensive Web Server Indexes; Comprehensive Information Resources on Australia; Australian Government; Australian Telecommunications; Tourism and Travel; Finance and Real Estate; Australian Sport; Australian Internet; Australian Education; Australian Employment; Australian Events, Conferences, etc.; and Other Australian Information. This is an excellent starting point for learning much more about Australia.

Australia

http://www.dpie.gov.au/dfat/genmnu.html

This text-only page from the Australian Department of Foreign Affairs and Trade provides links to a library of fact sheets about Australia. The Subject Directory lists links to papers under these headings: Trade, Government, General Information, Current Issues, Culture, and Geography. The Numerical Directory contains the same list; each entry is preceded by its Fact Sheet Number.

Guide to New Zealand

http://www.rmmb.co.nz/rmmbcont.html

The barristers, solicitors, and notaries public Russell McVeagh McKenzie Bartleet & Co provide an overview of New Zealand and an online document about doing business there. The overview (at http://www.rmmb.co.nz/rmmbgen.html) provides information about geography, climate, population, government, and business. The online article "A Guide for Foreign Investors in New Zealand," encompasses topics from taxation to trade practices to intellectual property. If you plan on

---

Terry Brainerd Chadwick on Web Page Graphics

I notice that some graphics seem to load more quickly than others. There must be ways of making graphics load faster.

It's called interlacing.

There are ways of coding that make it load faster?

I don't do these things, but I critique them. If a client has created a page with a graphic, I'll see how it loads. It's a combination of compression factors and a technique called interlacing. And the interlacing is what makes the entire graphic load and the resolution improve instead of coming up bit by bit so you only see the top or bottom of the graphic. Just go through an HTML beginner's tutorial, which explains interlacing and compression. If you do it online, you can view the differences in the pictures and see the differences between a JPEG and a GIF.

Some of the worst offenders are graphic designers. Many of them work on very fast computers that most of us don't have access to.

Statistics are showing the number of people who view the Web with their online images off, which means if you don't have an explanation of what that graphic is and an alternative to click on, you're alienating a whole bunch of people. What they're saying is OK, here's this explanation. That sounds interesting enough to make me turn my online images on or to download the image. But a lot of the most experienced Net surfers go with their images off. I'm not one of them because I do training and evaluation and I look at those things, but many of my colleagues don't have their images when they're surfing.

Some sites that I've critiqued look fine on the surface. However, if you look at them with images off or in text format, you may not know where to click. There would be image, image, image, with no alternative links. It's amazing.

doing business in New Zealand, you must read it. Click on Legal Update Publications to access a list of papers on particular areas of New Zealand law. Sites of Interest lists international legal sites, New Zealand resources, and many other interesting Internet sites.

World-Wide Web Virtual Library: Australia

http://www.psu.edu/research/anzsc/areas/au/Ausi.html

This site is composed of a variety of Australian resources. The table of contents has these links: Current News, Indexes, Electronic Publishing, Government, Education, Business, Academic Resources, Information Technology and Networks, General Information and References, and Aboriginal and Torres Strait Islander Information. Either scroll down the page or click on a link to jump to the desired category. You'll find good business resources under almost every category.

World-Wide Web Virtual Library: New Zealand

http://www.psu.edu/research/anzsc/areas/nz/NZi.html

Using the links at this one-page site, you can learn all about New Zealand, from today's news to active Internet sites to consular and trade offices in the U.S. Categories under which links are organized are Government, Academic, Business, Information Technology, General Information and References, Current News, Indexes, and Maori Interest.

European Resources

The cultures of the U.S. and the countries of Europe have been intertwined since the very beginning of U.S. history. After all, many of our grandparents immigrated to the U.S. from countries in this region. Economically, the U.S. and Europe also are interdependent. Using the resources in this section, you'll be able to keep track of this dynamic area of the world—the European Community (EC), European Union (EU), the former satellites of the Soviet Union, and particular countries.

Baltic Business Directory

http://www.massoc.com/bbd/

This attractive site with a unique background pattern provides information about doing business in Estonia, Latvia, and Lithuania. Links on the home page include Companies Seeking Cooperation (a long list), Investment Opportunities (only one company), Trade Fairs, and Tourist Information (a list of hotels, restaurants, and entertainment in all three countries). Also included are several links under the heading Lithuanian Business Practice, links to other Internet resources for Estonia, Latvia, and Lithuania, and an excellent list of Useful Business Links.

The European Business Directory

http://www.europages.com/

This valuable site—with English, French, German, Spanish, and Italian pages—provides a variety of information and resources for those doing business in Europe. The links on the home page include Consult Europages (a search index of what they claim are 150,000 companies listed here), European Economic Data, and the Business Information Service.

Clicking on Consult Europages results in a search index with which you can search for a product or service or for a company. Simply type a keyword and click on the Validate button.

The European Economic Data page allows you to access "over 100 pages of economic analysis" that you can download in Adobe Acrobat PDF format. Included is a European macroeconomic analysis, including updates, and Economic indicators.

The <u>Business Information Service</u> provides links to European resources: fairs and exhibitions, Chambers of Commerce, international standards bodies, and international dialing codes.

European Commission Host Organization (ECHO)

http://www.cec.lu/

The European Union (EU) is "preparing the way for economic and monetary union (EMU) and a single currency." Under the Maastricht Treaty on European Union, the 15 member states are continuing to pool their industries and markets. At this site, you can learn about the EU, its members, and their plans for the future.

European Union (EU)

http://www.chemie.fu-berlin.de/adressen/eu.html

This page not only provides links to information about the European Union but also links to home pages for EU members as listed in Table 12.1. Note that the Austrian link is inactive.

Also included are links to other European resources, some of which you can find in this section.

Friends and Partners

http://solar.rtd.utk.edu/friends/home.html

http://solar.rtd.utk.edu/fp/friends/

Friends and Partners is a project developed by Greg Cole at the University of Tennessee and Natasha Bulashova, a computer scientist in Russia. The pages at this site provide information about both the U.S. and Russia. Topics include history, geography, the arts, health, science, education, business, and more.

At the home page, you will find 12 buttons surrounding a clickable map as well as links scattered through the text on the page. In addition, you are invited to join the Friends and Partners Listserv and visit the coffee house, at which you can send messages and participate in online discussions.

The Information Market Policy ACTions (IMPACT) Programme

http://www.echo.lu/impact/en/impacthome.html

IMPACT was founded in 1988 to "establish an internal market for electronic information services and to improve the competitiveness of European firms by promoting the use of advanced information services." At this site, you'll learn about IMPACT and its programs. Of particular interest are <u>Information Services for Business and Industry</u> (articles about IMPACT programs) and <u>Information Market Observatory (IMO)</u>; (in particular, the working papers).

Table 12.1: Home Pages for Selected European Union (EU) Members

Country	URL
Belgium	http://info1.vub.ac.be:8080/Belgium_map/index.html
Denmark	http://www.daimi.aau.dk/denmark.html
Finland	http://www.funet.fi/resources/map.html
France	http://web.urec.fr/france/france.html
Germany	http://www.leo.org/demap/
Greece	http://www.forthnet.gr/
Ireland	http://itdsrv1.ul.ie/Information/ServerMapIreland.html
Italy	http://www.pi.cnr.it/NIR-IT
Luxembourg	http://www.restena.lu/luxembourg/lux_welcome.html
Netherlands	http://www.eeb.ele.tue.nl/map/netherlands.html
Portugal	http://s700.uminho.pt/homepage-pt.html
Spain	http://www.uji.es/spain_www.html
Sweden	http://www.sunet.se/map/sweden.html

Terry Brainerd Chadwick on Planning Web Pages

I understand that you use style sheets to plan Web pages.

I try to. Otherwise, the coding is not standard throughout the pages.

The whole point of a style sheet is to help you remember the commands that you are using for indents, italics, and so on. For example, you can either start italics with the letter *I* or the word *emphasis*. Or, you can indicate boldface with the letter *B* or the word *strong*. You also have to code everything so that it works better with more browsers. You don't want to use one command in half your document and another command in the other half. These are just standard style issues that anybody should be using.

Note that many IMPACT programs are still in the planning and demonstration stages.

St. Petersburg Business Way '94

http://www.spb.su/bw/index.html

This online document describes, in detail, how to do business in St. Petersburg, Russia. Included is information on the business environment, how to set up a company, important names and addresses of officials, government agencies, and St. Petersburg businesses. Although this document was posted early in 1994 and conditions in Russia seem to change day by day, this document is a very valuable starting point for doing business in Russia.

Top 500 German Companies

http://www.welt.de/extra/500/500.htm

This German language page lists the top 500 firms in Germany. Each entry on the list shows the current ranking, last year's ranking, the name and location of the company, its product or service, and financial information.

World-Wide Web Virtual Library: Russian and East European Studies

http://www.pitt.edu/~cjp/rees.html

This site, which is sponsored by the University Center for Russian and East European Studies of the University of Pittsburgh, is a long and comprehensive page of Internet resources. Countries covered here include the former Soviet Union, Albania, Armenia, Azerbaijan, Belarus, Bulgaria, Croatia, Czech Republic, Estonia, Hungary, Kazakhstan, Latvia, Lithuania, Macedonia, Moldova, Poland, Romania, Slovakia, Slovenia, Tajikistan, the Ukraine, and Yugoslavia. At the top of the page is a table of links to the rest of the page. Links here include Resources by Discipline, Resources by Type, National Hoepages and Major Sites, WWW Servers in the Former Soviet Union, and Some New Items This Month.

Latin and South American Resources

The Internet contains many resources that concern our closest neighbors—the countries of Latin America, the Caribbean, and South America. This section documents some of these resources—most created by students and academics throughout the Western Hemisphere, including the U.S.

Doing Business in Mexico

http://www.tpusa.com/nafta/nafta_facts/mexico.html

This text-only site, from Trade Point USA, provides links to papers on Mexico and its business resources. Simply click on a link to reveal a page of valuable resources. Links are arranged under five headings: Basic Information on Mexico and the Mexican Market, Other Offices to Contact for Information on the Mexican Market, Marketing Your Products and Services in Mexico, Preparing Your Product for Shipping and Sale to Mexico, and Legal and Tax Issues.

Foreign Trade Information System—SICE

http://www.sice.oas.org/

The Organization of American States presents pages (in English, Spanish, and Portuguese) that "provide foreign trade information to the public and private sectors of member states." Since 1984, SICE (Sistema de Información al Comercio Exterior) has had an online system. The top part of the home page is devoted to describing SICE. To get to the resources, scroll down the page. Links include both the text and summary of agreements, regulations, sources of trade-related information, trade data, tariff schedules, and miscellaneous Latin American resources.

How to Do Business in Mexico FAQ

http://daisy.uwaterloo.ca:80/~alopez-o/busfaq.html

With NAFTA now in effect, more companies are deciding whether to do business with or in Mexico. This comprehensive document, written by Alex López-Ortiz and Daniel M. Germán of CanAmMex Consulting & Translation Services, is a good way to start your research. At the top of the page is a table of links: General Mexican Business Practices (working hours and dress codes), More Mexican Business Practices (including negotiating, personal relationships, using

Terry Brainerd Chadwick on Choosing a Provider

Do you find Internet service providers for clients?

We try to place them with the provider that best meets their needs. Some of them already have their own servers; others don't. And I'm finding that a lot of people are selecting whoever gives the best story without asking really relevant questions.

What are some of the questions?

The type of connection is very important: Does the provider offer a T1 line? How many T1's per customer? For example, a provider for my higher-end customers says that it won't have any more than 50 customers per T1 line. Does the provider differentiate between commercial and noncommercial accounts? Does it provide free Listservs and free Gopher space? How much memory does it give? Does it charge a flat fee? Does it charge clients for storage? Does it charge for the number of hits or accesses, which isn't a good idea necessarily. Some things sound good, but you have to look at the overall picture before deciding.

the telephone and fax, hiring, and so on), The Mexican Wage Structure, General Tips, Getting a Distributor in Mexico, Social Practices, Getting Help, Information Sources, Acronyms, Literature on Business Trading, and Keeping Abreast of Economic/Politics and Social Changes. Either click on a link or scroll down the page to read the document.

LATCO Tools of the Trade

http://www.teleport.com/~tmiles/tools.htm

This text-only page lists links to many trade resources for Mexico, Central America, and South America. At the top of the page are the links that jump to major categories: New, Latin News, International Business and Trade, Other Latin America, Oregon—Washington, General Trade and Economics, and Internet Utilities.

Latin American Network Information Center (LANIC)

http://lanic.utexas.edu/

This well-organized site provides information about Spanish-speaking countries of the Caribbean, Latin America, and South America. The list of countries is Argentina, Barbados, Belize, Bolivia, Brazil, Chile, Colombia, Costa Rica, Cuba, Dominican Republic, Ecuador, El Salvador, Guatemala, Guyana, Haiti, Honduras, Jamaica, Mexico, Nicaragua, Panama, Paraguay, Peru, Suriname, Uruguay, Venezuela, and other places in the Caribbean (Aruba, Cayman Islands, French Guyana, Guadeloupe, Martinique, Puerto Rico, and U.S. Virgin Islands).

On the home page are two tables, the first of the countries and the second of subjects. Click on a country or a subject to obtain information. Under the tables are links to topics for the entire region. At the bottom of the page is a search index with which you can search the site.

When you click on a link in the country table, the contents of the page are arranged under two major headings: Reference Desk (economic data, general resources, news and newsgroups, and travel and tourism) and Resources by Type of Service (for example, World Wide Web and Gopher). On the other hand, if you click on a link in the subject table, links are alphabetically arranged under subject headings.

Latin American/Spanish Language Resources

http://www.uwm.edu:80/People/annepres/anne7.htm

This imaginatively designed page provides a variety of valuable resources. At this site are Spanish language and Latin American sites: Gophers, mega lists, country pages, language resources (dictionaries), and other miscellaneous resources. The pages are not limited to a particular region; here you'll find as many U.S. sites as those for Latin America.

The Latino Connection

http://www.webspace.com/~pedro/index95.html

The well-researched and good-looking Latino Connection presents links to Latin American and South American pages as well as other Latino Links and more. Click on a country link to reveal a page filled with links to Country Information, Travel & Tourism, Education, Arts & Entertainment, Food & Beverage, and Other Web Links.

Countries covered at this site are Argentina, Bolivia, Brazil, Chile, Colombia, Costa Rica, Cuba, Dominican Republic, Ecuador, El Salvador, Guatemala, Honduras, Mexico, Nicaragua, Panama, Paraguay, Peru, Puerto Rico, Spain, Uruguay, and Venezuela.

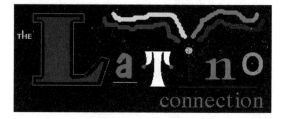

LatinoWeb

http://www.catalog.com/favision/latnoweb.htm

LatinoWeb "is a virtual information center for Latino businesses, non-profit organizations, and the community." The home page lists links from Art and Music to Resources. Links of interest to businesses include Business, Events, Government Agencies, Non-Profit Organizations, and Resources (links of all types).

Canadian Resources

Canada and the U.S. are very important trading partners and neighbors, with goods and services flowing steadily over our common border. Now, the passing of the North American Free Trade Agreement (NAFTA) makes it more important than ever for U.S. and

Canadian companies to consider doing business together.

Canada

http://www.cybersmith.net/compuguide/canada/

This text-only page provides a variety of links to information about Canada, from currency to tourism; about half the links are related to travel and tourism. Clicking on most links results in a concise but complete article about the selected topic.

Doing Business in Canada

http://www.tpusa.com/nafta/nafta_facts/canada.html

This text-only site, from Trade Point USA, provides links to papers on Canada and its business resources. Simply click on a link to reveal a page of valuable resources. Links are arranged under five headings: Basic Information on Canada and the Canadian Market, Other Offices to Contact for Information on the Canadian Market, Marketing Your Products and Services in Canada, Preparing Your Product for Shipping and Sale to Canada/Customs Issues, and Legal and Tax Issues.

Ernst & Young (Canada)

http://www.inforamp.net:80/ey/

Ernst & Young, a professional organization with 40 locations in Canada and 600 cities around the world, provides this commercial site with excellent information about Canada. Included on this long page are press releases, news stories, analysis, job opportunities, and links to many other Canadian resources, from associations and corporate sites to government pages in Canada and worldwide.

KPMG Online (Canada)

http://www.kpmg.ca/

This site, presented by KPMG, "Canada's largest firm of chartered accountants and management consultants," provides an enormous amount of information about doing business in Canada, whether you are a Canadian or live outside the country. The home page is loaded with links to survey results, publications that you can download or to which you can subscribe, analyses, and business resources. If you are planning on doing business in Canada, be sure to explore this site.

Chapter Thirteen

Coming Attractions

Travel

This chapter is not the only source of travel sites in *The Internet Business-to-Business Directory*. For example:

- In the *Corporations and Industry* chapter, look for companies located in the area that you plan to visit. Or in the *Law and Government* chapter, look at government agencies—federal, state, and local. Many corporate and government home pages include travel directions, favorite hotels and restaurants, and even local maps.

- Many colleges and universities provide a variety of travel resources on their pages. In the *Education and Training* chapter, look for an educational institution in a particular city or town.

- Newspaper home pages often include links to local travel sites. Just look at the newspaper tables in the *News and Events* chapter.

- What if you plan to travel outside the United States? The *Trade and Markets* chapter provides specific country information, including current travel conditions, culture and etiquette, and places to stay.

H ave you ever found yourself in a new place without information on where to stay, where to eat, or where to go for entertainment? Or have you had to make a last-minute trip without knowing air schedules or having a hotel reservation? In both cases, the Internet can come to the rescue.

In this chapter, you'll be able to find both generic and specific resources. For example, if you're taking a long business trip around the U.S., tour the state tables in this chapter; then visit sites from which you can gather information—to choose particular hotels, restaurants, or after-hours fun. Or if you've just gotten some vacation time and want to choose a destination, start with the general resources at the beginning of the chapter.

General Resources

This section presents travel-related sites that contain a variety of resources—within the U.S., outside the U.S., or worldwide. Here, you'll find two types of sites: those with links to many travel pages and those that cover a particular type of activity or topic, from fun in the great outdoors to your health while traveling to finding zoos all over the world.

@USA

http://emporium.turnpike.net/A/atLA/@usa/

At the @U.S.A. site, you will find a listing of guides to the largest cities and popular tourist destinations in the United States and Canada. @USA does not list every site for each city but tries to link you to those that have the most detailed information.

A la Carte Guide to North America

http://www.westweb.com/alacarte/index.html

This online guide reviews restaurants and hotels/motels in Canada and the U.S. To start a search at this site, click on a flag graphic or a link. Then click on a state, province, commonwealth, or district link. To complete the search, select Cuisine, City, and/or Lodging from the scroll boxes, fill in the text box, and click on the Search button. The resulting page lists restaurants or lodgings, their addresses, and telephone numbers. If the restaurant or lodging has a Web site, click on the name to go to its home page. At this site, you also have the opportunity to review or add an entry.

The Climbing Archive!

http://www.dtek.chalmers.se/Climbing/contents.html

Interested in recreational climbing? If the answer is yes, this is the place for you.

Guidebooks, grouped by continent, will aid in planning your next climb. A Climbing Directory is an alphabetical list of climbers, from which you can find a partner wherever you might want to go. Climbing stories, songs, pictures, and poems are available as well as information on the latest equipment. Advice on preventing accidents, frequently asked questions (FAQs), and workouts in preparation for climbing will help everyone from novice to expert. Finally, you can link to Ravage— Swiss Climbing Journal here.

Dr. Memory's Favorite Travel Pages

http://www.access.digex.net/~drmemory/cyber_travel.html

Although you will find information on transportation, travel agents, tours, favorite destinations, lodging, and more here, you also will find travel links that are different from those on other Internet travel pages. Some of the links, such as Travel Weekly News and TravelGram, are devoted to travel-related news, which you may not think is of value. Search a little deeper, and you will find up-to-date news about travel discounts. Look especially for the TravelGram VIP subscription service on the TravelGram page, or check out the Give Yourself a Break Newsletter.

Ecoventure

http://134.121.164.23/ecoventure.htm

This excellent site provides information for those exploring the possibility of a "great vacation in the great outdoors." Links include the BaseCamp Database (a search index of many outdoor resources), Links (many links to outdoor resources: commercial, organizations, books, and other information), and Other On-Line Sources (non-Web Internet resources).

Galaxy—United States

http://www.einet.net/galaxy/Community/World-Communities/
North-America/United-States.html

Galaxy provides another alphabetized listing of U.S. states and some major cities. The information found under the states can include travel but also is likely to be geared toward government, business, and organizations.

GardenNet Guide to Gardens of the USA

http://www.olympus.net/gardens/guide1.htm

This site lists U.S. gardens that are open to the public. To search this site, either click on <u>Browse Gardens by State</u> or <u>Browse Gardens by Type</u>. After clicking on a link, click on a state or type link. The resulting page provides some or all of the following information for each garden: name, address and telephone numbers, type of garden, size, hours, closed, best season, gardens, historic buildings, and special collections.

GNN TC Country Guides— United States

http://nearnet.gnn.com/gnn/meta/travel/res/countries/
cgus.html

The GNN TC Country Guide for the United States contains an alphabetical listing of the states with links to information about the states. In addition, this site also has a short but insightful review of what you will find at each link. This guide is refreshingly frank and might provide you with more unconventional links than you would find elswhere.

GoSKI!

http://www.goski.com/

This site has links to all the information you might need if you are a ski enthusiast.

GoSKI has a 600+ resort database, including reviews and trail maps, for ski resorts throughout the world. Also found here is weather information, including snow conditions and winter forecasts. The Travel Center will help you decide on accommodations and airlines and offers travel tips. Links to the latest ski-related news can be found here, including ski competitions and the 2002 Salt Lake City Olympic Winter Games. Links to Nordic skiing and snowboarding are also available. Finally, there are extensive links to the latest in ski equipment.

Great Outdoor Recreation Pages (GORP)

http://www.gorp.com/default.htm

GORP contains information on what to do and where to go in the outdoors. The attractions listed include national parks, forests, wilderness areas, wildlife refuges, and national monuments. Virtually all outdoor sports can be found in the activities section. Information about travel and outdoor recreation are listed geographically. If you are searching for books, maps, videos, trips, and gear related to the outdoors, you'll find it here.

Hotels & Travel on the Net

http://www.webscope.com/travel/homepage.html

Covering a great deal more than hotels on the Internet, Hotels & Travel on the Net is a public service of WebScope. There are links to airlines, hotels, and resorts around the world, a link to commercial airports on the Internet, and cruiseline information. Also found here are references for travelers and travel-related services. Look at the link to <u>AESU</u> for "Low Cost Airfares from the USA to Europe" or <u>The Travellers Diary</u> for current information on international events.

The Internet Sleuth—Travel

http://www.intbc.com/sleuth/trav.html

The Travel section of the Internet Sleuth (http://www.intbc.com/sleuth/index.html) has links and search indexes for various travel resources: accommodations, cruise ships, airlines, weather, travel health, a travel agency, and so on. Simply type a keyword in one of the text boxes, click on the Search button, and wait for the results. This is an excellent starting point for your travel research.

Interstate 95

http://interstatelink.com/isl/i95/i95-us.html

Interstate 95 (I-95) traverses the eastern United States from rural Maine through the urban centers of New York and Washington, D.C., to Florida. This virtual Interstate links you to hotels, motels, cities, and points of interest that you might encounter along the way.

L. L. Bean's Park Search

http://www.llbean.com/parksearch/

L. L. Bean, the sporting goods company, has compiled a guide to nearly 900 national parks and forests, state parks, and other outdoor locations. You can search by park name, activity, or state. Choose a park, and you will see a photo of the park, a summary of what you will find at the park, information about the park, and a chart that will tell you about activities there. This is a beautifully done, extremely informative site!

MCW International Travelers Clinic

http://www.intmed.mcw.edu/travel.html

This site, provided by the Medical College of Wisconsin, contains links to Travel Health Information and the ASTMH Directory of Travel Clinics and Physicians. Also included are links to other travel and travel health sites on the World Wide Web—particularly those devoted to international travel.

Perhaps the most valuable resource at this site is the ASTMH (American Society of Tropical Medicine & Hygiene) Directory. Here, you can peruse a text-only list of physicians arranged by state, Canadian province, or foreign country. Each entry contains the name and the town or city in which the physician is located. Unfortunately, street addresses and telephone numbers are not included.

Metroscope—Web Sites by City

http://isotropic.com/metro/scope.html

Metroscope, a well-designed and comprehensive site, has links to "almost 5,000 different Web sites." Both U.S. and international links are included. To find out about a location, scroll down the page, and click on a button that has the name of a state or a major city. U.S. sites are listed first, followed by international sites. When you click on a button, a pageful of links appears, arranged under Art and Entertainment, Business, Media, Towns, Sports, Colleges, Government, Professional Services, Internet Services, Financial, Organizations and Groups, and Other Sites. At the bottom of each page are links to major resources on the World Wide Web.

National Park Service

http://www.nps.gov/parks.htm/

http://woodstock.rmro.nps.gov/index.html

This National Park Service Web Site provides a comprehensive listing of the national parks in the U.S. The Preserving America's Heritage section delves into the past well and explains why the national parks are important to conserve the nation's natural resources. Specific information on entrance fees, camping, concessions, park phone numbers, weather, and preparations you should take before visiting the parks is also provided.

New England Online

http://ftp.std.com/NE/index.html

New England Online is a compendium of information links for the six-state New England region. Here you will find general information about the area, such as weather and the economy, as well as information about tourism.

Planet Earth—United States of America

http://white.nosc.mil/states.html

This site has a tremendous amount of information about the United States. Major

links are Comprehensive United States Servers, Washington D.C. and The 50 States, Census and Demographics, Maps and Imagemaps, Geography, Travel, Weather, Reference, Search Engines, and Earth Related Issues. Those sections that apply to the topic of travel are Virtual Tourist and Virtual Tourist II, National Parks, United States Travel, United States—GNN, United States—Galaxy, United States—City Net, United States—Yahoo, United States—GORP, United States—Welcome, United States—List of Sites, USA CityLink, See the USA in Your Virtual Chevrolet, Around America by Rail, United States Travel, and Dr. Memory's Favorite Travel Pages. All the above travel sites are evaluated in other parts of this chapter. Also included is an extensive map collection.

Rec.Travel Library: Worldwide Travel and Tourism Information

http://rec-travel.digimark.net

Referred to as "one of the Web's most extensive databases of travel information" by the *New York Times*, this site will aid you in deciding where to go on your next trip. Preparations, mode of transportation, and what you might want to do after your arrival are all included. Travel advice and reviews, even honeymoon travel suggestions, round out the features at this site.

Rec.Travel—USA

http://www.digimark.net/rec-travel/north_america/usa/

Rec.Travel contains an alphabetical listing of the states. Click on a state, and you will be shown a small map, the state motto and symbols (such as the state flower), a "Daily Travel Factoid" (something unusual about the state), and regional information. Special events and festivals, business information, and travelogues can also be included in the state's data. Many of the remaining topics are personal stories of travel adventures.

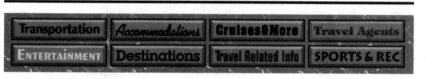

Figure 13.1 Click on a button to obtain travel information.

Starting Point—Travel

http://www.stpt.com/travel.html

This site is truly a starting point for anyone interested in travel. Here you will find information on places close to home and places on the other side of the world. There is a comprehensive listing of hotels, motels, and resorts, as well as international airlines.

State Parks Online

http://www.crl.com/~ddickson/parks.html

This site provides many links to state parks throughout the country, miscellaneous state park links, and historical information and statistics related to state parks. Either click on the U.S. map or a text link to get specific information. The resulting page contains a brief article and links to specific parks or regions.

TEN-IO

http://www.ten-io.com/

At this site, presented by Travel & Entertainment Network—Internet Operations, are travel services and information for travelers. Click on a button (see Figure 13.1) to go to a particular travel page. Click on <u>Transportation</u>, and you will find data on airlines on the Web, airports throughout the world, motorcoach services, trains, and auto rentals. Clicking on <u>Accommodations</u> gives you a listing of hotels, motels, bed and breakfasts, and hostels. <u>Destinations</u> will link you to travel and tourism companies as well as information on various locations. <u>Entertainment</u> and <u>Sports & Rec</u> will connect you to activities at the various destinations. Links to cruise information, travel-related information, and travel agents are also included here.

Travel Page

http://www.woi.com/travel.html

Use the Travel Page to find out more about a place you plan to visit. Click on <u>The Vatican</u>, and see 325 images of the Sistine Chapel. Visit <u>On Broadway</u> to find out about current on- and off-Broadway plays. This site also has links to guides, magazines, directories, reports, and other travel-related information.

Travel the USA

http://pathfinder.com/@@1PuxPOG@QQMAQLIr/Travel/indexusa.html

Pathfinder's (that is, Time-Warner's) site for U.S. travel includes ratings of car rental agencies and airlines. What makes this site different is that it not only links to travel sites but it also tells you what is worth seeing and helps you find the best restaurants and lodging. Here you also can find restaurants by price and cuisine at 30 destinations, travel activities for children, a selective guide to the best U.S. events each month, travel news, and a listing of 11,000 golf courses. Also included are Travelon, a commercial clearing house of daring and unusual travel, and Trip Planner, a travel agency.

Travelers' Health

http://www.cdc.gov/travel/travel.html

Before you take an international trip, be sure to visit this Centers for Disease Control (CDC) site to learn about precautions and vaccination requirements for the region that you'll be visiting. On this page are links arranged under these headings: Reference Material for International Travel, Geographic Health Recommendations, Disease Outbreaks, and Additional Information (about specific diseases).

United States Community Page Index

http://www.nsbol.com/nsbol/comindex/us_index.htm

This index is made up of community pages from every state in the U.S. A community page gives general information about the town and describes local events, area commerce, and tourism. Links are provided if you would like more information. The index also lists resources common to many communities.

U.S. State Department Travel Warnings

http://www.stolaf.edu/network/travel-advisories.html

As you know, the state of the world changes from day to day. The U.S. State Department tracks world conflicts and issues advisories for travelers.

This page contains a long list of links; each entry includes the date that the advisory was posted, and most provide a map of the country. Either click on a country link, or click on Search US-State-Department-Travel-Advisories to use a search index.

U.S. Travel and Tourism Administration (USTTA) Publications

http://www.doc.gov/resources/ustta/pubcat.html

On this page, you can learn about subscribing to or getting free publications. Subscriptions or low-cost publications include:

◆ USTTA Office of Research Information Updates and Alerts (including the USTTA Catalog of Selected Publications, Abstract of International Travel to and from the U.S., and other statistical and research data)

◆ *Summary and Analysis of International Travel to the United States*

◆ *Customized Profiles of International Travel to and/or from Canada*

◆ *In-Flight Survey of International Air Travelers*

◆ *Pleasure Travel Markets to North America*

◆ *Tourism USA* ($5)

Free publications include:

◆ *Outlook for International Travel to and from the United States*

◆ *Abstract of International Travel to and from the United States*

◆ *Historical Arrivals Data Base*

◆ *Impact of International Visitor Spending on State Economies, 1991 and 1992*

- *Analysis: Potential of International Pleasure Travel Markets to the U.S.*
- *Marketing Tourism Abroad: A Manual of International Cooperative Marketing Opportunities*
- *The United States Welcomes Handicapped Visitors*
- *World Tourism at the Millennium*
- *Tourism in the Caribbean Basin*
- *Business America*
- *The Implications of the North American Free Trade Agreement (NAFTA) for the Tourism Industry*
- *Traveler Safety and Security: Statistical Results of Industry Survey*
- *On the Road*

The USA CityLink Project

http://banzai.neosoft.com/citylink/default.html

This site is a comprehensive listing of World Wide Web pages featuring U.S. states and cities. After choosing a state, you can read general information about the state as well as information about specific cities in that state. A special feature is a relocation service, linking you with a local realtor.

The Virtual Tourist 2

http://www.vtourist.com/vt

This is a "map-based interface to City.Net, the Web's most extensive library of community." Click on an area of the world map, and you will be shown a map of just that area. Selecting a country from that area will take you to the City.Net directory for that country.

World-Wide Web Virtual Library: Zoos

http:www.mindspring.com/~zoonet/www_virtual_lib/zoos.html

This site's simple title does not convey its wealth of information about zoos and animals. Here you will find links to commercial and public zoos throughout the world, as well as links to private zoos and those zoos with specialized collections. Information on animals and insects, including pictures (see Figure 13.2) and audio, is also provided.

Entertainment Guides

Whether you're at home or on the road, finding concerts, games, and other events or places to go to is often a matter of searching through the local newspaper or listening to the radio. Using the Internet resources in this section, however, you can get right to it: look for an event or place, maybe check a seating diagram, and buy tickets—all online.

All American Events

http://cybermart.com/american/

All American Events, a ticket broker, links to "some of the hottest sports and events and concert tours in the country." At this attractive site, click on Weekly Special, SportsPage, ConcertPage, or ShowPage (Broadway Shows and Las Vegas Shows) to find out about the events (and team, performers, or theater) for which you might want to order tickets. Then call 1-800-270-6457 to place your order.

Disney Parks

http://www.best.com/~dijon/disney/parks/

This very simple site provides links to Disneyland, Walt Disney World, Tokyo Disneyland, and Disneyland Paris. You'll also find an extra link for the Hidden Mickey List, a compendium of Mickey Mouse shapes—not the obvious ones—that people have found while visiting these resorts.

Figure 13.2 An image from the ZooNet™ Bird and Fowl Gallery

Night Map

http://deck.com/entertain/nightmap/welcome.html

This site contains a growing list of nightspots in many major cities of the world. Much is under construction; so check back to see whether this attractive page expands.

Performing Arts on the Web

http://www.fdesigns.com/frcpa/perform.htm

This page contains links to other sources of information about the performing arts. It includes links to Boston Information Server Arts and Entertainment, Playbill On-Line™, Headquarters Entertainment Corporation Internet Entertainment Guide (professional, commercial theater productions), Yahoo Entertainment Listings (all types of entertainment from Amusement Parks to Virtual Reality), the Home Page of Theater, Royal Shakespeare Company, Theatre Central, ArtsNet Performing Arts Sites, the Galaxy Performing Arts Page, and the Performing Arts Information Web.

Theatre Central

http://www.theatre-central.com/

This site, the "hub of theatre resources on the Internet," has links to many theater or theater-related pages worldwide. You can start here to find the name of a theater in a city to which you will travel. Scroll down the page to see the table of contents under which you can link to many theater resources: New Links; Commercial & Non-Profit Theatre Companies; Specialty Professional Theatre Companies; Non-Professional Theatre Companies; Still Unclassified Theatre; Current Theatre, Shows & Facilities; Contacts and Associations; People; Scholastic and Educational Resources; Stagecraft; Literature and Playwright

Resources; Publications and Discussions; General Theatre Resources; and Film Resources. Click on a link to reveal a page of links; the small graphics to the left of each entry identify the type of site (for example, Web) and the country in which it is located.

Ticketmaster™ Online

http://www.ticketmaster.com:80/

Ticketmaster Online claims that it is "Ground Zero for Live Events." At this site, you can learn about popular events that have just occurred or are about to happen, get entertainment news, and even participate in a survey. Included here are the TM-Zagat Best of NY-LA Guide, Clubland, and Ticketmaster Travel.

Click on Events to browse a list of upcoming events—by category or by region of the U.S. Or click on Connections to find out about a particular venue. Click on the clickable map, select a venue, and click on Seating Chart before you buy your tickets.

Note
Another site at which you can find seating diagrams—primarily for sporting events and outdoor concerts—is the Stadiums and Arenas site at http://www.wwcd.com/stadiums.html.

World-Wide Web Virtual Library Museum Pages

http://www.comlab.ox.ac.uk/archive/other/museums.html
http://www.museum.state.il.us/vlmp/index.html

This site provides links to museums, galleries, and archives throughout the world. The museums are arranged by country or region. You can also search for museums by keyword. And be sure to look for the virtual exhibitions. At least one museum is added to this site each day; so plan to visit this site often.

Lodging

Looking for a place to stay for a night or a week? In this section, you'll find lists of resorts, databases with many hotels, and information about hostels. These lodging sites either include telephone numbers or links to online reservation systems.

All the Hotels on the Web

http://www.digimark.net/dundas/hotels/

As the title states, this is an index of hotels on the World Wide Web. When I visited, there were almost 7,000 listings, and the number continues to grow. Hotels are listed by geographical region and then further broken down by cities and countries within the region. Also featured are hotel chains around the world. Select a hotel, and you are likely to get a photograph of the hotel, address, phone number, rates, and additional features that the hotel offers.

Go Hosteling!

http://northcoast.com/~ebarnett/gohosteling.htm

This site is described as "The WWW Guide to Hosteling Culture, Itineraries and Services." Created by Gene Barnett, co-owner of the Avenue of the Giants/Ell River Redwoods Hostel, in Leggett, California, this site contains featured articles (Hostel-Hopping the Pacific Northwest, Cycling the Pacific Northwest, Hostel Reviews, Photographs), a listing of hostels in ski areas (with more special interest groups to come), as well as links to hostels throughout the world. If you are unfamiliar with hosteling, check the section called Hosteling for Newbies. This is a very informative site for those who would like to try this type of lodging.

Promus Hotels

http://www.promus-hotel.com/

At this site, you can find out about Promus Hotels: Embassy Suites, Hampton Inn, Hampton Inn & Suites, and Homewood Suites. Click on a logo to get descriptions and location information and to make reservations.

Resort Electronic Access Link (REAL)

http://www.realinfo.com:80/~bbrad/real.usa.html

REAL is an online, graphical information database of resort information for upper-income clients. Broken down by state and specific resort destination, this site features businesses, groups, and organizations in each market. This site is under construction.

TravelNow's Hotel and Motel Search

http://www.travelnow.com/tnow2.html

TravelNow provides links, by state, to accommodations in each state as well as British Columbia and Alberta, Canada. Here you also will find travel information and attractions.

World Wide Travel Exchange

http://www.pope.com/travelex

This promising site provides listings of accommodations: homes for exchange, vacation rentals, resort homes, and beds and breakfasts. Click on a link on the home page to reveal a page of links arranged by state and/or city. Sample listings included a photograph, a description of the site, links to or information about the area in which the lodging is located, and the name and telephone number of a contact.

Interesting Site

Resort Cam (at http://www.rsn.com/cam.html) from Resort Sports Network (RSN) not only provides almost up to date photographs of selected resorts but furnishes weather reports and snow conditions for ski areas—both well-known and obscure. Also included are links for college students looking for vacation spots. RSN also provides a link to the official home page for the U.S. Ski & Snowboard Team.

Maps

Maps show you features about an area. Depending on the type of map, you can see whether a region is relatively flat, hilly, or mountainous; or you can find out how to get from here to there. The sites in this section are just a few of the many map sites on the Internet.

Maps and References

http://www.cgrer.uiowa.edu/servers/servers_references.html

The University of Iowa Center for Global and Regional Environmental Research presents a page full of links to maps and desktop references arranged under these headings: Topics (a table of contents for the rest of the page), Map Sources and Information, Geographic References and Gazetteers, On-line Libraries and Book Information, Dictionaries/Glossaries, Telephone Directories, Searchable Bibliographies, and Other References. Many of these links are not to be found in other map and reference lists on the Internet.

Here you can find all sorts of maps, including United States national, state, regional, and city maps; foreign national and city maps; interactive maps; maps using the latest technologies (including Java and VRML); and even map stores. In the reference section are links to many online books, such as the classic *Elements of Style* and several foreign language to English dictionaries.

Interesting Site

Although the Texas Map Collection (at http://www.state.tx.us/maps.html) is a Texas site, you will find an extensive collection of maps for all over the world. Some of the maps in this collection are: static maps (including the On-line Map Exhibit, Texas Telephone Exchange Carriers Map, Surface Weather Map, and the U.S. Department of Agriculture Plant Hardiness Zone Map), clickable local and federal maps (Houston Real-Time Traffic Report Maps, the Digital Atlas, County Maps, the U.S. Census Bureau Data Map, and so on), and Clickable Private Organization Maps (including a U.S. Map, Dave's Map Collection, Endangered Species Map, Color Shaded Relief Map of US, and US Thematic Maps).

Map-Related Web Sites

http://www.lib.utexas.edu/Libs/PCL/ Map_collection/map_sites.html#state

This site provides links to map-related sites: Electronic Cartographic Reference Resources, General Map Sites, Country Map Sites, State Map Sites (U.S.), City Map Sites (International), and Weather Map Sites.

Ski Map Server

http://www.cs.umd.edu/~regli/ski.html

The Ski Map Server is brought to you by the University of Maryland Department of Computer Science. The goal of this site is to "serve images of ski resorts around the world." You can download from a growing list of resort photos, maps, and postcards. Information is available from the United States, Canada, and Europe. There is also a long list of other Internet sources for ski information. This site is invaluable for anyone interested in downhill skiing.

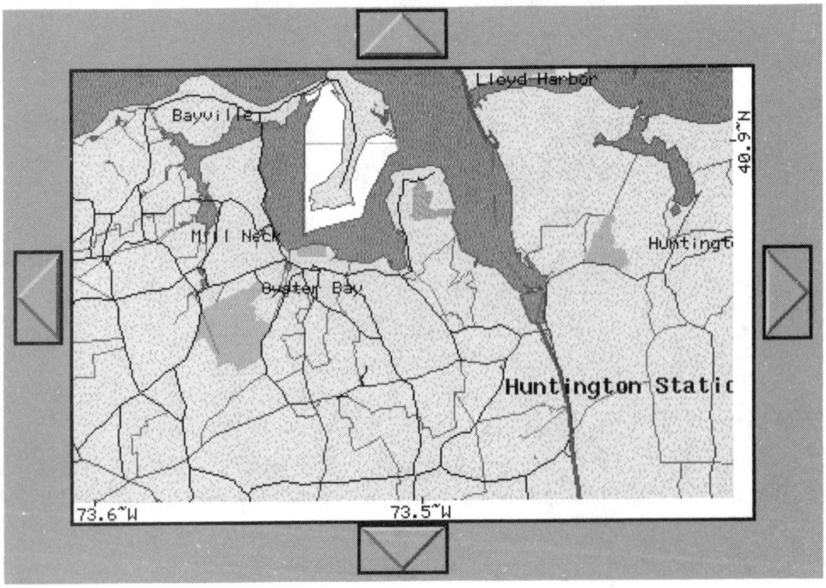

U.S. Gazetteer

http://tiger.census.gov/ cgi-bin/gazetteer

Type the name of a town or a city or the zip code in the searchable index, and this site will provide you with 1990 Census information as well as a map of the area. Click on the code location link to reveal the map (see Figure 13.3). Then click on one of the large arrows surrounding the map to go to an adjacent map. You can also zoom in and out and type longitudes and latitudes to show other maps.

Figure 13.3 Click on an arrow to reveal an adjacent map.

Xerox PARC Map Viewer

http://www.xerox.com/map

Click on a place on the world map to zoom in on the area. To zoom in again, click again. Various options allow you to add color, change projection, and add features.

Weather

Weather sites are some of the most innovative on the Internet. For example, if you have the appropriate viewers on your computer, you can see satellite images, animations, and movies. Or, if you have the most up to date browser, you'll find weather maps that change as you click on checkboxes. Of course, on the practical side, using the sites in this section, you can view a local weather map or a five-day forecast. You'll even find the *Old Farmer's Almanac* online.

The Daily Planet

http://www.atmos.uiuc.edu/

The Daily Planet is a very busy site managed by the Department of Atmospheric Sciences at the University of Illinois. The major links on the home page include The Weather Visualizer, UIUC—CoVis Geosciences Web Server (geoscience resources and archived weather data, etc.), Weather (maps, images, animations, and forecasts), Climate, Textbook (tutorials about weather), Horizon, and Servers.

The Weather Visualizer presents a clickable weather map of the U.S. A special feature is an experimental satellite map for those with Java browsers; check or clear a checkbox to change the look of the map instantly. This site is well worth exploring.

Environment Canada

http://www.on.doe.ca/

This site is the central place for Canadian weather forecasts, climate trends, and other weather services. Major headings under which links are organized are Welcome; What's New; Canadian Meteorological Centre; National Weather Services; Climate and Atmospheric Research; Policy, Program, and International Affairs; and Communications. To obtain a forecast for a province, click on Forecasts under Canadian Meteorological Centre, and click on the map (see Figure 13.4) or on a link in the list following the map. Then repeatedly click to narrow the forecast area.

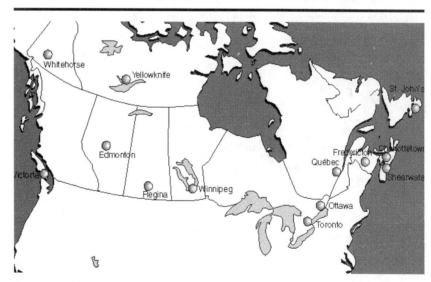

Figure 13.4 Click on the map to reveal a regional forecast.

INTELLiCast

http://www.intellicast.com/

NBC News presents INTELLiCast, which provides links to USA Weather, World Weather, Skiing, and NBC News. On the USA Weather page, you can get a national outlook, forecast for selected cities, images, and links to weather-related news stories—many that you can reach by scrolling down the page. If you click on a link, you might have to wait to jump down the page; this site is usually busy. To obtain weather information for a particular city, click on a city name, on the Complete Cities List, or on the two-letter state abbreviation following that list. The next set of links are weather images and movies. Before clicking on a link, look at the date and time that it was downloaded as well as its size. You can then make a choice based on how recently it was downloaded as well as the time that you are willing to wait for the image to appear.

Live Access Climate Data

http://ferret.wrc.noaa.gov/ferret/

This site provides climate conditions for any region in the world. You can find out the sea surface temperature, air temperature, wind speed, sea level pressure, or specific humidity for a particular place. You can zoom in to select a specific region, select the type of output, and select the data set from which you obtain the data. After selecting variables (see Figure 13.5), click on the Plot/Send Data button. Figure 13.6 shows a graph of COADS Monthly Climatology (1946–89) for sample longitudes and latitudes.

NJOnline Weather

http://www.nj.com/weather/index.html

From this handsome home page, you can obtain a five-day forecast and current conditions for U.S. cities and read history and pronouncements from the *Old Farmer's Almanac*, including Weather Ahead, Heavenly Details, and Ask the Almanac.

To find out the forecast and current conditions for a particular city, select it from one of the drop-down list boxes, and click on the Here button. To view the *Old Farmer's Almanac* prediction for your region, click on Weather Ahead, and click on your region on the map (see Figure 13.7).

The NOAA Weather Page

http://www.esdim.noaa.gov/weather_page.html

The National Oceanic and Atmospheric Administration (NOAA) presents a page of links

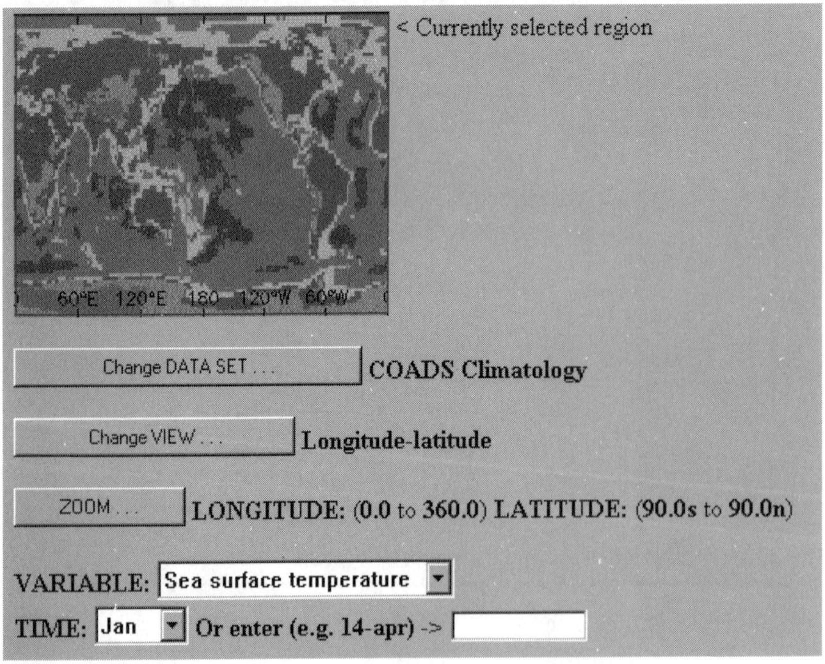

Figure 13.5 Select options to obtain specific data.

that not only provides weather information but also talks about NOAA and its plans for the future, provides links to National Weather Service (NWS) home and regional offices, and enables you to view geophysical images (aurora, biomass burning, city lights at night, hurricanes and tropical storms, and snow and ice). Also included are links to other weather pages from universities, organizations, and individuals. Links are arranged under the type of Internet resource: World Wide Web, Gopher, Telnet, Finger, FTP, and WAIS.

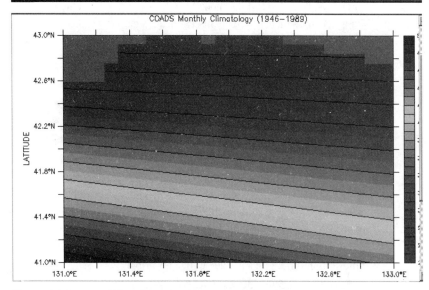

Figure 13.6 A graph of COADS Monthly Climatology (1946-89) for sample longitudes and latitudes

Purdue Weather Processor

http://thunder.atms
.purdue.edu/

The highlight of this well-designed site, from Purdue University, is a very clearly marked U.S. weather map on which you can click to display detailed information. Immediately preceding the map is a bar of links to forecast models and other weather data: Quick (links to images), SAT (satellite images), SFC (surface data), UPA (upper air data), MOS (Model Output Statistics), NGM (Nested Grid forecast Model), ETA (the planned successor to NGM), AVN (Aviation/MRF model forecasts), RUC (Rapid Update Cycle model forecasts), ECMWF (European Center for Medium

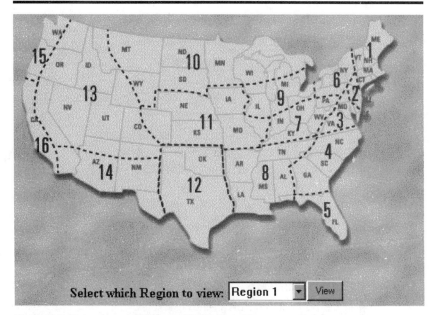

Figure 13.7 Click on a region to get an Old Farmer's Almanac prediction.

range Weather Forecasting model), <u>MRF</u> (Medium Range Forecast model), <u>MISC</u> (miscellaneous weather information: sea surface temperatures, hurricanes, U.S. Geological Survey maps, archives, and so on), <u>ARC</u> (image and map archive), <u>INT</u> (current data and forecasts for particular cities), and <u>HUR</u> (recent hurricanes and links to the NHC database).

UIUC Weather Machine

gopher://wx.atmos.uiuc.edu/

This very busy site from the University of Illinois at Urbana-Champaign is the source of other Internet weather pages. At this site, you can get information about the site itself and weather conditions all over the world. Links include <u>Canada</u>, <u>Caribbean</u>, <u>Case Studies</u>, <u>Documents</u>, <u>Hurricane Advisories and Images</u>, <u>Illinois</u>, <u>Images</u>, <u>International</u>, <u>Latin America</u>, <u>Other Servers</u>, <u>Regional</u>, <u>Satellite Discussion</u>, <u>Severe</u>, <u>States</u>, and <u>Status</u>.

U.S. Geological Survey Global Change Research Program

http://geochange.er.usgs.gov/pub/info/gch.html

The U.S. Geological Survey Global Change Research Program provides "reliable predictions of future climate changes and their effects." At this site, you can learn about research, access data sets, look at abstracts and the full text of papers, and search the site using a search index. <u>Data Sets</u> cover many topics, including the surface temperature of oceans, polar ice concentrations, various climates, analysis of the Arctic, volcano emissions, and glaciers.

U.S. Satellite Image and Conditions

gopher://atm.geo.nsf.gov/11/weather/North_America

This site, from the American Meteorological Society, presents the weather forecast and severe weather warnings for Washington, D.C. Also included are meteograms (graphs of weather conditions), for the area surrounding Washington, and surface statistics for the U.S. states.

U.S. Weather by State

gopher://ashpool.micro.umn.edu/11/Weather

Although this site has a link to Weather Service Satellite Maps, the other information found here is a text-based state-by-state listing of current weather conditions, today's weather forecast, and an extended weather forecast. Canadian weather, as well as information on earthquakes, tropical storms, and auroral activities is also available here.

Weather

gopher://groundhog.sprl.umich.edu/1/

This site provides weather information (some viewable by Macintosh computers running software that is compatible with the Moov format) with an educational point of view. Some of the features at this site include <u>Air Pollution</u>, <u>Curriculum Materials</u>, <u>Exploring the Internet</u>, <u>Famous Weather Events</u>, <u>Interactive Weather Maps</u>, <u>International Weather Maps</u>, <u>International Weather Watchers</u>, <u>K-12 School Weather Observations</u>, <u>Ozone Hole</u>, <u>Weather Animations</u>, and <u>Weather Images</u>.

The Weather Channel®

http://www.weather.com/

This commercial site allows you to choose a text-only or graphics home page. If you are new to this site, select the text-only page so that you can get an idea of the many choices here. For example, under <u>Weather Information</u>, you can choose from <u>current conditions and forecast</u>, <u>national maps</u>, <u>aviation maps</u>, <u>weather links</u>, <u>Atlantic tropical storm & hurricane maps</u>, or submit a question by clicking on <u>Met on the Net</u>. You can also <u>Get to know The Weather Channel</u>

(and look at a program guide) or link to Cool stuff from The Weather Channel (including the Meteorologist's Toolbox of weather-related articles and charts).

Weather Information Superhighway

http://thunder.met.fsu.edu:80/nws/public_html/wxhwy.html

The National Weather Service in Tallahassee, Florida, presents this comprehensive list of weather and meteorology sites. At the top of the page is a group of major links: USENET FAQs, Weather, WWW Virtual Library: Meteorology, University Weather Services, Government Weather Services, World Weather, U.S. Climate, Maps and Images, Tropical Weather, and Other Information (commercial weather sites and other weather-related sites). Either click on a link or scroll down the page (the best choice for a first-time visitor). Two advantages of using this site are that it is fast-loading, with only one graphic, and almost every link is accompanied by a short description.

Weather Underground

http://blueskies.sprl.umich.edu/

The University of Michigan presents a very popular and attractive weather site. Links on the home page include Blue-Skies™ (weather images), K-12 Activities, International Weather Watchers (links to an organization of weather watchers), Questions, Weather Underground, Who Are We? and WeatherNet.

Click on WeatherNet to access many weather-related sites. Just click on a menu bar with 10 buttons, from Main Menu to Software Archive and from Tropical Weather to Weather Servers.

Weather World

http://www.atmos.uiuc.edu/wxworld/html/top.html

Weather World is the World Wide Web counterpart to the popular University of Illinois Weather Machine Gopher site. Links on the home page are General Menu, Detailed Menu, First Time User, About Weather World, and Return to The Daily Planet (the home page for the Department of Atmospheric Sciences at the University of Illinois).

At the home page, click on General Menu to display a list of links to satellite images, MPEG animations, and weather maps. Detailed Menu presents links to images, maps, and additional weather forecasts and information. If you are a first-time visitor, be sure to click on First Time User, which summarizes the features of this site.

World-Wide Web Virtual Library: Meteorology

http://www.met.fu-berlin.de/DataSources/MetIndex.html

This long page of links could be the cornerstone of a meteorologist's or forecaster's weather resources. At this site, you can find links to Maps, Forecasts, Reports, RAW Data, Satellite Images, Movies, Climate, Interactiv [sic], Groups/Activities, and Libraries/Pointers for sites all over the world. Also included are statistics, commercial sites, and an index of images.

Restaurant Guides

One of the best things about travel is finding new restaurants. However, sometimes the results are mixed—from five-star to the pits. In this section, you can search for restaurants in a particular area and, in many cases, read a review before committing yourself.

Digital Dining® Directory and Guide

http://www.menu-net.com/

This promising but sparsely populated commercial site is a graphical home page with links to The Digital Dining! Directory, Best Restaurants, Celebrity Restaurants (a short list of celebrity-owned restaurants), All Restaurants (the same as clicking on The Digital Dining! Directory), and Cyber Cafés Worldwide. Clicking on The Digital Dining! Directory or All Restaurants reveals a page with a very small clickable U.S. map, a link to a page of state names, and links to selected cities. At this point, because the site seems very new, choose one of the selected cities;

otherwise, you may find pages with no information. When you obtain a list of restaurants, click on the first letter of a restaurant name to get a little more information—the name, address, and telephone number. Because this looks like an ambitious project, visit every once in a while to see whether more restaurants have been added.

Dining Out on the Web

http://www.ird.net/diningout.html

This excellent site presents many links to other Internet-based restaurant guides, organized under these headings: Comprehensive Sites, US Sites, and International Sites. Along with most entries is a short description or a mini-review of the site.

Essential Restaurant Guide

http://www.epicurious.com/epicurious/guide/guide.html

This promising and well-designed site not only reviews restaurants but also provides links to *Bon Appétit* and *Gourmet* magazines. On the home page, click on a city (Boston, Chicago, Houston, Los Angeles, Miami, New Orleans, New York, San Francisco, Seattle, and Washington DC), as shown in Figure 13.8. On that city's home page, click on a link to a restaurant and read a well-written review. Included in a typical review are the restaurant's history, the best items on the menu, setting (that is, decor), service, whether you should make a reservation, price range, and hours.

Clicking on the Drinking link reveals a searchable wine directory, a forum, and articles. The Playing page includes In Polite Company (how to eat particular foods), Victual Reality (articles),

epicurious
THE ESSENTIAL RESTAURANT GUIDE
Our critics share their favorite eating options in the cities below

Figure 13.8 Click on a graphic to read restaurant reviews for a particular city.

and Hot Links (links to diet, nutrition, and other pages, such as The American Heart Association Diet (at http://www.reg.uci.edu/UCI/CARDIOLOGY/PREVENTIVE/DIET/), Dr. Art Ulene's To Your Health (at http://www.vitamin.com/), and the Mail Order Gifts page (at http://www.epicurious.com/epicurious/play/links/links_gifts.html).

Kerry's Restaurant World

http://www.kerrymenu.com/Restaurants/index.html

Kerry's Restaurant World contains listings for restaurants in Atlanta, Boston, Chicago, Dallas, Los Angeles, Miami, New Jersey, New York, San Francisco, and Washington, D.C. To search this site, click on a city graphic. Then select a cuisine, price range, or neighborhood. Or you can look for a particular restaurant by using the search index or browsing the alphabetically arranged listing for the chosen city. The latter is the best choice if you want a complete selection of restaurants. For each entry on the list are its address, telephone number, cuisine, price, and neighborhood. To view a list of items on the menu, simply click on the name of the restaurant.

Kosher Restaurant Database

http://shamash.nysernet.org/kosher/krestquery.html

This large database enables you to search for kosher restaurants throughout the world. To find a restaurant, fill in the search form with as much information as you can. For example, to find restaurants in a particular U.S. state, type the two-letter U.S. Postal Service code; to look outside the U.S., type the country name. The results, which come almost instantly, show the name, address, telephone number, neighborhood, metropolitan area in which it is located, cuisine, price range, kosher category, and so on. If the entry is more than six months old, you are encouraged to update it.

The ULTIMATE Restaurant Directory

http://www.orbweavers.com/ULTIMATE/

This site provides a search index with which you can look for restaurants worldwide. On the home page, fill in the form: select from a long list of cuisine and type the name of a city (optional), zip code (optional), the two-letter state code (required if you are searching the U.S.), and country (required). Then click on the Submit Query button.

If you have the latest version of Netscape, one of the graphics at the top of the page changes to show a series of restaurant advertisements.

World Guide to Vegetarianism— USA

http://www.veg.org/veg/Guide/USA/index.html

This site provides extensive information on vegetarianism. Restaurant chains that include vegetarian menus as well as vegetarian restaurants listed by state are included here. The names of vegetarian organizations, magazines, newsletters, mail-order companies, travel agencies, and cooking schools are also provided.

Transportation

How do you get from here to there? In this section, you'll get some of the answers. You can obtain a variety of information about international airlines, railroads, highways, and more.

Airlines of the Web

http://haas.berkeley.edu/~seidel/airline.html/

This site, called "The Airlines of the WEB page," is a listing of all airline pages found by Marc-David Seidel, a graduate student at the University of California Berkeley. Here you can find information on passenger carriers throughout the world. Also included is information on Frequent Flyer Programs and other airline-related data.

Airline Toll-Free Numbers

http://www.princeton.edu/Main/air800.html

This text-only page provides a list of toll-free numbers for airlines worldwide. Also included are links to the AT&T 800 Directory and Airlines of the Web (see the entry in this section).

Amtrak

http://www.amtrak.com

This commercial site provides company information, generic travel hints, and information about railroad accommodations, checking luggage, the time to arrive at the station, and so on. Click on Amtrak's Routes to access route maps (see Figure 13.9). Unfortunately, you can't get schedule information here, but check Online Amtrak Schedules at http://libertynet.org/~dvarp/Amtrak. See its entry in this section.

Aviation Servers

http://acro.harvard.edu/GA/

If you're interested in aviation, you'll want to visit Harvard University's hierarchical and comprehensive list of aviation sites, ranging from the history of aviation to the Royal British Air Force Web page. Also included is an aviation archive, general aviation information, image archives, and weather information. The aviation archive contains valuable information

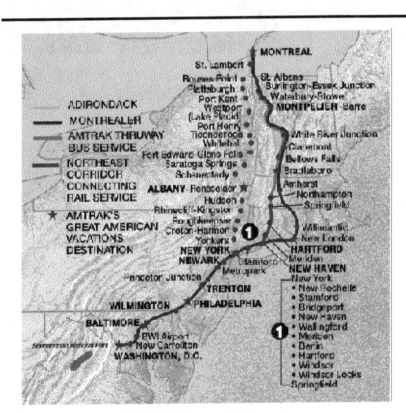

Figure 13.9 Amtrak route maps for the northeastern U.S.

such as federal aviation regulations and military aircraft information. The general aviation information area addresses topics such as planning databases and N number search engines. Those planning flights can check out current weather information via infrared maps, humidity images, and pressure patterns.

Federal Aviation Administration

http://www.faa.gov/faasites.htm

Interested in the latest aviation regulations? You can find the most up to date information online and free of charge at this site. This site provides links to FAA centers, groups, and laboratories; the FAA library and regional offices; and other flight-related information.

How Far Is It?

http://www.indo.com/distance/

This unique service tells you the straight-line, as-the-crow-flies distance between two points, usually in the U.S. So, if you are planning a trip, you can get a rough estimate of the time that it will take to get from point A to point B. In the From text box, type the name of the city or town and state (such as Boston, MA or Ivyland, PA), zip code, or longitude and latitude from which you will be traveling. In the To text box, type your destination, using the town/state, zip code, or longitude/latitude. Then click on the Look It Up button. After you have completed a search, you can click on these places on the map to use the Xerox PARC Map Viewer to look at your route.

Tip
To get a more accurate mileage, consider mapping out your route and finding intermediate points. Then run a series of searches from the beginning to the first intermediate city or town, ending with the last intermediate point and your destination.

Interesting Site

The Smithsonian Institution (at http://www.nasm.edu/) provides an excellent Web site for the National Air and Space Museum. Not only is the site educational, but it is very entertaining. Here, you can find an exhibition gallery, a calendar of events, department information, a resource page, educational programs, and statistical information. When visiting this site, don't miss the exhibition gallery. When you click on an exhibit, a new page containing full-color photographs and a complete description appears. Each of the exhibits at this site offer students of all ages an enormous amount of research information.

Online Amtrak Schedules

http://libertynet.org/~dvarp/Amtrak/

The Delaware Valley Association of Railroad Passengers provides this site for nationwide Amtrak information. The U.S. is divided into areas, and those areas are further broken down into local Amtrak service. Commuter rail connections to Amtrak are also available here.

Road Trip USA

http://www.moon.com/rt.usa/rdtrip/rdtrip.html

This site is described as a compendium of highways off the beaten path. Although this site is under construction, its developers aim is to compile those routes that would take the traveler to attractions, historic sites, and out of the ordinary Americana.

Subway Navigator

http://metro.jussieu.fr:10001/bin/cities/english

This popular and very busy site enables you to route a subway trip in a selected city. If a city has a subway system, you will probably find it here.

To find out about a particular subway system, click on a city name. The resulting page tells a little about the history of the selected subway system and contains text boxes in which you can type the name of the station from which you are departing and the station to which you plan to travel. If you don't know the names of the stations, click on *stations* to get a list. You can also click on *map* to view a clickable map of the system.

WWW Speedtrap Registry

http://www.nashville.net/speedtrap/

This site is a registry of sites, by state, where a motorist might encounter speed enforcement. Also included are sites in Australia, Canada, United Kingdom, and Sweden.

U.S. Travel Guide

If you've decided on a particular city, region, or state to visit, be sure to check out the resources in this section. Here you'll find 51 tables of resources—one for each state and for the District of Columbia. Those who have created the sites are usually experts: longtime residents; travel gurus; federal, state, or local government travel agencies; or businesses that either want to publicize their area at the same time they are publicizing themselves or help visitors and prospective employees find their way around.

Tables 13.4 to 13.54 present alphabetically arranged lists of travel sites for each state and the District of Columbia. In each table, statewide sites are listed before city, town, and regional sites.

Our Bookmarks, Which Are Ours

After a writer has worked for a few months on a book, he or she has explored his or her subject quite thoroughly and has formed definite opinions—both good and bad. When the book deals with the Internet, it's natural for an author to accumulate many outstanding and helpful sites on a Bookmark list or a Hot list.

Sandra E. Eddy is a full-time computer book writer. Her SYBEX books include *The Compact Guide to Lotus SmartSuite, Mastering Q&A for Windows* (with Michael M. Swertfager), and the upcoming *Mastering Lotus SmartSuite for Windows.* Table 13.1 reveals many of Sandy's bookmarks.

During the day, Michael M. Swertfager works at Mpath Interactive, Inc., as its Web Site Administrator. In the evenings, he runs his Internet presence provider company, Internet Presence and Publishing Services (IPPS). In addition to this book, Michael coauthored *Mastering Q&A for Windows* (SYBEX). Table 13.2 lists Michael's bookmarks.

Margaret M.E. Cusick acknowledges that she is a newcomer to the Internet and says, "I think that my getting to know the Internet shows that you don't have to know much about computers to take advantage of the Net. In the relatively short time that I have been on the Internet, the graphics have vastly improved, and the scope of information has grown by leaps and bounds. I hope that you find the Internet as intriguing and informative as I do." Table 13.3 lists just a few of Margaret's favorites.

Table 13.1: Sandy's Hot List

Site	URL	Description
Alta Vista	http://www.altavista.digital.com/	When SavvySearch is busy, Alta Vista is the one! It should almost always be available, thanks to its parent, Digital Equipment Corporation.
The Devil's Dictionary	http://www.wonderland.org/Works/ Ambrose-Bierce/The.Devils.Dictionary	A cynic's book of quotations. If the shoe fits…
Find It	http://www.cam.org/~psarena/find-it.html	Another search tool using many other Internet search indexes and master lists.
FTP search	http://ftpsearch.unit.no/ftpsearch	A fast FTP site search tool.
Hugh Chou	http://ibc.wustl.edu/~hugh/	And the calculators that show whether you can afford that house.
L. L. Bean	http://www.llbean.com/	An online version of its print catalog and information about national parks.
Martindale's 'The Reference Desk'	http://www-sci.lib.uci.edu/HSG/Ref.html	A group of every desktop reference known to man (or woman).
Money Quick Quotes—NSCP	http://www.pathfinder.com/money/quote/ qc?symbols=NSCP	How's Netscape doing today?
Netscape	http://home.netscape.com/	How's Netscape doing today?
NJOnline Weather	http://www.jm.com/weather/index.html	Weather forecasts and *Old Farmer's Almanac* predictions.
Not Just Cows	http://www.lib.lsu.edu/sci/njc.html	Agriculture, gardening, and so on.
Planet Access Networks	http://www.planet.net/	A pageful of the best Internet starting points.
Rocky Mountain Institute	http://solstice.crest.org/efficiency/rmi/ index.html	If you're planning on building an energy-efficient house, this is a top site.
SavvySearch Query Form	http://guaraldi.cs.colostate.edu:2000/form	My favorite search tool—it looks through several indexes and lists at once.
Scout Report	http://rs.internic.net/scout_report-index.html	Another excellent what's new site.
The Virtual Daily News	http://www.infi.net/~opfer/daily.htm	Links to virtually every source of news on the Net.
What's New with NCSA Mosaic	http://www.ncsa.uiuc.edu/SDG/Software/ Mosaic/Docs/whats-new.html	A long list of new World Wide Web sites, updated three times a week.
World-Wide Web Virtual Library: Subject Catalogue	http://www.w3.org/pub/DataSources/ bySubject/Overview.html	A source of comprehensive lists of sites.
Yahoo	http://www.yahoo.com/	The super master list that demonstrates that two grad students from Stanford can make it—big!

Table 13.2: Michael's Bookmarks

Site	URL
CGI Programming Tutorial	http://www.catt.ncsu.edu/~bex/tutor/index.html
CNN Interactive News Page	http://www.cnn.com/
HTML Verifier (checks for errors in HTML documents)	http://www.ijs.si/cgi-bin/htmlchek
Mastering Q&A for Windows	http://www.sybex.com/mastering.html#0-7821-1397-4
Mpath	http://www.mpath.com/
Mpath's Interactive Games	http://www.mplayer.com/
My Company	http://www.ipps.com
NCSA Web Server Site	http://hoohoo.ncsa.uiuc.edu/
Online PERL Manual	http://www-cgi.cs.cmu.edu/cgi-bin/perl-man
The President's Cabinet (index of all government departments online)	http://www.whitehouse.gov/White_House/Cabinet/html/cabinet_links.html
Unix Is a Four-Letter Word	http://tempest.ecn.purdue.edu:8001/~taylor/4ltrwrd/html/unixman.html

Table 13.3: Margaret's Top Eight List

Site	URL	What It's About
All the Hotels on the Web	http://duncas.digimark.net/hotels/	At this site, you will find a growing list of lodgings worldwide. The detail is amazing—you will usually be shown a photo of the hotel, its address, telephone number, cost, check-in and check-out times, the number of rooms, and so on. Many hotels allow you to make online reservations, and some include their restaurant's menu.
Amazon.com Books	http://www.amazon.com/	Amazon.com Books is self-described as the "Earth's biggest bookstore." It contains more than one million books, and you can select by author, subject, or keyword. Ordering is very easy, and shipment is prompt.
Folkworks Home Page	http://iquest.com/~virtual/folkworks/	This site is a compilation of work done by New England artisans and is an example of what a group can do to make their products available to the world. You will find photos and a short description of each item, including the price, and you can order online.
Museums	http://www.museum.state.il.us/vlmp/index.html	This site can connect you to museums, galleries, zoos, exhibitions, and archives throughout the world.
Peeping Tom Home Page	http://www.ts.umu.se/~spaceman/camera.html	This site links you to video camera views that are available on the Internet. You can look at a live picture of the Manhattan skyline; see what the weather is like in Stockholm; and view Sydney, Australia, from Matthew Perkins' living room. Fascinating—but the potential is a little scary.
Project Vote Smart	http://www.vote-smart.org/	Project Vote Smart was created to "provide voters with factual information on candidates and elected officials." Also included are government resources, elections (with all known candidates listed), and candidate information (biographical data, stands on the issues, campaign finances, and how to contact him or her).
Ticketmaster	http://www.ticketmaster.com/	As you can imagine, the Ticketmaster home page is your link to upcoming events in entertainment. Also included are features about the entertainers, a store, and much more. The best feature is the ability to view the seating arrangements at the arenas.
Views of the Solar System	http://bang.lanl.gov/solarsysy/	This site contains images and information about the solar system. The information is interesting, but the pictures are what makes this site special to me.

Table 13.4: Selected Alabama Travel Sites

Region [Site]	URL	Links
State of Alabama [City.Net—Alabama]	http://www.city.net/countries/united_states/alabama/	Cities, Counties, Education, Food and Drink, Government, Parks and Outdoors, State Information (Alabama's Information Center), and Television and Radio
State of Alabama [National Park Service—Alabama]	http://www.nps.gov:80/parklists/al.html	National Park Service Sites
Auburn [Auburn, Alabama]	http://www.viper.net/Auburn/	Introduction, Statistical Information, City Government, Alabama's Interactive Map, Community Information (Location, Population, Municipal, Education, Health, Recreation, General, Utilities, Transportation, Taxes, Plants, Industrial Expansions, Unions, and Industrial Incentives), Auburn University, and Auburn Chamber
Auburn [City.Net]	http://www.city.net/countries/united_states/alabama/auburn/	Auburn, Auburn Chamber of Commerce
Birmingham [The Birmingham Web Project]	http://www.the-matrix.com/	Web Page Locators, Matrix WWW Favorites (Birmingham Post-Herald, and more), News/Updated Local Pages, Events, Attractions, Museums, Historical Sites, Schools & Libraries, Government Agencies, Chambers of Commerce, Central Alabama Media, Arts, Non-Profit Organizations, Local Churches, Central Alabama Sports, and Other Alabama Cities on the WWW
Huntsville [City.Net—Huntsville, Alabama]	http://www.city.net/countries/united_states/alabama/huntsville/	Huntsville (Huntsville Chamber of Commerce), Travel and Tourism (Huntsville Convention and Visitors Bureau)
Huntsville [Huntsville, Alabama]	http://isotropic.com/metro/hunts.html?	Search, Metroscope, Alabama State W3, U.S. Government W3, World W3, Art and Entertainment Sites, Huntsville Business, Huntsville Media, Huntsville Internet Services, Huntsville Sports, Huntsville Colleges, Huntsville Guides, Huntsville Government, Professional Services, Huntsville Financial, Organizations and Groups, Other Huntsville Sites, Other Alabama Sites, American Universities, All Usenet FAQs, GNN Catalog, List of Lists, NCSA What's New, Multimedia Resources, Nonprofit Organizations, WWW Development, All in One Search, Virtual Library, World Art Resources, Yahoo's Index, Submit to Metroscope, What's New Sites
Tuscaloosa [Tuscaloosa Online]	http://www.dbtech.net/tuscaloosa	Business (Shop Online, Convention & Visitors Bureau, West Alabama Chamber of Commerce)Recreation (Movies, Sports, Entertainment, Clubs & Organizations), Education, Government, News and Internet Connections

Table 13.5: Selected Alaska Travel Sites

Region [Site]	URL	Links
State of Alaska [Alaska, USA]	http://isotropic.com/metro/alaska.html?	Search, Metroscope, Alaska State W3, U.S. Government W3, World W3, Art and Cultural Sites, Alaska Business, Alaska Media, Alaska Internet Services, Alaska Outdoors, Alaska Colleges, Alaska Guides, Alaska Government, AK Professional Services, Alaska Financial, Organizations and Groups, Other Alaska Sites, American Universities, All Usenet FAQs, GNN Catalog, List of Lists, NCSA What's New, Multimedia Resources, Nonprofit Organizations, WWW Development, All in One Search, Virtual Library, World Art Resources, Yahoo's Index, Submit to Metroscope, What's New Sites
State of Alaska [The Alaskan Center]	http://alaskan.com/	Visit the Alaskan Mall; Alaskan Adventures; Accommodations; Search Our Server; Alaskan Information; Alaskan Calendar of Events; Planning Your Visit; Travel Information (ISMPA); Community Profiles; Cities, Towns and Villages; Scenic Attractions; Government; Alaska Internet Sites; Current Alaska Weather; Free Visitors Guide: ACVB (Anchorage Convention and Visitors Bureau); Alaska's People Magazine
State of Alaska [Alaskana]	http://www.alaska.net/alaskana.html	An alphabetically arranged list of resources: travel, commercial, entertainment, from Adak to Vernair Flight Tours
State of Alaska [City.Net—Alaska]	http://www.city.net/countries/united_states/alaska/	Cities, Regions, Education, Events, Food and Drink, Government, Other Guides (Alaska's Cities, Towns and Villages), Parks and Outdoors, State Information, Television and Radio, Transportation, Travel and Tourism, and Travelogues
State of Alaska [Neptune's Alaska]	http://www.alaska.net:80/~akcache/	Neptune, Travel, Market, Great Outdoors, Accommodations, Source Book, Services, Greetings
Anchorage [City.Net—Anchorage]	http://www.city.net/countries/united_states/alaska/anchorage/	City Guides (Anchorage Community), Travel and Tourism (Alaska Internet Travel Guide, Anchorage CityLink)
Fairbanks [City.Net—Fairbanks]	http://www.city.net/countries/united_states/alaska/fairbanks/	General Information—The Falcon's Nest (Greetings, Where We Are, What It's Like Here, About Our School, Fairbanks Weather Conditions, Feature Articles, Alaskan Keypal, School District WWW Page)
Juneau [City.Net—Juneau]	http://www.city.net/countries/united_states/alaska/juneau/	City Guides (The Juneau Web), Government (The Capital City Home Page), Travel and Tourism (Juneau CityLink)

Table 13.6: Selected Arizona Travel Sites

Region [Site]	URL	Links
State of Arizona [Arizona Destinations]	http://www.amdest.com/	Arizona Internet Yellow Pages (Merchants and Global Shopping from The Arizona Marketplace), Arizona Attractions (Fun Things to See and Do), Arizona Lodging, Computer Services, Shopping, Sports, Children (Arizona Kids Net), Photography, Native American Pages, Politics, Celebrities, More Great Arizona Travel Pages, Current Market & Finance, Daily News, Magazines, and The World
State of Arizona [Arizonaguide]	http://www.arizonaguide.com/index.html	Festivals & Fiestas, 101 Things to Do, Golf, Maps, The Grand Canyon, Canyon Country, Indian Country, Arizona's West Coast, Central Territory, High Country, Valley of the Sun, and Old West Territory
State of Arizona [Arizonaguide Maps]	http://www.arizonaguide.com/maps/index.html	Arizona State Map, Phoenix & Valley of the Sun Map, Tucson Map, Detail Maps (Phoenix Street Map, Downtown Phoenix, Tempe Map, Scottsdale Shopping District Map, Mesa Map, Tucson City Center Map)
State of Arizona [City.Net—Arizona]	http://www.city.net/countries/united_states/arizona/	Cities, Counties, Arts and Entertainment, Education, Food and Drink, Government, Other Guides (Arizona's WebHub), Parks and Outdoors, Television and Radio, and Travel and Tourism
State of Arizona [National Park Service—Arizona]	http://www.nps.gov:80/parklists/az.html	National Park Service Sites
Flagstaff [Flagstaff CityLink]	http://banzai.neosoft.com/citylink/flagstaf/	What to See, What to Do, Where to Stay, Where to Eat, Where to Shop, and More Information
Flagstaff [Flagstaff Infoguide]	http://www.primenet.com/~iink/flag/nn.html	Calendar of Events; About Flagstaff; Current Weather and Forecast; Forest Activities: Kaibab National Forest, Coconino National Forest; Flagstaff Attractions; City Facilities; and Area Attractions
Phoenix [City.Net—Phoenix]	http://www.city.net/countries/united_states/arizona/phoenix/	City Guides, Other Guides, Parks and Outdoors, and Maricopa County
Phoenix [Phoenix, Arizona]	http://isotropic.com/metro/phoenix.html?	Search, Metroscope, Arizona W3, U.S. Government W3, World W3, Phoenix Art and Culture, Phoenix Business, Phoenix Media, Phoenix Internet Services, Phoenix Sports, Phoenix Colleges, Phoenix Guides, Phoenix Government, Professional Services, Phoenix Financial, Organizations and Groups, Other Phoenix Sites, Other Arizona Sites, American Universities, All Usenet FAQs, GNN Catalog, List of Lists, NCSA What's New, Multimedia Resources, Nonprofit Organizations, WWW Development, All in One Search, Virtual Library, World Art Resources, Yahoo's Index, Submit to Metroscope, What's New Sites

Table 13.6: Selected Arizona Travel Sites (continued)

Region [Site]	URL	Links
Scottsdale [City.Net—Scottsdale]	http://www.city.net/countries/united_states/arizona/scottsdale/	Businesses, Other Guides
Tucson [City.Net—Tucson]	http://www.city.net/countries/united_states/arizona/tucson/	Books and Libraries (Scenic Tucson), Businesses, City Guides, Other Guides, and Sports
Tucson [Tucson]	http://isatropic.com/metro/tucson.html?	Search, METROSCOPE, Arizona State W3, U.S. Government W3, World W3, Art and Entertainment Sites, Tucson Business, Tucson Media, Tucson Internet Services, Tucson Sports, Tucson Colleges, Tucson Guides, Tucson Government, Professional Services, Tucson Financial, Organizations and Groups, Other Tucson Sites, Other Arizona Sites, American Universities, All Usenet FAQs, GNN Catalog, List of Lists, NCSA What's New, Multimedia Resources, Nonprofit Organizations, WWW Development, All in One Search, Virtual Library, World Art Resources, Yahoo's Index, Submit to METROSCOPE, What's New Sites
Tucson [Welcome to Tucson]	http://www.tucson.com/tucson/	News, Dating, Parks, Community, Restaurants, Business Directory, Housing, Schools, Economy/Jobs, Government, Mover's Aid, and Calendar of Events

Table 13.7: Selected Arkansas Travel Sites

Region [Site]	URL	Links
State of Arkansas [City.Net—Arkansas]	http://www.city.net/countries/united_states/arkansas/	Cities, Education, Food and Drink, Government, Parks and Outdoors, Television and Radio
State of Arkansas [National Park Service—Arkansas]	http://www.nps.gov:80/parklists/ar.html	National Park Service Sites
Little Rock [Little Rock CityLink]	http://banzai.neosoft.com/citylink/lit-rock/	What to See, What to Do, Where to Stay, Where to Eat, Where to Shop, and More Information

Table 13.8: Selected California Travel Sites

Region [Site]	URL	Links
State of California [City.Net—California]	http://www.city.net/countries/united_states/california/	Cities, Counties, Islands, Regions, Education, Food and Drink, Government, Other Guides, Parks and Outdoors, Sports, Television and Radio, and Transportation
State of California [California Highway Conditions]	http://www.amdahl.com/internet/general/travel/ca-highway.html	Current Information (Construction, Closures, and Restrictions)
State of California [National Park Service—California]	http://www.nps.gov:80/parklists/ca.html	National Park Service Sites
State of California [Planet Earth Home Page—California]	http://www.nosc.mil/planet_earth/california.html	Sports Features, California Servers, Educational Resources, California State Government, California Images, Other California Resources, Search Engines and All Kinds of Numbers, Cities, Countries, and Images of the World
State of California [Regional Weather Forecasts]	http://www.svpal.org/weather.html	Weather Forecasts
State of California [Silicon Valley Pizza List]	http://WWW.Billboard.com/Pizza/PizzaList.html	San Jose, Milpitas, Sunnyvale, Campbell, Cupertino, Los Gatos, South Africa
State of California [Wine Country]	http://www.freerun.com/	Livermore Valley, Monterey, Napa Valley, Sonoma County, Temecula, Reference Library, What's New, Text Mode
Anaheim [Anaheim CityLink]	http://banzai.neosoft.com/citylink/anaheim/	What to See, What to Do, Where to Stay, Where to Eat, Where to Shop, and More Information
Berkeley [City.Net—Berkeley]	http://www.city.net/countries/united_states/california/berkeley/	Community Networks, Transportation
Berkeley [inBerkeley]	http://www.ci.berkeley.ca.us/	What's New in Berkeley; City Government, Agencies and Related Services; Arts and Entertainment, Businesses, and Community Resources; Bay Area Information; California State Information; and U.S. Federal Government Information
Big Bear Lake [Big Bear Lake, California]	http://www.web-link.com/bb-home.htm/	How to Get to Big Bear, Community Services Directory, Lodging Guide, Activities Guide, Events Calendar, and Real Estate Information
Burbank [Burbank Community Link]	http://linkto.burbank.k12.ca.us/	City of Burbank Home Page, Burbank Unified Schools Home Page, and Chamber of Commerce Tourist Information
Carlsbad [Carlsbad, California, USA]	http://www.bluebird.com/carlsbad/	Background, Local Information, Places to Go, Carlsbad on WWW and Internet, City Government, and Neighbors
Fresno [Fresno]	http://www.cybergate.com/~csjv/fresno/fresno.html	Free Fresno Brochure, Welcome Message, Visit Cityhall, Local Attractions, Map, Weather, California State University Home Page, Convention & Visitors Bureau, Chamber of Commerce, Veterans Memorial Auditorium, Medical Archives, Business Community, The Farmlands, Yosemite National Park, Kings Canyon National Park, Sequoia National Park, and Sequoia Gigantes

Table 13.8: Selected California Travel Sites (continued)

Region [Site]	URL	Links
Lake Tahoe [Lake Tahoe South Shore]	http://www.virtualtahoe.com/	Hotel/Casinos, Entertainment, Pillows for Your Head (Bed & Breakfast, Cabins, Casino Hotels, Guest Ranches, Hotels, Motels, Inns, Vacation Rentals), Ski Tahoe, Tahoe Emporium (Merchants), What's New, Tahoe-Douglas Chamber, South Lake Tahoe Chamber, Frequently Asked Questions, Year 'Round Recreation, Bon Appetit, Weddings & Honeymoons, Artistic Endeavors, Taking in the Sights, Real Estate, The Time Machine (The Area's History), Golden Opportunities (Information for Seniors), Getting Around, Child's Play, and Jump City (Internet Links)
Los Angeles [@LA]	http://emporium.turnpike.net/A/atLA/index.html/	Full Text Search of @LA, Go to the Full Index, Add a link/suggest a correction, What's New+User Guide, Reviews, Statistics+Feedback, Link of the Week, SuperLotto Results since 1986, @USA: Directory of City Directories, Arts_Sciences, Business, Classifieds, Community, Education, Entertainment, Government, News_Events, Online_Reference, Recreation, Sports, and Tourism
Los Angeles [City.Net—Los Angeles]	http://www.city.net/countries/united_states/california/los_angeles/	Arts and Entertainment, City Guides, Government, History and Literature, Magazines and Zines, Museums and Galleries, Other Guides, Transportation, and Travel and Tourism
Los Angeles [Fountainhead's Los Angeles Superstation]	http://www.fountainhead.com/super.html	Santa Monica BeachCam., Hot Site of the Moment, What's New, Home Pages, Traffic and Transportation, Weather, Sports, Disaster Information, Images From LA, Cruising LA, Visitor Information, Culture and Education, Business and Jobs, Community and Politics, Cities of Greater Los Angeles, and Other Useful Information
Los Angeles [Los Angeles, including Long Beach, Pasadena, & Santa Monica]	http://isotropic.com/metro/lamet.html	Search; Metroscope; California W3; U.S. Government W3; World W3; L. A. Art and Culture; Movies, TV, and Music; L. A. Business; L. A. Media; L. A. Internet Services; L. A. Sports; L. A. Colleges and Schools; L. A. Guides; L. A. Government; L. A. Professional Services; L. A. Financial; Groups & Organizations; Other L. A. Sites; Other California Sites; American Universities; All Usenet FAQs; GNN Catalog; List of Lists; NCSA What's New; Multimedia Resources; Nonprofit Organizations; WWW Development; All in One Search; Virtual Library; World Art Resources; Yahoo's Index; Submit to Metroscope; What's New Sites
Los Angeles [Things to do in L.A.]	http://cad.ucla.edu/repository/UCLA/TODO-off/TODO-off.html	Clubs, Restaurants, Coming Week, Foreseeable Future
Los Angeles [Virtually California- Los Angeles]	http://www.virtually.com/los_angeles/	Virtually Sightseeable, The Plaza, Virtually Academic, Virtually Entertaining, Virtually Hospitable, Virtually Delectable, and Locals Only
Marin County [Sally's Restaurant Listings]	http://www.bpe.com/dining/listings.marin100.html	List of recommended restaurants

Table 13.8: Selected California Travel Sites (continued)

Region [Site]	URL	Links
Monterey [Monterey]	http://www.monterey.com/california/mty/monterey.htm/	Things of Interest (Accomodations, Restaurant Guide, Arriving and Departing, Transportation, Convention Services, Weather, Climate, Time and Date, Cookbooks, Government, Chamber of Commerce, Travel and City Links), Museums, Calendar of Events, Play by the Bay, Shopping, Attractions, and Camping
Monterey [Monterey Bay Aquarium]	http://www.ucsc.edu/mb/mba/./	General Information, Our Purpose, Exhibits, Deadly Beauties, the New Wing, Education, Research, and Gift & Bookstore
Oakland [Oakland, California (including Berkeley, El Cerrito, & Hayward)]	http://isotropic.com/metro/oakland.html?	Search, Metroscope, California State W3, U.S. Government W3, World W3, Art and Cultural Sites, Oakland Business, Oakland Media, Oakland Internet Services, Oakland Sports, Oakland Metro Colleges, Oakland Metro Guides, Oakland Metro Governments, Oakland Metro Professional Services, Oakland Area National Laboratories, Organizations and Groups, Other Oakland Area Sites, Other California Sites, American Universities, All Usenet FAQs, GNN Catalog, List of Lists, NCSA What's New, Multimedia Resources, Nonprofit Organizations, WWW Development, All in One Search, Virtual Library, World Art Resources, Yahoo's Index, Submit to Metroscope, What's New Sites
Palo Alto [Palo Alto Chamber of Commerce]	http://www.persimmon.com/palo/chamber/home.html	What's New, Events, Guides (Entertainment, Shopping, Lodging, Resources)
Palo Alto [Palo Alto Downtown Restaurarnts]	http://www.persimmon.com/palo/chamber/entertainment/restaurants/map-downtown.html	Select an eatery from the Palo Alto map, a clever way to find out about a restaurant and its location.
Sacramento [Artdirect Guide to Sacramento]	http://www.artdirect.com/california/sacramento/homepage/	Art Galleries, Performing Arts, What's New, Museums, Regional Arts & Artists, Festivals, Music, Architecture, Parks, and Gardens
Sacramento [City.Net—Sacramento]	http://www.city.net/countries/united_states/california/sacramento/	City Guides, Travel and Tourism
Sacramento [Sacramento CityLink]	http://banzai.neosoft.com/citylink/sacramento/	What to See, What to Do, Where to Stay, Where to Eat, Where to Shop, and More Information
San Diego [City.Net- San Diego]	http://www.city.net/countries/united_states/california/san_diego/	San Diego Guide, San Diego Information at UCSD, Traffic Report, Photographs, InfoPost, City Guides, Government, Museums and Galleries, Other Guides, Parks and Outdoors, Travel and Tourism

Table 13.8: Selected California Travel Sites (continued)

Region [Site]	URL	Links
San Diego [San Diego]	http://isotropic.com/metro/sandiego.html?	Search, METROSCOPE, California W3, U.S. Government W3, Art and Entertainment Sites, San Diego Business, San Diego Computer Sites, San Diego Media, San Diego Internet Services, San Diego Sports, San Diego Colleges, San Diego Guides, San Diego Government, SD Professional Services, Organizations and Groups, Other San Diego Sites, Other California Sites, American Universities, All Usenet FAQs, GNN Catalog, List of Lists, NCSA What's New, Multimedia Resources, Nonprofit Organizations, WWW Development, All in One Search, Virtual Library, World Art Resources, Yahoo's Index, Submit to METROSCOPE, What's New Sites
San Diego [San Diego CityLink]	http://banzai.neosoft.com/citylink/sandiego/	What to See, What to Do, Where to Stay, Where to Eat, Where to Shop, and More Information
San Francisco Area [Bay Area Restaurant Guide]	http://www.w3.com/food	City/Type Listings, Search Reviews, Search Restaurants, Interactive Map, Alphabetical Listings, All Restaurants by Type, Top Reviewers, Restaurant w/ Home Pages or Photos, Your Restaurant List, New Reviews, Add a Restaurant
San Francisco [City.Net—San Francisco]	http://www.city.net/countries/united_states/california/san_francisco/	Arts and Entertainment, Books and Libraries, City Guides, Events, General Information, Government, Magazines and Zines, Maps, Museums and Galleries, News, Other Guides, Transportation, Travel and Tourism
San Francisco [Golden Gate National Recreation Area]	http://www.nps.gov/parklists/index/goga.html	Visitation, Location, Address, Telephone, Operating Hours, Climate, Directions, Transportation, Fees, Facilities and Opportunities, Additional Attractions, Trails, Roads, Programs/Activities, Lodging and Camping Facilities, Food/Supplies, Accessibility, Special Needs, Recommended Activities/Park Use, Reservations/Permits, Basic Visit Recommendations, Special Events, Adjacent Attractions
San Francisco [San Francisco Bay Area Transit Information]	http://server.berkeley.edu/Transit/index.html	Announcements, Transit Agencies (Map of Bay Area Transit Agencies, Map by County, Local & Regional Transit Services, Amtrak, Greyhound), Regional Information (Airport Service, Service to Sporting Events/Concerts, Bicycle and Commuter Information, More About Bay Area Public Transit), and Administrivia
San Francisco [San Francisco]	http://isotropic.com/metro/sanfran.html?	Search, METROSCOPE, California W3, U.S. Government W3, San Francisco Art Sites, San Francisco Business, San Francisco Media, SF Internet Services, San Francisco Sports, San Francisco Colleges, San Francisco Guides, San Francisco Government, SF Professional Services, San Francisco Financial, Organizations and Groups, Other San Francisco Sites, Other California Sites, American Universities, All Usenet FAQs, GNN Catalog, List of Lists, NCSA What's New, Multimedia Resources, Nonprofit Organizations, WWW Development, All in One Search, Virtual Library, World Art Resources, Yahoo's Index, Submit to METROSCOPE, What's New Sites

Table 13.8: Selected California Travel Sites (continued)

Region [Site]	URL	Links
San Francisco [Virtually California—San Francisco]	http://www.virtually.com/san_francisco/	Virtually Sightseeable, The Plaza, Virtually Academic, Virtually Entertaining, Virtually Hospitable, Virtually Delectable, Locals Only
San Francisco Area [Bay Area Restaurant Guide]	http://www.sfbay.com/food	Restaurants by City/Type, Reviews, Restaurant Search, Interactive Map, Alphabetical Listings
San Francisco Area [Waiters on Wheels]	http://www.ird.net/cgi/get?wow/index.f12pjo_zl~s/	Atherton, Belmont, Burlingame, Campbell, Concord, Cupertino, Foster City, Hillsborough, Lafayette, Los Altos, Menlo Park, Millbrae, Mountain View, Palo Alto, Pleasant Hill, Redwood City, Redwood Shores, San Carlos, San Francisco, San Jose, San Mateo, Santa Clara, Saratoga, Sunnyvale
San Jose [San Jose, California]	http://isotropic.com/metro/sanjose.html?	Search, METROSCOPE, California W3, U.S. Government W3, Art and Entertainment Sites, San Jose Business, San Jose Computer Web Sites, San Jose Media, San Jose Sports, San Jose Internet Services, San Jose Colleges, San Jose Guides, Professional Services, San Jose Financial, Organizations and groups, Other San Jose Sites, Other California Sites, American Universities, All Usenet FAQs, GNN Catalog, List of Lists, NCSA What's New, Multimedia Resources, Nonprofit Organizations, WWW Development, All in One Search, Virtual Library, World Art Resources, Yahoo's Index, Submit to METROSCOPE, What's New Sites
Santa Cruz [City.Net—Santa Cruz]	http://www.city.net/countries/united_states/california/santa_cruz/	Arts and Entertainment, City Guides, General Information, Other Guides, and Sports
Santa Cruz County [Santa Cruz County]	http://www.cruzio.com/	Feature Articles, Community Information (Arts, Business, Community Indexes, Online Library, Community Service Groups, Education, Government, Leisure & Entertainment, County Online Resources, WWW White Pages, Weather, Tides and Surf
Santa Monica [City.Net—Santa Monica]	http://www.city.net/countries/stataes/california/santa_monica/	City Guides, Travel and Tourism
Santa Monica [Santa Monica Web]	http://www.smweb.com/	What's Up, Visitors Info, City Home Page, Community, Marketplace, Calendar of Events, Entertainment, Restaurants, Lodging and Shopping
Sonoma County [Sonoma County Wine and Visitors Center]	http://www.geninc.com/geni/USA/CA/Sonoma/travel/index.html	Visitor & Convention Bureaus, About the Area (Area Map), What to See and Do, Visitors Guides, Helpful Information (Location, Weather), Conference/Convention Facilities, Helpful Organizations, and Nearby Cities
Sonoma County [Sally's Restaurant Listings]	http://www.bpe.com/dining/listings.sonoma.html	List of recommended restaurants
Yosemite [Yosemite National Park—National Park Service]	http://www.nps.gov:80/parklists/index tose.html/	Visitation Statistics; Location; Telephone; Operating Hours, Seasons; Climate; Directions; Transportation; Fees; Facilities and Opprtunities (Visitor Center/Exhibits, Trails, Roads, Programs/Activities, Lodging and Camping Facilities, Food/Supplies, Other Concessions); Recommended Activities; Reservations

Table 13.9: Selected Colorado Travel Sites

Region [Site]	URL	Links
State of Colorado [City.Net—Colorado]	http://www.city.net/countries/united_states/colorado/	Cities, Counties, Community Networks, Education, Events, Food and Drink, General Information, Government, Other Guides, Parks and Outdoors, Sports, Television and Radio
State of Colorado [Colorado State Parks]	http://www.aaeo.com/co_parks/cospmenu.html	Northern Region, Metro Region, Southern Region, and Western Region
State of Colorado [Detailed Colorado Weather]	gopher://weather.colorado.edu:361/1	Climatic Summary for Alamosa, Climatic Summary for Colorado Springs, Climatic Summary for Denver, Climatic Summary for Grand Junction, Climatic Summary for Pueblo, Colorado Avalanche Warnings, Colorado Regional Weather Forecasts, Colorado River Statement, Colorado Road Report, Colorado Ski Area Report, Colorado Temp. and Precip. Table, Current Metro Area Forecast, Denver Climatological Summary for 1993, Denver Climatological Summary for 1994, Hourly Colorado Weather Roundup, Last Record Weather Event, Limon Radar Summary, Monthly Climate Summary for Denver, Special Weather Statement, Stapleton Climate Report, State Forecast for Colorado, Today in Metro Denver Weather History
State of Colorado [National Park Service—Colorado]	http://www.nps.gov:80/parklists/co.html	National Park Service Sites
Aspen [Aspen Snowmass OnLine]	http://www.aspenonline.com/aspenonline/	News, Events, & Special Features; Visitor and Activity Guide; Reservations & Vacation Packages; The Aspen Catalog; Community Information; Weather; Ski Conditions; and Great Links
Boulder [Boulder Home Page]	http://www.boulder.org/	Recreation, Ski Conditions, Guide Lines (Dining, Shopping, Lodging, Professional Services, Real Estate, Recreation, University of Colorado at Boulder, and Boulder Media), Events This Week, Profile of the Month
Boulder [CU/Boulder Temperature Gateway]	http://www.cs.colorado.edu/htbin/temp/	Current Temperature, Weather Forecast, and Ski Area Reports
Denver [Denver Area Restaurant Guide]	http://www.w3.com/denver	City/Type Listings, Search Reviews, Search Restaurants, Interactive Map, Alphabetical Listings, All Restaurants by Type, All Reviews, Top Reviewers, Your Restaurant List, New Reviews, Add a Restaurant
Denver [Denver CityLink]	http://banzai.neosoft.com/citylink/denver/	What to See, What to Do, Where to Stay, Where to Eat, Where to Shop, and More Information
Denver [Denver, Colorado]	http://isotropic.com/metro/denver.html?	Search, Metroscope, Colorado W3, U.S. Government W3, World W3, Art and Entertainment Sites, Denver Business, Denver Media, Denver Sports, Colleges & Universities, Denver Internet Services, Denver Web Guides, Groups and Organizations, Other Denver Sites, Other Colorado Sites, American Universities, All Usenet FAQs, GNN Catalog, List of Lists, NCSA What's New, Multimedia Resources, Nonprofit Organizations, WWW Development, All in One Search, Virtual Library, World Art Resources, Yahoo's Index, Submit to Metroscope, What's New Sites
Vail [Vail Valley, USA]	http://www.realinfo.com/real/vail.home.html	Vail Daily News; Hotels and Restaurants; Real Estate; Roads and Weather; Catalogs, Retail, Guides, and Outfitters

Table 13.10: Selected Connecticut Travel Sites

Region [Site]	URL	Links
State of Connecticut [City.Net—Connecticut]	http://www.city.net/countries/united_states/connecticut/	Cities, Arts and Entertainment, Businesses, Economics, Food and Drink, Government, Parks and Outdoors, State Information, Television and Radio
State of Connecticut [Connecticut]	http://isotropic.com/metro/conn.html?	Search, Metroscope, Connecticut State W3, U.S. Government W3, World W3, Art and Entertainment Sites, Connecticut Business, Connecticut Media, Connecticut Towns, CT Internet Services, Connecticut Sports, Connecticut Colleges, Connecticut Guides, Connecticut Government, CT Professional Services, Connecticut Financial, Organizations and Groups, Other Connecticut Sites, American Universities, All Usenet FAQs, GNN Catalog, List of Lists, NCSA What's New, Multimedia Resources, Nonprofit Organizations, WWW Development, All in One Search, Virtual Library, World Art Resources, Yahoo's Index, Submit to Metroscope, What's New Sites
State of Connecticut [The Connecticut Guide]	http://ctguide.atlantic.com	Information, News, New Servers, Web Sites, Connecticut Winning Lottery Numbers
State of Connecticut [Connecticut Maps]	http://www.connecticut.com/maps/	Small, Large and Huge
State of Connecticut [Connecticut State Parks]	http://www.connecticut.com/parks/	Camping in Connecticut, River Camping, Connecticut State Parks Addresses, and Connecticut State Forests
State of Connecticut [Connecticut Tourism Guide]	http://ctguide.atlantic.com/vacguide/	Coast & Country, The Crossroads, Gateway to New England, Litchfield Hills, The Quiet Northeast Corner, River Country, and The Valleys
State of Connecticut [National Park Service—Connecticut]	http://www.nps.gov:80/parklists/ct.html	National Park Service Sites
Hartford [Welcome to Hartford, CT!]	http://www.hartford.edu/city/hartford.html	About Hartford (History, Area, and Climate), Business, Economy, Entertainment, Sports, Attractions, Schools, Health Services, Restaurants, Government, Getting Around, and Shopping
Mystic [Welcome to Mystic Seaport]	http://www.mystic.org/	Bark Charles W. Morgan, Catboat Breck Marshall, Ship Joseph Conrad, Visiting the Museum, Educational Programs, Collections and Research, Products and Services, About the Museum, About This Site

Table 13.11: Selected Delaware Travel Sites

Region [Site]	URL	Links
State of Delaware [City.Net Delaware]	http://www.city.net/countries/united_states/delaware/	Newark; Wilmington; Delaware State Chamber of Commerce; Delaware K-12 Schools (Web66); Delaware Trade Shows, Conferences, and Exhibitions (EXPOguide); Delaware Restaurants (A la Carte Guide); Delaware Vegetarian Restaurants (World Guide to Vegetarianism); Delaware Internet Directory (Virtual Enterprises); Delaware State and Local Government (Library of Congress); Delaware Members of the U.S. House of Representatives; State of Delaware; Bigshout Magazine; Index of Delaware Web Sites; Botanical Gardens in Delaware (GardenNet); Delaware Public Broadcasting Stations; At the Beach—Delaware; World Beat—Rough Guide—Delaware (HotWired); United States
State of Delaware [Delaware Public Transit]	http://www.state.de.us/tourism/transit.htm	Buses, Rail Systems, and Water Ways
State of Delaware [Delaware Tourism]	http://www.state.de.us/tourism/intro.htm	Attractions & Historic Sites, Scenic Towns & Drives, Outdoor & Sports Facilities, State Parks, Performing Arts, Guide Services, Travel Information, Airline & Airport Information, and Public Transit
State of Delaware [Delaware State Parks]	http://www.state.de.us/tourism/stparks.htm	General Information, Alphabetical Listing

Table 13.12: Selected District of Columbia Travel Sites

Region [Site]	URL	Links
District of Columbia [City.Net—Washington, D. C.]	http://www.city.net/countries/united_states/district_of_columbia/washington/	Arts and Entertainment, City Guides, Events, Food and Drink, Government, Museums and Galleries, Other Guides, Sports, Transportation, Travel and Tourism
District of Columbia [D.C. Restaurant List]	http://www.ngen.com/nextgen/restaurant/	Restaurants by Area, Type of Food, or Price Range
District of Columbia [Downtown Washington]	http://www.whitehouse.gov/White_House/EOP/html/DC_map.html	Detailed maps showing Government Buildings and Tourist Sites
District of Columbia [National Park Service—Nation's Capital]	http://www.nps.gov:80/parklists/dc.html/	National Park Service Sites
District of Columbia [National Zoo]	http://www.si.edu/organiza/museums/zoo/homepage/nzphome.htm	Zoo Highlights, Zoo Views (Behind the Scenes Look, New Exhibits, Newsletters), Zoo News (Coverage of National Zoo People, Programs, Plants, and Animals), Animal Photo Library, and Survey Questionnaire

Table 13.12: Selected District of Columbia Travel Sites (continued)

Region [Site]	URL	Links
District of Columbia [Smithsonian Air & Space Museum]	http://ceps.nasm.edu/	Exhibition Galleries; Calendar of Events; Departments; Resources; Educational Programs; About the Museum; Online Resources; and Info, Stats, etc.
District of Columbia [Smithsonian Institution]	http://www.si.edu/start.htm	Welcome (Overview of Smithsonian Museums, Navigating the Electronic Smithsonian, Smithsonian Search, Answers to Frequently Asked Questions, Planning a Visit), View from the Castle (Topical Issues, News Releases, Secretary of the Smithsonian Speeches), What's New (New and Temporary Exhibitions, Additions), You and the Smithsonian (Membership, Fellowship, Internship, and Volunteering Information), Departments (Places-Information on Locations, Hours, Exhibits, Events, etc.), People (Staff), Activities (Listing of Exhibitions, Events, Travelling Exhibitions), Perspectives, Resources (Smithsonian Magazine, Radio Smithsonian, Discussion Groups), and Products (Shopping Mart, Shopping Mall)
District of Columbia [United States Holocaust Memorial Museum]	http://www.ushmm.org/	General Information, Planning Your Visit, Research Institute, Education, and Other Resources, Conferences, Calendar, Camp Song, Readings, About the Archives & the Query System, and Query the Archives Data
District of Columbia [Washington, D. C.]	http://isotropic.com/metro/washdc.html?	Search, METROSCOPE, D. C. W3, U.S. Government W3, Art and Cultural Sites, D. C. Business, D. C. Internet Services, D. C. Media, D. C. Sports, Washington D.C. Guides, Washington Financial Sites, Washington Colleges, Government Sites, Professional Services, Organizations and Groups, Medical and Scientific Sites, Other D. C. Sites, American Universities, All Usenet FAQs, GNN Catalog, List of Lists, NCSA What's New, Multimedia Resources, Nonprofit Organizations, WWW Development, All in One Search, Virtual Library, World Art Resources, Yahoo's Index, Submit to METROSCOPE, What's New Sites
District of Columbia [Washington DC Area Multi-Scale Map]	http://www.c3.lanl.gov/~cjhamil/Browse/dc1.html	Map of the District of Columbia and Surrounding Suburbs (Click on Area or Select Site for Detail)
District of Columbia [The Washington DC City Pages]	http://dcpages.ari.net/	Arts, Commerce, Dining, Computing, Education, Entertainment, Government, recreation, Regional, Tourist, Travel, Weather, What's New, Search Options, HTML 2.0 Version, DC Pages Info
District of Columbia [Washington, DC, Metro Area Art Calendar]	http://www.dc202.com/artcal.html	Science and History, National Gallery of Art, American Art Museum, Arthur M. Sackler Gallery, National Air and Space Museum, National Museum of Women in the Arts, National Portrait Gallery, National Museum of American Art, Corcoran Gallery of Art, National Building Museum, Hirshhorn Museum and Sculpture Garden, National Museum of African Art, Freer Gallery of Art, Phillips Collection, Calendars for Upcoming Art Exhibits
District of Columbia [Washington DC Transportation]	http://www.proxima.com/dc/tourist/transport.html	Railroads, Subways, Car Rental, Downtown Washington Map, Tourist Map, Union Station, Virginia Map, and D.C. Satellite Map

Table 13.12: Selected District of Columbia Travel Sites (continued)

Region [Site]	URL	Links
District of Columbia [Washington Tourism]	http://www.proxima.com/dc/tourist/	Attractions, Museums, Memorials, Sports, Transportation, Places to Stay, Restaurants, Entertainment, Area Day Trips, Washington, D.C. Virtual Tour, and Trade Tips (What to See and Where to Go)
District of Columbia [The White House]	http://www.whitehouse.gov/	The Executive Branch, The First Family, What's New, Publications, Comments, and Tours (White House, Executive Office Building, and First Ladies' Garden)
District of Columbia [WorldNet—Washington, District of Columbia]	http://www.goworldnet.com/cgi-gin/rbox/gohtml?U.S.A.&District_of_Columbia&Washington/	Accommodations, Attractions, Dining, Nightlife, Performing Arts, Points of Interest, Sports, Tours, and Visitor Information

Table 13.13: Selected Florida Travel Sites

Region [Site]	URL	Links
State of Florida [City.Net—Florida]	http://www.city.net/countries/united_states/florida/	Cities, Counties, Islands, Regions, Businesses, Education, Food and Drink, Government, Magazines and Zines, Other Guides, Parks and Outdoors, Television and Radio, Travel and Tourism
State of Florida [Florida Camping Directory]	http://florida.com/parkwel.htm	RV Parks and Campgrounds by Regions
State of Florida [Florida State Parks]	http://www.dep.state.fl.us/parks/index.html	Recreational Activities/Interests, Parks by Geography, Parks by Special Calendar Events, Index of Parks, Other US Parks and Forests, and Special Park Programs
State of Florida [infoGuide]	http://infoguide.com/	South Florida, Central Florida, Florida's West Coast, Travel Needs, Attractions, Business Center, Real Estate, Internet Classified, and the Bahamas
State of Florida [National Park Service—Florida]	http://www.nps.gov:80/parklists/fl.html	National Park Service Sites
Daytona Beach [Daytona Beach CityLink]	http://banzai.neosoft.com/citylink/daytona	What to See, What to Do, Where to Stay, Where to Eat, Where to Shop, and More Information
Fort Lauderdale [Greater Fort Lauderdale Home Page and Visitors Guide]	http://www.introweb.com/fortlauderdale/mainmenu.htm	Accommodations, Restaurants, Attractions, Where We Are and What It's Like, and Local Businesses
Jacksonville [Jacksonville CityLink]	http://banzai.neosoft.com/citylink/jackvill/	What to See, What to Do, Where to Stay, Where to Eat, Where to Shop, and More Information

Table 13.13: Selected Florida Travel Sites (continued)

Region [Site]	URL	Links
Key West [Discover: Key West]	http://discover.key-west.fl.us/	Accommodations, Events & Festivals, Discount Coupons, Diving & Snorkeling, Fishing & Boating, Museums, Real Estate, Weather, Tours, Transportation, Theaters & Art Galleries, Shopping, Services, Restaurants & Bars
Miami [Greater Miami Convention & Visitors Bureau]	http://www.neptune.com/bureau/bureau.html	The Arts, Lodging, Attractions & Museums, Recreation, Restaurants, Festival Fever, Shopping, Getting Around, Visitor Information, What's Happening, Neighborhoods, Sightseeing, Maps, Nightlife, and Sports
Miami [Miami, Florida]	http://isotropic.com/metro/miami.html?	Search, Metroscope, Florida State W3, U.S. Government W3, World W3, Art and Entertainment Sites, Miami Business, Miami Media, Miami Internet Services, Miami Web Publishers, Miami Sports, Miami Colleges, Miami Guides, Professional Services, Miami Financial, Miami Government, Organizations and Groups, Other Miami Sites, Other Florida Sites, American Universities, All Usenet FAQs, GNN Catalog, List of Lists, NCSA What's New, Multimedia Resources, Nonprofit Organizations, WWW Development, All in One Search, Virtual Library, World Art Resources, Yahoo's Index, Submit to Metroscope, What's New Sites
Miami [Miami Maps]	http://www.neptune.com/cgi-bin/imagemap/bureau?345,104	Miami Reference Maps
Miami [Subway System of Miami]	http://metro.jussieu.fr:10001/bin/select/english/usa/miami	MetroRail and MetroMover Stations
Orlando [Welcome to Orlando]	http://intpro.com/orlando/	Accommodations, Attractions, Business Directory, Real Estate, City of Orlando, Entertainment, Events, Shopping, and Travel Information
South Florida [XSO's South Florida Restaurant Locator]	http://www.xso.com/permanent/search_restaurants.htm	Restaurant Reviews by Type, by Location
Tallahassee [Tallahassee, Florida]	http://isotropic.com/metro/talla.html?	Search, METROSCOPE, Florida State W3, U.S. Government W3, Art and Cultural Sites, Tallahassee Business, Tallahassee Media, Tallahassee Internet Services, Tallahassee Sports, Tallahassee Colleges, Tallahassee Guides, Tallahassee Government, Professional Services, Organizations and Groups, Other Tallahassee Sites, Other Florida Sites, American Universities, All Usenet FAQs, GNN Catalog, List of Lists, NCSA What's New, Multimedia Resources, Nonprofit Organizations, WWW Development, All in One Search, Virtual Library, World Art Resources, Yahoo's Index, Submit to METRO-SCOPE, What's New Sites
Tampa [Tampa]	http://isotropic.com/metro/tampa.html?	Search, METROSCOPE, Florida State W3, U.S. Government W3, Art and Entertainment Sites, Tampa Business, Tampa Media, Tampa Internet Services, Tampa Sports, Tampa Colleges, Tampa Area Guides, Tampa Government, Professional Services, Organizations and Groups, Other Florida Sites, American Universities, All Usenet FAQs, GNN Catalog, List of Lists, NCSA What's New, Multimedia Resources, Nonprofit Organizations, WWW Development, All in One Search, Virtual Library, World Art Resources, Yahoo's Index, Submit to METROSCOPE, What's New Sites

Table 13.14: Selected Georgia Travel Sites

Region [Site]	URL	Links
State of Georgia [City.Net—Georgia]	http://www.city.net/countries/united_states/georgia/	Cities, Counties, Islands, Education, Food and Drink, Government, Parks and Outdoors, Television and Radio
State of Georgia [Georgia Web Guide]	http://www.ajc.com/atl/gaweb.htm	General, Regional, Entertainment, Music, Sports and Recreation, Media, Groups, Education, Technology, Government
State of Georgia [National Park Service—Georgia]	http://www.nps.gov:80/parklists/ga.html	National Park Service Sites
Atlanta [Atlanta Area Restaurant Guide]	http://www.w3.com/atlanta/	City/Type Listings, Search Reviews, Search Restaurants, Interactive Map, Alphabetical Listings, All Restaurants by Type, All Reviews, Top Reviewers, Your Restaurant List, New Reviews, Add a Restaurant
Atlanta [Atlanta, Georgia]	http://isotropic.com/metro/atlanta.html?	Search, Metroscope, Georgia State W3, U.S. Government W3, World W3, Atlanta Art and Cultural, Atlanta Business, Atlanta Media, Atlanta Internet Services, Atlanta Sports, Atlanta Olympic Sites, Atlanta Colleges, Atlanta K-12 Schools, Atlanta Guides, Atlanta Government, Professional Services, Atlanta Financial, Organizations and Groups, Other Atlanta Sites, Other Georgia Sites, American Universities, All Usenet FAQs, GNN Catalog, List of Lists, NCSA What's New, Multimedia Resources, Nonprofit Organizations, WWW Development, All in One Search, Virtual Library, World Art Resources, Yahoo's Index, Submit to Metroscope, What's New Sites
Atlanta [Atlanta Open Directory]	http://www.netoffice.com/open/	Arts & Entertainment, Business Desktop, Computer Services, Government Services, MARTA Scheduler, Perimeter Map, Housing & Real Estate, Schools and Universities, Sports and Recreation, Weather Radar, What's New?, What's on Tonite?
Atlanta [The Atlanta Restaurant Review]	http://www.gatech.edu/3020/restaurants/atlanta.restaurants.html	Restaurants by Price, by Food Type
Atlanta [City.Net—Atlanta]	http://www.city.net/countries/united_states/georgia/atlanta/	Art, Arts and Entertainment, City Guides, Community Organizations, Events, General Information, Government, Museums and Galleries, Other Guides, Parks and Outdoors, Transportation, Travel and Tourism
Atlanta [Jeremy and Richard on Gay Atlanta]	http://userwww.service.emory.edu/~librpj/atlanta.html	General Info (Phoning, Safety, Neighborhoods, Transportation, Weather), Georgia GLB Folks on the Web, Gay Bars and Dance Clubs, The Drag Scene, The Male Stripper Scene, A Bathhouse in Our Fair City, Restaurants, Places to Spend Your Money, Places to Hang Out, Culture and Activities, Gay and Gay-Friendly Businesses, Atlanta Publications, Other Atlanta Guides, Other Gay City Guides
Atlanta [Menu's On-Line Home Page]	http://menus.atlanta.com/	Search by Area, Search by Cuisine, List of Restaurants, Buckhead Gourmet Delivery
Atlanta [TransporT]	http://www.gatech.edu/3020/travelink/transprt.html	Airport, Buses, Public Transport, Rentals, Taxis, and Trains

Table 13.14: Selected Georgia Travel Sites (continued)

Region [Site]	URL	Links
Atlanta [Virtual Atlanta]	http://virtual.atlanta.com/index.html	Atlanta Interactive Calendar, Music Scene, Shops, On-Line Magazines, Channel Surf, Vat'l Survey
Atlanta [Welcome to Atlanta]	http://www.tourist.com/atlanta/atlanta.htm	Hotels, Restaurants, Nightclubs, Shopping, Private Olympic Housing, Tourist Attractions & Parks, Business & Services, Rental Cars, and Entertainment
St. Simons and Jekyll Islands [Golden Isles at a Glance]	http://www.webrunner.com/webrun/lcmn/lcmn.html	Places to Visit, Calendar of Events, Art Associations/Galleries, Theater, Lectures, Concerts, Cultural Events, Fishing, and Sports
Savannah [Savannah Entertainment]	http://wce.com/entertai/entertai.htm	Savannah has numerous places to go and things to do. Here you will find theater listings as well as area festivals arranged by month.
Savannah [Travel and Tourism in Savannah]	http://wce.com/tourist/tourist.htm	Tourist Agencies, Bed and Breakfasts, Places to Visit, Tour Guides, and Tours

Table 13.15: Selected Hawaii Travel Sites

Region [Site]	URL	Links
State of Hawaii [City.Net—Hawaii]	http://www.city.net/countries/united_states/hawaii/	Islands, Culture and Language, Education, Food and Drink, Government, Government Information, Magazines and Zines, Other Guides, Parks and Outdoors, Regional Information, Sports, State Information, Television and Radio, Travel and Tourism
State of Hawaii	http://isotropic.com/metro/hawaii.html?	Search, Metroscope, Hawaii State W3, World W3, U.S. Government W3, Art and Cultural Sites, Hawaii Business, Hawaii Media, Hawaii Internet Services, Hawaii Sports, Hawaii Colleges, Hawaii Vacations, Hawaii Guides, Hawaii Government, Hawaii Professional Services, Organizations and Groups, Other Hawaii Sites, American Universities, All Usenet FAQs, GNN Catalog, List of Lists, NCSA What's New, Multimedia Resources, Nonprofit Organizations, WWW Development, All in One Search, Virtual Library, World Art Resources, Yahoo's Index, Submit to Metroscope, What's New Sites
State of Hawaii [Hawai'i Hotlinks]	http://planet-hawaii.com/redroad/hotlink.hawaii.html	Nation of Hawai'i; Photo Tour of Hawai'i; Cascades Volcano Observatory Home Page; H4, Hawai'i's Data SuperHighway; Island of Hawaii Current Earthquake Map; Destination Highlights—Island of Hawaii; Virtually Hawaii; Virtually Hawaii: Kilauea Virtual Field Tips; The Blue Room
State of Hawaii [The Hawaii InfoWeb]	http://www.outrigger.com/infoweb/	Home, Hotels, Dining, Shopping, Reservations, Contests & Discounts, Guest Book
State of Hawaii [Hawai'i Visitor Bureau]	http://www.visit.hawaii.org/	Japanese, Hokeo, Enter to win, Islands, Activities, Accommodations, Calendar, Links, Feedback

Table 13.15: Selected Hawaii Travel Sites (continued)

Region [Site]	URL	Links
State of Hawaii [This Week]	http://www.thisweek.com/	Up to Date News in Hawaii, Experience Hawaii, Accommodations, Activities, Mail Order and Shopping, Dining and Entertainment, Links to the Internet Universe
State of Hawaii [Virtually Hawaii]	http://satftp.soest.hawaii.edu/hawaii/index_orig.html	What's New, Virtual Field Trip, Remote Image Navigator, Real Time Satellite Data and Weather, Information, Guest Book
Hawaii (island) [Big Island of Hawaii]	http://bookweb.cwis.uci.edu:8042/Books/Moon/hawaii.html	The Land; Flora and Fauna; People; Sports and Recreation; Festivals, Holidays, and Events; and Special Topics
Maui (island) [Maui Weather Today]	http://www.satlab.hawaii.edu:80/weather/	Weather Reports, Live Camera—Maui's Iao Valley, Iao Images, View of Kihei, Weather Trivia/Weather History/Nature Poem, Satellite Image of the Hawaiian Islands, Underwater, Surf, and Windsurfing

Table 13.16: Selected Idaho Travel Sites

Region [Site]	URL	Links
State of Idaho [City.Net—Idaho]	http://www.city.net/countries/united_states/idaho/	Cities, Education, Food and Drink, Government, Parks and Outdoors, State Information, Television and Radio
State of Idaho [Idaho's Official Recreation and Tourism Information Web Site]	http://www.IDOC.state.id.us/	Regional Directory, Ski Idaho, Outdoor Recreation, Accommodations, State Parks, Site of the Day, Statewide Calendar, Adobe Acrobat Documents Download Page, Recreation Report, Links to Related Sites, and River Trip Applications
State of Idaho [National Park Service—Idaho]	http://www.nps.gov:80/parklists/id.html	National Park Service Sites
Boise [Boise CityLink]	http://banzai.neosoft.com/citylink/boise/	What to See, What to Do, Where to Stay, Where to Eat, Where to Shop, and More Information
Sun Valley [Sun Valley Guide]	http://www.svguide.com/	Local News and Features, Visitor and Activity Guide, Community Information, and Other Information

Table 13.17: Selected Illinois Travel Sites

Region /Site	URL	Links
State of Illinois [City.Net—Illinois]	http://www.city.net/countries/united_states/illinois/	Cities, Counties, Community Networks, Education, Food and Drink, Government, History and Literature, Parks and Outdoors, Regional Information, State Information, Television and Radio, Travel and Tourism
Chicago [Chicago and Illinois Forecasts and Current Conditions]	gopher://huinfo.nwu.edu/11/weathernews/weather	Chicago & Illinois Forecasts and Current Conditions
Chicago [Chicago Area Restaurant Guide]	http://www.w3.com/chicago	City/Type Listings, Search Reviews, Search Restaurants, Interactive Map, Alphabetical Listings, All Restaurants by Type, All Reviews, Top Reviewers, Your Restaurant List, New Reviews, Add a Restaurant
Chicago [Chicago, Illinois]	http://isotropic.com/metro/chiago.html?	Search, Metroscope, Illinois State W3, U.S. Government W3, World W3, Art and Cultural Sites, Chicago Business, Chicago Media, Internet Services, Chicago Sports, Colleges & Universities, Chicago Guides, Professional Services, Chicago Financial Sites, Chicago Government, Groups and Organizations, Other Chicago Sites, Other Illinois Sites, American Universities, All Usenet FAQs, GNN Catalog, List of Lists, NCSA What's New, Multimedia Resources, Nonprofit Organizations, WWW Development, All in One Search, Virtual Library, World Art Resources, Yahoo's Index, Submit to Metroscope, What's New Sites
Chicago [Chicago Web by Gordon Lake]	http://www.chiweb.com/	Chicago Web Yellow Pages, Chicago Sports Teams, Lake Shore Drive (an online soap opera), Chicago Weather Forecast, Shopping Cart, Chicago Web Movie Guide, Sandra Keeley's Internet Newstand, Chicago Reader Online Features, Ticketmaster, Concerts and Shows, Classic Concerts, Singles Choice, Restaurants, Jokes of the Day, Digital Coffee (Chicago Sun-Times), Discovery Center, IDOT Travel Report, Chicago Mosaic, Blues in Chicago, EL Guide to Chicago, Centerstage Chicago, Chicago Subway System, Michael Jordan Page, Bob Allison (of BOBAworld fame), Theater Directory, Chicago Nightlife, Gay and Lesbian Sites, Activities, Studs on the Web, Transportation, Hotels, The Sandra Kelley Chicago Motherlode, Infoseek Guide, Lycos, DejaNews (slow-loading)
Chicago [Chicago WebGuide]	http://chicago.chi.il.us/webguide/	Arts and Entertainment, Business, Computers, Education, Government and Politics, Health and Medicine, News and Media, Regional Information and Maps, Science and Technology, Shopping
Chicago [Metra Information Center]	http://www.metrarail.com/	Metra Train General Information, Ticket Information, News and Promotions, Schedules, and Metra Maps

Table 13.17: Selected Illinois Travel Sites (continued)

Region [Site]	URL	Links
Chicago [This Is Chicago!]	http://www.ncsa.uiuc.edu/SDG/IT94/Venue.html	Hotels (Downtown Chicago), Restaurants, Activities, Shopping, Sporting Events, Theater, Chicago Night Life, Transportation, International Services, and Important Telephone Numbers
Chicago [The Web Wanderer's Chicago Guide]	http://www.xnet.com/~blatura/chicago.shtml	General Info, Entertainment, Sightseeing, Around Town, The Burbs, Sports, Health and Medicine, Organizations, Computing in Chicago, Media, Additional Chicago WWW Resources, The Rest of the World, The Web Wanderer Directory, Feedback (comprehensive and fast-loading site)
Evanston and Chicago [Evanston and Chicago]	http://www.nwu.edu/activity/evanston-chicago.html	Shopping and Dining; Arts, Performance, and Entertainment; Chicago Highlights; Evanston Highlights; Public Transportation; and Northwestern University Information
Evanston [Evanston Restaurants]	http://www.nwu.edu/ev-chi/evrestaurants/	Restaurants by Type
Peoria [Peoria Area Visitors Guide]	http://PeoriaCVB.Peoria.Il.US/home.html	Weather, Search Peoria, Historic Sites, Accommodations, Calendar of Events, Maps, Dining, Attractions, Shopping, and Services

Table 13.18: Selected Indiana Travel Sites

Region [Site]	URL	Links
State of Indiana [City.Net—Indiana]	http://www.city.net/countries/united_states/indiana/	Cities, Education, Food and Drink, Government, Parks and Outdoors, Regional Information, Television and Radio
State of Indiana [National Park Service—Indiana]	http://www.nps.gov:80/parklists/in.html	National Park Service Sites
Columbus [The City Web]	http://isc.cphx.net/	Maps, News & Sports, Business & Finance, City Hi-Lites, Schools, Entertainment & Recreation, Arts, Social Scene, and Government
Evansville [City of Evansville Home Page]	http://www.evansville.net/eville/	Welcome, Area Profile, Entertainment, Education, History, Accommodations, Churches, Area Services, and At the Mall
Indianapolis [Indianapolis, Indiana]	http://isotropic.com/metro/indianap.html?	Search, Metroscope, Indiana State W3, U.S. Government W3, World W3, Art and Entertainment Sites, Indianapolis Business, Indianapolis Media, Indianapolis Internet, Indianapolis Sports, Indianapolis Colleges, Indianapolis Guides, Professional Services, Indianapolis Government, Other Indianapolis Sites, Other Indiana Sites, American Universities, All Usenet FAQs, GNN Catalog, List of Lists, NCSA What's New, Multimedia Resources, Nonprofit Organizations, WWW Development, All in One Search, Virtual Library, World Art Resources, Yahoo's Index, Submit to Metroscope, What's New Sites
Lafayette [Lafayette Online]	http://www.mdn.com/LafOnline/	About Lafayette, Community Calendar, Business, Virtual Tour, Area History, and Useful Links

Table 13.19: Selected Iowa Travel Sites

Region [Site]	URL	Links
State of Iowa [National Park Service—Iowa]	http://www.nps.gov:80/parklists/ia.html	National Park Service Sites
State of Iowa [City.Net—Iowa]	http://www.city.net/countries/united_states/iowa/	Cities, Regions, Education, Food and Drink, Government, Parks and Outdoors, Television and Radio
Des Moines [Des Moines—The New Style American City!]	http://www.ioweb.com/desmoines/	Area Attractions, Lodging Accomodations, That's Entertainment, Convention Information, Shopping Information, Interesting Trivia, and Dining Guide
Iowa City and Coralville [Visitors Guide to Iowa City & Coralville]	http://www.biz.uiowa.edu/iapages/iowacity/iccvb/index.html	Local Treasures, Historic Treasures, Area Attractions, Entertainment, Recreation, Camping, Shopping, Transit Information, and Annual Events

Table 13.20: Selected Kansas Travel Sites

Region [Site]	URL	Links
State of Kansas [City.Net—Kansas]	http://www.city.net/countries/united_states/kansas/	Cities, Education, Food and Drink, Government, History and Literature, Other Guides, Parks and Outdoors, Television and Radio
State of Kansas [Interactive Map of Kansas]	http://gisdasc.kgs.ukans.edu/dasc/inter-map.html	Interactive Map by County, Digital Elevation Map
State of Kansas [National Park Service—Kansas]	http://www.nps.gov:80/parklists/ks.html	National Park Service Sites
State of Kansas [Sights of KANSAS, USA!]	http://falcon.cc.ukans.edu/~nsween/europa.html	Weather, Interactive Map, Distances Between Towns, Cities, Exploring Kansas (Community Networks, Towns & Cities, Robinson Observatory, The Prairie Falcon), Lake and Fishing Report, The Prairie, Accommodations, Biking, Highways, Native American Homepages, Government, and Sports
Dodge City [Dodge City CityLink]	http://banzai.neosoft.com/citylink/dodge/	What to See, What to Do, Where to Stay, Where to Eat, Where to Shop, and More Information

Table 13.20: Selected Kansas Travel Sites (continued)

Region [Site]	URL	Links
Manhattan [Manhattan Travel and Tourism]	http://www.mnedia.com:80/manhattan/mankansas2.html#travel	Community Information (Maps, White Pages, Weather, Organizations, Media, Education, Libraries, History, Emergency Services), Business Information, Travel and Tourism (Chamber of Commerce Visitor's Bureau, Travel Agencies), Leisure (Movies, Culture, Parks & Recreation, Night Clubs, Calendar of Events, Retail Shops, Arts Council), Government Information, Overnight Lodging, On the Menu, Places to Worship, Periodicals, Real Estate, and Schools
Topeka [Topeka WEB]	http://lawlib.wuacc.edu/topeka/topeka.html	Attractions, Camping, Eating Out, Entertainment, Events, General Information, Government, Kansas Internet, Kansas, Law, Libraries, Lodging, Map, Medical, Transportation, Topeka Zoo
Wichita [Welcome to Wichita]	http://www.southwind.net/ict/index.html	Business, Community, Education, Government, History, Things to See & Do, What's New, and Other Information (slow-loading)

Table 13.21: Selected Kentucky Travel Sites

Region [Site]	URL	Links
State of Kentucky [City.Net—Kentucky]	http://www.city.net/countries/united_states/kentucky/	Cities, Businesses, Education, Food and Drink, Government, Parks and Outdoors, Television and Radio
State of Kentucky [Commonwealth of Kentucky Web Server–Virtual Tour]	http://www.state.ky.us/tour/tour.htm	What's Happening, Travel Guide (Western Waterlands, Bluegrass Heartlands, Scenic Wonderlands, East Highlands), Outdoors, Home Video, and Home Audio
State of Kentucky [Kentucky Atlas & Gazetteer]	http://www.uky.edu/KentuckyAtlas/kentucky-atlas.html	Clickable Kentucky Map (by County), Relief Map, Physiographic Map
State of Kentucky [National Park Service—Kentucky]	http://www.nps.gov:80/parklists/ky.html	National Park Service Sites
Lexington [Lexington CityLink]	http://banzai.neosoft.com/citylink/lexing/	What to See, What to Do, Where to Stay, Where to Eat, Where to Shop, and More Information
Louisville [Louisville Restaurant Guide]	http://www.iglou.com/restaurants/eats.html	Dining Establishments by Type, New and Noteworthy Restaurants
Louisville [Louisville Visitor Center]	http://www.iglou.com/lou/	Visitor Information, Attractions, Area Organizations, Economic and Business Information

Table 13.22: Selected Louisiana Travel Sites

Region [Site]	URL	Links
State of Louisiana [City.Net—Louisiana]	http://www.city.net/countries/united_states/louisiana/	Cities, Education, Food and Drink, Government, Parks and Outdoors, Television and Radio
State of Louisiana [Louisiana Office of Tourism]	http://www.state.la.us/cgi-bin/imagemap.exe/button3?542,288	State Overview, Welcome Centers, State Phone Numbers and Addresses, Safety Tips, Climate, Our Culture Abounds (African American Heritage), Greater New Orleans Region, Plantation Country, Cajun Country, Crossroads, Sportsman's Paradise, Statewide Information (many links)
State of Louisiana [National Park Service—Louisiana]	http://www.nps.gov:80/parklists/la.html	National Park Service Sites
New Orleans [New Orleans]	http://isotropic.com/metro/no.html?	Search, Metroscope, Louisiana State W3, U.S. Government W3, World W3, Art and Cultural Sites, New Orleans Business, New Orleans Media, N. O. Internet Services, New Orleans Sports, New Orleans Guides, New Orleans Colleges, New Orleans Government, N. O. Professional Services, Organizations and Groups, Other New Orleans Sites, Other Louisiana Sites, American Universities, All Usenet FAQs, GNN Catalog, List of Lists, NCSA What's New, Multimedia Resources, Nonprofit Organizations, WWW Development, All in One Search, Virtual Library, World Art Resources, Yahoo's Index, Submit to Metroscope, What's New Sites
New Orleans [New Orleans Virtual Dining Guide]	http://www.vatcom.com/neworl/dining/restop.html	What's New, New Orleans Cuisine Basics, Featured Restaurants, Restaurant Listings, Restaurants by Neighborhood, Restaurants by Cuisine
New Orleans [Virtually New Orleans]	http://vatcom.com/neworl/vno.html	Hot Topics; Feature Photo of the Week; Weather; History and Politics; Media; Restaurant Guide; Cooking and Recipes; Entertainment; Ernest N. Morial Convention Center; On-Line Shopping; Getting Around Town; Sightseeing; Museums and Galleries; Shopping Guide; Neighborhood Guide; New Orleans Lifestyle; Sports; Libraries, Schools, Colleges, Universities; Literary New Orleans; Mardi Gras; Jazz and Heritage Festival

Table 13.23: Selected Maine Travel Sites

Region [Site]	URL	Links
State of Maine [City.Net—Maine]	http://www.city.net/countries/united_states/maine/	Cities, Counties, Islands, Businesses, Education, Food and Drink, Government, Parks and Outdoors, Regional Information, Television and Radio, Travel and Tourism
State of Maine [National Park Service—Maine]	http://www.nps.gov:80/parklists/me.html	National Park Service Sites
State of Maine [Travel Maine]	http://www.sourcemaine.com/TravelMaine/	Maine–Vacationland (Overview), Maine by Region, What's New, Calendar of Events, Accommodations, Maine Towns, Seasons, Skiing, and travel-related resources
Camden [Welcome to Camden, Maine]	http://www.camden.lib.me.us/cpl3.htm	About Camden, Government Information, Camden Mall, Community Activities, and Cultural Activities
Portland [Portland CityLink]	http://banzai.neosoft.com/citylink/portland/	What to See, What to Do, Where to Stay, Where to Eat, Where to Shop, and More Information
Old Orchard Beach [Old Orchard Beach Area]	http://www.sourcemaine.com/TravelMaine/oob.html	Town Info, Attractions, Recreation, Golf Courses, Annual Events, Lodging, Campgrounds, Restaurants, Shopping, Activities, Day Trips Services, and Regional Chambers of Commerce

Table 13.24: Selected Maryland Travel Sites

Region [Site]	URL	Links
State of Maryland [City.Net—Maryland]	http://www.city.net/countries/united_states/maryland/	Cities, Counties, Metropolitan Areas, Education, Food and Drink, Government, Television and Radio, Travel and Tourism
State of Maryland [National Park Service—Maryland]	http://www.nps.gov:80/parklists/md.html	National Park Service Sites
State of Maryland [Welcome to Maryland]	http://www.mdisfun.org/mdisfun/	History, Chesapeake Bay & Maritime Activity, Recreation & Parks, Cultural Activities and Museums, Shopping & Outlets, Accommodations, Sports Facilities, Transportation, Other Maryland Resources, Calendar of Events, and Baltimore Link
Annapolis [Historic Annapolis]	http://www.umcp.umd.edu/CampusMaps/Annapolis/Welcome.html	Historic Sites and Homes, Accommodations, and Dining
Baltimore [Baltimore CityLink]	http://banzai.neosoft.com/citylink/baltimor/	What to See, What to Do, Where to Stay, Where to Eat, Where to Shop, and More Information

Table 13.24: Selected Maryland Travel Sites (continued)

Region [Site]	URL	Links
Baltimore [Julie's Restaurant Reviews]	http://gdbdoc.gdb.org/~jbouzoun/food.html	Restaurants by Area and Type
Baltimore [Subway System of Baltimore]	http://metro.jussieu.fr:10001/bin/select/english/usa/baltimore	MTA Subway and Light Rail Stations
Eastern Shore [Eastern Shore and the Chesapeake Bay]	http://www.covesoft.com/eastern	Delmarva Peninsula, Delaware, Maryland, Virginia, Historic Towns & Places, to Visit, Area Attractions & Things to Do, Visit the Chesapeake Bay via Pictures, The Weekly Chesapeake Bay Fishing Report, Eastern Shore Property, The Annapolis Maryland Home Page, The Marine Market, Great Oak Manor B&B Chestertown MD, Holland Island Preservation Foundation, Wicomico County Home Page, The Chesapeake Bay Trust, Chesapeake Bay Maritime Museum Home Page, The Maritime History Virtual Archives, Chesapeake Wildlife Heritage, A Walk through Chesapeake Bay, Chesapeake Bay Region Map, Maryland Sea Grant, The Coastal Marsh Project Website, The Chesapeake Free-Net
Ocean City [Ocean City Chamber of Commerce]	http://www.intercom.net/oceancity/	Chamber Information, Lodging, Recreation, Transportation, Sightseeing, Events Calendar, Dining, and Weather

Table 13.25: Selected Massachusetts Travel Sites

Region [Site]	URL	Links
State of Massachusetts [City.Net—Massachusetts]	http://www.city.net/countries/united_states/massachusetts/	Cities, Counties, Islands, Metropolitan Areas, Regions, Businesses, Education, Food and Drink, Government, Other Guides, Television and Radio
State of Massachusetts [Massachusetts]	http://ftp.std.com/NE/mass.html	Agriculture, Amateur Radio, Bicycling, Boston Online, Business, Communities and Regions, Consumer Issues, Dining/Eats, Education, Fishing, Employment, Queer Resources Directory, Government/Politics, History, Literature, Massachusetts/Boston-Area Maps, Massachusetts Media Outlets, Movies, Pets, Public Libraries, Travel, The Quiz, clari.local.massachusetts, clari.local.massachusetts.briefs
State of Massachusetts [Massachusetts/Boston Maps]	http://ftp.std.com/NE/maps.html	Downtown Boston, Massachusetts and Its Counties, Greater Boston, Interactive Boston Map, Cambridge, Harbor Islands, Harvard Square, Harvard Yard, MBTA Subway Lines, MBTA Commuter Lines, Charles River Running
State of Massachusetts [Massachusetts Diner Directory]	http://www.neb.com/noren/diner/MA_diner_dir.html	Alphabetical list of diners

Table 13.25: Selected Massachusetts Travel Sites (continued)

Region [Site]	URL	Links
State of Massachusetts [National Park Service—Massachusetts]	http://www.nps.gov:80/parklists/ma.html	National Park Service Sites
State of Massachusetts [Travel Massachusetts]	http://ftp.std.com/NE/masstravel	Boston/Cambridge, The Berkshires, Cape Ann, Cape Cod and the Islands, Central Massachusetts, Minuteman National Historic Park, Plymouth Colony, Salem, Fishing, State Parks and Forests
Boston [Boston, Massachusetts (including Brookline, Cambridge, and Waltham)]	http://isotropic.com/metro/boston.html	Search, Metroscope, Massachusetts State W3, U.S. Government W3, World W3, Art and Cultural Sites, Boston Business, Boston Media, Boston Sports, Boston Colleges, Boston Internet Services, Boston Guides, Boston Medical Sites, Boston Professional Services, Boston Financial, Organizations and Groups, Other Boston Sites, Other Massachusetts Sites, American Universities, All Usenet FAQs, GNN Catalog, List of Lists, NCSA What's New, Multimedia Resources, Nonprofit Organizations, WWW Development, All in One Search, Virtual Library, World Art Resources, Yahoo's Index, Submit to Metroscope, What's New Sites
Boston [Boston Online]	http://ftp.std.com/NE/boston.html	Many links, including Boston Winter Misery Center, Nor'easterCam, Roslindale Snowcam, Travel Boston, Electronic Post Cards, Neighborhoods of Greater Boston, Wicked Good Guide to Boston English, NetForums
Boston [The Boston Restaurant Guide]	http://www.hubnet.com/	Restaurants by Cuisine, Location, Detailed Search, Features, What's New, and Quick Search (By Name)
Boston [Boston Restaurant Reviews]	http://genoa.asf.org:8001/boston-food/boston-by-cuisine.html	Select a Cuisine, Restaurants Organized by Area, Review a Restaurant
Boston [Boston Travel]	http://ftp.std.com/NE/bos.html	Arts and Entertainment, Calendar of Events, Eats, Lodging, Public Transportation (two links), Recreation, Newbury Street League, Boston, Cambridge, The Freedom Trail, The Black Heritage Trail, Transportation, Local Weather, The Wicked Good Guide to Boston English, Travel Massachusetts, Mass. Online
Boston [BostonWeb]	http://www.bweb.com/bostonweb/ or http://www.bweb.com/slowroad/index.html	Find out what's new on the BostonWeb, TownNet, MenuNet, ShopNet, Help (slow-loading)

Table 13.25: Selected Massachusetts Travel Sites (continued)

Region [Site]	URL	Links
Boston [Museum of Science Web Server]	http://www.mos.org/	Museum Directions; Hours, Costs, and Phone Numbers; Visitor Services; History; Exhibits; Today's Programs; Museum Store; News; Tour; Online Exhibits; and Other Museum Offerings
Boston [Subway System of Boston]	http://metro.jussieu.fr:10001/bin/select/english/usa/boston	MBTA Subway Stations, Streetcar Stations, AMTRAK Commuter Rail Stations
Boston [Virtually Boston]	http://www.cybercom.net/~kiwicove/vboston/index.htm	New at Virtually Boston, UB Netforums, Boston, History, General History, Photo Album, On the Web
Cambridge [City of Cambridge]	http://www.ci.cambridge.ma.us/	Selected links include A Historical Background, Arts/Entertainment, Education, Employment, Environment, Health Care, Libraries/Bookstores, Museums, Tourism/Recreation, Transportation and Maps, Area Real Estate and Apartment Listings, Survey of Community Networks
Cape Ann [Cape Ann WebSite]	http://wizard.pn.com/capeann/	Events, Quarries, Fishing, Map, Cape Ann Communities (Gloucester, Rockport, Manchester-by-the-Sea, Essex), Attractions, Arts, Restaurants, Accommodations, Shops & Galleries, Real Estate, Marinas, Weather, and related sites
Cape Cod [The Cape Cod Connection]	http://turnpike.net/emporium/M/mkron/capec_re/inf_cape.htm	Cape Cod by Area
Martha's Vineyard [Welcome to Martha's Vineyard!]	http://www.tiac.net/users/prowten/	Vineyard Map, Transportation (Steamship, Bus), Accommodations, Local Events, Weather, Local Sites
Nantucket [Nantucket Island Information Center]	http://www.oneweb.com/infoctrs/NIIC.html	Lodging, Vacation Rentals, General Information, Weather & Tides, Education, History, Island Businesses, Real Estate, Scientific Studies, Entertainment, News, Literature, Travel and Sightseeing, Politics, Miscellaneous, and Nearby Areas
Plymouth [America's Home Page]	http://media3.com/plymouth/	First Thanksgiving Story, New England Style Recipes, Plimoth Plantation, Museums/Historical Sites, Historical Reference, Plymouth Schools
Plymouth [Plimoth Plantation]	http://media3.com/plymouth/plant.htm	Virtual Tour, Index, Shops, Dining, Lodging, Activities, Museums, Beaches, Events, and Maps
Provincetown [Provincetown Business Guild]	http://www.ptown.com:80/ptown/	History, Travel Tips, Free Guide, The Lodging Locator©, Calendar of Events, Restaurants, Art Galleries, Travel Services, Retail Shops & Services, Real Estate & Rentals, Links to Other Cape Cod Sites
Sturbridge [Old Sturbridge Village]	http://www.osv.org/	Explore an 1830s Village, Christmas in Early New England, Planning Your Visit, Calendar of Events, Membership, Kids Club, Frequently Asked Questions, Gift Shop, Lodging, Educational Programs, Accessibility, and Regional Links

Table 13.26: Selected Michigan Travel Sites

Region [Site]	URL	Links
State of Michigan [City.Net—Michigan]	http://www.city.net/countries/united_states/michigan/	Cities, Counties, Regions, Education, Food and Drink, General Information, Government, News and Weather, Parks and Outdoors, Regional Information, Sports, State Information, Television and Radio
State of Michigan [National Park Service—Michigan]	http://www.nps.gov.80/parklists/mi.html	National Park Service Sites
Ann Arbor [Ann Arbor Online]	http://online.ann-arbor.mi.us/ann-arbor/online.html	Photo Tour, Shopping, Universities, Around Town (Weather, Events Calendar, Food, Entertainment, Books, Music, Places to Visit, Arts, Jobs, Sports, Recreation, Places to Stay, Transportation, Government), Hot Spots, Directory, Michigan and the Great Lakes
Detroit [Detroit CityLink]	http://banzai.neosoft.com/citylink/detroit/	What to See, What to Do, Where to Stay, Where to Eat, Where to Shop, and More Information
Detroit [Detroit, Michigan (including Ann Arbor, Dearborn, and Pontiac)]	http://isotropic.com/metro/detroit.html?	Search, Metroscope, Michigan State W3, U.S. Government W3, World W3, Art and Entertainment, Detroit Business, Detroit Media, Detroit Sports, Detroit Colleges & Universities, Detroit Government Sites, Internet Services, Detroit Guides, Professional Services, Detroit Financial Sites, Other Detroit Area Sites, Michigan Newsgroups, Other Michigan Sites, American Universities, All Usenet FAQs, GNN Catalog, List of Lists, NCSA What's New, Multimedia Resources, Nonprofit Organizations, WWW Development, All in One Search, Virtual Library, World Art Resources, Yahoo's Index, Submit to Metroscope, What's New Sites
Grand Rapids [Grand Rapids Area]	http://www.mswco.com/wmich/wmich.htm	Entertainment, Business, Organizations, Education, Tourism, and Government
Keweenaw Peninsula [Keweenaw Traveler]	http://www.portup.com/traveler/home.html	Featured Attractions, About Bears, and Calendar

Table 13.27: Selected Minnesota Travel Sites

Region [Site]	URL	Links
State of Minnesota [City.Net—Minnesota]	http://www.city.net/countries/united_states/minnesota/	Cities, Counties, Metropolitan Areas, Education, Food and Drink, Government, Museums and Galleries, Other Guides, Parks and Outdoors, Regional Information, Television and Radio, Travel and Tourism
State of Minnesota [Fun Stuff in Minnesota]	http://www.primenet.com/~kennyb/mn-fun.htm	Indoor Activities, Casinos and Misc. Gambling, Restaurants, Outdoor Activities, and Professional Sports Activities
State of Minnesota [Minnesota Special Interests]	http://www.rconnect.com/special.htm	Yahoo Search, Mall of America, Missing Children, Valleyfair Amusement Park

Table 13.27: Selected Minnesota Travel Sites (continued)

Region [Site]	URL	Links
State of Minnesota [National Park Service—Minnesota]	http://www.nps.gov:80/parklists/mn.html	National Park Service Sites
State of Minnesota [Travel Perks]	http://www.wp.com/perks/	Minnesota Resorts, Travel Advisories
Minneapolis [Meet Minneapolis]	http://designstein.com/gmcva/	General Information, Convention Center, Events, Accommodations, Minneapolis Facts, Dining, Entertainment, Multi-Cultural, and Shopping
Minneapolis [Minneapolis Institutes of Art]	http://www.mtn.org	Museum Index, The Permanent Collection, Special Exhibitions, General Information, What's Hot, Exhibitions and Galleries, Events, Educational Programs and Quiz, Membership, Museum Shop, Opportunities for Involvement, Services and Resources, and Institute Telephone Directory
Minneapolis-St. Paul [Fallon McElligott Faves]	http://www.fallon.com/faves/faves.html	Restaurants, Shopping, Rest and Relaxation
Minneapolis-St. Paul [Minneapolis-St. Paul]	http://isotropic.com/metro/minnean.html?	Search, Metroscope, Minnesota W3, U.S. Government W3, World W3, Minneapolis Art Sites, Minneapolis Business, Minneapolis Media, Internet Services, Minneapolis Sports, Minneapolis Colleges, Minneapolis Guides, Professional Services, Minneapolis Financial, Organizations and Groups, Minneapolis Government, Other Minneapolis Sites, Other Minnesota Sites, American Universities, All Usenet FAQs, GNN Catalog, List of Lists, NCSA What's New, Multimedia Resources, Nonprofit Organizations, WWW Development, All in One Search, Virtual Library, World Art Resources, Yahoo's Index, Submit to Metroscope, What's New Sites
Minneapolis-St. Paul [Minneapolis/St. Paul Map & Travel Center]	http://www.tgimaps.com/minneapolis-st.paul.html	Points of Interest by Map, Information by Category (Lodging; Shopping & Dining; Events, Attractions and Entertainment; Golf; Parks & Recreation; Travel & Tourism Information)
Minneapolis-St. Paul [Twin Cities Restaurant Guide]	http://www.w3.com/twin	City/Type Listings, Search Reviews, Search Restaurants, Interactive Map, Alphabetical Listings, All Restaurants by Type, All Reviews, Top Reviewers, Your Restaurant List, New Reviews, Add a Restaurant
St. Paul [City of Saint Paul]	http://www.stpaul.gov	Greetings, Breweries, Business, Education, Fun, Jobs, Sports, Virtual St. Paul, Government and Visitors Information

Table 13.28: Selected Mississippi Travel Sites

Region [Site]	URL	Links
State of Mississippi [City.Net—Mississippi]	http://www.city.net/countries/united_states/mississippi/	Cities, Regions, Education, Food and Drink, Government, Parks and Outdoors, Television and Radio
State of Mississippi [National Park Service—Mississippi]	http://www.nps.gov:80/parklists/ms.html	National Park Service Sites
Biloxi [Biloxi CityLink]	http://banzai.neosoft.com/citylink/biloxi/	What to See, What to Do, Where to Stay, Where to Eat, Where to Shop, and More Information
Gulf Coast [Mississippi Gulf Coast Home Page]	http://www.datasync.com/trebor/index.html	Restaurants, Featured Recipe, Entertainment, Accommodations, Casinos, Coast Coliseum and Convention Center, Sightseeing, Charter Boats, Golf Courses, Museums and Galleries, Shopping, Real Estate, Colleges and Universities
Vicksburg [Vicksburg]	http://www.southernnet.com/vicksburg/cvb/	Attractions, Accommodations, Restaurants, and Other (Annual Events, Major Routes to Vicksburg)

Table 13.29: Selected Missouri Travel Sites

Region [Site]	URL	Links
State of Missouri [City.Net—Missouri]	http://www.city.net/countries/united_states/missouri/	Cities, Regions, Economics, Education, Food and Drink, Government, Parks and Outdoors, State Information, Television and Radio
State of Missouri [National Park Service—Missouri]	http://www.nps.gov:80/parklists/mo.html	National Park Service Sites
Branson [Access Branson]	http://www.travelnow.com/branson/	Motels & Hotels, Shows & Tickets, Information Center, Roads & Weather, Fishing & Lake Conditions, Dining, Amusement Parks, and Shopping
Hannibal [Welcome to Hannibal, Missouri!]	http://www.webcom.com/~twainweb/	Visitor's & Convention Bureau Home Page, Chamber of Commerce, Visitor and Historical Information, Health Care, Education, and Businesses
Kansas City [Kansas City, Missouri]	http://isotropic.com/metro/kancity.html?	Search, Metroscope, Missouri State W3, U.S. Government W3, World W3, Kansas City Business, Kansas City Media, Kansas City Internet Services, Kansas City Sports, Kansas City Colleges, Kansas City Guides, Kansas City Government, Organizations and Groups, Other K C Sites, Other Missouri Sites, American Universities, All Usenet FAQs, GNN Catalog, List of Lists, NCSA What's New, Multimedia Resources, Nonprofit Organizations, WWW Development, All in One Search, Virtual Library, World Art Resources, Yahoo's Index, Submit to Metroscope, What's New Sites

Table 13.29: Selected Missouri Travel Sites (continued)

Region [Site]	URL	Links
Lake of the Ozarks [The Official Lake of the Ozarks Home Page]	http://www.odd.net/cgi-win/loto.exe	LakeCam (Lake of the Ozarks State Park Photo), Camdenton, Lake Ozark, Osage Beach, Sunrise Beach, Gravois Mills, Greenview, Laurie, Churches, Lakeside Dining, State Parks, Lodging, Weather, Maps, Calendar, and What's New
St. Louis [Low BS Guide to St. Louis]	http://www.inlink.com/~jbhicks/stlguide.html	What St. Louis Looks Like; Getting Into, Around In, and Out of St. Louis; What You Must See In St. Louis; Crime; The People; Food; Cultural Geography; Moving to St. Louis? (Jobs, Housing, Cost of Living, Media); Finding Weirdness; and Addendices
St. Louis [Restaurants of St. Louis, Missouri]	http://stlweb.basenet.net/restaurants/index.html	Restaurants listed alphabetically
St. Louis [St. Louis, Missouri]	http://isotropic.com/metro/stlouisa.html?	Search, METROSCOPE, Washington W3, U.S. Government W3, Art and Cultural Sites, St. Louis Business, Internet Services, St. Louis Sports, St. Louis Colleges, St. Louis Guides, St. Louis Media, Other St. Louis Sites, Other Missouri Sites, American Universities, All Usenet FAQs, GNN Catalog, List of Lists, NCSA What's New, Multimedia Resources, Nonprofit Organizations, WWW Development, All in One Search, Virtual Library, World Art Resources, Yahoo's Index, Submit to METROSCOPE, What's New Sites

Table 13.30: Selected Montana Travel Sites

Region [Site]	URL	Links
State of Montana [City.Net—Montana]	http://www.city.net/countries/united_states/montana/	Cities, Counties, Education, Food and Drink, Government, Magazines and Zines, Other Guides, Parks and Outdoors, State Government, Television and Radio
State of Montana [Montana Big Sky Country]	http://travel.mt.gov/	Camping & Lodging, Events & Attractions, Recreation & Adventure, Welcome & Guestbook, What's New, Travelers' Services, and Other Information (under construction)
State of Montana [Montana State Library Montana Natural Resource Information System]	http://nris.msl.mt.gov/gis/mtmaps.html	Maps of Montana by Counties, Cities, Lakes & Streams, Highways, Railroads, 1990 Population Density, Elevation, Land Use, River Basins, National Forest Land, National Park Service Land, Indian Reservations, U.S. Fish & Wildlife Service Lands, and Legislative Districts

Table 13.30: Selected Montana Travel Sites (continued)

Region [Site]	URL	Links
State of Montana [Montana Web]	http://www.netrix.net/montanaweb/	Artists and Galleries, Businesses, Entertainment, Government & Information, Lodging & Travel, Montana Images, Outdoor Recreation, Personal Home Pages, Publications, Real Estate, Rural Offerings, School and Education
State of Montana [National Park Service—Montana]	http://www.nps.gov:80/parklists/mt.html	National Park Service Sites
Billings [Billings CityLink]	http://banzai.neosoft.com/citylink/billings/	What to See, What to Do, Where to Stay, Where to Eat, Where to Shop, and More Information
Missoula [Welcome to the City of Missoula!]	http://www.ism.net/missoula/index.html	About Missoula, City Government, Weather, Public Library, MCAT (Community Access Television), The Missoulian (Daily Newspaper), University of Montana, and Businesses

Table 13.31: Selected Nebraska Travel Sites

Region [Site]	URL	Links
State of Nebraska [City.Net—Nebraska]	http://www.city.net/countries/united_states/nebraska/	Cities, Education, Food and Drink, Government, Other Guides, Parks and Outdoors, State Information, Television and Radio, Travel and Tourism
State of Nebraska [National Park Service—Nebraska]	http://www.nps.gov:80/parklists/ne.html	National Park Service Sites
State of Nebraska [Nebraska Travel & Tourism]	http://www.ded.state.ne.us/tourism.html	Governor's Welcome, Travel Information, Other Information on Nebraska, Tourism Information from Other States, Other Nebraska Servers
Lincoln [Lincoln Online]	http://www.inetnebr.com/	Organizations, Government, Education, City Map, Arts & Entertainment, Employment, Financial Services, Food & Lodging, News, Weather, Sports, Health & Fitness, KidzStuff, Real Estate, Shopping, and Tourism
Omaha [The Omaha Page]	http://www.novia.net/~cmeyers/omaha.html	Arts and Entertainment, Attractions, History, Recreation Parks, New Resident Information, Misc Omaha Info (Omaha Web page, Area Events, Food, Omaha Photo, Map, Weather, Lodging, Shopping, Photo Tour), Real Estate, Radio Stations, Schools,
Scottsbluff/Gering [United Chamber of Commerce—Scottsbluff/Gering]	http://www.prairieweb.com/scb_gering_ucc/	Highways to History, Events of Interest, Tourist Information, Area Attractions, Area Accommodations, Economic Development, City of Gering, and City of Scottsbluff

Table 13.32: Selected Nevada Travel Sites

Region [Site]	URL	Links
State of Nevada [City.Net—Nevada]	http://www.city.net/countries/united_states/nevada/	Cities, Regions, Education, Food and Drink, Government, Parks and Outdoors, Television and Radio
State of Nevada [National Park Service—Nevada]	http://www.nps.gov:80/parklists/nv.html	National Park Service Sites
Las Vegas [Las Vegas]	http://isotropic.com/metro/lasvegas.html?	Search, Metroscope, Nevada State W3, U.S. Government W3, World W3, Las Vegas Gambling and Shows, Las Vegas Business, Las Vegas Media, Las Vegas Internet Services, Las Vegas Sports, Las Vegas Colleges, Las Vegas Reservations, Las Vegas Guides, Professional Services, Other Las Vegas Sites, Other Nevada Sites, American Universities, All Usenet FAQs, GNN Catalog, List of Lists, NCSA What's New, Multimedia Resources, Nonprofit Organizations, WWW Development, All in One Search, Virtual Library, World Art Resources, Yahoo's Index, Submit to Metroscope, What's New Sites
Las Vegas [Las Vegas Leisure Guide]	http://www.pcap.com/lasvegas.htm	Feature Stories, Features Archive, New Areas, Tours, Lodging, Shows, Dining, Recreation, Night Life, Shopping, Attractions, Maps, Convention/Business, and Other Info Sources
Las Vegas [Las Vegas Maps]	http://www.pcap.com/lvmaps.htm	Street and Area Maps (Las Vegas Strip & Airport, Downtown, West Side, North Las Vegas & Nellis AFB, Las Vegas & Surrounding Area Highways, Laughlin)
Las Vegas [Vegas.COM]	http://www.vegas.com/	Discount Dining, 106.5 FM Radio, Local News, Government, Tourism, Hotels, Restaurants, Shows, On-line Guide to Reno and Surrounding Areas, Gaming, Sports, Businesses, Real Estate, and Entertainment
Reno [Reno Net]	http://www.vegas.com/Reno-net/	Reno/Tahoe Territory, Hotels/Casinos, Dining, Business Connection, and Sports Info

Table 13.33: Selected New Hampshire Travel Sites

Region [Site]	URL	Links
State of New Hampshire [City.Net—New Hampshire]	http://www.city.net/countries/united_states/new_hampshire/	Cities, Businesses, Education, Food and Drink, General Information, Government, Parks and Outdoors, State Information, Television and Radio, Travel and Tourism
State of New Hampshire [National Park Service—New Hampshire]	http://www.nps.gov:80/parklists/nh.html	National Park Service Sites
State of New Hampshire [The Un-Official New Hampshire Travel Guide]	http://VintageDB.com/guide.htm	Travel Guides by Region, State-wide Information (Events, Covered Bridges, Ski Areas, and Lodging)
Atlantic Coast [seacoast.nh]	http://www.star.net/people/~marshall/summer95.htm	The Towns (Dover, Durham, Exeter, the Hamptons, Newmarket, Portsmouth, Rye, Seabrook), The Area (Entertainment, Recreation, Food, Lodging, News and Weather, Nynex Yellow Pages, Information and Tourism, Real Estate and Rentals, NH Resources), Regional Media, and Shopping (under construction)
Londonderry [Londonderry Home Page]	http://www.netis.com/members/londonderry/	An Overview of the Town of Londonderry, Brief History, Information about Our Town (Government, Business, Religious Organizations, Housing and Lodging, Leach Public Library, Local Festivals, Media, Medical Facilities, Recreational Facilities, Transportation), Organizations, and Map (under construction)
Portsmouth [Bridge to the Seacoast]	http://www.nh-meseacoast.com/	Newstand, Tourism, Calendar, Enterprise, Marketplace, and Other Cool Sites

Table 13.34: Selected New Jersey Travel Sites

Region [Site]	URL	Links
State of New Jersey [CAMPING New Jersey]	http://www.beachcomber.com/Nj/campnj.html	Index of New Jersey's Campgrounds by Region
State of New Jersey [City.Net—New Jersey]	http://www.city.net/countries/united_states/new_jersey/	Cities, Counties, Arts and Entertainment, Education, Food and Drink, General Information, Government, Television and Radio, and Transportation
State of New Jersey [National Park Service—New Jersey]	http://www.nps.gov:80/parklists/nj.html	National Park Service Sites

Table 13.34: Selected New Jersey Travel Sites (continued)

Region [Site]	URL	Links
State of New Jersey [New Jersey]	http://isotropic.com/metro/njersey.html?	Search, Metroscope, New Jersey State W3, World W3, U.S. Government W3, World W3, Art and Entertainment Sites, New Jersey Business, New Jersey Media, New Jersey Internet Services, New Jersey Sports, New Jersey Colleges, New Jersey Guides, New Jersey Government, N. J. Professional Services, N. J. Organizations and Groups, Other New Jersey Sites, American Universities, All Usenet FAQs, GNN Catalog, List of Lists, NCSA What's New, Multimedia Resources, Nonprofit Organizations, WWW Development, All in One Search, Virtual Library, World Art Resources, Yahoo's Index, Submit to Metroscope, What's New Sites
State of New Jersey [NJ Transit Train Schedules]	http://www.eclipse.net/~scheurle/njt/	NJ Transit Commuter Train Schedules (by Rail Line, Direction, and Day of the Week), New Jersey Association of Railroad Passengers Site, All-Time NJT/NJDOT Locomotive Roster, Fares to Upstate New York
State of New Jersey [What's Happening in New Jersey]	http://diamond.davison.net/whnj/	Current Issue and Back Issues
Atlantic City [Atlantic City CityLink]	http://banzai.neosoft.com/citylink/atlantic/	What to See, What to Do, Where to Stay, Where to Eat, Where to Shop, and Other Information
Atlantic City [Atlantic City CityLink]	http://banzai.neosoft.com/citylink/atlantic/	What to See, What to Do, Where to Stay, Where to Eat, Where to Shop, and Other Information
Burlington [Welcome to Historic Burlington!]	http://bc.emanon.net/	City History, Events, Community Groups, Schools, Shops, and Tours
Cape May County [Beachcomber.com]	http://www.beachcomber.com/	Cape May County Department of Tourism, Chamber of Commerce Calendar of Events, Mid-Atlantic Center for the Arts, Avalon, Cape May, Graphical Tour, North Wildwood, Ocean City, Sea Isle City, Stone Harbor, Wildwood, Wildwood Crest, Cape Map County Zoo, Beaches, New Jersey Camping and RV Information, and Rainy Day Activities
Cape May [Cape May, New Jersey]	http://www.covesoft.com/capemay/	History, Historical Sights, Attractions, Events, Maps of Cape May and Surrounding Area, Images of Cape May Area, Local Shore Forecast, Churches, Accommodations, Restaurants & Lounges, Shopping, Activities, Services, Classifieds, Internet Links to the Cape May Community Information Pages, Other Interesting Web Sites

Table 13.34: Selected New Jersey Travel Sites (continued)

Region [Site]	URL	Links
Jersey City [Liberty Science Center]	http://www.lsc.org/	The Yuckiest Site on the Internet, Exhibits, New Jersey Institute of Technology
Ocean County [Discover Ocean County NJ]	http://www.vitinc.com/~bohh/oceanco/oc_home.html	Information Directory, Activities (Free Activities, Time Travel Historical Trail, Historical Sites, Parks, Music and Arts, Local Events, Sports), General Information (Amusement Parks, Zoos & Aquariums, Airports, Boardwalks, Campgrounds, Golf Courses, Water Activities, Weather)
Princeton, New Jersey, and Philadelphia, PA [Local Hotels and Restaurants]	http://www.princeton.edu/Main/restaurant.html	Princeton area inns, hotels, restaurants, desserts, NJ Smokefree Dining, Philadelphia area restaurants
Trenton [Trenton Web Page]	http://www.prodworks.com/trenton/index.htm	Events, Restaurants, Local Government, Cultural, Web Sites, Business, Shops, Featured Events, Restaurant Feedback, New Jersey Activities, Travel Schedules, and Weather

Table 13.35: Selected New Mexico Travel Sites

Region [Site]	URL	Links
State of New Mexico [City.Net—New Mexico]	http://www.city.net/countries/united_states/newmexico/	Cities, Education, Events, Food and Drink, Government, Parks and Outdoors, State Information, Television and Radio, Travelogues
State of New Mexico [National Park Service—New Mexico]	http://www.nps.gov:80/parklists/nm.html	National Park Service Sites
State of New Mexico [New Mexico Travel Guide]	http://www.viva.com/nm/regions.html	Mileage Index; New Mexico by Region; Forest, Parks, Monuments, Recreational Areas; Recreational Activities; General Information; Travel to New Mexico (Accommodations, Tours, Travel Agents, Book Your Own Travel)
State of New Mexico [New Mexico Web]	http://www.nets.com/newmextourism/	Current Features (Maps, Mileage, Climate, and Chambers of Commerce), Visitor Information, Culture and Calendar, and Skiing
State of New Mexico [VIVA New Mexico!]	http://www.viva.com/nm/nmhome.html	What's New; Event Calendar; Travel Guide: Culture & Cultural Events; Art and Pictures; Almanac; Schools, Universities, & Libraries; Science and Technology; New Mexico Books; El Mercado; Food & Drink; About VIVA; Commerce; Comments to VIVA

Table 13.35: Selected New Mexico Travel Sites (continued)

Region [Site]	URL	Links
Albuquerque [Albuquerque Information Index]	http://rt66.com/abqinfo/index.html	History, Attractions/Activities, Accommodations, Shopping, Self-Guided Tours, Events, Dining/Nightlife, Native American Culture, Arts & Culture, Tours/Transportation, Media/News Releases, and Meetings/Conventions
Albuquerque [Albuquerque, New Mexico]	http://isotropic.com/metro/albnm.html?	Search, Metroscope, New Mexico State W3, U.S. Government W3, World W3, Art and Cultural Sites, Albuquerque Business, Albuquerque Media, Albuquerque Internet Services, Observatories, Albuquerque Colleges, Albuquerque Guides, Albuquerque Government, National Laboratories, Professional Services, Organizations and Groups, Other Albuquerque Sites, Other New Mexico Sites, American Universities, All Usenet FAQs, GNN Catalog, List of Lists, NCSA What's New, Multimedia Resources, Nonprofit Organizations, WWW Development, All in One Search, Virtual Library, World Art Resources, Yahoo's Index, Submit to Metroscope, What's New Sites
Las Cruces [Las Cruces, New Mexico, USA]	http://www.weblifepro.com/lascruces/	History, Outdoors, General Information, Bus Tour Info, Annual Events, Lodging, The Good Life (Dining and Entertainment), All Around Las Cruces (Recreation, Cultural Attractions, Art), and Day Trips (excellent site)
Santa Fe [Santa Fe Convention and Visitors Bureau Web Site]	http://www.nets.com/santafe.html	What's New & Happening, Santa Fe Profile (Climate, Geography, and more), Getting To and Around, Arts & Culture, Pueblo Indian Culture, History, Historic Downtown Sites, Lodging, Dining & Cuisine, and Meetings and Convention Services
Taos [TaosWebb]	http://taoswebb.com/nmusa/index.html	Skiing, Vacationing, The Arts, and Business

Table 13.36: Selected New York Travel Sites

Region [Site]	URL	Links
State of New York [City.Net—New York]	http://www.city.net/countries/united_states/new_york/	Cities, Counties, Islands, Regions, Businesses, Education, Food and Drink, General Information, Government, Parks and Outdoors, Regional Information, Television and Radio
State of New York [I Love NY—Tourism in New York State]	http://www.iloveny.state.ny.us/	Thousand Islands-Seaway, The Adirondacks, Capital-Saratoga, Central Leatherstocking, Finger Lakes, Niagara Frontier, Chautauqua-Allegheny, The Catskills, Hudson Valley, New York City, Long Island, Commissioner's Message, Accommodations, Events Calendar, NY State Facts, Weather, Major New York State Attractions, Ballooning, Bicycling, Camping, Canoeing, Cross-Country skiing, Downhill Skiing, Dude Ranches, Fishing, Hunting, Snowmobiling, Whitewater Rafting, Family Vacations, History NY, New York City Weekends, I Love the Outdoors, Road Trips, Romantic Getaways, Water Vacations, Empire State Development Travel Information, New York Convention and Visitor's Bureau, Local and Regional Tourism Promotion Agencies
State of New York [Maps of Buffalo, Erie County, Western New York, and the Northeast]	http://www.moran.com/buffalo/maps.html	Maps of Downtown Buffalo, Erie County, Eight-County Western New York Area, and Northeastern United States
State of New York [National Park Service—New York]	http://www.nps.gov:80/parklists/ny.html	National Park Service Sites
State of New York [NuWeb, N.Y.]	http://www.nuwebny.com/	Areas, Cities and Map; Businesses; Attractions; Business Card Directory; Events; News & Weather; History; General Information; Related Web Sites; Related Newsgroups; What's New; NuWeb, NY Museum (Featured Photos); NY Picture Slide Show (excellent site)
State of New York [Online Travel Guide for Upstate New York]	http://www.roundthebend.com/	Regions (Adirondacks, Capital/Saratoga, Catskills, Central Leatherstocking, Chautauqua/Allegheny, Finger Lakes, Hudson Valley, Niagara Frontier, Thousand Islands/Seaway), Activities (Camping, Skiing, Fall Foliage, Golfing, Museums and Galleries, Snowboarding, Spiritual Sites)
Adirondacks [AdirondackNET]	http://www.adirondack.net/	Arts, Media, Current Events, History, Industry, Organizations, Professsional Services, Real Estate and Construction, Retail, Sports, and Tourism
Albany Area [About the Capital Region of New York State]	http://www.crisny.org/about/about_capreg.html	About, Camping, Community Calendar, Computer Resources, Demographics, Environment, Hobbies and Interests, Lodging, Movie Theaters, Museums & Historic Sites, Music, Parks, Publications, Real Estate, Restaurants, Services, Shopping, Sports, Television, Theaters, Transportation, Weather

Table 13.36: Selected New York Travel Sites (continued)

Region [Site]	URL	Links
Buffalo [Buffalo Official Online Information Service]	http://www.moran.com/buffalo/bflotop.html	Attractions, Sports & Recreation, Architecture, Visitor Information, Events & Festivals, Shopping, Theater & Arts, and Regional Attractions
Glens Falls [Glens Falls Restaurants]	http://www.rpi.edu/~vanzad/food.html	Restaurants by Type, Glens Falls Home Page, Glens Falls from A to Z, Events, Local Maps, Parks and Recreation Guide, Local Entertainment, Shopping, Art and Museums, Lodging, and Other Web Sites
Long Island [Long Island Virtual Restaurant Guide]	http://www.macroserve.com/livrg/guide.htm	Restaurants by Location, By Type
Long Island [The Long Island Web Site]	http://www.webscope.com/li/info.html	What's New; Discover Long Island; The Seasons; Recreation; Food, Fun and Lodging; Transportation and Excursions; Business; and Points of Interest
New York City [The Best Restaurants of New-York]	http://www.cam-orl.co.uk/~hs/restos-GB/New-York/GBmain New_York.html	All the different tastes in New-York, The different areas in New-York, All prices in New-York, Index, The authors
New York City [Explore New York]	http://email.com/ExploreNY/NY1.html	Manhattan (Downtown, Midtown, Broadway, Upper West Side, Upper East Side, Uptown)
New York City [New York City]	http://isotropic.com/metro/newyork.html?	Search, Metroscope, New York State W3, U.S. Government W3, World W3, New York City Art and Culture, New York City Business, New York City Media, New York City Sports, New York City Colleges, N Y Internet Services, New York Guides, New York City Government, Professional Services, Organizations and Groups, New York City Financial, Other New York City Sites, Other New York State Sites, American Universities, All Usenet FAQs, GNN Catalog, List of Lists, NCSA What's New, Multimedia Resources, Nonprofit Organizations, WWW Development, All in One Search, Virtual Library, World Art Resources, Yahoo's Index, Submit to Metroscope, What's New Sites
New York City [New York City Reference]	http://www.panix.com/clay/nyc/	Index, What's Cool, What's New
New York City [New York New York]	http://www.WWW.BMCC.CUNY.EDU/NYNY_HTML/bmcc4.htm/	Weather, Locators, Sights, Visual Arts, Performance, Restaurants, Business, Other NY Links, Media, Politics, Introduction, Downtown, Point Survey, Borough of Manhattan Community College, New York New York's Creators
New York City [The Neighborhood]	http://www.nfit.columbia.edu/about_Dalton/Neighborhood/bronx.shtml	Bronx Map
New York City [The New York Botanical Garden]	http://pathfinder.com/@@/u5J@m2EbtAlADlRf/vg/Gardens/NYBG/	About the Botanical Garden, Garden and Plant Collections, Educational Programs, Research, Events and Calendar, Plant Information, and The Shop in the Garden

Table 13.36: Selected New York Travel Sites (continued)

Region [Site]	URL	Links
New York City [New York City Restaurant Finder]	http://www.riar.com/people/sib/foodfind.html	Restaurants by Location and by Cuisine
New York City [New York City's Famous Parks]	http://www.users.interport.net/~jerdugal/nycpark.html	Special Events Calendar, West 59th Recreation Center, Summer Arts in the Parks, Central Park Homepage, Friends of Van Cortlandt Park, Prospect Park Alliance, Times Square History
New York City [New York Opera]	http://plaza.interport.net/nycopera/	Season Information and Tickets, Gift Shop, NYCO Quiz, On-Line Library, Archives, Join the Friends of City Opera, Education and Community Service, Volunteer and Intership Oppurtunities, New York State Theater Information and Technical Data, General Information and Phone Numbers, Related Sites, and Season Highlights
New York City [On Broadway WWW Information Page]	http://artsnet.heinz.cmu.edu/OnBroadway/	On Broadway (Shows currently playing), Off Broadway (Shows currently playing), Tony Award Listings, Broadway Season Summary, WWW Theater Sites (other Theater related WWW Sites), Reviews
New York City [The Paperless Guide to NYC]	http://www.mediabridge.com/nyc/	Holiday Guides, HOW (History & Facts, General Info, Transportation, Navigator, Survival), WOW (Food & Dining, Shopping, Sightseeing, Hotels, Museums), NOW (Current Events, Sports & Fitness, Entertainment, Media, Headlines), Marketplace
New York City [Subway System of New York City (United States of America)]	http://metro.jussieu.fr:10001/bin/select/english/usa/new-york	NYCTA Subway Stations; LIRR, Metro-North and PATH Railways Stations
Rochester [@ Rochester]	http://www.roccplex.com/atroch/welcome.html	Arts and Culture, Hotels, Business, Movies, Education, Recreation, Events, Shopping, Food and Drink, and Sports
Rochester [Rochester, New York]	http://isotropic.com/metro/rochest.html?	Search, Metroscope, New York State W3, U.S. Government W3, World W3, Art and Cultural Sites, Rochester Business, Rochester Media, Rochester Internet Services, Rochester Sports, Rochester Colleges, Rochester Guides, Rochester Government, Rochester Professional Services, Other Rochester Sites, Other New York Sites, American Universities, All Usenet FAQs, GNN Catalog, List of Lists, NCSA What's New, Multimedia Resources, Nonprofit Organizations, WWW Development, All in One Search, Virtual Library, World Art Resources, Yahoo's Index, Submit to Metroscope, What's New Sites

Table 13.36: Selected New York Travel Sites (continued)

Region [Site]	URL	Links
Rochester [Virtual Tourist Guide to Rochester, New York]	ftp://spectrum.xerox.com/pub/map/www/monroe/index.html	Photos, Universities, Eastman Kodak Company, Current Weather, Regional Library Access, Local Coffee Houses
Rochester [The World's Image Centre, Rochester, N.Y.]	http://www.vivanet.com/rochester/visitor.html	Most Asked Questions; History; Museums, Galleries and The Arts; Sights; Sounds and Fun Things; Dining; Clubs and Pubs; Calendar; Business; Hotels and Inns; Shopping; Colleges; Services; Exhibits; and Maps
Saratoga Springs [Saratoga Travel Guide]	http://www.infovantage.com/NY/Saratoga/index.html	Horse Racing, Arts & Entertainment, Museums & Historic Sites, Calendar of Events, Recreation Guide, Restaurant & Pub Guide, Accommodations, Business & Shopping, Regional Weather, How to get to Saratoga, Saratoga Web Links

Table 13.37: Selected North Carolina Travel Sites

Region [Site]	URL	Links
State of North Carolina [City.Net—North Carolina]	http://www.city.net/countries/united_states/north_carolina/	Cities, Counties, Islands, Regions, Education, Food and Drink, Government, Parks and Outdoors, Television and Radio, Travel and Tourism
State of North Carolina [National Park Service—North Carolina]	http://www.nps.gov:80/parklists/nc.html	National Park Service Sites
State of North Carolina [North Carolina Department of Transportation]	http://itre.uncecs.edu/dot/projmap.html	Interactive Highway Construction Project Locator Map
State of North Carolina [North Carolina Department of Transportation Ferry Schedules]	http://itre.uncecs.edu/dot/ferry/ferry.html	Schedules (Southport-Fort Fisher, Cherry Branch-Minnesott, Aurora-Bayview, Ocracoke-Swan Quarter, Cedar Island-Ocracoke, Hatteras-Ocracoke, Currituck-Knotts Island)

Table 13.37: Selected North Carolina Travel Sites (continued)

Region [Site]	URL	Links
State of North Carolina [North Carolina Department of Transportation: Rail Division]	http://tire.uncecs.edu/dot/rail/	Piedmont Daily Schedule (Raleigh to Charlotte), Carolinian Daily Schedule, Overview, Railroad Facts, Internet Railroad Resources, Schedules and Fares
State of North Carolina [Southern Eastern United States Map]	http://sunsite.unc.edu/dykki/ncweather.html	Weather for North Carolina and the southeast, Weather Map with Key, Triangle Area Forecast, State-wide Extended Forecast, Current N.C. Conditions, All N.C. Weather Data, Visual Eastern United States, Infrared Eastern United States, Visual United States, Infrared United States, Visualizations, Recent Severe Weather Advisories, UIUC Weather Machine
Blue Ridge Parkway [Blue Ridge Parkway: A Guided Tour]	http://ncnet.com/ncnw/brp-intr.html	Map: Northern Section, Map: Southern Section, Parkway by Milepost (with Activities)
Charlotte [Charlotte Local]	http://www.webserve.com/charlocal/charlocal.htm	Feature Stories, People & Places, Entertainment
Charlotte [Charlotte, N.C.]	http://isotropic.com/metro/charlot.html?	Search, Metroscope, North Carolina State W3, U.S. Government W3, World W3, Art and Entertainment Sites, Charlotte Business, Charlotte Media, Charlotte Internet Services,Charlotte Sports, Charlotte Colleges, Charlotte Guides, Charlotte Government, Professional Services, Organizations and Groups, Other N. Carolina Sites, American Universities, All Usenet FAQs, GNN Catalog, List of Lists, NCSA What's New, Multimedia Resources, Nonprofit Organizations, WWW Development, All in One Search, Virtual Library, World Art Resources, Yahoo's Index, Submit to Metroscope, What's New Sites
Hickory [Greater Hickory]	http://www.hickory.nc.us/ncnetworks/hkr-intr.html	Calendar of Events; Arts, Culture, and History; Hickory Furniture ONLINE; Business; Lodging and Restaurants; Hickory Crawdads Baseball
Raleigh [Raleigh CityLink]	http://banzai.neosoft.com/citylink/raleigh/	What to See, What to Do, Where to Stay, Where to Eat, Where to Shop, and More Information
Raleigh [User's Guide to the Triangle]	http://nando.net/triguide/	Take It Outside, The Critic's Picks, Entertainment and Nightlife, Raleigh: A Bicentennial History, The Arts, Colleges and Schools, Restaurants, Hotels and Motels, Shopping, Clickable Map of the Triangle, Triangle Public Libraries, Living in North Carolina, Health Care, The News and Observer
Winston-Salem [Welcome to Winston-Salem]	http://www.hickory.nc.us/ncnetworks/ws-intr.html	Things to Do and See (Calendar; Arts, Culture, & History; Sports & Recreation; Business & Industry; Wake Forest University; Lodging and Restaurants), Nearby Cities of Interest

Table 13.38: Selected North Dakota Travel Sites

Region [Site]	URL	Links
State of North Dakota [National Park Service—North Dakota]	http://www.nps.gov:80/parklists/nd.html	National Park Service Sites
State of North Dakota [City.Net—North Dakota]	http://www.city.net/countries/united_states/north_dakota/	Cities, Education, Food and Drink, Government, Parks and Outdoors, Television and Radio

Table 13.39: Selected Ohio Travel Sites

Region [Site]	URL	Links
State of Ohio [City.Net—Ohio]	http://www.city.net/countries/united_states/ohio/	Cities, Education, Food and Drink, Government, History and Literature, Regional Information, Television and Radio
State of Ohio [National Park Service—Ohio]	http://www.nps.gov:80/parklists/oh.html	National Park Service Sites
State of Ohio [Tr@vel.Ohio]	http://www.travel.state.oh.us/	Home, Events, Feature, Lodging, Trips, Club, Search, Welcome to Ohio, What's New, Traveling the Heartland, Buck's Connections
Cincinnati [The Best of Greater Cincinnati]	http://cinci.com/contents	For Your Information, Recreation & Entertainment, Visiting & Relocating, News & Commentary, New, Live, Feedback, About
Cincinnati [Cincinnati, OH CityLink]	http://banzai.neosoft.com/citylink/cincinnati/	What to See, What to Do, Where to Stay, Where to Eat, Where to Shop, and More Information
Cincinnati [Cincinnati, Ohio]	http://isotropic.com/metro/cincinn.html?	Search, Metroscope, Ohio State W3, U.S. Government W3, World W3, Cincinnati Business, Cincinnati Media, Cincinnati Internet Services, Cincinnati Sports, Cincinnati Colleges, Cincinnati Guides, Professional Services, Organizations and Groups, Other Cincinnati Sites, Other Ohio Sites, American Universities, All Usenet FAQs, GNN Catalog, List of Lists, NCSA What's New, Multimedia Resources, Nonprofit Organizations, WWW Development, All in One Search, Virtual Library, World Art Resources, Yahoo's Index, Submit to Metroscope, What's New Sites
Cleveland [Cleveland.net]	http://www.cleveland.net/cleveland/	General Information, Lifestyles, Business, Reference Directory, What's New, Entertainment & Dining, Sweepstakes, Rock & Roll Hall of Fame

Table 13.39: Selected Ohio Travel Sites (continued)

Region [Site]	URL	Links
Cleveland [Cleveland, Ohio]	http://isotropic.com/metro/cle.html?	Search, Metroscope, Ohio State W3, U.S. Government W3, World W3, Art and Entertainment Sites, Cleveland Business, Cleveland Media, Cleveland Internet Services, Cleveland Sports, Cleveland Colleges, Cleveland Guides, Cleveland Government, Professional Services, Organizations and Groups, Other Cleveland Sites, Other Ohio Sites, American Universities, All Usenet FAQs, GNN Catalog, List of Lists, NCSA What's New, Multimedia Resources, Nonprofit Organizations, WWW Development, All in One Search, Virtual Library, World Art Resources, Yahoo's Index, Submit to Metroscope, What's New Sites
Cleveland [CLEVE.NET: The North Coast Post]	http://antares.en.com/cleve.net/	Arts & Entertainment, Commerce, Education, General, Government, Other Organizations
Cleveland [Facts about the Rock and Roll Hall of Fame+Museum]	http://www.rocknroll.org/	The Inductees, The Architect, Exhibit Facts, Collection Facts, Highlights
Cleveland [TRAVELCLEVE-LAND]	http://www.webcom.com/~infoserv/traicleveland/travel.html	Accommodations, Calendar, Community (Programs, Organizations, History, and General Information), Cultural Activities, Cyberspace Cleveland, Education, Food, Recreation/Entertainment, Search (Word search of information in Travel/Cleveland), Shopping, Sports, Transportation, and Weather
Cleveland and Cuyahoga County [Regional Transit Authority]	http://www.cwru.edu/Cleve/rta/rta.html	Bus and Rail Lines (Information and Other Transportation Services, Downtown System Loops, Fares and Ticket Pricing)
Columbus [The Columbus Home Page]	http://www.ohiocap.com/columbus/	Arts & Entertainment, Business, Today's News, Television, Magazines, Weather, Comics, For Columbus Visitors, Local News, Map of Downtown, Regional Map (with Shopping Areas), Government, Ohio State University (Campus Tour)
Columbus [Columbus, Ohio]	http://isotropic.com/metro/columbus.html?	Search, Metroscope, Ohio State W3, World W3, Art and Cultural Sites, Columbus Business, Columbus Media, Columbus Internet Services, Columbus Sports, Columbus Colleges, Columbus Guides, Columbus Government, Professional Services, other Columbus Sites, Other Ohio Sites, American Universities, All usenet FAQs, GNN Catalog, List of Lists, NCSA What's New, Multimedia Resources, Nonprofit Organizations, WWW Development, All in One Search, Virtual Library, World Art Resources, Yahoo's Index, Submit to Metroscope, What's new Sites

Table 13.39: Selected Ohio Travel Sites (continued)

Region [Site]	URL	Links
Columbus [ColumbusPages™]	http://www.columbuspages.com/	Welcome, Currents (Weather, Calendar, and Club Gigs), Community (Art and Culture, Media, Personal Pages, Organizations, Sports, Nightlife, Government, and Education), Marketplace, Guides (Restaurants, Theaters, Lodging, and Malls)
Dayton [The Dayton Home Page]	http://www.dayton.net/dayton/	History, Tourism, Calendar of Events, Accommodations, Restaurants, Shopping, Transportation, Suburbs, Financial Information, Hospitals, Universities, Wright Patterson Air Force Base, Sports, Local Business, Media, Weather, and Realty
Toledo [Toledo, Ohio—"The Heart of It All"]	http://www.toledolink.com/~matgerke/toledo/toledo.html	Information about Toledo's Resources (Businesses, Educational Institutions, Culture); News (Recent Press Releases, Ohio News); Weather, Maps, and Travel; History; Suburbs; and Statistical Information

Table 13.40: Selected Oklahoma Travel Sites

Region [Site]	URL	Links
State of Oklahoma [City.Net—Oklahoma]	http://www.city.net/countries/united_states/oklahoma/	Cities, Education, Food and Drink, Government, Parks and Outdoors, Television and Radio
State of Oklahoma [National Park Service—Oklahoma]	http://www.nps.gov:80/parklists/ok.html	National Park Service Sites
Oklahoma City [Oklahoma City Home Page]	http://www.netplus.net/okc/	Attractions, Events, History, Downtown, Accommodations, Business Highlights, What's New, and Chamber of Commerce

Table 13.41: Selected Oregon Travel Sites

Region [Site]	URL	Links
State of Oregon [City.Net—Oregon]	http://www.city.net/countries/united_states/oregon/	Cities, Counties, Metropolitan Areas, Regions, Community Organizations, Education, Food and Drink, Government, Internet Access Providers, Other Guides, Parks and Outdoors, Television and Radio
State of Oregon [National Park Service—Oregon]	http://www.nps.gov:80/parklists/or.html	National Park Service Sites

Table 13.41: Selected Oregon Travel Sites (continued)

Region [Site]	URL	Links
State of Oregon [Oregon Community Resources]	http://www.state.or.us/quality.htm	Albany, InterAshland, Cave Junction & Illinois Valley, Cottage Grove, Douglas County Home Page, Eugene Home Page, The Eugene Pages, Gold Beach, Grants Pass, Hillsboro, Lkamath County Home Page, Lincoln City, Marion County, McKenzie River Valley, Rogue River, Roseburg, Salem, Springfield, Sweet Home, Portland (several sites), InterRogue, Visit Southern Oregon, Southern Oregon, Pacific Harbor, Yahoo's Guide to Oregon by Region, CityNet's Guide to Oregon by Region, Seniors On-Line, Go to the Natural Resources, Great Outdoor Recreation Pages, Oregon Climate Service Home Page, ODOT Highway Report, Environmental Issues
State of Oregon [State Map of Oregon]	http://www.cse.ogi.edu/ oregon-map.html	Map of Oregon
Eugene [Welcome to Eugene, Oregon!]	http://www.efn.org/~sgazette/ eugenehome.html	General Information (Business Pages, Community Pages (Facts & Figures, Governmental Agencies, History, Media, Education, Surrounding Area, Weather), Things to Do (Arts & Entertainment, Events/Festivals, Museums, Parks, Recreation, Restaurants & Cafes, Shopping, Sports, Travel, Young at Heart, Getting Around (Airport, Auto Rentals, Bicycles, Buses, Maps, Taxis, Trains), Visitor Information (Bed & Breakfast Inns, Hotels & Motels, University of Oregon), and What's New
Portland [Portland Area Restaurants]	http://www.teleport.com/~ronl/ restrnt.html	Alphabetical Listing of Restaurants, Reviews
Portland [Portland, Oregon]	http://isotropic.com/metro/ portland.html?	Search, Metroscope, Oregon State W3, U.S. Government W3, World W3, Art and Cultural Sites, Portland Business, Portland Media, Portland Internet Services, Portland Sports, Portland Colleges, Portland Guides, Portland Government, Professional Services, Portland Financial, Organizations and Groups, Other Portland Sites, Other Oregon Sites, American Universities, All Usenet FAQs, GNN Catalog, List of Lists, NCSA What's New, Multimedia Resources, Nonprofit Organizations, WWW Development, All in One Search, Virtual Library, World Art Resources, Yahoo's Index, Submit to Metroscope, What's New Sites
Portland [Sally's Restaurant Listings]	http://www.bpe.com/dining/listings/ portland20.html	List of recommended restaurants
Portland [seethecity InterPortland]	http://www.eek.com/eek/portland/ ?CityAd	Arts & Entertainment, City & Regional Information, Businesses & Organizations, Visitor Information & Attractions
Portland [A Visual Tour of Downtown Portland, Oregon]	http://www.fpa.pdx.edu/depts/fpa/ html/portlandtour.html	Photos of Portland, Featured Areas (South Park Blocks, Oregon Historical Society, Cultural District), Weather Today, and School of Fine and Performing Arts (slow loading)
Portland Area [Transit Station]	http://www.tri-met.org/	News (Rider Alerts, Special Events, Press Releases, Construction Update), Routes, Fares, Easy Riding (Using the Bus, Using MAX Light Rail, Fares, Personalized Trip Planning), Visitors (Around Town, Vintage Trolley, Visitors Association), and Other Information

Table 13.42: Selected Pennsylvania Travel Sites

Region [Site]	URL	Links
State of Pennsylvania [City.Net—Pennsylvania]	http://www.city.net/countries/united_states/pennsylvania/	Cities, Counties, Education, Food and Drink, Government, Parks and Outdoors, Regional Information, State Information, Television and Radio
State of Pennsylvania [Commonwealth of Pennsylvania]	http://www.state.pa.us/	Coming Attractions and Recent Additions, Visitors Guide, Government and Services, Education, Weather, Lottery Results, Business, and Technology
State of Pennsylvania [National Park Service—Pennsylvania]	http://www.nps.gov:80/parklists/pa.html	National Park Service Sites
State of Pennsylvania [Pennsylvania Maps]	http://mtmis1.mis.semi.harris.com/maps.html	Mountaintop Map, Pennsylvania Map, Luzerne County Map, Pennsylvania Highway Map, Map of Pennsylvania Counties
Bucks County [Bucks County, Pennsylvania]	http://www.covesoft.com/Bucks_County	Attractions, Shopping, Restaurants, Lodging, Services, Activities, Special Events, More Information, Pictures of the Area, Local Philadelphia Forecast, Maps of Bucks County and Surrounding Environs
Gettysburg [Gettysburg, Pennsylvania]	http://gettysburg.welcome.com/	The Battle of Gettysburg, The Gettysburg Address, Gettysburg's Location, Calendar of Events, Attractions, Accommodations, Shopping, Dining, Information Booklet, and Video Preview
Lancaster County [Welcome To The Pennsylvania Dutch Country!]	http://padutch.welcome.com/	General Information (The Amish, An Overview of the Area, Covered Bridges, Quilts and Quilting, Free Things to Do, Calendar of Events, Map and Visitors Guide, Video Preview), Specific Information (Attractions, Accommodations, Shopping, Dining, Sightseeing/Tours, Publications/Information, Strasburg Area Information)
Mountaintop [Mountaintop Home Page]	http://mtmis1.mis.semi.harris.com/welcome.html	What's New, Weather and Time, Harris E-mail/Phone Dir, Other Servers, Semiconductors, Reference Data, News, PC, FTP Sites, Financial, Entertainment, Miscellaneous Information about N.E. Pennsylvania, Area Maps, General Internet Info, Mountaintop Master Index
Philadelphia [Fun in the Philadelphia Region]	http://www.libertynet.org:80/fun/	Convention and Visitors Bureau; Restaurants and Hotels; Sightseeing, History, and Culture; Museums, Galleries, and Performing Arts; Radio, TV, Newspapers, and Magazines; Hobbies, Recreation and Professional Sports; and Weather
Philadelphia [Joe's Links to Philadelphia Information]	http://cwis.usc.edu/dept/cs/personal/jdevlin/Philly.html	Maps of Philadelphia, Outdoor Attractions, Philadelphia Convention and Visitor's Bureau, The latest Philly weather report, SEPTA Rail Schedules, Philly Foods, Where to Eat in Historic Philadelphia, Philly's Finest Foods, The Philadelphia Eagles, The Philadelphia Phillies, The Philadelphia 76ers, Philadelphia Flyers, Sporting Activities, Education & Culture, Music & Dance, Media, Non-Profit Organizations, Moving to Philly?, General Philadelphia Guides, Other Local Information

Table 13.42: Selected Pennsylvania Travel Sites (continued)

Region [Site]	URL	Links
Philadelphia [Maps of the Philadelphia Area]	http://www.upenn.edu/img/maps/philly-maps.html	Maps (Center City East, Center City West, Greater Philadelphia Area, Penn's Landing and Historic Area), Videos (City Hall, Penn's Landing, Independence Hall and the Liberty Bell)
Philadelphia [Philadelphia, PA]	http://isotropic.com/metro/philly.html?	Search, Metroscope, Pennsylvania State W3, U.S. Government W3, World W3, Art and Entertainment Sites, Philadelphia Business, Philadelphia Media, Philadelphia Internet Services, Philadelphia Sports, Philadelphia Colleges, Philadelphia Guides, Philadelphia Government, Professional Services, Organizations and Groups, Other Philadelphia Sites, Other Pennsylvania Sites, American Universities, All Usenet FAQs, GNN Catalog, List of Lists, NCSA What's New, Multimedia Resources, Nonprofit Organizations, WWW Development, All in One Search, Virtual Library, World Art Resources, Yahoo's Index, Submit to Metroscope, What's New Sites
Pittsburgh [Pittsburgh]	http://isotropic.com/metro/pittsbrg.html?	Search, Metroscope, Pennsylvania W3, U.S. Government W3, World W3, Art and Entertainment Sites, Pittsburgh Business, Pittsburgh Media, Pittsburgh Internet Services, Pittsburgh Sports, Pittsburgh Colleges, Pittsburgh Guides, Professional Services, Pittsburgh Financial, Organizations and Groups, Other Pittsburgh Sites, Other Pennsylvania Sites, American Universities, All Usenet FAQs, GNN Catalog, List of Lists, NCSA What's New, Multimedia Resources, Nonprofit Organizations, WWW Development, All in One Search, Virtual Library, World Art Resources, Yahoo's Index, Submit to Metroscope, What's New Sites
Pittsburgh [Pittsburgh...South Side]	http://www.maya.com/Local/sahside/sahside.html	Calendar of Events, Food & Drink (by Type), Fun, Shops, and Miscellaneous
Scranton [Listening@the.socket]	http://www.scranton.com/	CafeNews (guestbook), Arts and Culture, The Anthracite Region, Media, Institutions, Entertainment, Users Home Pages, Regional Web Sites, Our Supporters, The Gate
Wilkes-Barre [Wilkes-Barre, Pennsylvania, and Surrounding Areas]	http://mtmis1.mis.semi.harris.com/wb.html	Weather, Local News and Info, Maps (Mountaintop, Luzerne County, and Pennsylvania Maps, Wilkes-Barre Street Map), History (Wilkes-Barre, Scranton and Steamtown NHS), Parks and Recreation, Universities, Skiing, Cultural Resources, Museums and Historic Sites, Shopping Malls, Motels, and Airport

Table 13.43: Selected Rhode Island Travel Sites

Region [Site]	URL	Links
State of Rhode Island [City.Net—Rhode Island]	http://www.city.net/countries/united_states/rhode_island/	Cities, Businesses, Education, Food and Drink, Government, Parks and Outdoors, State Information, Television and Radio
State of Rhode Island [National Park Service—Rhode Island]	http://www.nps.gov:80/parklists/ri.html	National Park Service Sites
State of Rhode Island [Rhode Island Online]	http://www.ids.net/ri/	Local Weather, Business, Entertainment, Recreation and Tourism, Government, From the State House (State Archives), and Other Local Attractions (under construction)
Providence [Providence CityLink]	http://banzai.neosoft.com/citylink/providen/	What to See, What to Do, Where to Stay, Where to Eat, Where to Shop, and More Information

Table 13.44: Selected South Carolina Travel Sites

Region [Site]	URL	Links
State of South Carolina [City.Net—South Carolina]	http://www.city.net/countries/united_states/south_carolina/	Cities, Islands, Education, Food and Drink, General Information, Government, Parks and Outdoors, State Information, Television and Radio, Travel and Tourism
State of South Carolina [National Park Service—South Carolina]	http://www.nps.gov:80/parklists/sc.html	National Park Service Sites
State of South Carolina [Scenic]	http://scenic.ricommunity.com/	Tourism, SC Info, Entertainment, News/Sports, Marketplace, Guide, What's New, South Carolina White Pages, South Carolina Yellow Pages
State of South Carolina [South Carolina]	http://isotropic.com/metro/sc.html?	Search, METROSCOPE, South Carolina W3, U.S. Government W3, Art and Entertainment Sites, S. C. Business, S. C. Resorts, S. C. Media, S. C. Internet Access, S. C. Web Builders, S. C. Sports, S. C. Colleges, S. C. Guides, S. C. Government, S. C. Professional Services, Organizations and Groups, Other S. C. Sites, American Universities, All Usenet FAQs, GNN Catalog, List of Lists, NCSA What's New, Multimedia Resources, Nonprofit Organizations, WWW Development, All in One Search, Virtual Library, World Art Resources, Yahoo's Index, Submit to METROSCOPE, What's New Sites
State of South Carolina [South Carolina Home Page]	http://www.state.sc.us/	Greetings from the Governor, State Agencies, Government in the Palmetto State, History, Commerce & Tourism (Department of Commerce, South Carolina Business Gateway, Tourism, State Parks, Guide to Olympic Games), Education, Network & Information Services, Other Interesting Information

Table 13.44: Selected South Carolina Travel Sites (continued)

Region [Site]	URL	Links
State of South Carolina [South Carolina Smiling Faces, Beautiful Places]	http://www.prt.state.sc.us/sc/home.html	Clickable Map of South Carolina (by Region: Historic Charleston, Capital City and Lake Murray Country, Olde English District, Grand Strand and Myrtle Beach Area, Lowcountry and Resort Islands, Old 96 District, Pee Dee Country, Santee Cooper Country, Thoroughbred Country, Discover Upcountry Carolina), Golf Guide, Calendar of Events, Things to Do, History, Accommodations, International Offices, Additional Information, and Free Travel Guide and Map
Charleston [Welcome to Charleston]	http://www.ricommunity.com/scenic/tourism/charles.htm	Activities, Beaches, Parks, Historic Sights, Historic Homes, Plantations and Gardens, Golf, Accommodations, Dining Guide (under construction)
Myrtle Beach [Myrtle Beach Live!]	http://www.myrtlebeach-info.com/	Lodging, Golf, Entertainment, Amusement, Shopping, Dining, Real Estate, News-Weather, Public Info, Golf Packages, Show Packages, Speed Traps, Beach Sounds, Photo Gallery
Myrtle Beach [Myrtle Beach, SC]	http://www.hickory.nc.us/ncnetworks/mb-intr.html	Myrtle Beach Area Map, Calendar of Events, Entertainment, Shopping, Furniture OnLine, Area Golf Courses, Lodging and Restaurants

Table 13.45: Selected South Dakota Travel Sites

Region [Site]	URL	Links
State of South Dakota [City.Net—South Dakota]	http://www.city.net/countries/united_states/south_dakota/	Cities, Education, Food and Drink, Government, Government Information, Parks and Outdoors, Regional Information, Television and Radio, Travel and Tourism. Note: Unlike other states, when you select a city from the South Dakota Cities Listings, you will only find the site created by the South Dakota Tourism Council. Because of this, you will find more cities covered but less variety.
State of South Dakota [Maps of South Dakota]	http://www.state.sd.us/state/executive/tourism/maps/maps.htm	Map of the Midwest (Interstate Highways), South Dakota Road Map, Black Hills Area Map, Mt. Rushmore Map, Custer State Park Maps, Black Hills Caves Map, Maps/Mileage Charts, SD Snowmobile Maps, State Park and Recreation Areas Maps
State of South Dakota [National Park Service—South Dakota]	http://www.nps.gov:80/parklists/sd.html	National Park Service Sites
State of South Dakota [South Dakota Department of Tourism]	http://www.state.sd.us/tourism/	Information by Region (Black Hills, Badlands & Lakes Region; Great Lakes Region; Glacial Lakes & Prairies Region; Dakota Heritage & Lakes Region), Accommodations and Services, American Indian, Attractions/Sites, Cities, Events, Fun Facts, Tour Planning Guide, Maps, National and State Parks, Outdoor Recreation, Travel Tips, What's New, and More Information

Table 13.45: Selected South Dakota Travel Sites (continued)

Region [Site]	URL	Links
Black Hills [Regional Information for the Black Hills]	http://www.sfsml.edu/regional/regional.html	Photo (Very nice!), Visitor Attractions, Local Weather
Madison [Madison The Heart of Lake County]	http://www.dsu.edu/projects/madison/	Government, History, Feature Stories, Photos, Labor, Lake Herman State Park, Mass Media, Prairie Village, Recreation, Schools, Police
Sioux Falls [Sioux Falls A Good Thing Going]	http://www.iw.net/sioux_falls/index.htm	Photo, Churches, Education, Festivals, Golf Courses, Indian Culture, Magazines, Organizations, Rooms/Inns, Waterparks, Weather, Western Art, Zoo, Graphical Sioux Falls
Sisseton Wahpeton Sioux Tribe [Sisseton Wahpeton Sioux Tribe]	http://swcc.cc.sd.us/homepage.htm	Language Homepage (Lessons 1-3), Points of Interest (Dakota Art, Calendar of Events, Dakota Culture, Education, Historic Sites, South Dakota Web Page)

13.46: Selected Tennessee Travel Sites

Region [Site]	URL	Links
State of Tennessee [City.Net— Tennessee]	http://www.city.net/countries/united_states/tennessee/	Cities, Counties, Education, Food and Drink, Government, Parks and Outdoors, State Information, Television and Radio, Travel and Tourism
State of Tennessee [National Park Service—Tennessee]	http://www.nps.gov:80/parklists/tn.html	National Park Service Sites
Chattanooga [Chattanooga CityLink]	http://banzai.neosoft.com/citylink/chat/	What to See, What to Do, Where to Stay, Where to Eat, Where to Shop, and More Information
Memphis [City of Memphis]	http://www.vidosplk.com/memphis/	Memphis Weather, Concerts, Exhibits, Theater, Miscellaneous Events, Downtown, Map
Memphis [Memphis, Tennessee]	http://isotropic.com/metro/memphis.html?	Search, Metroscope, Tennessee State W3, U.S. Government W3, World W3, Art and Cultural Sites, Memphis Business, Memphis Media, Memphis Internet Services, Memphis Education, Memphis Guides, Professional Services, Other Tennessee Sites, American Universities, All Usenet FAQs, GNN Catalog, List of Lists, NCSA What's New, Multimedia Resources, Nonprofit Organizations, WWW Development, All in One Search, Virtual Library, World Art Resources, Yahoo's Index, Submit to Metroscope, What's New Sites

13.46: Selected Tennessee Travel Sites (continued)

Region [Site]	URL	Links
Nashville [Nashville]	http://isotropic.com/metro/nash.html?	Search, Metroscope, Tennessee W3, World W3, U.S. Government W3, World W3, Music and Entertainment Sites, Nashville Business, Nashville Music Sites, Nashville Media, Nashville Internet Access, Nashville Sports, Nashville Colleges, Nashville Guides, Nashville Government, Professional Services, Organizations and Groups, Other Nashville Sites, Other Tennessee Sites, American Universities, All Usenet FAQs, GNN Catalog, List of Lists, NCSA What's New, Multimedia Resources, Nonprofit Organizations, WWW Development, All in One Search, Virtual Library, World Art Resources, Yahoo's Index, Submit to Metroscope, What's New Sites
Nashville [Nashville Music City Vacation Guide]	http://nashville.musiccityusa.com/tour/index.html	Index of Offerings, Free Copy of Vacation Guide, Convention and Meeting Planning Information, and Hot Picks

Table 13.47: Selected Texas Travel Sites

Region [Site]	URL	Links
State of Texas [City.Net—Texas]	http://www.city.net/countries/united_states/texas/	Cities, Metropolitan Areas, Education, Food and Drink, Government, Other Guides, Parks and Outdoors, Regional Information, State Government, Television and Radio, Travel and Tourism
State of Texas [National Park Service—Texas]	http://www.nps.gov:80/parklists/tx.html	National Park Service Sites
State of Texas [State of Texas Tourist Information]	http://www.texas.gov/tourist.html	Texas State Parks, Welcome to Texas, Texas Resource Listings
State of Texas [Texas Monthly]	http://www.texasmonthly.com/	Steppin' Out (Texas Events and Entertainment Info), Hit the Road (Texas Travel Info), What's Cooking (Texas Restaurant Reviews, Texas Recipes), Texas Talk (Bulletin Board), What's New (Marketplace, Texas Monthly Store), Hot Spot, and Texas Monthly's Current Issue
State of Texas [TEXAS—The REAL Guide]	http://www.amarillo-tx.com/realtex.html	Doing Business in Texas, Having Fun in Texas (includes calendars of events and outdoors), Best Places (Texas Towns & Cities)
State of Texas [Welcome to Texas]	http://traveltex.com/	Texas Search List (Name, Topic, Region), Ordering Information (Travel Guide, Texas Highways Magazine), Texas Tours, Interactive Map, Texas Postcards (Photos), Scavenger Hunt Game, Tour Tex 2000 (Information by City or Town), and Texas Calendar
Abilene [Abilene Online]	http://www.abilene.com/	What's New, Convention & Visitors Bureau, Arts and Entertainment, Business and Industry, Community Services, Dining, Education, Health Care, Local Government, Media, Real Estate, Religion

Table 13.47: Selected Texas Travel Sites (continued)

Region [Site]	URL	Links
Austin [Austin City Limits]	http://www.quadralay.com/Austin/austin.html	Antone's Home of the Blues; Armadillos; Business; Community Calendar; Education; Fine Arts; Food, Drink, and Lodging; Government; Image Map; Media; Movies; Music Scene; Online Services; Organizations; Recreation; Reference, General; Services, General; Southwest Airlines
Austin [Austin Information Center]	http://www.tech.net/austin/	Public Service Listings, Commercial Listings, Dining Guide, New Dining Guide, Alphabetic Index
Austin [Austin, Texas]	http://isotropic.com/metro/austin.html?	Search, Metroscope, Texas State W3, U.S. Government W3, World W3, Art and Cultural Sites, Austin Business, Austin Media, Austin Internet Services, Austin Sports, Austin Colleges, Austin Guides, Austin Government, Professional Services, Austin Financial, Organizations and Groups, Other Austin Sites, Other Texas Sites, American Universities, All Usenet FAQs, GNN Catalog, List of Lists, NCSA What's New, Multimedia Resources, Nonprofit Organizations, WWW Development, All in One Search, Virtual Library, World Art Resources, Yahoo's Index, Submit to Metroscope, What's New Sites
Austin [Austin Visitor's Guide]	http://visit.ci.austin.tx.us/	Texas Welcome (Frequently Asked Questions), Austin Phone Numbers, History, Super Sights, Entertainment, Touring the Area, Festivals and Events, Shopping, and Accommodations
Austin [An Engineer's Guide to Austin Restaurants]	http://www.quadralay.com:80/www/Austin/AustinFood/engineer.html	Asian, Barbeque, Beer, Breakfast, Burgers, Dessert, Mediterranean, Mexican, Pizza, Sandwiches, Seafood, Steak, Texas, Vegetarian, OtherEthnic, Eclectic, Late Night
Austin [Entertain Austin]	http://www.websrc.com/enteryn.htm	Food and Dining (by Cuisine, by Price Range, by Location)
Austin [Entrees on Trays]	http://entrees.com/	Home delivery: Register with Entrees, Information, Restaurants, Comments, Restaurant Map
Austin [Hotel Guide of San Antonio & Austin]	http://www.dcci.com/HotelGuide/HotelGuide.html	Accommodations, Relocation Information, Events, Texas Pages, Golfing in Texas, and More
Austin [Metropolitan Austin Interactive Network]	http://www.main.org/	Metropolitan austin Community Pages, Austin Area Visitor Information, Events in the Austin Area, austin City Connection, Austin Free-Net, Community Networks and Infrastructure, Parent's Guide, and more
Austin [Places to Eat in Austin]	http://www.quadralay.com:80/www/Austin/AustinFood/AustinFood	Asian, BBQ, Brunch, Cajun, Italian, Latin, Pizza, Steak Houses, Sushi, Tamales, TexMex, Vegetarian Burgers, Vegetarian Restaurants, An Engineer's Guide to Austin Restaurants, TechNet Austin Dining Guide
Austin [T.A.B. Net Travel Guide—Austin, Texas]	http://www.tab.com/Travel/Austin/Austin.html	Pictures of Austin, Hotels (by Area), Restaurants (by Type), Car Rental Agencies, Limo Services, Places to See (Austin Night Clubs, Golf Courses), Radio Stations, Additional Information about Austin, Austin Area Maps

Table 13.47: Selected Texas Travel Sites (continued)

Region [Site]	URL	Links
Austin [WebSource, Inc.]	http://www.websrc.com/	Listing of all Austin restaurants, Check out zoos in and around Texas, A listing of all Austin area apartments, and more
Dallas [Dallas Area Restaurant Guide]	http://www.w3.com/dallas/	City/Type Listings, Search Reviews, Search Restaurants, Interactive Map, Alphabetical Listings, All Restaurants by Type, Top Reviewers, Restaurant w/ Home Pages or Photos, Your Restaurant List, New Reviews, Add a Restaurant
Dallas [Dallas Entertainment Guide]	http://www.wn.com/dallas/	Upcoming Events, Business Guide, Dining, Clubs & Live Music, Roadshows, Hotels, Museums, Shopping, Attractions, In the Spotlight (Featured Festivals, Museums, etc.), Of Special Interest (Businesses, Media, Local Bands, Sports, Magazines/Publications, Restaurants & Bars)
Dallas-Ft. Worth [Dallas-Ft. Worth]	http://isotropic.com/metro/dallas.html?	Search, Metroscope, Texas State W3, U.S. Government W3, World W3, Art and Cultural Sites, Dallas Business, Dallas Media, Internet Services, Dallas Sports, Colleges & Universities, Professional Services, Financial Sites, Clubs and Groups, Other Dallas Sites, Other Texas Sites, American Universities, All Usenet FAQs, GNN Catalog, List of Lists, NCSA What's New, Multimedia Resources, Nonprofit Organizations, WWW Development, All in One Search, Virtual Library, World Art Resources, Yahoo's Index, Submit to Metroscope, What's New Sites
El Paso [El Paso, Texas]	http://cs.utep.edu/elpaso/main.html	History, Dining, Location, Climate, University of Texas, Surrounding Sites, Event Calendar, Hotels and Motels, Museums and Historic Sites
Galveston [Virtual Tour of Galveston Island]	http://www.utmb.edu/galveston/welcome.html	Attractions, Beaches, Community, Entertainment, Festivals, Map, Historic Homes, Hotels, Restaurants, Universities, and Slide Show (Photos)
Gulf Coast [Gulf Coast Region Restaurants]	http://www.texasmonthly.com/resto/gulf-coast.html	Restaurant Reviews by City
Houston [Houston Entertainment Web]	http://www.compassnet.com/entertainment/	Music Club Calendar and Directory, Movies, Restaurants, What's Happening Today, and Fine Arts
Houston [Houston Real-Time Traffic Map]	http://herman.tamu.edu/traffic.html	Houston Map with Clickable Roadway Segments
Houston [Houston Restaurant Database]	http://ngsa.rice.edu/restdb.html	Clickable map, List, Search, Submit

Table 13.47: Selected Texas Travel Sites (continued)

Region [Site]	URL	Links
Houston [Houston, Texas]	http://isotropic.com/metro/houston.html?	Search, Metroscope, Texas State W3, U.S. Government W3, World W3, Art and Entertainment Sites, Houston Business, Houston Internet Services, Houston Sports, Houston Colleges, Houston Guides, Houston Media, Houston Government, Professional Services, Houston Financial, Organizations and Groups, Other Houston Sites, Other Texas Sites, American Universities, All Usenet FAQs, GNN Catalog, List of Lists, NCSA What's New, Multimedia Resources, Nonprofit Organizations, WWW Development, All in One Search, Virtual Library, World Art Resources, Yahoo's Index, Submit to Metroscope, What's New Sites
Houston [Sally's Restaurant Listings]	http://www.hpe.com/dining/listings/houston20.html	List of recommended restaurants
San Antonio [Hotel Guide of San Antonio & Austin]	http://www.dcci.com/HotelGuide/HotelGuide.html	Accommodations, Relocation Information, Events, Texas Pages, Golfing in Texas, and More
San Antonio [Passport Gateway Magazine]	http://www.gadsby.com/passport/index.html	Hotel Reservations, Attractions, Calendar of Events, Dining, Dining Reservations, Discount Program, Golf, Tournament And Tee Time Reservations, Relocation, River Walk, Shopping, Touring Texas, and Travel Weekly
San Antonio [San Antonio, Texas]	http://isotropic.com/metro/sa.html?	Search, METROSCOPE, Texas W3, U.S. Government W3, Art and Entertainment Sites, San Antonio Business, San Antonio Media, San Antonio Internet Access, San Antonio Web Builders, San Antonio Sports, San Antonio Colleges, San Antonio Guides, San Antonio Government, Professional Services, Organizations and Groups, Other San Antonio Sites, Other Texas Sites, American Universities, All Usenet FAQs, GNN Catalog, List of Lists, NCSA What's New, Multimedia Resources, Nonprofit Organizations, WWW Development, All in One Search, Virtual Library, World Art Resources, Yahoo's Index, Submit to METROSCOPE, What's New Sites
San Antonio [What's in San Antonio]	http://www.gadsby.com/	San Antonio Airport; Amusement Parks; The City of Boerne, Texas; Dateline; Fast Food; Local Government; Fly Fishing; Hospitals; Hotels & Motels; Libraries; Military Bases; Museums; City Parks; Real Estate; Restaurants; Schools, Shopping Malls; Weather; and Shopping
Waco [Waco Web]	http://www.acm.org/waco/	Upcoming Events, Annual Events, What's New, Historic Houses, Shopping, Waco History, Community Facts, Universities/Education, Theaters/Centers, Art/Culture, Parks/Zoos/Outdoors, Museums/Libraries, Activities/Things to Do, Organizations, Hospitals, Churches, Businesses, Tourism, Weather, Sports, and Politics

Table 13.48: Selected Utah Travel Sites

Region [Site]	URL	Links
State of Utah [City.Net—Utah]	http://www.city.net/countries/united_states/utah/	Cities, Counties, Arts and Entertainment, Education, Food and Drink, Government, Maps, Other Guides, Parks and Outdoors, Regional Information, Television and Radio, Travel and Tourism
State of Utah [National Park Service—Utah]	http://www.nps.gov:80/parklists/ut.html	National Park Service Sites
State of Utah [Utah Travel Guide]	http://www.netpub.com/utah/	Ski Utah, Welcome to Utah, At a Glance, Adventures, Playgrounds, Travel Regions, Where's Dave (What's Going on This Week, Current Plays, Upcoming Events, Reminders and On-going Events, 1996 Events), Campground Locator, and Winter Olympic Games Information
State of Utah [Utah Geography]	http://www.nr.usu.edu/geography-department/utgeog/utgeog.html	Utah Maps (Utah From Space, Flora and Fauna, Utah Climate, Demographic, Physiography), Virtual Utah, Images of Utah, Vascular Plants of Utah, and Virtual Tourist of Utah (clickable map showing WWW sites in Utah)
Heber Valley [Welcome to Beautiful Heber Valley]	http://www.ditell.com/~heberce/	Heber Valley Profile and Business Statistics, Hiking Opportunities, Gliding over Heber Valley, Calendar of Events and Local Attractions, Read about Lost Gold of the Uinta Mountains, Online Newspaper—The Wasatch Wave, and Sites of Interest
Park City [Park City! Online]	http://www.ditell.com/ParkCity/ParkCityMainStreet.html	Government, Guest Services, Local News Groups, Lodging, Media, Personal Web Pages, Professional & Business, Real Estate, Restaurants & Clubs, Schools, Shops & Boutiques, Events & Entertainment, Sports & Activities, Transportation & Travel
Salt Lake City [Salt Lake Convention & Visitors Bureau]	http://www.saltlakecvb.com/	Utah Ski Report, Today's Weather, Photo and Area Information, Myths About Salt Lake City, Calendar, Salt Lake City News, Winter Olympics, Transportation, Accommodations, Attractions & Tours, Sports & Recreation, Dining & Nightlife, Shopping, Convention Planning & Miscellaneous
Salt Lake City [Salt Lake City, Utah (including Ogden, Park City, and Provo)]	http://isotropic.com/metro/salt.html	Search, METROSCOPE, Utah State W3, U.S. Government W3, Art and Entertainment Sites, Salt Lake Business, Salt Lake Media, Salt Lake Internet Services, Salt Lake Sports, Salt Lake City Colleges, Salt Lake Guides, Salt Lake Government, Professional Services, Organizations and Groups, Other Salt Lake Area Sites, Utah Outdoors, Other Utah Sites, American Universities, All Usenet FAQs, GNN Catalog, List of Lists, NCSA What's New, Multimedia Resources, Nonprofit Organizations, WWW Development, All in One Search, Virtual Library, World Art Resources, Yahoo's Index, Submit to METROSCOPE, What's New Sites

Table 13.49: Selected Vermont Travel Sites

Region [Site]	URL	Links
State of Vermont [City.Net—Vermont]	http://www.city.net/countries/united_states/vermont/	Cities, Businesses, Community Networks, Education, Food and Drink, Government, Magazines and Zines, Other Guides, Parks and Outdoors, Television and Radio
State of Vermont [National Park Service—Vermont]	http://www.nps.gov:80/parklists/vt.html	National Park Service Sites
State of Vermont [Scenes of Vermont Contents Page]	http://www.pbpub.com/vermont/contents.htm	Weather, Woodstock-Quechee and the Valley, Area Inns and Bed & Breakfasts, Visit Sugarbush Farm, Taftsville General Store, Real Estate and Rentals, Northeast Kingdom—an Overview, East Burke, Real Estate and Rentals in the Northeast Kingdom Lakes, Montgomery, Jay Peak Area Association, Inns and Bed & Breakfasts in the Northeast Kingdom, Visit Cabot Cheese, Outdoor Recreation (Alpine Skiing, Cross Country Skiing, Snowmobiling, and Other Stuff
Brattleboro [Welcome to Brattleboro, Vermont]	http://www.sover.net/~hratchml/	Welcome, History, About Brattleboro, Outdoor Recreation Guide, Businesses and Attractions, Upcoming Events, and Photographs
Northeast Kingdom [Welcome to Vermont's Northeast Kingdom]	http://www.pbpub.com/vermont/vtnek1.htm	Downhill Skiing, Snowmobiling, Hunting, Bed & Breakfasts, Inns, Sugaring Houses (Maple Syrup), Bread and Puppet (Outdoor Politic Theater), How to Get Here, Northeast Kingdom Lake Pages, East Burke, Montgomery, and Jay Village, and Fairbanks Museum and Planetarium
Quechee [Welcome to Quechee, Vermont]	http://www.pbpub.com/vermont/quechee.htm	Location, Events, Attractions, and Real Estate
Woodstock [Welcome to Woodstock]	http://www.pbpub.com/vermont/valley.htm	Welcome, Cultural Attractions, Inns and Bed & Breakfasts

Table 13.50: Selected Virginia Travel Sites

Region [Site]	URL	Links
State of Virginia [City.Net—Virginia]	http://www.city.net/countries/united_states/virginia/	Cities, Counties, Islands, Metropolitan Areas, Regions, Community Networks, Education, Food and Drink, Government, Parks and Outdoors, Television and Radio
State of Virginia [National Park Service—Virginia]	http://www.nps.gov:80/parklists/va.html	National Park Service Sites
Blue Ridge Parkway [Blue Ridge Parkway: A Guided Tour]	http://ncnet.com/ncnw/brp-intr.html	Map: Northern Section, Map: Southern Section, Parkway by Milepost (with Activities)

Table 13.50: Selected Virginia Travel Sites (continued)

Region [Site]	URL	Links
Hampton Roads [Guide to Hampton Roads]	http://www.abel-info.com/regguide/	Welcome, Users Guide, History, Museums and Attractions, Outdoor Recreation, Entertainment, Local Information, Economy and Population, Maps, Internet Links, Search The Guide
Norfolk [Norfolk CityLink]	http://banzai.neosoft.com/citylink/norfolk/	What to See, What to Do, Where to Stay, Where to Eat, Where to Shop, and More Information
Portsmouth [Portsmouth Weather Records Service]	http://www.infi.net/~bsmoot/	Forecasts (Our Forecast for Southeastern Virginia, Marine Forecasts for Nearby Waterways, Additional Forecasts), Observations (Portsmouth Weather Observations, Virginia's Hourly Observations) Summaries (Latest Mid-Atlantic Surface Plot, Virginia's Climate Summaries, Virginia Meteograms, National Weather & Storm Summaries, Global Summary), Local/National Radar Images, Hot Links (Weather Sites)
Richmond [Style Weekly]	http://www.infi.net/style/	Classifieds, Personals, Restaurants, Calendar, and About Style
Virginia Beach [Virginia Beach]	http://hampton.roads.net/nhr/vabeach/	City Government, Climate, Communications, Community Facilities, Economy, Education, Housing, Location, Population, Transportation, Utilities, History, News, Weather, Events, Entertainment, Attractions, Business, and Shopping
Williamsburg [Williamsburg Online]	http://www.williamsburg.com/wol/wol.html	Tourism Guide, Yellow Pages, and Maps

Table 13.51: Selected Washington Travel Sites

Region [Site]	URL	Links
State of Washington [City.Net—Washington]	http://www.city.net/countries/united_states/washington/	Cities, Counties, Islands, Regions, Education, Food and Drink, Government, Parks and Outdoors, Television and Radio, Transportation
State of Washington [National Park Service—Washington]	http://www.nps.gov:80/parklists/wa.html	National Park Service Sites
Bellingham [Welcome to Bellingham]	http://www.pacificrim.net/~chamber/	Location, Business, Recreation, Visitor Information, Transportation, Business Relocation, and Weather
Federal Way [Welcome to Federal Way]	http://www.nbs.net/~federal-way/	Chamber of Commerce, Government Center, Schools, Community Services, Local Churches, Business Directory, Shopping Values, Organizations & Clubs, Dining and Entertainment, Local WWW Sites, and Other Web Pages
Friday Harbor/San Juan Island [Welcome to Friday Harbor]	http://pacificrim.net/~islodge/	Friday Harbor (History, Wildlife, Beaches and Museums, Nature and Fishing Charters, Map), Island Lodge, How to Travel Here, Fun Stuff, and Photos

Table 13.51: Selected Washington Travel Sites (continued)

Region [Site]	URL	Links
Olympic Peninsula [Olympic Peninsula]	http://olympus.net/	Life on the Peninsula, Out and About, Travel Information, Stop Here First, OlympusNet, Feedback, Reciprocal Sites
Seattle [Caustic Seattle Compendium]	http://www.oz.net/~eval/	Eats (by Area), Drinks (Coffeehouses, Cocktail Lounges, Taverns), Shops, Etc. (Art Scene, Local Links, Other Links)
Seattle [City of Seattle Public Access Network]	http://www.pan.ci.seattle.wa.us/	Government, Art/Entertainment, Jobs/Business, Education, Transportation, Environment, Social/Health, News/Weather, What's Hot, What's New, and Help/Search
Seattle [MotherCity Espresso Virtual Magazine]	http://www.halcyon.com/zipgun/mothercity/mothercity.html	Coffee Culture, Latest Reviews, Capitol Hill, Downtown, Around Seattle
Seattle [Seattle, Washington]	http://isotropic.com/metro/seattle.html	Search, METROSCOPE, Washington W3, U.S. Government W3, Seattle Art and Culture, Seattle Business, Seattle Media, Seattle Internet Services, Seattle Sports, Seattle Colleges, Seattle Guides, Seattle Government, Professional Services, Seattle Financial, Organizations and Groups, Other Seattle Sites, Other Washington Sites, American Universities, All Usenet FAQs, GNN Catalog, List of Lists, NCSA What's New, Multimedia Resources, Nonprofit Organizations, WWW Development, All in One Search, Virtual Library, World Art Resources, Yahoo's Index, Submit to METROSCOPE, What's New Sites
Seattle [Seattle Webspace]	http://www.eskimo.com/seattle2.html	Geography/Weather, Government, Business, Universities and Schools, Libraries, World Wide Web
Seattle [Waiters on Wheels]	http://www.ird.net/cgi/get?wow/index:R2zpjo_zl~s	Restaurants with delivery services
Spokane [Spokane]	http://www.THENEWS.COM/news/public/spokane/	Visitor's Guide, General (Spokane on the Map, Weather, Spokane Information), Government and Public Institutions, Education, Entertainment and Events, Businesses, and The News
Spokane [Waiters on Wheels]	http://www.ird.net/cgi/get?wow/index:R2zpjo_zl~s	Restaurants with delivery services
Yakima [The Yakima Virtual Valley]	http://www.yakima.net/	What's New, General Information, City and County Government, Educational Resources, Tourism Center, Yakima Valley Agricultural Products, Market Square (Businesses), Local Organizations, and Yakima Web Pages

Table 13.52: Selected West Virginia Travel Sites

Region [Site]	URL	Links
State of West Virginia [City.Net—West Virginia]	http://www.city.net/countries/united_states/west_virginia/	Cities, Counties, Education, Food and Drink, Government, Parks and Outdoors, State Information, Television and Radio
State of West Virginia [National Park Service—West Virginia]	http://www.nps.gov:80/parklists/wv.html	National Park Service Sites
State of West Virginia [West Virginia University Health Sciences Center West Virginia Information]	http://www.hsc.wvu.edu/wv.htm	Information, Government, Recreation, Rovert C. Byrd Health Sciences Center of West Virginia University, Schools, WWW Sites in West Virginia
Charles Town [Welcome to Charles Town, West Virginia]	http://www.intrepid.net/~jsantos/~ctown.html	History, Places to Visit (Culture and Recreation), Calendar of Events, Merchants, Accommodations, Directions, Shepherdstown (History, Culture, Merchants, and Directions), Harpers Ferry National Park, Jefferson County, and Jefferson County Development Authority
Charleston [Charleston, West Virginia]	http://www.city.net/countries/united_states/west_virginia/charleston	Map; Weather; Sports, Charleston Chamber of Commerce; Arts, Culture, and History; Recreation; and Yearly Local Events
Morgantown [Welcome to Morgantown, West Virginia]	http://www.dmssoft.com/mrgntwn/	Site of the Week, History, Yellow Pages, Classified Ads, Upcoming Civic Events, Upcoming Commercial Events, Places to Eat, Hotels, Motels, Real Estate, Transportation, WVU Sports, City of Morgantown, Weather, Area Concert Info, and Clickable Downtown Morgantown Map (Photograph and Information)

Table 13.53: Selected Wisconsin Travel Sites

Region [Site]	URL	Links
State of Wisconsin [City.Net—Wisconsin]	http://www.city.net/countries/united_states/wisconsin/	Cities, Counties, Education, Food and Drink, Government, Government Information, Other Guides, Parks and Outdoors, Regional Information, Television and Radio, Travel and Tourism
State of Wisconsin [National Park Service—Wisconsin]	http://www.nps.gov:80/parklists/wi.html	National Park Service Sites
State of Wisconsin [Wisconsin Destinations by Area]	http://badger.state.wi.us/agencies/tourism/places/Map.html	Clickable Map (Northwest, Southwest, Northeast, and Southeast)
Door County [Door County Chamber of Commerce]	http://198.150.175.123/innline/innline.htm	Lodging, Food and Spirits, Recreation, Arts, Shopping, and Services
Fond du Lac County [Fond du Lac County: A Great Place to Live]	http://www.uscyber.com/virtual/landnet/fdlhome.htm	Recreation, Business and Industry, Demographics, Education, and Cities of Fond du Lac County

Table 13.53: Selected Wisconsin Travel Sites (continued)

Region [Site]	URL	Links
Madison [The Greater Madison Home Page]	http://www.inmarket.com/madison/	Greater Madison Convention & Visitors Bureau, Greater Madison Home Page; Community Profile; Calendar of Events; Natural Madison; Dining and Shopping; Arts, Entertainment, and Museums; Recreation and Lakes; Conference Facilities, Madison Facts; History; Maps; and Other Information
Milwaukee [Milwaukee]	http://isotropic.com/metro/mil.html?	Search, Metroscope, Wisconsin State W3, U.S. Government W3, World W3, Art and Entertainment Sites, Milwaukee Business, Milwaukee Media, Milwaukee Internet Access, Milwaukee Web Builders, Milwaukee Sports, Milwaukee Colleges, Milwaukee Guides, Milwaukee Government, Professional Services, Milwaukee Financial, Organizations and Groups, Other Milwaukee Sites, Other Wisconsin Sites, American Universities, All Usenet FAQs, GNN Catalog, List of Lists, NCSA What's New, Multimedia Resources, Nonprofit Organizations, WWW Development, All in One Search, Virtual Library, World Art Resources, Yahoo's Index, Submit to Metroscope, What's New Sites

Table 13.54: Selected Wyoming Travel Sites

Region [Site]	URL	Links
State of Wyoming [City.Net—Wyoming]	http://www.city.net/countries/united_states/wyoming/	Cities, Education, Food and Drink, General Information, Government, Parks and Outdoors, State Information, Television and Radio
State of Wyoming [National Park Service—Wyoming]	http://www.nps.gov:80/parklists/wy.html	National Park Service Sites
State of Wyoming [The Windy Wyoming Web]	http://www.uwyo.edu/lib/Wyoming/index.html	Clickable Map (Topographic Map; County Map; Links to Yahoo, City Net, Virtual Tourist), Wyoming Virtual Map, Art, Business, Cities and Counties, Communication and Media Services, Education, Entertainment, Environment and Nature, Events, Geography, Government, Health, History, Images, Maps, News, Organizations, People, Recreation, Reference, Science, Services, Society and Culture. Weather, and General Wyoming Information

Table 13.54: Selected Wyoming Travel Sites (continued)

Region [Site]	URL	Links
Casper [Welcome to Casper, Wyoming]	http://www1.trib.com/AOS/CASPER/	Sites to See, Events, History & Art, Wildlife, Western Fun, Conventions & Groups, and Accommodations
Cheyenne [Cheyenne: Live the Legend]	http://jackalope.lcc.whecn.edu/scc/html/cheyenne.html	Places to See, Things to Do, City Government, Cheyenne Frontier Days
Cody [In 1896, Buffalo Bill founded Cody, Wyoming]	http://wave.park.wy.us/~chamberc/chamber.html	Points of Interest, Calendar of Major Events, 1996 Centennial Events, How to Get There, Accommodations, Dining Guide, Economic Development Opportunities, Community Audit and Relocation Information, History, "Buffalo Bill" Cody Biography, Road Report, and Weather
Laramie [Laramie, Wyoming]	http://www.uwyo.edu/wyoming/laramie/default.html	Map, University of Wyoming, Location, History, Economy, and Recreation

Appendix A

An Introduction to the Internet

information and provides it to client computers upon request. Thus, if you use your personal computer to connect to an online information service or Internet service provider, your PC is the *client,* and the computer to which you connect is the host, which in turn may be connected to other hosts via the Internet.

You need two things to get information from Internet sites: an Internet connection and client software.

T his book has introduced you to a vast array of Internet sites, particularly Web sites. But just as a road map is designed with the assumption that you know how to drive a car, an Internet guide must assume you have some experience connecting to the Net. In case you don't, this appendix will give you a brief introduction to the basics of connecting to and navigating the Internet.

What is the Internet anyway? Despite what you might think, the Internet is not the information that can be accessed online, just as the motels, restaurants, and shopping centers that can be accessed via a freeway are not the Interstate Highway System. Rather, it's the conduit itself that makes up the Net. Simply stated, the Internet is a network of networks, an interconnection of millions of computers around the globe.

There are two types of computers in a network: servers and clients. The *server*, also known as the host, stores

Getting Connected

Unless your office or school provides a direct connection to the Internet, you will need to establish an account with an Internet service provider for dial-up access. Computers connected to the Internet communicate with one another using a common set of *protocols*, or communication rules, called *TCP/IP* (Transmission Control Protocol/Internet Protocol). To use TCP/IP with a modem over phone lines, you'll need to establish a *PPP* (Point-to-Point Protocol) or *SLIP* (Serial Line Interface Protocol) connection. Of these, PPP is the newer technology and is generally preferable.

Your Internet service provider should give you a TCP/IP software package that will allow you to dial, log in to the host, and establish a SLIP or PPP connection. If not, you can purchase a commercial TCP/IP package, such as Super TCP/IP from Frontier Technologies, or obtain a shareware package such as Trumpet Winsock; however, you will need to configure it to work with your provider. If you are using Microsoft Windows, its built-in TCP/IP software typically includes a module called a Winsock and a dialer program, Dial-Up Networking, which is in the Accessories group. The Winsock acts as an interface between Windows and the dialer, which actually makes the connection. In most cases, when you launch an Internet application, it will search for a Winsock in memory; if one is not loaded into memory, it will search for a Winsock on disk and launch it, which in turn launches the dialer program.

Note

If you are using more than one service provider, each with its own uniquely configured Winsock and dialer, you must be careful to store these files in the proper directories; otherwise an application could invoke the wrong Winsock and dialer and connect to the wrong provider. For this reason, it is generally advisable to establish the TCP/IP connection before launching client applications.

Destinations

You can access information through the Internet in several ways. This appendix discusses the following ways:

- ◆ World Wide Web
- ◆ Gopher
- ◆ FTP
- ◆ Usenet
- ◆ Telnet
- ◆ E–Mail

To access the various resources on the Internet, your computer needs to run programs called *client applications*. Typically, a separate client application is required for each of these Internet areas, though the programs may be integrated into a suite of applications. In the following sections, you'll see examples of popular client applications used to access the Web, Gopher, Usenet, FTP, Telnet, and electronic mail (*e-mail*). Though the examples illustrate programs that run under Microsoft Windows 95, similar applications are available for use with other platforms, including MS-DOS, Macintosh, and Unix.

The World Wide Web

The fastest growing area of the Internet is the World Wide Web, which was designed to add *hypertext* capabilities to the network. This means that documents can contain *links* with which you can jump to other documents and resources on the Internet. A coding system called HyperText Markup Language (HTML) is used to embed links in Web documents. (See *Appendix B* for more details on HTML.)

Clicking on an embedded link automatically calls up the linked document, no matter where it is on the Internet. For example, you might be viewing a document stored on a system in Dallas that contains a link to a document stored on a system in Finland, Australia, or Los Angeles.

To view a coded Web document and activate its links, you need a software package called a Web reader or browser. Table A.1 lists selected Web browsers, their developers, the platforms on which they run, and brief descriptions.

Tip

To learn more about Internet browsers or to obtain lists or reviews of browsers, visit some of these sites: <u>Browsers</u> (at http://miso.wwa.com/~boba/browsers.html), <u>BrowserWatch</u> (at http://www.browserwatch.com/), <u>HotWired: Browser Acceptance Sheet</u> (at http://www.hotwired.com/browsers.html), <u>Picking the Perfect Web Browser</u> (at http://www.cnet.com/Content/Reviews/Compare/Browsers/), and the <u>Web Developer's Virtual Library: Browsers</u> (at http://www.charm.net/~web/Vlib/Users/Browsers.html).

Table A.1: Selected Web Readers

Reader (Developer)	URL	Platform(s)	Description
Aficionado/Web Surfer [Web Surfer Software and BlackBird Systems]	http://www.blackbird.co.uk/websurfer	Windows 95, Solaris 2.4, and all 32-bit platforms	Downloadable evaluation software will be available soon. Compliant with HTML 3.0, extensions, HTTPD compatible.
Alis [Alis Technologies]	http://www.alis.com/P_NET/P_MCP/P_MCP.EN.HTML	Windows 3.1, Windows NT, Windows 95	Downloadable evaluation copy of commercial software. Multilingual (French, Italian, German, Spanish, Russian, English and many more); easily switch from one language to another.
ArcWeb [Stewart Brodie]	http://louis.ecs.soton.ac.uk/~snb94r/arcweb.html	Acorn RISC OS computers	Downloadable freeware. WWW browser for RISC OS 3.1 or greater.
Cello [Thomas R. Bruce, Legal Information Institute, Cornell Law School]	ftp://ftp.law.cornell.edu/pub/LII/Cello/default.htm or http://www.law.cornell.edu/cello/cellotop.html	Microsoft Windows	Downloadable freeware. Accesses Web, Gopher, FTP, CSO/ph/qi, and Newsnet News groups.
Charlotte [BC Systems Corp.]	gopher://p370.bcss.gov.bc.ca/11/vmtools	VM CMS platform	Downloadable freeware.
Dancer [Smiale]	http://www.cs.indiana.edu/hyplan/smiale/dancer.html	Unix, requiring Python and the tkinter module	Downloadable freeware. Program made up of easily changed modules: agents and viewers.
Delrina Cyberjack [Delrina (Canada) Corporation]	http://www.cyberjack.com/	Windows 95	Downloadable beta version of commercial software. Includes Delrina WinComm™ PRO and pre-loaded Web sites, FTP files, Usenet newsgroups, IRC chat channels, and so on; intelligent setup; Usenet News, FTP, GOpher, Archie, Telnet, Ping, Finger, IRC.
Emacs-W3 [William M. Perry, Spry]	http://www.cs.indiana.edu/elisp/w3/docs.html	Macintosh, Windows 95, Windows NT, Unix (Linux, SGI, SunOS, Solaris, HP/UX, etc), XWindows, NextStep, VMS, OS/2, DOS, AmigaDOS	Downloadable freeware. Supports FTP, NNTP, Gopher, Gopher+, HTTP, HTTPS.

Table A.1: Selected Web Readers (continued)

Reader (Developer)	URL	Platform(s)	Description
Emissary™ [The Wollongong Group, Inc.]	http://www.twg.com/emissary/emiss1.html	Windows	Downloadable evaluation version of commercial software. Supports email, newsgroups, FTP, Telnet, Web editor.
Fountain [Caligari Corporation]	http://www.caligari.com/	Windows	Downloadable evaluation copy of freeware. A VRML (virtual reality modeling language) authoring tool that also allows you to browse 3D resources on the Internet. (Caligari also offers trueSpace2 and trueSpace/SE, which are graphics, raytracing, modeling, and animation tools.)
Grail [Corporation for National Research Initiatives (CNRI)]	http://monty.cnri.reston.va.us/grail/	Unix systems with Python and Tk	Downloadable freeware. Supports HTTP, FTP, HTML and can support other protocolors or file formats.
HotJava™ [Sun Microsystems, Inc.]	http://java.sun.com/ and http://paladin.cs.cf.ac.uk/Java/	Windows NT, Windows 95, Solaris	Downloadable beta program that supports Java applets.
Internet in a Box for KIDS [Spry]	http://www.spry.com:80/products/kidbox.html	Windows 3.1, Windows 95	Commercial software for children. Includes SurfWatch, software that monitors Internet sites.
Internet with an Accent [Accent Software]	http://www.accentsoft.com/	Windows	Downloadable working model of commercial software. Multilingual Internet software: Accent Multilingual Publisher, Accent Multilingual Mosaic, Accent Multilingual MailPad, Accent Multilingual Viewer.

Table A.1: Selected Web Readers (continued)

Reader (Developer)	URL	Platform(s)	Description
The Internet Workhorse [MarketNet]	http://mkn.co.uk/help/system/horse	Windows 95, Windows 3.1	Downloadable freeware. A secure client for UK companies that are not allowed to import Netscape for its security features.
Microsoft Internet Explorer [Microsoft Corporation]	http://www.microsoft.com/windows/ie/ie.htm	Windows 95, Windows 3.1, Macintosh	Downloadable released and beta freeware. Supports multimedia, newsgroups, FTP, etc.
MMM [Francois Rouaix, INRIA]	http://pauillac.inria.fr/~rouaix/mmm/	Unix (Tcl/Tk)	Downloadable freeware. Implemented in Caml Special Light; Japanese version is available; users are encouraged to write applets for MMM.
Mosaic in a Box [Spry]	http://www.spry.com:80/products/mosaic.html	Windows 95	Commercial software. CompuServe access.
NCSA Mosaic for Microsoft Windows [National Center for Supercomputing Applications, University of Illinois at Urbana-Champaign]	http://www.ncsa.uiuc.edu/SDG/Software/WinMosaic/HomePage.html	Windows 95, Windows NT, Windows for Workgroups, Windows 3.1 or greater	Downloadable freeware. Supports Telnet, FTP, Gopher.
NCSA Mosaic for the Macintosh [National Center for Supercomputing Applications, University of Illinois at Urbana-Champaign]	http://www.ncsa.uiuc.edu/SDG/Software/MacMosaic/MacMosaicHome.html	Macintosh	Downloadable freeware. Supports FTP, Gopher, WAIS, and more.

Table A.1: Selected Web Readers (continued)

Reader (Developer)	URL	Platform(s)	Description
NCSA Mosaic for the X Window System [National Center for Supercomputing Applications, University of Illinois at Urbana-Champaign]	http://www.ncsa.uiuc.edu/SDG/Software/XMosaic/	X Window system.	Downloadable freeware. Supports Gopher, WAIS, FTP, NNTP/Usenet news, Telnet, tn3270.
Netscape Navigator [Netscape Communications Corporation]	http://home.netscape.com/	Windows 3.1, Windows 95, Mac, Unix	Downloadable beta version of commercial software. Supports e-mail, newsgroups, chat, FTP, and Gopher.
NetShark [Intercon Systems]	http://netshark.inter.net/netshark/	Mac, Windows 3.1, Windows 95	Downloadable "lite" version of commercial software. Supports e-mail; supports graphics, sound, Quicktime movies, and tables.
OLIAS [HaL Computer Systems]	http://www.hal.com/products/sw/olias/index.html	Unix	Commercial software. Retrieves SGML and World Wide Web documents, contains Query Editor with which you can search your collection of saved Web documents.
Opera [Opera Software]	http://opera.nta.no/opera/	Windows 3.1 or greater	Commercial software with English and Norwegian versions. Bases design on Windows; customizable in many ways.
Quarterdeck InternetSuite [Quarterdeck Corporation]	http://www.qdeck.com/qdeck/products/ISuite/	Windows	Commercial software. Supports FTP, Telnet, e-mail, Usenet newsgroups.
Quarterdeck Mosaic [Quarterdeck Corporation]	http://www.qdeck.com/qdeck/demosoft/QMosaic	Windows	Downloadable demo version of commercial software. Supports HTML extensions, etc.

Table A.1: Selected Web Readers (continued)

Reader (Developer)	URL	Platform(s)	Description
SuperHighway Access 2 [Frontier Technologies Corporation]	http://www.frontiertech.com/	Windows 95	Commercial software. Web browser, Multimedia (MIME) Email, FTP, newsreader, Telnet, Gopher+, WWW, WAIS, CSO Phone Book, and security features. Also you can subscribe to the Lycos CD-ROM catalog for off-line searches, preloaded Internet locations.
Surfit! [Steve Ball, PASTIME Project of the CRC for Advanced Computational Systems, Tcl Group at Sun Microsystems]	http://pastime.anu.edu.au/Surfit/	Unix with Tcl 7.5 alpha2/Tk 4.1 alpha2	Downloadable freeware. Can download and execute applets written in Tcl/Tk.
TkWWW	http://tk-www.mit.edu:8001/tk-www/help/overview.html	Unix, based on the tk toolkit	Downloadable freeware. Combines browser with hyper-text editor.
TradeWave MacWeb [TradeWave Corporation]	http://galaxy.einet.net/EINet/MacWeb/MacWebHome.html	Macintosh	Downloadable evaluation copy of commercial software. Supports FTP, Gopher, and a news reader.
TradeWave winWeb [TradeWave Corporation]	http://galaxy.einet.net/EINet/WinWeb/WinWebHome.html	Windows 3.1	Downloadable evaluation copy of commercial software. Supports FTP and Gopher.

When you display a Web document, a link typically appears as a highlighted term, usually underlined and/or in a contrasting color. Icons and other graphical images can also be links. Clicking on a link brings up the referenced resource.

Tip
To see whether a term or a graphic is a link, look in the status bar at the bottom of the computer screen. If any type of text appears when you move the mouse pointer over a term or a graphic, chances are you are pointing to a link.

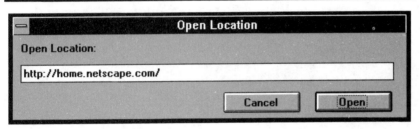

Figure A.1   Entering a URL

Figure A.2   Part of the Netscape home page

To locate documents and other resources on the Internet, the Web reader uses an address format called a Uniform Resource Locator, or URL. This specifies the resource or server type, host name, directory path, and document or resource filename. Web documents typically have the resource type of *http*, which indicates that HyperText Transfer Protocol is used. Here's an example of a URL for a Web document:

http://home.netscape.com/

This address indicates you are seeking a hypertext document located on the http://home.netscape.com/ World Wide Web server. The slash at the end of the address indicates that you might be able to go to lower level pages linked to this document.

To reach a desired address, type the URL, as shown in Figure A.1, in the Location text box above the work area. The Web reader will attempt to contact the appropriate host and retrieve the desired resource.

After typing the address http://home.netscape.com/, the Netscape home page (see Figure A.2) appears. As you can see in this illustration, this page contains several graphical elements as well as underlined terms, each of which is a link to another resource.

You may see the term *home page* used a lot on the Internet. Generally, if a user or a company has a single page on the World Wide Web, it is referred to as the home page. If the user or company has several linked pages, the top or the main page is called the home page.

As you'll see, Web readers give you access to resources other than HTML documents. But to specify a resource or location, you'll need to know the proper URL format. Table A.2 shows a list of URL prefixes called *resource type designators* and what they mean.

Graphical images and links to multimedia resources, such as movie and sound files, can be embedded within a Web document. To access these resources, however, you'll need *helper applications* that can execute these files. For example, you may need a program that can display a certain type of image, view a movie file, or play an audio file. If you specify the names of helper applications in the options or preferences settings for your Web browser (see the manual that came with your browser for instructions), the browser starts the appropriate application automatically when it encounters a file that requires a helper applicaion. You'll also need a terminal emulation helper application for Telnet sessions, as described below.

Gopher

Gopher, developed at the University of Minnesota (whose mascot is the gopher), is a menulike system of folders and files. It's a quick way to present typically nongraphical documents to researchers and other Internet surfers. When you reach a Gopher site, simply click on a folder to see more folders or documents, or click on a document to view its contents. In Netscape, folders and documents are represented by icons in the left margin. Some other browsers show a hierarchical "tree"; you can click on a folder icon to see the documents in each folder.

Table A.2: Resource Type Designators

Designator	Resource
file://	Local file on your computer
ftp.//	FTP site
gopher://	Gopher resource menu
http://	World Wide Web page, hypertext document
telnet://	Telnet site
wais://	WAIS database search

FTP

FTP stands for File Transfer Protocol, the method used to transfer files between computers on the Internet. You can use FTP to download a file from a host to your system or to upload a file from your system to a host. Typically, you use an FTP client application to perform either of these functions. Many Web browser applications, however, provide the capability of downloading files using FTP.

One popular shareware FTP application for Microsoft Windows is called WS_FTP. The following example shows how to download or upload a file using WS_FTP.

As shown in Figure A.3, enter the name of the host you want to connect to in a session profile. In most cases, you can retrieve publicly accessible files using *anonymous FTP*, which merely means that you do not need to provide your name or have an account on the host system to log in. Typically, you type **anonymous** as the User ID and your e-mail address as the password.

WS_FTP displays a directory listing for your system in the left half of the window (see Figure A.4). Once you are connected to the host, WS_FTP displays a list of host system directories in the right half of the window. Choose the host directory containing the file you are seeking. Many file libraries have a public directory (for example, \PUB) that contains files accessible to the general public.

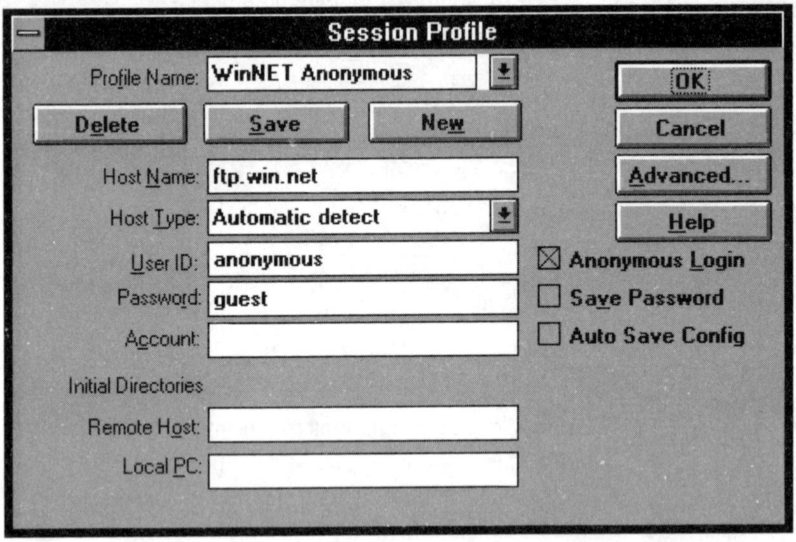

Figure A.3 Entering session profile information for anonymous FTP

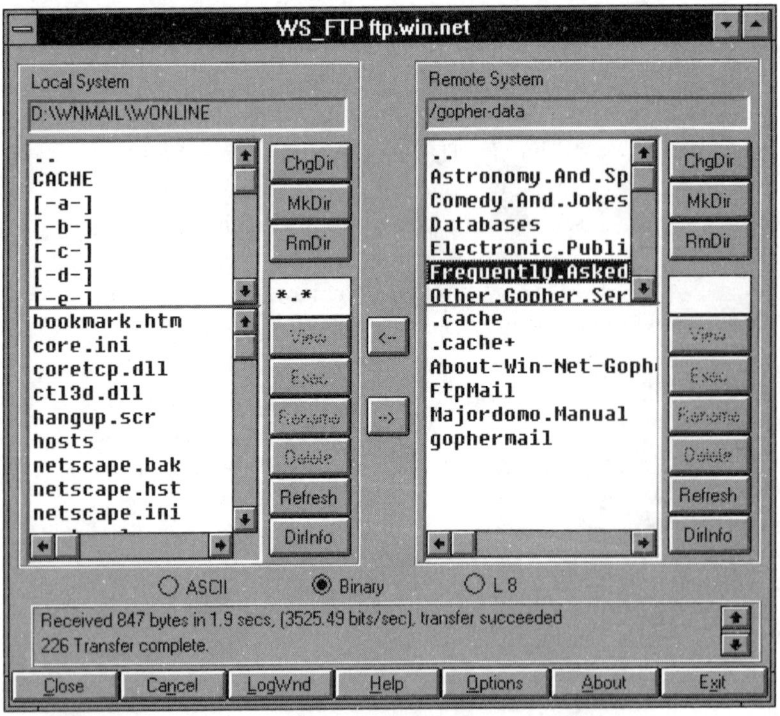

Figure A.4 Transferring files with WS_FTP

To retrieve a file, once you have located it in the host directory listing, highlight the filename and click on the left arrow button (←) to indicate that you want to copy the file to your system.

To upload a file to the selected host directory, select the file in your directory listing in the left half of the window, and then click on the right arrow button (→) to copy the file to the host system. Generally, you will need an account or special access privileges on the host system to be able upload files to it.

Most Web browsers allow you to download files using FTP. You might get to an FTP site through a link from a Web page, or you can specify an FTP site using the ftp:// prefix in the address. As Figure A.5 illustrates, directories and files are shown in Web browsers as links. Click on the desired file to retrieve it.

Some files may be compressed (archived) to save disk space and reduce transmission time. For example, in Figure A.5, the file WS_FTP.ZIP is being selected. As indicated, this is a "zip compressed file"; so you will need an application such as PKUNZIP or WinZip that is capable of decompressing the archive before you can install the software on your system. These applications are widely available on the Internet and through online services. See the sidebars in the *Computing and Software* chapter for information about many compression utilities.

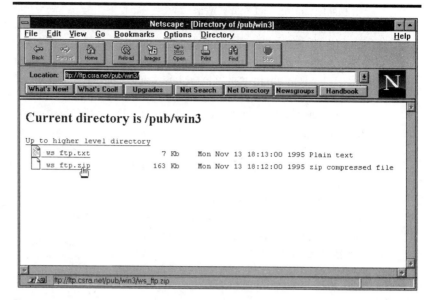

Figure A.5 Using a Web browser to retrieve a file from an FTP site

Usenet

Usenet is an area of the Internet made up of thousands of topical discussion groups called *newsgroups*. Each newsgroup is like an electronic bulletin board where participants post and read messages related to a particular topic. A message posted to a newsgroup is called an *article*.

The range of subjects discussed in newsgroups is as wide as you can imagine. The name of a newsgroup generally indicates the topic at hand. Here are three examples:

alt.animals.dolphins

comp.publish.cdrom.multimedia

rec.music.classical.guitar

As you can see, newsgroup names have a hierarchical structure. Each segment of the name is separated by a period (although it's pronounced "dot"—for example, "alt dot animals dot dolphins"). The top-level hierarchy indicates a general category of newsgroups and is always shown first. Table A.3 lists some of the most widely used top-level hierarchies and what they mean. Many others are used,

including some that indicate a geographic location for regional groups—that is, nyc.jobs.wanted for Jobs Wanted in New York City, or utexas.lbj.forum for the LBJ Forum at the University of Texas.

To access newsgroups, you need a piece of client software called a *news reader*. Many news readers are

Table A.3: Top-Level Newsgroup Hierarchies	
Prefix	*Represents*
alt	Alternative information
biz	Business, marketing, advertising
comp	Computer topics
misc	Miscellaneous topics
news	Discussion of Usenet
rec	Recreational topics, such as art and sports
sci	Scientific discussions
soc	Social issues
talk	Debate, discussion of controversial topics

available, and in fact many Web browsers, such as Netscape, include a news reader. The news reader gives you the ability to perform these operations:

Subscribe and Unsubscribe—Subscribing to a newsgroup simply means indicating to the host system that you want access to the articles posted in it. The news reader keeps a list of groups to which you are subscribed and tracks the messages you read in each group. From the subscription list, you can choose which newsgroups to read. Unsubscribing means to remove a newsgroup from your subscription list.

Browse and Read Articles—The news reader will display a list of article topics in the current newsgroup. Select a topic to read the articles sharing that topic. Articles include a header, which shows the user that posted the article and the subject of the article, and the message text (see Figure A.6).

Reply to Articles—You can respond to an article in two ways: by posting a follow-up article or e-mailing a personal reply. A follow-up article can, of course, be read by everyone in the newsgroup; a personal reply is read only by the person who posted the article (unless she or he shares it with others).

Post a New Article—You can start a new topic of discussion within a newsgroup by creating a new article, assigning a subject to it, and posting it to the newsgroup.

Be aware that articles do not remain in newsgroups indefinitely. Articles scroll off the board as they are replaced by new ones. In a busy newsgroup—one to which many articles are posted—articles may disappear in a few days, but typically they remain for a week or more. It's a good idea to check your favorite newsgroups regularly to keep current.

When you are just starting out, you should check out a few newsgroups to get answers to your questions about Usenet newsgroups. These are listed in Table A.4.

Telnet

Using special terminal emulation software, you can access remote host systems connected to the Internet. This allows your computer to act as if it were directly connection to the remote host. Perhaps you have visited a library that uses terminals to access the computerized card catalog system. Imagine, then, that your computer is a terminal connected to the same library computer system, allowing you to browse the catalog without leaving your home or office. Telnet makes such things possible.

You will need to use a Telnet terminal emulation program to establish a Telnet connection. To launch a Telnet session from a Web reader such as Netscape Navigator or Mosaic, you'll need a Telnet helper application. Specify this application in the options or preference settings for your Web reader. Figure A.7 illustrates a Telnet session established using Trumptel, a Telnet helper application for Windows.

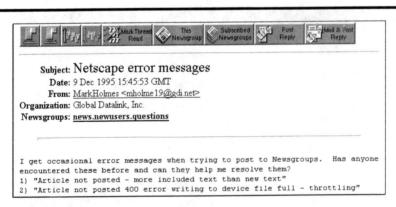

Figure A.6   Reading a newsgroup article

When you connect to a Telnet site, you may be asked to specify your terminal type. Most Telnet applications provide VT100 terminal emulation; so in most cases, you can select the VT100 terminal type. The system commands vary by site; so follow the on-screen instructions carefully. To log off the remote host, use the proper exit command for that system.

Table A.4: Usenet Newsgroups for New Users	
Newsgroup	*Description*
news.announce.newusers	Read announcements related to Usenet newsgroups.
news.newusers.questions	Post questions and get answers about Usenet newsgroups.
news.announce.newgroups	Get information about new or proposed newsgroups.
news.answers	Browse a list of articles with answers to Frequently Asked Questions (FAQs) about various newsgroups.

Electronic Mail

Perhaps the most widely used service on the Internet is electronic mail, or *e-mail*. Using a piece of client software called a *mail reader*, you can receive, read, and reply to electronic mail messages from anyone connected to the Internet, including those using online services that provide Internet mail capabilities. You can also create your own e-mail messages and send them across the Internet, allowing you to distribute information around the globe in a matter of minutes.

Most mail reader programs will let you perform the following operations:

♦ Check for new e-mail messages addressed to you and retrieve them

♦ Read e-mail messages and reply to them

♦ Forward received messages to other users

♦ Create new e-mail messages and post them over the Internet

Some mail readers also let you:

♦ Attach files to e-mail messages. This is helpful if you want to send the contents of a disk file along with an explanatory note.

♦ Read and reply to messages offline (that is, when you are not connected to the Internet)

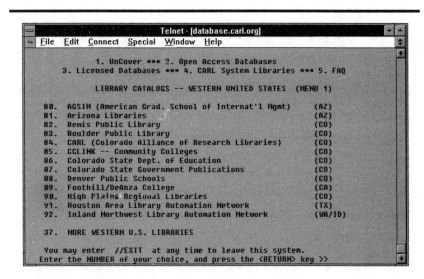

Figure A.7 A Telnet session

◆ File incoming and outgoing messages in folders or In/Out baskets for handling at a later time

◆ Maintain an electronic address book containing the e-mail addresses of persons with whom you regularly correspond

A number of Internet mail reader applications are available, but one of the most widely used mail readers is Eudora for Windows, which is illustrated in the following examples.

Before accessing your online mailbox, you'll need to configure your mail reader, entering your Internet e-mail address and the name of the mail server. Your Internet service provider can give you this information.

When you have established an Internet connection, start the mail reader client application. To see if you have new messages waiting in your online mailbox, instruct the mail reader to check for new mail. For example, using Eudora, choose File ➤ Check Mail or press Ctrl+M. If you have any new messages, a list of them will be displayed in the In Box window (see Figure A.8).

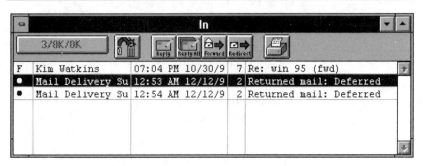

Figure A.8 Checking for new mail

To read a message, select it from the list to display the message contents (see Figure A.9). You may want to print out the message or file it in a folder for future reference if your news reader provides this option.

If you'd like to send a copy of the message to another user, choose the Forward option. In Eudora, you'd choose Message ➤ Forward. The message text will be placed in a new message window. Address the message by typing the Internet e-mail address of the intended recipient at the To prompt. If you want, you can change the entry at the Subject prompt and add your own comments in the text window before sending the message on its way.

To reply to an e-mail message, choose Message ➤ Reply or press Ctrl+R. A new message window will appear, pre-addressed to the

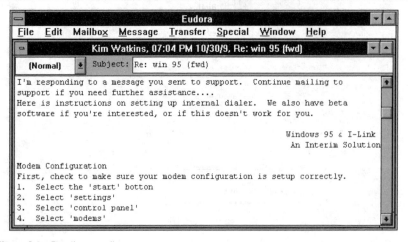

Figure A.9 Reading a mail message

person to whom you are responding. The Subject line of the message will be automatically filled in with the topic of the original message. Type your response in the text window, and then send the message.

Creating a new mail message is similar to forwarding and replying, except that you must provide both the recipient address and the subject. Select the option to create mail (choose Message ➤ New Message or Ctrl+N in Eudora) to open an empty mail message window. Type the recipient's address carefully at the To prompt, and then enter a brief description of the message topic at the Subject prompt (see Figure A.10). After typing the text of the message, select Send to post it.

When you select Send (click on the Send button in Eudora), the message will be sent immediately if you are online. If not, the message may be temporarily stored in an Out Box folder so that you can send it later.

Internet email addresses typically are formatted username@hostname.domaintype, where username is the user ID or account name of the recipient, hostname is the name of the recipient's host system, and domaintype is the type of organization that controls the host. Some domain types include com for commercial enterprises, edu for educational institutions, and net for networks. (See Table 1.2 for more information about domains.) Here are some examples of Internet mail addresses:

johndoe@nyuniv.edu

sandys@ilink.net

AAA123@prodigy.com

78900.0000@compuserve.com

Most Web browsers include the ability to send e-mail, although you can't use them to retrieve

incoming e-mail. In general, you can post e-mail using a browser such as Netscape Navigator in several ways. One way is to select the Mail option (choose File ➤ Mail Document in Netscape). This opens a Send Mail/Post News dialog box (see Figure A.11). Type the recipient's e-mail address and the subject and message text, and then choose Send. Optionally, you can copy the contents of the current Web page into the message or attach a disk file.

Sometimes in a Web page, you encounter a link that is designed to allow you to send e-mail to the administrator of the page or another user. For example, when visiting a particular home page, you may see something like this:

To send feedback, contact info@sandy.net.

Clicking on such a link will bring up the Mail To dialog box, allowing you to send a message to the e-mail address attached to that link. This kind of link uses a special URL prefix, mailto:. Entering this prefix with an e-mail address as a URL is another way of sending mail from a Web browser. For example, entering the URL

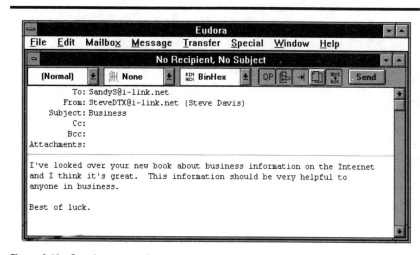

Figure A.10   Creating an e-mail message

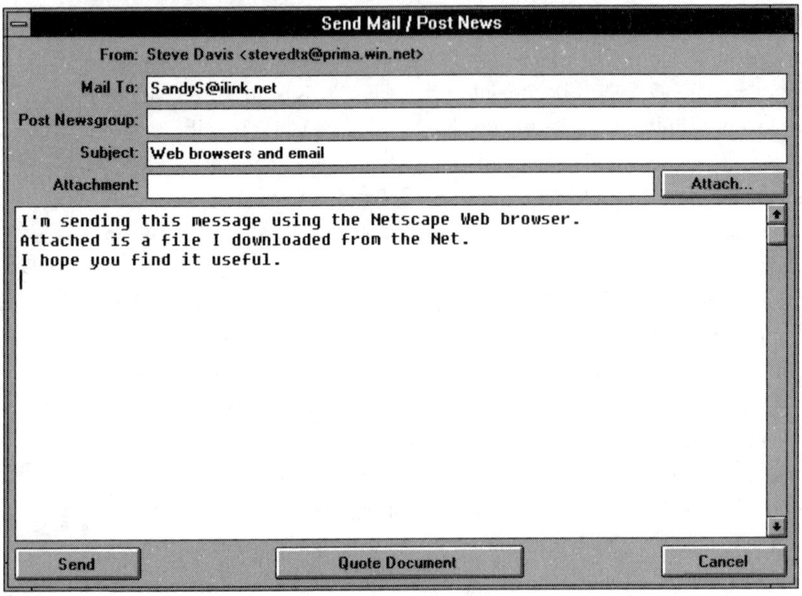

Figure A.11   Sending mail with a Web browser

mailto:info@sandy.net will open the Mail To dialog box, with your new message pre-addressed to the specified user.

Finally, you can send e-mail replies to people posting newsgroup articles using any news reader, including those integrated into Web browsers. When you reply to an article, instead of posting your reply in the newsgroup, you can choose to send it as a private e-mail message. Your response will be sent to the address of the user who posted the article.

Appendix B

Putting Your Business on the Internet

Is a World Wide Web Site Cost-Effective for Your Business?

The most important question that a business asks when considering the Web as a means of mass communication to the world is, Why should I build a World Wide Web presence? If you're a World Wide Web–savvy business person, you can answer with many, many reasons. No matter how many reasons you give, however, the even more important question remains: Are any of these reasons cost-effective for your business?

Although a World Wide Web site offers many benefits to a company at a relatively low price, it is not for everyone. To decide if you and your company want to invest in a Web site, you need to analyze the benefits versus the costs. This is no simple task since understanding the benefits and costs can be very difficult in such a new and rapidly growing technology. Nobody can completely understand all the benefits since they are what you make of them. Right now, many Internet specialists will tell you that the possibilities are endless. And it definitely seems that way. Every month a new application for Web technology is announced, and many are wooed with the new idea.

The costs are a little simpler to identify than the benefits. Most can even be broken down to dollar amounts that are easily quantified.

After a year or two of doubting the value of the World Wide Web, businesses have finally accepted the inevitable: It's here to stay. Although some are intimidated by the new technology, those who are more progressive have benefited from the Web. Thousands of businesses have created Web sites as solutions to various company needs: marketing, sales, personnel management, customer service, and more. Your business can also benefit from an online presence.

This appendix focuses on the key issues of developing a World Wide Web presence for your business: the benefits of an online presence, components of a site, basic page creation with HTML programming, interactivity, add-ons, and outsourcing the work. After reading this appendix, you will have a basic understanding of all issues involved in creating a valuable Web site for your business. Then, you can make confident decisions in managing the construction of your company site.

Three Benefits of Having a Web Site

The benefits of having a World Wide Web site are many. The three most important are:

◆ Its massive audience

◆ Its graphical and informative nature

◆ Its interactivity

The World Wide Web has acquired a huge following that is increasing at an amazing rate. Every month, the World Wide Web audience increases by about 10 percent. Not even television gathered such an initial following. It is this growing audience that is the most powerful asset of a company Web site. Every person using the World Wide Web can access your site. Think of all the information you can provide about your company to potentially millions.

One reason the World Wide Web is so popular is that it can attractively present graphics and text together. Online information is no longer restricted to boring text. Just as a magazine is more exciting to read when it incorporates pictures, online information is more appealing with graphics. Beside the aesthetics, the incorporation of text and graphics provides more functionality to the users. Now customers can view maps, pictures of people, demonstrations of products, charts and graphs, and the latest pictures of those in the news. Think of what your company can present to the world in bright new colors: brochures, the company logo, maps to the facilities, and illustrations of products or services.

Television shows and radio commercials are not interactive; a Web site is. Through the World Wide Web, you can perform many interactive tasks not possible through television, radio, magazines, or even the telephone. A well-crafted site provides many avenues for a user to respond to company forms, send messages directly to employees, receive customized information, and more. This interactivity is extremely important because it allows users to perform the tasks needed to conduct normal business: register for seminars, purchase items, change bank account information, order magazine subscriptions, and make appointments, to name only a few.

Another way of determining what a Web site can do for your company is to see what other companies offer to the World Wide Web audience. Visit some sites on the Web. You may want to investigate sites of your competitors as well as those of major companies.

With all this in mind, you can determine all the applications for which your company can use a World Wide Web site. And don't forget about the internal uses for employees: phone directories, employee handbook, internal company newsletters, and so on. Now you can compare the value for these applications with the estimated costs of creating a Web site.

The Costs of Creating a Web Site

To determine if a Web site is cost-effective, you need to understand all the costs involved, not just the monetary costs. A cost is any expenditure, such as time, money, labor, and so on. The following section discusses the components of building a basic Web presence. You can use the costs of these components to determine whether a Web site is a worthwhile solution for or an addition to your business. Although all the costs listed are necessary, you may be able to reduce them by having an Internet presence provider handle them rather than hiring or training one or more employees. An Internet presence provider offers a full range of services such as creating, maintaining, and hosting Web sites on its server and connection to the Internet. In exchange, a subscribing company pays the Internet provider a monthly rental rate for use of the server and connection. This is often a very financially reasonable route for smaller businesses that want a presence on the Web. The last section of this appendix addresses outsourcing work to presence providers.

How to Build a Basic Web Presence

Building a basic World Wide Web presence requires five components:

◆ Hardware to host the information

◆ Software to present the Web pages to the public

◆ A connection to the Internet from a host computer

◆ Registration of your Web site on the Internet

◆ Development of your Web pages

Server Hardware

A *server* is a computer that hosts or distributes information to other computers, and a *Web server* is a computer that hosts or distributes information to users on the World Wide Web. To create your Web presence, you need to acquire or have access to a Web server. The first concern when building a Web server is hardware.

Web servers can be almost any brand of computer and the accompanying operating systems: Unix, Windows NT, Windows 3.1, Windows 95, OS/2, and Macintosh. When deciding which to use, keep in mind certain issues: The computer should be fast, easy to maintain, reliable, and be able to run the desired Web server software.

If your Web site becomes popular, you can easily receive as many as 2,000 connections a day. Many of these connections are condensed into *peek times* (a quick visit), resulting in multiple server requests at once. The more quickly the server can handle these requests, the less time the users must wait. As you may have already experienced yourself, it takes patience to wait for a server that is overloaded or slow. Many Internet users will not wait. Therefore, it is important

for the more popular sites to have a fast computer serving their Web pages. All the computers listed earlier in this section can serve your Web pages. The Unix and Windows NT systems, however, are designed to handle multiple tasks at once. With true multitasking built into their software and hardware design, these two systems are often the quickest. Of course, the speed at which your computer microprocessor processes data, the speed at which the hard disk is accessed, and size of *RAM* (random access memory) come into play as well.

Keep in mind that if your connection to the Internet is slow, it can easily slow performance, no matter how fast your computer is. Often this is the case when you visit a slow site on the Internet. Sending many responses using a 28.8 baud connection to the Internet can quickly slow your speedy delivery to the next user. (For a home computer, 28.8 baud seems fast; however, it is slow for a busy Internet site.) We will discuss the connection to the Internet in the section entitled *The Internet Connection*.

Some Web sites demand more from their systems than others. Many interactive sites perform processor-demanding tasks such as database searches, automatic page creation, animation, and so on. If your site will offer such functionality, beef up the system to handle such tasks quickly.

Another important issue is whether the site is easily maintained. Many World Wide Web administrators claim that a Unix system is best suited to deliver Web pages to users. If the administrator maintaining the site knows Windows NT, however, he or she will probably be able to squeeze more power out of an NT server. This is an especially important consideration if the administrator will not have much time to learn a new system.

It is imperative that the system used to distribute the Web site is reliable. Internet users often try to access a site just once. If your server locks up, nobody can access the Web site. Quite possibly the user will not return. Older operating systems such as Windows 3.1 have a reputation for memory leaks and general protection faults, both of which will cause problems. An ideal system is one that can run for months through hundreds of thousands of connections without any problems. Unix and Windows NT servers have the best reputation for reliability.

You can choose to deliver your Web presence from many Web server software programs. Web server software runs on your server and presents the Web pages to the Internet users. Unix seems to have the most Web server software available as well as the most add-on programs, which provide database connectivity, statistical programs, prewritten scripting programs, and so on. For more information about Web server software, see the section entitled *Web Server Software*.

Server hardware also includes components that send the information across the Internet. After all, the Internet connection needs to interface through some type of hardware to your system. These components include modems, ISDN modems, networks, and routers. The peripherals that you use depend on the Internet connection that you choose. Connections are discussed in greater detail in the section entitled *The Internet Connection*.

Web Server Software

Web server software, which is available for all the main operating systems, performs a variety of services. Deciding on Web server software is not like choosing a word processor. The decision requires a solid understanding of the technology and how it applies to your needs. For instance, will your company be using electronic commerce, multiple domain names, statistics, CGI programming, and so on? The best way to decide on the Web server software that will best work for you is to get the information directly from developers. You can bet that they have a World Wide Web site from which to retrieve the information. You can obtain more information about Web servers by going to Paul Hoffman's Web Server Comparison page at http://www.proper.com/www/servers-chart.html.

Paul Hoffman surveyed the servers used at more than 2,000 sites and found that the free Unix servers dominate the Internet and that the NCSA and CERN servers were used most often.

The Internet Connection

After you choose the server hardware and software, you need to decide on the type of connection that the server will have to the Internet. The link to the Internet is routed from your server to a provider company onto the Internet. The provider is necessary because very complex computers are used to tap directly into the "backbone" of the Internet.

Unless you have an unlimited budget, choosing your connection to the Internet requires a great deal of research. Installing a larger connection than you need can waste thousands of company dollars. If you choose a type of connection that does not meet your company needs, however, World Wide Web users will encounter difficulties (such as long waits and failures to connect) when they attempt to access your site. So, to decide on a type of connection, you need to investigate a few issues: the load, the cost, your company's location, and site maintenance.

The Expected Load

When building a Web site, you need to predict the *load*, the amount of data sent to users at one particular moment. The load is a function of the number of connections to your site and the number of bytes being transferred over the line. Some sites have a heavy load of more than 100,000 connections a day with many graphic transfers. Be sure that your connection can handle all the requests to your server during peak hours. Remember, graphics use significantly more *bandwidth*, or transfer capacity, than text. A useful analogy is to think of your connection as a busy country road that is a shortcut to a four- or eight-lane highway—the more cars and trucks on the shortcut, the longer it takes to get to the highway. The more requests the server responds to, the longer it takes each request to get to a site. You can even think of graphics as extra-large trucks with wide loads. Too many requests or too many large graphics can cause a traffic jam, which slows everything down.

To deal with a larger expected load, find a connection with greater bandwidth.

Table B.1: Types of Internet Connections	
Type of Connection	*Transfer Speed*
Modem	0–28.8 baud
ISDN	56 or 112 kilobytes(Kb)/second
Frame Relay	56 kilobytes(Kb) to 1.5 megabits(Mbps)/second
T1	1.54 megabits(Mbps)/second
T3	44.736 megabits(Mbps)/second

The Cost

Money is always an important consideration. Serving information on the Internet is much more expensive than setting up a personal Internet connection to surf the Net. Hosting a site requires a dedicated connection of significantly larger bandwidth, which can be expensive. Fortunately, if you offer great services and intense marketing on your site, the return on investment (ROI) can be significantly more than marketing through television, magazines, or newspapers. The cost of your link to the Internet can range from about $200 a month for a dedicated modem connection to several thousand for a high-speed T3 connection.

You can choose from a variety of connections to get the bandwidth and price that are right for your business. Call local providers or link to their sites to investigate services and prices in your area and to get information about connecting your server to the Internet. The following sites contain comprehensive lists of Internet providers: Internet Access by Area Code (http://helpdesk-www.cit.cornell.edu/IAP/ZC.html), Internet Access Providers (http://helpdesk-www.cit.cornell.edu/IAP/INAccess.html), The List (http://thelist.com/), and U.S. Internet Service Providers (http://www.primus.com/providers/). To help with your search, Table B.1 lists the types of connections available.

The Location

Building facilities and location can be an issue when installing an Internet connection, especially if a company is either not near a major metropolitan area or is leasing an office or a building. Many places in the world and in the United States do not have high-speed connections to the Internet. For instance, T1 or T3 connections are not available in most rural areas. If your company is outside a metropolitan area, check your local service providers. At the very least, you should have access to a modem connection, since it uses the telephone lines to connect to the Internet provider.

If you rent an office, a frame relay, T1, or T3 connection may pose a problem to the building owners since the connection may require mounting bulky hardware and cabling. Both modem and ISDN lines connect through the telephone lines. ISDN lines, however, use a special telephone cable that not all areas have.

Maintenance

Maintenance is an important consideration when setting up a Web site. Someone who understands your particular server and the Internet needs must oversee the Web site. A *webmaster*, the Web site administrator, must ensure that the server software is running well, watch for breaches in security, monitor the Internet connection, and more. This usually requires constant attention from a full-time employee. If you are now going to hire a webmaster to maintain your server, consider hiring someone with HTML programming experience. *HTML* (HyperText Markup Language) is the programming language used to create Web pages.

Creating Web Pages

Although HTML is not a very complex language, new versions arrive quickly. In three years, the HTML standard has changed three times: from HTML 1.0 to HTML 2.0 to HTML 3.0. The first two versions were adopted by the World Wide Web Consortium (http://www.w3.org/), but the third version was adopted by default: The Netscape Web browser (http://www.netscape.com/) became so popular that its version of HTML, HTML 3.0, has become the new standard.

When creating a Web site, first decide on the HTML version that you will use. All World Wide Web *browsers*, the software that a person uses to visit your site, are compatible with a particular version of HTML; some with HTML 2.0 and others with HTML 3.0. Later versions of HTML include the same basic programming features as the earlier versions of HTML, but features have been added with each new version. Thus, you can create a site using HTML 3.0, and browsers with only HTML 2.0 capabilities can still access and view your site. The browser ignores HTML 3.0–specific features, however. Most of these extra features are for aesthetics and are not essential to the content of the Web page.

By late 1995, from 70 to 80 percent of Internet users were using Netscape browsers running HTML 3.0, and most Web pages were created with 3.0 as a standard. Therefore, it is a good idea to create a Web site using HTML 3.0. After creating your pages, however, test-view the pages using a browser that is compatible only up to HTML 2.0. In this way, you can be sure that the ignored HTML 3.0 codes do not render the page unreadable. Usually, you'll find that the page will be quite legible.

HTML As a Language

HTML is essentially a word-processing language and is very easy to learn. The whole structure is based on marking sections of text to be displayed in a special format. For example, to bold the word SYBEX, all you need to do is put a start bold mark <b> at the beginning of the word and an end bold mark </b> at the end of the word (<b>SYBEX</b>). The entire language consists of such markups (hence the name HyperText Markup Language). The word *HyperText* in HTML describes the ability to click on a hypertext *link* (that is, text that will connect you to a different page, section of the page, or to another site).

HTML does not need to be compiled or to be saved in a special file format. HTML works as a simple ASCII or text file. Many people even write their code using the DOS editor or Windows Notepad.

Each Web page that you create is a separate file. If you create a Web site with three Web pages (such as an introduction page linked to a services page and a products page), you will actually have three HTML files on your server.

HTML files must be saved with the extension *html* or *htm*. Any Web page without the extension html (for the Unix or Macintosh environment) or htm (for the Windows environment) may not be read correctly by a Web browser.

A Step-by-Step Guide to Creating a Web Page

Creating your first Web page is exciting. This section tutors you on creating a very basic Web page. Throughout the creation of this page, you will want to check your work and see what it looks like through a Web browser. Almost all Web browsers can view HTML files from a local hard disk. For example, if you are using Netscape, choose File ➤ Open File or press Ctrl+O. Using the Open dialog box, select the file that you want to check and press Enter. In seconds, your newly created Web page is displayed on the screen.

Building a Skeleton Page

A Web page consists of a header section and a body section starting with an `<html>` marker and ending with an `</html>` marker. Note that most markers, which are called *tags*, come in pairs— one that starts a section and one that ends the section. The header tags are represented by `<head>` and `</head>`. Note that the only difference between starting and ending tags is the slash in the end tag. Below is a skeleton HTML file.

```
<html>
<head>
</head>
<body>
</body>
</html>
```

So, go ahead and create a text file with any text editor. If you are using Windows, you can create this skeleton HTML file with the Notepad program in the Accessories group. If you are using DOS, use the DOS editor program. Unix users can use vi.

In the example, the sections are indented for aesthetics. Large blank spaces such as extraneous carriage returns and tabs are ignored by HTML browsers. In fact, to create a new line or paragraph on the actual Web page, special tags (`<>` and `<p>`, respectively) are used.

Now that you have created the skeleton HTML file, add some text. Our sample Web page will be an advertisement for a new coffee shop called Caffeine Rush.

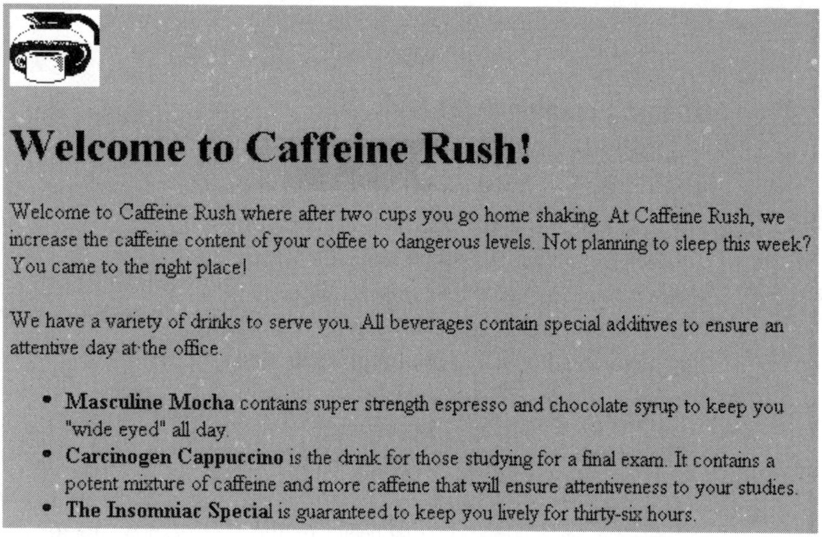

Welcome to Caffeine Rush!

Welcome to Caffeine Rush where after two cups you go home shaking. At Caffeine Rush, we increase the caffeine content of your coffee to dangerous levels. Not planning to sleep this week? You came to the right place!

We have a variety of drinks to serve you. All beverages contain special additives to ensure an attentive day at the office.

- **Masculine Mocha** contains super strength espresso and chocolate syrup to keep you "wide eyed" all day.
- **Carcinogen Cappuccino** is the drink for those studying for a final exam. It contains a potent mixture of caffeine and more caffeine that will ensure attentiveness to your studies.
- **The Insomniac Special** is guaranteed to keep you lively for thirty-six hours.

Figure B.1   The top of the Caffeine Rush tutorial Web page

Figure B.1 shows an example of the finished Web page that we are going to create. The components include a title in the title bar, a graphic logo, a large-font welcome, general text, a couple of paragraph markers, an unnumbered list, **boldface** words, *italic* text, and a link to another Web site.

Adding a Title

First, add the title to your Web page. The title is inserted into the header section. Type `<title>Caffeine Rush</title>` between the lines `<head>` and `</head>`. Your Web page should now look something like:

```
<html>
<head>
<title>Caffeine Rush</title>
</head>
<body>
</body>
</html>
```

Pretty simple! That's all we need to put into the <head>|</head> section.

Adding a Graphic to the Body

Now let's concentrate on the <body>|</body> section, which is analagous to the work area of the Web page. First, add a graphic to capture the audience's attention. To insert a graphic, add a line that specifies that an image is being inserted and then specify the graphic file being inserted. Simply type **<img src="">**. Then insert the location and filename of the graphic file between the quotation marks:

<img src="bean.gif">

In this case, we instruct the browser viewing the Web page to display the picture BEAN.GIF that is stored in the same directory as the HTML file. Always use a graphic that is saved with the GIF extension. All Web browsers can display GIF images directly on the Web page.

What if you can't create your own graphics? As you might guess, the Internet is loaded with collections of icons, rule (horizontal) lines, buttons, and other graphics. Simply download a file and insert it on your Web page. Table B.2 lists some of the best graphics sites on the Internet.

Inserting a Welcome Message

Next, add a new line that welcomes the viewer to the Web page. Now we want to be sure that this welcome stands out; so we increase its font size by using a heading command. HTML provides many headings that use different fonts and font (point) sizes. For the example, use heading style number one (<h1>|</h1>). Simply enclose the welcome between the tags <h1> and </h1> At this point, your HTML file should look like this:

<html>
<head>
<title>Caffine Rush</title>
</head>
<body>
<img src="bean.gif">
<h1>Welcome to Caffeine Rush!</h1>
</body>
</html>

There is no space between the graphic and the welcome heading because HTML assumes that you want a new line for your heading. As you will see later, you need to add a new line or paragraph tag when dealing solely with text.

Adding Text to the Page

Next, add some text. Text does not need to be encapsulated in markers. Simply type your text directly into the body as you want it. You don't need to worry about word wrapping text within the HTML file because the browser does that automatically. Insert text into your HTML file so it looks like this:

<html>
<head>
<title>Caffine Rush</title>
</head>
<body>
<img src="bean.gif">
<h1>Welcome to Caffeine Rush!</h1>

Table B.2: Online Graphics Collections		
Title	*URL*	*Description*
ASU Graphics Warehouse	http://www.eas.asu.edu/~graphics	Graphics, backgrounds, and links to other graphics pages
Daniel's Icon Archive	http://www5.biostr.washington.edu/icons/dans-icons.html and http://www.cs.monash.edu.au/icons/dicons	A well-organized and gigantic site of icons
Directory and Demos	http://www.mind.net/xethyr/demos/gfx.htm	A directory of all types of computer graphics resources, including links to sites for three-dimensional graphics, fractals, and stereograms
GIF Image Locator	http://www.nova.edu/Inter-Links/cgi-bin/wugif.pl	A search index of more than 2,000 GIF images at Washington University
Graphics 4 Your Page	http://www.rfhsm.ac.uk:70/0/people/gifs/index.html	Horizontal lines (rules), Stanford University logos, icons, arrows and buttons, and so on (slow connection)
Planet Earth Images	http://www.nosc.mil/planet_earth/images.html	Links to many image servers, images (particularly space-related), icons, flags, and miscellaneous
RGB Hex Triplet Color Chart	http://phoenix.phoenix.net/~jacobson/rgb.html	Codes for background colors
Rutgers Network Services WWW Icons and Logos	http://ns2.rutgers.edu/doc-images/	Icons, buttons, small buttons, and Rutgers logos
Timo's WWW GIF's Gallery	http://reimari.uwasa.fi/~ts/gifst/	Many small GIF files and icons, such as New, Under Construction, and many more
Transparent Background Images	http://melmac.corp.harris.com/transparent_images.html	How to make a GIF transparent
Transparent/Interlaced GIF Resource	http://dragon.jpl.nasa.gov/~adam/transparent.html	How to use transparent and interlaced GIFs, links to other similar pages, and downloadable graphics programs and tools
The Wallpaper Machine	http://www.ccsf.caltech.edu/cgi-bin/wallpaper.pl	Randomly created page backgrounds
The Web Rules	http://www.ECNet.Net/users/gas52r0/Jay/GIFs/rules/the_web_rules.htm	Horizontal rules and dividers
Xmorphia	http://www.cacr.caltech.edu/ismap/image.html	Randomly created page backgrounds
Yahoo Backgrounds	http://www.yahoo.com/Computers_and_Internet/Internet/World_Wide_Web/Programming/Backgrounds	Links to page backgrounds
Yahoo Icon Collections	http://www.yahoo.com/Computers_and_Internet/Internet/World_Wide_Web/Programming/Icons/	Many links to icon collections and other GIF files

Welcome to Caffeine Rush where after two cups you go home shaking. At Caffeine Rush, we increase the caffeine content of your coffee to dangerous levels. Not planning to sleep this week? You came to the right place!

\<p\>We have a variety of drinks to serve you. All beverages contain special additives to ensure an attentive day at the office.

\</body\>

\</html\>

Notice the \<p\> at the beginning of the second paragraph. The \<p\> acts as a paragraph marker, dropping the text to the next line. If there were no \<p\> tag, the browser would present the text as one complete paragraph because HTML ignores added space.

Inserting an Unnumbered List

Now we will spice things up by adding an unnumbered list. Start an unnumbered list with the \<ul\> tag and end it with \</ul\>. Each item in the list is marked with the \<li\> tag. Add three list items describing the different beverages.

\<html\>

\<head\>

\<title\>Caffine Rush\</title\>

\</head\>

\<body\>

 \<img src="bean.gif"\>

 \<h1\>Welcome to Caffeine Rush!\</h1\>

Welcome to Caffeine Rush where after two cups you go home shaking. At Caffeine Rush, we increase the caffeine content of your coffee to dangerous levels. Not planning to sleep this week? You came to the right place!

\<p\> We have a variety of drinks to serve you. All beverages contain special additives to ensure an attentive day at the office.

 \<ul\>

\<li\> Masculine Mocha contains super strength espresso and chocolate syrup to keep you "wide eyed" all day.

 \<li\>Carcinogen Cappuccino is the drink for those studying for a final exam. It contains a potent mixture of caffeine and more caffeine that will ensure attentiveness to your studies.

\<li\>The Insomniac Special is guaranteed to keep you lively for thirty-six hours.

\</ul\>

\</body\>

\</html\>

Enhancing the Page

Now, add the last line and more aesthetics to the page. First, add the following line after the closing unnumbered list tag: ***Warning: these drinks are not recommended for those with heart conditions***. To italicize (enhance) this line, we will enclose it with enhancement tags \<em\>|\</em\>. Next, apply boldface to the names of the drinks in the unnumbered list by enclosing them within bold markers \<b\>|\</b\>.

Warning: these drinks are not recommended for those with heart conditions.

The Coffee Journal

Adding a Link

The last component of the HTML file will be a link to another Web site, the Coffee Journal. Create a link by inserting the hyperlink tags \<a href=""\> and \</a\>. Within the quotes, type the URL of the Coffee Journal Web page. Between \<a href=""\> and \</a\>, type the text you want the user to see and click on to link to the other Web page.

The finished HTML file should look like this:

\<html\>

\<head\>

\<title\>Caffine Rush\</title\>

\</head\>

\<body\>

 \<img src="bean.gif"\>

 \<h1\>Welcome to Caffeine Rush!\</h1\>

Welcome to Caffeine Rush where after two cups you go home shaking. At Caffeine Rush, we increase the caffeine content of your coffee to dangerous levels. Not planning to sleep this week? You came to the right place!

<p>We have a variety of drinks to serve you. All beverages contain special additives to ensure an attentive day at the office.

<ul>

<li>Masculine Mocha contains super strength espresso and chocolate syrup to keep you "wide eyed" all day.

<li>Carcinogen Cappuccino is the drink for those studying for a final exam. It contains a potent mixture of caffeine and more caffeine that will ensure attentiveness to your studies.

<li>The Insomniac Special is guaranteed to keep you lively for thirty six hours.

</ul>

Warning: these drinks are not recommended for those with heart conditions.

<p>

<a href="http://www.bid.com/coffeejrnl/">The Coffee Journal</a>

</body>

</html>

For more information on how to program in HTML, visit one of the HTML tutorial sites on the Internet, as listed in Table B.3.

Another Sample Page

This section illustrates a typical Web home page and shows the code that makes it look that way.

The top of the page (see Figure B.2) contains the information that appears in the browser's title bar as well as the company logo.

◆ The first code (<html>) indicates the beginning of an HTML page.

◆ The title (<title> and </title>) is inserted.

◆ Then the body begins (<body).

◆ The white background color is defined (bgcolor="#FFFFFF">).

Table B.3: Selected Online HTML Tutorials and Aids	
Title	*URL*
A Beginners Guide to HTML	http://www.ncsa.uiuc.edu/demoweb/html-primer.html
Composing Good HTML	http://www.cs.cmu.edu/~tilt/cgh
The Cossack's Home Page/HTML Creation Page	http://www.utoledo.edu/www/homepages/dechelb/html.html
Extensions to HTML 2.0	http://home.netscape.com/assist/net_sites/html_extensions.html
Extensions to HTML 3.0	http://home.netscape.com/assist/net_sites/html_extensions_3.html
Home Page Construction Kit	http://gnn.com/gnn/netizens/construction.html
Home Page Improvement	http://www.boston.com/common/cimprove.htm
HTML Quick Reference	http://www.ncsa.uiuc.edu/General/Internet/WWW/HTMLQuickRef.html
The Planet Access HTML Page	http://www.murraymedia.com/pa2html.html
Style Guide for Online Hypertext	http://www.w3.org/hypertext/WWW/Provider/Style/Introduction.html
Tips for Web Spinners	http://gagme.wwa.com/~boba/tips1.html
The Web Designer	http://www.kosone.com/people/nelsonl/nl.htm
The Web Developer's Virtual Library	http://www.charm.net/~web/

- The location of this part of the page (<a name="Top">) enables a user to jump here after clicking on a link (<a href="#Top">[Top of Page]</a>).

- The logo (<img src=ippslog4.gif alt="IPPS Logo"></a>) and a line break (<br>) follow.

The code looks like this:

```
<html>
<head>
<title>
Internet Presence and Publishing Services
</title>
```

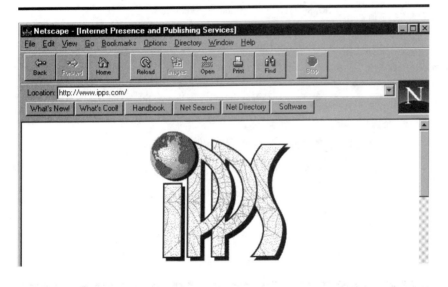

Figure B.2   The top of a sample Web page

```
<body bgcolor="#FFFFFF">
<center>
<a name="Top"><img src=ippslog4.gif
alt="IPPS Logo"></a><br>
```

The next section (Figure B.3) contains an image map on which you can click to go to one of three pages.

- At the beginning of the line is the code (<a href= "http://www.ipps.com/cgi-bin/ imagemap/ipps">) that names the location of a page of image map programming.

- The image map is a centered (<center>|</center>) GIF file, its width, border, and a description (<img src="choices.gif" height="165" width="457" border="0" alt="Image Map display of three balls" ISMAP>). ISMAP is the program with which you define the areas of the image map on which you click to go to particular pages.

Figure B.3   The image map on which you click to go to a particular page

The code looks like this:

```
<center>
<a href="http://www.ipps.com/cgi-
bin/imagemap/ipps"><img src="choices.gif"
height="165" width="457" border="0"
alt="Image Map display of three balls"
ISMAP></IMG></a>
</center>
```

Finally, the end of the page (Figure B.4) contains these codes and text:

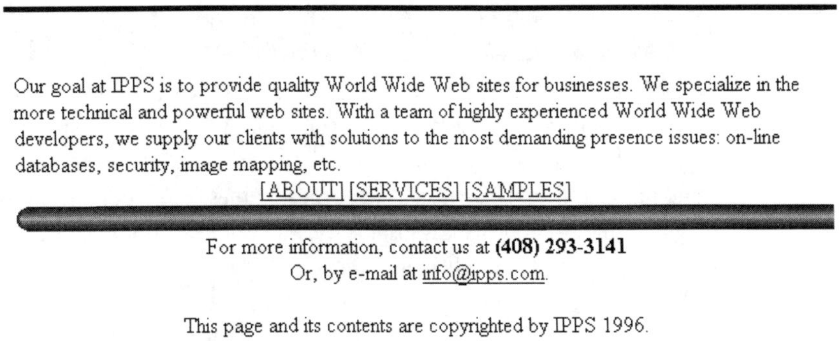

- The body text starts with a paragraph break (<p>) and ends with a line break (<br>).

- HTML pages should contain text links for users with nontext browsers or browsers that do not support image maps. Links include <a href="about.html"> (the code for the link), [ABOUT] (the actual text for the link), </a> (the end of the link), <a href="services.html">[SERVICES]</a>, and <a href="samples.html">[SAMPLES]</a>.

- A centered rule and a line break (<center><img src="line.gif">
) follow. Notice that "centered" is not turned off because the remaining lines on the page are centered.

- Text follows. For emphasis, the telephone number is enhanced with boldface (<b>|</b>).

- A link for the e-mail address (<a href="mailto:info@ipps.com">info@ipps.com</a>) is inserted.

- The page ends with two codes (</body> and </html>).

Our goal at IPPS is to provide quality World Wide Web sites for businesses. We specialize in the more technical and powerful web sites. With a team of highly experienced World Wide Web developers, we supply our clients with solutions to the most demanding presence issues: on-line databases, security, image mapping, etc.

[ABOUT] [SERVICES] [SAMPLES]

For more information, contact us at **(408) 293-3141**
Or, by e-mail at info@ipps.com.

This page and its contents are copyrighted by IPPS 1996.

Figure B.4   The bottom of the sample page

The code looks like this:

```
<p>
Our goal at IPPS is to provide quality World Wide Web sites for businesses. We
specialize in the more technical and powerful web sites. With a team of highly
experienced World Wide Web developers, we supply our clients with solutions to
the most demanding presence issues: on-line databases, security, image mapping,
etc. <br>
<center><a href="about.html">[ABOUT]</a> <a
href="services.html">[SERVICES]</a>
<a href="samples.html">[SAMPLES]</a> </center>
<center><img src="line.gif"><br>
For more information, contact us at <b>(408) 293-3141</b>
<br> Or, by e-mail at <a
href="mailto:info@ipps.com">info@ipps.com</a>.<p>
This page and its contents are copyrighted by IPPS 1996.
</center>
</body>
</html>
```

HTML Editors

Although HTML is not a difficult language to learn, you may still require a little assistance in creating your Web pages. Fortunately, several companies have created freeware that helps you create HTML pages. Most of these programs allow you to add text just the way you would in a word processor while clicking on buttons to create HTML markers. If you are new to any form of programming or if you are having a particularly difficult time using HTML, try one of the programs listed in Table B.4.

HTML Verification

Successfully following the many rules of HTML programming can get confusing. With so many tags, it is easy to accidentally misplace a tag or forget to close a section. To make matters worse, an incorrectly programmed Web page may look good when viewed with your browser but fail on another's browser. If you are making a site public, it is imperative that you double-check. Fortunately, you can check your programming by going to a verification site. Put your HTML pages on

Table B.4: Selected HTML Editors and Lists of Editors

Editor [Freeware/Commercial]	URL	Operating Environment
Alpha-Text [Freeware]	http://www.cs.umd.edu/~keleher/alpha.html	Macintosh
Ant HTML/Ant PLUS [Freeware]	http://www.w3.org/hypertext/WWW/Tools/Ant.html	Windows or Macintosh
Arachnid [Freeware]	http://sec-look.uiowa.edu/about/projects/arachnid-page.html	Macintosh
ASHE [Freeware]	ftp://ftp.cs.rpi.edu/pub/puninj/ASHE/README.html	X-Windows
HotDog Web Editor [Freeware]	http://www.sausage.com/	Windows
HoTMetaL Free Version [Freeware]	http://www.sq.com/products/hotmetal/hm-feat.htm	Windows
HoTMetaL PRO [Commercial]	http://www.sq.com/products/hotmetal/hm-org.htm	Windows
HTML Assistant Pro [Commercial]	http://fox.nstn.ca/~harawitz/index.html	Windows
HTML Assistant Pro—Freeware Edition [Freeware]	http://cs.dal.ca/ftp/htmlasst/htmlafaq.html	Windows
HTML Easy [Freeware]	http://www.trytel.com/~milkylin/htmleasy.html	Windows
HTML Editor [Freeware]	http://dragon.acadiau.ca/~giles/HTML_Editor/Documentation.html	Macintosh
HTML Grinder [Freeware]	http://www.matterform.com/mf/grinder/htmlgrinder.html	Macintosh
HTML Pro [Freeware]	http://www.ts.umu.se/~r2d2/computers/package/htmlpro_help.html	Macintosh
HTML Web Weaver [Freeware]	http://www.northnet.org/best/Web.Weaver/HTMLWW.html	Macintosh
HTML.edit [Freeware]	http://ogopogo.nttc.edu/tools/HTMLedit/HTMLedit.html	Macintosh

Table B.4: Selected HTML Editors and Lists of Editors (continued)		
Editor [Freeware/Commercial]	*URL*	*Operating Environment*
HTML Editors	http://www.money.com/htmleditors.html	List of HTML editors, links, and descriptions
HTMLed Pro [Freeware]	http://www.ist.ca/htmledpro/htprdemo.html	Windows
Microsoft Internet Assistant for Word 6.0 for Windows [Freeware]	http://www.microsoft.com/msoffice/freestuff/msword/download/ia/	Windows
Navigator: Windows-Based HTML Editors Revised	http://www.ziff.com/~pcweek/navigator/htmled.html	List and reviews of HTML editors
WebDoor [Freeware]	http://www.opendoor.com/webdoor/	Macintosh
Web Weaver [Freeware]	http://www.northnet.org/best/	Macintosh
WordPerfect Internet Publisher [Freeware]	http://wp.novell.com/elecpub/intpub.htm	Windows
World Wide Web Weaver for Macintosh [Freeware]	http://www.northnet.org/best/Web.Weaver/WWWW.html	Macintosh

your Web server, visit the verification site, specify the URLs to your pages, and press Enter. In a short time, the server checks your site and responds with a list of errors and suggestions. You can validate your site using HALsoft HTML Validation Service (at http://www.halsoft.com/html-val-svc/), Dr. HTML (http://imagiware.com/RxHTML.cgi), Weblint (http://www.unipress.com/web-lint), or Webtest Tools (http://web.gmu.edu:80/admin/webtest).

Interactive Web Sites

World Wide Web sites are not limited to static text and graphics. A well-crafted site may incorporate interactive features allowing form registration, animation, database searches, automated stock updating, electronic commerce, and more. Without interactive communication, World Wide Web sites would be nothing more than online magazines. In this section, you'll learn about form submission and Java programming.

About Forms

Forms are excellent ways to integrate interactivity into a Web site. Forms are sections of a Web page in which a user can type information into a field and submit the entered values for processing by the server computer (see Figure B.5). The server can process the submitted information through various programming languages: C, Unix shell scripts, PERL scripts, and so on. What the server does with the submitted information is totally up to the programmer:

◆ Generate a new Web page from the information and display valuable graphs and charts to the user

◆ Debit the submitted credit card and instruct the shipping department to send a product to the customer

◆ Link to a company database and register the user for a conference

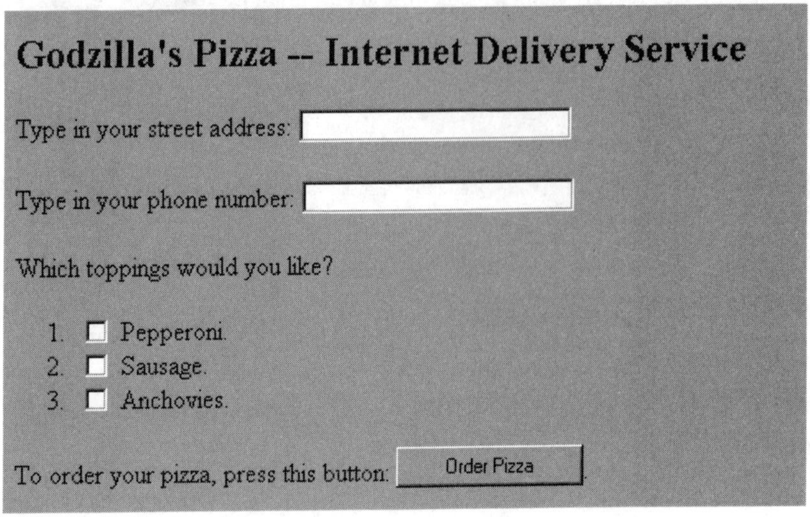

Godzilla's Pizza -- Internet Delivery Service

Type in your street address:

Type in your phone number:

Which toppings would you like?

1. ☐ Pepperoni.
2. ☐ Sausage.
3. ☐ Anchovies.

To order your pizza, press this button: Order Pizza

Figure B.5 An example of a form page (at http://www.ncsa.uiuc.edu/SDG/Software/Mosaic/Docs/fill-out-forms/example-3.html)

Creating an interactive form page is much more difficult than writing an HTML file. To produce a form page, follow these steps:

1. Set up the links from the HTML page.

2. Use the Common Gateway Interface (CGI) protocol to manage the data as it is passed to the server.

3. Configure the Web server to run a server side program.

4. Write a program to accept and process the information.

5. If you are returning information to the user, create an HTML page with its hidden MIME settings and return it to the Web server for delivery.

If you are interested in creating form HTML pages, consult an HTML/CGI programming book or read the Beginner's Guide to HTML at http://www.ncsa.uiuc.edu/demoweb/htmlprimer.html.

Programming Pages with Java

Another way to create an interactive site is to use Java programming. Java is an innovative programming concept created by Sun Microsystems. It allows programs stored on the server to download to the browser and run on the client (that is, the user's) computer. Good Java programs can, for example, constantly update current stock market quotes, manage online video games so that people can play others across the Internet, or simply download a word processor and execute it for your use. Java has been recognized by the larger progressive companies as the high-tech future of the World Wide Web. Companies such as Netscape have even licensed the Java language from Sun Microsystems and incorporated the technology into their browsers. For more information, visit the very busy Java Web site at http://java.sun.com/.

Add-Ons for Web Servers

When running your Web server, consider installing some add-on applications such as statistics or counter programs. These programs work in conjunction with your Web server to manage or enhance your site. Statistical programs allow you to measure *hits* (visits to) at your site. Depending on the statistical program installed, you can receive a wide variety of information such as the number of hits on each page and who is contacting your site.

Counter programs measure the number of hits you get on a particular page, and they enable you to display that number to anyone visiting your site.

Tip

To automatically place your site in several Internet master lists and search indexes simultaneously, go to the free Submit It service at http://www.submit-it.com/. Simply fill in a form and select the resources to be notified.

Using an Internet Presence Provider

Now that you understand the basics of creating a World Wide Web presence, you will want to begin developing your site. After investigating the costs, you may decide to outsource the work with a *presence provider*, a company that specializes in developing World Wide Web sites and hosting the sites on its servers. Don't confuse a presence provider with an Internet provider. Remember, an Internet provider mainly supplies end users with connections to access the Internet. For a list of Internet presence providers, go to Yahoo (http://www.yahoo.com/ Business_and_Economy/Companies/Internet_Service_Providers/ Internet_Presence_Providers/National_U_S_/).

Outsourcing the Development of Your Site

Many business people create their own Web sites since basic HTML programming is easy. For large, complex, and well-visited sites, consider leaving the work to a professional. An Internet presence provider has the following: a great deal of experience in developing many sites; advanced knowledge of the tools, computer systems, and peripherals needed for a good and reliable site; and programming knowledge. In addition, a presence provider keeps current with new and upcoming technologies.

Many presence providers make their services available to the general public, but be cautious! Many of these companies are run by hobbyists who only have a few months' experience. To determine if an Internet presence provider has enough experience to build your site, ask if he or she has interactive programming knowledge such as CGI and Perl.

An important question for a potential presence provider is, Do you outsource any of your work to other presence providers or consultants? If the presence provider farms out work, someone (namely you) may have to pay for the higher consulting rates. And if you have a problem with the site months after its development, the presence providers who actually did the work do not have any loyalty to you; they may not be available or may charge for maintenance.

Also ask, Who owns the developed pages? Some presence providers don't mention that they consider themselves the owners of the Web site. This can turn into a major problem if they host your pages on their server and you decide to move the pages to your new server. You may actually have to rebuild the pages.

Outsourcing the Hosting of the Web Site

It is often more efficient to rent space from a presence provider to host your Web site rather than to do it yourself. Many presence providers have sophisticated, expensive connections to the World Wide Web. In addition, hosting your own site requires installing the connections to the Internet, buying and setting up a server, and maintaining the connection and the server.

When considering a presence provider to host your site, ask these questions:

◆ How many other sites are also located on my server?

◆ What level of access will I personally have for managing the site?

◆ How many are sharing the connection to the Internet?

These questions will help you determine if your bandwidth and control will be worth the money.

Summing Up

Building a Web site is an important and time-consuming task. A Web site serves as the company's front page to a potential audience of millions; so choose very carefully when developing the site. Deciding on the correct hardware, software, and connection requires dedicated research. And don't forget to analyze the possibility of outsourcing.

Glossary of Internet Terms

acknowledgment (ACK) an automatic or manual response that an e-mail message has arrived at its destination. See *e-mail*.

address the location of an individual, a computer, or an organization to which e-mail is sent; a location on the Internet or on a network; a location on a particular computer. See *e-mail, Internet protocol address*.

address resolution the conversion of a four-byte internet address (for example, 204.71.16.10) to its physical address (for example, sover.net).

Advanced Research Projects Agency Network (ARPAnet) the internet run by the Defense Advanced Research Projects Agency (DARPA), formerly known as the Advanced Research Projects Agency (ARPA). ARPAnet has connected educational institutions, laboratories, and government agencies across the United States since the end of the 1960s and is the foundation for today's Internet. See *internet, Internet*.

agent a search tool that looks for and gathers information from all or part of the Internet, using one or more search indexes, lists, and other search tools. See *search index, search tool*.

alias a nickname; a short and simple name that usually is a substitute for a long and complicated name.

American National Standards Institute (ANSI) a U.S. standards organization affiliated with the International Organization for Standardization (ISO), a voluntary international organization that creates many international standards including those for computers and telecommunications; a coding standard for characters, numbers, and symbols. See *International Organization for Standardization*.

American Standard Code for Information Interchange (ASCII) a coding standard for characters, numbers, and symbols. The first 128 characters of the ANSI character set coincide with the first 128 characters of the ASCII character set.

anonymous FTP a file transfer protocol (FTP) that allows users to access, read, and/or download data, such as documents, programs, and other files, from a public part of a remote site. Using anonymous FTP, an assigned user identification (user ID) or password is not required to log on to the remote system. The remote system accepts a user ID of anonymous and a password of your e-mail address. Today, many Internet sites include links to FTP files, thereby eliminating the need to log in. See *File Transfer Protocol, password*, and *user identifier*.

ANSI See *American National Standards Institute*.

Appletalk an Apple Computer networking protocol. See *protocol*.

archie ARCHIve sErver; a keyword search tool with which you can search for files from anonymous FTP sites and other sites on the Internet. See *anonymous FTP, archive, keyword*, and *search tool*.

archive a collection of data, usually a combination of historical and up-to-date.

ARPAnet See *Advanced Research Projects Agency Network*.

artificial intelligence a category of computing in which human experts provide information to untrained or novice users through computer programs.

ASCII See *American Standard Code for Information Interchange*.

ASCII file a text file; an almost-universal file format. ASCII files contain very few formats beyond spaces, punctuation, and end-of-line marks, thereby being easy to transfer and to read by dissimilar applications and operating systems.

Asynchronous Transfer Mode (ATM) fast packet, or cell relay; an ISDN, high-speed transmission protocol that supports multimedia file transfer in fixed-size packets. See *Integrated Services Digital Network, multimedia, packet, protocol.*

backbone the top-level connections or cables in a network; the main connections to which many networks attach to the Internet. See *midlevel network, stub network.*

bandwidth the capacity, measured in bits per second (bps), of a particular path in a network; that is, how much data you can send per second. Sending a text-only page (about 16,000 bits) requires far less bandwidth than sending a photograph, a sound file, or a video. See *bits per second, modem.*

baud the number of bits that a modem can send or receive per second; the number of times a carrier signal changes per second, which normally exceeds the stated baud rate since each change can represent the sending of many bits of data.

BBS See *Bulletin Board System.*

binary a numbering system that consists of 0's and 1's (or Offs and Ons), which computers use in processing. A value of 0 closes an electronic circuit, and a 1 opens a circuit. See *bit.*

bit binary digit; a single value (a 0 or a 1) and the smallest unit of computer information.

bitmap a graphic image made up of pixels (pels), which are tiny dots.

BITNET an internet that provides e-mail and file transfer capabilities for thousands of educational institutions and laboratories throughout the world. The BITNET once was separate from the Internet. Since 1989, Computer Research and Education Network (CREN) has operated BITNET.

bits per second (BPS) the speed at which data move from the sending computer to the receiving computer. See *bandwidth, modem.*

bookmarks also known as *Hot lists.* With most Internet browsers, you can save the addresses of sites to which you return frequently. Then you can open a menu (for example, Bookmarks in Netscape) and click on the name of the site to go to it.

bounce the return of an undeliverable e-mail. See *e-mail.*

BPS See *bits per second.*

broadband a means of transmission that allows multiple signals at various frequencies to be sent simultaneously.

broadcast sending a message to a distribution list of recipients.

browser a program with which you can travel the Internet, particularly the World Wide Web but often Gopher and FTP sites. Popular browsers include Netscape, Mosaic, and Internet Explorer.

buffer a temporary storage area in computer memory. Buffers allow data to be transferred at high speeds; information is stored in buffers and then transferred to a permanent storage area at a lower speed.

Bulletin Board System (BBS) a system that you dial in to in order to participate in discussion groups, download and upload files, and learn about upcoming events. BBS's come in all sizes, from those run by one or two individuals as a hobby to large systems, such as Fedworld, a BBS that has links to various U.S. government departments. A Campus-Wide Information System (CWIS) is a type of BBS. See *Campus-Wide Information System.*

byte a set of 8 to 10 bits representing a single character. See *bit.*

CAD See *Computer-Aided Design.*

CAM See *Computer-Aided Manufacturing.*

Campus-Wide Information System (CWIS) a BBS for an entire educational institution, laboratory, or business with hookups for privately owned and publicly available computers. See *Bulletin Board System.*

CCITT See *Consultative Committee International Telephone and Telegraph.*

cell relay See *Asynchronous Transfer Mode.*

CEPT See *Conference on European Post and Telegraph.*

CERN Conceil Européen pour la Recherche Nucleaire (The European Laboratory for Particle Physics), which developed the World Wide Web, HTTP, and HTML. See *HTML, HTTP,* and *World Wide Web.*

CERT See *Computer Emergency Response Team.*

CGI See *Common Gateway Interface.*

channel a path over which data travel from a starting point to an ending point.

Class A network an Internet-connected network that allows up to 254^3 local machines and a large Internet Protocol (IP) address. Class A addresses start with decimal numbers ranging from 1 to 126; the network address comprises the first byte in the four-byte IP address, and a network node is assigned the last three bytes. See *Internet, Internet Protocol address, node.*

Class B network an Internet network that allows up to 254^2 local machines and a somewhat smaller Internet Protocol (IP) address than Class A networks. Class B addresses start with decimal numbers ranging from 128 to 191; the network address comprises the first two bytes in the four-byte IP address; a network node is assigned the last two bytes. See *Internet, Internet Protocol address, node.*

Class C network an Internet network that allows 254 local machines and a somewhat smaller Internet Protocol (IP) address than Class B networks. Class C addresses start with decimal numbers ranging from 192 to 223; the network address comprises the first three bytes in the four-part IP address, and a network node is assigned the last byte. See *Internet, Internet Protocol address, node.*

Class D network an Internet network used for multi-casts. Class D addresses start with decimal numbers ranging from 224 to 239. See *Internet, Internet Protocol address, multicast.*

client a program that requests information from a server program on a remote computer. A particular client must be programmed to communicate with the server. See *server.*

Common Gateway Interface (CGI) a program or script with which a user can search for information in the databases on your server. A CGI must run quickly to satisfy the users searching your system, and it must be secure to limit access to only those files that you want to have available.

compression data compression or data compaction; making files smaller by replacing commonly used words and combinations with codes, which take up less space.

Computer-Aided Design (CAD) using computers in manufacturing and architectural design; often combined with Computer-Aided Manufacturing (CAM) and known as CAD/CAM.

Computer-Aided Manufacturing (CAM) using computers to design and manufacture; often combined with Computer-Aided Design and known as CAD/CAM.

Computer Emergency Response Team (CERT) an organization, now located at Carnegie Mellon University, that oversees security issues and emergencies on the Internet.

Conference on European Post and Telegraph (CEPT) a European telecommunications standards organization.

congestion a "traffic jam" of data in which the amount of data to be sent is greater than the capacity to send it.

connect time the measurement of hours and minutes between the time at which you log on to a network or BBS and the time at which you log off.

Consultative Committee International Telephone and Telegraph (CCITT) Comite Consultatif International de Telegraphique et Telephonique; an international telecommunications standards organization and part of the United National International Telecommunications Union (ITU).

Corporation for Research and Educational Networking (CREN) the organization that has operated BITNET since 1989. See *BITNET.*

CREN See *Corporation for Research and Educational Networking.*

CWIS See *Campus-Wide Information System.*

cyberpunk a cyberspace inhabitant who dresses and behaves in a certain way in order to conform to the social culture of the Internet and computers. See *cyberspace.*

cyberspace the name given by William Gibson in his novel *Neuromancer* to the society surrounding computers, especially the computer culture of the future. Now, the Internet and its culture is known as cyberspace.

daemon a utility that is always available to correct problems and errors and to run commonly used functions on a Unix system.

DARPA See *Defense Advanced Research Projects Agency*.

decode convert a text file that has been encoded back to its original binary format. See *encode, uudecode, uuencode*.

dedicated connection a connection with a network that is almost always (except for maintenance and power outages) in effect. See *dialup*.

Defense Advanced Research Projects Agency (DARPA) the U.S. Department of Defense office that develops new military technology and runs ARPAnet, the internet of educational institutions, laboratories, and government agencies across the United States and the foundation for today's Internet. See *Advanced Research Projects Agency Network, internet, Internet*.

Defense Data Network Network Information Center (DDN NIC or NIC) part of the Defense Data Network, which connects U.S. military bases. This NIC and NICs throughout the world assign Internet network addresses and administer other parts of the Internet. The DDN NIC also manages a repository of Requests for Comments (RFCs). See *Network Information Center, Request for Comments*.

dialup a temporary connection to a network or to the Internet made by dialing a modem and logging in. In contrast, a dedicated connection is almost always (except for times of maintenance or power outages) in effect. See *dedicated connection*.

digerati digital literati; those cool individuals (or those who think they are) leading the rest of us along the "information superhighway."

DNS See *Domain Name System*.

domain the two- or three-character specifications of the type of organization or the region in which the organization is located.

domain name the identifer of an Internet site, which includes the name of a particular site (such as mit, which represents the Massachusetts Institute of Technology, or digital, which represents Digital Equipment Corporation) and its domain (which indicates the type of organization or the region in which it is located). A domain name looks like this: mit.edu or digital.com.

Domain Name System (DNS) the standard for naming Internet sites, including domain names and the preceding components of a physical Internet address (for example, www.ibm.com or eddygrp@sover.net) of a particular server or individual using that server. See *Internet Protocol address, server*.

dotted quad See *Internet Protocol address*.

download transfer a file from a larger computer (usually a remote computer) to a smaller one (your PC) using anonymous ftp (file transfer protocol). See *upload*.

DS1 digital service hierachy level 1, which is another term for T1. See *T1*.

E1 European T1, which transmits data at 2.04 megabits per second. See *T1*.

Ebone the European backbone. See *backbone*.

electronic mail See *e-mail*.

e-mail electronic mail, in the form of messages or files, from an individual to another individual or from an individual to more than one individual.

e-mail address the electronic mailing address of a particular individual, usually formatted as follows: eddygroup @sover.net (the individual's user ID, the @ sign, and the domain name). See *domain name, user identifier*.

encode convert a binary file to text format before sending it from one computer to another. Most, if not all, computers can read text files; so users can encode binary files to make them readable by the receiving computer system. See *decode, uudecode, uuencode*.

encryption the changing of characters in a file to other characters so that data will be secure while it is transferred. At the receiving computer, an encryption program translates the encrypted characters back to the original characters.

emoticons also known as smileys; combinations of characters such as :), which indicates happiness, or ;l, which shows a wink, added to an e-mail message to indicate the emotions of the individual sending the message.

ethernet A local area network (LAN) standard by which computers in the network are connected with coaxial cables and data are transferred at about 10 million bits per second (Mbps).

European Academic and Research Network (EARN) an internet, similar to BITNET, that provides e-mail for educational institutions and laboratories in Europe. See *BITNET*.

FAQ See *Frequently Asked Questions*.

fast packet See *Asynchronous Transfer Mode*.

FDDI See *Fiber Distributed Data Interface*.

Fiber Distributed Data Interface (FDDI) a very high speed fiberoptics transmission protocol that transmits data at about 100 million bits per second (Mbps).

File Transfer Protocol (FTP) a protocol that allows users to access, read, and/or download data, such as documents, programs, and other files, from a remote computer. A user can log on to permissible parts of the remote computer using either an assigned user ID and a password or anonymous FTP, which requires a user ID of anonymous and a password of your e-mail address. Today, many Internet sites include links to FTP files, thereby eliminating the need to log in. See *anonymous FTP*.

finger a client program that displays information about a particular user logged on a particular host system. Information can include the user ID, the user's full name, if the user is logged in now or the last time the user was logged in, a telephone number, address, and other information that the user wants to make public. The host system determines the information that is released.

firewall an imaginary wall of software and hardware that prevents unwanted visits to all or part of a network.

flame an impolite and inflammatory comment about an e-mail message, sometimes due to the content but often due to the host from which the message came. For example, when America Online began access to the Internet, many new users (newbies) who asked "ignorant" questions were flamed.

flame war a series of flames back and forth among two or more flamers.

frame the beginning (header) and end (trailer) of a packet. Headers and trailers announce the beginning and end of a packet and include other information, such as the names of the sending and receiving computers. See *header, packet*.

freenet a bulletin board system (BBS) that is community-based and offers e-mail, file transfer, other Internet access, and forums for little or no cost.

freeware public-domain programs; programs that are available at no charge. See *shareware*.

Frequently Asked Questions (FAQs) documents, sometimes text-only and sometimes with links, that list commonly asked questions and the accompanying answers for a variety of subjects. Before asking a human a question about a particular subject, search for the FAQ.

FTP See *File Transfer Protocol*.

gateway an entry to a network, usually requiring software that enables translating from one or more communications protocol to another.

GIF Graphics Interchange Format; a format for graphics files that can be used to illustrate World Wide Web pages.

Gopher a fast menu-based system of data presentation developed at the University of Minnesota. Most World Wide Web browsers enable access to Gopher sites.

Gopherspace all Gopher sites across the Internet.

hacker an individual who wants to learn all there is to know about computers, programs, and/or networks. Most hackers hack to answer what-if questions. A very small minority hack to cause trouble and havoc.

header the top part of a packet or a message; the area that contains packet information—the addresses of the computer from which the packet is sent and the computer to which it is sent; the area of a message that contains the address of the message creator, the date, and the time.

history list a list of documents and addresses that a browser keeps during a session on the Internet.

home page (1) the top hypertext document at a World Wide Web site. Typically, the top hypertext document at a site introduces the organization sponsoring the site and links you to lower-level pages at the site. (2) The first site automatically displayed when you start your browser. For example, by default Netscape points to the Netscape home page using this line in the NETSCAPE.INI file: Home Page=http://home.netscape.com/. You can change this line to make any Internet site (including Web, Gopher, and FTP) your home page.

host a server; a computer that "hosts" other computers; a computer that provides data or services, such as e-mail or World Wide Web, Gopher, FTP, and other Internet sites.

host name the name of a host computer. Host names identify a particular computer on a network.

Hot list See *bookmarks*.

HTML HyperText Markup Language; a language with which you create World Wide Web pages that have hypertext links. Most HTML documents have an HTML or HTM file extension. HTML is a subset of Standard Generalized Markup Language (SGML). See *hypertext*, *link*, *Standard Generalized Markup Language*, and *World Wide Web*.

HTTP HyperText Transport Protocol; the rules and standards used to make World Wide Web hypertext files on host computers readable by client programs. See *client*, *host*, *hypertext*, and *World Wide Web*.

hyperlink See *link*.

hypermedia See *multimedia*.

hypertext a document with a variety of media (multimedia): text, graphics, audio, and/or video along with links to other documents. Typically, World Wide Web pages are hyptertext. See *link*, *multimedia*, and *World Wide Web*.

ICMP See *internet control message protocol*.

icon a small graphic that represents a folder, a document, a file, or a program. Click on an icon to access a new page of folders or documents, to open a document, or to download a file. Double-click on an icon to start a program.

identifier the label of a computer or computer component, a person, or a procedure or variable in a computer program. See *user identifier*.

in-line image a graphic on a World Wide Web page.

Integrated Services Digital Network (ISDN) a digital data service that allows high-speed (128,000 bits per second) movement of voice and digital messages over conventional telephone lines, which ordinarily move data at half that speed. CCITT has set ISDN standards. See *Consultative Committee International Telephone and Telegraph*.

International Organization for Standardization (ISO) an international, voluntary organization that sets standards for computing, telecommunications, and many other areas. The American National Standards Institute (ANSI) is the U.S. affiliate. See *American National Standards Institute*.

internet two or more networks connected into a single network.

Internet the largest internet in the world made up of networks connecting educational institutions, laboratories, government agencies, businesses, and individuals. The Internet comprises three levels of networks: the backbones (national and international), the mid-level (regional) networks, and the stub (local) networks. All the networks on the Internet use the TCP/IP communications protocol. See *backbone, midlevel network, stub network, Transmission Control Protocol/Internet Protocol*.

Internet access provider a company or an organization that provides user access to the Internet. Now, for many users, the terms *Internet service provider* and *Internet access provider* both represent the same thing: a company or organization that provides user access to the Internet and that may provide Web page development and other services. See *Internet service provider*.

Internet address See *domain name, Domain Name System, Internet Protocol address*.

internet control message protocol (ICMP) the rules and standards used to correct errors and control messages sent to remote computers.

Internet Protocol (IP) the connectionless, best-effort packet-switching protocol that defines a packet and manages packet deliveries among unlike networks and pathways on the Internet.

Internet Protocol address IP address, Internet address, or dotted quad; the unique 32-bit address consisting of four numbers separated with periods (for example, 204.71.16.10) assigned to every host computer on the Internet and translated into a domain name. See *address resolution, domain name, Domain Name System*.

Internet Relay Chat (IRC) talk; a facility that allows people from all over the world to communicate (chat) in real time, publicly or privately.

Internet service provider (ISP) a company or an organization that provides services such as Web page development. Now, to many users, the terms *Internet service provider* and *Internet access provider* have merged into one meaning: a company or an organization that provides user access to the Internet and that may provide Web page development and other services. See *Internet access provider*.

IP See *Internet Protocol*.

IP address See *Internet Protocol address*.

IRC See *Internet Relay Chat*.

ISDN See *Integrated Services Digital Network*.

ISO See *International Organization for Standardization*.

JPEG Joint Photographic Expert Group; a standard for compressing a gray-scale or color graphic file.

Kbps See *kilobits per second*.

keyword a word or phrase stored in a database record enabling you to find that record using a search index or to sort selected records in a database. See *search engine, search index, search tool*.

kilobits per second (Kbps) 1,000 bits per second.

kilobyte kb, KB, or Kbyte; 1,024 bytes.

LAN See *Local Area Network*.

LD-1 a type of T1, which is capable of transmitting voice, video, and data. See *T1*.

leased-line a rented telephone line that is dedicated 24 hours a day exclusively to a particular connection to the Internet.

link an underlined or highlighted word or phrase, part of a graphic, or an icon or a button on which you click to jump to another document. Links are most commonly found on World Wide Web hypertext documents and at Gopher sites. See *Gopher, hypertext, World Wide Web*.

Linux a freeware version of Unix named after Linus Torvalds. See *freeware, Unix*.

Listserv list server; a mailing list and discussion group to which you can subscribe. Listservs can be moderated or unmoderated. See *mailing list, moderator*.

Local Area Network (LAN) a network of computers, workstations, and/or computer peripherals in a small area, such as a room, floor, or building. See *Wide Area Network*.

log in the act of typing a user ID and, optionally, a password to access a computer or a network.

lurk view the messages in a discussion group without writing or responding to them. Most experienced Internet users think that newbies (beginners) should lurk for a while and learn the conventions before joining in the "conversation" in a discussion group.

mailbox a place on a network or a computer in which messages are stored. Some mail storage areas include an inbox and an outbox to differentiate between incoming and outgoing messages.

mail bridge mail gateway; an area through which mail is sent from one network to another ensuring that unlike systems can communicate and that security is maintained.

mail gateway See *mail bridge*.

mailing list Maillist; a distribution list of e-mail addresses, used to send messages to members of a discussion group. You can subscribe to mailing lists. Mailing lists can be moderated or unmoderated. See *Listserv, moderator*.

maillist See *mailing list*.

master list mega-list or meta-list; one or more pages of Internet links usually arranged under subject headings. Yahoo, The Whole Internet Catalog, and the World-Wide Web Virtual Library are well-known sets of master lists. Some of the better master lists also include a search index. See *search index, search tool*.

Mbps See *megabits per second*.

megabits per second (Mbps) 1,000,000 bits per second.

megabyte 1 million bytes; 1,000 kilobytes.

mega-list See *master list*.

meta-list See *master list*.

midlevel network a regional network; a second level network on the Internet. Midlevel networks connect stub (local) networks to the backbone networks (the top level). See *backbone, stub network*.

MIME See *Multipurpose Internet Mail Extensions.*

modem MOdulator|DEModulator; a computer peripheral that is a telephone with which the computer dials and connects with remote computers.

moderator one or more individuals that control the content of a discussion group by reviewing e-mail messages and deciding whether they will be included in the discussion.

MOO See *Mud, Object-Oriented.*

Mosaic the first World Wide Web browser for several platforms. Mosaic was developed by the National Center for Supercomputing Applications (NCSA) at the University of Illinois.

Moving Pictures Experts Group (MPEG) a standard for compressing video and audio files.

MPEG See *Moving Pictures Experts Group.*

MUD See *Multi-User Dungeon.*

Mud, Object-Oriented (MOO) a role-playing textual game in which several players participate.

multicast a broadcast of a message to many or all recipients on a distribution list.

multimedia a file made up of text, graphics, video files, and/or audio components. On the World Wide Web, a multimedia file may contain links to any of these components.

Multipurpose Internet Mail Extensions (MIME) also Multiple Internet Mail Extensions; the ability of Internet e-mail to send and receive graphics, audio files, video files, and other nontextual information.

Multi-User Dungeon (MUD) a text-based, role-playing, virtual reality adventure. MUDs—which can be used for gaming, education, or software development—enable users to create permanent objects with which other players and users can play. See *Mud, Object Oriented; MUSE.*

MUSE a type of MUD with very little or no violence. See *Multi-User Dungeon.*

National Center for Supercomputing Applications (NCSA) the developer of the Mosaic World Wide Web browser and a major center for computing and telecommunications located at the University of Illinois.

NCSA See the *National Center for Supercomputing Applications.*

netiquette Internet etiquette; good manners when communicating over the Internet.

netizen Internet citizen; a mannerly citizen of the Internet.

network two or more computers and peripherals, such as printers, connected with cables, telephone lines, and/or network adapter cards. Networked computers share common resources, and users on the network can communicate.

network address the portion of an Internet Protocol (IP) address assigned to the network. The network address for a large Class A network is the first byte of the four-byte address. The network address for a Class B network is the first two bytes, and for a Class C network is the first three bytes. The remaining byte or bytes are assigned to a particular node. See *Internet Protocol address, network, node.*

Network Information Center (NIC) an office that provides administrative help for users of a network. The InterNIC administers the Internet and assigns new domain names.

newbie a somewhat disparaging term representing a newcomer to the Internet.

newsgroup a discussion group on the Usenet; analogous to a mailing list on a Listserv. See *Usenet.*

NIC See *Network Information Center.*

node a device, such as a computer, printer, or another peripheral, that can be communicated with and attached to a network.

node address the portion of an Internet Protocol (IP) address assigned to a node on a network. The node address for a large Class A network is composed of the three rightmost bytes of the four-byte address. The node address for a Class B network is composed of the two rightmost bytes, and for a Class C network is the last byte. The other byte or bytes are assigned to the network. See *Internet Protocol address, network.*

packet a unit of data and accompanying identifying information sent across a network.

Packet InterNet Groper (pint) a utility that tests whether a remote computer or a node on a network is running and available. Think of the ping sound made by a submarine's sonar system to detect other submarines.

packet switching the act of moving packets from the sending computer to the receiving computer using paths that are not always the shortest distance between two points, depending on whether hosts are running or are down for a variety of reasons.

password a combination of letters, numbers, and special symbols that you type or that is automatically entered in order to gain access to a protected computer or network.

PGP See *Pretty Good Privacy*.

ping See *Packet InterNet Groper*.

Point of Presence (POP) the physical location at which an Internet provider attaches its network to telephone company leased lines and one or more new local telephone numbers.

Point-to-Point Protocol (PPP) a standard that enables the transmission of packets from a serial port of a sending computer to a receiving computer over synchronous (one frame at a time followed by a set period of time) and asynchronous (one character at a time followed by any period of time) paths. PPP is newer and an improvement over SLIP. See *Serial Line IP*.

polling a network node ensuring that incoming information arrives at the network or that outgoing information departs.

POP See *Point of Presence, Post Office Protocol*.

port (1) A communications port, a connection on a computer into which a modem, mouse, printer, or other peripheral is attached. (2) Part of a URL following the colon (:) after the domain name and representing a particular server, often used for Gopher servers and less often for World Wide Web servers. See *Gopher, server, Uniform Resource Locator, World Wide Web*.

post send a message.

Post Office Protocol (POP) an e-mail account with your provider and the way in which your e-mail software receives incoming mail.

PostScript Adobe Systems' page description language, a standard for some Internet documents; it is also used for sophisticated desktop publishing.

PPP See *Point-to-Point Protocol*.

Pretty Good Privacy (PGP) a popular freeware program, created by Phil Zimmermann, that encrypts data to be sent across the Internet. PGP is available for U.S. and Canadian citizens living in their respective countries and to citizens of other countries, depending on their anticryptography laws. See *encryption*.

protocol rules, regulations, and standards that guide the interaction between a program and a computer, two computers, two networks, and so on.

Protocol Data Unit (PDU) another name for packet. See *packet*.

provider See *Internet access provider, Internet service provider*.

public domain See *freeware*.

rank a value or score assigned to an entry in a WAIS search results list. A high rank indicates that the result closely fits the keywords and criteria that you entered, according to the way in which the search index has been programmed to evaluate results. See *Wide Area Information Servers*.

Request for Comments (RFC) the published official standards for the Internet developed by the Internet Engineering Task Force (IETF). Reading RFCs provides a good background and detailed information about using the Internet—from e-mail to Internet Protocol addressing.

RFC See *Request for Comments*.

route the potential path or the real path along which packets travel from the sending computer to the receiving computer.

router a hardware device or program that "routes" or sends packets from a sending computer to a receiving computer.

search engine See *search index*.

search index a form with which you set the parameters for an Internet search. A search index is composed of a text box in which you type one or more keywords, usually a button on which you click to start the search, and optional checkboxes, text boxes, and option buttons with which you can select the conditions for a search. See *search tool*.

search tool a program or set of commands with which you search for an Internet site. Search tools encompass both master lists and search indexes. See *search index*.

Serial Line IP (SLIP) a standard that enables the transmission of packets from a serial port of a sending computer to a receiving computer over synchronous (one frame at a time followed by a set period of time) and asynchronous (one character at a time followed by any period of time) paths. Point-to-Point Protocol (PPP) is a newer and improved protocol of this type. See *Point-to-Point Protocol*.

server a computer or software that serves client computers; a single machine on which files are stored and which client computers can access; the software that communicates with client computers and that enables access to files. See *client*.

SGML See *Standard Generalized Markup Language*.

shareware programs that are available at a small charge. Typically, you can download and try a program before buying. When you license a shareware program, the author will send you a full version of the program as well as a manual. Some large companies provide a shareware "lite" version of a program in the hopes that you will buy a full-featured version.

signature after an e-mail message, a short (fewer than five lines is the standard) message or biography of the sender.

Simple Mail Transfer Protocol (SMTP) a server-to-server standard for transferring e-mail messages from a sending computer to a receiving computer.

Simple Network Management Protocol (SNMP) the standard that is used to manage nodes ranging from common nodes (such as computers and printers) to rare ones (for example, coffee makers, vending machines, and cameras taking real-time pictures of aquariums or harbors) on a TCP/IP network. See *node, Transmission Control Protocol/Internet Protocol*.

site a home page and all linked pages at a particular Internet address. See *address, home page*.

SLIP See *Serial Line IP*.

smileys See *emoticons*.

SMTP See *Simple Mail Transfer Protocol*.

snail mail mail sent through the U.S. Postal Service. For users of e-mail, snail mail, which is measured in days, travels much too slow.

SNMP See *Simple Network Management Protocol*.

spam use a mailing list or a newsgroup to broadcast e-mail messages that may not be related to that mailing list or newsgroup and that attempt to sell goods or services. Most Internet users believe that spammers must be flamed. For a list of flagrant spams, see the Blacklist of Internet Advertisers at http://math-www.uni-paderborn.de/~axel/BL or http://www.cco.caltech.edu/~cbrown/BL. Spam® is a canned meat product of the Hormel Corporation.

SQL See *Structured Query Language*.

Standard Generalized Markup Language (SGML) a text-processing language with codes for various levels of headings, paragraphs, links, and line and page breaks. HTML is a form of SGML. See *HTML*.

Structured Query Language (SQL) a standard query language for finding records or sets of records in databases. Internet users can use SQL to access large databases on the Net.

stub network a local network attached to a midlevel network, which in turn is attached to a backbone. Smaller Internet service providers are usually connected to a stub network. See *backbone, midlevel network*.

subnet part of a network, which can be assigned its own unique part of the network address.

sysop See *system operator*.

system operator sysop; one or more individuals responsible for maintaining a network, including repairs, troubleshooting, backing up files, and upgrading hardware and software. A sysop may report to a system administrator, who may set schedules for maintenance, order hardware and software, and make other decisions.

T1 also known as T-1; a leased high-speed telephone line that can transmit data at more than 1.544 million bits a second.

T3 also known as T-3; a leased high-speed telephone line that can transmit data at more than 44.736 million bits a second.

talk See *Internet Relay Chat.*

TCP See *Transmission Control Protocol/Internet Protocol.*

Transmission Control Protocol/Internet Protocol (TCP/IP) sometimes known as TCP; the standard set (or suite) of protocols that rules how data is broken into packets and transferred from a sending computer to a receiving computer. TCP/IP covers e-mail, login onto remote computers, and file transfer.

Telnet an application with which you can log on to a remote computer on the Internet and access the computer as though you were connected locally.

terminal a monitor and a keyboard with which you interact with a remote computer. Communications software emulates (imitates) certain terminals. (VT100 and VT102 are two examples.)

terminal emulation imitating the behavior and other attributes of popular terminals using communication software.

terminal server a computer that connects many terminals to a network through one connection.

thread an e-mail message and all the replies to it.

timeout a broken connection to a remote computer, due to user inactivity for a certain amount of time.

topology a map of a network with all attached computers, peripherals, and other nodes.

Uniform Resource Locator (URL) an address made up of four parts: the protocol type (for example, http:, ftp:, gopher:, and so on), the name of the server (for example, www.sover.net or gopher.usda.mannlib.cornell.edu:70), the directories or folders (for example, /11/data-sets/general), and the optional filename (for example, contents.html or homepage.htm).

Universal Time Coordinated (UTC) Zulu or Greenwich Mean Time; the time zone that starts at 0 degree longitude and the time from which all other times around the world are calculated.

Unix a very stable operating system that can be used by more than one user at a time. Unix, which is the most commonly used operating system for Internet servers, has a built-in version of TCP/IP. See *server, Transmission Control Protocol/Internet Protocol.*

Unix-to-Unix CoPy (UUCP) a protocol that enables a sending computer using the Unix operating system to use dial-up telephone lines to send packets to a receiving computer using the Unix operating system. See *Unix.*

upload a file transfer from a smaller computer (your PC) to a larger one (usually a remote computer) using anonymous ftp (file transfer protocol). See *download.*

URL See *Uniform Resource Locator.*

Usenet thousands of discussion groups, known as newsgroups, about half of which are on the Internet. Participants in Usenet newsgroups discuss various topics, from business to fun. Usenet newsgroup discussion groups are arranged by hierarchies, including alt (alternative), biz (business), comp (computers), rec (recreation), sci (science), soc (social issues), and more.

user identifier user ID or userid; the unique assigned name by which a user is known to a network. Examples of user identifiers are *eddygrp* and *73510.3154* in the addresses eddygrp@sover.net and 73510.3154@compuserve.com.

username See *user identifier.*

UTC See *Universal Time Coordinated.*

UUCP See *Unix-to-Unix CoPy.*

uudecode a program that decodes (converts a text file that has been converted from binary format back to binary format) a file that has been sent from one computer to another. See *decode, encode, uuencode.*

uuencode a program that encodes (converts a binary file to text format) a file that will be sent from one computer to another. See *decode, encode, uudecode.*

Veronica Very Easy Rodent Oriented Net-wide Index to Computerized Archives; a search engine for searching a database of all Gopher sites in Gopherspace. Veronica was developed at the University of Nevada. See *Gopher, Gopherspace.*

W3 See *World Wide Web.*

WAIS See *Wide Area Information Servers.*

WAN See *Wide Area Network.*

The Web See *World Wide Web.*

webmaster the individual who administers a Web site, including solving problems, coding World Wide Web pages, and checking that links are still active.

Whois an Internet program with which you can search for individuals, organizations, networks, and companies on the Internet. You can use Whois to search the Internet registry at the Defense Data Network Network Information Center (DDN NIC) server at whois.internic.net and at other Whois servers found using an FTP search tool such as Archie or FTP search. See *Defense Data Network Network Information Center.*

Wide Area Information Servers (WAIS) a commercial program, developed by WAIS, Inc., with which information can be indexed so that users can access it using a search engine. The results of each search is arranged by rank; the program scores the results, and the information that is more relevant is placed at the top of the list and given a high score (ranging from 0 to 100). See *rank, search index, search tool.*

Wide Area Network (WAN) a network of computers, workstations, and/or computer peripherals in a large area or region—even worldwide; a network that is not a Local Area Network (LAN). See *Local Area Network.*

World Wide Web WWW, W3, or the Web; the fastest-growing part of the Internet; a hypertext-based and multimedia system that supports the use of text, hypertext links that enable users to jump to other Internet sites, graphics, and sound files. The World Wide Web was developed by a group at the European Laboratory for Particle Physics (CERN) in Switzerland. See *CERN, HTML, HTTP,* and *hypertext.*

WWW See *World Wide Web.*

Index

Note to the Reader:
First level entries are in **bold**. Page numbers in **bold** indicate the principal discussion of a topic or the definition of a term. Page numbers in *italic* indicate illustrations.

I

N

Search Tools

Search Tool	URL
ALIWEB	http://www.nexor.co.uk/public/aliweb/doc/search.html
All-in-One Search Page	http://www.albany.net/allinone
Alta Vista	http://altavista.digital.com/
Comprehensive List of Sites	http://www.netgen.com/cgi/comprehensive
CUI W3 Catalog	http://cuiwww.unige.ch/w3catalog
Dave's WEB Page	http://www.connix.com/~dberry/search.html
DejaNews	http://www.dejanews.com/
Excite	http://www.excite.com/
Find It	http://www.cam.org/~psarena/find-it.html
Harvest Demonstration Brokers	http://rd.cs.colorado.edu/harvest/demobrokers.html
InfoSeek	http://www2.infoseek.com/
INTAC FAQ Index	http://www.intac.com/FAQ.html
The Internet Sleuth	http://www.intbc.com/sleuth/
Lycos	http://www.lycos.com/
Magellan	http://www.mckinley.com/
NCSA Experimental Meta-Index	http://www.ncsa.uiuc.edu/SDG/Software/Mosaic/Demo/metaindex.html
Netscape Internet Search	http://home.netscape.com/internet-search.html
The Otis Index	http://www.interlog.com/~gordo/otis_index.html
Quarterdeck: Net Search	http://www.qdeck.com/cusi.html
Robot List	http://info.webcrawler.com/mak/projects/robots/active.html
Savvy Search	http://guaraldi.cs.colostate.edu:2000/
Wandex, the World Wide Web Wanderer	http://wandex.netgen.com/cgi/wandex
The Way	http://www.infohiway.com/way or http://www.csn.net:80/way/
Web Crawler	http://webcrawler.com/
WWWW—World Wide Web Worm	http://wwwmcb.cs.colorado.edu/home/mcbryan/WWWW.html
Yahoo's Best of the Web Page	http://www.yahoo.com/Computers_and_Internet/Internet/World_Wide_Web/Best_of_the_Web/index.html